Principles of Banking Regulation

An accessible, comprehensive analysis of the main principles and rules of banking regulation in the post-crisis regulatory reform era, this textbook looks at banking regulation from an inter-disciplinary perspective across law, economics, finance, management and policy studies.

It provides detailed coverage of the most recent international, European and UK bank regulatory and policy developments, including Basel IV and Brexit, and considers the impact on bank governance, compliance, risk management and strategy.

Kern Alexander is Professor of Banking and Financial Market Regulation and Chair for Law and Finance at the University of Zurich. He teaches the Principles of Financial Regulation course at the University of Cambridge and is Senior Fellow in Financial Regulation at the University of London School of Advanced Study. He has taught international economics and law, banking and financial regulation and corporate law at the University of Cambridge, Queen Mary University of London and University of Warwick. He has authored numerous books, articles and research reports. He was Specialist Adviser to the British Parliament's Joint Select Committee on the Financial Services Act 2012, Member of the European Parliament's Expert Panel on Financial Services (2009–14), Adviser to the United Nations and the G20 Secretariat on banking regulation. He also advised the UK Treasury, Foreign and Commonwealth Office and Serious Fraud Office on bank governance, financial sanctions and regulatory and compliance issues.

Principles of Banking Regulation

KERN ALEXANDER

University of Zurich

CAMBRIDGE
UNIVERSITY PRESS

University Printing House, Cambridge CB2 8BS, United Kingdom

One Liberty Plaza, 20th Floor, New York, NY 10006, USA

477 Williamstown Road, Port Melbourne, VIC 3207, Australia

314–321, 3rd Floor, Plot 3, Splendor Forum, Jasola District Centre, New Delhi – 110025, India

79 Anson Road, #06–04/06, Singapore 079906

Cambridge University Press is part of the University of Cambridge.

It furthers the University's mission by disseminating knowledge in the pursuit of
education, learning, and research at the highest international levels of excellence.

www.cambridge.org
Information on this title: www.cambridge.org/9781108427265
DOI: 10.1017/9781108551557

© Kern Alexander 2019

First published 2019

Printed in the United Kingdom by TJ International Ltd, Padstow Cornwall

A catalogue record for this publication is available from the British Library.

Library of Congress Cataloging-in-Publication Data
Names: Alexander, Kern, 1962- author.
Title: Principles of banking regulation / Kern Alexander, University of Zurich.
Description: Cambridge, United Kingdom ; New York, NY, USA : Cambridge University Press, 2019. |
    Includes bibliographical references and index.
Identifiers: LCCN 2018048592| ISBN 9781108427265 (hardback : alk. paper) | ISBN 9781108447973
    (paperback : alk. paper)
Subjects: LCSH: Banking law. | Banks and banking, International–Law and legislation.
Classification: LCC K1066 .A952 2019 | DDC 346/.082–dc23
LC record available at https://lccn.loc.gov/2018048592

ISBN 978-1-108-42726-5 Hardback
ISBN 978-1-108-44797-3 Paperback

Contents

Detailed Contents

Figures

Tables

Preface

Banks are important because they bring communities together by accepting deposits from savers and lending to borrowers to start businesses, buy houses, pay university fees or engage in a number of other socially useful activities. In doing so, banks provide credit and liquidity for their customers which supports the economy. To do this effectively, banks must manage financial risks, including credit, market, liquidity and operational risks, which if managed effectively, benefit society economically, but if mismanaged may result in costs for society. Banking regulation is therefore important to ensure that banks manage these risks efficiently and that they do not create social costs. This book is about the regulatory principles, standards and legal frameworks that govern the banking business and why it is important to society.

Banking regulation has undergone dramatic transformation in recent years following the financial crisis of 2007–2008. International regulatory reforms have resulted in major changes in the regulation and supervision of the banking and financial services industries. Banks are now required to hold more loss-absorbent capital and liquid assets and to have more stable sources of funding. Banks are also required to have living wills (resolution plans) to ensure that if they fail they do so without imposing significant costs on society. Regulators now scrutinise more closely bank business strategies, including the financial products they sell to customers, and they approve the appointments of senior management and board positions and control certain aspects of their compensation. They require stricter stress tests and oversight of risk management practices. They also are concerned with the integrity of banks as organisations and the conduct of their staff. Moreover, banks are required to cap their overall leverage, and certain 'systemically important' banks are required to hold more capital depending on their size and interconnectedness with other institutions. Banking regulation has become more comprehensive and the relationship between banks and regulators since the crisis has become more adversarial. This book analyses the main principles and rules that govern this relationship and whether they are achieving their objectives.

Despite extensive reforms, regulators face uncharted waters. Across major economies (i.e. United States, China and Germany) house prices are increasing again and banks and non-bank lenders (so-called shadow banks) are lending much more to meet growing demand. Bank regulators are monitoring whether an asset price bubble may be growing that cannot be explained by underlying economic fundamentals, and although they do not foresee any imminent threat to financial stability, it is clear that they want to avoid the mistakes that regulators and policymakers made in the 1990s and 2000s that led to the last crisis.

This book examines some of the uncertainties surrounding the scope of banking regulation and whether post-crisis reforms are achieving their objectives. The topic of banking regulation has been written about from a number of perspectives. This book adds to the literature by explaining the rationale and economic and legal theories of banking regulation in an accessible format for the general reader with an interest in public affairs and for the student and specialist. The book analyses all of the main post-crisis regulatory reforms including the 2017 amendments to Basel III, known as Basel IV, regulatory initiatives concerning environmental sustainability and climate change, risk culture, financial technology, and misconduct and mis-selling. The book also ties together the post-crisis regulatory reforms with the newly emerging theory of financial regulation known as 'macroprudential' regulation and supervision. Indeed, most regulatory authorities are now empowered with macroprudential tools to monitor and minimise the risks of instability across the financial system. An effective application of these tools, however, requires that in globalised financial markets national regulators cooperate and agree on certain 'rules of the game' with their counterparts in other countries regarding how and to what extent the 'rules' should be applied. This book aims to analyse the 'rules of the game', that is, the principles, standards, norms and laws that govern the banking business.

An overarching theme in the book is that banking regulation has evolved from a focus on individual institutions that assumed that they could manage their risks efficiently to a broader focus on the banking systems as a whole, that is, its organisational and institutional structure and how it manages and controls systemic risks across the financial system. Although banking regulation has undergone significant changes since the crisis, it is submitted that the banking system may still be exposed to systemic risks from a number of new sources including shadow banking and environmentally sustainable activity. Banking regulation in its current form should not ignore the development of fundamental market failures that could likely lead to the next financial crisis.

This book attempts to provide an analysis of the concepts and practices of banking regulation that have emerged post-crisis and to analyse critically the new regulatory terrain as of January 2018 and whether it is achieving its objectives. The book will be especially useful for academics, students, regulators and practitioners.

The book has benefited from the inspiration and influence of many individuals and organisations. I am particularly grateful to Sir William Blair QC, Philip Wood QC and CBE, Dr Paul Fisher, Lord Eatwell, Niamh Moloney FBA, Danny Ralph, Christos Gortsos, Guido Ferrarini, Gudula Deipenbrock, Mads Andenas, Nikoletta Kleftouri, Danny Busch, Richard Herring, Alexandra Balmer, Rosa Lastra, Francesco de Pascalis and Steven Schwarcz, all of whose insights and comments helped hone my ideas. I am also grateful to the University of Zurich, especially Barbora Castell, Bruce Pollock, Aleksandra Gebicka, Leonardo Gelli, Vivienne Madders, Sara Hampel, Fabrizio Wyss and Annina Melliger. Special thanks to Cambridge University Press, including Valerie Appleby, Toby Ginsburg, Rosie Crawley and Denise Bannerman for their invaluable contribution to publishing the book. All errors and omissions are my responsibility. Finally, I would like to thank my family for their support and devotion, Kern IV, Natalia and Ruth Alexander.

Table of Cases

The below table of cases is divided in the following manner: UK, US, EU, ECtHR, Other National Jurisdictions, International Court of Justice.

UK

US

EU

EUROPEAN COURT OF HUMAN RIGHTS

OTHER

INTERNATIONAL COURT OF JUSTICE

Introduction

We shape our buildings; thereafter, they shape us.

Winston Churchill

This book analyses how the principles of banking regulation, including the regulatory standards, norms and legal frameworks, develop and interact with the institutional and organisational structure of banking. The fractional reserve banking system discussed in Chapter 2 allows the banking system collectively to create and allocate credit – which means they decide who gets access to scarce economic resources. This means that banks have control over the redistributive process in the economy and as a result have become essential to the political settlement of a country. Banking regulation reflects the very nature of this settlement.

The global financial crisis of 2007–2008 has been the subject of much debate and analysis. The causes of the crisis have been attributed to over-expansive monetary policies in developed countries which led to property and share price bubbles in the United States, the United Kingdom and many other countries. Most large banks and financial institutions failed to measure and manage the risks to which their highly leveraged balance sheets were exposed. Regulators and supervisors also played a role by failing to require that banks hold adequate levels of capital while also failing to detect the serious liquidity exposures of financial institutions in the wholesale funding markets and the large build-up of leverage in the financial system. Few observers paid attention to systemic risks which had arisen from global macroeconomic imbalances and a substantial increase in leverage and debt across the financial system. Bank regulatory capital models were heavily dependent on risk-weightings of assets on bank balance sheets, which were based on historic default and loss data that were inadequate for estimating the institution's future credit, market and liquidity risks or for estimating systemic risks across the financial system. Moreover, banks and their interconnected financial agents and institutions in the wholesale capital markets devised and traded complex collateralised debt obligations and credit default swaps that contributed significantly to systemic risk. Also, accounting standards impeded adequate provisions and valuation of assets when wholesale markets suddenly collapsed.

In addition, the crisis management measures of regulators and central banks failed to manage the fallout from the crisis. Central banks, including the Bank of England and the

Board of Governors of the Federal Reserve, were slow to recognise dangers from the collapse of confidence in inter-bank markets in mid to late 2007. In August 2007, the Bank of England refused to provide the British bank Northern Rock with lenient lending terms after the bank, which was solvent at the time, had lost access to the wholesale funding markets.[1] A few months earlier, in March 2007, at a time when US mortgage loan defaults were increasing sharply and when mortgage lenders were going out of business, Federal Reserve Chairman Ben Bernanke testified before the US Congress that '[t]he impact on the broader economy and financial markets of the problems in the subprime market seems likely to be contained'.[2] Similarly, William Poole, former President of the Federal Reserve Bank of St Louis, stated in late 2007 that '[m]y own bet is the financial market upset is not going to change fundamentally what's going on in the real economy'.[3] This suggests that UK and US central bankers had very little, if any, understanding of the risks that were threatening the financial system nor how to respond to a crisis once it began.

The regulators of the world's most sophisticated banking and financial markets failed to learn the lessons from previous banking crises in Japan and Scandinavia in the early 1990s and from the Asian financial crisis of the late 1990s, including that banking sector losses must be recognised early and sometimes separated from viable assets in so-called 'bad' banks.[4] Market panic and the collapse of confidence in counterparties should have triggered faster official guarantees. For instance, it was not until December 2007 after the crisis had intensified that the US government established the Term Auction Loan Facility, the first in a series of government-subsidised loans to the financial sector. Later, US authorities failed to pre-empt the collapse of Lehman Brothers in 2008 or to limit the fallout, while most European states had inadequate legal frameworks to allow the restructuring of their largest and most systemically important banks.

The fall of Lehman Brothers demonstrated that in an increasingly interconnected world, a localised economic shock (such as a market or institutional failure) can affect financial institutions and markets in other countries, even causing the global financial system to collapse like a row of dominos. Such a chain of failures that threatens all or part of the financial system epitomises 'systemic' risk. Prior to the global financial crisis, regulators

---

1   See House of Commons Treasury Committee, 'The Run on the Rock' (2008) 38ff.
2   See Federal Open Market Committee of the Board of Governors of the Federal Reserve System, Transcript of Minutes of Meeting of 7 August 2007 (Federal Open Market Committee meeting transcript, Board of Governors of the Federal Reserve System 2018) www.federalreserve.gov/monetarypolicy/files/FOMC20070807meeting.pdf accessed 3 January 2018, with Ben Bernanke stating after the crisis had begun, '[m]y own feeling is that we should try to resist a rate cut until it is really very clear from economic data and other information that it is needed', and he went on 'I'd really prefer to avoid giving any impression of a bailout or a put, if we can.'
3   See Poole W, President of the Federal Reserve Bank of St Louis, stating '[m]y own bet is the financial market upset is not going to change fundamentally what's going on in the real economy', Binyamin Appelbaum, 'Days Before Housing Bust, Fed Doubted Need to Act', *New York Times* (New York, 18 January 2013) www.nytimes .com/2013/01/19/business/economy/fed-transcripts-open-a-window-on-2007-crisis.html accessed 3 January 2018.
4   See Fujii M and Kawai M, 'Lessons from Japan's Banking Crisis – 1991–2005', in Alexander K and Dhumale R (eds), *Research Handbook on International Financial Regulation* (Edward Elgar 2012), 259, 284.

focused almost entirely on 'micro-prudential' regulation: correcting market failures that threaten economic efficiency at the level of the individual firm, such as by maintaining competition, protecting investors against fraud and other abuses, preventing standard externalities, and preserving the viability of individual banks and other financial institutions. The crisis revealed that regulation must also focus on correcting market failures that cause systemic risk both from within the banking sector and from the broader financial system. Such regulation is often called 'macro-prudential'.

In the relatively few years since the crisis, no overall conceptual framework has emerged for designing a macro-prudential regulatory regime to control financial market failures that cause systemic risk. In some cases, macro-prudential regulation – as exemplified by the US Dodd-Frank Act and European legislative reforms – remains constrained by its predominant focus on standard externalities caused by individual banking institutions but without adequate focus on the market failures across the financial system that create systemic risk. And although it is now apparent that both financial institutions and financial markets can be triggers and transmitters of systemic risk, macro-prudential regulation in its current form rarely addresses the systemic risks that arise from the regulatory arbitrage that results in the business of borrowing and lending and the trading of risky financial instruments that increasingly takes place in the so-called shadow banking markets.

A large part of the problem is that regulators and policymakers view macro-prudential regulation in an *ad hoc* manner – as a collection of 'tools' in their regulatory 'toolkit'. This results in either overly specific regulatory proposals without realistic guidance as to their application or use, or overly broad propositions that provide no concrete regulatory guidance at all. Furthermore, the misapplication of these tools – such as stricter restrictions on leverage and credit growth – may be as likely to increase financial risk-taking, however, as to control it. At an October 2015 US Federal Reserve conference, regulators themselves recognised that 'policymakers have made little progress in figuring out how they might actually' prevent another financial crisis and that both monetary and macro-prudential policies are not really effective.[5]

This book argues that to develop a coherent and consistent approach to banking regulation the regulator's objectives must be clear and guided by certain principles that aim to correct the fundamental types of market failures that undermine banking sector stability and threaten the legitimate interest of bank customers, depositors and investors and other stakeholders who depend on the banking sector for their economic livelihood. It also attempts to build on recent academic and policy-based literature that analyses the need to design a more coherent regulatory framework that links the objectives and theory of micro-prudential regulation and macro-prudential regulation.[6] Indeed, Ingves (2011) has identified the need to have a better conceptual framework that strikes a balance between macro-prudential regulation and micro-prudential regulation: both are necessary

5 See Appelbaum B, 'Skepticism Prevails on Preventing Crisis' *New York Times* (New York, 5 October 2015).
6 See Brunnermeier M, Crockett A, Goodhart C, Persaud A and Shin H, *The Fundamental Principles of Financial Regulation* (Princeton University Press 2009).

for maintaining financial stability and the conditions for sustainable economic growth.[7] But other principles of regulation such as accountability and transparency that aim at protecting bank customers and investors are also important and should be recognised in the analysis.

The first part of the book covers Chapters 1–5. Chapter 1 provides a general discussion of the banking business and its origins and evolution in modern financial markets. It considers the historic differences between commercial banks and other deposit-taking institutions, such as savings banks/building societies and credit unions, by explaining when and why they were created and what functions they serve. The evolution of the banking business has often responded to regulatory changes. For instance, the chapter discusses how the primary economic function of banking – credit intermediation – has evolved in response to financial innovation, such as securitisation, and regulatory changes that resulted in bank disinter-mediation – alternative forms of credit – outside the formal regulated banking sector. It also discusses the role of banks in payment systems and the implications for systemic risk and competition, while exploring how banks use low-margin lending to attract other higher-margin business, such as underwriting. The chapter will also discuss the advantages and disadvantages of direct and indirect finance and the role of technology. Also discussed is the importance of bank organisational structure and how different organisational structures have evolved in different jurisdictions.

Chapter 2 discusses the main theories and institutional models of banking regulation, including how asymmetric information within banks and across the financial system can result in moral hazard and adverse selection, thereby leading to negative externalities that can undermine financial stability. The chapter considers some of the main theories of regulation, including public interest and capture theories. It traces the recent development of prudential regulatory concepts and supervisory practices and the move from a primarily micro-prudential supervisory perspective to a macro-prudential perspective that focuses on risks across the financial system and the role of banks in payments systems. Regulation has to do with rule-making, while supervision involves monitoring institutions' compliance with regulatory rules and enforcement by imposing sanctions. The chapter discusses the economic importance of banks and the importance of effective regulation to curb the costs of banking failures and crises. The evolving regulatory concepts are also relevant for understanding the different institutional models of banking regulation (e.g. Twin Peaks, sectoral or mixed approach) and the advantages and disadvantages of certain models. In this regard, the national institutional models will be analysed in terms of their interaction with regional (i.e. EU ESAs/ESRB/SSM) and international institutional structures, with particular focus on the Financial Stability Board and G20 policy framework. The experiences of different jurisdictions, including the US, UK, Australia, China and EU, will be considered.

Chapter 3 analyses global policy developments in banking regulation and the role of international soft law norms and standards, with particular focus on the Basel Committee

---

7   See Ingves S in Brunnermeier et al. (n 6), 96.

on Banking Supervision and the Core Principles for Banking Supervision and the importance of the financial stability objective in international banking regulation. The chapter discusses the role of the Financial Stability Board (FSB) in fostering macro-prudential regulatory practices and its important influence on the development of bank resolution regimes. It also discusses how the FSB coordinates its responsibilities with the G20 and the International Monetary Fund in promoting international standards to safeguard financial sector stability.

Chapter 4 analyses bank capital regulation and risk management. The chapter discusses the role of regulatory capital and how the risk management function is essential for calculating the bank's regulatory capital. It will also discuss the evolution of bank capital and liquidity requirements under Basel II and Basel III, and how Basel III adopts stricter regulatory capital and risk governance standards. It will also provide critical discussion of the risk-weights used by banks to calculate regulatory capital and how reliance on risk-weighting has come to be perceived as a major weakness in prudential regulation. It discusses the application of higher capital requirements to so-called Systemically Important Financial Institutions (SIFIs) and the systemic risks they pose. The chapter also addresses the amendments to Basel III (so-called 'Basel IV') that were adopted in 2017 which, among other things, reduce the extent to which banks can rely on their internal risk-weightings to calculate regulatory capital. Moreover, the chapter will also discuss how risk management has evolved from a micro-prudential approach to assessing risks to a macro-prudential approach that focuses more on the stability of the financial system and the inter-linkages and operations of the financial system.

Chapters 5 will analyse the law and regulation of bank corporate governance and how governance processes for banks have undergone greater formalisation since the financial crisis of 2007–2008. Governance reforms are a response to pre-crisis breakdowns that led to excessive risk-taking in bank lending and derivatives trading and to criminal activity in the case of LIBOR manipulation and other market abuse. The chapter will provide a comprehensive discussion of the unique governance issues associated with banks arising from the inherent complexity of bank business models and their risk profile. It will provide an understanding of the duties and responsibilities of directors and the behaviour required from them and well-functioning boards. Inadequate credit assessment was identified as a key contributor to the banking crisis and governance issues in relation to risk will receive attention in this chapter.

The next part covers Chapters 6–10. **Chapter 6** analyses deposit guarantee schemes and bank recovery and resolution frameworks. It considers the importance of depositor protection regulation with a particular focus on UK and EU regulations and comparison with the United States. The inadequacy of deposit protection schemes in Europe became apparent during the crisis and led to substantial reforms of bank deposit guarantee regulation in the European Union. The UK's experience with depositor guarantee reform will be discussed along with a case study involving the bank run on Northern Rock in 2007. The conceptual basis of deposit guarantee schemes is analysed along with the position of the depositor as an unsecured creditor. The different types of deposit guarantee schemes (e.g. risk-based) and pre-pay versus post-pay will be compared. The chapter will consider whether bank deposit guarantee schemes are complementary to achieving regulatory objectives and the relationship between deposit guarantee schemes and bank resolution. The chapter also reviews the main resolution tools in several jurisdictions and the main principles of bank resolution adopted by the Financial Stability Board. It also considers the Dodd-Frank Act's resolution framework and the operation of the US Organised Liquidation Authority. The importance of the bail-in principle is discussed in the context of the EU Bank Resolution and Recovery Directive and the legal and regulatory issues raised by the bail-in tool. It also analyses the requirements for total loss-absorbent capital on the bank's capital structure and operations.

Chapter 7 discusses structural regulation of banks and why this has become important for achieving regulatory and resolution objectives. The chapter will discuss the conceptual basis of structural regulation and how it has been applied in some countries. It compares the main structural regulatory approaches – the UK, France, Germany and the US – and how they are designed to meet regulatory objectives and their impact on bank governance. In particular, the UK Banking Reform Act 2013 requires that banking groups with more than £25 billion in deposits segregate their retail banking operations and payment services into a separate subsidiary subject to higher capital requirements and different governance arrangements than the rest of the banking group, while allowing other subsidiaries in the group to engage in risky proprietary trading and other trading and investment activities. The UK's so-called ring-fenced banking regime has significant implications for the governance and strategy of the UK banking group, but does not apply to non-UK banking groups that operate retail branches in the UK. The chapter concludes that the use of different structural regulatory approaches across jurisdictions has important implications for the regulatory level playing field in Europe and internationally.

Chapter 8 analyses the regulation and law of bank mis-selling of financial products with particular focus on the sale of risky financial products and investments to non-professional customers and how the EU, UK and US legal and regulatory frameworks have been called into question because of widespread mis-selling. The legal concept of the duty of care is discussed and how it impacts bank management and decision-making regarding the design of retail financial products. It also discusses recent developments in EU regulation (e.g. MiFID II) that require banks to create organisational structures to review the development of financial products and to ensure that products and sales processes are suitable for bank customers. Chapter 9 addresses the growing regulatory challenges for banks regarding misconduct risk and financial crime. The chapter reviews the large number of fines imposed on many banks post-crisis for misconduct in their business practices and the extent of administrative liability for banks and bankers who engage in market abuse including manipulation of benchmarks such as LIBOR. It also considers the criminal law investigations of the UK Serious Fraud Office of many international banks for manipulating LIBOR and related criminal investigations and trials which led to both convictions and acquittals for LIBOR manipulation.

Chapter 10 analyses the growing regulatory concern with shadow banking. Shadow banking has been described as another form of bank disintermediation – that is, maturity transformation, borrowing short and lending long – outside the formal regulated banking sector. The risks associated with shadow banking will be discussed and evaluated. The chapter suggests that regulators should take a functional approach to finance which would involve them identifying what functions the banking system performs (i.e. maturity transformation) and attempting to promote the benefits of the function while curbing the externalities associated with financial risk-taking. The chapter will also consider the potential new risks that post-crisis regulatory reforms may be spawning as they relate to bank trading of derivatives and their involvement in derivatives clearing houses.

The final part of the book covers Chapters 11–15. **Chapter 11** explores the meaning of risk culture and its contribution to bank governance and responsibility. Systemic failures and the perception of a widespread culture of misconduct in UK, European and US banking practices have led to a number of high-profile investigations into the culture of banking. The chapter will discuss international initiatives to regulate risk culture in banking and financial institutions and recent developments in EU regulation. Among G20 countries, the UK has taken the lead by introducing a Senior Manager's Certification Regime that attempts to enhance ethics and risk culture in British financial institutions. Regulatory reforms are also built on the initiatives of industry and professional bodies, such as the Banking Standards Board, FICC Market Standards Board and the Chartered Banker Professional Standards Board, to enhance banking culture and professional standards. The chapter will conclude by considering what further organisational and regulatory initiatives can support the maintenance of ethical behaviour and responsible attitudes that will induce bank employees to engage in higher ethical standards and appropriate levels of risk-taking in the future.

Chapter 12 considers recent developments in financial technology and its potential to transform the banking business and related regulatory challenges. The chapter reviews recent regulatory and legal developments in open banking and how it may transform the banking business by allowing third-party data firms to have access to bank customer data and to offer them a multitude of financial services. This could lead to the unbundling of the banking industry and could have important ramifications for regulation and policy. The chapter also discusses the growing importance of digital currencies and Bitcoin, and whether this is causing disintermediation in the banking sector. The chapter further considers how certain international initiatives are promoting fintech solutions to support the spread of digital financial technologies in order to increase financial inclusion. It also discusses some areas of regulation that can support the establishment of responsible digital practices to protect financial customers and improve financial literacy and awareness so that digital financial products are better understood by end users.

Chapter 13 analyses recent developments in financial policy that have put environmental sustainability on the regulatory reform agenda. This chapter addresses how environmental sustainability is related to banking regulation and how banks have incorporated sustainability objectives into governance and strategic objectives.

Chapter 14 analyses the growing use of administrative sanctions and civil liability imposed on banks for breaching prudential regulatory standards and rules. It analyses the administrative sanctions regime under EU and US law and discusses the administrative process and legal principles and standards that regulators must comply with in order to impose administrative and regulatory sanctions on banking institutions and their employees. Administrative and constitutional law are relevant for the analysis of how regulatory sanctions and the importance of the proportionality principle are vital for understanding how the EU and UK go about enforcing financial regulation. Similarly, US regulatory authorities are constrained by the constitutional principle of due process in applying and enforcing regulatory standards. The importance of the European Convention of Human Rights' protection of property rights is essential for understanding the scope of authority of regulators. Indeed, the legal foundation of financial regulation and the administrative law principles (e.g. proportionality) that apply to its enforcement are an important focus. The principles governing regulatory investigations and enforcement are essential for understanding how bank compliance strategies can be used to support risk management and overall bank governance.

Chapter 15 concludes by summarising the overall themes and major regulatory issues of the book; it considers the impending challenges of building a more effective banking regulatory regime and some of the important issues raised by recent regulatory reforms. It identifies future prospects, challenges and tensions in developing an effective regulatory and policy framework. The chapter also considers some of the different approaches to banking regulation adopted by the European Union, the United States and some other jurisdictions, and whether these differences are significant enough to hinder the development of an effective cross-border banking framework to control systemic risks and achieve other regulatory objectives.

Also discussed are the implications for banking regulation of the Brexit negotiations and how some of the mooted principles of regulation emerging from the Brexit debate are relevant for international banking regulation. In particular, future market access between the UK and EU – for cross-border banking in the context of Brexit – will likely be governed by a trade agreement that contains the regulatory principles of equivalence and/or parity. Also, the chapter suggests that important future developments in banking regulation will involve efforts by regulators and bankers to manage environmental and social risks and to understand the extent that sustainability risks can constitute material financial risks. Indeed, understanding the linkages between environmental sustainability and social inclusion risks and the banking sector will be a major challenge for regulators.

The reader should come away from this book with a deeper understanding of the objectives and function of banking regulation and its vital importance to our economy and society. Financial regulation cannot simply eliminate the market failures that threaten banking stability and bank customers, depositors and investors. In a market-based financial system where most decisions on the allocation of capital are based on the pursuit of private gain, financial crises will be inevitable. The book will show instead how a shift in focus in traditional banking regulation towards a more macro-prudential perspective can nonetheless reduce the risks associated with market failures and reduce the impact of crises when they occur. To achieve this, banking regulation should be designed to operate both *ex ante*, based on a coherent and consistent application of certain regulatory measures or tools, and *ex post*, by stabilising parts of the financial system afflicted by systemic shocks and reducing the impact of those shocks. This book attempts to elucidate the main principles and standards that guide regulators in fulfilling their tasks.

1

The Business of Banking

History, Function and Organisational Structure

Table of Contents

INTRODUCTION

1.1 This chapter provides an overview of the banking business and its origins and evolution in modern financial markets. It discusses the historical development of banking in medieval and early modern Europe and how certain restrictions on banking, such as usury, led to innovations in the banking business and in ways to manage risks. The chapter also analyses the primary *economic* function of banking – credit intermediation – and how financial innovation, such as securitisation, has facilitated bank disintermediation and other forms of credit provision outside the formal regulated banking sector. Finally, it examines the organisational structure of banks and banking groups and how different organisational structures evolved in different jurisdictions and with different strategic objectives.

I THE ORIGINS OF BANKING

1.2 In ancient societies, the temple was usually the location for much of what we would associate today with the banking business. Indeed, sanctuaries and temples in ancient Greece served to provide safe custody for bullion and other valuables.[1] In Mesopotamia, borrowing and lending took place at the temple,[2] while in Jerusalem temples served as fora for money dealers to trade currencies and to take deposits and make loans with interest. The money trading business within temples and their precincts provided a sense of security for traders and an effective system of regulation and dispute resolution. For example, the temples in Jerusalem were known as centres of money changing as depicted in biblical passages.[3] The first codified restrictions on lending and borrowing included the prohibition on usury and guarantees of privacy rights for parties to loan transactions as set forth in the Code of Hammurabi between 2084 BC and 2081 BC.[4]

1.3 The term 'bank' derives from the medieval Italian *banco*, which denoted a merchant's bench in a marketplace. The bench would often serve as a place where merchants and money dealers would agree loans, and if a merchant defaulted on a loan or other obligation the money dealer was entitled to break the bench in front of the merchant.[5] This was the origin of the term 'bankruptcy'. During the Middle Ages, bankers came to play an important role in providing innovative forms of finance to supply credit to monarchs, merchants and traders. For example, some of the large Florentine and Siennese banks founded around 1250 were family-owned (i.e. by the Bardi, Peruzzi and Acciaiuoli families) and played an important role in providing loans to merchants and traders across Europe in the eleventh and twelfth centuries.[6]

1.4 In the thirteenth and fourteenth centuries, the prohibition on usury restricted how Christian bankers could be repaid for loans. Indeed, usury had been considered an odious practice in antiquity. In the *Politics*, Aristotle described usury 'as a most hated sort' of wealth

---

1 See Kurke L, *Coins, Bodies, Games, and Gold: The Politics of Meaning in Archaic Greece* (Princeton University Press 1999). See also Von Reden A, *Exchange in Ancient Greece* (Duckworth 1995) and E. Cohen E, *Athenian Economy and Society: A Banking Perspective* (Princeton University Press 1992).
2 See Millett P, *Lending and Borrowing in Ancient Athens* (Cambridge University Press 1991). See also Duggan A and Lanyon E, *Consumer Credit Law* (Butterworths 1999).
3 See the Book of Matthew 21:12–13.
4 Maloney R, 'Usury and Restrictions on Interest-Taking in the Ancient Near East', 36 Catholic Biblical Quarterly, 1, 1–20, 4–7. See also Thier A, 'Money in Medieval Canon Law', in Fox D and Ernst W (eds), *Money in the Western Legal Tradition* (Oxford University Press 2016).
5 See Tyree AL, *Banking Law in Australia* (5th edn, Butterworths 2005), chapter 2.
6 Hunt E, *The Medieval Supercompanies: A Study of the Peruzzi Company of Florence* (Cambridge University Press 1994), 38.

accumulation.[7] Similarly, Islamic sharia law has always prohibited usury or interest on loans, known as *riba*, defined as an 'increase or excess' above the principal amount of a loan.[8] In medieval Europe, the charging of interest on loans was considered a sin and a crime, and bankers in Florence, Siena, Venice and other Italian city states imposed conditions on sovereign debtors that involved the pledging of royal revenues directly to the bankers.[9] Also, the Kingdom of Naples had by 1325 pledged all of its revenues to repay loans owed to the Florentine Peruzzi bank.[10] It was common practice for the Italian banks of this period to enter into arrangements with sovereign debtors that allowed the bank to collect duties and taxes, appoint government officials, and sell most of the kingdom's grain to ensure that loans were repaid and that the bank was compensated for its services. Similarly, the Peruzzi bank avoided restrictions on usury by requiring the English Crown (under Edward II and Edward III) to pay large gifts or 'compensations' to it for loans and other credits. Across Europe during this period, the large banking houses acquired control over royal licences and revenues as payment for loans to sovereigns. This allowed the banks to control the production of important commodities, agricultural goods, wool, clothing, salt and iron, which had previously been produced and taxed under royal licence.

1.5 Italian bankers also loaned aggressively to farmers, merchants and other tradesmen, and landowners. By the 1330s, this had led to the banking practice of collecting 'perpetual rents' on land rather than accepting usurious interest payments. Perpetual rents involved farmers calculating the expected lifetime rental value of their land and selling that value to a bank for cash along with the bank taking a collateral interest in the land. These cash sales of the land's expected future rental value often resulted in the debt not being fully paid and the bank seizing the land.

1.6 Essentially, the prohibition on usury for European bankers during the Middle Ages led to innovation in how bankers compensated themselves (i.e. the debtor pledging and assigning future revenues) for issuing loans and by structuring the provision of credit so that lenders and bondholders could invest in collateralised assets of the debtors and ensure repayment by allowing the creditor banks to take control of valuable land and the revenues from a wide range of economic activity. This was an example of how legal and regulatory restrictions could be a source of financial innovation which would lead banks to expand their activities and adjust their business models to ensure that their core business of raising capital and making loans remained viable.

---

7   See Aristotle, *Politics* (Benjamin Jowett tr., revised edn, Aeterna Press 2015) Book I, Chapter 10, 1258b.
8   The Quran, Sura Al-Baqarah (The Cow) 2:275–279, http://islamicstudies.info/reference.php?sura=2&verse=275&to=279. See Saleh NA, *Unlawful Gain and Legitimate Profit in Islamic Law: Riba, Gharar and Islamic Banking* (Cambridge University Press, 1996), 47–48.
9   Hunt (n 6), 40.
10   Ibid., 41.

1.7 By the sixteenth and seventeenth centuries, merchants, goldsmiths and scriveners were active in providing a simple form of banking in many European countries. Merchants provided short-term credit to other merchants for the period between buying and reselling goods. Merchants and goldsmiths acted as money changers and foreign exchange dealers. Scriveners were scribes or notaries who copied legal documents and who also in many European countries held funds on deposit for clients and invested those funds for profit and made loans secured by property or other collateral. Gold was deposited with goldsmiths for safekeeping and was expected to be kept on hand and returned to the owners on demand. In England, the emergence of goldsmiths as small deposit takers began to grow significantly in the 1630s after King Charles I seized the hard currency that many depositors held in safe repositories in the Tower of London. The role of goldsmiths and scriveners as deposit takers who also extended credit grew further when Charles II closed the Exchequer, where many savers had deposited their gold and other currencies, in 1672.

1.8 As goldsmiths monitored and kept detailed accounts of deposited gold, the actual amount withdrawn on demand by all the owners at any one time was only a small fraction of all the gold that was held on deposit. Instead of lending only their own gold to borrowers, they began to loan the gold they held on deposit to others as well. In doing so, they would issue promissory notes to depositors that detailed how much they would be paid in principal and interest on a certain date. These notes were the forerunners of the notes that banks began to issue in the late seventeenth and eighteenth centuries that were redeemable in gold coin and circulated instead of gold. This was the beginning of the fractional reserve banking system that continues to operate today in modern financial markets.

1.9 Fractional reserve banking involves a bank holding only a small proportion of its short-term deposit liabilities in liquid money form while loaning the rest out at longer maturities. This type of leveraged lending allowed many European banks in the late eighteenth and nineteenth centuries to channel 'pools' of their depositors' savings (rather than hoarding them) to viable investment projects that played an important role in driving economic development. Indeed, Walter Bagehot, the first editor of *The Economist*, famously described in the nineteenth century how the British banking system was more successful than continental European banks in making depositor savings 'borrowable' by entrepreneurs to invest in the economy.[11] The growth of a fractional reserve banking system in Europe, the United States and other developing industrialised economies in the nineteenth century greatly increased the provision of credit and purchasing power in the economy because banks only had to keep a small ratio of their total deposits available for withdrawal at any one time while loaning the rest of the depositors' capital out to borrowers. This resulted in the banking system having the capacity to create credit and purchasing power for borrowers at a high ratio relative to the value of depositors' savings.

---

11 Bagehot B, *Lombard Street: A Description of the Money Market* (Kegan Paul 1878), 5.

1.10 Earlier in the seventeenth century, however, merchant and goldsmith bankers were constrained by limited resources and the scale of their operations. There was a need for banking institutions that could operate on a larger scale by raising larger amounts of capital and lending it to the Crown and other borrowers to support the expansion of European commerce and to settle payments by issuing 'bank money'. One of the first large banking institutions to play this role was the Dutch Amsterdamsche Wisselbank (the Bank of Amsterdam), which was issued a royal charter in 1609 as a municipal exchange bank that accepted coin deposits in return for issuing bank notes and settling payments through an account ledger that recorded its customers' debits and credits, thus avoiding the need for its customers (especially merchants) to pay foreign bills of exchange with common or foreign currency that was 'clipt and worn' and of uncertain value. In *The Wealth of Nations*, Adam Smith famously discussed the rationale for establishing the Bank of Amsterdam:

> to receive both foreign coin, and the light and worn coin of the country at its real intrinsic value in the good standard money of the country, deducting only so much as was necessary for defraying the expense of management. For the value [of the coin] which remained, it gave a credit in its books. This credit was called bank money, which, as it represented money exactly according to the standard of the mint, was always of the same real value, and intrinsically worth more than current money. It was at the same time enacted, that all bills drawn upon or negotiated at Amsterdam of the value of six hundred guilders and upwards should be paid in bank money, which at once took away all uncertainty in the value of those bills. Every merchant, in consequence of this regulation, was obliged to keep an account with the bank in order to pay his foreign bills of exchange, which necessarily occasioned a certain demand for bank money.[12]

1.11 Later, the Bank of Amsterdam issued fiat money to increase the provision of credit and to support commercial growth in the Netherlands and the Dutch Crown's commercial ventures, wars and colonial expansion, including the Dutch East India company, in the Far East and the Caribbean.[13] Other European countries recognised the importance of establishing banking institutions to support industrial development and colonial expansion. In 1611, Sweden's King Gustav II Adolph and his Chancellor Axel Oxenstierna proposed 'a bank in every town or at least in the foremost' cities.

1.12 In 1656, Sweden's King Gustav X issued a charter to Johan Palmstruch to establish an exchange and loan bank that would provide financing for Sweden's wars against Poland and other Baltic countries.[14] The new bank, Stockholms Banco, was a private company that

---

12 See Smith A, *The Wealth of Nations* (first published 1776, Bantam Dell 2003) Part I, Chapter III, 603–614.
13 See Quinn S and Roberds W, 'An Economic Explanation of the Early Bank of Amsterdam, Debasement, Bills of Exchange and the Emergence of the First Central Bank', in Atack J and Neal N (eds), *The Origins and Development of Financial Markets and Institutions from the Seventeenth Century to the Present* (Cambridge University Press 2009), 32–70. See also Smith (n 12), 320.
14 Wetterberg G, *Money and Power: The History of the Sveriges Riksbank* (Atlantis 2010).

was subject to strict state regulation and was authorised to raise capital from investors and depositors and to extend credit to the king and merchants. After King Gustav died in 1660, the Swedish currency suddenly depreciated, thus precipitating a depositor run on the bank. The bank responded by embarking on a risky strategy of issuing more credit notes to investors to support the bank's finances, but public confidence did not recover and the bank was liquidated in 1664, and its founder Johan Palmstruch was convicted of mismanagement and sentenced to prison in 1668.[15] Although Stockholms Banco had been subjected to strict regulation when it was established, this was not enough to protect it from mismanagement that resulted in excessive risk-taking that led to its demise. The bank's failure demonstrates how the economic benefits and synergies of large banking institutions should be considered carefully in light of the systemic risks they pose.

1.13 The collapse of Stockholms Banco resulted in the loss of a large banking institution that had played an important role in raising revenue for the Crown and issuing notes for merchants and other traders. To fill the void, the Swedish Parliament enacted legislation in 1668 to re-establish the Stockholms Banco under the name the Bank of the Estates of the Realm (the 'Riksbank'), which resumed the majority of the functions of its predecessor except that most of its shares would be owned by the Crown and other public bodies. Although the Riksbank was subjected to greater public control over its activities than the previous banking company, it would still be hampered by weak governance and management and was used by Kings Karl XI and Karl XII to issue fiat paper money to finance costly wars. It would not be until the nineteenth century that the Riksbank would become more financially stable.[16]

1.14 The creation of large banking institutions by royal charter was considered necessary to put state finances on a firmer footing and to create a more unified system of money and credit for countries that were undergoing industrialisation. The English Parliament followed this approach by enacting a statute in 1694 that authorised the Crown to issue a royal charter to a group of investors who had subscribed capital of £1.2 million in return for being incorporated into the Governor and Company of the Bank of England.[17] To induce investors to subscribe to the Bank's share capital, Parliament granted the Bank limited liability company status. The Bank was created primarily to raise capital for the Crown but also accepted deposits, maintained large government accounts and acted as the Crown's banker and debt manager, and was granted monopoly note issuance powers in the City of London. Also, the Bank of Scotland had been formed in the late seventeenth century by an Act of the Scottish Parliament. The Bank of Scotland, however, was different from the Bank of England to the extent that it was forbidden from lending to the Scottish government unless approved by the Scottish Parliament.

---

15   Ibid.
16   See Wetterberg (n 14).
17   See Bank of England, Charter Incorporating the Governor and the Company of the Bank of England (27 July 1694) www.whatdotheyknow.com/request/6134/response/14050/attach/5/1998charter%201.pdf accessed 18 May 2018. See Clapham J, The Bank of England – A History, 1694–1797 (Cambridge University Press 1943) 17–20.

1.15 Moreover, the financial crisis that arose from the South Sea Bubble of the early 1700s resulted in the Bank of England becoming a lender of last resort for other banks and institutions (i.e. merchant banks) who had suffered massive losses in the crisis, but the Bank's emergency loans, though issued on generous terms, required borrowers to provide high-quality financial instruments as collateral which the Bank could sell easily in the market to cover any default. The Bank's role as lender of last resort in the South Sea Bubble crisis became a model for other large European banks and for modern-day central banks in managing the fallout from a financial crisis.

1.16 Royal charters had become extremely important across Europe in shaping the practice and objectives of the banking business, especially for larger banks that were established to raise revenue for the state and to raise capital to invest in large commercial ventures. By the late eighteenth and early nineteenth centuries, however, banking services (e.g. accepting deposits, lending and currency exchange) that had been provided previously by merchants, goldsmiths and scriveners began increasingly to be provided by specialised enterprises that were skilled in managing the se banking transactions. For instance, the British banking system by 1760 had spawned the creation of over 500 banks that were mostly small partnerships. Legislation permitted these institutions to accept deposits, issue notes and discount bills of exchange to finance domestic trade, but limited the number of partners to six and they could only operate outside London and could not have overseas branches. Despite banking crises in 1815 and 1825, the growing demand for banking services in the country and regions led to a sharp increase in their numbers to over 700 by 1825.[18] In 1826, Parliament enacted the Act for the better regulation of Co-partnerships of certain Bankers in England, which allowed banking co-partnerships with the right of note issuance outside a 65-mile radius of London to have an unlimited number of shareholders, but they were liable jointly and severally for debts of the partnership. Banking partnerships were thus free to operate outside London as joint stock companies with an unlimited number of shareholders. This contributed to a significant consolidation in the domestic banking industry from over 700 banks in 1825 to 450 in 1850.[19]

1.17 At the same time, specialist discount houses were emerging in London that bought and sold bills of exchange, which were used to finance domestic trade. Later in the nineteenth century, the discount houses began to work more with the merchant banks in discounting international bills and supporting the issuance of government and railway debt.[20] These institutions, however, were not principally in the business of accepting deposits, issuing notes and making loans, as they performed other intermediary functions that supported corporate finance and international trade.

1.18 In the nineteenth century, there was a geographic separation between the banking services provided by British multinational banks and those provided by English domestic banks.

18   See Collins M, *Money and Banking in the UK: A History* (Croom Helm 1988), chapter 3, 55.
19   Ibid., 65.
20   Jones G, *British Multinational Banking 1830–1990* (Oxford University Press 1993), 5.

Multinational banks were established in the nineteenth century to support commerce and further expansion in the British empire. Most of these multinational banks were created by royal charters that prescribed their business functions and geographical areas of operation. They were prohibited from conducting banking business in England but most had their headquarters in London and were governed by boards of directors consisting of British citizens who held their meetings in London; capital subscriptions were mainly from British investors. The timing of the banks' promotion and the regions of their operations were largely related to the needs of British imperial policy. By 1860, there were fifteen British multinational banks with 132 overseas branches.[21]

1.19 As these banks began to grow rapidly in size and scope of operations, their size and importance to British imperial policy made them systemically important institutions whose failure could result in major economic and political repercussions. As a result, the UK Treasury developed in the 1830s the colonial banking regulations that applied to British multinational banks with operations in the empire. The regulations were forerunners of modern prudential banking regulation in so far as they were designed to prevent bank failures and to limit the impact of failure. Indeed, these regulations were deemed necessary to protect the City of London's reputation as a growing international financial centre and to limit the political risks for British imperial policy if one of these chartered multinational institutions were to fail.

1.20 The colonial banking regulations influenced the organisational structure of the multinational banks, restricting their business activities to 'banking' broadly defined and, significantly, imposed limits on note issuance to a ratio of the value of paid-up equity capital in the bank. These regulations provided a level of confidence for investors but did not provide stock owners with limited liability. In order to induce more investors to subscribe to capital from the multinational banks, Parliament authorised the Crown to issue royal charters in the 1840s that offered a type of limited liability for investors in certain banks that were operating in specialised geographical regions deemed important to British policy. The royal charters adopted many of the requirements of colonial banking regulation, including limiting the ratio of notes issued to share capital, required banks to disclose annual accounts, increased controls on the opening and closing of branches and required banks to renew their charter periodically. The royal charters were a way of ensuring that banks fulfilled public objectives while creating profitable opportunities for British investors. However, some multinational banks were created under English companies legislation or colonial legislation without royal charters. For instance, the Oriental Bank Corporation of India was an example of a multi-national bank that was not created by royal charter and therefore was not subject to geographic restrictions. In the 1840s, the bank expanded beyond India to open branches in Colombo, Singapore and Hong Kong before later expanding its branch network to eastern and southern Africa and Australia.[22] This allowed it to operate without the restrictions that were imposed by charters, such as geographic restrictions on operations, and by controls imposed by the Treasury's colonial banking regulations.

---

21 Ibid., 23.
22 Ibid., 20–21.

1.21 The UK 1857 Joint Stock Banking Companies Act (20 and 21 Vict. c. 49) provided a simpler and more liberal set of provisions to allow the formation of a joint stock banking company, but expressly excluded limited liability for members of banking companies. This was reversed, however, by the 1858 Joint Stock Banks Act (21 and 22 Vict. c.91), which allowed banks to be formed with limited liability so long as they published a statement of assets and liabilities twice a year. This led to increased stock investment in British banks so that they could grow in scale and scope to accommodate the growing demands of British industry and commerce. However, the limited liability structure incentivised the owners of British banks to take greater risks that resulted in some bank failures. For instance, the failure of the London discount house Overend Gurney in 1866 had systemic consequences, necessitating emergency intervention by the Bank of England as a lender of last resort.

1.22 Limited liability also facilitated a substantial increase in investment in British overseas banks, with an increase of nearly thirty new banks operating in the colonies between 1858 and 1866. Some private multinational banks were permitted to combine domestic and overseas banking and because they were exempt from the colonial banking regulations, they financed many speculative investments. The Agra and Masterman's Bank – established in the 1830s as a private bank in India without a royal charter – increased its branch operations to over three continents by the early 1860s and had financed a number of speculative ventures in Australasia. As it was not constrained by the functional or geographical limits that applied to overseas banks with a royal charter, its expansion across continents and its degree of note issuance was unprecedented. As a result, during the British banking crisis of 1866, Agra and Masterman collapsed and was restructured under the oversight of the Bank of England into a bank with more limited geographic and functional reach, but in 1900 – after experiencing further financial distress – it was liquidated.

1.23 The banking business in other countries, such as the United States, was heavily regulated during this time according to function and geographic operation. The US experience with a national bank ended in 1832 when President Andrew Jackson allowed the charter of the Bank of the United States to expire without renewal, much to the consternation of northeastern industrialists, merchants and politicians who had wanted the bank to continue as a national bank with authority to issue notes, take deposits and extend credit to the US government. As a result, the US banking system remained – and became even more – fragmented between the states, and was even fragmented within certain states that prohibited banks from having branches in more than one county. Banks were licensed and regulated primarily by the states and could not establish branches in other states. Banks in most states could sell securities to their customers and extend credit to their customers to invest in the stock market.[23] By the early twentieth century, the US had over 9,000 deposit-taking banking institutions, most of which were small and medium-sized community

---

23 See Galbraith JK, *The Great Crash 1929* (Penguin Press 2009), 69–79.

banks. In states where there were big financial centres, such as New York, banks could grow to a large size and become more easily involved in the securities business.

1.24 In the early twentieth century, banks across Europe and the United States began to exhibit similar traits in that they accepted deposits, issued notes, discounted bills of exchange, exchanged foreign currency and notes, and provided payments services (by issuing cheques) for their customers. They remained subject to heavy regulation and limited in their geographic scope. In the early 1970s, the breakdown of the International Monetary Fund's fixed exchange rate regime resulted in a dramatic liberalisation of global financial and capital markets. Combined with technological advances, many banks began to diversify and speculate against currency risks through the use of innovative instruments such as derivatives and alternative forms of debt finance such as securitisation that allowed borrowers to access credit outside traditional banking channels.

1.25 As discussed later in this chapter, modern financial market developments – liberalisation and regulatory changes – incentivised banks to innovate in how they were performing their credit intermediation function. Further, liberalisation has allowed them to expand their activities across states and national borders and to become multi-functional institutions with global reach that can provide their customers with a wide variety of financial services. This creates substantial synergies for banks, their customers and the broader economy, yet it introduces risks which, if not managed efficiently, can create substantial social costs. These social costs are known as negative externalities in regulatory jargon. As discussed in subsequent chapters, the main objective of banking regulation is to control and mitigate the negative externalities created by bank risk-taking. The next section will discuss in more detail the economic function of banks as credit intermediaries and some of the challenges for bankers in managing the banking business.

II THE ECONOMIC FUNCTION OF BANKS AS INTERMEDIARIES

1.26 The conventional theory of banking holds that banks are mere financial intermediaries whose core activities are to make loans to borrowers and to collect deposits from savers, thereby supporting the economy and a more efficient allocation of resources, while providing banks with a profit margin arising from the difference between loan and deposit rates.[24] However, the financial intermediation theory is only one of three main theories of banking: the other two are the fractional reserve theory of banking and the credit creation theory of banking. The fractional reserve theory of banking provides that although each bank individually is an intermediary that collects deposits and lends them out, all banks acting collectively create money through the process of 'multiple deposit expansion', also known

---

24   See Greenbaum S and Thakor A, *Contemporary Financial Intermediation* (2nd edn, Academic Press 2007), 43–44. See also Golin J and Delhaise P, *Bank Credit Analysis Handbook: A Guide for Analysts, Bankers and Investors* (2nd edn, Wiley 2013), 67–71.

as the money multiplier. The third theory – the credit creation theory – does not consider banks as intermediaries, but holds that they create credit and money in their accounts when they grant loans.[25]

1.27 The financial intermediation theory has attracted the most adherents and is based on the idea of *maturity transformation*. Maturity transformation is what makes the banking business distinctive and special and an object of policymaker and regulatory concern because along with the positive value it brings to society in allocating callable funds from savers and investors to borrowers, there are substantial risks and potential social costs if market demand for a bank's liabilities suddenly declines because of a loss of confidence by depositors and investors.[26] This could lead to a bank run in which a bank sells its assets suddenly and at a steep discount in order to meet depositors' repayment demands, potentially resulting in a contagion-like effect on other banks with exposure to the distressed bank. Confidence is essential, therefore, for the banking business to flourish and for banks to play their intermediary role in channelling surplus savings to borrowers in need of loans.

1.28 Similarly, other financial institutions, such as securities brokers and investment banks, are also intermediaries between buyers and sellers of securities, but they invest their customers' money mainly in tradable securities that are held in segregated customer accounts. Investment banks also act as intermediaries when offering services such as underwriting, advice on mergers and acquisitions, asset management and global custody. However, it is a different form of intermediation than the maturity transformation undertaken by deposit-taking banking institutions. This form of credit intermediation involves the bank taking the proceeds from short-term deposits and other liabilities and then leveraging its own balance sheet to grant longer-term loans for the bank's customers or other longer-term investments. This is what makes the banking business distinctive and, if managed effectively, beneficial for the economy and society.[27]

1.29 But banks are exposed to liquidity risks of both an institution-specific and market nature. Liquidity risk of an institution-specific nature can take the form of *funding risk*; that is, a bank will not be able to attract adequate funding from lenders or investors to continue its operations. Liquidity risk of a market nature involves the risk that a bank will not be able to sell enough assets to continue funding its operations.

1.30 The liquidity risks of banks are a public concern because of their fundamental role in credit intermediation that integrally involves them in the payment system.[28] Indeed, bank balance

---

25   McLeay M, Radia A and Ryland T, 'Money Creation in the Modern Economy' (2014 Q1), Bank of England Quarterly Bulletin, 14–27, 15–17. See also Werner R, 'A Lost Century in Economics: Three Theories of Banking and the Conclusive Evidence' (2016) 46 *International Review of Financial Analysis* 361–379, 363–364.
26   See Diamond DW and Dybvig PH, 'Bank Runs, Deposit Insurance, and Liquidity' (1983) 91 *Journal of Political Economy* 3 401–419.
27   Heffernan S, *Modern Banking* (Wiley 2005), 1.
28   Greenbaum and Thakor (n 24), 55.

sheets are fragile – customer deposits may be available for instant withdrawal, while bank loans are committed over years – and prone to sudden losses of funding. Even a well-run bank could suffer an unexpected loss of liquidity. Central banks usually are able to serve as a 'backstop' provider of liquidity for commercial banks, and therefore can provide liquidity support to both creditworthy individual banks and to the banking system as a whole. In providing liquidity support, however, central banks should take account of the potential for *moral hazard* – the incentive for banks to take greater risks than would be the case if central bank support were unavailable.[29] This requires that central banks balance the benefits of providing liquidity for an individual bank or the banking system subject to the central bank's objective not to take such risks onto its balance sheets.

1.31 Another important feature of the banking business involves the bank holding a small ratio of its deposits as reserves with the central bank.[30] This supports the second theory of banking that holds that most banking systems are based on fractional reserve banking, whereby banks or credit institutions maintain reserves (in cash, coins or deposits at the central bank) that are only a small fraction of their customers' deposits. Although most funds deposited into a bank are loaned out, a small fraction of a bank's quantity of deposits (called a 'reserve ratio') are kept at the central bank.[31] Central banks often attempt to control the supply of money and the credit creation process in the banking system by adjusting interest rates and the reserve ratio that influence the cost of funding for banks and indirectly affect the rates and terms by which banks lend to their customers.[32]

1.32 Similarly, deposit-taking banks provide liquidity support to the wider economy by providing a type of liquidity insurance to their customers in the form of deposits that provide flexibility for them to meet unexpected cash flow demands. By providing liquidity in the form of a liability – a bank deposit – to their customers, banks incur debts that can come due on short notice. As discussed above, this can occur if there is a sudden shift in demand for a bank's liabilities, which can be especially disruptive for a bank that is using most of its liabilities to fund longer-term lending projects, such as property purchases. Moreover, banks' liquidity function provides economic benefits to society by allowing longer-term loan projects to be funded through a constantly changing group of short-term depositors. Although banks' intermediary role generates positive externalities, it exposes banks and society at large to liquidity risks. The management of this risk is the core of the banking business.

1.33 In contrast, investment banks do not offer liquidity as a service in the same way as a deposit-taking banking institution. They contribute to increased liquidity in the system by arranging new forms of finance for companies and other firms, but this is quite different from meeting the liquidity demands of depositors. However, many investment banks do

---

29   Goodhart CAE, 'What Do Central Banks Do?', in Goodhart CAE, *The Central Bank and the Financial System* (Palgrave Macmillan 1995), 205–215. See discussion of 'moral hazard' in Chapter 2.
30   See Mishkin F, *The Economics of Money, Banking and Financial Markets* (11th edn, Pearson 2015), 57–59.
31   Ibid.
32   Heffernan (n 27), 37.

offer the core services of deposit-taking, chequing, ATM and loan facilities to a selected group of very-high-net-worth individuals. Though these services form a small part of their business, it does mean they do in limited circumstances perform traditional deposit-taking intermediary functions.

1.34 The core functions of banks therefore and, thus, their defining features are the provision of credit intermediation and liquidity.[33] Payment facilities are a by-product of these two services. Banks require a payment system to process the debits and credits arising from their transactions. In most advanced developed economies, central banks operate a real-time gross settlement system (RTGS) in which a bank's payment instructions are credited or debited electronically through its accounts at the central bank in real time or during the same day that the instruction is issued.[34] 'Settlement' refers to the actual transfer of funds from a sending to a receiving bank. 'Finality' means the settlement is unconditional and irrevocable. And 'real time' means that payment orders are continuously executed, while 'gross settlement' means that for each payment order, the total gross amount of funds is transferred.

1.35 The central bank payment system facilitates the transfer of ownership claims directly between banks and indirectly across the broader financial sector.[35] An efficient inter-bank payment is necessary to control credit and settlement risk. Given the sheer growth in the number and the large volume of transactions processed through inter-bank payment systems, participating banks incur significant intraday credit risk exposure to other banks. Such credit exposures can give rise to settlement failures and result in systemic risk. These credit exposures between banks are particularly acute in foreign exchange transactions in which one bank will settle its side or 'leg' of a transaction while the other bank will fail to do so. This is often referred to as Herstatt risk, named after *Bankhaus Herstatt*, a small German bank, that was active in the foreign exchange market before becoming insolvent in 1974 after the German leg of its transactions was irrevocably settled in favour of the Herstatt bank but before the US leg of its transactions was settled, leaving Herstatt's US counterparty banks with huge losses. The US bank exposures were temporarily covered by the US Federal Reserve in the Clearing House Inter-bank Payment System (CHIPS) to prevent a systemic crisis in the US payment system, with the German central bank (the *Bundesbank*) eventually covering Herstatt's liabilities.[36] This type of cross-currency settlement risk occurs because the respective payment systems are operated by central banks during non-overlapping hours as a result of different time zones.

1.36 The Herstatt case demonstrated that credit and settlement risk in inter-bank payment systems can threaten financial stability, and that central banks will act as the ultimate

---

33 Ibid., 15.
34 See generally Alexander K, Dhumale R and Eatwell J, *Global Governance of Financial Systems: The International Regulation of Systemic Risk* (Oxford University Press 2006), 1884–1886.
35 Heffernan (n 27), 9.
36 See Alexander et al. (n 34), 188.

guarantor for payment exposures to protect against payment system failure because of bank counterparties failing to meet their payment obligations. It is necessary therefore to foster a greater sense of responsibility through appropriate regulation. This involves a trade-off between ensuring adequate liquidity and reducing unnecessary credit exposures between banks. As a result, many countries have debated the appropriate design of payment systems, which often reflects different approaches to regulation by national authorities. For example, the US Federal Reserve operates a RTGS 'daylight' overdraft system, which allows banks to run an overdraft with the central bank, but it prices the risk of bank default by charging a fee which varies depending on the riskiness of the bank and the amount of overdraft. In contrast, the European Central Bank (ECB) operates what is known as 'Target 2' RTGS that is implemented by the nineteen central banks of the Eurozone. Target 2 has a collateralisation requirement for bank overdrafts in which each bank is required to deposit in advance high-grade securities (funds or government bonds) to cover any daily credit exposures arising from banks' payments. The ECB Target 2 system links bank payments across the nineteen central banks of the Eurozone, as explained in the hypothetical example below:

1.37 A German investor sells an office building in Athens to a Greek property investor for €10 million. The €10 million cash is transferred from a bank account in Greece to a bank account in Germany. Yet, the money does not really change hands. The German bank receives a €10 million credit in its central bank account with the German central bank (the Bundesbank). The Greek bank has the same sum deducted from its account with the Greek central bank.

1.38 The ECB and the Federal Reserve each utilise a different regulatory mechanism to manage credit and settlement risks in the inter-bank settlement system. The Committee on Payment and Market Infrastructure (CPMI) established in 2014 and formerly known as the Committee on Payment Settlement Systems has adopted recommendations to national authorities to promote the safety and efficiency of payment, clearing, settlement and related arrangements, including managing credit and settlement risk in inter-bank payment systems.[37] The CPMI Recommendations provide flexibility for national authorities to decide whether to use an RTGS or multilateral netting system – the latter involves the netting out between participating banks of their net exposures at the end of each working day. The CPMI recognises that the financial stability risk inherent in any payment and settlement system requires the establishment of minimum regulatory standards, whether in terms of interest charges, collateralisation requirements or loss-sharing agreements.

III ADVANTAGES OF BANKING INTERMEDIATION OVER DIRECT FINANCE

1.39 Arguably, savers and borrowers do not need banks to intermediate their funds: in direct finance borrowers obtain funds directly from lenders in financial markets. However, two

---

37 See Committee on Payments and Market Infrastructure, 'Charter' (Bank for International Settlements, September 2014) paras. 1 and 2 www.bis.org/cpmi/publ/d174.pdf accessed 28 May 2018.

types of barriers can be identified to the direct financing process: (1) the difficulty and expense of matching the complex needs of individual borrowers and lenders; (2) the different financial needs and objectives of borrowers and lenders. In summary, the majority of lenders want to lend their assets for short periods of time and for the highest possible return. In contrast, the majority of borrowers demand liabilities that are cheap and for long periods.[38] Banks bridge the gap between the needs of lenders and borrowers by performing a size, maturity and risk transformation function.[39]

1.40 Financial intermediaries help minimise the costs associated with direct lending – particularly transaction costs and those derived from information asymmetries. Transaction costs relate to the costs of searching for a counterparty to a financial transaction; the costs of obtaining information about them; the costs of negotiating the contract; the costs of monitoring the borrowers; and the eventual enforcement costs should the borrower not fulfil their commitments. In addition to transaction costs, lenders are also faced with the problems caused by asymmetric information. These problems arise because one party has better information than the counterparty. In this context, the borrower has better information about the investment (in terms of risk and returns of the project) than the lender. Information asymmetries create problems in all stages of the lending process. Transaction costs and information asymmetries are examples of market failures; they act as obstacles to the efficient functioning of financial markets. One solution is the creation of organised financial markets. However, transaction costs and information asymmetries, though reduced, still remain. Another solution is the emergence of financial intermediaries. Organised financial markets and financial intermediaries coexist in most economies.[40] Therefore, one of the main features of banks is that they reduce transaction costs by exploiting scale and scope economies while often owing their extra profits to superior information.[41]

1.41 In his classic analysis, Coase argued that the firm acted as an alternative to market transactions, as a way of organising economic activity, because some procedures are more efficiently organised by 'command' rather than depending on a market price.[42] The existence of the 'traditional' bank, which intermediates between borrower and lender, and offers a payments service to its customers, fits in well with the Coase theory. The core functions of a bank are more efficiently carried out by a command organisational structure, because loans and deposits are internal to a bank. Such a structure is also efficient if banks are participating in organised markets. These ideas were developed and extended by Alchian and Demsetz, who emphasised the monitoring role of the firm and its creation of incentive

---

38 Casu B, Girardone C and Molyneux P, *Introduction to Banking* (Pearson Education Limited 2006), 5.
39 Ibid., 7–8.
40 Heffernan (n 27), 5.
41 Casu et al. (n 38), 8.
42 See Coase RH, *The Firm, the Market and the Law* (University of Chicago Press 1988), 13–17. See Alchian A and Demsetz H, 'Production, Information Costs, and Economic Organization' (1972) 62 *American Economic Review* 5 777–795.

structures through the design of contracts.[43] Similarly, Williamson argued that under conditions of uncertainty, a firm (e.g. a bank) could economise on the costs of outside contracts.[44]

IV LIBERALISED FINANCIAL MARKETS AND BANK DISINTERMEDIATION

1.42 For most of the twentieth century, the availability of credit has been segmented into two markets: the banks and mutual savings associations and what may be described as the informal lending sector – a plethora of unregulated direct lending mechanisms (person to person, credit cooperatives, micro-lending and so on).[45] While a significant proportion of lending to retail customers and small businesses has gone through these direct lending markets, the majority of all borrowing and almost all large corporate borrowing has gone through banking institutions.

1.43 Since the 1970s, however, the liberalisation of foreign exchange controls and cross-border capital movement has led to the development of a global capital market in which investors are able to invest in credit exposures across jurisdictions and markets in order to obtain higher yields and risk diversification. This has led to a new source of credit provided directly to corporate and other borrowers without channelling their investment capital through banks. This is generally referred to as 'bank disintermediation'. The whole corporate bond market effectively disintermediated the banks by directly pairing off non-bank providers of liquidity with corporate and sovereign borrowers. The banks themselves benefited from the growth of non-bank bond investors by tapping this sector for their own senior and subordinated liquidity needs. Having established a huge investor base of non-bank credit investors, the next step in the bank disintermediation process was to allow assets traditionally funded on bank balance sheets (corporate loans, mortgages, etc.) to be moved into separate companies and then financed by these same non-bank liquidity providers.

1.44 It is this second development that has seen enormous growth over the last decade as bank loans, bonds, credit derivatives and a growing array of retail asset-backed securities (ABSs) were packaged into collateralised debt obligations (CDOs) and structured investment vehicles (SIVs) and sold to non-bank investors. Understanding the drivers for this change and whether these trends continue requires consideration of the motivations of the banks and the fixed-income investors, as well as the impact of the development of new products.

---

43   See Alchian A and Demsetz H, 'Production, Information Costs, and Economic Organization' (1972) 62 *American Economic Review* 5, 777–795.
44   Williamson OE, 'Economics of Organization: A Transaction Cost Approach' (November 1981) 87 *American Journal of Sociology* 3 548–577.
45   See generally, Alexander K, Eatwell J and Persaud A, 'Modern Banking and Securitization', chapter 1 in Alexander K and Dhumale R (eds), *Research Handbook on International Financial Regulation* (Elgar 2012).

V BANK MOTIVATION

1.45 Traditionally, the basic economics of lending have focused on the returns generated by raising money from depositors, the inter-bank or wholesale debt markets and the ability to lend it at a wider margin to corporate and retail borrowers. A certain amount of equity capital is needed to allow a bank to do this and – given the high operating costs of running a bank, the credit losses associated with lending, the costs imposed by banking regulations such as capital adequacy requirements and the generally competitive bank environment – the return to equity investors from pure lending was traditionally less than 10 per cent. Prior to the crisis of 2007–2008, however, banks were able to increase their return on equity to nearly 20 per cent by supplementing the low return, high-risk business of lending with the high return, low- or no-risk business of advisory and transactional services such as cash management, foreign exchange and mergers and acquisitions.

1.46 However, to enjoy these high margin businesses, the bank needs client relationships and these normally come with a requirement to lend. So, the high margins of non-lending businesses are normally diluted by the low margins of the supporting loan book. With bank disintermediation, the need to hold expensive assets disappears. For the first time in banking history, banks were able to enjoy all of the benefits of their franchise without some of the balance sheet costs.

VI FIXED-INCOME INVESTORS

1.47 It is impossible to discern whether the supply of fixed-income assets created the demand or vice versa. But it is certainly the case that the disintermediation revolution in the banking sector coincided with a revolution in the demand for credit fixed-income assets. In part, this demand was supported by a combination of several developments. The first was the regulatory strain on long-term financial institutions like pension and insurance providers to match their liabilities with fixed-income assets. This pressure has often come in the form of mark-to-market valuation and solvency requirements. Second was a requirement to provide financial benefits that matched earnings and economic growth at a time when government bond yields were being weighed down by the impact on inflation levels stemming from the introduction of China and India into the world's trading system and the recycling of Middle East and Asian surpluses into government bond markets. The structured finance markets – mainly ABSs, CDOs and SIVs – allowed investors in developed countries to gain exposure to economic growth in many emerging market economies.

1.48 Finally, the role of securitisation in driving the bank disintermediation revolution should be considered in the broader context of liberalised financial markets that began in the 1970s following the breakdown of fixed exchange rate controls. Historically, the risk associated with lending was distributed via bank balance sheets and was available to fixed-income investors in the form of bank senior and subordinated debt. However, in comparison to the innovative, tailored structures used in the structured credit markets, bank debt lacks granularity. This is because there is generally no transparency regarding the bank's underlying portfolio. Investors can be more easily persuaded to invest in bank-originated credit that is structured into different risk tranches that are more transparent and flexible for them to adjust their exposures based on risk and return. Securitisation was also ideal for banks that were seeking to provide more transparent structured credit investment products that allowed banks to have more flexibility in separating risk from the banks' franchise value.

VII FINTECH AND PEER-TO-PEER LENDING

1.49 Since the crisis, financial technology ('Fintech') and the internet have further facilitated bank disintermediation by bringing together borrowers, such as small businesses and start-up entrepreneurs, with potential investors, such as institutions and individuals willing to invest their surplus capital directly to borrowers without channelling it through traditional banking institutions. In Europe, over a dozen 'peer-to-peer' lending platforms have been established for small and medium-sized businesses and fledgling entrepreneurs to obtain credit. In 2017, the two largest peer-to-peer lending firms in Europe are Funding Circle – a company with over $1 billion valuation – and Zopa – which facilitated over $700 million in loans in 2016 and over $1.8 billion in loans since 2005.[46] Peer-to-peer lending platforms provide a venue so that investors and business borrowers can identify one another and agree credit terms. They do not meet the definition of banks – and therefore are not regulated as such – because they do not accept deposits and do not leverage their own balance sheets to make loans. They provide alternative sources of credit for many small businesses and start-up entrepreneurs – many of whom have had difficulty after the crisis in obtaining credit from traditional banks because of the economic slowdown and stricter regulatory requirements.

1.50 Although peer-to-peer lending appears to be gaining market share from traditional banks and thus contributing to bank disintermediation, some platforms are restricting the amount of money they accept from investors because there is inadequate demand from creditworthy borrowers to support the growing number of lending platforms. However, competition between platforms has led some to accept funding from investors with a greater appetite for credit risk who are seeking to place loans with riskier borrowers while charging a higher interest rate for the risk. This raises the question of whether the investors have adequate information to assess the risks they are exposed to. For instance, investors

---

46   See Hesse M, 'Angriff der Finanzzwerge' *Spiegel.de* (20 October 2015) www.spiegel.de/wirtschaft/ unterneh men/fintech-fusion-funding-circle-uebernimmt-konkurrenten-zencap-a-1058522.html accessed 18 March 2018; 'Breaking: Zopa Will Launch a Bank' (16 November 2016) www.p2p-banking.com/tag/bank/ accessed 18 March 2018. See also Bernegger MP, 'Die digitale Revolution – Neue Geschäftsmodelle für die Finanzindustrie', in Strebel-Aerni B (ed.), *Finanzmärkte im Banne von Big Data* (Zurich Schulthess Juristische Medien AG 2012), 302–303.

in peer-to-peer loans may be providing financing for risky borrowers without adequate disclosures as to the relevant risks. Also, the amount of credit provided by peer-to-peer lending is growing and there is an incentive for some platforms to become too big too quickly, with the result that certain risks will be ignored or under-priced by investors. The question arises: should such types of alternative finance attract the same degree of regulation as traditional banking?

1.51 The above forms of bank disintermediation are transforming how credit is provided to the broader economy and have shifted the risks that banks once posed to the economy to other sectors of the financial system that may not be as capable as banks in managing those risks. Nevertheless, bank disintermediation is a form of financial innovation that brings benefits to the economy by providing more diverse and cost-efficient sources of credit for borrowers as well as greater risk-adjusted returns for creditors who provide alternative sources of funding. That is why efforts to regulate the risks associated with the provision of disintermediated credit should be considered carefully in terms of the benefits and costs they bring to the economy.

VIII THE ORGANISATIONAL STRUCTURE OF BANKING

1.52 This section generally discusses the organisational structure through which banks conduct their business. In most developed market economies, the banking business is conducted through corporate or other legal entities with limited liability based on the value of common equity shares or other participation instruments. Across most developed countries, and particularly in continental Europe, the universal banking model has provided the predominant form of organisational or institutional structure for the commercial banking business.[47] The traditional approach to universal banking involved a single bank offering a variety of financial services across the main financial sectors of commercial banking, securities trading and insurance. This is known in some European countries as *bancassurance*, in which the banking corporation is permitted to take deposits, make loans and provide payment services, while also providing insurance services and products. Universal banks often operate in a corporate group or conglomerate structure from which they provide a wide range of financial services through a network of subsidiaries and branches that are controlled by the group's holding company or affiliated banking institution.

A 'financial conglomerate' has been defined as any corporate group under common control whose exclusive or predominant activities consist of providing a significant level of services in at least two of the financial sectors of banking, securities and insurance.[48]

---

47 See Canals J, *Universal Banking* (Oxford University Press 1997), 6–11.
48 See Tripartite Group of Bank, Securities and Insurance Regulators, 'The Supervision of Financial Conglomerates' Report (July 1995), 1 www.bis.org/publ/bcbs20.pdf accessed 21 February 2018.

1.53 The growing operations of universal banks in corporate groups and conglomerate structures is a response to the globalisation of financial markets and the competitive pressures of providing financial services to corporate clients with cross-border operations, and the pooling of capital and investment services to achieve greater returns for clients. Moreover, the group or conglomerate structure of universal banks allows them to provide affiliates and subsidiaries of the group with financial products (i.e. derivatives and swaps) and risk mitigation techniques (i.e. securitisation) that allow them to manage their risks more efficiently.

1.54 The universal banking model arose to dominance in continental Europe because historically bank loans were the main source of funding for companies, while in the US and UK companies sourced considerably more of their funding directly from the capital markets. The recent trend in Europe, however, is for companies to source more and more of their funding in capital markets.[49] Also, the regulatory and legal restrictions on banks have evolved differently across European countries. For instance, the organisational structure of British banks in the nineteenth century was influenced by legal restrictions on the size and operations of domestic and multinational banks.[50] As discussed in 1.16, before 1826, banks in England and Wales were not permitted to have more than six partners. In contrast, the Bank of England, whose original charter in 1694 had been re-enacted by Parliament time and again on terms that provided it with the sole right among English banks to be a joint stock company and to have more than six members.[51] The Bank's exclusive privilege to have joint stock organisation status, however, ended in 1826 when Parliament enacted legislation allowing private banks outside London to adopt the joint stock organisation form, though it was not until 1834 that banks with joint stock organisation status that did not issue notes could be established in London.[52] Parliamentary legislation in 1887 introduced limited liability for joint stock banks.[53] Thereafter, the number and size of joint stock banks grew rapidly and substantially – both multinational and domestic – far surpassing in number the hundreds of smaller private banks already in existence throughout the country. One way the British multinational banks expanded in the late nineteenth century occurred in Australia, where the strategy was to establish both a trading bank to provide credit for exporters and importers and a savings bank in which the trading bank could make deposits and obtain credit.[54] By the mid-twentieth century, through a variety of strategies, British multinational banking groups had grown in size and scope by offering a wide array of

49   See European Commission, Communication from the Commission to the European Parliament and the Council on 'Long-Term Financing of the European Economy' (27 March 2014) COM(2014) 168 final www.ec .europa.eu/internal_market/finances/docs/financing-growth/long-term/140327-communication_en.pdf accessed 21 February 2018.
50   Crick WF and Wadsworth JE, *A Hundred Years of Joint Stock Banking* (Hodder & Stoughton 1935) and Jones (n 20), 76–82.
51   See Clapham J, *The Bank of England: A History* vol. 1, 1694–1797 (Cambridge University Press 1944), 79–86.
52   Joint Stock Companies Act 184 (7 and 8 Vict. c. 110). See also Crick and Wadsworth (n 50), 18.
53   Joint Stock Banks Act 1858 (21 and 22 Vict. c. 91).
54   See Jones (n 20), 297.

banking and financial services akin to the continental universal banks, with extensive cross-border operations through multiple subsidiaries and branches operating in countries across the world.

1.55 By the late twentieth century, European-based banking groups, such as Barclays PLC, Société Générale SA, UBS AG and the Royal Bank of Scotland PLC, had become some of the largest banking groups in the world with their cross-border financial and investment services provided through multiple and geographically diverse subsidiaries and branches. The synergies brought about by such conglomerations of banking and financial activity contributed to the dramatic growth of these institutions.

1.56 In 2007–2008, however, large banks and financial institutions – including many universal banking groups – experienced severe financial distress and were rescued with taxpayer-funded bailouts and/or supported with central bank and government guarantees.[55] Large banking groups and conglomerates were criticised for investing in high-risk structured finance assets and for speculating in credit default swaps and other credit-linked derivatives which recklessly increased their risk exposure at the expense of their depositors, creditors, shareholders and *ultimately* the taxpayers.[56] In the United Kingdom, large banking groups, such as the Royal Bank of Scotland, Lloyds TSB and Halifax Bank of Scotland, received direct taxpayer bailouts during the crisis that took the form of equity capital injections and guarantees of their liabilities. In October 2008, at the height of the global banking crisis, the UK Treasury injected £45 billion of equity capital directly into one of Britain's largest banks – the Royal Bank of Scotland PLC (RBS) – and became an 82 per cent owner of that banking group. The UK Treasury also injected capital into Lloyds Banking Group PLC in 2008 to become a 25 per cent equity owner after Lloyds had incurred huge losses on its acquisition of the Halifax Bank of Scotland (HBOS) in 2008 during the crisis. The UK Treasury has managed its ownership interests in British banks through the entity UK Financial Investments Ltd (now UK Government Investments Ltd) and began in 2016 to re-privatise its shares in Lloyds resulting in the Treasury selling all of its shares by 2018. In contrast, it has only more recently begun to sell off its shares gradually in RBS by announcing in June 2018 that it would reduce its stake in RBS by 7.7 per cent from 71 per cent to 62.4 per cent. The government intends to sell another £15 billion worth of RBS shares by 2023.[57]

1.57 The collapse of many large and interconnected European banking and financial institutions, the extent of the taxpayer bailouts and the subsequent severe impact on the economy have led to a re-evaluation of the benefits of the universal banking model and

---

55 See *BaFin Journal*, 'Systemrelevante Finanzunternehmen – G20 sehen Fortschritte bei nationalen und internationalen Lösungsansätzen zum "Too Big to Fail" – Problem' (October 2013), 30. See also Alistair Darling, *Back from the Brink: 1,000 Days at No. 11* (Atlantic Books Limited 2011), 130–149.
56 See *BaFin Journal* (n 55), 31.
57 See HM Treasury (5 June 2018), 'Disposal of Approximately 7.7% of The Royal Bank of Scotland Group PLC' (5 June 2018) www.londonstockexchange.com/exchange/news/market-news/market-news-detail/other/13666278.html accessed 20 December 2018.

to calls for structural regulation of financial groups that would require, *inter alia*, legal separation – or ring-fencing – of certain financial services into separate subsidiaries. For instance, as discussed in Chapter 7, the United Kingdom's Financial Services (Banking Reform) Act 2013 requires banking groups with more than £25 billion in deposits to separate retail banking and payment services into a separate subsidiary.[58] Germany and France have also adopted legislation that would require certain risky investment banking activities to take place in a separate subsidiary of the group.

1.58 Despite the stricter regulations (discussed in later chapters) for multi-functional and universal banks, the benefits of universal banking for the economy and bank customers are recognised: banks are more diversified across business lines and, through cross-selling, can provide customers with more efficiently priced products and services. Greater diversification and larger balance sheets allow them to provide the entire financial system with more liquidity. This allows them to play a central role for the economy by providing funding to institutions and individuals to invest in viable assets that might otherwise not obtain funding in a difficult economic climate. The array of financial services which they provide can also facilitate and enhance cross-border trade and investment and assist local companies with more competitive terms of finance for their cross-border operations. The banking industry and regulators recognise that these benefits outweigh the risks to society and therefore universal banking – especially as it is conducted in corporate group and conglomerate structures – will continue to be recognised as a viable organisational structure for the business of banking.

CONCLUSION

1.59 This chapter analysed the foundations and evolution of important aspects of the banking business. In doing so, it explored the historical origins of banking and how its role in providing credit intermediation evolved. Banks have traditionally followed the business model of borrowing short and lending long – maturity transformation – which if managed effectively can generate economic gains for banks and their owners and the economy at large. If not managed well, however, it can lead to substantial losses for bank owners as well as potentially high social costs. The chapter then discusses the evolution of banking markets and how financial innovation and technology brought about bank disintermediation in the form of securitisation along with more recent trends in advanced financial technology and the rise of alternative credit disintermediation in the form of peer-to-peer lending.

58 See generally the recommendations of the Independent Commission on Banking, 'Final Report – Recommendations' (September 2011), 252 http://webarchive.nationalarchives.gov.uk/20131003105424/https:/hmt-sanctions.s3.amazonaws.com/icb%20final%20report/icb%2520final%2520report%5B1%5D.pdf accessed 21 February 2018. See also European Commission, 'Report of the High-Level Expert Group on Reforming the Structure of the EU Banking Sector', chaired by Erkki Liikanen (2 October 2012) www.ec.europa.eu/internal_market/bank/docs/high-level_expert_group/report_en.pdf accessed 21 February 2018.

1.60 The chapter also considered the organisational and institutional development of the banking business. It traced the growth of the universal banking model in continental Europe with that of domestic and multinational banks in the United Kingdom. It also discussed the benefits and risks of multi-functional banking groups and conglomerates and their significance as global financial institutions.

QUESTIONS

1. How was banking conducted in sixteenth and early seventeenth-century Europe?
2. What main functions do banks fulfil in the modern economy?
3. What types of risks do banks pose to the economy?
4. What are the main risks in inter-bank payments and what are some regulatory approaches for addressing these risks?
5. What regulatory or legal developments contributed to the growth of UK multinational banks?

Further Reading

Admati A and Hellwig M, *The Bankers' New Clothes* (Princeton University Press 2013), assuming the financial intermediation theory of banking, that 'the use of deposits to fund loans has been a standard practice in banking for centuries'.

Alexander K, Eatwell J, Persaud A and Reoch R, 'Financial Supervision and Crisis Management in the EU', IP/A/ECON/IC/2007–069 Brussels, European Parliament, 2–4, discussing the early liquidity phase of the global financial crisis that began in 2007 in which many banks despite having adequate regulatory capital experienced serious funding difficulties because they failed to managed their liquidity risk effectively.

Cassel G, *The Theory of Social Economy* (T. Fisher Unwin 1923), supporting the credit creation theory of banking.

Choudhry M, *An Introduction to Banking* (2nd edn, Wiley 2018)

Cohen EE, *Athenian Economy and Society: A Banking Perspective* (Princeton University Press 1992), arguing that lenders in the ancient Greece classical period were not merely money changers, but were more sophisticated intermediaries that took deposits and made loans and provided wealth planning.

Diamond P and Dybvig P, 'Bank Runs, Deposit Insurance, and Liquidity' (1983) 91 *Journal of Political Economy* 3 401–419, discussing the risks arising from depositors' loss of confidence in a bank that can cause a bank run and devising a model of the bank performing the intermediary function of information gatherer and monitor.

Fox D and Ernst W, *Money in the Western Legal Tradition – Middle Ages to Bretton Woods* (Oxford University Press 2016)

Goodhart CAE, *Monetary Theory and Practice: The UK Experience* (Macmillan 1984)

Guttentag JM and Lindsay R, 'The Uniqueness of Commercial Banks' (September–October 1968) *Journal of Political Economy* 76 991–1014, supporting the fractional reserve banking theory.

Kashyap AK, Rajan R and Stein JC, 'Banks as Liquidity Providers: An Explanation for the Co-Existence of Lending and Deposit-Taking', *Journal of Finance* (2002) 57 33–73, supporting the financial intermediation theory of banking by presenting a model of banking in which banks use funds obtained from deposits and issuance of equity and bonds to purchase longer-term assets.

Kurke K, *Coins, Bodies, Games, and Gold: The Politics of Meaning in Archaic Greece* (Princeton University Press 1999), and political institutions and practices.

Kynaston D, *Till Time's Last Sand: A History of the Bank of England 1694–2013* (Bloomsbury 2017), discussing history of the Bank of England's evolution into a modern central bank.

Ruefner T, 'Money in the Roman Law Texts', in Fox D and Ernst W (eds), *Money in the Western Legal Tradition* (Oxford University Press 2016)

Samuelson P and Nordhaus W, *Economics* (McGraw-Hill 1995), 490, 492, supporting fractional reserve theory of banking, that central banks create 'reserves' that are used by banks 'as an input' which are transformed into a much broader amount of bank credit for lending, and that all banks together can create a 'multiple expansion of reserves'.

Werner R, *New Paradigm in Macroeconomics* (Palgrave Macmillan 2005)

Werner R, 'Can Banks Individually Create Money Out of Nothing? – The Theories and Empirical Evidence', *International Review of Financial Analysis* 36 (2014) 1–19

Werner R, 'A Lost Century in Economics: Three Theories of Banking and the Conclusive Evidence' (2016) 46 *International Review of Financial Analysis* 361 363–364, providing a comprehensive literature review of three main theories and an empirical analysis of a bank creating credit in its loan books.

2

Economic Theories and Institutional Design

Table of Contents

INTRODUCTION

2.1 Banking regulation traditionally has had three main objectives: financial stability; depositor and customer protection; and market integrity.[1] This chapter discusses some of the

---

1   See Bank of England Act 1998, section 2A (as amended by the Financial Services Act 2012) and the Financial Services and Markets Act 2000, sections 3–6: market confidence, public awareness, protection of consumers and reduction of financial crime. Other secondary objectives have been recognised and include investor protection and competition.

main theories of financial regulation that explain the rationale of banking regulation. It also analyses the economic concept of externalities as it relates to systemic risk in financial markets and how regulating systemic risk supports the financial stability objective.[2] The chapter analyses how prudential regulatory concepts have evolved to address the changing nature of financial risks and how a careful combination of market innovation and policy frameworks are desirable for designing an effective and efficient banking regulation framework. The chapter then discusses the economic importance of banks and the importance of effective regulation in curbing the costs of banking failures and crises. It considers the various definitions of systemic risks and how they have evolved from firm-level microprudential risks, to broader system-wide macro-prudential risks. It discusses the changing philosophy of banking regulation that has developed to include both micro-prudential supervision as well as macro-prudential supervision. At the outset, it should be emphasised that banking regulation refers to the body of rules and standards established by regulatory authorities or self-regulatory bodies to limit or control the risk assumed by banks or other financial institutions, while supervision refers to the process of ensuring and monitoring compliance with regulatory rules and standards.[3] For our discussion, the terms will be used interchangeably. The chapter concludes that banking supervision and regulation has become a rich and multi-faceted concept that has taken on a deeper meaning in response to recent crises and regulatory reforms.

I BANKING AND AGENCY PROBLEMS

2.2 The role of banks is integral to most economies. They collect deposits and provide loans for retail and commercial customers, and provide access to payment systems and a variety of other financial services for the economy. Some banks serve a broader function for the economy by transmitting monetary policy through the provision of credit and liquidity – sometimes under difficult market conditions.[4] The integral role that banks play in economies is demonstrated by the almost universal practice of states regulating the banking industry and providing, in many cases, governmental safety nets in the form of deposit insurance and other guarantees. Banks are also eligible for central bank support in the form of lender of last resort for short-term financing if they are solvent but experiencing funding or liquidity problems. Banks are commonly referred to as special because of the multiplier effect that they have on the economy. The large number of stakeholders, such as employees, customers, suppliers, etc., whose economic well-being depends on the health of the banking industry, depend on a well-regulated and supervised banking sector. Effective banking regulation involves the promulgation of substantive standards (e.g. capital adequacy and liquidity, corporate and risk governance, disclosure) and risk management procedures and

---

2 The depositor protection objective is addressed in Chapter 6, while the market integrity objective is addressed in Chapter 9.
3 See Lastra RM, 'Central Banking and Banking Regulation' (1996), LSE Financial Market Group.
4 See Hawkins J and Turner P, 'Managing Foreign Debt and Liquidity Risks in Emerging Economies: An Overview' (September 2000), BIS Policy Papers No. 8 www.bis.org/publ/plcy08a.pdf accessed 21 February 2018.

risk assessments within financial institutions that allow banks to measure and manage their risks.[5]

2.3   Banking regulation is considered necessary because banks are disproportionately affected by agency problems, which arise from imperfect or *asymmetric* information. The theory of modern information economics holds that the conditions for a competitive equilibrium (where no one can be made better off without making someone else worse off) do not hold if information between market participants is imperfect or *asymmetric*. Agency problems are at the core of market failures and usually arise from two sources: (1) imperfect information between the owners of assets (principals) and their managers (agents) who are delegated responsibility to manage the assets, and (2) misaligned incentives between the principal and agent that allow the agent to utilise the principal's assets opportunistically. It is argued that contract design can address agency problems by aligning the incentives of the agent with those of the principal (i.e. shareholder wealth maximisation or debt repayment) as efficiently as possible.[6]

2.4   Another form of the agency problem arises in what Arrow classified as *hidden action* and *hidden information*.[7] According to Arrow, if the agent's actions are not observable, it is impossible to design a contract based on these actions, and, similarly, if the agent's decision-making is based on information that is only available to the agent, the principal cannot then infer the agent's actions based on available information. Arrow's theory of hidden action and hidden information reveals the limitations of using contract design to address agency problems, as perfect alignment of interests is very difficult (if not impossible) to achieve because the unobservable actions of the agent cannot be perfectly inferred based on observable information. For example, the agent's amount of effort or level of output cannot provide an adequate measure of performance because other random factors may contribute to the level of output independent of the agent's effort.

2.5   The agency problems that arise from hidden action and hidden information manifest themselves in the form of *moral hazard* (involving hidden action) and adverse selection (involving hidden information). Moral hazard can be defined as actions of economic agents to maximise their own utility to the detriment of others in situations where they do not bear the full costs or consequences of their actions. This may be due to the uncertainty and incomplete or restricted nature of contracts which prevent the assignment of full costs or benefits to the responsible agent. Moral hazard is a form of *post-contractual* opportunism that involves the agent choosing to pursue his or her self-interest at the expense of the principal by deviating from the course of conduct that the principal would prefer the agent to take. Moral hazard therefore is associated with *hidden action* in a contractual

---

5   See Chapter 4 'Capital Adequacy and Risk Management' and Chapter 5 'Bank Corporate Governance: Law and Regulation' in this volume.
6   See Ross SA, 'The Economic Theory of Agency: The Principal's Problem' (1973) 53 *American Economic Review* 2 134–139.
7   Arrow KJ, *Essays in the Theory of Risk-Bearing* (Markham Publishing Co. 1971).

relationship. Hidden action involves actions that cannot be accurately observed or inferred by others, thus making it impossible to condition contracts on these actions.

2.6 *Adverse selection* is another form of the agency problem that applies to a market in which the products or services of varying qualities are exchanged, and only sellers know the quality of the goods. In contrast to moral hazard, adverse selection refers to a form of pre-contractual opportunism which arises when the agent has private information about something which affects the net benefit that the principal derives from the bargain. Adverse selection is associated therefore with *hidden information*. This means that the agent has some information (possibly incomplete) which determines the appropriateness of the agent's actions, but which is imperfectly observable by others. For instance, a borrower is likely to know a lot more about their ability to repay a loan than the lending bank. This means that high-risk borrowers can exploit this informational advantage by portraying themselves as low-risk borrowers in order to obtain improved conditions on a bank loan.

2.7 The traditional principal–agent framework has been used to analyse bank risk-taking and how the incentives of shareholders, creditors and managers can diverge and thus undermine allocative efficiency and potentially impose significant costs on society.[8] The main characteristic of the agency problem is that some managers have the incentive and opportunity to engage in unobserved behaviour that is costly to the firm and to society.[9] The agency problem can result in different risk preferences for bank managers as compared to shareholders or creditors, such as depositors, and other stakeholders including employees, borrowers and other customers. Overcoming agency problems involves reducing information asymmetries between these parties and aligning their incentives through contracting to mitigate the potential social costs. This can be difficult, however, because of transaction costs and institutional barriers that prevent the parties from contracting in an optimal manner with each other to allocate the risk burden more efficiently.[10] Banking regulation has therefore been considered necessary to overcome the transaction costs and institutional barriers to more efficient contracting by ensuring that the incentives of these groups are properly aligned and that adequate information is available to shareholders, creditors and other stakeholders in order to enhance their monitoring of institutions and individuals to achieve sustainable profitability of the bank and minimise the negative externalities for society.

2.8 Moreover, as discussed above, agency problems can develop within the context of the bank playing the role of external monitor over the activities of third parties to whom it grants loans. When banks make loans, they are concerned about two issues: the interest rate they receive on loans and the risk level of the loan. The loan's interest rate, however, has two effects. First, it distinguishes between potential borrowers (adverse selection), and second, it affects the actions

---

8 Stiglitz JE, 'Principal–Agent', in Eatwell J, Milgate M and Newman P (eds), *The New Palgrave: Allocation, Information and Markets* (Macmillan Press 1989), 241.

9 See Allen F and Gale D, *Comparing Financial Systems* (MIT Press 1997), 93–97.

10 Coase RH, 'The Problem of Social Cost', in Coase RH, *The Firm, The Market, and the Law* (University of Chicago Press 1992), 118.

of the borrowers (moral hazard). These effects derive from the hidden information present in the loan markets and hence the interest rate may not be the efficient rate to clear the market, as higher-risk borrowers will drive lower-risk borrowers out of the market over time.[11]

2.9 Another important challenge posed by agency problems within financial institutions concerns how hidden action (moral hazard) and hidden information (adverse selection) problems can also result in market failures that can lead to widespread financial instability and systemic crises in the banking sector. This means that banking regulation should be concerned not only with creating an incentive framework that induces managers and employees to achieve the objectives of bank principals, such as shareholders (e.g. wealth maximisation) and creditors (debt repayment), but also to enable the regulator to balance the interests of the various societal stakeholder groups that are affected by bank risk-taking and to reduce the social costs that are inevitably associated with poorly managed banks.

2.10 The foregoing illustrates the wide range of potential agency problems in financial institutions involving several major stakeholder groups including, but not limited to, shareholders, creditors, including depositors (see Chapter 7), management (see Chapter 4) and supervisory bodies. Agency problems arise because responsibility for decision-making (and the risks associated with these decisions) is directly or indirectly delegated from one stakeholder group to another in situations where objectives between stakeholder groups differ and where complete information which would allow further control to be exerted over the decision-maker is not readily available. As discussed above, examples of agency problems in banking institutions involve shareholders and management, creditors and shareholders, and supervisors and bank shareholders. While that perspective underpins the major features of the design of regulatory structures – capital adequacy (Chapter 4), corporate and risk governance (Chapter 5) – incentive problems that arise because of conflicts of interests between bank shareholders and management were a focus of recent regulatory reforms. It is suggested in Chapter 4 that such a focus on conflicts between bank shareholders and management is not sufficient to address the substantial negative externalities posed by bank risk-taking and that a new theory of bank governance is necessary to address systemic risks in banking and financial markets.

II EXTERNALITIES AND SYSTEMIC RISK

2.11 As discussed above, the problem of imperfect information in markets can result in significant social costs, also known as *negative externalities*. Externalities are spillover costs from a private transaction that affect third parties who were not directly involved in the transaction. The theoretical foundation in neo-classical economics for externalities was

11 See Akerlof GA, 'The Market for "Lemons": Quality Uncertainty and the Market Mechanism' (1970) 84 *The Quarterly Journal of Economics* 3 488–500. See also Stiglitz JE and Weiss A, 'Credit Rationing in Markets with Imperfect Information' (1981) 71 *American Economic Review* 3 393–410, 409.

originally set forth by Adam Smith in the *Wealth of Nations*; he asserted that the 'invisible hand' of the market would lead self-interested individuals promoting their own economic welfare to promote the total welfare of society without intending to do so.

> He generally, indeed, neither intends to promote the public interest, nor knows how much he is promoting it. By preferring the support of domestic to that of foreign industry, he intends only his own security; and by directing that industry in such a manner as its produce may be of the greatest value, he intends only his own gain, and he is in this, as in many other cases, led by an invisible hand to promote an end which was no part of his intention. Nor is it always the worse for the society that it was not part of it.[12]

Smith's idea was that an increase in the economic welfare of private entrepreneurs should be taken as equivalent to an increase in total societal welfare. He recognised, however, that the 'invisible hand' can break down in the presence of externalities or public goods that could cause a divergence between economic welfare and total welfare, thereby justifying some type of corrective intervention.

2.12 Arthur C. Pigou later built on Smith by making the important distinction between marginal private net product and marginal social net product.[13] Marginal private net product was the individual or private return that resulted from the pursuit of economic self-interests, which in a competitive equilibrium equalises among firms and individuals. Marginal social net product was the collective benefit or cost that is the private product plus or minus the indirect benefits or costs at the margin that are not internalised in the calculation of private net product. Pigou used the example of the manufacturer's smoking chimney that imposes the uncompensated loss of welfare, of ill-health and soiled laundry on third parties who live near the chimney. According to Pigou, the social cost, as measured in money, of the manufacturer's marginal unit of output exceeds his private cost of production by making necessary the provision of additional health care and cleaning services for third parties who have suffered the spillover or negative externality of dirty smoke. Because the manufacturer does not internalise the full cost of its production, it will produce and pollute more than what would have been socially optimal if the manufacturer had fully been internalising its costs of production.

2.13 Pigou's solution for requiring the manufacturer to absorb the social costs caused by the dirty smoke was to impose 'an appropriately devised system of bounties and duties' on the items produced by the manufacturer where the marginal social costs of production exceeded the private costs.[14] However, in devising such a bounty, duty or tax, he recognised that 'the practical difficulty of determining the right rates of bounty and of duty would be extraordinarily great'. Indeed, the difficulty of determining an efficient 'bounty' and 'duty'

---

12 Smith A, *The Wealth of Nations* (first published 1776, Bantam Dell 2003), 572.
13 Pigou AC, *The Economics of Welfare* (Macmillan and Co. 1920).
14 Pigou AC, *Socialism versus Capitalism* (Macmillan and Co. 1937), 41–42.

to equalise private and social costs was formidable and was criticised by Coase as poten-tially creating other social costs or introducing further distortions (or costs) to the market.[15] Coase argued that it would be less socially costly to allow the third parties who had suffered the costs of the dirty smoke to bargain with the polluting firm to agree a price that could compensate the polluting firm for not polluting as much, thereby using contracting to find a socially optimal amount of pollution rather than the distortionary 'bounties' and 'duties' proposed by Pigou.

2.14 Nevertheless, the notion of externalities or social costs is useful for explaining why financial regulation is necessary to control systemic financial risks. The International Monetary Fund and Financial Stability Board have defined systemic risk as the risk of threats to financial stability that impair the functioning of a large part of the financial system with significant adverse effect on the broader economy.[16] The financial system includes banks, other financial intermediaries, financial markets and payment and settlement systems. The European Central Bank (ECB) defined systemic risk as the 'trigger that causes massive damages to the financial system and the broader economy through the development of severe threats within the financial system or break-down of a financial institution'.[17] The European Systemic Risk Board (ESRB) has defined systemic risk as 'the risk of disruption in the financial system with the potential to have serious negative consequences for the internal market and the real economy'.[18] Systemic risk has also been defined as 'the clear and present danger that problems in financial institutions can be transmitted rapidly to other institutions or markets, inflicting damage on those institutions, their customers, and ultimately, the economy at large'.[19] Similarly, the Group of 10 (G10) advanced industrial countries defined systemic risk as 'the risk that an event will trigger a loss of economic value or confidence in, and attendant increases in uncertainty about, a substantial portion of the financial system that is serious enough to quite probably have significant adverse effects on the real economy'.[20]

15   Coase (n 10), 118–120.
16   International Monetary Fund, 'Global Financial Stability Report – Navigating the Financial Challenges Ahead' (October 2009) World Economic and Financial Surveys www.imf.org/external/pubs/ft/gfsr/2009/02/pdf/ text.pdf accessed 21 February 2018; European Central Bank, 'Recent Developments in the Balance Sheets of the Eurosystem, the Federal Reserve System and the Bank of Japan', Monthly Bulletin (October 2009) www.ecb .europa.eu/pub/pdf/other/art2_mb200910_pp81-94en.pdf accessed 21 February 2018. See also European Central Bank, 'The Concept of Systemic Risk' (June 2009) Financial Stability Review www.ecb.europa.eu/pub/pdf/ other/financialstabilityreview200906en.pdf accessed 21 February 2018.
17   Trichet J-C, 'Systemic Risk' (speech at the European Central Bank, 10 December 2009) www.ecb.europa.eu/ pub/pdf/other/financialstabilityreview200906en.pdf accessed 21 February 2018.
18   Regulation (EU) No. 1092/2010 of the European Parliament and of the Council of 24 November 2010 on European Union macro-prudential oversight of the financial system and establishing a European Systemic Risk Board OJ L 331.
19   Gart A, *Regulation, Deregulation, Regulation: The Future of Banking, Insurance, and Securities Industries* (Wiley 1994).
20   G10, 'Report on Consolidation in the Financial Sector' (January 2001), 126 www.bis.org/publ/gten05.pdf accessed 21 February 2018.

2.15 Systemic risk can originate in any part of the financial system and is especially associated with institutions involved in maturity transformations (borrowing short and lending long) that have high leverage and rely predominantly on short-term financing for day-to-day operations. The adverse impact on the economy of systemic risk is generally attributed to disruptions in inter-bank payment systems and credit flows leading to substantial deterioration in asset values. Systemic risk arises from negative externalities associated with excessive financial risk-taking that can have severe disruptions in the financial system and that can result in substantial shocks on the broader economy. If there were no spillover effects, or negative externalities, there would be, arguably, no role for public policy intervention in regulating systemic risk. However, precisely because a systemic risk event (i.e. banking crisis) is defined as very likely to induce undesirable real economic effects, such as substantial reductions in output and employment, in the absence of appropriate policy responses, policymakers are concerned about systemic risk and how it can impose substantial externalities on the economy.[21] In this definition, a financial disruption that does not have a high probability of causing a significant disruption of real economic activity is not a systemic risk event.

2.16 Systemic financial risks are analogous to dirty smoke, and regulating it to limit the costs it imposes on society is an important policy objective. The crisis demonstrated that, given the nature of financial institutions' business models and the increasingly complicated and internationally linked financial markets, the transmission of risk can become an immediate financial stability threat. From domestic to international markets, economies are not immune from financial sector risks. Risks that are systemic affect the economy and society at many levels. For example, as a result of the global economic slowdown of 2008–2010,[22] less credit was made available to the general public due to the deterioration of financial institutions' balance sheets. There was an effect on household wealth due to job losses and unaffordable mortgages. Governments bailed out financial institutions with taxpayer money and there was a decrease in household spending and consumption (which in turn affects other sectors of an economy). Overall, systemic crises put the economy in severe distress and led to a general economic slowdown. This was demonstrated by the negative impact on global economic growth of the financial crisis of 2007–2008 (see Figure 2.1).

2.17 After the crisis, the social cost of systemic risk required policy intervention to limit its spillover effects. Mitigating the impact of systemic crises became the focal point of the regulatory agenda. The main challenge for policymakers and regulators is what type of regulatory instruments, including taxes, should be used to incentivise financial institutions to internalise the costs associated with their risk-taking, and how regulators can monitor and identify the accumulation of financial risks that pose systemic risks to the financial

---

21   Ibid. The G10 further observes that '[s]ystemic risk events can be sudden and unexpected, or the likelihood of their economic occurrence can build up through time in the absence of appropriate policy responses'.
22   See Figure 2.1.

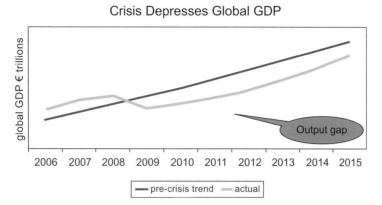

Figure 2.1 Crisis depresses global GDP. This shows the significant drop in economic growth between late 2007 and mid-2009 coinciding with the onset of the global credit and financial crisis that began around August 2007 and reached an apex in September 2008 with the collapse of Lehman Brothers bank.

system and the economy. When risk-taking costs are not internalised, society will have to pick up these costs with taxpayers' money. Before the crisis, there was a lack of appreciation by policymakers, regulators and bankers about the potential social costs of bank risk-taking and how this contributes to systemic risks. The broad goal of regulation and policy is not to eliminate risk-taking, but rather to require banks and other financial market actors to price their risk-taking efficiently (i.e. through equity finance and collateral requirements) to control and limit the associated costs for third parties (society) who are not directly involved in the risk-taking.

2.18 Although it is difficult to identify the actual or estimated cost of financial institutions' risk-taking, it is submitted that it is still important to take it into account and ask this fundamental question: is such risk-taking socially appropriate? And does its overall benefit to society outweigh the harm it will cause? The banking community neglected this line of discussion. However, as a result of the crisis, a combination of regulatory focus, public pressure and political processes revealed the social cost imposed by systemic risk. Prior to the crisis, discussions on banking and banking regulation were limited to those who were directly concerned (i.e. financial institutions, their representative bodies and regulators). There was inadequate representation of societal stakeholders who were directly affected by excessive risk-taking.

2.19 Therefore, it is argued that the definition of systemic risk should include a reference to the social cost that systemic risk imposes on society as a whole. Such costs can take the form of direct taxpayer financial support for a failing institution, while other costs are incurred indirectly by the economy, as a whole, as measured by economic slowdowns. It is suggested that systemic risk should be defined to include the societal impact and economic costs imposed by excessive risk-taking by financial institutions and other entities, and such risks can be propagated by the interlinkages between institutions and entities across the financial system. On that basis, systemic risk can be considered as risk that can cause severe damage to the financial system through its potential to expose the economy and the public to excessive risk and thereby impose severe costs on the economy and society as a whole.

2.20 The sole justification for regulating systemic risk is maximising economic efficiency by limiting the negative externalities associated with financial risk-taking. Without regulation, the externalities caused by systemic risk would amount to a tragedy of the commons, as the motivation of market participants is to protect themselves but not the financial system or commons. Thus, even if market participants were able to act collectively to protect the financial market commons by controlling systemic risk, they might not choose to do so as the externalities of systemic failure include social costs that are not fully incurred by market participants but, rather, are imposed on other third parties in society at large.

2.21 The financial crisis of 2007–2008 demonstrated that systemic risk can threaten global financial stability, and that systemic risk is not confined to the banking sector, as it can also arise in securities and derivatives markets. Indeed, during the crisis, systemic risks stemmed from non-bank financial institutions and from complex financial instruments that traditionally fell outside the regulatory perimeter of the banking sector. Furthermore, systemic risks are not bounded by jurisdictional frontiers; they have a tendency to spread rapidly across geographical borders. The dichotomy between global markets and institutions and national law, on the one hand, and national policies, on the other, is particularly acute in the management of systemic risk and in the design of adequate institutional and regulatory solutions to deal with its negative spillover effects.

III THE ECONOMIC IMPORTANCE OF BANKS AND THE COSTS OF CRISES

2.22 Banks play an important economic role as they, as financial intermediaries, aid in economic growth by providing funds to those engaged in the production of goods and services vital to economic growth.[23] They are a source of funds for many businesses and without banks commercial activities would grind to a halt.[24] Although the importance of banks as a source of credit varies between countries depending on whether they are bank-led or capital market-led financial systems, a stable banking system is considered for most economies to be essential for economic growth and development and for the smooth functioning of the financial system. By monitoring the repayment of loans, banks exert sound governance over funded firms, they foster innovation and growth by lending to entrepreneurs, they also

---

23   Levine R, 'Finance and Growth: Theory and Evidence' (2004) NBER Working Paper No. 10766; Brownbridge M and Kirkpatrick C, 'Financial Regulation in Developing Countries' (2000) Finance and Development Research Program Working Papers Series, Paper No. 12/2006.
24   Goodhart CAE, 'The Macro-Prudential Authority: Powers, Scope and Accountability' (2011) LSE Financial Markets Group Paper Series, Special Paper 203.

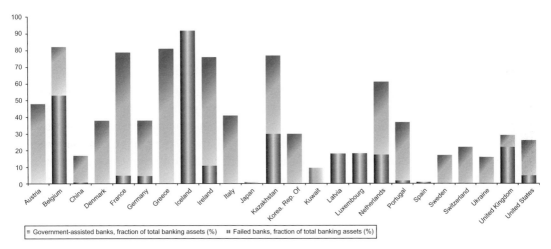

Figure 2.2 Bank failures and interventions in selected countries.
Source: Laeven and Valencia (2012)

allocate and mobilise savings efficiently by allocating capital to those endeavours with the highest expected social return.[25] Moreover, central bank liquidity and lending facilities allow banks to create credit that can support large lending projects in the economy but which can have negative economic effects if left unchecked. The power to create credit allows banks to provide liquidity to the broader economy and banking system; but excessive liquidity resulting in too much money chasing too few goods can lead to inflation, necessitating the intervention of the central bank by withdrawing excess liquidity through open market operations.[26]

2.23 Studies have shown that economies with strong financial institutions or banks record greater levels of growth than those with weak banks.[27] The UK economy is an example of how the banking sector can contribute to economic growth. In 2015, the UK financial services and insurance sectors accounted for 6.5 per cent of UK GDP, the highest of all G7 economies.[28] However, the ability of banks to aid in economic growth or mobilise and allocate savings efficiently is largely dependent on how well capitalised they are and the liquidity of their balance sheets. Sound banks promote the efficient allocation of resources, the efficiency of investment and economic growth in an economy, while weak banks slow down growth and put a strain on economic resources as public funds are utilised to bail them out of crises or to pay off depositors in order to maintain confidence in the financial system. Figure 2.2 depicts

25   Levine R, 'Bank Regulation and Supervision' (2005) NBER Reporter, Research Summary Fall 2005.
26   Spong K, *Banking Regulation: Its Purposes, Implementation, and Effects* (5th edn, Federal Reserve Bank of Kansas City Division of Supervision and Risk Management 2000).
27   Favara G, 'An Empirical Reassessment of the Relationship Between Finance and Growth' (2003) IMF Working Paper WP/03/123 www.imf.org/external/pubs/ft/wp/2003/wp03123.pdf accessed 21 February 2018.
28   Rhodes C, 'Financial Services: Contribution to the UK Economy' (25 April 2018) House of Commons briefing paper 6193, 5, http://researchbriefings.files.parliament.uk/documents/SN06193/SN06193.pdf accessed 18 March 2018.

the substantial costs of intervening to bail out banks as a proportion of total bank assets for the advanced developed countries affected by the crisis of 2007–2008.

2.24 Subsequent studies show that the negative externality associated with a systemic financial crisis can be measured by output losses and fiscal costs to resolve failed financial institutions. Laeven and Valencia (2012) show that fiscal costs and output losses vary across country and the mix of policy responses is an important determinant of outcomes.[29] Regulatory and policy responses include recapitalisation, separating the institution into a good bank with viable assets and a bad bank with unviable assets, persuading other banks or investors to purchase the viable assets and/or assume some of the liabilities of an ailing bank, and restructuring or bailing in creditor claims to absorb a bank's losses as a going concern. The variety of policy responses to a systemic banking crisis demonstrates the complexity of the challenge for the regulator and the risk that some responses may be inappropriate for particular institutions and might even result in greater social costs for the banking system and the economy. This is why some regulators and policymakers are reluctant to deal promptly with banks experiencing financial distress in the hope that they will ultimately recover if market conditions improve.

2.25 Banking crises tend to occur in waves and within each of these waves are regional clusters associated with contagion effects,[30] suggesting that systemic risk is not constant over time. This can be demonstrated through the range of crises beginning with crisis activity in the early 1980s, the four clusters of crises in the 1990s involving the Nordic banking system, Eastern European transitional economies, the Mexican banking crisis (1994–1995), and the East Asian crisis (1998–1999). In the early 2000s until 2007, financial markets were relatively calm but experienced an asset price bubble that was generated by an excessive supply of credit and leverage that was channelled through the wholesale asset-backed securities markets and which culminated in a global financial crisis. The latter crisis was particularly virulent because of its overreliance on asset securitisation as a vehicle to generate an increased supply of credit and leverage and to spread risks through the financial system, thereby creating cross-exposures among financial institutions.[31]

2.26 The justification for governmental intervention in banking regulation is strongly linked to the economic importance of banks, systemic issues and consumer protection. Sheng, for instance, cites the ability of banks to create money, the involvement of banks in credit allocation, fostering competition and innovation through the prevention of cartels, consumer protection and banks' vulnerability to crisis and collapse as the main rationales for

---

29 Laeven L and Valencia F, 'Systemic Banking Crises Database: An Update' (2012) IMF Working Paper WP/12/163 www.imf.org/en/Publications/WP/Issues/2016/12/31/Systemic-Banking-Crises-Database-An-Update-26015 accessed 21 February 2018.
30 Reinhart CM and Rogoff KS, *This Time is Different: Eight Centuries of Financial Folly* (Princeton University Press 2009).
31 Shin HS, 'Securitisation and Financial Stability' (2009) 119 *Economic Journal* 536 309–332.

bank regulation.[32] The economic consequence of bank failures can be viewed as further justification for regulation, as bank failures are costly and dissipate vital economic resources that should have been channelled into more productive ventures. Since most governments undertake the responsibility of preventing bank failures or rescuing ailing banks by acting as a lender of last resort and operating a deposit insurance scheme, it's only natural that they regulate banks to reduce the potential for a call on the deposit insurance funds.

2.27 Bank failures impact negatively on a country's gross domestic product (GDP) and fiscal position as taxpayer money is used to recapitalise and restructure ailing financial institutions. In a cross-country survey involving Indonesia, Chile, Thailand and Uruguay, it was discovered that governments spent an average of about 13 per cent of GDP restoring financial systems after banking crises,[33] while more generally banking problems cost developing and transition economies between 1980 and 1998 roughly $250 billion.[34]

IV THEORIES OF FINANCIAL REGULATION

2.28 Corporate finance theory holds that in a perfectly competitive market without market failures, bankruptcy and taxes, profit-maximising banks and other financial intermediaries would provide credit to and invest in all sustainable economic projects that have positive net present values, and that the capital structure of the firm (its mix of debt and equity) is irrelevant to the firm's value.[35] In the real world, however, there are bankruptcy, taxes and market failures that can lead firms to take on excessive amounts of debt resulting in negative externalities for the market and undermining the efficient operation of financial markets. The public interest theory of regulation holds that policy or regulatory intervention is justified to manage or control the negative externalities that arise from these market distortions. Evidence suggests that market discipline, on its own, cannot adequately control the externalities in financial markets associated with excessive financial risk-taking.[36]

2.29 In contrast, Stigler (1971) set forth what became known as the private interest theory of regulation, which postulated that regulation is a commodity demanded by consumers and producers and supplied by a regulatory agency. According to Stigler, regulation is designed and operated by industry primarily for its own benefit. This private interest theory or

---

32   Sheng A, *From Asian to Global Financial Crisis: An Asian Regulator's View of Unfettered Finance in the 1990s and 2000s* (Cambridge University Press 2009), 23–26.
33   Honohan P and Klingebiel D, 'Controlling the Fiscal Costs of Banking Crises' (September 2010) World Bank Policy Research Working Paper WPS 244 http://documents.worldbank.org/curated/en/109971468741329122/pdf/multi-page.pdf accessed 21 February 2018.
34   Ibid.
35   See Modigliani F and Miller MH, 'The Cost of Capital, Corporation Finance, and the Theory of Investment' (1958) 48 *American Economic Review* 3 261–297.
36   See Basel Committee on Banking Supervision, The Joint Forum, 'Review of the Differentiated Nature and Scope of Financial Regulation, Key Issues and Recommendations' (January 2010), 85.

capture theory of regulation was further developed by Pelzman (1976) who showed how industries could use regulation to capture rents from the public sector. For producers, the cost benefit of lobbying is favourable when the government can produce subsidies (i.e. bank bailouts), reduce competition by restricting entry or decrease production costs. Bank regulators could provide a subsidy for certain types of activity by, for instance, reducing capital requirements for bank loans that are hedged with credit default swaps that are AAA rated. The probability of 'collusion' and rent redistribution between the regulatory agency and interest groups creates associations among politicians, regulatory agencies and regulated firms that reward special interests that are often prejudicial to the public interest.

2.30 More recently, legal scholars have joined the debate over the theory of financial regulation. One view holds that 'four interwoven propositions' underlie the legal theory of finance: (1) that financial markets are made up of private contracts and public rules; (2) that the public rules (and associated legal institutions) support these contracts and their enforcement; (3) that the financial system is inherently hierarchical in that the only true lenders of last resort are sovereign states that control their own currency and are able to issue debt, in that currency and rights and obligations under contracts, private rules and public laws to which market participants are subject may not be strictly enforced if, in a crisis, non-enforcement is needed to protect the financial system; (4) and that while these rules and laws are necessary to support the development of financial markets, they are also a potentially significant source of financial instability.[37]

2.31 These theories suggest that policy and regulatory intervention, if not calibrated properly, can produce its own distortions in the market that can result in further externalities and misallocations of capital and investment. A careful combination of market innovation and regulatory frameworks that suit institutional and market structures may be necessary for controlling externalities while encouraging a reallocation of capital through financial intermediaries to its most efficient use in the economy.

V FINANCIAL STABILITY AND THE BANKING SYSTEM

2.32 Monetary and financial stability are important governmental objectives and fundamental economic goals.[38] Defining financial stability is difficult as it encompasses several disparate elements, but it has been defined as the 'absence of stresses that have the potential to cause measurable economic harm beyond a strictly limited group of customers and

---

37 Elliott DJ, Feldberg G and Lehnert A, 'The History of Cyclical Macroprudential Policy in the United States' (2013) Federal Reserve Board of Governors, Finance and Economics Discussion Series No. 2013–2029, 2, 5 www.federalreserve.gov/pubs/feds/2013/201329/201329pap.pdf accessed 21 February 2018.
38 Spong (n 26) and Lastra LM, *International Financial and Monetary Law* (2nd edn, Oxford University Press 2015), 59.

counterparties'.[39] Financial stability has also been defined as 'a condition in which the financial system would be able to withstand shocks, without giving way to cumulative processes, which impair the allocation of savings to investment opportunities and the processing of payments in the economy'.[40] Defining financial stability is difficult, as it encompasses several disparate elements that are typically the subject of regulatory control and oversight by supervisory authorities.[41]

2.33 Financial stability and stable banks are interrelated concepts with both impacting equally on the stability of the other. The presence of financial stability enhances the process of intermediation and the efficient allocation of resources, while the presence of unsound banks in an economy threatens financial stability. It is however ironic that long periods of financial stability often induce greater risk-taking by banks. Banks all over the world, especially in the developed countries, buoyed by long periods of financial stability prior to the 2007–2008 crisis, took risks in a manner that was unprecedented.[42] The subprime mortgage loan crisis in the US is an example of how financial innovation and technology could create a seemingly efficient and stable network for transferring credit risks from the originating bank balance sheets in one country through securitisation and complex derivative instruments to investors in other markets under the mistaken belief that the risks had been adequately measured and controlled, and were not a threat to financial stability.[43]

2.34 The substantial costs imposed on economies by banking and financial crises demonstrates that the overriding objective of banking regulation should be to safeguard financial stability and build resilience to financial shocks, wherever they may come from, and provide a sustainable source of credit, savings products and payment services to the broader economy. Banking regulation can potentially play an important role in mitigating the institutional and market impediments to the banking sector's ability to provide adequate capital and liquidity for the economy so that it can grow sustainably. Economic theory holds that policy and regulatory intervention in the banking sector is justified by market failures, which can arise from negative externalities resulting from moral hazard and asymmetric information, and competitive distortions.[44] Evidence suggests that market discipline, on its own, cannot adequately control the externalities in financial markets

---

39   Crockett A, 'Why is Financial Stability a Goal of Public Policy?' (1997) Proceedings – Economic Policy Symposium – Jackson Hole, Federal Reserve Bank of Kansas City, 9–10.

40   See Schioppa TP, 'Central Banks and Financial Stability: Exploring a Land in Between' (October 2002), European Central Bank Second Central Banking Conference 'The Transformation of the European Financial System', 269–310 www.ecb.europa.eu/pub/pdf/other/transformationeuropeanfinancialsystemen.pdf accessed 21 February 2018.

41   Lastra (n 3), 92.

42   See *The Economist*, 'Financial Stability: The Better You Do, the Greater the Risk' (*The Economist*, 26 April 2007) www.economist.com/node/9086520 accessed 18 March 2018.

43   See US Financial Crisis Inquiry Commission, 'Financial Crisis Inquiry Report – Final Report of the National Commission on the Causes of the Financial Crisis in the United States' Official Government Edition (January 2011), 77–91 www.gpo.gov/fdsys/pkg/GPO-FCIC/pdf/GPO-FCIC.pdf accessed 21 February 2018. See also *The Economist*, 'Subprime Lending: Rising Damp' (*The Economist*, 8 May 2007) www.economist.com/node/8829612 accessed 18 March 2018.

44   See Basel Committee on Banking Supervision, The Joint Forum (n 36), 85.

associated with excessive banking and financial risk-taking. Accordingly, policy or regulatory intervention may be necessary to prevent a misallocation of resources to unsustainable economic activity that relies on excessive financial risk-taking and to support a reallocation of capital to sustainable economic activity. Policy intervention, however, if not calibrated properly, can also produce its own distortions in the market which can result in further externalities and misallocations of bank capital and investment. A careful combination of market innovation and policy frameworks that suit national circumstances may be desirable for designing an effective and efficient banking regulation framework. In this way, banking policy can support the efficient operation of the economy by encouraging banks to harness more credit and investment for profitable and sustainable economic activity.

VI CHANGING PHILOSOPHY OF FINANCIAL REGULATION

2.35 A major weakness in financial regulation prior to the crisis was that banking supervision and regulation were disproportionately focused on bank balance sheets and less concerned with systemic risks across the broader financial system. There was a conventional view that the shifting of risks through off-balance sheet entities, through the use of credit default swaps and securitisation structures, reduced banking sector instability because other market participants (i.e. long-term institutional investors) were willing to invest in bank credit and absorb the related risks. The spreading of risk throughout the wholesale securitisation and structure finance markets was viewed to be beneficial for financial stability and was thought to lead to a more resilient financial system.[45] The micro-prudential focus on institutions, however, failed to take account of the systemic risks that had arisen across the financial system because of bank involvement and exposure to the securitisation and derivatives markets.

2.36 The micro-prudential approach to regulation and supervision was predominantly concerned with the stability of individual financial institutions and their responses to risks that are external to their operations ('exogenous' risks).[46] However, by focusing on individual institutions, such forms of regulation tend to ignore the impact of individual institutions' risk-taking on the broader financial system. For example, the micro-prudential approach often failed to incorporate into regulatory assessments the impact of a bank's size, degree of leverage and interconnectedness with the rest of the financial system. Moreover, bank supervisors generally assumed that banks were primarily exposed to exogenous risks;

---

45   See International Monetary Fund, 'Global Financial Stability Report – Market Developments and Issues' (April 2006), www.imf.org/en/Publications/GFSR/Issues/2016/12/31.pdf accessed 18 May 2018. See critique in Alexander K, Eatwell J, Persaud A and Reoch R, 'Financial Supervision and Crisis Management in the EU' (2007) Policy Study IP/A/ECON/IC/2007-069, Brussels: European Parliament, 5–7 www.augurproject.eu/IMG/pdf/ JEatwellEtAl_FinancialSupervisionYCrisisManagement_EUreport-2.pdf accessed 21 February 2018.
46   See Padoa-Schioppa T, Regulating Finance (Oxford University Press, 2004) 116–118.

that is, risks that are generated externally to the bank's operations, and that any change, for example, in their credit or market risk exposures, would require them to make balance sheet adjustments (i.e. by buying or selling assets) in a more or less similar manner.[47]

2.37 Although each bank, individually, might be adjusting its balance sheet risk in a prudent manner, the cumulative effect of all banks acting in the same manner would be to increase system-wide risks across the financial sector. This could have the effect of exacerbating a market upturn or downturn. Indeed, the Turner Review (2009),[48] published in the aftermath of the crisis, argued that this sort of regulation mistakenly and fatally relied on an underlying philosophy and an ill-placed faith in market prices and estimations of bank capital as accurate indicators of risk. In seeking to focus their risk assessment at the level of the individual institution, regulators failed to take account of a number of internal amplifying processes which propagated the effects of one institution's risk-taking to other institutions' balance sheets.

2.38 The financial crisis demonstrated weaknesses in the micro-prudential regulatory approach and the need for the supervisor to have broader oversight of risks across the financial system, the capacity to take measures (i.e. adjust capital requirements) that support the stability of the financial system as a whole, and to take into account the interconnectivity of financial institutions and their effects on the global economy in times of crisis.[49] Macro-prudential regulation consists of three main areas: (1) adjusting the application of regulatory rules to institutions according to developments in the broader economy (i.e. counter-cyclical capital requirements); (2) imposing economy-wide controls on the financial sector to limit aggregate risk-taking (i.e. capital controls to limit foreign exchange risk or system-wide leverage limits); and (3) prudential requirements for financial infrastructure or firms providing infrastructure services (i.e. capital requirements for derivative clearing houses).[50] After reviewing the growing literature on macro-prudential regulation, the British House of Lords Committee on Economic Affairs observed in a 2009 report that 'macro-prudential supervision is the analysis of trends and imbalances in the financial system and the detection of systemic risks' and '[t]he focus of macro-prudential supervision is the safety of the financial and economic system as a whole, the prevention of systemic risk, and [m]icro-prudential supervision is the day-to-day supervision of individual financial institutions and imbalances in the financial system and these different areas of macro-prudential regulation'.[51] What is

---

47   See discussion in Alexander et al. (n 45) 8–14.
48   Financial Services Authority, 'The Turner Review – A Regulatory Response to the Global Banking Crisis' (March 2009) www.fsa.gov.uk/pubs/other/turner_review.pdf accessed 21 February 2018.
49   See European Commission, 'Report of the High-Level Expert Group on Financial Supervision in the EU', chaired by Jacques de Larosière (25 February 2009) www.ec.europa.eu/internal_market/finances/docs/de_laro siere_report_en.pdf accessed 21 February 2018. See also FSA, The Turner Review (n 48).
50   Basel Committee on Banking Supervision, 'Macroprudential Policy Tools and Frameworks – Progress Report to G20' (October 2011) www.bis.org/publ/othp17.pdf accessed 21 January 2018.
51   See House of Lords European Union Committee, 'The Future of EU Financial Regulation and Supervision' (17 June 2009), 14th Report of Session 2008–2009, Vol. 1 www.publications.parliament.uk/pa/ld200809/ ldselect/ldeucom/106/106i.pdf accessed 21 February 2018.

clear in the macro-prudential regulatory literature thus far is the need to strike a balance between macro-prudential regulation and micro-prudential regulation: both are necessary for maintaining financial stability and the conditions for sustainable economic growth.[52]

2.39 Despite the enthusiasm for macro-prudential regulation, it is certainly not a panacea, as it does not eliminate credit cycles in an economy. Nor does it address regulatory failure and government subsidies for banks and financial firms which create moral hazard and can induce unsustainable risk-taking. Ultimately, whereas the macro-prudential approach focuses on risks across the financial system as a whole, regulatory and policy measures must be introduced at the level of individual banks. The micro-prudential approach will continue therefore to be important – if not primary – and serve as the foundation for prudential financial regulation. Although it was largely rules-based and backward-looking prior to the crisis, it now will involve regulators asking themselves strategic questions about where risks are being shifted in the system, where capital can be found in the system to limit system-wide losses and how various forms of bank capital can be bailed-in to a bank restructuring.[53] This will be supplemented by macro-prudential supervision, which is largely forward-looking and involves the regulator monitoring risks across the system and markets and forecasting how they might evolve; it requires discretionary authority to take measures that address risks that may not threaten the market today but which may lead to substantial risks in the future.[54]

2.40 Despite their different approaches, micro-prudential regulation and supervision *and* macro-prudential regulation and supervision are not mutually exclusive and their tools will overlap considerably. Indeed, by recognising the links between micro-prudential and macro-prudential regulation, a more coherent and effective framework can be developed for mitigating excessive risk-taking and ensuring that banks hold adequate loss-absorbent capital.

VII INSTITUTIONAL DESIGN OF FINANCIAL REGULATION

2.41 The institutional design of financial regulation has historically differed between states and jurisdictions. Generally, four main supervisory models of financial regulation provide the canvas on which states develop their institutional structures of financial regulation and

---

52 See Padoa-Schioppa (n 46) 117–118. See also Ingves S, 'Challenges for the Design and Conduct of Macroprudential Policy' (speech at BOK-BIS Conference, Seoul, Korea, 18 January 2011) www.riksbank.se/Upload/Dokument_riksbank/Kat_publicerat/Tal/2011/110118e.pdf accessed 18 May 2018.

53 Bank of England Prudential Regulation Authority, 'The Prudential Regulation Authority's Approach to Banking Supervision' (April 2013), 5 www.bankofengland.co.uk/-/media/boe/files/prudential-regulation/approach/banking-approach-2013.pdf accessed 23 May 2018. See also Tucker P, 'Macro and Microprudential Supervision' (speech at British Bankers' Association Annual International Banking Conference, London, 29 June 2011) www.bis.org/review/r110704e.pdf accessed 18 May 2018.

54 See Goodhart CAE, 'Bank Resolution in Comparative Perspective: What Lessons for Europe?', in Goodhart CAE, Gabor D, Vestergaard J and Ertürk I (eds), *Central Banking at a Crossroads* (Anthem Press 2014).

supervision. These models are known as the *functional, institutional, integrated* and *Twin Peaks* approaches.[55] According to the *functional* approach, supervisors are responsible for the type of financial business or function of a firm or institution. Generally, the financial business is divided into banking, investment securities and products, and insurance and pensions. Different supervisors would have responsibility for different lines of financial business. Financial policymakers often define lines of business according to different sectors of the financial system, such as banking, investment securities and insurance. An institution authorised to write insurance policies would, for example, be supervised by the insurance regulator, whereas a financial institution authorised to provide a broader array of financial services – such as under the universal banking model – would be supervised by several regulators – generally, banking, securities and insurance supervisors, respectively.

2.42 In contrast, the *institutional* model of supervision attributes competences or powers to a regulatory body depending on the type of financial institution subject to supervision. The legal classification of the institution, for instance, whether it is defined as a bank or credit institution, investment or securities firm, or insurance company, determines which regulator has competence to supervise it. Where the institution is authorised to engage in a number of different financial activities, the regulator is empowered to supervise all these activities. This could result in complexity and difficulties for the regulator as it attempts to monitor and enforce certain behaviour that falls outside its traditional remit. The integrated approach generally involves a regulator with full or consolidated authority to supervise all financial institutions and approved individuals in the financial sector regarding their discharge of all functions in the financial services industry. The integrated model was popular in the 1990s, with many countries (i.e. UK, Korea, Japan and Germany) adopting it because of the perceived synergies that a single regulator would have in supervising financial markets that were becoming increasingly integrated and liberalised.[56] The *Twin Peaks* approach involves the division of supervisory powers between (usually) two regulators: one with responsibility for prudential supervision of all financial institutions and the financial stability objective, and the other responsible for conduct of business and investor and consumer protection in the marketing and sale of securities and other financial products. The Twin Peaks approach was first promoted in the 1990s but has become increasingly used by countries post-crisis because the financial crisis demonstrated the importance of having one regulatory authority solely devoted to financial stability and other prudential oversight issues and another regulator with responsibility for investor and consumer protection in light of the scandals involving mis-selling of investments and financial products.[57] The Twin Peaks approach has been made more complex by the

---

55   See Ferran E, 'Institutional Design: The Choices for National Systems', in Moloney N, Ferran E and Payne J (eds), *The Oxford Handbook of Financial Regulation* (Oxford University Press 2015), 99–128. See also G30, 'The Structure of Financial Supervision: Approaches and Challenges in a Global Marketplace' (Group of Thirty report, 2008).
56   Briault C, 'The Rationale for a Single National Financial Services Regulator', FSA Occasional Paper No. 2 (May 1999).
57   Taylor MW, 'Twin Peaks: A Regulatory Structure for the New Century' (London: CSFI, 1995); and Taylor MW, 'The Road from "Twin Peaks" and the Way Back' (2000) 1 *Connecticut Insurance Law Journal* 16 61.

splitting of the financial stability objective into micro-prudential supervision and macro-prudential supervision, the latter of which is often carried out by a central bank while the former is often the responsibility of a prudential supervision authority.[58] And in some countries the Twin Peaks approach has taken a new dimension as regulators are given some responsibility for ensuring competition in the financial services industry.

2.43 Although some states have adopted a version of one of the above models in practice, most states have experimented with hybrid institutional forms that are the product of historical evolution and the design of constitutional structures (i.e. federalism), and the design of economic and financial institutions.[59] States are continuing to experiment with different institutional structures of supervision post-crisis as they did prior to the crisis. No one size appears to be optimal for all countries, as financial and political systems vary between states. Although the crisis did not demonstrate conclusively what the optimal form of supervisory model should be, it did demonstrate the practical importance of having a strong central bank and finance ministry which is capable of injecting adequate liquidity and (if necessary) capital into banks to keep them solvent in order to prevent the financial system from imploding. For example, to prevent a total collapse of the British financial system, the UK had to part nationalise two of its largest banks and provide additional support for other smaller institutions. This involved financial sector interventions costing hundreds of billions of pounds.[60]

2.44 Although national regulatory bodies have been identified as being partly responsible for the crises because of weak supervision and inadequate regulations,[61] most regulatory reforms at the national level invested greater powers in national regulators – particularly in central banks – who now have a wider regulatory remit. Indeed, the move towards macro-prudential regulation has resulted in the empowerment of regulatory institutions so they have greater powers to monitor and collect data from across the financial system and to intervene where deemed necessary by applying supervisory measures and tools. Micro-prudential regulation has depended to a great extent on the collection and assessment of data from individual institutions and on applying supervisory measures to the risk-taking of individual institutions. In contrast, macro-prudential regulation and supervision will necessarily involve the collection and analysis of data from across the financial system and the application of measures based on assessments of risk across the system. Central banks are generally the main repositories of macroeconomic and financial data. This means that central banks will play some type of role in the macro-prudential supervision process – whether indirectly by providing data and analysis to the competent supervisory authorities or by acting directly as the competent authority themselves. In either case, central banks

58   Ibid.
59   Ferran (n 55), 100.
60   See HM Treasury, 'A New Approach to Financial Regulation: Judgment, Focus, Stability' (July 2010) Report presented by HM Treasury to Parliament by Command of Her Majesty www.frc.org.uk/directors/corporate-governance-and-stewardship/uk-corporate-governance-code accessed 7 January 2019.
61   See The Economist, 'The Origins of the Financial Crises: Crash Course' (The Economist, 7 September 2013) www.economist.com/news/schoolsbrief/21584534-effects-financial-crisis-are-still-being-felt-five-years-article accessed 18 March 2018.

will play a significant role in macro-prudential policy and in monitoring system-wide risks and by working closely with micro-prudential supervisors to ensure that risk-taking at the entity level does not cumulatively undermine financial stability across the system.

2.45 In Europe, the institutional restructuring of financial regulation and supervision has played a major role in macro-prudential regulatory reforms. The European Union has embarked on a major institutional restructuring of financial regulation by creating a European System of Financial Supervision (ESFS) consisting of three micro-prudential supervisory authorities – the European Banking Authority, the European Securities and Markets Authority and the European Insurance and Occupational and Pension Authority – and a European Systemic Risk Board (ESRB), which became operational in December 2010 in order to conduct macro-prudential oversight of the European financial system.[62] However, the ultimate authority over macro-prudential powers and policies rests with Member State authorities, though their macro-prudential monitoring and decision-making will be coordinated through their membership in the ESRB and other ESFS bodies.

2.46 The European System of Financial Supervision attempts to establish a more coherent institutional framework that links the ESRB's macro-prudential supervision and oversight function with the three European Supervisory Authorities' (ESAs) function for coordinating the harmonised implementation of EU financial law and the supervisory practices of Member States.[63] Indeed, this linkage is essential for building an efficient EU supervisory regime that allows Member States to exercise more effective oversight of individual firms and investors, while monitoring, measuring and issuing recommendations and warnings about systemic risk in the broader European financial system and across global financial markets. Moreover, the ESFS and the three ESAs will ensure that Member State regulatory and supervisory authorities can work more effectively together at the micro-prudential level to control and manage systemic risk and develop a harmonised regulatory code and implementation across all EU states.[64]

2.47 Regarding macro-prudential oversight, the ESRB's scientific committee conducts research and collects data from Member State central banks. Decision-making is vested in the ESRB Board whose members include the central bank governors of EU Member States. Bearing in mind the different jurisdictional domains of the EU Member States (consisting of Member State authorities and the monitoring function of the ESRB) and the euro area (for which the ECB has supervisory jurisdiction), responsibility for macro-prudential supervision is thus overlapping and not well coordinated between the ECB, national regulatory authorities and

---

62 Regulation (EU) No. 1092/2010 of the European Parliament and of the Council of 24 November 2010 on European Union macro-prudential oversight of the financial system and establishing a European Systemic Risk Board OJ L 331.

63 See Alexander K, 'Reforming European Financial Supervision: Adapting EU Institutions to Market Structures', *European Law Academy Forum* (2011) 229–252, 239–240 (ERA Trier DE).

64 Ibid., 243–244.

central banks, and the ESRB – whose powers are limited to issuing recommendations and warnings.[65]

2.48 The ESRB has set out five intermediate objectives that macro-prudential policy should aim to achieve. These intermediate objectives are (1) mitigating and preventing excessive credit growth and leverage; (2) mitigating and preventing excessive maturity mismatch and market illiquidity; (3) limiting direct and indirect exposure concentrations; (4) limiting the systemic impact of misaligned incentives with a view to reducing moral hazard; and (5) strengthening the resilience of financial infrastructures.[66] The ESRB considers that 'identifying intermediate objectives makes macro-prudential policy more operational, transparent and accountable and provides an economic basis for the election of instruments'.[67] These five objectives provide the basis for the development of the ESRB's future macro-prudential monitoring function.

A Redesigning UK Regulation

2.49 Following the crisis of 2007–2009, the UK undertook a review of the institutional structure of financial regulation and concluded that the former Tripartite model based on coordination among the Bank of England, the Financial Services Authority and the UK Treasury had failed to fulfil their responsibilities of protecting the financial system against systemic risks and fulfilling other regulatory objectives.[68] A newly elected government proposed draft legislation in 2010 that ultimately became the Financial Services Act 2012, which created a 'Twin Peaks' institutional structure for micro-prudential regulation consisting of a Prudential Regulation Authority, responsible for supervising individual banks, insurance firms and large investment banks, and a Financial Conduct Authority, responsible for investor protection, exchanges and market conduct.[69] The Prudential Regulation Authority (PRA) was based in the Bank of England, where a Financial Policy Committee (FPC) was established to be responsible for macro-prudential oversight of systemic risks and with the authority to adopt directives and recommendations to the two micro-prudential supervisors and to regulated institutions to take certain actions (i.e. apply counter-cyclical capital requirements) to achieve macro-prudential objectives.[70]

---

65 Ferran E and Alexander K, 'Can Soft Law Bodies be Effective? The Special Case of the European Systemic Risk Board' (2011) 12 *The European Law Review* 751–777, 759.

66 European Systemic Risk Board, Recommendation of the European Systemic Risk Board of 4 April 2013 on intermediate objectives and instruments of macro-prudential policy (ESRB/2013/1) OJ L 170, 15.06.2013 1 (4 April 2013) www.esrb.europa.eu/pub/pdf/recommendations/2013/ESRB_2013_1.en.pdf accessed 21 February 2018.

67 Ibid., para. 4.

68 See House of Lords, House of Commons, Joint Committee on the Draft Financial Services Bill, 'Draft Financial Services Bill – Session 2010–12' Report, together with formal minutes and appendices (December 2011), 9, para. 13 www.publications.parliament.uk/pa/jt201012/jtselect/jtdraftfin/236/236.pdf or www.publications.parliament.uk/pa/jt201012/jtselect/jtdraftfin/236/23602.htm accessed 21 February 2018.

69 See Financial Services Act 2012, section 6 'The New Regulators'. See also House of Lords, House of Commons, Joint Committee on the Draft Financial Services Bill (n 68), 7, para. 1.

70 See Financial Services Act 2012, section 4(1)(9A) and (9B) as well as the Financial Policy Committee website: www.bankofengland.co.uk/financial-stability accessed 18 March 2018.

2.50 The Financial Services Act 2012 provides that the strategic objective of the UK regulators – the FCA and PRA – is to 'protect and enhance confidence in the UK financial system'.[71] For the FCA, this primary objective is complemented by three operational objectives: (1) securing an appropriate degree of protection for consumers; (2) protecting and enhancing the integrity of the UK financial system; and (3) promoting efficiency and choice in the market for certain types of services. Parliament recognised that to achieve its strategic objective, the FCA should aim to promote fair, efficient and transparent financial services markets that work well for the users of these markets, including not only the banks but also bank customers, consumers and investors. This would better reflect the Treasury's intended purpose in the legislation that the FCA should ensure that business across financial services and markets is conducted in a way that advances the interests of all users and participants.

2.51 As mentioned above, the FPC is tasked with coordinating and directing macro-prudential policy by making recommendations and issuing directives regarding the use of macro-prudential measures and instruments and assessing macro-prudential conditions in the financial sector. Both the FCA and PRA are subject to directions and recommendations on a 'comply or explain' basis by the FPC in regard to how they apply macro-prudential measures or tools to entities they supervise.[72] The FPC is expected to conduct research on macro-prudential risks and to challenge conventional wisdom in micro-prudential regulatory practices to ensure that generally accepted principles are continually tested. For instance, by challenging conventional wisdom, the FPC is also expected to challenge the judgements of other supervisors and international organisations, such as the International Monetary Fund, which had failed to detect and assess the risks that toppled the financial system in 2007 and 2008. Thus, the IMF issued a report in 2006 that stated that 'dispersion of credit risk by banks to a broader – group of investors – helped make the financial system more resilient'.[73]

B US Dodd–Frank Act of 2010

2.52 After the financial crisis, the United States acknowledged widespread failures in financial regulation and supervision that destabilised financial markets by allowing weak bank corporate governance and risk management practices that ignored the build-up of risks across the financial system, particularly in the structured finance and securitisation markets, and the inadequate and inconsistent response of policymakers once the crisis began.[74] Congress responded by enacting the Wall Street Reform and Consumer Protection Act of 2010 (the Dodd-Frank Act), the preface of which states that it is '[a]n Act to promote the financial stability of the United States by improving accountability and transparency in

---

71 House of Lords, House of Commons, Joint Committee on the Draft Financial Services Bill (n 68), 26, referring to Draft Financial Services Bill, Clause 5 (new Financial Services and Markets Act clause 1B).
72 See Financial Services Act (2012), sections 4 and 6.
73 See International Monetary Fund, 'Global Financial Stability Report – Market Developments and Issues' (April 2006), chapter 1.
74 Financial Crisis Inquiry Commission, 'The Financial Crisis Inquiry Report' (Public Affairs, 2011), xvii–xxi.

the financial system, to end "too big to fail", to protect the American taxpayer by ending bailouts, to protect consumers from abusive financial services practices, and for other purposes'.[75] Title I of the Dodd-Frank Act attempts to set the groundwork for a more comprehensive future macro-prudential framework by creating the Financial Stability Oversight Council (FSOC), which brings together top regulators from across the government in order to identify and address systemic risk.[76] A new Office of Financial Research (OFR) supports FSOC's mission by collecting data across regulators in order to identify potential macro-prudential risks.[77] In addition to its general oversight and advisory role, FSOC can make recommendations on a 'comply or explain' basis to other government agencies.[78] These institutional reforms are deemed to be crucial elements in building a more effective macro-prudential supervisory system.

2.53 In contrast, Australia follows a version of the Twin Peaks approach with the Reserve Bank of Australia (the central bank) responsible for monetary policy, oversight of payment systems and maintenance of full employment and the welfare of the overall economy, while the two main supervisory bodies – the Australian Prudential Regulatory Authority (APRA) and the Australian Investment and Securities Commission (AISC) – are responsible, respectively, for carrying out integrated prudential supervision of individual financial institutions (commercial banks, approved depository institutions and insurance firms), regulating the conduct of business and investor protection in the capital markets and bringing enforcement actions for market misconduct.[79] The ASIC's investor protection remit also involves oversight of securities issuance by money market funds, finance companies and public unit trusts. The Australian Competition and Consumer Commission does not generally regulate financial firms but through the regulation and approval of mergers and acquisitions has a significant impact on the structure of the banking sector, and investigates and can approve the pricing of payment services and other charges of banks and financial institutions. In comparison with other advanced developed countries, Australia weathered the financial crisis relatively well.[80] This has been attributed not so much to the institutional architecture of its regulation, but to a 'regulatory culture in Australia' that emphasised more hands-on scrutiny of institutions and their risk-taking activities prior to the crisis than what was the case in other jurisdictions.[81]

---

75 See Dodd-Frank Act 2010, Preface.
76 Ibid., section 111, 112.
77 Ibid., section 152, 153.
78 Ibid., section 120.
79 Davis K, 'Financial Reform in Australia', in Maximilian Hall JB (ed.), *The International Handbook on Financial Reform* (Edward Elgar, 2003), 9.
80 See Edey M, Assistant Governor (Financial System) of the Reserve Bank of Australia, Oral Evidence to British Parliament Joint Select Committee on the Financial Service Bill 2011 (15 September 2011), see House of Lords, House of Commons, Joint Committee on the Draft Financial Services Bill, 'Draft Financial Services Bill – Session 2010–12' Report, together with formal minutes and appendices (December 2011).
81 Ibid.

2.54 Despite many efforts across Europe and globally to reform the institutional design of financial regulation, it should be emphasised that policymakers and regulators often conflate the need for regulatory reforms with the need for a particular institutional design of financial regulation – or, at least, they assume that the latter obviates the need for the former. Indeed, international financial authorities have observed that although countries recognise the need for a system-wide perspective, the 'main disagreement is on the importance of carving out a specific macroprudential [supervisory] framework'.[82] It is true that the institutional structure of administrative supervision can influence the degree of regulatory consistency and completeness.[83] For example, a philosophically sound approach to macro-prudential regulation can be misapplied in practice by fragmented supervisory authorities, especially if some of the authorities lack a legislative mandate to promote financial stability. Nonetheless, even a particular supervisory structure may fail if it administers regulatory standards and rules in a way that is not based on a coherent regulatory philosophy and set of values that have a consistent focus. This is supported by the case of Canada, a country with a unified single regulator (like the Japanese Financial Services Agency or the German BaFin), but which like Australia had a stricter approach to regulation that required higher bank capital requirements and the use of softer powers of persuasion to put pressure on banks to follow less risky business practices. It is the combination of stricter regulatory rules and supervisory practices, rather than the regulatory architecture, that explains most why Canada and Australia were much less affected by the global financial crisis than other countries.[84]

2.55 A single regulatory authority that is tasked with overseeing financial stability can fail to fulfil its objectives if that authority lacks a coherent and consistent regulatory philosophy and the power to implement adequately its regulations. For example, the main macro-prudential oversight body in the US created under the Dodd-Frank Act is the Financial Stability Oversight Council (FSOC). The FSOC, however, lacks the power to directly supervise financial entities and market practices.[85] In contrast, the UK Financial Policy Committee – the main British macro-prudential oversight body – has the power to issue directives or recommendations to other UK financial regulators to act to address macro-prudential risks developing in the financial system. The UK legislative framework describes how the regulators will interact with one another, but does not elucidate nor prescribe how the primary macro-prudential supervisor will approach macro-prudential policies or use macro-prudential instruments.[86]

---

82 Financial Stability Board, International Monetary Fund, Bank for International Settlements, 'Macroprudential Policy Tools and Frameworks – Progress Report to G20' (27 October 2011), 4.
83 See House of Lords House of Commons Joint Committee on the draft Financial Services Bill, Session 2010–2012 (HL Paper 236, HC 1447) (13 December 2011), 10.
84 Ibid.
85 Dodd-Frank Act 2010, 12 USC § 5322 (2010).
86 See Walker GA, 'U.K. Regulatory Revision – A New Blueprint for Reform' (2012) 46 *The International Lawyer* 3 793. See also Financial Services Act 2012, section 4(1)(9A) and (9B).

2.56 Aside from the issue of who should actually exercise macro-prudential regulatory and supervisory authority, the macro-prudential supervisory approach involves, among other things, the following activities: devising regulatory standards to measure and limit leverage levels in the financial system as a whole, requiring financial institutions to have enhanced liquidity reserves against short-term wholesale funding exposures, and, more generally, counter-cyclical capital regulation whereby capital requirements are linked to points in the macroeconomic and business cycle. Moreover, macro-prudential regulation may also involve linking monetary policy (interact rates and money supply), fiscal policy (i.e. government taxation and spending) and exchange rate policy (i.e. influencing the value of the currency) to the regulation of institutions by monitoring how these policies affect prudential supervisory risks across the financial system; this could involve taking supervisory measures that support the stability of the financial system as a whole and account for the interconnectivity of financial institutions and their effects on the global economy in times of crisis.

2.57 In addition, the wide scope of macro-prudential regulation requires a broader definition of prudential supervision to include both *ex ante* supervisory powers, such as licensing, authorisation and compliance with regulatory standards, and *ex post* crisis management measures, such as recovery and resolution plans, deposit insurance and lender of last resort. Indeed, the objectives of macro-prudential regulation – to monitor and control systemic risks and related risks across the financial system – will require greater regulatory and supervisory intensity that will necessitate increased intervention in the operations of cross-border banking and financial groups, and a wider assessment of the risks they pose. For example, as discussed in Chapter 6, recovery and resolution of failing banks will involve authorities in restructuring and disposing of banking assets and using taxpayer funds to bail out and provide temporary support '[t]o enable the continued operations of systemically important functions' and if necessary 'to require that these functions be segregated in legally and operationally independent entities'.

2.58 The exercise of macro-supervision and regulation will require that national authorities coordinate with each other in order to monitor the cross-border activities of large or interconnected financial groups and to ensure that their risk-taking complies with the macro-prudential objectives of the countries in which they operate. In some situations, it may be necessary for regulatory authorities that are not central banks to coordinate with central banks and finance ministries regarding the use of macro-prudential economic measures such as exchange rates, interest rates and fiscal policy alongside the traditional tools of micro-prudential supervision (i.e. capital and governance). And, under the Financial Stability Board's attributes for effective resolution regimes, countries will be expected to intervene in a bank's or financial firm's business practices at an early stage to require prompt corrective action to comply with regulatory requirements and if necessary to alter the organisational structure of the institution to make it more amenable to resolution by local authorities acting in coordination with the home country authorities of the financial group.

CONCLUSION

2.59 The chapter discussed the main theories of banking regulation and the concept of financial stability. It also examined how banking sector instability can be caused by market failures that arise from imperfect or asymmetric information that can lead to agency problems. Agency problems can exist between parties to a contract (creditor and debtor) or between owners of a firm and their employees. Imperfect information can result in *ex post* contract monitoring problems when the principal cannot sufficiently monitor the agent's actions (moral hazard) or *ex ante* information problems when the agent has inadequate information to assess the risks (adverse selection). For example, imperfect information can lead to misaligned incentives between bank shareholders (owners) and bank managers (agents), making it difficult for the shareholders to monitor adequately the activities and conduct of the managers and other employees (i.e. bank risk-takers such as traders) to ensure that the bank is managed in a profitable and sustainable manner. The chapter considered how agency problems can cause externalities in financial markets resulting in systemic risk. The chapter discusses how the control and mitigation of systemic risk has become a major financial policy and regulatory objective. The chapter also considers how the financial crisis of 2007–2008 led to major regulatory reforms and a change in the philosophy of banking and financial regulation to include macro-prudential principles and objectives.

2.60 The chapter considers the main theories of financial regulation – public interest, capture and legal theories – and then discusses the post-crisis evolution of the philosophy of banking regulation from a micro-prudential perspective to a macro-prudential perspective. The lack of a macro-prudential focus in banking supervision and regulation resulted in massive amounts of leverage building up across the financial system and an overreliance by banks on short-term wholesale funding. Moreover, central bankers failed to understand the linkages between monetary policy and prudential financial regulation and, in particular, how accommodative interest rate policies can cause asset price bubbles and excessive debt in the financial system. The prevailing approach to prudential regulation was essentially micro-prudential; that is, it was concerned mainly with the stability of individual financial institutions and the response of individual banks to exogenous risks, while ignoring the correlation of risks across asset classes and counterparty credit and liquidity risks in wholesale securities and derivatives markets. Indeed, the crisis has led to regulatory reforms that aim not only to identify and control risks at the level of individual institutions, but also across the financial system. This means that the concept of prudential regulation has expanded beyond the regulation and supervision of individual credit institutions to include a broader supervisory mandate to monitor and control system-wide risks in the securitisation and structured finance markets, maturity transformation risks in the shadow banking markets, and the risks associated with centralised trading and clearing of OTC derivatives and oversight of securities settlement systems.

QUESTIONS

1. What is the economic rationale of banking regulation?
2. What are the main institutional models of financial regulation?
3. Is the institutional design of financial regulation relevant to regulatory objectives?
4. Why are macro-prudential risks a concern for financial regulators?
5. Consider the main theories of financial regulation and argue which one you believe is most viable.
6. Discuss the similarities and differences between micro-prudential supervision and macro-prudential supervision.

Further Reading

Andenas M and Chu I, *Regulating Financial Markets* (Routledge 2015)

Andenas M and Deipenbock G, *Regulating and Supervising European Financial Markets* (Springer 2016)

Brunnermeier M, Crockett A, Goodhart CAE, Shin H and Persaud A, *The Fundamental Principles of Financial Regulation* (Princeton University Press 2009)

Conac P-H, 'Mastering the Financial Crisis – The French Approach Discussion Report' (2010) ECFR 297

Financial Crisis Inquiry Commission, 'Financial Crisis Inquiry Report (Public Affairs 2011)

Freixas X and Rochet J-C, *Microeconomics of Banking* (2nd edn, MIT Press 2008)

3

International Banking Regulation

Table of Contents

INTRODUCTION

3.1 The global financial crisis of 2007–2008 demonstrated serious weaknesses in international financial regulation and led to comprehensive reforms of international standard-setting and the design of banking regulation. The G20 and the Financial Stability Board have taken the lead post-crisis with efforts to make international financial standard-setting more accountable and legitimate by involving more countries in the standard-setting process and by making deliberations more transparent and reflecting the views of a broader number of stakeholders. Moreover, the G20 initiated at the Pittsburgh Heads of State Summit in September 2009 an extensive reform of international financial regulation with the overall aim 'to generate strong, sustainable and balanced global growth'. An important feature of the international regulatory reforms has been the G20's stated objective to make financial regulation more 'macro-prudential'; that is, to address risks and vulnerabilities across the financial system and broader economy that might threaten the stability of the financial system, and hence imperil the stability and sustainability of the economy.

3.2 Since the 1970s, the liberalisation of foreign exchange markets and subsequent increase in cross-border capital flows have contributed to the development of a global financial system but have also resulted in greater financial risks and more channels for contagion to spread risks during periods of fragility and crisis. These cross-border linkages between national financial systems have led to the emergence of a globalised financial market in banking, wholesale securities and asset management. Indeed, the move from segmented national financial systems to a liberalised and globalised financial system has posed immense challenges to financial regulators and supervisors, including the need to adopt more effective regulation and supervision across financial systems and to enhance coordination between states in supervising on a cross-border basis and internationally.

3.3 International financial regulation is primarily a system of 'international soft law' – meaning standards, guidelines, interpretations and other statements that are not legally binding or enforceable according to formal techniques of international law, but nevertheless are capable of exerting powerful influence over the behaviour of countries, public entities and private parties.[1] Despite its legally non-binding nature, international financial 'soft law' has had an enormous impact on state regulatory practices,[2] especially in the area of prudential bank regulation. This chapter will discuss several of the international bodies responsible for developing and overseeing the implementation of international banking regulation standards. The Basel Committee is responsible for the Basel Capital Accord and the Basel Concordats – probably the most important and influential international financial regulatory agreements – that establish, respectively, regulatory capital standards for banking institutions that operate on a cross-border basis and the principle of consolidated supervision that allocates jurisdictional authority over a bank's cross-border operations between home and host state supervisory authorities.[3]

---

1   See Brummer C, *Soft Law and the Global Financial System* (Cambridge University Press 2012), 121–134. See also Alexander K, Dhumale R and Eatwell J, *Global Governance of Financial Systems: The International Regulation of Systemic Risk* (Oxford University Press 2006), 138–150.
2   The international standards governing English cricket provide an analogy to the governance of international financial soft law. In cricket, the international equivalent to the Basel Committee or Financial Stability Board is the International Cricket Council, which promulgates the Code of Conduct and appoints umpires and referees for international matches; at the national or regional (i.e. EU) level are the umpires who specify the precise rules of play to ensure these rules are followed; and, finally, the players (i.e. market participants) who wield bat and ball under the umpire's eagle eye!
3   See Alexander K, 'Global Financial Standard Setting, the G10 Committees, and International Economic Law' (2009) 34 *Brooklyn Journal of International Law* 3 861.

3.4 The crisis demonstrates the need to adopt a more holistic approach to international financial regulation and supervision that involves linking the micro-prudential supervision of individual institutions to a broader oversight of the financial system and to macroeconomic policy. This chapter argues that the 'macro-prudential' dimension of financial regulation will have important implications for international banking regulation and will require more accountability and legitimacy in the international financial standard-setting process. First, the chapter traces the development of international banking regulation standard-setting from the 1960s to the reforms following the 2007–2008 crisis. Second, the chapter considers the post-crisis international regulatory reforms and whether they adequately address regulatory weaknesses and represent relevant stakeholder interests. Third, the chapter suggests that although international reforms have begun to address the interests of wider stakeholder groups through macro-prudential regulation, more work should be done to address stakeholder concerns regarding the impact of environmental and social risks on financial stability.

I INTERNATIONAL BANKING REGULATION AND THE RISE OF G10 COMMITTEES

3.5 In international finance, the globalisation of financial services has necessitated that regulators develop cooperative relations to facilitate their oversight and regulation of banking and financial services. Cooperative relations between national regulatory authorities have depended heavily for institutional support on the Bank for International Settlements (BIS) in Basel, Switzerland. The BIS is an international organisation with separate legal personality created under The Hague Agreements of 1930 and the Constituent Charter of the Bank for International Settlements of 1930. It was established in the context of the Young Plan, which restructured the reparation payments imposed on Germany by the Treaty of Versailles following the First World War. The BIS served as the payment agent for the European Payments Union between 1950 and 1958 which facilitated bank payments and currency convertibility between Western European countries following the Second World War.[4]

3.6 Beginning in 1962, the central banks of the ten leading industrialised nations began to meet regularly at the BIS to coordinate central bank policy and to organise lending to each other through the General Arrangements to Borrow.[5] These ten countries became known as the Group of Ten or G10. During the 1960s, the G10 central banks were primarily involved in settling payments in international transactions and buying and selling currencies between one another with a view to maintaining each country's fixed exchange rate parity within

---

4   See Gros D and Thygesen N, *European Monetary Integration, from the European Monetary System to Economic and Monetary Union* (2nd edn, Addison Wesley Longman 1998), 4–8.
5   See Alexander K, 'The Fund's Role in Sovereign Liquidity Crises', in *Current Developments in Monetary and Financial Law*, Vol. 5 (International Monetary Fund 2008), 131, 140–146.

the International Monetary Fund's (IMF) foreign exchange rate regime. In the 1960s, the G10 central bank governors established two committees whose secretariats were based at the BIS. The first of these committees was the Eurocurrency Standing Committee (also known as the Markets Committee). Founded in 1962, it was formed to monitor and assess the operations of the then newly established euro currency markets. This Committee later became the Committee on the Global Financial System in 1971. It now deals with broader issues of systemic risk and financial stability. The Committee on Payment and Settlement Systems was formed in 1990 to negotiate and set standards to support the continued functioning of payment and settlement systems.[6]

3.7 In the early 1970s, after the IMF exchange rate regime collapsed, the G10 was confronted with extreme volatility in the foreign exchange markets and imbalances caused by 'petro dollar' flows from oil-producing countries following the Arab oil embargo. These market developments led the G10 to establish the Basel Committee on Banking Regulation and Supervisory Practices in December 1974 in response to the collapse of the German bank *Herstatt*, whose insolvency in 1974 had created severe foreign exchange settlement problems between US and European banks, and the Franklin National Bank of New York, whose insolvency later in 1974 because of mismanaged foreign exchange rate risks threatened US banking stability. These bank collapses required central bank intervention to cover bank liabilities and to prevent contagion within the banking sector and broader financial system. These bouts of financial instability exposed substantial gaps in the ability of central bankers and national regulators to control and manage banking sector instability on a cross-border basis.

3.8 The creation of the Basel Committee on Banking Supervision was intended to address cross-border coordination issues between central banks and bank supervisors in overseeing international banking activity. Indeed, Goodhart described the relationship of the G10 with the Basel Committee as one of delegated authority to engage in regulatory standard-setting:

> Having established a standing committee of specialists in this field, the G10 Governors would find it difficult to reject a proposal from them, especially on a technical matter. The relationships between the G10 Governors and the BCBS emerge from the analysis of what the BCBS actually did and were quite complex. The G10 Governors set priorities for work, and frequently required papers to be revised and reconsidered. But at the same time they often gave the BCBS considerable freedom to decide its own agenda, and frequently rubber-stamped the papers emerging; basically the Governors did not have the time or the desire for textual criticism. They had a general oversight role; the detail was to be hammered out in the BCBS.[7]

6 See Baker JC, *The Bank for International Settlements: Evolution and Evaluation* (Praeger 2002), 32.
7 Goodhart CAE, *The Basel Committee on Banking Supervision: A History of the Early Years, 1974–1997* (Cambridge University Press 2011), chapter 14.

3.9 Between the 1970s and 2007, three international committees with G10 membership emerged to lead international financial standard-setting: the Basel Committee on Banking Supervision, the Committee on Payment and Settlement Systems and the Committee on the Global Financial System.[8] These committees still exert tremendous influence over the development of international regulatory standards for banking, currency and market operations, and payment system law and regulation. Specifically, the Basel Committee has produced a number of important international agreements that regulate the amount of capital that banks must set aside against their risk-based assets and the allocation of jurisdictional responsibility for bank regulators in overseeing the international operations of banks. Although the Committee's early agreements in the 1970s and 1980s were viewed by policymakers and commentators to be necessary to stabilise international banking markets, its efforts in the early 2000s to adopt Basel II and to extend its application to all countries where international banks operate attracted significant critical comment and brought its work under close scrutiny by leading policymakers and regulators.

3.10 The Committee on Payment and Settlement Systems has produced important agreements setting forth principles and recommendations for the regulation of bank payment systems and has worked with the International Organization of Securities Commissions (IOSCO) to adopt principles and standards for the regulation of clearing and settlement of securities and derivatives trading. The Committee on Global Financial Systems, though it has not adopted regulatory principles or recommendations, has produced a number of reports that have influenced the debate over macro-prudential financial reforms post-crisis to control systemic risk across financial systems, and the interrelationship with monetary policy.

3.11 These committees have examined many important central banking and financial regulatory issues, as well as attempted to elaborate and promulgate best practices in supervision and regulation, the functioning of payment and settlement systems and the overall operation of financial markets. The committees are usually chaired by senior officials of member central banks and are composed of experts from central banks, regulatory authorities and finance ministries. In the case of the Basel Committee on Banking Supervision, members also include non-central bank supervisory authorities and other regulatory and economic policy experts. Members of the committees have voting power and decision-making authority, while non-member country representatives are often consulted for their views on a variety of regulatory and economic issues. Frequently, special initiatives are undertaken to share experience with, and invite the opinions of, those not directly involved in the work of the committees. In promoting cooperation in their respective areas, the committees determine their own agenda and, within their mandate, operate independently from their host organisation, the BIS, which only provides its good offices for meetings as well as administrative and research support.

---

8 Walker GA, *International Banking Regulation: Law, Policy, and Practice* (Kluwer 2001), preface, xxii.

3.12 Significantly, these committees have resolved not to adopt legally binding international standards in a public international law sense, but rather to influence domestic regulatory practices and standards by adopting what has become known as 'international soft law'.[9] The Basel Committee has been the most influential of the G10 committees with respect to its impact on developing legally non-binding international financial norms of banking regulation standards, especially through the adoption of the *Capital Accord, the Concordat* and *the Core Principles for Effective Banking Supervision* which have an impact on domestic regulatory and supervisory practices. Indeed, as an international legal matter, the Basel Capital Accord and its amended versions, Basel II and III, are not legally binding for the countries that adhere to it, but the Accord has tremendous effect on the behaviour of states in implementing banking regulatory and supervisory standards.[10]

3.13 The Basel Committee's Concordat – adopted in February 1975 – established principles of information exchange and cross-border coordination for the oversight of international banking operations. The Concordat was amended in 1983 in response to the collapse and insolvency of the Italian bank Banco Ambrosiano. The 1983 Revised Concordat was entitled Principles for the Supervision of Banks' Foreign Establishments and contained the principle of consolidated supervision; this principle provides that home country regulators shall have responsibility for ensuring that the transnational operations of their home country banks are sound regarding credit risk exposure, quality of assets and the capital adequacy of the banking group's global operations, while the host country authority will mainly be responsible for the provision of local liquidity to foreign banks.[11]

3.14 Following the Latin American debt crisis of the early 1980s and the near collapse of several major US banks, the Basel Committee adopted the 1988 Capital Accord, which established a minimum 8 per cent capital adequacy requirement calculated against risk-based assets that applied only to internationally active banks that were based in G10 country jurisdictions.[12] The Capital Accord was originally calculated based on a bank's credit risk exposure, but was later amended in 1996 to include a bank's market risk exposure (i.e. the so-called Market Risk Amendment), thereby extending the 8 per cent capital adequacy requirement to a bank's trading book activities.[13] Between 1999 and 2004, the Committee engaged in a lengthy and radical revision of the Accord known as 'Basel II'. The final text was concluded in 2004, and resulted in changes in how the largest and most sophisticated banks calculated their regulatory capital: Basel II would permit them to use their own historic loan loss and

9   See Alexander et al. (n 1), 138–141.
10   Ibid., 135–137,
11   Ibid., 47–48.
12   The 1988 Capital Accord was entitled 'International Convergence of Capital Measurement and Capital Standards' and it was applied based on the principle of home country control to banks based in G10 countries with international operations (Basel Committee on Banking Regulation and Supervisory Practices, 1988), Report of the Committee on Banking Regulations and Supervisory Practices, International Convergence of Capital Measurements and Capital Standards (Basel: Bank for International Settlements).
13   See Alexander et al. (n 1), 38–39.

trading book data as a basis to estimate the riskiness of their assets and hence to determine their regulatory capital.

3.15 In doing so, Basel II aimed to make regulatory capital more sensitive to the risks which banks face in the marketplace. It allowed banks, under most conditions, to hold less regulatory capital for their credit, market and operational risk exposures than what was required under Basel I. The global credit crisis of 2007–2008, however, revealed that banks are also exposed to significant liquidity risks, especially in their off-balance sheet exposures, and that banks should hold more loss-absorbent capital. Basel II failed to address the liquidity risks to which banks are exposed and also did not require banks to hold adequate levels of loss-absorbent capital. Moreover, Basel II's excessive reliance on risk-weighting of assets to calculate regulatory capital resulted in procyclicality – that is, banks holding too little capital during market upturns and too much capital during downturns.[14] It also favoured large banks with sophisticated databases over small banks with less data in that it allowed larger banks to hold less capital as a percentage of risk-weighted assets compared to medium-sized and smaller banks. It also advantaged the banking systems of advanced economies at the expense of less developed and emerging market economies, as banks in advanced economies had access to large amounts of default data on borrowers and counterparties, therefore were in a better position to devise risk models based on these data that would qualify the bank for a lower capital requirement. Moreover, the procyclicality of Basel II had pernicious effects on economies that were more prone to volatility and booms and busts – specifically, developing and emerging market economies.

3.16 The Basel Committee responded to the 2007–2008 financial crisis by adopting further amendments to Basel II, which became known as Basel III. As discussed in Chapter 4, Basel III requires an increased level of Tier 1 regulatory capital to 4.5 per cent from 2 per cent, plus a 2.5 per cent capital conservation buffer, a tighter definition of Tier 1 capital to include mainly ordinary common shares and retained earnings, and up to an additional 2.5 per cent counter-cyclical capital ratio that will be adjusted across the economic cycle.[15] Basel III also contains liquidity requirements that include a ratio for stable wholesale funding, liquidity coverage ratios and an overall leverage ratio. Also, an additional capital charge of up to 2.5 per cent will be required for large and interconnected systemically important financial institutions (SIFIs).

3.17 Despite significant increases in capital and liquidity requirements, Basel III essentially builds on the edifice of Basel II by leaving in place the Basel II risk-weighting regime. However, Basel III requires regulators to challenge banks more in the construction of their

14 Alexander K, Eatwell J, Persaud A and Reoch R, 'Financial Supervision and Crisis Management in the EU' (2007) Policy Study IP/A/ECON/IC/2007-069, Brussels: European Parliament www.augurproject.eu/IMG/pdf/ JEatwellEtAl_FinancialSupervisionYCrisisManagement_EUreport-2.pdf accessed 21 February 2018.
15 See Basel Committee on Banking Supervision, 'Regulatory Consistency Assessment Programme (RCAP): Handbook for Jurisdictional Assessments' (March 2016) www.bis.org/bcbs/publ/d361.pdf accessed 21 February 2018.

models and broadens regulatory authority to require banks to undergo more frequent and demanding stress tests. The Pillar 2 review also consists of a supervisory review enhancement process (SREP) that includes separate assessments of bank capital and governance. The SREP can be utilised to forecast the bank's exposure to systemic risks and related macro-prudential risks. The SREP is also designed to address bank corporate governance and risk management. The corporate governance dimension of Pillar 2 is important for assessing the effect of Basel III on broader stakeholders who are affected by the regulation and supervision of banks. Enhanced bank corporate governance is designed not only to promote bank shareholder value but also to control and limit the potential social costs of weak bank management and the deleterious effect on the broader economy. In other words, Pillar 2 of Basel III – especially through the SREP process – is concerned with the effect of bank governance and risk management on stakeholders – those in the economy who are directly and indirectly affected by banks.

3.18 Other international supervisory bodies have also played a key role in developing international standards and rules for the regulation of financial markets. The International Association of Deposit Insurers meets at the BIS and discusses and adopts international principles and standards that govern deposit insurance regulation (Chapter 6). In the area of money laundering and terrorist financing, the OECD's Financial Action Task Force (FATF) has attained a high-profile role in setting international standards (so-called recommendations) of disclosure and transparency for the regulation of banks, financial service providers and other businesses in order to combat the global problem of financial crime (Chapter 9). The International Accounting Standards Board (IASB) and the International Federation of Accountants (IFAC) are bodies composed of professional accountants and academics who devise international accounting standards for the accounting industry. Similarly, the International Auditing and Assurance Standards Board (IAASB) sets standards for international financial reporting.

3.19 The FATF and the Basel Committee have each played a much more prominent role in their respective international regulatory standard-setting functions as compared to the International Organization of Securities Commissions (IOSCO) and the International Association of Insurance Supervisors (IAIS). IOSCO, however, adopted its most important post-crisis regulatory reform standards in February 2012 when it published guidelines for national authorities to implement the principle of central clearing of standardised over-the-counter derivatives, and later adopted, with the Committee on Payment and Financial Market Infrastructure, twenty-four principles for the regulation of risk management in financial market infrastructure (e.g. payment systems).

3.20 As discussed above, these international standard-setting bodies have been characterised as 'networks' of international technical experts, which are not concerned with broader public policy or international political economy issues. Rather, they are at the 'coal face' of technical and regulatory standard-setting. The goal of these regulatory technicians in international bodies is to coordinate regulatory and supervisory oversight of international banks and financial conglomerates with operations across financial sectors. These networks are composed of national regulators and supervisors – mainly from developed countries – who have established several international bodies to coordinate communication and the exchange of ideas among regulators on common issues of concern. These regulatory networks play an important role in disseminating information among regulators across financial sectors in different jurisdictions.

3.21 Before the 2007–2008 crisis, the Financial Stability Forum (FSF) coordinated activities relating to issues common to the banking, securities and insurance sectors. As the common body of three international financial standard setters, the BCBS, the IAIS, and the IOSCO and the Joint Forum on Financial Conglomerates set soft law in the form of guidance[16] and reports in the form of broad principles, which serve to establish a minimal standard. The FSF was established in 1999 in response to the Asian financial crisis and was composed of regulatory officials from advanced developed countries and a few developing countries. It relied on the work of the other international financial standard-setting bodies, the central banks and the various departments of the OECD for information and regulatory and financial market analysis. The FSF compiled a Compendium of Standards (CoS) with a summary and classification of the most significant rules, best practices, principles and guidelines of international financial regulation that had a direct impact on the regulatory practices of many countries. Crucially, FSF membership included the representatives of the banking and financial services industry in its deliberations and they played an important role in FSF working groups that published papers on regulatory reform, such as Basel II, that had significant influence on the work of the BCBS, the IAIS and the IOSCO and which contributed to an overall weakening of regulation prior to the crisis. The influence of the banking and financial services industry on the FSF working groups and standard-setting processes was substantial and was a form of regulatory capture.

II INTERNATIONAL DECISION-MAKING: ACCOUNTABILITY AND LEGITIMACY

3.22 The international financial bodies lack the requisite attributes of an international organisation, namely, they are not subject to international law, and do not have international personality, the capacity to conclude treaties or international legal immunities. In so far as these organisations are neither composed of states nor founded upon an international treaty, they also do not meet the traditional legal definition of an international organisation and therefore are not subject to minimum rules of transparency regarding, for example, the keeping of meeting minutes and other records concerning decision-making and deliberations. It is argued in some quarters that this lack of accountability in decision-making and operational processes can potentially undermine the effectiveness and legitimacy of the IFIs. On the other hand, other commentators suggest that precisely because these international

---

16   See Alexander et al. (n 1), 74–76.

standard-setting bodies are devoid of legal personality and excluded from the potential discipline of international law, they gain in flexibility and enhanced coordination benefits by not being subject to formalistic rules of decision-making process and consultation, and therefore are in a position to devise international norms that turn out to be more effective in influencing state practice than traditional methods and procedures of public international law-making.[17] The worldwide credit crisis of 2007–2008, however, called into question the efficacy of this flexible and unstructured decision-making framework and in particular raised concerns regarding the accountability and legitimacy of the IFI standard-setting processes.

3.23 In assessing whether the Basel Committee's standard-setting process complies with the principles of accountability and legitimacy as discussed above, a closer look at the Basel Committee's deliberation and decision-making process is necessary. The Basel Committee addresses issues that are of global concern to regulators and supervisors through a set of committees established to address particular issues of concern to bank regulators. After committees deliberate, they issue recommendations to the Basel Committee Secretary General and Deputy Secretary General who are in a position to table recommendations or issues of concern (including reports by external bodies) to the senior representatives of members of the Basel Committee. Its decision-making operates on a consensus basis. Although the Committee's decision-making has traditionally been secretive and reliant on personal contacts, it has become more formalised in recent years because of the considerable criticism of its deliberations over Basel II. For instance, during the Basel II negotiations, the Committee put a number of issues for consultation on its website and engaged in a public dialogue through the publication of its quantitative impact studies, which measured the impact of Basel II on a hypothetical basis based on the reports of a number of banks in both G10 and non-G10 countries.

3.24 As discussed above, the Committee's decisions are *legally non-binding* in a traditional public international law sense and place a great deal of emphasis on decentralised implementation and informal monitoring of member compliance. The Committee has sought to extend its informal network with banking regulators outside the membership through various consultation groups. The Core Principles Liaison Group remains the most important forum for dialogue between the Committee and systemically relevant non-G20 countries. Moreover, the BIS established the Financial Stability Institute to conduct outreach to non-member banking regulators by holding seminars and conferences on implementing international banking and financial standards. Most recently, it has conducted seminars and consultations with banking regulators from over 100 countries as part of the deliberations over adopting the Basel II Agreement.

3.25 Although some have viewed the informality of the Committee's decision-making process as effective for developing international banking regulatory standards,[18] others have

17   See Alexander et al. (n 1), 136–139.
18   Jackson P, 'Amending the Basel Capital Accord' (unpublished paper, Cambridge Endowment for Research in Finance Seminar, 22 January 2000).

considered it a constraint on effective implementation.[19] As Goodhart has observed, 'The way that the BCBS, under its various Chairmen, interpreted this constraint was that all proposals for forward transmission to the G10 Governors, and thence to the wider community of regulators/supervisors around the world, had to be accepted consensually by all country members of the Committee.'[20] As a consensus of all Committee members was required to adopt any standards or agreement, each country had a veto. According to Goodhart, however, this was in practice 'somewhat less of a constraint than it might seem at first sight'.[21] The smaller countries, for example, Benelux, Canada, Italy, Sweden and Switzerland, were reluctant to object to proposals by the United States and the United Kingdom and rarely took a minority position, 'except on a matter of extreme national importance, an example of [which is] ... banking secrecy for Switzerland'.[22] Despite Japan's substantial economic and financial influence, Goodhart notes that Japanese representatives on the Committee 'usually remained quiet and withdrawn ... partly due to their rapid turn-over of personnel, so they had little opportunity to build up expertise'.[23]

3.26 Monitoring non-compliance has generally been a decentralised task that is the responsibility of Member States themselves, not international organisations, such as the BIS, or other international bodies.[24] Nonetheless, the Committee monitors and reviews the Basel framework with a view to achieving greater uniformity in its implementation and convergence in substantive standards. Moreover, the Committee claims that the legitimacy of the international standards it adopts derives from a communiqué issued by the G7 heads of state in 1998 that encouraged emerging economies to adopt 'strong prudential standards' and 'effective supervisory structures'.[25] To ensure that its standards are adopted, the Committee expects the IMF and World Bank to play a surveillance role in overseeing Member State adherence through its various conditionality and economic restructuring programmes. In addition, because some G10 countries are members of the European Union, they are required by EU law to implement most of the Capital Accord's requirements into domestic law.[26] Other European countries obliged to implement the Accord into domestic law as a matter of EU/EEA law include Austria, Luxembourg, Belgium, Ireland, Finland, Norway, Poland, Hungary, Czech Republic, Latvia, Lithuania and Estonia, Bulgaria, Romania, Lichtenstein, Iceland, Greece and Cyprus.

---

19 Goodhart (n 7).
20 Ibid.
21 Ibid.
22 Ibid.
23 Ibid.
24 See generally Norton J, *Devising International Bank Supervisory Standards* (Kluwer 1995).
25 Ibid.
26 See Directive 2013/36/EU of the European Parliament and of the Council of 26 June 2013 on access to the activity of credit institutions and the prudential supervision of credit institutions and investment firms, amending Directive 2002/87/EC and repealing Directives 2006/48/EC and 2006/49/EC [2013] OJ L 176/338 (Capital Requirements Directive IV, 'CRD IV'), and Regulation (EU) No. 575/2013 of the European Parliament and of the Council of 26 June 2013 on prudential requirements for credit institutions and investment firms and amending Regulation (EU) No. 648/2012 [2013] OJ L 176/1 (CRR).

3.27 In fact, the only G10 countries not required by local law to implement the Capital Accord are Canada, Japan and the United States. In fact, this has posed a serious implementation problem at times when large and influential countries, such as the US, have decided not to implement fully the Capital Accord. This occurred in 2005 when the United States announced that it would apply Basel II only to its bank and financial holding companies, while small and medium-sized banks that would have been subject to the Standardised Approach of Basel II for measuring credit and market risks would instead be subjected to a type of Basel I+ because Basel II's standardised approach (discussed in Chapter 4) would have been more costly to comply with.[27]

3.28 The extended application of the Basel Committee's standards to non-G10 countries, however, has raised questions regarding the accountability of its decision-making structure and its suitability for application in developing and emerging market economies.

3.29 The Basel Committee's capital adequacy standards and rules on consolidated supervision were originally intended to apply only to credit institutions based in G10 countries that had cross-border operations. But this changed in 1998 during the Asian financial crisis when, at the urging of the G7 finance ministers and the world's largest financial institutions, which were lobbying for more market-sensitive capital standards, the Basel Committee stated its intent to amend the Capital Accord and to begin working on Basel II with a view to making it applicable to all countries where banks operate on a cross-border basis. At the time, many non-member countries had incorporated the Basel standards into their regulatory frameworks for a variety of reasons, including strengthening the soundness of their commercial banks, raising their credit rating in international financial markets and achieving a universally recognised international standard. The IMF and World Bank have also required many countries to demonstrate adherence or a realistic effort to implement the Basel Accord in order to qualify for financial assistance as part of IMF Financial Sector Assessment Programmes (IMF FSAPs) and World Bank Financial Sector Adjustment Programmes. Moreover, as a condition for obtaining a bank licence, all member countries require foreign banks to demonstrate that their home country regulators have adopted the Capital Accord and other international agreements. International reputation and market signals are also important in creating incentives for non-member countries to adopt the Capital Accord. Many non-member countries (including developing countries) have found it necessary to require their banks to adopt similar capital adequacy standards in order to attract foreign investment as well as to stand on an equal footing with international banks in global financial markets.

---

27 See Department of the Treasury Office of the Comptroller of the Currency, Federal Reserve System, Federal Deposit Insurance Corporation, Department of Treasury Office of Thrift Supervision, 'Risk-Based Capital Guidelines; Capital Adequacy Guidelines; Capital Maintenance: Domestic Capital Modifications' (October 2005) draft www.federalreserve.gov/bcreg20061205a1.pdf accessed 21 February 2018.

III REGULATORY CAPTURE IN INTERNATIONAL BANKING REGULATION

3.30 Although the flexible and secretive manner in which the G10 international financial standard-setting bodies conducted their deliberations and standard-setting was generally considered a strength in the effectiveness of their governance structures and decision-making processes,[28] it also had the unfortunate result of exposing them to special interest group pressure from major banks and international finance associations, such as the Institute for International Finance in Washington, DC. For example, most of the major international banks and their advocates lobbied and pressured the Basel Committee to incorporate lower capital adequacy requirements that reflected the economic capital models that banks were using at the time to measure their risks. In allowing banks to use more market-sensitive risk measurement models, these processes resulted in lower levels of regulatory capital held by banks. This left the banking system seriously undercapitalised and exposed to liquidity risks that could topple a bank if there was a sudden loss of confidence in the banking sector or with an individual institution that was systemically important. Indeed, as the crisis of 2007–2008 unfolded, it became apparent that the market-sensitive regulatory capital measurement processes approved under Basel II undermined financial stability and destabilised the global financial system.[29] Basel II had permitted regulators to approve more market-risk sensitive capital models, which led to lower levels of regulatory capital and created an incentive for banks to increase their leverage levels in the structured finance and securitisation markets.[30] The Basel Committee's failure to adopt regulatory capital standards that would protect the global financial system from systemic risk contributed significantly to the regulatory failings that caused the worst financial crisis since the Great Depression of the 1930s. In other words, the lack of transparency, accountability and legitimacy in the Committee's decision-making structure and the bank industry's disproportionate influence on the regulators who were members of the Committee resulted in the leading G10 countries adopting weak bank capital standards, thereby significantly contributing to the largest global financial crisis since the 1930s that resulted in a worldwide economic recession, from which the global economy has not fully recovered.

3.31 International financial standards produced by international bodies, such as the Basel Committee, have raised important questions regarding their accountability and legitimacy. The growing importance of international financial standards, such as the Basel Capital Accord, and their acceptance by most countries for their domestic regulatory systems, demonstrated the importance of international financial soft law in influencing state regulatory practice. Nevertheless, international financial soft law and its development through global financial governance structures failed to produce effective regulations and supervisory standards because the countries and the banking industry that developed the standards

---

28   See Jackson (n 18).
29   See Alexander et al. (n 14), 2–7.
30   Ibid.

did not consult countries that were not members of the Basel Committee (mainly developing and emerging market economies), including their banking industries, and did not consider the interests of broader stakeholders in society who were affected by the operations of the banking and financial system. As a result, Basel II was inadequate for the needs of most countries' economies and their banking sectors and broader financial systems. In particular, it demonstrated a lack of accountability and legitimacy for the non-members of the Basel Committee and their banking sectors who were subject to these international financial norms. Also, because the standard-setting process was opaque and subject to excessive influence by some stakeholder groups (e.g. the large banking groups) it failed to adopt efficient regulatory standards that would promote regulatory objectives for the countries that were members of the Basel Committee.

A The G20 Response

3.32 The financial crisis triggered intense efforts internationally, regionally and nationally to enhance the monitoring of systemic stability and to strengthen the links between macro- and micro-prudential oversight, supervision and regulation. One such response is the widening of the international forum in which worldwide economic and financial policy issues are discussed from G8, the Group of Eight leading industrialised countries, to G20 in 2008. The transition from G8 to G20/Financial Stability Board (FSB) is of great importance because at all G20 meetings of 2008 to 2010, notably those in London (2009), Pittsburgh (2009) and Seoul (2010), the financial crisis and the international response to it were the dominant topics. And it was indeed decisions taken by the assembled twenty heads of state which kick-started many of the national and regional responses to the crisis that are discussed in this section of the chapter. For instance, in motivating the steps it has taken to avoid a repetition of the crisis, or at least to mitigate the negative effects that a new financial crisis might have, the EU authorities regularly referred to commitments made at G20 meetings.

3.33 Since the crisis, the philosophy of prudential financial regulation has shifted away from a sole focus on micro-prudential regulation and supervision – the regulation of individual banks and financial firms – to a broader focus on the whole financial system and how it relates with the broader economy. This is called macro-prudential regulation. The redesign of international financial regulation – and the main objective of global financial governance – and the regulatory challenge posed by the financial crisis will be how regulators and central bankers can strike the right balance between micro-prudential regulation and supervision with macro-prudential controls on the broader financial system and economy. The international regulatory reform efforts were initially led by the G20 Washington Action Plan and the London and Pittsburgh Summit Statements on strengthening the financial system. The London and Pittsburgh Summit Communiqués provided a roadmap on financial supervision and regulation, and set forth principles for a more robust supervisory and regulatory framework based on new rules not only for financial institutions but also other actors, markets and supervisors.

3.34 An overriding theme of the international financial reform initiatives has been how to devise effective regulatory frameworks that durably link micro-prudential supervision with broader macro-prudential systemic risk concerns. Indeed, a major reform of global financial governance has been the shift in regulatory and supervisory focus from micro-prudential to macro-prudential regulation. The focus on macro-prudential regulation has involved, for instance, devising regulatory standards to measure and limit leverage levels in the financial system and to require financial institutions to have enhanced liquidity reserves against short-term wholesale funding exposures. Macro-prudential regulation also involves capital regulation that is counter-cyclical – requiring banks to hold more regulatory capital during good times and permitting them to hold less than what would be usually required during bad times. Counter-cyclical capital requirements would link capital charges to points in the macroeconomic and business cycle. The Basel Committee has introduced a framework for national authorities to consider how to implement counter-cyclical capital buffers. The Committee reviews the appropriate set of macroeconomic indicators (e.g. credit variables) and micro-indicators (banks' earnings) to determine how and when counter-cyclical regulatory charges and buffers should be imposed. This will necessarily involve banks using more forward-looking provisions based on expected losses.

B The Financial Stability Board

3.35 The Financial Stability Board (FSB) is the international body that has been given the responsibility by the G20 to develop international financial standards that control systemic risk and provide more effective oversight of the global financial system.[31] The FSB was created at the G20 London Summit in 2009 and was later established with legal personality by the G20 in the Cannes 2010 Summit Communiqué that stated that the Financial Stability Board will have 'legal personality', which could dramatically change the present system of legally non-binding international financial soft law standards. The Cannes Communiqué also provided for enhanced G20/FSB coordination with the International Monetary Fund on macro-prudential financial regulation and oversight of the global financial system. This raises important issues regarding the binding nature of G20/IMF macroeconomic policy regulatory objectives and their decision-making and standard-setting processes.

3.36 The FSB has adopted twelve key standards for sound financial systems, all of which are legally non-binding soft law, but nevertheless are expected to be incorporated into the national regulatory regimes of all countries. Since its establishment, the FSB has been addressing a diverse range of regulatory issues. Initially, the FSB addressed the significant regulatory gaps in overseeing the failure of banks with cross-border establishments and operations by introducing resolution principles in late 2009 that aimed primarily at controlling systemic risk when a bank fails. Also, banks were required under Basel III to

---

31 See Financial Stability Board, 'Declaration on Strengthening the Financial System – London Summit' (2 April 2009) www.fsb.org/wp-content/uploads/london_summit_declaration_on_str_financial_system.pdf accessed 21 February 2018. The FSB consists of twenty-four member countries, the European Central Bank and the International Monetary Fund.

'move expeditiously' to raise the level and quality of capital, but in a manner that 'promotes stability of national banking systems'. For example, the G20/FSB adopted a protocol to establish colleges of supervisors for all major cross-border financial institutions.[32] It has developed guidance notes and draft bank recovery and resolution plans to assist with its advice to national authorities for implementing the FSB 'Principles for Cross-Border Cooperation on Crisis Management'.[33] It has established 'Principles for Sound Compensation Practices',[34] and has coordinated with other international financial bodies such as IOSCO to develop a consistent regulatory framework for the oversight of hedge funds.[35] It is also overseeing the emergence of national and regional frameworks for the registration, regulation and oversight of credit rating agencies and encouraging countries to engage in bilateral dialogues to resolve home–host country issues, involving inconsistencies and disagreements that may arise because of different regulatory approaches.

3.37 To enhance the legitimacy of FSB standard-setting, the G20 and FSB increased their membership to include twelve additional member countries compared to the previous membership of the Financial Stability Forum and the G10 standard-setting committees. The additional membership includes large developing and emerging market countries, such as China, South Africa, India and Brazil. The move to a more macro-prudential regulatory regime has led the FSB to work more closely with the International Monetary Fund. The FSB-IMF have undertaken collaborative early warning exercises to strengthen assessments of systemic risks and to identify possible regulatory controls and supervisory practices as a response to the changing face of systemic risk in financial markets.[36] These exercises are aimed at providing policymakers with policy options and, as such, they add to the data-gathering, analysis and evaluation work and information-sharing activity that the IMF already conducts with a view to preventing crises by identifying policies to control macroeconomic and systemic risks.[37] It is argued that the combination of the IMF's macro-financial expertise with the FSB's regulatory perspective will provide an important link between the micro-prudential regulatory perspective and the macro-prudential

32   See Financial Stability Board, 'Overview of Progress in Implementing the London Summit Recommendations for Strengthening Financial Stability' Report of the Financial Stability Board to G20 Leaders (25 September 2009), 2–3 www.fsb.org/wp-content/uploads/r_090925a.pdf accessed 21 February 2018; and Financial Stability Board, 'Progress since the Pittsburgh Summit in Implementing the G20 Recommendations for Strengthening Financial Stability' Report of the Financial Stability Board to G20 Finance Ministers and Governors (7 November 2009), 13 www.fsb.org/wp-content/uploads/r_091107a.pdf accessed 21 February 2018. Other FSB initiatives include its 'Principles for Cross-Border Cooperation on Crisis Management' (2 April 2009) www.fsb.org/wp-content/uploads/r_0904c.pdf accessed 21 February 2018.
33   Financial Stability Forum, *FSF Principles for Cross-Border Cooperation on Crisis Management*, 2 April 2009 (Basel: Bank for International Settlements).
34   Financial Stability Board, 'FSB Principles for Sound Compensation Practices: Implementation Standards' (25 September 2009) www.fsb.org/wp-content/uploads/r_090925c.pdf accessed 21 February 2018.
35   International Organization of Securities Commissions, Technical Committee, June 2009, *Hedge Funds Oversight – Final Report* www.fsb.org/source/iosco accessed 21 February 2018.
36   International Monetary Fund, 'IMF-FSB Early Warning Exercise' Factsheet (ordered November 2008, current as of October 2017) www.imf.org/About/Factsheets/Sheets/2016/08/01/16/29/IMF-FSB-Early-Warning-Exercise accessed 21 February 2018.
37   The IMF's 'Global Financial Stability Reports' and 'World Economic Outlook Reports' are its 'flagship' global surveillance publications.

supervisory perspective.[38] These exercises are expected to be incorporated into the IMF's surveillance activities and this could serve as a way by which findings and policy recommendations may acquire more concrete effect.

3.38 The success of the FSB-IMF collaboration in macro-prudential regulation raises concerns about the effectiveness, accountability and legitimacy of its standards and recommendations. For instance, Lord King, former Governor of the Bank of England, raised important questions regarding the accountability and legitimacy of FSB standards for countries not represented in the G20. He observed that 'the legitimacy and leadership of the G20 would be enhanced if it were seen as representing views of others countries too'.[39] Close collaboration between the FSB and the IMF is a step towards addressing this concern. However, the involvement of the IMF does not address fully the existing weaknesses in the international financial architecture as the IMF itself has been subject to extensive criticism on legitimacy grounds, because of its allocation of Special Drawing Rights and the related allocation of weighted voting rights. Also, the IMF's practice of appointing Europeans as Managing Director has perpetuated the image that the IMF is governed by and for the interests of the advanced industrial economies. The IMF's Executive Board should therefore adopt internal governance reforms to enhance its accountability and legitimacy and to re-orient its financial policy advice to support alternative financial regulatory frameworks that allow developing and emerging market countries more discretion in how they implement international regulatory standards and to experiment more with macro-prudential policy tools, such as cross-border capital controls. This would partially address the concern of many developing and emerging market countries that the implementation of harmonised international financial standards provides a competitive advantage for advanced industrial countries and, based on the principle of home country control, can potentially expose host state countries to undue financial risks.

IV CONSEQUENCES OF INTERNATIONAL FINANCIAL REGULATORY REFORMS

3.39 The crisis has led to significant changes in regulatory standards, stricter supervisory practices and institutional restructuring of financial regulation. Nevertheless, weaknesses remain. Basel III continues to allow global banking groups to use risk-weighted internal models to calculate credit, market and liquidity risks that rely on historic data and risk parameters that are based on individual bank risk exposures and not to systemic risk across the financial system. Although Basel III contains higher capital requirements, liquidity requirements and a leverage ratio, it remains essentially dependent on risk-weighted

---

38 International Monetary Fund, 'Initial Lessons of the Crisis for the Global Architecture and the IMF' (18 February 2009) www.imf.org/external/np/pp/eng/2009/021809.pdf accessed 21 February 2018.
39 Mervyn King, Speech at the University of Exeter (19 January 2010), see www.bankofengland.co.uk/archive/Documents/historicpubs/speeches/2010/speech419.pdf accessed 28 August 2015.

models that were proven to be unreliable prior to the crisis because of their disproportionate focus on risk management at the level of the individual firm. As discussed above, the G20 and the Financial Stability Board have adopted the overall objective of refocusing financial regulation along macro-prudential lines. This requires not only stricter capital and liquidity requirements for individual institutions, but also monitoring risk exposures across the financial system, including the transfer of credit risk to off-balance sheet entities and the general level of risk across the financial system. For example, the G20/FSB objective of requiring systemically significant financial instruments (that is, over-the-counter (OTC) derivatives) to be traded on exchanges and centrally cleared with central counterparties is an important regulatory innovation to control systemic risk in wholesale securities markets. Also, systemically important financial institutions will be subjected to more intensive prudential regulatory requirements, including higher capital requirements and more scrutiny of their cross-border operations.

3.40 The Financial Stability Board and the Basel Committee on Banking Supervision have taken the lead in adopting international regulatory standards to address macro-prudential risks. Since the financial crisis both international bodies have cooperated in developing proposals for macro-prudential reforms by encouraging countries to assess the risks outside the banking sector that can threaten banking and financial stability. In particular, the FSB has analysed the shadow banking market involving non-bank financial firms engaged in maturity transformation – borrowing short and lending long – and the systemic risks that this may pose to the financial system. The FSB has also adopted principles that states are encouraged to follow for the orderly resolution of large systemically important financial institutions. The FSB's principles and objectives are designed to broaden the scope of prudential supervision to include systemic risks that can arise from excessive lending in the shadow banking industry as well as the risks in the trading, clearing and settlement of securities and derivatives.

3.41 Moreover, the macro-prudential standards adopted by the Financial Stability Board and International Organization of Securities Commissions provide that regulators and supervisors should be monitoring risk exposures across the financial system with particular focus on the transfer of credit risk to off-balance sheet entities and the trading book risks related to the OTC derivatives market. For example, the G20/FSB objective of requiring systemically significant financial instruments (i.e. OTC derivatives) to be traded on exchanges and centrally cleared with central counterparties (CCPs) or clearing houses is an important regulatory innovation to control systemic risk in wholesale securities and derivatives markets, but raises important questions about whether or not central clearing of derivatives might lead to a concentration of risks in CCPs and clearing houses that creates financial stability risks, especially if one of these institutions were to fail. The overriding theme of international initiatives (e.g. the G20/Financial Stability Board and IOSCO) has been how to devise effective regulatory frameworks that durably link micro-prudential supervision with broader macro-prudential systemic concerns of controlling systemic risks.

3.42 The exercise of macro-supervision and regulation along with overseeing bank recovery and resolution programmes (Chapter 6) will require a greater role for host country authorities to ensure that the risk-taking of cross-border financial groups complies with the host country's macro-prudential objectives. Most host countries will be able to achieve macro-prudential objectives in part by utilising traditional tools of macroeconomic policy – exchange rates, interest rates and fiscal policy – and by applying, under certain circumstances, tools of micro-prudential supervision, such as the use of counter-cyclical capital requirements, loan-to-value ratios and debt-to-income ratios. Moreover, as discussed in Chapter 6, under the FSB/G20 proposals, countries will be expected to intervene in a bank's or financial firm's business practices at an early stage to require prompt corrective action to comply with regulatory requirements and, if necessary, to alter the organisational structure of the institution by requiring, for instance, that the local operations of a cross-border bank be placed in a separately capitalised subsidiary or independent legal entity so that the local operations of a large systemically important institution could be compelled to undergo restructuring and/or recapitalisation by local authorities. Indeed, a key element of any bank resolution regime is that the local authority can have tools at its disposal to intervene in bank management (i.e. restrict dividends), restructure creditor claims, use taxpayer funds to recapitalise a systemically important institution or facilitate the transfer of assets to a private purchaser in a bank insolvency.

V REFORMING AND RESTRUCTURING FINANCIAL SUPERVISION

3.43 In addition to enhancing prudential oversight of cross-border financial groups, the FSB has encouraged host state supervisors to participate voluntarily in supervisory colleges to oversee the cross-border operations of financial groups. The main function of colleges will be to exchange information between supervisors, coordinate communication between supervisors of the financial group, voluntary sharing and/or delegation of tasks, joint decision on model validation, e.g. Basel II/III. The colleges will also be involved in joint risk assessment and joint decisions on the adequacy of risk-based capital requirements, planning and coordination of supervisory activities for the financial group and preparation for and during emergency situations (i.e. crisis management).

3.44 The use of supervisory colleges is expected to modify the existing principle of home country control, with limited host country intervention of a bank's cross-border operations by recognising that host state authorities should play a greater role in approving the risk models and engaging in other supervisory practices of cross-border banking groups. This is a departure from existing principles of home–host coordination under the Basel Concordat, which places most of the responsibility for supervising the cross-border operations of a banking group with the group's home country supervisory authority.[40] For example, the

---

40   See discussion in Alexander et al. (n 1), 27–38.

global banking group's risk models are ordinarily assessed and approved by the home country supervisory authority and applied on a global basis without much adjustment by host country authorities in whose jurisdiction the bank operates. By contrast, international and European regulatory regimes should focus on equipping host country regulatory authorities with greater powers to implement macro-prudential tools to control excessive risk-taking by global banking groups. For instance, national regulatory authorities should require cross-border banking groups to maintain subsidiaries in every jurisdiction where they have significant operations and to hold minimum capital in these subsidiaries. This would have the effect of subjecting the global bank's risk management practice to a local assessment by the host supervisor. The assessment would require the bank to show how its local operations are holding adequate capital and liquidity that are appropriate for the host country's macro-prudential objectives. This would result in global banking groups moving away from a centralised approach to risk management at the global level to a decentralised approach for measuring and managing risks at the national or host state levels. This would have important implications for Basel III's present approach to cross-border supervision that encourages and rewards global banking groups with more favourable capital and liquidity requirements for centralising and consolidating risk management and measurement in the jurisdiction (or few jurisdictions) where the banking group is based. Moreover, increased host country authority in supervising cross-border banking militates against the principle of home country supervisory oversight contained in the Basel Concordat and the Basel III principles of home–host country control. Although not legally binding, these principles support limiting a host country supervisory authority's discretion to apply prudential regulatory controls to a foreign bank's operations in the host country.

3.45 In contrast, macro-prudential regulation will necessarily involve host countries in playing a more proactive role in prudential supervision because the design of macro-prudential regulation must fit the particular attributes of the local economy where the banking group operates. There is no one-size-fits-all macro-prudential regulatory approach. Moreover, macro-prudential regulation is not well defined in practice and there needs to be a period of experimentation by national authorities before tested approaches are adopted by international standard setters. Countries must be given discretion to experiment with different macro-prudential tools whose effectiveness will vary from country to country based on differences in economic and financial systems. This means that bank capital management should be decentralised from the group level and based on diverse approaches across countries and different economies. This would give host country authorities a wider array of regulatory tools to address the particular risks that different banking groups and conglomerates pose to their financial system. It would be an important step in creating incentives for bank management to take more efficient financial risks that promote more sustainable economic growth for the country or region in question. Effective macro-prudential regulation therefore will require that host countries intervene and challenge risk management and measurement models that global banks use and which have been approved by their home regulatory authorities, but which may be inappropriate in a macro-prudential regulatory sense for some host countries. Moreover, regulators working through IOSCO and the FSB will have agreed a consistent regulatory framework for hedge funds oversight; and there will be adopted consistent frameworks for registration, regulation and oversight of credit rating agencies for consideration by national legislatures.

VI ENVIRONMENTAL AND SOCIAL RISKS AND BANKING STABILITY

3.46 An important question arises whether international financial regulation adequately addresses systemic environmental risks – for example, the macro-prudential economic risks associated with the banking sector's exposure to high carbon and other fossil fuel assets.[41] As discussed above, Basel III has already taken important steps to address both micro-prudential and macro-prudential systemic risks in the banking sector by increasing capital and liquidity requirements and requiring regulators to challenge banks more in the construction of their risk models, and for banks to undergo more frequent and demanding stress tests. Moreover, under Pillar 2, banks must undergo a supervisory review of their corporate governance and risk management practices that aims, among other things, to diversify risk exposures across asset classes and to detect macro-prudential risks across the financial sector. Regarding environmental risks, Basel III already requires banks to assess the impact of specific environmental risks on the bank's credit and operational risk exposures, but these are mainly transaction-specific risks that affect the borrower's ability to repay a loan or address the 'deep pockets' doctrine of lender liability for damages and the cost of property clean-up. These transaction-specific risks are narrowly defined and do not constitute broader macro-prudential or portfolio-wide risks for the bank that could arise from its exposure to systemic environmental risks.

3.47 Recent research suggests that Basel III is not being used to its full capacity to address systemic environmental risks and that such risks are in the 'collective blind spot of bank supervisors'.[42] Despite the fact that history demonstrates direct and indirect links between systemic environmental risks and banking sector stability and that evidence suggests this trend will continue to become more pronounced and complex as environmental sustainability risks grow for the global economy, Basel III has yet to take explicit account of, and therefore only marginally addresses, the environmental risks that could threaten banking sector stability.[43]

3.48 In a related area, the Basel Committee has formed a committee to address whether financial inclusion should be addressed by bank regulators. In 2015, it published a survey of international state practice regarding how countries regulate banks and other financial

---

41 See Alexander K, 'Stability and Sustainability in Banking Reform: Are Environmental Risks Missing in Basel III?' (2014) United Nations Environment Programme and University of Cambridge Institute for Sustainability Leadership www.unepfi.org/fileadmin/documents/StabilitySustainability.pdf accessed 21 February 2018.
42 Ibid.
43 See Chapter 13 for a discussion of environmental and social risks in banking.

institutions in respect of the financial risks associated with financial exclusion.[44] The issue of environmental and social sustainability risks and the banking sector has been taken up by the World Bank's International Finance Corporation (IFC), which has established a network of bank regulators and global banks to discuss good regulatory and bank governance practices that address the environmental and social risks that are material to the banking sector. This network is the Sustainability Banking Network (SBN, see Chapter 13) which consists of many developing and emerging market countries, including China, Brazil, Bangladesh and Peru, and some of the world's largest international banks, which, acting under the guidance of the SBN, have embarked on innovative risk assessment programmes to identify environmental and social risks that are material to the banking sector. The SBN is analysing environmental systemic risks from a macro-prudential perspective to consider whether or not these risks are material risks to banking and financial stability. A strong case can be made that these efforts of the SBN should be coordinated with the banking risk assessments being done by the traditional international financial standard-setting bodies, such as the Basel Committee.

CONCLUSION

3.49 The global financial crisis of 2007–2008 called into question the efficacy of the traditional approach to international bank regulatory standard-setting that involved a flexible and legally non-binding standard-setting process. This has also raised concerns more generally about the accountability and legitimacy of international financial standard-setting processes and how international standards are negotiated and implemented across different countries and jurisdictions. Major weaknesses in international banking regulation that resulted in the adoption of Basel II suggest that the international financial standard-setting processes should be more accountable and legitimate. Moreover, it suggests that the flawed economic policies and regulatory frameworks and practices of the world's major advanced economies (the G10 countries, including the US, Europe/UK and Japan) cannot be relied upon by other countries to provide sustainable models for economic and financial development. This means that the development of international financial regulatory standards should be influenced more by countries outside the G10 club of advanced developed countries and that international regulatory standards should address broader risk factors – environmental and social risks – that can have a significant effect on financial stability, thereby contributing to more sustainable economic growth and financial development. The overall message – welcomed in many reform circles – is that economic policymakers should consider building institutional mechanisms that transcend national borders and which establish solidarity between the banking sector and all parts of society that are affected by financial risk-taking.

3.50 This chapter also suggests that future international regulatory reform must be built on a more holistic approach to financial regulation and supervision that involves linking

---

44   See generally, Basel Committee on Banking Supervision 'Range of Practice in the Regulation and Supervision of Institutions Relevant to Financial Inclusion' (January 2015) www.bis.org/bcbs/publ/d310.pdf accessed 21 February 2018.

micro-prudential supervision of individual banks with broader oversight of the financial system and to macroeconomic policy. Not only should regulation focus more on macroeconomic factors, such as liquidity risks and leverage requirements for banks, but it should also develop capital adequacy standards that have linkages and reference points in the broader macroeconomy, such as counter-cyclical capital ratios. Macro-prudential regulation will necessarily require a more rules-based approach to regulation at both the national and international levels in order to be effective. Effective international regulatory reform will require a more intrusive approach to regulation, supervision and crisis management that will necessarily require enhanced measures to control excessive risk-taking whilst mitigating and paying for the tremendous social costs imposed by financial crises.

QUESTIONS

1. Discuss the origins of modern international banking regulation in1970s and 1980s.
2. How was Basel II different from Basel I?
3. Discuss how financial liberalisation in the 1970s led to changes in banking regulation.
4. Why was the Basel Committee formed?
5. What were the two main objectives of the first Basel Accord (Basel I)?
6. Why does the Basel Committee represent a form of flexible decision-making?
7. Discuss the role of the Financial Stability Board.
8. How are international regulatory objectives different post-crisis from pre-crisis?

Further Reading

Avgouleas E, *Governance of Global Financial Markets* (Cambridge University Press 2012)

Goodhart CAE, *The Basel Committee on Banking Supervision: A History of the Early Years, 1974–1997* (Cambridge University Press 2011), providing a detailed history of the negotiations and issues addressed by the Basel Committee on Banking Supervision.

Gold, Sir J *Interpretation: The International Monetary Fund and International Law* (Kluwer Law International 1996), discussing how soft law emerges in the provisions of binding treaties, such as the IMF Articles of Agreement, or other binding legal instruments.

Lastra R, *The Legal Foundations of International Monetary Stability* (Oxford University Press 2006)

Mayer C and Gordon JN, 'The Micro, Macro and International Design of Financial Regulation' (2012) Columbia Law and Economics Working Paper No. 422 https://papers.ssrn.com/sol3/Delivery.cfm/SSRN_ID2047436_code69460.pdf?abstractid=2047436&mirid=1 accessed 25 May 2018

Quaglia L, *The European Union and Global Financial Regulation* (Oxford University Press 2014), discussing how the European Union downloads international financial standards in areas where it does not have regulatory capacity and uploads its regulatory standards to international bodies where it does have regulatory capacity.

4

Capital Adequacy and Risk Management

Table of Contents

INTRODUCTION

4.1 The chapter discusses the concept of regulatory capital and how it has evolved under the Basel Capital Accord. It discusses what bank capital is and why it is important. It then discusses the evolution of bank capital requirements and how they are influenced by risk management processes, including risk-weightings, that determine the amount and quality of regulatory capital. The chapter will discuss how Basel II allowed banks to use more refined risk measurement techniques to calculate their regulatory capital and to optimise on the amount and type of capital they were required to hold against their business risks. Basel II's heavy reliance on value-at-risk statistical models to estimate the riskiness of credit and market risks resulted in banks holding inadequate regulatory capital, which contributed substantially to the severity of the financial crisis of 2007–2008. The chapter then discusses how Basel III increases the level and quality of regulatory capital and takes account of certain macro-prudential risks in the banking sector. The recent amendments to Basel III (known by some as 'Basel IV') which increase capital for trading book risks and significantly limit the extent to which risk models can be used to lower capital requirements are also discussed.

I BANK CAPITAL: DEFINITIONS, CONCEPTS AND IMPORTANCE

4.2 The banking business is distinctive and a source of regulatory concern because unlike most other industries a bank's balance sheet is highly leveraged: its liabilities consist almost entirely of debt with a very low percentage of equity capital.[1] In many cases, the limited liability of bank shareholders and the short-term compensation structure of bankers create an incentive for them to maximise the bank's leverage. As a result, banks are particularly exposed to the possibility of insolvency because their liabilities consist overwhelmingly of debt: most of the large global banking groups based in advanced developed countries operated from the early 2000s to around 2010 (when Basel III was agreed) with less than 3 per cent equity capital as a percentage of their total assets. This meant that defaults or losses of only 3 per cent on their assets would have left the bank with no equity capital and thus insolvent. This is why bank capital regulation has attracted great attention and controversy after the 2007–2008 global financial crisis because so many banking institutions – especially the largest banking groups – based in advanced developed countries were undercapitalised and highly leveraged at the time of the crisis. When the crisis hit, many systemically important banks were unable to borrow from other banks in the inter-bank loan markets and from other wholesale investors in the securitisation markets. As a result, taxpayer bailouts and generous central bank liquidity schemes were necessary to avoid a collapse of the banking system.

---

1 Heffernan S, *Modern Banking* (Wiley 2005), 2. See also Greenbaum S and Thakor A, *Contemporary Financial Intermediation* (Elsevier-Academic Press 2007), 55.

4.3 To understand the role of bank capital, it is necessary first to focus on a bank's organisational structure and balance sheet. In market economies, banks are typically joint stock companies, with their shares listed and traded on a stock exchange.[2] Investors who purchase the shares of a bank are its owners, who also own the bank's profits and losses. One side of the bank's balance sheet describes its assets (for example, loans, investments, cash, buildings and equipment), while the other side of the balance sheet lists its liabilities, which include mainly debt and capital. Debt liabilities include deposits, bonds and other borrowings. Capital includes shareholder equity in the form of paid-in capital (i.e. the amount paid for the bank's stock upon issuance) that provides rights to all residual assets including ownership of the bank. A bank that is owned by shareholders can have different classes of shares with different financial returns and ownership and voting rights.

4.4 Capital also consists of retained earnings, which is the bank's income at the end of the fiscal year (net of expenses) earned during that year, less any dividends paid to shareholders. Capital also consists of preferred stock (or preference shares) that are entitled to specific dividends that may accrue if unpaid, but which afford limited ownership rights, and whose value may be perpetual or have a fixed duration. As discussed below, preference shares are a less pure or hybrid form of capital because they do not typically absorb losses for the bank as a going concern and instead more closely resemble debt. Capital can also be the surplus gain from the sale of shares for more than their par value or stated value. Reserves – such as equity reserves – can also constitute capital when they are set aside from revenues to pay, for example, dividends on preferred shares or to retire preferred shares or senior debt.

4.5 Although most banks or credit institutions in European countries today are limited liability companies, some take the legal form of *Mutuals* or *Credit Unions* – whose owners are its members and customers, not shareholders. In Australia and the UK, building societies and credit unions are mutuals whose business lines are restricted to retail banking-type services such as mortgage loans, credit cards and current accounts. Similarly, credit unions in the US are restricted in the loans they can make and their customers or members are limited to those who share a common bond, such as an employer or university alumni. However, a financial firm that operates as a mutual or credit union is still required to hold reserves, known as capital, that can absorb losses.

4.6 Bank capital has four main purposes: (1) to absorb losses against asset value declines because of non-performing loans, expected losses arising from inadequate loan loss reserves, and ultimately bank failure; (2) to provide start-up funding for a bank's early operations; (3) to reduce losses to deposit insurance schemes by providing a means to repay the claims of depositors and creditors of a failed bank; and (4) to create incentives for shareholders, directors and managers to exercise more prudence in overseeing the bank's operations.

---

2 Greenbaum and Thakor (n 1) 57. See also Crick W and Wadsworth J, *A Hundred Years of Joint Stock Banking* (Hodder & Stoughton 1935), 3, 16, 19.

4.7 Prior to the 1980s, however, most countries with market-led banking systems used *equity to deposits* or *liabilities to deposits* ratios as measures of bank capital strength. From the early twentieth century until 1983, the United States used *equity to deposit ratios* in the form of a 1 to 10 ratio of equity capital to deposits. These regulatory capital rules were increasingly seen as constraints on the growth and development of the US banking sector.[3] Similarly, Australia relaxed maturity controls on deposits and lending restrictions for banks in 1982 and 1984 respectively and later in 1999 enacted legislation that replaced minimum liquidity requirements with an 'agreed liquidity policy'.[4]

4.8 As discussed below, the Basel Accord and most countries implementing it adhere to the following definitons of regulatory capital. *Core Equity Tier 1* (CET1) consists primarily of equity or common stock (i.e. shares) and equivalent instruments which are considered to be the highest quality or loss-absorbent forms of capital. Banks consider CET1 to be the most costly form of capital because its issuance can dilute existing shareholders in terms of their monetary interests and control rights (voting rights) in the governance of the bank. However, regulators prefer banks to issue more CET1 and equivalent instruments because these instruments allow the bank owners to absorb more of the bank's losses as a going concern.[5] But banks prefer to issue less CET1 to count as regulatory capital and instead to issue more debt-like instruments (e.g. other Tier 1 and Tier 2 capital) for regulatory capital because these instruments are generally not dilutive of existing shareholders and also attract tax benefits (deductible interest) and will only absorb losses if the bank becomes insolvent, which rarely happens for most banks because governments perceive them as 'special' and worthy of bailouts and other taxpayer subsidies.

4.9 *Tier 1 capital* consists of CET1 and disclosed reserves (or retained earnings), but may also include *other less loss-absorbent* capital (less favoured by regulators), such as non-redeemable or non-cumulative preferred stock, which does not as readily absorb losses compared to common stock or profits, and thus functions more like debt, rather than equity capital. *Tier 2 capital* is less loss-absorbent than *Tier 1 capital* because Tier 2 instruments generally can only absorb losses if the bank is being restructured or becomes insolvent. Tier 2 instruments can include revaluation reserves, subordinated bonds with extendable terms, undisclosed reserves, hybrid instruments (i.e. convertible capital instruments) with cumulative coupon interest rates and subordinated term bonds. Although banks are allowed to fund Tier 2 with CET1 or other Tier 1 instruments, they prefer to fund Tier 2 capital with debt and debt-like instruments, such as subordinated bonds with extendable terms, or convertible capital instruments (Cocos) that have equity-like properties but are issued and priced as debt instruments which pay cumulative coupon interest rates that are tax deductible.

---

3   Golin J and Delhaise P, *The Bank Credit Analysis Handbook: A Guide for Analysts, Bankers and Investors* (Wiley 2013), 264–265.
4   See Davis K, 'Financial Reform in Australia', in Hall MJB, *The International Handbook on Financial Reform* (Edward Elgar 2003), 1–30, 12–13, 20.
5   See Golin and Delhaise (n 3), 405–411.

4.10 Another type of regulatory capital that some EU Member States treat as Tier 1 capital are tax assets; that is, an entititlement by a bank under its home jurisdiction's tax laws to claim a deduction or credit against its income tax in future years (contingent on the bank earning taxable profits in future years) when it has inadequate profits against which to claim the deduction or credit in the earlier year. This latter type of Tier 1 capital is generally frowned upon by regulators because of its future contingent-like quality, and is often used by undercapitalised banks to meet minimum capital requirements in jurisdictions which have had serious banking sector weaknesses, such as, among others, Greece, Italy, Portugal and Cyprus.

4.11 Another type of regulatory capital (discussed in Chapter 6) is *bail-inable debt*, often used in bank resolution, which converts to capital if bank capital falls below some contractual or regulatory determined trigger point. The contractual terms on bail-inable debt differ but generally the bank resolution authority may extinguish certain eligible creditor claims (i.e. subordinated bonds) including claims for coupon payments (i.e. interest rate payments) on bond or debt instruments. Bail-inable debt is also known as Total Loss-Absorbent Capital (TLAC) and the Financial Stability Board expects countries to hold a minimum amount of TLAC of 18 per cent of risk-based assets by 2022.[6] In addition to Tier 1 and Tier 2 capital under Basel III, the TLAC standard requires at a minimum that banks hold additional loss-absorbent capital consisting of subordinated bonds and convertible capital instruments (Cocos). The FSB expects that subordinated bonds have loss-absorbent capacity so that if the bank is put into bankruptcy or resolution the value of the bonds can be reduced or extinguished in the queue of creditor claims following the wiping out of shareholders and before imposing losses on senior creditors. Cocos also constitute TLAC but involve a conversion of the face value of the bond into an equivalent amount of shareholder equity prior to the bank going into resolution or bankruptcy upon the bank's share price or capital level dropping to a pre-defined trigger point.[7] Under EU capital rules, banks are required to hold Cocos in the form of Additional Tier 1 capital (AT1) that automatically convert to equity if the bank's capital level drops to 5.125 per cent of risk-based assets. Other jurisdictions (i.e. Switzerland) require that some additional capital bonds are converted into equity at a higher trigger point (7.5 per cent) while other additional capital bonds convert at lower trigger points (5.125 per cent or less) (SR 952.03, Art 27(3)).

4.12 Under the Basel Accord, a bank's capital requirements will depend mainly on the riskiness or risk classification of its loan assets and the riskiness of its trading positons. The riskiness of its assets will determine how much in common equity shares or equivalent instruments (CET1) the bank is required to hold. Most assets will require (depending on their riskiness) a combination of Tier 1 and Tier 2 capital. And international TLAC standards require at a

---

6 Financial Stability Board (2015), *Summary of Findings of TLAC Impact Assessment Studies* (November) Basel, BIS www.fsb.org/2015/11/summary-of-findings-from-the-tlac-impact-assessment-studies/ accessed 21 December 2018.

7 See Chapter 6.

minimum banks to hold 18 per cent of risk-based assets in the form of bail-inable capital (bonds or Cocos).

4.13 A bank's capital serves as a buffer from which any losses are taken, and provides a reserve from which bank depositors and creditors may ultimately be repaid when losses can no longer be absorbed in case of a bank failure. For instance, if a bank has negative income for the year, the capital account is reduced by the amount of the loss. A bank is insolvent if its liabilities exceed its assets. Regulators require a bank's balance sheet to balance, and the difference between the assets and liabilities is the main measure of the bank's net worth and viability. This is why regulators and bank deposit insurers are very concerned about the amount of a bank's capital buffer. In the event of a bank insolvency and liquidation, the deposit insurer would pay the bank's depositors the amount of the depositors' effective deposit insurance coverage.[8] The bank's assets would be sold and the proceeds used to reimburse the deposit insurer first and then to pay the bank's uninsured creditors, usually leaving shareholders with a worthless investment. If the bank has a severe insolvency problem, its assets may not be enough to reimburse fully the deposit insurer for its payments to insured depositors. A greater equity buffer, however, would give the bank the ability to absorb greater losses before it becomes insolvent and the deposit insurer would be less likely to suffer losses as a result of the bank's liquidation. Essentially, the level of loss-absorbent capital is important for a bank because it sends a signal to the market as to the bank's solvency, affects its cost of funding (i.e. the spread it has to pay to borrow short term from banks and other lenders) and can be used in a restructuring to pay the claims of bondholders, depositors and other creditors.

4.14 Nevertheless, if a bank's capital is reduced to zero, its assets could in theory still be sold to satisfy the claims of depositors and other liability holders. It is difficult to judge, however, the exact value of a bank's assets, especially during times of market stress when there could be widespread borrower defaults. This is where bank risk management becomes important, especially as it relates to the amount of capital held by the individual banking institution.

II THE BASEL ACCORD AND RISK-BASED SUPERVISION

4.15 From around the mid-1980s until the collapse of the US investment bank Lehman Brothers in 2008, bankers and investors were presumed to understand the risks they were taking through increased lending and investment in asset-backed securities and other structured credit products, and in trading complex over-the-counter derivatives to manage risks. The risk-based approach to banking regulation was designed to incentivise banks and other institutions to manage more efficiently their balance sheet risks in a financial system where

---

8   See Kleftouri N, 'Rethinking UK and EU Bank Deposit Insurance' (2013) 24 *European Business Law Review* 1 95–125.

capital movements, interest rates and exchange rates were liberalised and deregulated. Risk-based supervision rewarded banks with lower capital requirements if they could show the supervisor that they had diversified their risk exposures, especially on a cross-border basis.

A Basel I

4.16 Risk-based supervision was largely based on the notion that if bank supervisors could ensure that banks and other financial firms were managing their risks well on an individual basis, they would be profitable and stable and systemic risks across the financial system would also be negligible. International financial regulation encouraged this approach with the adoption of the 1988 Basel Capital Accord (Basel I) that required internationally active banks to hold a miimum of 8 per cent capital against their credit risk exposures. It classified credit risks into a few simple categories of balance sheet exposures known as risk-weights.

4.17 According to Figure 4.1, the Basel I risk-weighting regime required a bank that had loaned money to a country that was a member of the Organisation for Economic Co-operation and Development (OECD) to classify that loan with a zero risk-weighting, which meant it did not have to hold any regulatory capital against the value of the loan. Countries outside the OECD were subject to the full 100 per cent risk-weighting which required banks to hold 8 per cent capital against loan exposures to these countries. Similarly, all loans to businesses and individuals were subject to 100 per cent risk-weightings, thereby requiring the bank to hold 8 per cent regulatory capital against the full value of these loan exposures. Basel I, however, treated residential mortgage lending more favourably than business and retail loans as mortgage loans were subject to a 50 per cent risk-weighting (or 4 per cent – one half of the 8 per cent) of the regulatory capital requirement.

4.18 For most credit risk exposures, Basel I required banks to hold 8 per cent regulatory capital. The 8 per cent capital requirement consisted of Tier 1 and Tier 2 capital. As discussed above, Tier 1 capital was primary and more favoured by regulators because it consisted mainly of common equity shares, equivalent instruments and retained earnings, which could absorb losses for the bank as a going concern. Tier 1 capital had to be at least 4 per cent of risk-based assets, and of that 4 per cent at least 50 per cent – or 2 per cent of risk-based assets – had to be *core equity* Tier 1 capital (CET1), consisting of common equity shares (or

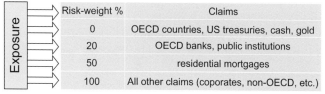
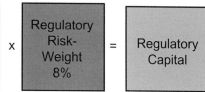

Figure 4.1 Basel I capital calculations

equivalent instruments) and retained earnings. In contrast, Tier 2 capital consisted mainly of subordinated debt and other bonds and debt-like instruments, such as preference shares, and convertible instruments. Tier 2 capital was less flexible for regulators because it could not impose losses on the bank as a going concern. This is why Basel I required that Tier 2 capital not constitute more than 50 per cent – or 4 per cent of risk-based assets – of the 8 per cent regulatory capital requirement.

4.19 The regulatory capital requirements for these exposures applied only to loans that were booked on the bank's balance sheet; this led banks to develop ways to shift these assets or risks off their balance sheets in order to reduce their regulatory capital requirements, thus freeing up more capital for lending and investment. Banks responded to these regulatory requirements by developing credit risk transfer methods, such as securitisation and credit derivatives, to spread risk to third-party investors and others seeking risk exposure to these assets. Central bankers and regulators applauded these financial innovations as a way for banks to encourage investors to invest in loan or credit assets without the bank having to hold regulatory capital against the loan exposure,[9] thereby motivating the massive growth of the securitisation and credit derivatives markets in the 1990s and 2000s.

4.20 Basel I also favoured short-term (less than one year) lending to banks with a 1.75 per cent risk-weighting as opposed to the standard 8 per cent risk-weighting for such loans that had a maturity of one year or more. This contributed to a substantial increase in short-term cross-border lending to banks in developing and emerging market economies that were especially vulnerable to sudden reversals of capital flows and lending during periods of market instability. Indeed, these Basel I risk-weightings incentivised banks to make more short-term loans (less than one year) to banks in developing countries than they would have otherwise made, thereby contributing to the intensity of the Asian financial crisis in the late 1990s when foreign investors and lenders lost confidence in certain East Asian countries and refused to rollover short-term loans. Although Basel I achieved its main objective of increasing the level of regulatory capital and providing a more or less level playing field for the capital regulation of cross-border banks, it contained many national discretions, loopholes and incentives for banks to make riskier short-term loans and to transfer less risky assets off their balance sheets that ultimately put the financial system at great risk.[10]

4.21 Basel I contained another gap in that it had initially applied only to bank loan books or credit risk and not to other risky areas of the banking business. The rationale for this was

9 See HM Treasury, 'Review of HM Treasury's Response to the Financial Crisis' (March 2012), 5 www.gov.uk/government/uploads/system/uploads/attachment_data/file/220506/review_fincrisis_response_290312.pdf accessed 21 February 2018, stating '[b]efore the 2007–09 financial crisis, regulators across the international financial system championed the economic benefits of rational, self-correcting markets and the merits of financial innovation. A global consensus emerged that new modes of finance had reduced systemic risks.'
10 See Goodhart CAE, *The Basel Committee on Banking Supervision: A History of the Early Years, 1974–1997* (Cambridge University Press 2011), 351–353.

that the maturity transformation in the bank loan book (borrowing short from depositors and lending long to borrowers) created externalities or social costs for the economy that should be internalised or covered by banks in the form of regulatory capital requirements. By contrast, a bank's trading book – trading securities or derivatives for clients or for its own book (proprietary trading) – was viewed to be less socially risky because banks could trade in and out of positions at market prices that reflected approximately the value of assets held in their trading books. As a result, regulators did not require banks to hold capital for the growing amount of assets that they were trading in the capital markets because the potential negative externalities were considered to be minimal, if not non-existent. This changed, however, with the collapse of Barings Bank in 1995 (discussed in Chapter 5) that arose from the British bank's failure to cover its trading book loses in derivatives markets and to disclose its actual losses in a timely manner to its regulator, the Bank of England. After the Bank of England became aware of the extent of Barings' losses, it guaranteed most of the bank's trading positions while winding down the rest of its operations before selling the remainder of the bank's net assets to the Dutch bank ING for 1 pound sterling.

4.22 As part of the international response to the Barings collapse, the Basel Committee adopted the Market Risk Amendment to Basel I in 1996 which expanded regulatory capital requirements to include a bank's market risk (or trading book) exposures. The real significance of the Market Risk Amendment, however, was that it allowed banks for the first time to use their own data and value-at-risk (VaR)[11] models as a basis for calculating their regulatory capital for the trading book. This resulted in banks with the largest trading book operations (usually large systemically important banks) using their extensive data and risk management resources to develop statistically sophisticated models to persuade regulators to approve a lower regulatory capital charge than what regulators had originally intended when they adopted the Market Risk Amendment. This model-based approach for determining trading book regulatory capital was the basis upon which the banking industry began to lobby regulators and policymakers for amendments to Basel I which would allow banks to use their own economic capital models that relied on their historic loan loss data and VaR models to calculate regulatory capital for their credit risk exposures.

B Basel II

4.23 The Basel Committee proposed in 1999 revisions to the 1988 Capital Accord, which became known as Basel II that was finally agreed in 2005. Basel II was designed to enhance the capital and risk governance of banks by creating incentives for banks to hold lower levels of regulatory capital if they could show that they were measuring and managing their risks more efficiently. Basel II addressed some of the risks associated with off-balance sheet exposures by requiring banks to hold some additional capital based on a small fraction of

11   See Hull JC, *Risk Management and Financial Institutions* (3rd edn, Wiley 2012), 183–201, 266, 279.

the assets shifted off the balance sheet. More generally, however, Basel II supported the conventional view at the time among some academics, regulators and bankers that the shifting of risks to off-balance sheet entities and the use of credit default swaps and securitisation structures reduced banking sector instability because other market participants (i.e. long-term institutional investors) were willing to invest in bank credit and absorb the related risks.[12] As discussed in 2.35, the spreading of risk throughout the wholesale structured credit markets was viewed to be beneficial for financial stability.[13] The regulator's focus on individual institutions, however, failed to take account of the systemic risks in these markets and how that was related to the highly leveraged balance sheets of banks.

4.24 Basel II was proposed in 1999 to address many of these gaps and weaknesses. In doing so, Basel II introduced the 'three pillars' concept – (1) minimum capital; (2) supervisory review; and (3) market discipline – designed to reinforce each other and to create incentives for banks to enhance their risk measurement and management. Basel II's overall objective was to make regulatory capital more sensitive to the credit, market and operational risks that banks faced as measured on their balance sheets and to align regulatory capital with the economic capital that banks were already holding. Basel II's risk-based framework remains relevant today because it forms the edifice upon which subsequent bank capital regulatory requirements under Basel III and its amendments are based.

4.25 Pillar 1 allows banks to calculate their regulatory capital by using statistical models that rely mainly on their own historic default and loss data to estimate their credit, market and operational risks. Pillar 2 set forth principles of supervisory review that authorise regulators to require banks to comply with broad principles of corporate governance and to adopt an internal capital adequacy assessment process (ICAAP) designed to enhance risk measurement and management. Pillar 3 uses market discipline to require banks to disclose more information to the market so shareholders and creditors can monitor bank management more effectively to ensure the bank's soundness and future prospects.

4.26 Pillar 1 calculates regulatory capital differently depending on the type of risks being assessed; for example, credit risk, market risk (e.g. interest rate, foreign exchange or equity price) and operational risk. The results are effectively additive; for example, credit risk plus market risk plus operational risk. A risk-based capital regime requires a bank to hold capital

---

12 Dudley WC and Hubbard G, 'How Capital Markets Enhance Economic Performance and Facilitate Job Creation' (Goldman Sachs Markets Institute 2004), 3, 17. See also Greenspan A, 'Risk Transfer and Financial Stability', Federal Reserve Bank of Chicago's Annual Conference on Bank Structure, Chicago, IL USA (5 May 2005), 2 www.federalreserve.gov/boarddocs/speeches/2005/20050505/ accessed 21 February 2018; International Monetary Fund, 'Global Financial Stability Report: Market Developments and Issues' (April 2006), 51 www.imf.org/en/Publications/GFSR/Issues/2016/12/31/Market-Developments-and-Issues3 accessed 21 February 2018.

13 See Alexander K, Dhumale R and Eatwell J, *Global Governance of Financial Systems: The International Regulation of Systemic Risk* (Oxford University Press 2006), 5–7.

against some proportion of the total risk of the asset measured against the possibility of unexpected losses. This is based on the assumption that all assets will not default at once. For example, a risk-based capital requirement will increase when the probability of default (PD) of an asset increases, or the bank's exposure at the point of default (EAD) increases, or the loss given default on an asset or asset class increases (LGD).

4.27 Basel II expanded the use of risk-weightings for banks to estimate the riskiness of their assets. A number of parameters determine an asset's risk-weighting, including the maturity of the loan, the probability of default, and the bank's loss and exposure given default. Assets with lower risk-weightings generally attract lower capital charges, whereas assets with higher risk-weightings generally attract higher capital charges. Corporate loans with short-term maturities attract lower risk-weightings (lower capital charges), while corporate loans with long-term maturities (seven years or more) attract higher risk-weightings (higher capital charges).

4.28 The use of risk-weights for assessing credit risk involves specifying relative weights for broad asset classes based on factors such as PD, LGD and EAD. These factors or metrics add together the assets across all risk-weighted asset exposures, providing a total of 'risk-weighted assets', known as RWA. The capital requirements are then calculated as a ratio to RWA.

4.29 The idea is that the capital requirement ('or capital charge') is proportional to the risk; that is, it is neutral in so far as it requires more capital for riskier assets and less capital for less risky assets, as risk-based regulatory capital should be neutral and not encourage nor discourage particular levels of risk-taking. Nevertheless, some banks use their own internal data to calculate unrealistically low risk-weights in order to justify building a very large balance sheet based on a relatively very low level of regulatory capital. This has been an express risk management strategy for some banks, such as UBS, which call it 'capital optimisation'.[14]

4.30 It should be borne in mind that the capital optimisation strategy will vary between banks and involve different approaches to measuring risks. Generally, smaller, less complex banks will measure their risks based on the Basel III standardised approach (SA). The *standardised approach* uses standard industry credit risk-weights, and includes some risk-weightings that are determined by external credit assessment institutions (ECAIs) (i.e. credit rating agencies). The ECAI's rating (e.g. A+ or BBB+) will determine the SA risk-weighting for the particular bank credit risk exposure.

4.31 Under the SA, the ECAI rating can fall into one of five categories, AAA to AAA+ (20 per cent); A+ to A- (50 per cent); BBB+ to BB- (100 per cent), Below BB- (150 per cent) and

---

14 See Ita A, Head of Group Economic Performance and Capital Optimization, UBS AG, Presentation at the University of Zurich University Finance Research Program (9 June 2017).

Table 4.1 Basel III Standardized Approach ECAI Risk-Weights

Credit assessment	AAA to AAA+	A+ to A−	BBB+ to BB−	Below BB−	Unrated
Risk weight	20%	50%	100%	150%	100%

Unrated (100 per cent) (see Table 4.1). The SA's five categories of risk-weights are supplemented by retail credit portfolios consisting of credit risk exposures to individual and small business customers that are subject to a 75 per cent risk-weighting.[15]

4.32 The SA also allows banks to lower their credit risk-weightings if they conduct credit risk mitigation (CRM) techniques to mitigate their risk exposure – such as collateralised exposures or exposures guaranteed by third parties. Banks can obtain further capital relief when these techniques meet legal certainty standards.

4.33 The largest most complex banking and financial groups utilise the *Advanced* approach, in which the banks use their own internal risk models to estimate their risk expsoures on different asset classes and to create firm-specific risk-weights. As discussed above, *internal risk models* are usually based on extensive past data to assess the pattern and extent of defaults (PD, EAD, LDG) in the particular risks that the individual bank takes. The bank supervisor must approve these risk models so that the bank can use them to calculate its regulatory capital. The bank sets up and validates the model and the supervisor approves (or disapproves) it. These models are expensive to establish and maintain but in most cases allow the largest and most sophisticated banks to reduce their regulatory capital levels substantially in comparison to what they would have been required to hold under the standardised approach.

4.34 Basel II and II.5 (latter adopted in 2008) also apply to market risk exposures (also known as trading risk). In assessing market risks, banks often use *value-at-risk* models which look at the historical variation in asset prices over a certain period of time. These can be misleading, especially just before a crisis when volatility is likely to be low. So, Basel II.5 requires 'stressed VaR', to be measured based on particularly volatile periods over recent years. The old Basel II approach to measuring market risk used a model that estimated the current risk at a particular *point in time.* A more macro-prudential approach that focuses on inter-temporal volatility of market risks focuses more on averaging the risk using conditions *through the (business) cycle.* Both approaches have advantages and disadvantages, and under Basel II.5 regulators have discretion to adopt a hybrid middle way.

4.35 The capital requirements for a bank's market risk are calculated through either the *standardised approach* or the *Internal Models Approach (*IMA – typically *VaR* and *stressed VaR-*

---

15 Basel II Agreement, see Basel Committee on Banking Supervision, Basel III: A Global Regulatory Framework for More Resilient Banks and Banking Systems (Basel III Accord) (December 2010, revised June 2011), No. 69–71, 23.

based models). The capital requirements for market risk consist of the sum of capital requirements for the following market risk-weighted categories: Foreign exchange risk; Commodities risk; Treatment of options; Equity position risk (general market risk and specific risk); Interest rate risk (general market risk and specific risk). The resulting total capital requirements for total market risk exposures are then multiplied by 12.5 to obtain the market risk RWA-equivalent.

1 Operational Risk RWA

4.36 The operational risk capital requirements are calculated through either *the Basic Indicator Approach* (BIA), *Standardised Approach* or the *Advanced Measurement Approach* (AMA). Capital requirements under the BIA are calculated as 15 per cent (the alpha factor) of the bank's annual positive gross income averaged over the previous three years. Capital requirements under the standardised approach are calculated in a similar way, but instead of having a single alpha factor, the calculation is weighted utilising different beta factors (ranging from 12–18 per cent) for various business lines (e.g. corporate finance, trading and sales, retail banking, etc.). Capital requirements under the AMA are calculated based on internal and external data on various risk drivers spanning a five-year observation period, as well as corrections for control factors and risk mitigation. Similar to the calculation of RWAs for market risk, the RWA-equivalent for operational risk is determined by multiplying the operational risk capital requirements by a factor of 12.5.

4.37 The use of internal models to calculate regulatory capital became controversial in the aftermath of the crisis because many of the largest and most sophisticated banks were manipulating or at least stretching the assumptions in their models to reduce unduly their regulatory capital levels. Under Basel III, the internal models are treated more sceptically by regulators but are essentially still used to calculate risk-weightings and remain similarly flawed (as discussed above) because they are based on backward-looking data that are used to estimate future credit and market risks. Moreover, the past data are more often inadequate and do not properly ascertain the risks of actual losses. Small and medium-sized banks are at a disadvantage because they do not have enough data to satisfy the regulator in order to qualify for lowering capital requirements and so must use the standardised approach, which results in a much higher capital requirement. Also, new challenger banks have no data and would be relegated to the SA. Small and new banks complain that internal models give the big banks an unfair competitive advantage.

2 Leverage Limits

4.38 US regulators have generally been sceptical of heavy reliance on bank risk models to calculate regulatory capital and have historically (pre-crisis) limited their use by applying a leverage ratio for banks and financial holding companies. A leverage ratio is an unweighted capital requirement that is measured in the numerator with core equity Tier 1 capital divided by the bank's total assets (plus some off-balance sheet exposures) in the denominator. The leverage ratio is designed to capture the whole of a bank's exposures on an unweighted basis. It is therefore not risk-neutral but instead provides a minimum capital floor beneath which the bank cannot reduce its capital requirements based on risk-weightings. As discussed below, the leverage ratio is now part of Basel III. A few EU states, including the UK, have implemented the leverage ratio, but it is not yet required by EU banking law.

4.39 The important point is that a risk-based regime permits an asset to be assessed for capital requirements depending on a variety of risk metrics (as discussed above) and the task for the regulator should be not to favour any particular risk appetite, but to charge regulatory capital according to the economic riskiness of the exposure and the estimated social costs or externalities that the risk exposures pose to the public. Regulatory capital should aim to have a minimum capital safeguard in the form of a leverage ratio but also focus on risk neutrality to stop firms arbitraging the rules.

3 Basel II and the Crisis

4.40 When the global banking crisis began in late 2007, however, the risk-weightings of most European and US banks were shown to be poor indicators of the financial risks to which banks were exposed.[16] Specifically, bank models estimated their counterparty credit and liquidity risks in the asset-backed securities and derivatives markets underestimated correlations across asset classes. Moreover, the opaqueness of the risk-weightings in the credit and trading books made it very difficult, if not impossible, for investors to understand the true risk exposure of a bank. These factors contributed significantly to an undercapitalisation of the banking system, which weakened its ability to absorb losses in the crisis.

4.41 Basel II allowed banks to use their own estimates of credit and market risks to lower their risk-weightings for certain asset classes with regulatory approval. This approach to calculating regulatory capital – involving the bank estimating its risks and calculating its regulatory capital to be approved by the bank supervisor – was criticised before the crisis as potentially leading to an undercapitalisation of the banking sector.[17] If the supervisor approved the bank's model for measuring and managing its risk, the bank could hold a significantly lower level of regulatory capital based on its model calculation. In theory, the Basel II process provided an incentive for banks to improve their risk management by offering them reduced regulatory capital if they could demonstrate that their risk-based models adequately controlled the risks that the bank individually faced against creditors and depositors. However, the risks that Basel II focused on were primarily micro-prudential risks; that is, risks that were largely exogenous – or external – to the bank's balance sheet and not the risks that the bank itself created for the financial system – so-called endogenous risks – because of its size, interconnectedness and exposure to liquidity risks.[18] Basel II

---

16 See discussion in Admati A and Hellwig M, *The Bankers' New Clothes: What's Wrong with Banking and What to do About It* (Princeton University Press 2013), 170.
17 See Alexander et al. (n 13), 31–33.
18 See Brunnermeier et al. (n 13), 10–11.

did not require, therefore, that banks hold adequate capital to address the systemic risks that the banks themselves create for the financial system.

4.42 Although Basel II was not formally adopted in Europe until January 2007 and only applied in the US to the largest US financial holding companies, its flawed model-based approach for measuring and managing risk had become an industry standard for most European and global financial institutions before it was actually adopted into national regulation. The model-based approach to measuring risk was already in use by financial institutions in the 1990s to determine their economic capital.[19] The economic capital models of these institutions assumed that volatility was a proxy for risk. This was based on conventional portfolio management theory, and involved the widespread use of volatility-based models, such as VaR. As it turned out in 2007 and 2008, with the onset of the crisis, these standardised VaR models badly underestimated the likelihood of significant falls in asset prices based on external shocks and failed to take into account the likelihood of numerous aftershocks. The use of these volatility-based models for determining bank economic capital was the essential basis for the development of Basel II, and remains an important factor for measuring risk under Basel III.

4.43 Moreover, Basel II did not contain liquidity requirements to ensure that banks held a minimum amount of liquid assets or that they had stable sources of funding. Basel II also increased the complexity of banking regulation and risk management by encouraging banks to rely heavily on their internal risk models to calculate regulatory capital, which ultimately resulted in an undercapitalised banking system. This was in keeping with the pre-crisis regulatory philosophy in Europe and the US, that financial markets were rational and self-correcting and that financial innovations (i.e. credit default swaps) and other new modes of finance had reduced systemic risks.[20] The financial crisis demonstrated that bank risk models failed to detect how financial innovation in the form of securitisation and derivatives can introduce systemic risks into the financial system.

4.44 Under Basel II, prudential regulation was structured to support market-based governance models of banks that regulators heavily relied on to ensure that the banking system was safe and efficient.[21] The financial crisis of 2007–2008 exposed bank models as seriously flawed in how they measured and managed financial risks.

C Risk Management

4.45 Financial liberalisation in the 1970s and 1980s transformed bank risk management by requiring banks to collect more data on the riskiness of their assets and to build models that

---

19   See de Weert F, *Bank and Insurance Capital Management* (Wiley 2011), 79.
20   See HM Treasury (n 9), 5.
21   Renner M, 'Death by Complexity: The Financial Crises and the Crises of Law in World Society', in Kjaer PF, Teubner G and Febbrajo A (eds), *The Financial Crises in Constitutional Perspective: The Dark Side of Functional Differentiation* (Hart Publishing 2011), 93.

estimated the level of capital they should hold to demonstrate their solvency and market performance. In many countries, regulators began to use risk classifications or weightings as a basis for calculating regulatory capital. Under Basel II, the calculation of bank regulatory capital has been based primarily on the estimated riskiness of bank assets. The determination of economic and regulatory capital is an important part of bank risk management. The main strategic objective of bank risk management is to measure and manage financial risks for a greater risk-adjusted return on equity for shareholders based on the firm's expected profits minus its expected costs for credit, market, liquidity and operational risks. Before the financial crisis, average risk-adjusted returns on capital for non-financial companies in developed countries amounted to approximately 9.5 per cent across most industry sectors, while average risk-adjusted returns for large banks and financial institutions averaged an excess of 20 per cent.[22] To achieve such returns, banks must take significant risks, which can potentially threaten financial stability.

4.46 Financial firms, however, have an incentive to hold economic capital only at a level required by the market to optimise their cost of funding. This is intended to protect the creditors of the firm against default, but it does not take into account the negative externalities or social costs of a potential bank default on the economy. This is exacerbated by the limited liability structure of most banks that incentivises shareholders to pressure management to take on greater leverage (i.e. debt) to achieve higher risk-adjusted returns but which could potentially put the firm's solvency at risk as well as impose significant externalities on the financial system. Indeed, Alan Greenspan, who had initially praised credit risk transfer innovations that shifted risk around the financial system as stability enhancing,[23] later came to recognise bank risk management failings prior to the crisis and the moral hazard problem for bank shareholders in pressuring bank management to take excessive risks when he stated:

> In August 2007, the risk management structure cracked. All the sophisticated mathematics and computer wizardry essentially rested on one central premise: that the enlightened self-interest of owners and managers of financial institutions would lead them to maintain a sufficient buffer against insolvency by actively monitoring their firms' capital and risk position.[24]

4.47 Indeed, the Financial Stability Forum observed in an April 2008 report that the 2007 credit crunch and ensuing global crisis was the result of massive failings in risk management in some of the largest and most sophisticated financial institutions.[25] Risk managers failed to

---

22   Admati A and Hellwig M (n 16), 100–109; see also Jackson P, 'Beyond Basel II' (presentation at Clare College, Cambridge, 12 September 2010); and Reilly D, 'From Wall Street to Crawl Street' (*Wall Street Journal*, Europe edition, 29 July 2011) www.wsj.com/articles/SB10001424053111904888304576474261732934454 accessed 18 March 2018.

23   Greenspan (n 12), 2.

24   Greenspan A, 'We Need a Better Cushion Against Risk' (*Financial Times* Opinion, 26 March 2009) www.ft .com/content/9c158a92-1a3c-11de-9f91-0000779fd2ac accessed 18 March 2018.

25   Financial Stability Forum, 'Report of the Financial Stability Forum on Enhancing Market and Institutional Resilience' (7 April 2008) www.fsb.org/wp-content/uploads/r_0804.pdf accessed 21 February 2018.

appreciate or understand the externality risks of the structured finance market and, in particular, to understand the extent of the risks of their undercapitalised positions in the mortgage-backed securities market and the OTC credit default swap market. This contributed to destructive speculation that fuelled the market bubble and exacerbated the fallout when the markets inevitably collapsed.

1 Balance Sheet Management

4.48 Any company is sensitive to the size of its balance sheet. Normally, the pricing of its liabilities is a function of the size of its balance sheet. Simply stated, the more assets a company has, the more liabilities are needed to finance these assets. To the extent that these liabilities are debt (as opposed to equity), this introduces more leverage, makes the company look riskier and hence pushes up the return expectations of both debt and equity investors. This ultimately translates into a higher cost of capital.[26]

4.49 Bank management is very sensitive to the expectations of investors and hence constantly monitors the size of the bank's balance sheet. When the decision is taken to reduce assets, the number of options available is limited. Outright sale is one option, but where the underlying assets are loans, this is hampered by two factors: first, illiquid loans can be hard to sell. Second, loans sales (normally to other banks) are never popular with the borrower, who normally prefers not to see its pool of creditors change. For these two reasons, beginning in the 2000s, banks were drawn to using certain types of structured finance instruments, such as collateralised debt obligations (CDOs), to manage their balance sheets. Illiquid loans can be sold into a CDO more easily than into the secondary loan market. Furthermore, borrowers are more comfortable with their loans being owned by a special purpose vehicle (SPV), which is normally operationally managed by an arranger who is also responsible for transferring the loans from the originator to the SPV as part of the securitisation process.

2 Economic Capital Management

4.50 Post-crisis market developments have placed an even greater importance on banks' ability to manage their 'economic capital' – that is, the equity capital needed for banks to support the risks of the unexpected losses associated with holding assets. Whereas Basel I used a few risk-weighted 'buckets' to calculate how much regulatory capital should be held, the economic capital approach uses a model to calculate how risky a portfolio of assets is and how much capital is needed. As discussed below, the intention of Basel II and Basel III is to link regulatory capital to risk ('risk-sensitivity') and hence represents a migration from the Basel I approach of increasing bank capital across the board based on broadly defined risk categories to an economic capital management approach that relies on more precise measures of risk. While this sounds sensible in principle, there are substantive definitional

---

26 See Adam A, *Handbook of Asset and Liability Management: From Models to Optimal Return Strategies* (Wiley 2007).

issues. Whose risk should the regulator focus on? – the bank's risk to bondholders or depositors, or the systemic risk that arises from externalities imposed on third parties who are not directly involved in transactions with the bank? How do we measure risk when we are worried about market failures – using historic prices, market forecasts or non-market measures?

4.51 From an economic capital perspective there are three main contributors to risk: the risk of a particular asset (for example, its issuer may go bankrupt tomorrow), the risk of holding too large an exposure to a particular issuer (1,000 loans of $1 are less risky than one loan of $1,000 if the one thousand loans are diversified), and the risk of being exposed to an industry sector that is correlated (during a severe oil price decline all oil company issuers tend to suffer and, because they are correlated, tend to look like one large exposure). Further, each of these risks changes with the length of the loan's holding period. While the first of these risks can be assessed independently, the other two require a portfolio analysis, as the risk of the whole is different from the risk of the parts.

4.52 Any transaction that results in the sale of assets that are risky for the institution to hold should have a risk management benefit. For example, a balance sheet CDO is an important instrument for allowing a bank to manage its regulatory capital position. CDOs are debt instruments that allow investors with differing risk appetites to invest in a broad range of assets that would normally reside on bank balance sheets. The CDO market evolved from the older CBO (bond) and CLO (loan) markets, the name change reflecting the fact that the underlying assets in CDO transactions include a broad range of debt-related products. The traditional CDO structure involves the issuance of bonds – 'debt obligations' – by an SPV such that the bonds are 'collateralised' by a portfolio of assets owned by the SPV. It is unlikely that the only rationale for a CDO is risk management; it is more likely to offer a combination of benefits. A bank may use a CDO to dispose of risky assets but is normally mindful of the fact that investors may share the same negative sentiment and hence there may be little net commercial advantage from the transfer. A bank may also use a CDO to manage its credit lines – the internal limits placed on the total credit exposure to any one issuer. Often, banks want to do more with a particular client, but are constrained by internal limits. Moving the risk (into a CDO or elsewhere) frees up the credit line. The bank's strategy in managing its economic capital is to allocate capital to its most profitable use on a risk-adjusted basis and to optimise its cost of capital by sending a signal to the market that it is solvent.

3 Regulatory Capital Management

4.53 As mentioned above, banks are required to hold regulatory capital that is measured against their risk-based assets. Banks monitor their risk-based capital ratio very closely and will take steps to manage it. The sale of certain assets is one way of managing it as the notional value of risky assets is reduced. As discussed above, a balance sheet CDO is a very effective way of managing a bank's risk-based capital, as a large number of loans are sold in one transaction. This is often referred to as 'freeing up capital' and is part of the overall process known as 'regulatory capital management'.[27] Since a bank has a finite amount of capital, there is a quantifiable maximum amount of corporate debt that can be taken on. Selling or hedging debt frees up the capital that was allocated and allows it to be used for new lending or other banking business, such as investing in securities.

Calculating Total Risk-Weighted Assets

4.54 Similar to Basel II, Basel III now requires that a bank's total risk-weighted assets (RWAs) are the sum of its credit risk RWA, market risk RWA and operational risk RWA. Of these, the credit risk RWA (RWA_{CR}) is accepted as the only genuine form of risk-weighted assets, whereas the market risk asset RWA (CAP_{MR}) and the operational risk asset RWA (CAP_{OpRisk}) are essentially 'RWA-equivalents', obtained by multiplying the calculated capital requirements for these risk categories by a factor of 12.5 (the inverse of the traditional 8 per cent capital ratio for determining capital requirements for credit risk). Besides these main components, additional surcharges to RWA may result from counterparty credit risk (RWA_{CCR}) for centrally cleared derivatives, credit valuation adjustment (CAP_{CVA}) for non-cleared derivative trades and settlement risk (RWA_{SR}):

$$RWA_{Total} = RWA_{CR} + RWA_{CCR} + RWA_{SR} + 12.5 \times \left(CAP_{MR} + CAP_{OpRisk} + CAP_{CVA} \right)$$

Equation 4.1

4.55 As discussed earlier, regulators consider credit risk-weighted assets as the main form of risk-weighted assets. At a basic level, every credit exposure is assigned a risk-weight to determine the RWA. Under Basel III, the RWA can be determined in four ways. The advanced approaches consist of the Advanced Internal Ratings Based Approach (AIRB), in which risk-weights are calculated with a bank's modelled PD, LGD and EAD, and the Foundation Internal Ratings Based Approach (F-IRB), in which risk-weights are calculated with a bank's modelled PD, while the regulator prescribes the LGD and EAD.

4.56 The two less data-driven approaches are the standardised approach (SA) and the *slotting approach*. As discussed above, the SA provides that an asset receives a fixed risk-weight depending on a particular industry classification or characteristic (e.g. a certain loan-to-value ratio for residential real estate, or credit rating for sovereign and corporate exposure). The slotting approach involves each asset class (e.g. retail, corporate, real estate, banks, sovereign, etc.) receiving a fixed risk-weight based on a combination of risk characteristics across several risk 'buckets' or 'slots' (e.g. Strong, Good, Satisfactory, Weak and Default).[28] Banks may utilise different approaches for different portfolios, subject to certain conditions

---

27   See Berger A, De Young R, Flannery M, Lee D and Öztekin Ö, 'How Do Large Banking Organizations Manage Their Capital Ratios?' (2008) 34 *Journal of Financial Service Research* 123–149.
28   The slotting approach is now used to calculate risk-weights in the commercial lending sector.

set by the supervisor. The total sum of the individual exposures multiplied by their respective risk-weights results in the credit risk RWA.

4.57 As discussed below, the statistical models utilised under Basel II and now under Basel III, however, continue to have serious flaws because they are mainly based on value-at-risk models (VaR) that rely on historic loss data that are too limited to capture the full range of asset price volatility and are based on the flawed assumption that the observation of past price movements could be used to estimate future price movements.[29] This assumption fails to recognise what Keynes observed, as 'human decisions affecting the future, whether personal or political or economic, cannot depend on strict mathematical expectations, since the basis for making such calculations does not exist'. The probability of future market developments is based on historic market data and excludes the possibility of extreme events that had never occurred before. Indeed, VaR models are misapplied to the calculation of economic and regulatory capital, as they assume 'that past price movements represent a random sample from a universe of possible patterns, and that future price movements will also be samples drawn from that unchanging universe'. As a result, they 'fail to recognize that the future is governed not by quantifiable probabilistic risk but by inherent uncertainty'.[30]

4.58 Specifically, the financial crisis showed how VaR models were flawed in estimating market risks in the trading of collateralised debt obligations and the related liquidity risks and counterparty credit risks in the wholesale securitisation markets. These factors contributed significantly to an undercapitalisation of the banking system, which weakened its ability to absorb losses when the crisis began. Moreover, overreliance on these flawed models and weak and haphazard governance in individual banks resulted in direct taxpayer-funded bailouts of large banking institutions, such as the US bank Citicorp and the Swiss bank UBS (as discussed in Box 4.1).

4.59 The severe write-downs by UBS in 2007 and by other banks, incuding Citi in early 2008, led to unprecedented taxpayer-funded bailouts of some of the most recognised global banks. These failures in bank risk management revealed a huge flaw in the Basel II framework: that the economic capital models used by banks and which were accepted by regulators as being valid reference points for the calculation of regulatory capital could be manipulated by the banks to support aggressive and excessively risky business practices. Moreover, the economic capital models under Basel II failed to anticipate systemic financial risks – e.g. drying up of bank liquidity in the wholesale funding markets and correlated declines in the value of asset-backed securities across different markets – and utilised risk-sensitive techniques that could exacerbate systemic risks in the face of extreme events. Moreover, Basel II's supervisory review process (Pillar 2) which could be used to test and challenge bank risk management practices was under-utilised and even ignored by many supervisors as a tool

---

29 Keynes JM, *The General Theory of Employment, Interest and Money* (Palgrave Macmillan 1936), 162–163.
30 Turner A, *Between Debt and the Devil* (Princeton University Press 2016), 102–103.

Box 4.1 UBS and Risk Management Failure

UBS had become one of the largest banking groups in the early 2000s. Under its chairman, Marcel Ospel, the bank embarked on an aggressive business strategy that was largely based on a substantial expansion of the fixed-income business (including asset-backed securities) and by the establishment of an alternative investment business (hedge fund). A major objective of the bank was to reduce its regulatory capital requirements, particularly for its fixed-income trading in asset-backed securities and alternative investment strategy. In July 2006, the UBS Group Board of Directors had approved the bank's business strategy and risk management as prudent. The Board's strategic focus for 2006–2010 was for 'significant revenue increases but the Group's risk profile was not predicted to change substantially with a moderate growth in overall risk weighted assets'. Aside from the change in business strategy, there was no specific decision by the Board either to develop business in or to increase exposure to subprime markets. UBS, however, later in 2008, acknowledged that in 2006 'there was amongst other things, a focus on the growth of certain businesses that did, as part of their activities, invest in or increase UBS's exposure to the US subprime sector by virtue of investments in securities referencing the sector'.

Although the Executive Board approved the strategy in March 2006, it stressed at that time that 'the increase in highly structured illiquid commitments that could result from this growth plan would need to be carefully analysed and tightly controlled and an appropriate balance between incremental revenue and VAR/Stress Loss increase would need to be achieved to avoid undue dilution of return on risk performance'. The plan was approved by the Group Board.

Having approved the strategy, the bank did not establish balance sheet size as a limiting metric. Senior management did not decide to impose hard limits and risk-weighted asset targets on each of its business lines until the third and fourth quarters (Q3 and Q4) 2007. In early 2007, however, the US housing market began to decline and the value of the asset-backed securities and other 'highly structured illiquid commitments' held by UBS had begun to drop precipitously. By the end of 2007, the bank needed to recognise losses of USD 18.7 billion and to raise new capital. What went wrong?

As it turned out, the strategy of the investment bank to develop the fixed-income and asset-backed securities business was disastrous. The bank followed a strategy of acquiring mortgage-based assets (mainly US subprime) and then packaging them for resale (holding them in the meantime, i.e. warehousing the assets). Each transaction was frequently in excess of USD 1 billion, normally requiring specific approval. In fact, it was later discovered in 2008 that senior management had only approved of these transactions *ex post*, after they had taken place, in violation of internal compliance rules. As much as 60 per cent of the value of the most complex and illiquid of these asset-backed securities, known as collateralised debt obligations (CDOs), were in fact retained on UBS's own books.

In a later report that investigated UBS's pre-crisis trading activities, it was noted that '[i]n undertaking the transactions, the traders benefited from the banks' allocation of funds that did not take risk into account. There was thus an internal carry trade but only involving returns of 20 basis points. In combination with the bonus system, traders were thus encouraged to take large positions. Yet until Q3 2007 there were no aggregate notional limits on the sum of the CDO warehouse pipeline and retained CDO positions, even though warehouse collateral had been identified as a problem in Q4 2005 and again in Q3 2006.'

'Further, the UBS strategy evolved so that the CDOs were structured into tranches with UBS retaining the Senior Super tranches. These were regarded as safe and therefore marked at nominal price. A small default of 4 per cent was assumed and this was hedged, often with monoline insurers. There was neither monitoring of counterparty risk nor analysis of risks in the subprime market, the credit rating being accepted at face value. Worse, as the retained tranches were regarded as safe and fully hedged, they were netted to zero in the value-at-risk (VaR) calculations used by UBS for risk management. Risk management and the Board expressed little concern about the growing risks in the subprime market. Moreover, senior management and the Board ignored the bank's exposure in its other lines of business to risks in the subprime market. There was no assessment of these risks until the third quarter (Q3) 2007, when the bank was in negotiations with the Swiss central bank for a bailout. In summary, UBS's Board, senior management and risk officers believed that they had a 'safe' risk management strategy, but their risks assessments were flawed and resulted in unprecedented write-downs on the value of assets of USD 18.7 billion and a taxpayer-supported bailout by the Swiss central bank and the Swiss government.'

Source: Shareholder Report on UBS's Write-Downs, 2008 (Blundell-Wignall A, Atkinson A and Lee SH, 1995)

to monitor and detect weak risk management and governance. Prior to the crisis, regulators failed to utilise Pillar 2 to challenge bank risk officers, senior management and the board in their oversight of bank risk-taking. Essentially, Basel II embodied the failure of financial policymakers and regulators to incorporate systemic risks into the design of regulatory capital and risk management.

D Basel III

4.60 The post-crisis amendments to the Basel II framework, known as Basel III,[31] raise important issues regarding whether bank capital regulation adequately limits systemic risks in the banking sector. Although Basel III is largely built on the edifice of Basel II, it attempts to address many of the weaknesses of Basel II that contributed to the crisis. Figure 4.2 shows how Basel III increases core Tier 1 regulatory capital from 2 per cent to 4.5 per cent of risk-based assets, plus adds a 2.5 per cent capital conservation buffer, and a tighter definition of Tier 1 capital to include mainly ordinary common shares and retained earnings (excluding most other equivalent instruments). It will also impose an additional 2.5 per cent

---

31 See Basel Committee on Banking Supervision, 'Basel III: A Global Regulatory Framework for More Resilient Banks and Banking Systems' (Basel III Accord) (December 2010, revised June 2011) www.bis.org/publ/bcbs189 .pdf accessed 21 February 2018.

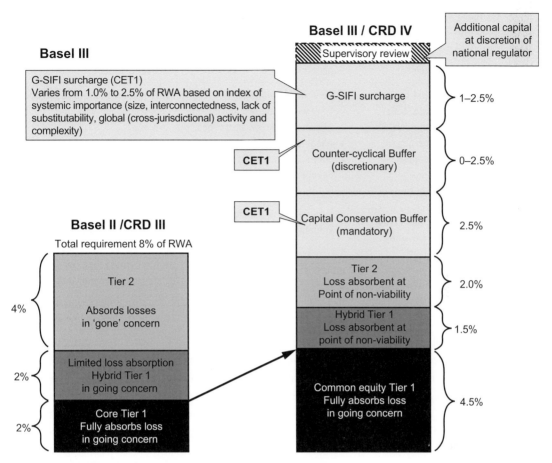

Basel III

G-SIFI surcharge (CET1)
Varies from 1.0% to 2.5% of RWA based on index of
systemic importance (size, interconnectedness, lack of
substitutability, global (cross-jurisdictional) activity and
complexity)

Basel II /CRD III

Total requirement 8% of RWA

4% — Tier 2 / Absorbs losses in 'gone' concern

2% — Limited loss absorption Hybrid Tier 1 in going concern

2% — Core Tier 1 Fully absorbs loss in going concern

Basel III / CRD IV

Additional capital at discretion of national regulator

Supervisory review

G-SIFI surcharge — 1–2.5%

CET1 — Counter-cyclical Buffer (discretionary) — 0–2.5%

CET1 — Capital Conservation Buffer (mandatory) — 2.5%

Tier 2 Loss absorbent at Point of non-viability — 2.0%

Hybrid Tier 1 Loss absorbent at point of non-viability — 1.5%

Common equity Tier 1 Fully absorbs loss in going concern — 4.5%

Figure 4.2 Comparing regulatory capital between Basel II and Basel III

counter-cyclical capital ratio that will be adjusted across the economic cycle.[32] Also, an additional capital charge of up to 2.5 per cent regulatory capital will be required for large and interconnected systemically important financial institutions (SIFIs).

4.61 As with Basel II, Basel III consists of three pillars: (1) minimum capital; (2) supervisory review; and (3) market discipline (see Table 4.2). Under Pillar 1, banks on the advanced approach are allowed to devise statistical models that rely mainly on their own internal historic default data and risk-weights to estimate their credit, market, liquidity and operational risks. Based on these risk estimations, the bank calculates the amount of regulatory capital it should hold against these risks.

32   See Basel Committee on Banking Supervision, 'Regulatory Consistency Assessment Programme (RCAP): Handbook for Jurisdictional Assessments' (March 2016) www.bis.org/bcbs/publ/d361.pdf accessed 21 February 2018.

Table 4.2 Basel III's three-pillar framework

Pillar 1	Pillar 2	Pillar 3
Minimum capital requirements	Supervisory review process	Market discipline
Additional/refined capital basis • liquidity coverage ratio (LCR) • Net stable funding ratio (NSFR) • OTC derivatives charge • Quality and level of capital • Leverage ratio • Capital conservation buffers • Counter-cyclical buffers • Enhanced loss absorption clause (write-off or debt conversion)	**Supervision (dialogue)** • Firm-wide corporate governance • Managing risk concentrations • Alignment of LT incentives • Sound compensation practices • Supervisory colleges **Capital (ICAAP)** • Firm-wide risk management • Valuation practice, stress tests **Supervisory review evaluation process (SREP)** • Capital governance	**Additional/enhanced disclosure** Risk Management Market Credit Operational • Regulatory capital components • Detailed reconciliation of capital • Regulatory capital ratios • Securitisation exposures

4.62 Under Pillar 2, states have discretion to impose a range of measures, including additional capital requirements, on individual institutions or groups of institutions to address corporate governance weaknesses and unsound risk management practices. Bank supervisors generally consider their discretion to adjust capital under Pillar 2 to be 'additive' only to the capital calculated under Pillar 1. Therefore, national supervisors should be able to impose higher capital requirements if they believe the bank has inadequate governance and risk management processes in place. If they determine that the bank has adequate governance structures and risk management processes, they would require no additional capital. As discussed below, this crucial linkage between the amount of regulatory capital and the quality of the bank's corporate governance will be assessed through Pillar 2's supervisory review enhancement process (SREP). Pillar 3 remains focused on regulatory disclosures by the bank to the market and the use of fair value accounting to value bank assets (known as IFRS 9) and trading positions in order to enhance market discipline of the bank risk-taking activities.

1 Pillar 1: Minimum Capital

4.63 In addition to increasing the level of core equity Tier 1 capital from 2 per cent to 4.5 per cent, along with an additional capital conservation buffer of 2.5 per cent that takes CET1 up to 7.0 per cent, Pillar 1 also prescribes a tighter definition of CET1 to include only ordinary common shares (or strict equivalents) and retained earnings. Pillar 1 also requires a leverage ratio of 3 per cent of a bank's total assets (unweighted for risk) in which Tier 1 capital is the numerator and total balance sheet assets plus certain off-balance sheet contingencies serve as the denominator (1/33). Pillar 1 also contains new liquidity requirements in the form of a net ratio for stable wholesale funding, and liquidity coverage ratios to ensure that the bank is holding a certain amount of high-quality assets that can be sold quickly to cover short-term liability exposures.

4.64 Moreover, large and interconnected SIFIs are required to hold an additional capital charge of between 1 per cent and 3 per cent depending on the institution's size and interconnectedness. Higher capital requirements for SIFIs are deemed necessary because banks have an incentive to grow larger, partly because by becoming larger they can reduce the relative costs of their funding since investors perceive an implicit guarantee by the state to provide direct or indirect financial support to them during times of market stress. The larger a banking group becomes, the lower the costs of its funding relative to its operations. Basel III attempts to address this moral hazard problem by imposing additional capital requirements according to the bank's size, interconnectedness and global reach. And as discussed below, amendments to Basel III in 2017 (known as 'Basel IV') have, among other things, increased the Tier 1 capital requirement for the top category of SIFI institutions to 3.5 per cent.

4.65 As discussed earlier, Pillar 1 offers banks three menus – Advanced Approach, Foundation Approach and Standardised Approach – by which they can measure their credit risks and calculate regulatory capital. The largest, most sophisticated financial institutions will opt for the Advanced Approach because it allows them to use their own default and loss data in a statistical model to estimate their unexpected losses and calculate a regulatory capital amount. Large and medium-sized banks with less data may opt for the Foundation Approach, which requires the bank to submit probability of default data but the supervisor would supply loss data and calculate the capital requirement. The third menu – the Standardised Approach – will be used by most small and medium-sized banks which do not have extensive default and loss data to estimate risk-weights; they will use risk-weightings provided by the regulator and industry that are matched to credit rating scores. This less flexible approach requires credit ratings to play the primary role in determining regulatory capital for small and medium-sized banks.

Liquidity Risks

4.66 Regulators began emphasising liquidity risk management during the crisis of 2007–2008 when it became apparent that many large and medium-sized banks had failed to manage their liquidity risk exposures, thus resulting in many institutions losing access to funding during the crisis and unable to sell assets from their balance sheets which they thought were liquid. Indeed, the banking business – borrowing short and lending long (maturity transformation) – is inherently fragile and the market's perception of a bank's liquidity is important for its soundness. As discussed in Chapter 1, fractional reserve banking has become the conventional business model for most banks in which a depository institution lends all but a fraction of its funding (except reserves held at the central bank) to borrowers. Most of that funding is short-term debt and can be called in generally on short notice. This makes banks vulnerable to the potential need for liquid funds that exceed what they have available. For instance, retail deposits are subject to immediate withdrawal, while most of a bank's loans are longer term. This is the Achilles heel of the banking industry: the inability to repay all depositors or other creditors should a high proportion withdraw their funds at once, plus the difficulty in predicting future cash requirements.

4.67 The Basel Committee responded to this concern by adopting in September 2008 seventeen principles of liquidity risk management for banks that are premised on the notion that lack of access to funding sources and weak liquidity management are typical factors that can lead to bank failures. The Basel Committee's Seventeen Principles of Liquidity Risk Management consist of five categories: a Fundamental Principle, Governance, Measurement and Management, Public Disclosure, and the Role of Supervisors.

4.68 The fundamental principle of liquidity management states that a bank should establish a robust *liquidity risk management framework* that ensures it maintains sufficient liquidity, including a cushion of unencumbered, *high-quality liquid assets*, to withstand a range of stress events, including those involving the loss or impairment of both unsecured and secured funding sources (Principle 2). Regarding bank governance, banks should articulate a liquidity strategy and develop a *strategy, policies and practices* to address liquidity risks. A bank's board of directors should review and approve the strategy, policies and practices related to the management of liquidity at least once a year (Principle 3).

4.69 A bank should incorporate *liquidity costs, benefits and risks* in the internal pricing, performance measurement and new product approval process (Principle 4). Other principles include that a bank should actively monitor and control liquidity risk exposures and funding needs within and across *legal entities, business lines and currencies*, taking into account legal, regulatory and operational limitations to the *transferability* of liquidity (Principle 6) and establish a *funding strategy* that provides effective diversification in the sources and the period of funding. It should maintain an ongoing presence in its chosen funding markets and strong relationships with fund providers and promote effective diversification of their funding sources (Principle 7). Banks should *publicly disclose* information on a regular basis that enables market participants to make an informed judgement about the soundness of its liquidity risk management framework and liquidity position (Principle 13).

4.70 And the role of the bank supervisor should be to supplement their regular assessments of a bank's liquidity risk management framework and liquidity positions by monitoring a combination of internal reports, prudential reports and market information (Principle 15). Bank supervisors should also ensure that banks manage their liquidity risk effectively. For instance, supervisors should intervene to require effective and timely remedial action by a bank to address deficiencies in its liquidity risk management processes or liquidity position (Principle 16). And bank supervisors should be coordinating with other public sector bodies – both at the national and international levels – to ensure effective liquidity oversight of banks and financial institutions and to have as few limitations as possible on the exchange of information between supervisors to ensure effective and informed liquidity oversight (Principle 17). Indeed, Principle 17 states in the relevant part:

> Supervisors should communicate with other relevant supervisors and public authorities, such as central banks, both within and across national borders, to facilitate effective cooperation regarding the supervision and oversight of liquidity risk management. Communication should occur regularly during normal times, with the nature and frequency of the information sharing increasing as appropriate during times of stress.

4.71 Based on the Basel Committee Principles for Sound Liquidity Risk Management, a bank should adopt a liquidity strategy that allows it to meet its obligations as they fall due (for example, honour deposit withdrawals) and to have *satisfactory liquidity*; that is, the ability to access sufficient cash or liquid assets from a number of sources to honour its liabilities. Essentially, the liquidity risk for a bank equals the risk of being unable to honour deposit withdrawals or to make repayments of other liabilities at maturity. Bank management should therefore engage in a robust liquidity 'gap analysis' that measures potential liquidity problems. The bank's gap analysis should follow an equation that the *difference must be greater* than 1 (> 1) between the volume of assets that will mature within a preset period (timeband) and the volume of liabilities that will mature within the same period.

$$\frac{\text{Volume of assets that will mature in a preset period (timeband)}}{\text{Volume of liabilities that will mature within the same period}} > 1 \qquad \text{Equation 4.2}$$

4.72 The bank board will be expected to conduct a liquidity gap analysis of the bank's asset/liability position that should not be static, but dynamic over time and an ever-moving tool to measure a bank's liquidity. Moreover, the board and executive management are expected to ensure that the bank's risk models allow risk managers to measure, monitor and control individual and portfolio risks subject to the board's approved risk appetite statement.

4.73 In addition, the Basel III Agreement also addresses liquidity risks with requirements under Pillar 1 that banks should comply with a Liquidity Coverage Ratio (LCR) and a Net Stable Funding Ratio (NSFR). The liquidity coverage ratio required banks by 2015 to hold an amount of high-quality, liquid assets (i.e. unencumbered highly rated government and corporate bonds) exceeding 100 per cent of the value of net cash outflows over a thirty-day period or other stress scenario prescribed by the regulator. For example, the LCR would allow the bank to sell assets in a stress scenario to cover net cash outflows over a thirty-day period. The stock of the highest-quality liquid assets would constitute about 20 per cent of the value of the bank's balance sheet assets and would be classified as Level 1 assets, while the bank would also be required to carry an additional 20 per cent of high-quality, unencumbered assets that would be known as Level 2 assets. Level 2 assets would consist of other highly rated government debt, high-quality corporate bonds and covered bonds and some simple and transparent asset-backed securities approved by the supervisor. The LCR ratio is:

$$\frac{\text{Stock of high-quality liquid assets}}{\text{Total net cash outflows over a 30-day period}} > 100\% \qquad \text{Equation 4.3}$$

4.74 The net stable funding ratio would require banks by 2018 to maintain a positive ratio of incoming funds to outgoing funds over a period of time – ordinarily thirty days – and to fund long-term credit exposures with liabilities that have a maturity of not less than one year. The NSFR is intended to promote longer-term wholesale market structural funding by requiring that the ratio of available stable funding to required stable funding exceeds 100 per cent over a one-year time horizon.

$$\frac{\text{Available amount of stable funding}}{\text{Required amount of stable funding}} > 100\% \text{ over 1 year} \qquad \text{Equation 4.4}$$

4.75 However, there is a lower required ratio of stable funding for residential mortgages designed to support banks in making home mortgage loans as follows:

$$\frac{\text{Available amount of stable funding}}{\text{Required amount of stable funding}} > 65\% \text{ over 1 year} \qquad \text{Equation 4.5}$$

4.76 These requirements are generally expected to reduce the reliance of banks on short-term sources of funding, such as from securitised notes, or limit the ability of banks to rely excessively on short-term funding that could be withdrawn quickly in a severe market downturn. And when there is a loss of short-term funding (for instance, funding from off-balance sheet entities in the securitisation markets), the bank will have at least 20 per cent of its risk-based assets in liquid, high-quality assets (i.e. AAA-rated government or corporate debt) that can be sold in the market at short notice to offset the loss of funding.

4.77 To comply with the Basel III liquidity requirements, banks will need to invest in more short-term, highly marketable, low-risk securities, and they will need to fund their assets with more stable, longer-term sources of capital. Empirical studies suggest that banks will incur a significant increase in costs to comply with the LCR and NSFR requirements based on the term structure of interest rates that varies by maturity.[33] The theory of the term structure of interest rates holds that short-term assets yield less than long-term assets because their yield does not include the credit risk premium or the liquidity premium that increases with maturity.[34] Similarly, bank funding that is based on longer-term, more stable sources of capital is more costly than short-term debt liabilities, as holders of longer-term debt

33   For Basel principles for liquidity management, see Basel Committee on Banking Supervision, *Principles for Sound Liquidity Risk Management and Supervision* (25 September 2008) (Basel: Bank for International Settlements); also see Handorf WC, 'Financial Implications of Transitioning to the Wall Street Reform and Consumer Protection Act 2010' (2017) 18 *Journal of Banking Regulation* 1, 7.
34   See Handorf WC, 'The Cost of Bank Liquidity' (2012) 15 *Journal of Banking Regulation* 1 1–13. See also Woodward S, 'The Liquidity Premium and the Solidity Premium' (1983) 73 *American Economic Review* 3 348–361.

liabilities require a higher yield than for short-term debt liabilities in order to compensate for the additional credit and liquidity risks.

Leverage Ratio

4.78 Another important feature of the bank capital framework will be the requirement of a leverage ratio of 3 per cent or 33 to 1 (total assets/total common equity).[35] The Basel Committee observes that one of the causes of the crisis was the build-up of excessive on- and off-balance sheet leverage in the banking system. In other words, banks were too heavily leveraged, even though their risk-based capital ratios complied with Basel II requirements.[36] The *leverage ratio* puts a cap on how much leverage a bank can have in relation to the size of its balance sheet.[37] Leverage is calculated as the value of assets divided by the value of equity, or in this case, Tier 1 capital. The leverage ratio is the inverse of this: the value of equity or Tier 1 capital divided by the value of assets. So, under Basel III, bank assets should not exceed thirty-three times the value of Tier 1 capital, or Tier 1 capital cannot fall below 3 per cent of the bank's total unweighted assets (including certain off-balance sheet exposures).

$$\frac{\text{Tier 1 capital}}{\text{Total exposure}} \geq 3\% \qquad\qquad \text{Equation 4.6}$$

4.79 The leverage ratio puts a floor of about 3 per cent (and up to 6 per cent for SIFIs) beneath which a bank's capital ratio as measured against its total asset exposures (including central bank reserves) may not drop. However, the introduction of the leverage ratio has been contentious. The leverage ratio encompasses low-risk and high-risk assets indiscriminately: it is a binding 3 per cent cap; which assets are included is irrelevant. In other words, the leverage ratio is risk insensitive. Therefore, it can be interpreted as an incentive for banks to hold riskier assets, which generally yield higher returns (higher interest rates). One cannot, however, conclude that banks will hold only high-risk assets, but that their asset composition will effectively become riskier.

4.80 By imposing a leverage requirement, actual bank capital requirements will increase substantially for the largest, most systemically important banks that have been relying heavily on risk-weightings to calculate their capital because banks will be required to hold capital against the nominal value of their asset exposures (including some off-balance sheet exposures), rather than against the risk-weighted value of the asset exposures. A binding leverage ratio, however, leads to some unintended consequences: first, a binding minimum capital requirement against a bank's total asset exposures can incentivise banks to substitute riskier (higher yielding on a risk-adjusted basis) assets for less risky assets (lower yielding, i.e. highly rated government debt securities) into their mix of total assets, thereby

---

35   See Basel Committee on Banking Supervision (n 31).
36   Ibid., 61.
37   Lee (2014), 42.

increasing the riskiness of the bank's total exposures. Second, for banks with growing balance sheets (increased lending) and for whom the leverage ratio is binding, identical marginal capital requirements make riskier assets with higher returns more attractive than assets with lower risk and lower returns. Third, the current leverage ratio definition requires high capital reserves even for bank deposits with central banks. And fourth, the leverage ratio has, in combination with the liquidity coverage ratio, an effect on the profitability of the lending side of the business, since required liquidity reserves need to be backed by capital reserves.

4.81 Moreover, even if bank substitutes riskier assets onto their balance sheet in order to chase a higher risk-adjusted return, these assets will still come with higher capital requirements. The introduction of the leverage ratio will force banks to reshuffle their assets until they find a balance between the higher returns associated with riskier assets and the costs generated by higher capital requirements.

4.82 Nevertheless, the leverage ratio serves as a bare minimum capital requirement or 'backstop' to ensure that banks are holding at least 3 per cent Tier 1 capital against all balance sheet and certain off-balance sheet exposures. It was introduced to address the weaknesses in risk-based capital models that relied heavily on risk-weightings to calculate regulatory capital. As discussed above, by simply using risk-based capital weightings to calculate regulatory capital, banks could hold substantially less capital than the nominal value of their asset exposures.

4.83 Basel III's focus on a significantly higher amount of core Tier 1 equity capital to constitute most of the regulatory capital total and the use of a minimum amount of Tier 1 capital in the leverage ratio as a minimum 'backstop' against all assets (risk-based) provides a significant departure in the design and purpose of regulatory capital. Under Basel II, banks were free to experiment with their risk measures and to utilise a wider array of financial instruments – i.e. common equity shares, participation rights, preference shares and subordinated debt – to constitute most of Tier 1 capital while Tier 2 capital (mainly debt instruments) provided 50 per cent of all regulatory capital. This approach to regulatory capital was deliberately aligned to the economic capital models that banks were already using, whose purpose was to signal bank solvency and performance to the market. By contrast, Basel III now requires banks to hold significantly more core Tier 1 and Tier 1 capital than what banks were holding in their economic capital models and a cap on leverage. This extra layer of high-quality, loss-absorbent capital is designed mainly to address the externality problem or the 'social costs' that bank risk-taking imposes on the financial system and broader economy.

4.84 In addition, regulatory capital will also have a 'counter-cyclical' component that will be measured against points in the economic cycle. Counter-cyclical capital regulation will require banks to hold more capital during good times and allow them to hold less capital than what would normally be required during a downturn in the economic cycle. For example, banks could let their capital levels fall beneath the 9.5 per cent capital requirement (including the counter-cyclical buffer) during a recession or financial crisis. This would encourage banks to lend more during an economic or financial downturn. The Basel Committee has introduced a framework for national authorities to consider how to implement counter-cyclical capital buffers and has approved a set of macroeconomic indicators (e.g. credit variables) and micro-indicators (i.e. bank earnings) to determine how and when counter-cyclical regulatory charges and buffers should be imposed.[38] This will necessarily involve banks using more forward-looking provisions based on expected losses.

4.85 Counter-cyclical capital requirements can be criticised on several grounds. First, that the regulatory authorities are not supposed to be any better at predicting the economic cycle than the markets. This is a less viable argument now than twenty years ago, as many countries have shifted the role of their central banks to control inflation numbers, and the central banks have adopted economic models of the cycle to help inform their interest rate decisions. However, as many have argued, predicting the cycle is not required if all that is desired is to lean against it.[39] Some authorities, such as the Bank of England, have selected a number of contemporaneous measures of the credit cycle, such as trend growth in credit or bank lending, against which to measure whether they should raise or lower capital adequacy requirements. These measures are unlikely to neutralise a boom, but they may keep the worst excesses in check, and perhaps even more importantly, they will mean that when the cycle turns down, the banks will have a stronger capital base to draw against. Regulatory forbearance from a high base is better than forbearance from a disappearing base.

4.86 A second argument against contra-cyclical measures is that they open the regulator up to political interference. There will be calls for regulators to reduce capital charges at the slightest hint of economic slowdown. Regulation could become a political football match. This was once said of monetary policy, but independence has worked relatively well in monetary policy, which is intrinsically more political than regulation. In addition to ensuring the political independence of regulators, another way to address the issue of politics is to make the contra-cyclical element as non-discretionary as possible.

4.87 Some commentators have recommended that bank capital requirements should be related to the rate of change of asset prices in the relevant sectors. For example, the capital adequacy requirement on mortgage lending could be linked to the rise in housing prices, and lending to construction and property companies to the rise in commercial property prices. Bank lending in other sectors where there are less reliable guides to asset prices could be linked to

---

38   See International Monetary Fund, 'Key Aspects of Macro-Prudential Policy' (10 June 2013), 61, para. 141 www.imf.org/external/np/pp/eng/2013/061013b.pdf accessed 21 February 2018.
39   Borio C and Lowe P, 'Asset Prices, Financial and Monetary Stability: Exploring the Nexus' (July 2002), BIS Working Papers No. 114 www.bis.org/publ/work114.pdf accessed 21 February 2018; Goodhart, C, Hofmann B and Segoviano M, 'Bank Regulation and Macroeconomic Fluctuations' (2004) 20 *Oxford Review of Economic Policy* 4 591–615.

price changes in the relevant equity market sector. The objective would be to build up bank reserves and to restrain bank lending during asset price booms, and to release the reserves into the economy through increased lending during asset price recessions or even depressions.[40]

4.88 Basel III has attracted substantial criticism from all quarters, including the banking industry, which asserts that the increase in Core Tier 1 capital requirements from 2 per cent to 7 per cent (4.5 per cent CET + 2.5 per cent CCB) plus a counter-cyclical and SIFI capital surcharge, liquidity requirements and leverage ratio are increasing the cost of bank funding and making it more expensive for banks to lend because they have to fund more of their lending by issuing more Tier 1 capital or through retained earnings (profits). Specifically, some criticism has been directed to its treatment of long-term lending, which might reinforce short-termism in bank lending.

2 European Union Bank Capital and Liquidity Requirements

4.89 The European Union adheres to the policy of implementing most of the Basel Capital Accord into binding EU legislation – either as Directives or as Regulations – for all EU Member States. The Basel III Agreement is implemented into EU law in the form of the Capital Requirements Directive IV (CRD IV).[41] CRD IV consists of the Capital Requirements Directive (CRD) and the Capital Requirements Regulation (CRR).[42] The CRR addresses the calculation and estimates of regulatory capital and liquidity requirements for EU-based banking institutions and certain investment firms. As a Regulation, it is directly applicable to EU Member States' regulatory law and administrative rulebooks. The CRR determines the prudential requirements for banks, and the relevant Article 92 sets the compulsory capital requirement as: Common Equity Tier 1 capital ratio of 4.5 per cent, Tier 1 capital ratio of 6 per cent and total capital ratio of 8 per cent. The banks are obliged to comply with these requirements at all times. In contrast, the CRD, as a Directive, is not directly applicable in Member States and must be implemented through the adoption of domestic legislation. As a Directive, the Member State is able to adapt the provisions of the Directive in a way that respects national legal requirements and practices, whereas the Regulation affords much less flexibility and must supersede, through direct application, existing provisions of Member State laws.

4.90 Most provisions of the Capital Requirements Regulation (CRR) and some provisions of the CRD dealing with the Pillar 2 issues of counter-cyclical capital requirements and risk

---

40 Ibid.
41 Directive 2013/36/EU of the European Parliament and of the Council of 26 June 2013 on access to the activity of credit institutions and the prudential supervision of credit institutions and investment firms, amending Directive 2002/87/EC and repealing Directives 2006/48/EC and 2006/49/EC OJ L 176, 27.6.2013, 338–436 (CRD IV).
42 Regulation (EU) No. 575/2013 of the European Parliament and of the Council of 26 June 2013 on prudential requirements for credit institutions and investment firms and amending Regulation (EU) No. 648/2012 OJ L 176, 27.6.2013, 1–337 (CRR).

governance became legally effective in EU Member States in January 2013 and apply to a wide range of banking activities, including bank capital and liquidity management, corporate governance and risk management. Basel III's bank corporate governance requirements and Pillar 3 market disclosure standards are implemented through the CRD and became legally effective in EU Member States on 31 December 2013. For example, Article 162 of the CRD requires the transposition into domestic law of the CRD's provisions requiring Member States to ensure the 'sound and prudent management' of credit institutions and certain investment firms, and that they apply dissuasive and proportionate administrative sanctions.

4.91 CRD IV requirements that relate to bank corporate governance and risk management practices are found in the CRD. The CRD affords much more discretion to Member States to devise rules governing bank corporate governance and risk management from within their existing domestic legal and regulatory regimes. Moreover, under both CRR and CRD, bank supervisors have wide discretion to address the particular risks that individual banks face and pose to the domestic banking system. As such, bank supervisors are not subject to a prescriptive framework of rules (although rules supplement the exercise of supervisory discretion). Supervisors may adopt stricter requirements with some banks, as opposed to others, where they decide that the institution has not devised a risk management model or implemented suitable corporate governance practices and strategies that address the risks that the bank faces and poses to the financial system.[43]

4.92 Nevertheless, the CRD IV (CRR and CRD) constitutes a maximum harmonisation regime in which capital and liquidity requirements (CRR) and the more general governance and risk management standards (including counter-cyclical capital), along with administrative sanctions, are expected to be applied in a substantially similar way across EU Member States. The European Banking Authority (EBA) was established in 2010 to promote enhanced harmonisation of supervisory practices across the EU Member States. The EBA is designated under CRD IV to develop regulatory technical standards (RTS) to give more precision to Member State authorities regarding how they define regulatory capital and liquidity and risk governance standards, and that administrative regulations to implement the CRD IV are imposed based on recognised principles of proportionality, legality and due process.

4.93 Despite the regulatory changes to capital regulation and risk governance, Basel III has been criticised as not raising capital and liquidity requirements enough.[44] These critics argue that despite the stricter capital and liquidity requirements, Basel III remains essentially based on a flawed risk-weighting approach to measuring bank risk exposures that relies

---

43   Alexander K, 'The EU Single Rulebook: Capital Requirements for Banks and the Maximum Harmonisation Principle', chapter 3 in Hinojosa LM and Beneyto J (eds), *European Banking Union: The New Regime* (Wolters Kluwer 2015), 24.
44   See Admati and Hellwig (n 16), 222–224.

disproportionately on assessments of risk by individual banks based on their own internal data that is not transparent to the market. This undermines the comparability of capital and liquidity standards between banks and undermines the concept of the level playing field. Moreover, risk-weightings do not take into account inter-linkages between banks that may cause systemic risk with other sectors of the financial system (i.e. shadow banking) and in financial infrastructure (i.e. clearing and settlement).[45] For example, the G20/FSB objective of requiring systemically significant financial instruments (i.e. OTC derivatives) to be traded on exchanges and centrally cleared with central counterparties is an important regulatory innovation to control systemic risk in wholesale securities markets. The G20 and the FSB expect all countries to require '[a]ll standardized OTC derivative contracts' to be 'traded on exchanges or electronic trading platforms, where appropriate, and cleared through central counterparties by end-2012 at the latest'. The OTC derivative contracts should be reported to trade repositories. Non-centrally cleared contracts should be subject to higher capital requirements.[46]

4.94 The G20 and FSB initiatives require regulators to address the systemic risks that can arise because of financial innovation and the shifting of risk to financial sectors to which banks are indirectly exposed, such as the risks of banks owning derivatives clearing houses and securities settlement institutions, and their ongoing exposure to derivatives trading and other trading book risks that are serious threats to financial stability.

4.95 Despite its shortcomings, Basel III expands the role for regulatory capital to be concerned not only with micro-prudential balance sheet risks of individual banks but also with the risks posed by banks to the broader financial system (i.e. counter-cyclical capital and liquidity requirements). It also links the application of capital requirements to governance practices in banking institutions and related market developments. Although these are significant enhancements to the bank capital regime, they do not go far enough in certain key areas in addressing macro-prudential financial stability risks. For instance, Basel III continues to allow global banking groups to use risk-weighted internal models to calculate credit, market and liquidity risks that rely on historic data and risk parameters that suffer from the same flaws as the models used by UBS and Citicorp that resulted in their respective collapses and government bailouts in 2007 and 2008.

4.96 A more effective capital regime should require not only enhanced quality of Tier 1 capital but also more transparency in the way that banks signal to the market the type of capital they are holding. This means that investors should have full information regarding what constitutes all types of bank regulatory capital. Although not included as regulatory capital,

---

45 G20, 'G20 Leaders Statement: The Pittsburgh Summit' (2009), University of Toronto G20 Research Group www.g20.utoronto.ca/2009/2009communique0925.html accessed 16 May 2018; Financial Stability Board, 'Implementing OTC Derivatives Markets Reform' (25 October 2010). See Balmer A, *Regulating Financial Derivatives* (Edward Elgar Financial Law Series 2018), 77.
46 Ibid.

bank loan loss reserves and provisioning for expected losses should be reported to the market.

E Basel IV and Future Challenges

4.97 The amendments to Basel III adopted in December 2017 have been referred to as 'Basel IV'. Basel IV attempts to reduce the reliance of banks on internal risk models to calculate their regulatory capital and imposes increased capital requirements in the trading book and stricter leverage requirements for SIFIs. In doing so, it aims to enhance the transparency and comparability of capital requirements between banks by reducing the extent to which banks can rely on internal risk models to calculate capital. It will reduce excessive variability in risk-weighted assets between banks and improve the comparability and transparency of banks' risk-based capital ratios. This will allow regulators to promote a more level playing field in bank regulatory capital requirements and to ensure that the standards are implemented consistently around the world.[47]

4.98 Basel IV also addresses weaknesses in risk assessment by adopting a revised standardised approach for credit risk, which will improve the robustness and risk sensitivity of the existing approach. For example, the Basel II standardised approach assigns a flat risk-weight to all residential mortgages. In the revised standardised approach, mortgage risk-weights will depend on the loan-to-value ratio of the mortgage, which is a better indicator of the credit risk to which the bank is exposed. Also, revisions to the internal ratings-based (A-IRB) approach for credit risk will restrict the use of the most advanced internally modelled approaches to only low-default portfolios. For example, banks will use the foundation IRB (F-IRB) approach for exposures to large and mid-sized corporates, banks and other financial institutions (i.e. asset classes that cannot be modelled in a robust and prudent manner) which applies fixed values to loss-given-default and exposure at default parameters.

4.99 In addition, Basel IV contains important changes to the credit valuation adjustment (CVA) framework, which includes the removal of the internally modelled approach to be replaced with the revised standardised approach. This will result in an increased capital charge for potential mark-to-market losses of derivative instruments as a result of deterioration in the creditworthiness of a counterparty. The revised framework consists of a standardised approach (based on fair value sensitivities to market risk factors) and a basic approach, which is benchmarked to the standardised approach.

4.100 Basel IV also changes the operational risk framework by adopting a revised (single, risk-sensitive) standardised approach for operational risk, which will replace the existing three

---

47   See Stefan Ingves Chairman of the Basel Committee, stating that '[t]he Committee, through its Regulatory Consistency Assessment Programme, will therefore continue to monitor closely the implementation of the Basel III standards': Ingves S, 'Basel III: Are We Done Now?', 29 January 2018 (Basel: Bank for International Settlements) www.bis.org/speeches/sp180129.htm accessed 21 February 2018.

standardised approaches and the advanced measurement approach (based on banks' internal models). The new operational risk framework determines capital requirements for operational risk on the basis of (1) a measure of a bank's income and (2) a measure of a bank's historical losses. Conceptually it assumes (i) operational risk increases at an increasing rate with a bank's income and (ii) banks which have experienced greater operational risk losses historically are assumed to be more likely to experience operational risk losses in the future.

4.101 The measurement of the leverage ratio will be revised. Jurisdictions may exercise national discretion in periods of exceptional circumstances to exempt central bank reserves from the leverage ratio exposure measure on a temporary basis. Jurisdictions will be required to recalibrate the minimum leverage ratio to offset the impact of excluding central bank reserves. And banks should disclose the impact of this exemption on their leverage ratios. This could have unintended consequences. For example, in circumstances where firms' balance sheets increase because of an expansion in central bank balance sheets, regulatory leverage requirements could effectively tighten. This could prompt banks to deleverage by shedding assets, cutting their supply of credit or withdrawing from other activities. This could affect the ability of the banking system to cushion shocks, and maintain the supply of credit to the real economy and support for market functioning.

4.102 At the same time, central bank reserves are a unique asset class. If matched by liabilities in the same currency and of identical or longer maturity, they typically do not represent an exposure to risk. Therefore, there is no need to build resilience against holdings of reserves.

4.103 Moreover, there will be an additional leverage ratio buffer for global systemically important banks (G-SIBs), which will take the form of a Tier 1 capital buffer set at 50 per cent of a G-SIB's higher risk-weighted capital requirement. For example, a G-SIB subject to a 2 per cent risk-weighted core Tier 1 requirement will be subject to a 1 per cent leverage ratio buffer. The leverage ratio buffer will be divided into five ranges. Capital distribution constraints will be imposed on a G-SIB that does not meet its leverage ratio buffer.

4.104 The part of Basel IV that attracted the most debate was the 'aggregate output floor', which is designed to ensure that banks' risk-weighted assets (RWAs) generated by internal models are no lower than 72.5 per cent of their risk-weighted assets as calculated by the Basel III framework's standardised approach. Banks will also be required to disclose their risk-weighted assets calculated by the standardised approaches.[48] The notion of an output floor is not new, as Basel II had introduced an output floor based on Basel I capital requirements that would have prevented banks from reducing capital beneath 80 per cent of what would have been required under Basel I. This proposed output floor was never adopted, however, in Basel II, because of inconsistent implementation due to differing interpretations of Basel

---

48   The Basel Committee will consult on what details should be disclosed in late 2018.

INTERNATIONAL COMPARISON OF RWA DENSITY
Risk-weighted assets in relation to total exposure, Q4 2015   Chart 10

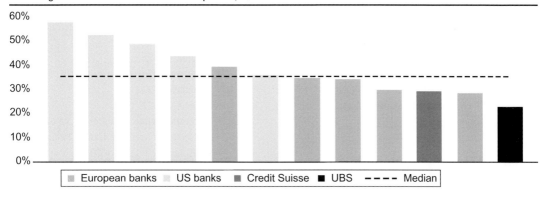

Figure 4.3 International comparison of RWA density
Source: Swiss National Bank Financial Stability Report 2016.

II and Basel I at the time. The Basel IV output floor, which must be implemented by 2022, places a limit on capital reduction benefits for a bank using internal models at 72.5 per cent of what would have been required under the standardised approach; it is more strictly defined and has fewer exceptions than the earlier proposal under Basel II. Jurisdictions may elect to implement accelerated transitional arrangements, as the Basel framework comprises minimum standards only.

1 The Rationale of the Output Floor

4.105 The reason why the Basel Committee decided to impose the Basel IV output floor is demonstrated in Figure 4.3. All the banks in the chart are holding capital ratios in excess of what is required by Basel III (including SIFI capital surcharges). However, it is submitted that an appropriate bank capitalisation should also depend on both the capital base held by the bank and how it determines its RWAs. This chart shows that the biggest US and European banks have very low RWA densities (the ratio of RWAs to total exposures). For example, the two Swiss banking groups UBS and Credit Suisse are indicated by the two darker blocks on the histogram. Although each bank is holding capital in excess of minimum Basel III requirements, the RWA density of UBS (22 per cent) and Credit Suisse (25 per cent) are significantly below the international average of 35 per cent RWA density for the largest banking groups in the US and Europe.[49] Similarly, three EU-based banks are beneath the international average of 35 per cent RWA density. Although all the banks in this sample make extensive use of internal models to calculate their RWAs, the two Swiss banks and the three EU-based banks with

---

49   Swiss National Bank Financial Stability Report 2016 (Swiss National Bank 2016), 12 www.snb.ch/en/mmr/reference/stabrep_2016/source/stabrep_2016.en.pdf accessed 5 March 2018.

Table 4.3 Transition and implementation schedule for Basel IV: implementation dates of Basel III post-crisis reforms and transitional arrangement for phasing in the aggregate output floor

Revision	Implementation date
Revised standardised approach for credit risk	• 1 January 2022
Revised IRB framework	• 1 January 2022
Revised CVA framework	• 1 January 2022
Revised operational risk framework	• 1 January 2022
Revised market risk framework	• 1 January 2022
Leverage ratio	• Existing exposure definition: 1 January 2018
	• Revised exposure definition: 1 January 2022
	• G-SIB buffer: 1 January 2022
Output floor	• 1 January 2022: 50%
	• 1 January 2023: 55%
	• 1 January 2024: 60%
	• 1 January 2025: 65%
	• 1 January 2026: 70%
	• 1 January 2027: 72.5%

the lowest RWA densities are heavily reliant on internal RWA modelling in order to push their capital requirements downwards.

4.106 The implementation of an output floor under Basel IV is designed to limit the ability of banks to use their internal models to push downwards their RWAs. It will require first that the RWA is calculated under the standardised approach, and that amount would subsequently be reduced by the use of IRB internal risk-weightings, but with the strict limitation that the IRB approach can only reduce the value of the total RWA by 27.5 per cent (the difference between the 100 per cent RWA under the standardised approach and the 72.5 per cent output floor). This expected increase of RWAs under Basel IV should result in a significant increase in the amount of regulatory capital held by the world's largest banks and thus contribute to banking sector and financial stability (see Table 4.3).

4.107 Regarding the EU-based banks in Figure 4.3, the European Union will almost certainly have to adopt new legislation to implement this framework into EU law. Implementation will inevitably require a lengthy and complex political process that could be further delayed by elections and other political developments. Regarding minimum standards, jurisdictions may elect to adopt more conservative – or stricter – standards and will be considered compliant if they do not implement any of the internally modelled approaches and instead implement the standardised approaches. The treatment of sovereign risk on bank balance sheets at zero risk-weightings (i.e. Greek sovereign bonds), on which the Basel Committee chose not to consult, will continue to linger as a long-outstanding reform initiative that regulators in many countries would like to see the Basel Committee or other national authorities (including the EU) address in the near future.

CONCLUSION

4.108 Since the crisis of 2007–2008, bank regulatory capital has become the key indicator of bank soundness. The crisis, however, raised important questions about how regulatory capital should be measured and monitored across the banking system and the overall utility of the risk-based capital regime in supporting financial stability. This chapter discusses what regulatory capital is, its rationale, and how it has become integral to bank risk management. The chapter discusses how the crisis demonstrated weaknesses in the Basel II model-based approach for calculating regulatory capital. The model-based approach to measuring risk, which regulators and bank management had accepted and embedded into their bank risk management practices, failed to estimate the amount of capital and liquidity banks should hold against systemic or macro-prudential risks in the financial system.

4.109 Moreover, as discussed in Chapter 2, a major weakness in financial regulation prior to the crisis was that banking supervision and regulation were disproportionately focused on bank balance sheets and less concerned with systemic risks across the broader financial system. There was a conventional view that the shifting of risks to off-balance sheet entities and the use of credit default swaps and securitisation structures reduced banking sector instability because other market participants (i.e. long-term institutional investors) were willing to invest in bank credit and absorb the related risks. The spreading of risk throughout the wholesale structured credit markets was viewed to be beneficial for a more resilient financial system.[50] The regulator's focus on individual institutions, however, failed to take account of the systemic risks in the structured finance and derivatives markets and how this was exacerbated by highly leveraged bank balance sheets.

4.110 The chapter also considers the main changes in Basel III that aim to address macro-prudential risks by, for example, requiring that core Tier 1 capital has a counter-cyclical component whose calculation is linked to broader developments in the economy. The SIFI capital surcharge also attempts to address macro-prudential risks by linking part of the bank capital requirement to the size and interconnectedness of the institution and whether it poses disproportionate risks to the financial system. The focus on macro-prudential regulation is also reflected in enhanced supervisory oversight of bank corporate and risk governance and a cap on overall bank leverage.

4.111 The chapter then discusses how Basel III continues to rely disproportionately on internal bank risk-weightings to determine regulatory capital and how the risk-weighted densities of the largest global banks continued to be very low, thus resulting in an under-capitalised banking system. The Basel Committee therefore has adopted amendments to

---

50   See Alexander et al. (n 13), 5–7. See also Brunnermeier M, Crockett A, Goodhart CAE, Persaud A and Shin H, 'The Fundamental Principles of Financial Regulation' (2009) Geneva Reports on the World Economy 11 (International Centre for Banking and Monetary Studies), 18.

Basel III (known as 'Basel III.5' or 'Basel IV'). The chapter discusses the main areas of reform under Basel IV, which include limiting the reduction of risk-weighted assets to 72.5 per cent of the value of risk-weighted assets calculated under the Basel III standardised approach. Basel IV also subjects SIFIs to more intensive prudential regulatory requirements, including stricter minimum leverage ratios requiring higher core equity Tier 1 capital requirements and more scrutiny of their cross-border operations. Nevertheless, the chapter suggests that Basel IV may still not be doing enough to address macro-prudential systemic risks. For instance, the Financial Stability Board has attempted to address some of the systemic risks by asking regulators to focus not only on stricter capital and liquidity requirements for individual institutions, but also to monitor risk exposures across the financial system, including the transfer of credit risk to off-balance sheet entities and the soundness of financial infrastructure, such as central counterparties or clearing houses.

QUESTIONS

1. Explain the concepts of economic and regulatory capital.
2. What is the purpose of regulatory capital?
3. How did capital adequacy standards change from Basel II to Basel III?
4. Understand Basel III's expanded definition of regulatory capital.
5. Understand how liquidity risks threaten bank stability and Basel III liquidity standards.
6. How does conduct risk relate to prudential regulatory requirements?
7. What is operational risk and why is it important?
8. How does Basel III regulate operational risk?
9. Describe liquidity risk and how banks can manage it.
10. How does Basel III address liquidity risks?

Further Reading

Admati AR, 'Fallacies, Irrelevant Facts, and Myths in the Discussion of Capital Regulation: Why Bank Equity is Not Socially Expensive' (2012) Stanford GSB Working Paper www.gsb .stanford.edu/faculty-research/working-papers/fallacies-irrelevant-facts-myths-discussion-capital-regulation-why accessed 25 May 2018

Admati A and Hellwig M, *The Bankers' New Clothes: What's Wrong with Banking and What to Do About It* (Princeton University Press 2014)

BCBS, 'The Interplay of Accounting and Regulation and its Impact on Bank Behaviour: Literature Review' (2015) Working Paper No. 28 www.bis.org /bcbs/publ/wp28.pdf accessed 25 May 2018

BCBS, 'Basel III: A Global Regulatory Framework for More Resilient Banks and Banking Systems – Revised Version June 2011' (2011) www.bis.org/publ/bcbs189.pdf accessed 25 May 2018

Blundell-Wignall A and Atkinson P, 'Thinking Beyond Basel III: Necessary Solutions for Capital and Liquidity' (2010) *OECD Journal of Financial Market Trends* 9, 1–23

Capie F and Wood G, 'Do We Need Regulation of Bank Capital? Some Evidence from the UK' (2013) IEA Current Controversies No. 40 www.iea.org.uk/sites/default/files/publications/files/Do%20we%20need%20regulation%20of%20bank%20capital.pdf accessed 25 May 2018

Cline WR, *The Right Balance for Banks: Theory and Evidence on Optimal Capital Requirements* (Peterson Institute for International Economics 2017), discussing the Miller-Modigliani Theory and its application to bank capital debate and concluding that increased capital requirements up to about 12 per cent of risk-based assets only marginally increases bank funding costs and is offset by the decline in the cost of bank equity based on financial stability considerations, and rejecting the argument of Admati and Hellwig (2013) for higher capital requirements of about 30 per cent and higher requirements proposed by the Minneapolis Federal Reserve Bank Plan (2016) of 53 per cent capital to risk-based assets and 38 per cent capital against unweighted assets as unnecessarily costly for the economy.

De Pascalis F, *Credit Ratings and Market Over-Reliance* (Brill/Nijhoff 2017), arguing that banking regulation has become over-reliant on credit ratings.

Federal Reserve Bank of Minneapolis, *The Minneapolis Plan to End Too Big To Fail*, November (Minneapolis: Federal Reserve Bank of Minneapolis 2016)

Fullenkamp C and Rochon C, 'Reconsidering Bank Capital Regulation: A New Combination of Rules, Regulators, and Market Discipline' (2014) IMF Working Paper www.imf.org/external/pubs/ft/wp/2014/wp14169.pdf accessed 25 May 2018

Gordon JN and Ringe W-G, 'Banking Resolution in the European Banking Union: A Transatlantic Perspective on What It Would Take' (2015) 115 *Columbia Law Review* 1297

Greenbaum SI and Thakor AJ, 'Bank Funding Modes: Securitization versus Deposits' (1987) 11 *Journal of Banking and Finance* 379

5

Bank Corporate Governance: Law and Regulation

Table of Contents

INTRODUCTION

5.1 Effective supervision and regulation require banks to have robust corporate governance arrangements that incentivise bank management and owners to understand the risks they are taking and to price risk efficiently in order to cover both the private costs that such risk-taking poses to bank shareholders and the social costs for the broader economy if the bank fails.[1] Corporate governance plays an important role in achieving this in two ways: to align the incentives of bank owners and managers so that managers seek wealth maximisation for owners, while not jeopardising the bank's franchise value through excessive risk-taking; and to incentivise bank management to price financial risk in a way that covers its social costs. The latter objective is what distinguishes bank corporate governance from other areas of corporate governance because of the potential social costs that banking can have on the broader economy. This chapter will examine the proposition that regulatory intervention is necessary in bank corporate governance because the regulator is uniquely situated to assert the varied interests of other stakeholders in society and to balance those interests according to the public interest.

5.2 The chapter will analyse the legal and regulatory dimension of bank corporate governance with particular emphasis on the board of directors and role of shareholders. It also considers the legal structure of banks as corporate entities that are owned by shareholders who are protected by limited liability and the duties of directors of banking institutions. The special position of banks in the economy and their capacity to generate externalities requires that bank director duties are interpreted to take account of the social impact of the banking business and the importance of the principle of sound and prudent management. The chapter examines the proposition that bank corporate governance should be regulated both to align the incentives of bank shareholders and managers to promote wealth maximisation of the bank, along with aligning the incentives of bank managers and shareholders with the broader interests of societal stakeholders in ensuring that systemic risks are limited.

I INTERNATIONAL STANDARDS OF BANK CORPORATE GOVERNANCE

5.3 Based on post-crisis international regulatory reforms, the regulation of bank corporate governance has become a major focus of regulators in most jurisdictions. Regulators now scrutinise most areas of bank management, including controls on remuneration that are linked to the long-term profitability of the bank, while restricting short-term bonuses. Regulators now have powers to approve bank director appointments and to ensure that directors have the knowledge and training to understand the bank's business and risk

---

1 See Mehran H, 'Introduction: Critical Themes in Corporate Governance' (2003), 9 *Federal Reserve Bank of New York Economic Policy Review* 1 www.newyorkfed.org/medialibrary/media/research/epr/2003/EPRvol9no1 .pdf accessed 21 February 2018.

models and the financial implications not only for the bank's shareholders, but for the broader economy. Bank management should be required to understand the technical aspects of stress-testing, which the regulator should ensure is done on a much more frequent basis than was the norm prior to the crisis.

5.4 In most countries where global banks operate, there were major weaknesses in bank corporate governance that not only reduced shareholder value, but also resulted in substantial externalities for the broader economy, resulting in significantly lower economic growth, higher unemployment, and massive taxpayer subsidies and bailouts for the banking sector. As discussed in Chapter 4, most bank senior managers and board members did not understand nor appreciate how the business models that drove bank lending were putting the financial system at risk. Moreover, they failed to grasp the true risks which their risk managers had approved based on faulty value-at-risk models that were used to calculate the market risk associated with investing in mortgage-backed securities and collateralised debt obligations. Equally important, they allowed irresponsible compensation packages to be awarded to bankers which incentivised them to book short-term profits based on excessively risky behaviour, which increased systemic risk in the financial system and weakened the medium and long-term prospects and profitability of the bank. Moreover, weak governance contributed to the poor performance of banks that resulted in publicly financed bailouts for many banks, such as UBS, Citi group, and the Royal Bank of Scotland, and insolvency for others, such as Lehman Brothers.

5.5 International initiatives to enhance standards and principles of bank corporate governance were led by the Organisation for Economic Co-operation and Development (OECD) and the Basel Committee. The OECD and Basel Committee corporate governance principles and standards have been influential in determining the shape and evolution of bank corporate governance in many advanced and developing countries and have influenced countries in establishing internal control systems and risk management frameworks for banks. Indeed, the OECD and Basel Committee standards on bank corporate governance have been implemented into the regulatory codes of most countries where international banks operate. It should be noted, however, that international standards and principles of corporate governance may result in different economic effects across different countries with different institutional and legal structures and with different business customs and practices. Therefore, the adoption of international standards and principles of corporate governance should be accompanied by domestic regulations that prescribe specific rules and procedures for the governance of financial institutions, which address national differences in institutional, economic and legal systems.

5.6 The Basel Committee's Core Principles for Effective Banking Supervision address bank governance in several principles, including major acquisitions (Principle 7), corporate governance (Principle 14), and internal control and audit (Principle 26). In addition, the Basel Committee adopted a revised set of bank corporate governance principles in 2014 which were subject to further consultation in 2015. Principles 6 to 8 emphasise the role of the board of directors in understanding the banking business and how financial risk affects it, and in establishing clear lines of accountability from line managers to senior management and the board.[2]

5.7 Although international standards of corporate governance should respect diverse economic and legal systems, the overriding objective for all financial regulators is to encourage banks to devise internal controls and compliance systems that require senior management and directors to identify and take measures to mitigate material risk exposures for the institution. Because different national markets have different types of economic risks, there are no universally correct legal and regulatory rules to govern bank management. Recognising this, sound governance practices for banking organisations can take place according to different forms that suit the economic and legal structure of a particular jurisdiction. Nevertheless, the organisational structure of any bank or securities firm should include four forms of oversight: (1) oversight by the board of directors or supervisory board; (2) oversight by non-executive individuals who are not involved in the day-to-day management of the business; (3) oversight by direct line supervision of different business areas; (4) and oversight by independent risk management and audit functions. Regulators should also utilise approximate criteria to ensure that key personnel meet fit and proper standards. These principles should also apply to government-owned banks, but with the recognition that government ownership may often mean different business strategies and objectives for the bank.

5.8 Chapter 4 discussed how the Basel III reforms changed the Pillar 2 framework of bank corporate and risk governance to include a more detailed assessment of a bank's internal processes and decision-making structure and compliance with procedural standards of assessment. Banks are expected to follow process-oriented rules in assessing the risk of assets and calculating capital and not merely rely on external standards and criteria of assessment. This involves the regulator working closely with banks and adjusting standards to suit the particular risk profile of individual banks. Indeed, Basel III emphasises that banks and financial firms should adopt, under the general supervision of the regulator, robust internal self-monitoring systems and processes that comply with statutory and regulatory standards. Pillar 2 provides for supervisory review that allows regulators to use their discretion in applying regulatory standards. This means that regulators have discretion to modify capital requirements depending on the risk profile of the bank in question. Also, the regulator may require different internal governance frameworks for banks and to set controls on ownership and asset classifications. Moreover, regulators are now expected to require banks to analyse their business models and whether their business strategies conform with stricter risk management controls. This will involve the regulator assessing the riskiness of financial products for retail and wholesale clients and whether the bank's

---

2 See Basel Committee on Banking Supervision, 'Guidelines: Corporate Governance Principles for Banks' (July 2015) www.bis.org/bcbs/publ/d328.htm accessed 21 December 2018. For example, see Principle 6 (Risk Management) and Principle 8 (Risk Communication).

business models are sustainable for the bank over the longer term. Bank boards are now expected to consult and, in most cases, obtain approval of regulators before making senior management and board appointments. As discussed below, the EU has required that bank supervisors have ultimate authority to approve a bank's appointment of a CEO and board chairman and to assess the role and influence of controlling shareholders and whether they are supporting (or undermining) the sound and prudent management of the bank.

II CORPORATE GOVERNANCE AND DIRECTORS' DUTIES

5.9 It is important to keep in mind that it is not merely the regulatory laws that apply to banking institutions. Company law rules are applicable to joint stock banks and other legislation applies to non-joint stock banks, such as building societies, savings banks and credit unions. Also, general contract, tort and fiduciary law principles apply to the internal and external relations of financial institutions and their members, including, but not limited to, compensation limits, personal liability for unreasonable risks and director and officer duties to the company.[3] In this respect, the role of legal issues is crucial for determining ways to improve corporate governance for banking institutions. There are several ways to help promote strong business and legal environments that support corporate governance and related supervisory activities. These include designing and enforcing contracts, clarifying supervisors' and senior managements' governance roles, ensuring that the corporation has controls in place to mitigate corruption and bribery, and aligning laws and other measures with the interests of managers, shareholders and employees.

A Directors' Duties

5.10 Generally, as a matter of corporate law, most jurisdictions adhere to the principle that directors owe a duty to the company, not to *individual shareholders*.[4] Many jurisdictions have interpreted this rule as meaning that directors owe duties of care and fiduciary duties to the shareholders *collectively* in the form of the company, and not to the shareholders *individually*.[5] However, the Australian and New Zealand courts have departed from this view in special circumstances by recognising that a fiduciary duty may be owed by directors to individual shareholders, particularly where the facts of the case show that directors had established a special relationship with shareholders by making certain representations to them directly.[6]

---

3 Gevurtz FA, 'The Role of Corporate Law in Preventing a Financial Crisis: Reflections on "In re Citigroup Inc. Shareholder Derivative Litigation"' (2010) 23 *Pacific McGeorge Global Business & Development Law Journal* 113 118–119.

4 For UK company law, see *Percival* v. *Wright* [1902] 2 Chapter 421, 425–426. See also Davies P and Worthington S, *Gower and Davies' Principles of Modern Company Law* (9th edn, Sweet & Maxwell 2012), 508, 1132.

5 *Foss* v. *Harbottle* [1843] 2 Hare 461, 67 ER 189.

6 See *Brunninghausen* v. *Glavanics* [1999] NSWCA 199; 46 NSWLR 538; 32 ACSR 294 37.

5.11 However, it is difficult to separate the interests of the company from those of the share-holders. Indeed, the interests of the company are, in an economic and legal sense, the interests of the shareholders, which can be divided further into the interests of the *present* and *future* shareholders, including a balance between the interests of the various share-holder classes. Therefore, discretionary exercise of directors' duties must be directed towards the maximisation of profits for the balance of shareholder interests.

5.12 This suggests that the principle that the director's duty is owed to the company raises important issues regarding how the interests of the company should be defined. Is the company merely an aggregate of the interests of the shareholders? Or does the company itself encompass a broader measure of interests that includes not only the shareholders' interests, but also the interests of other so-called 'stakeholders'? The UK Code of Corporate Governance states that every company should be headed by a board that is collectively responsible for the long-term success of the company.[7] The Code further provides that '[a]ll directors must act in what they consider to be the best interests of the company, consistent with their statutory duties', and that the board is responsible for determining the nature and extent of the principal risks faced by the company and to ensure sound risk management and internal controls.[8] And the board should develop a satisfactory dialogue with share-holders based on a mutual understanding of objectives.[9]

5.13 Regarding fiduciary duties, directors have the paramount duty of acting in the *bona fide* interest of the company. Specifically, this means that the director owes a duty of good faith to the company, which means that the director is a fiduciary or a trustee of the company's best interest. The fiduciary duties of directors are also known as the duty of loyalty in many jurisdictions and generally fall into the following categories: the directors may act only within the course and scope of duties conferred upon them by the company memorandum or articles, and they must act in good faith in respect to the best interest of the company, while not allowing their discretion to be limited in the decisions they make for the company. Moreover, a director who finds themselves in the position of having a conflict of interest will be required to take corrective measures. In the case of a bank manager or director who has breached a fiduciary duty by privately gaining from a transaction at the bank's expense without having disclosed or gained approval from the bank, most jurisdic-tions would require that the manager or director concerned should pay restitution or compensation to the company for the value of the property dissipated or lost.

5.14 In addition, some jurisdictions also recognise that directors have a specific duty to have regard to the interests of employees and societal stakeholders, including the environment.[10]

---

7   See Financial Reporting Council, 'The UK Corporate Governance Code' (April 2016), Section A.1: The Role of the Board www.frc.org.uk/directors/corporate-governance-and-stewardship/uk-corporate-governance-code accessed 7 January 2019.
8   Ibid., section C: Accountability.
9   Ibid., Relations with Shareholders.
10   See Neill L.J. in *Fulham Football Club* v. *Cabra Estates PLC* [1992] BCC 863 (CA).

The UK Companies Act 2006 section 172(1) provides that a director, while promoting success for the company as a whole, needs to consider long-term consequences and look after employees, community and the environment. This provision suggests that directors have a duty to consider broader stakeholder interests that are affected by the company's operations (including externalities) when making business and other strategic decisions for the firm.

5.15 Of particular relevance to financial companies are cases in which the court considers whether a director violated the duty of care and skill. In considering whether a director violated this duty, the courts will apply a reasonable person test. In *Dovey and The Metropolitan Bank (of England and Wales) Ltd* v. *Cory*[11] a third party brought an action in negligence against a bank director for malpractice and the court applied a reasonable person standard in deciding that the director had not acted negligently in receiving suspicious information from other company officers and in failing to investigate any further irregularities in company practice.[12] The significance of the decision was that the court ruled that a reasonable person test should be applied to determine whether a director had breached their duty of care and skill, and that the reasonable person test should not be that of a 'reasonable professional director', but rather a reasonable person who had possessed the particular ability and skills of the actual defendant in the case. This decision was later cited as authority in a case in which it was held that a director 'need not exhibit in the performance of his duties, a greater degree of skill than may reasonably be expected from a person of his knowledge and experience'.[13] The reasoning of these decisions supports the proposition that where a bank director or senior officer did not have the requisite skills to make an informed judgement, liability could be avoided on the grounds that the director or manager had little or no training for the specialised tasks in question and therefore could not have breached the duty of care. Conversely, liability could be imposed on a director or manager who did have the requisite skills and training for the task at hand, but failed to act in an informed way based on these skills and knowledge as a reasonable person would have been expected to do.

5.16 Similarly, in *Dorchester Finance Co Ltd* v. *Stebbing*,[14] the court found that the reasonable person test should apply equally to both executive and non-executive directors. More generally, UK company law sets forth three important standards regarding the duty of care and skill for directors. First, a director is not required to demonstrate a degree of skill that would exceed what would normally be expected of a person with the director's actual level of skill and knowledge (CA 2006, s 174).[15] Second, a director is not required to concern themselves on a continuous basis with the affairs of the company, as their involvement will

11 (1901) AC 477.
12 Ibid., 492–493.
13 *Re City Equitable Fire Insurance Co Ltd* [1925] 1 Ch. 407, 408.
14 *Dorchester Finance Co Ltd* v. *Stebbing* [1989] BCLC 498.
15 Hannigan B, *Company Law* (3rd edn, Oxford University Press 2012), n 10; see *Re Brian D. Pierson (Contractors) Ltd* [2001] 1 BCLC 275 at 302.

be periodic and will be focused mainly at board meetings and at other meetings at which they are in attendance, and they are not required to attend all meetings, nor to be liable for decisions that are made in their absence.[16] Third, a director may properly rely on company officers to perform any day-to-day affairs of the business while not being liable for any wrongdoing of those officers in the absence of grounds for suspicion.[17] Notwithstanding the courts' efforts to define further the reasonable person standard for company directors, it can be criticised on the grounds that it may create a disincentive, in the absence of regulatory standards, for skilled persons to serve as directors, especially for financial companies that often require more technical supervisory skills in the boardroom.

5.17 However, UK courts have shown willingness in recent years to develop a definition of what is expected of bank directors and senior management with governance responsibilities over a bank. Indeed, the case concerning the collapse of *Barings* bank[18] resulted in the court applying the Company Directors Disqualification Act 1986, which imposes personal liability on directors for failing to use due care and skill in overseeing the operations of a company that as a result collapses and causes losses to creditors and customers. In this case, directors were held accountable for their failure to perform their duty to oversee the bank's global operations,[19] specifically to ensure that there was a clear segregation of front- and back-office functions, to put proper risk limits in place and to investigate the large profits made by a single trader in Singapore. As discussed in the case study below, the court was not reluctant to define the reasonable person standard for imposing negligence on bank directors as including a professional level of skill and knowledge that every director of such a bank would be expected to possess.

5.18 The Barings case demonstrates how bank directors can be disqualified under the Company Directors Disqualification Act 1986 (CDDA).[20] Since the Barings case, the UK Companies Act 2006, section 174 was adopted and clarifies a director's duty to exercise 'reasonable care, skill and diligence', which combines both 'subjective' and 'objective' standards of care. The duty of care test in section 174 requires the standard of care exercised by a reasonably diligent person with the general knowledge, skill and experience that may reasonably be expected of a person carrying out the functions expected to be fulfilled by a director in relation to the company and the general knowledge, skill and experience that the director has. Liability under the CDDA, however, appears to be based more on serious misconduct such as fraud, insolvency-related matters and failures in relation to filing account records and annual returns. The section 174 standard, however, appears to be biased in favour of

---

16   *Re City Equitable Fire Insurance Co Ltd* [1925] 1 Ch. 408.
17   Hannigan (n 15) n. 10–31; *Re City Equitable Fire Insurance Co Ltd* [1925] 1 Ch. 408. Directors do retain a residual duty of supervision as was made clear by Jonathan Parker J. in *Re Barings PLC (No. 5), Secretary of State for Trade and Industry* v. *Baker (No. 5)*.
18   *Secretary of State for Trade and Industry* v. *Baker (No. 5)* [1999] 1 BCLC 433.
19   Ibid.
20   Section 9 of the CDDA refers to Schedule 1, Part 1, para. 1 which cites the grounds of 'misfeasance or breach of any fiduciary or other duty'.

less experienced directors who can potentially escape liability on the grounds of their incompetence.

5.19 In many civil law jurisdictions, company directors are also subject to duties of care and loyalty. The Swiss Code of Obligations creates a duty of care and a duty of loyalty (Article 717 para. 1 CO) for board members to oversee the company's operations in the best interest of the company. The best interest of the company is defined to be what is in the best economic interests of the shareholders as a class. Nevertheless, the awareness of Corporate Social Responsibility has increasingly gained relevance. The duties of care and loyalty are applicable to board members of Swiss banks that are joint stock companies (Article 39 Swiss Banking Act). The duty of care is defined by a minimum negligence standard stated as what a reasonable person in the position of the director or executive manager would have done or have been expected to do. Given their particular level of skill and knowledge, the negligence standard may be higher. The duty of loyalty prohibits directors and management from engaging in self-interested transactions involving the company unless the directors or the management concerned establish appropriate measures to ensure that such transactions will be carried out in the interest of the company, respectively 'at arm's length' (such measures include for example the order of a fairness opinion or the obligation to disclose the transaction in advance and require it to be approved by the board). Shareholders themselves can bring an action directly against board members or management for breaching their duties to the company and seek compensation in the form of losses or damages suffered or can bring an action derivatively on behalf of the company resulting from the alleged breach (Article 754 CO). The company itself also has a right to bring a liability action for damages suffered by the company (Article 754 para. 1 CO).

5.20 The Swiss law governing the liability of bank directors for violation of the duty of care and duty of loyalty was tested after the financial crisis of 2007 when new UBS board members considered an action against former members of UBS's board of directors for bank losses related to major failings in oversight of the bank's operations in 2006 and 2007 that resulted in its bailout by the Swiss government and the Swiss central bank in late 2007. Although UBS's new board members had a right to pursue – on behalf of UBS – the former executive and non-executive board members for losses related to the bank's collapse, the new board members decided for strategic reasons not to do so, as discussed below.

5.21 UBS's risk management failures and subsequent taxpayer-funded bailout shows that directors have an important role to play in overseeing the bank's operations and ensuring that internal systems and controls work effectively. Moreover, ignorance is no longer a defence against failing to perform the professional responsibilities reasonably expected of a director or senior manager in their particular position. Senior management and directors must make themselves aware of what is reasonably expected of them for their particular responsibilities and for any oversight of the performance of others in the bank.

5.22 Although the legal liability rules governing director duties varies between countries and jurisdictions, the general principle that directors owe duties directly to the company and indirectly to shareholders applies regarding the interpretation of director duties to banks that are incorporated legal entities. Following the financial crisis, legal actions were brought in the US, UK and elsewhere by investors against directors of major financial institutions, such as Citigroup, the Royal Bank of Scotland, Lloyds Bank and AIG. In the case against Citigroup, which ended in a large settlement paid to investors, the directors were alleged to have failed in their duty by failing to control and disclose the bank's investments in subprime mortgages.[21] In fact, Citigroup board member Robert Rubin, former Goldman Sachs partner and US Treasury Secretary, had approved the bank's investment strategy in subprime mortgage products, which resulted in substantial losses and the bank's bailout by the US government in 2008. Although the investors' lawsuit against AIG was ultimately unsuccessful, the court found that AIG directors were aware of fraudulent investment activities and had failed to prevent them.[22] In a pre-crisis case in Japan, the Osaka District Court in September 2000 ordered eleven of the directors of Daiwa Bank in a shareholder derivative suit to pay a total of US$775 million in damages related to the hiding of losses taking place in their New York office.[23] When faced with hidden losses of over US$1.1 billion in July 1995, senior management at Daiwa Bank did not inform US and Japanese regulators until three months later, resulting in the bank facing criminal charges and losing its licence in the US. Based on these cases, it is clear that corporate law and criminal law provide civil remedies and sanctions respectively for shareholders and regulators against bank directors for violating their duty of care in overseeing bank management.

5.23 Despite the UK court's ruling in the Barings case, imposing penalties and banning some of the bank's directors from serving on a company board, the legal remedies under company law or other non-regulatory law for holding directors and senior managers liable for breach of the duty of care and skill appears to provide limited redress for shareholders and other third parties seeking to recover damages or related compensation for negligent management and oversight of a bank. Therefore, it is questionable whether company law without more regulatory protection serves as a deterrent to negligent oversight of a banking institution.

Box 5.1 Bank Director Duties and Negligence: The Case of Barings Bank

The collapse of the UK's oldest investment bank, Barings, in February 1995 raised important issues regarding the scope and application of director's duties under the UK *Company Directors Disqualification Act 1986* (CDDA). The Barings case judgment established a three-limbed test for assessing the nature and scope of unfit conduct of directors in disqualification proceedings under the CDDA. Although this case was decided in 1998, it provides a timely and relevant case study to consider how directors' duties should

---

21 *Re Citigroup Inc. Shareholder Litigation*, 964 A2d 106 (Del. Ch. 2009).
22 *AIG Consolidated Derivative Litigation*, 965 A2d 763 (Del. Ch. 2009).
23 Aronson BE, 'Reconsidering the Importance of Law in Japanese Corporate Governance: Evidence from the Daiwa Bank Shareholder Derivative Case' (2003) 36 *Cornell International Law Journal* 1 11.

be interpreted in the context of bank failures in the financial crisis. The Barings case upholds the use of strong sanctions against bank directors for management misconduct in the form of financial penalties, regulatory de-authorisation, and banning orders against the directors from managing any company.

The conduct alleged in the claim involved the lack of director supervision and monitoring of the dealings of a rogue trader, Nick Leeson, who had been conducting a switching business (arbitrage in derivatives between markets) in Singapore. The business generated a substantial proportion of the Barings group's profits; however, it was conducted on margin and there were repeated calls for the transfer of funds from London to Singapore which in total amounted to £300 million. In fact, the business was not profitable but incurred losses in the order of £827 million, which caused the bank to collapse and the regulator, the Bank of England, to intervene to prevent a systemic crisis and facilitate its winding-up in insolvency. Later, the bank was bought for £1 by the Dutch banking and insurance group ING.

The Barings case consisted of a number of separate disqualification actions against its senior managers and directors; however, the principal proceeding heard before Mr Justice Parker related to the question of whether the conduct of three of the bank's directors, Andrew Tuckey (deputy group chairman), Ronald Baker (Leeson's product manager) and Anthony Gamby, amounted to a high degree of incompetence such that it rendered them unfit to be concerned in the management of a company under section 6, CDDA.

Section 6, CDDA requires a disqualification order to be made against a director of a company if the company at any time becomes insolvent and the director's conduct makes him unfit to manage a company. The purpose of section 6 is to protect the public against future conduct of directors who have proved unfit to manage a company in the past.

Pursuant to section 9, CDDA, Parker J. considered Schedule 1, para. 1 of the CDDA which *inter alia* requires the court to assess whether a director is unfit by reason of 'any misfeasance or breach of any fiduciary or other duty in relation to the company'. The crux of the case turned on the nature and scope of directors' duties of care, skill and diligence.

Parker J. expressed his three-limbed formulation of directors duties as follows:

(i) 'Directors have, both collectively and individually, a continuing duty to acquire and maintain a sufficient knowledge and understanding of the company's business to enable them properly to discharge their duties as directors.

(ii) Whilst directors are entitled (subject to the articles of association of the company) to delegate particular functions to those below them in the management chain, and to trust their competence and integrity to a reasonable extent, the exercise of the power of delegation does not absolve a director from the duty to supervise the discharge of the delegated functions.

(iii) No rule of universal application can be formulated as to the duty referred to in (ii) above. The extent of the duty, and the question whether it has been discharged, must depend on the facts of each particular case, including the director's role in the management of the company.'

The court emphasised that even when a director has delegated a function, he remains responsible for the delegated function and retains a residual duty of supervision and control.

The court characterised its approach to assessing incompetence as universal in that it would determine incompetence in any circumstances and at any management level. The exact nature and scope of the above duties will vary depending on the facts of the case, including: the size and business of the company, experience or skills of the director, organisation of the business, management role assigned to the director and their duties and responsibilities and remuneration (the higher the reward, the greater the responsibilities reasonably expected). For example, the duties expected of a high-earning executive director of a publicly listed company will be greater than of a less highly remunerated non-executive director of a small private company.

The key question of law in such disqualification cases is whether the director's conduct fell below the standards of probity and competence appropriate for a 'fit' director.

Parker J. held that a director could be deemed unfit by the court for breach of any statutory or common law duty, any dishonest conduct (want of probity or integrity) or a high degree of incompetence and examples of conduct showing unfitness including trading at creditors' risk or gross lack of judgement. Incompetence has been expressed invariably as 'total incompetence', 'very marked degree of incompetence' and 'really gross incompetence'. Parker J. noted, 'It is, I think, possible to envisage a case where a respondent has shown himself so completely lacking in judgement as to justify a finding of unfitness, notwithstanding that he has not been guilty of misfeasance or breach of duty.' Conversely, a misfeasance or breach of duty does not automatically mean a director is unfit.

The court also rejected a number of defences against a finding of unfitness, including: the director is unlikely to reoffend or the director would have performed another management role competently (lowest common denominator approach).

The court found that the directors' conduct involved serious incompetence in failing to understand and remain informed about the switching business. Tuckey was disqualified for four years, while Baker was disqualified for six years and found to have 'failed to make any serious attempt to discharge his management responsibilities'. Gamby was disqualified for five years and criticised for his 'culpable degree of inactivity'.

Parker J. found that the three directors failed to ensure that Leeson's proprietary trading activities were properly monitored and/or controlled in the following ways:

1. Leeson was left in full control of both the front and back offices of the bank's trading subsidiary in Singapore.
2. Prior to the bank's collapse, no objective assessment of Leeson's activities was ever made, despite unusually high levels of reported profitability.
3. Leeson's requests for funds on an increasingly massive scale were not challenged or investigated.

Parker J. concluded that '[i]t is a truism that if a manager does not properly understand the business which he is seeking to manage, he will be unable to take informed management decisions in relation to it'. Therefore, a director must keep informed of the conduct of the business to be able to manage it effectively, which includes supervising his delegates and if he fails to perform his duties of supervision and control, he exposes himself to the risk of disqualification from acting as a director of any company.

Box 5.2 UBS and the 'Décharge'

The Swiss Code of Obligations provides in Article 758 CO for a so-called 'Décharge', which is a discharge from liability of the board of directors (BoD) and management. Shareholders of large Swiss companies usually vote for such a discharge every business year. In case of UBS, after the crisis, this vote was postponed until 2010 when shareholders voted in a general meeting upon the discharge for the years 2007, 2008 and 2009. In 2008 and 2009, UBS had new management and BoD. The shareholders gave the discharge to the new management (including the BoD) in the years 2008 and 2009, but did not discharge the old management (former pre-crisis BoD Chairman Marcel Ospel and others) for their failure to act prudently in overseeing the bank in 2005–2007 just before it was bailed out by the Swiss government and central bank. This meant that UBS itself under its new management and BoD, or the shareholders, had the opportunity to bring a civil liability action against the old management and BoD for negligent oversight of the bank.

However, practically, only the company itself has the financial capacity to sue its former management. In case of UBS, the court fees would have reached millions of Swiss francs. If a shareholder or a group of shareholders sued UBS in a Swiss court, they would have to deposit in advance some of the substantial court fees. In addition, they would have had to bear the risk of losing the court proceedings and paying for all legal costs. So, it was clear that no shareholder (or even a group of shareholders) would bring a liability action against UBS's ex-management, unless the BoD authorised the bank itself to bring the action against the former management/BoD and thereby incur the legal expenses.

Under the leadership of its new management, however, UBS decided not to sue its former BoD/management. The main reason for this was that there were court proceedings at the time in the United States against UBS's former board and that the amount of the settlement payments UBS would have eventually to pay to US investors had not been settled in 2010. UBS expected that these payments would rise significantly if it filed a suit against its former managers in Switzerland and won the case. Its new management anticipated that if a Swiss court decided that UBS's ex-management was liable for the bank's earlier failure, then US investors could have used any admissions or factual determinations in Swiss courts to increase their claims in US courts and to seek greater settlement amounts. The new UBS management expected therefore that the price of the settlement payments the bank would have to pay to US investors would exceed the amount UBS could win in front of a Swiss court if it sued its former management. In addition, the new management feared that a suit against UBS's former management would result in lengthy court proceedings which would continue to harm the bank's reputation. The new management thus decided not to sue on behalf of UBS, in order to keep the expected settlement payments in the US as low as possible and to begin rebuilding the bank's tarnished image.

B Directors' Duties and Regulatory Law

5.24 Following the financial crisis of 2007–2008, the European Union drastically restructured its financial regulatory law by adopting a massive legislative programme of banking and financial law reform governing all areas of the financial services sector. The major objective of the legislative programme was to ensure that there would be no repeat of the banking collapses and public bailouts of privately owned banks that occurred across many EU Member States in 2007 and 2008 and which caused Europe to enter into its longest and most severe economic recession since the 1930s. As part of the financial market legislative reforms, the EU Council and Parliament adopted the Capital Requirements Directive IV (CRD IV) that consists of the Capital Requirements Regulation (CRR)[24] and the Capital Requirements Directive (CRD).[25] CRD IV substantially added to the requirements for the regulation of bank corporate governance and enhanced the powers of supervisory authorities to enforce governance principles based on more specific criteria for determining administrative sanctions to be imposed on banks and bank shareholders who fail to ensure that banks are governed in a sound and prudent manner.

5.25 Article 162 of the CRD requires the implementation into domestic law of the CRD's provisions dealing with 'sound and prudent management' of credit institutions and certain investment firms. The CRD affords considerable discretion to Member States to devise rules governing bank corporate governance and risk management from within their existing domestic legal and regulatory regimes.

5.26 Under the CRD, bank supervisors have wide discretion to address the particular risks that individual banks face and pose to the domestic banking system. As such, bank supervisors are not subject to a prescriptive framework of rules (although rules supplement the exercise of supervisory discretion). Supervisors may adopt stricter requirements with some banks, as opposed to others, where they decide that the institution has not devised or adhered to sound and prudent corporate governance practices and strategies.[26]

5.27 Moreover, the CRD provides Member State supervisory authorities with discretion to take all necessary measures to ensure the prudent and sound management of banks and certain investment firms, and that they may subject these institutions to remedial, business and recovery, and resolution plans whose content must be approved by the supervisor or other authority. The bank supervisor may also regulate and approve the risk management practices and business strategies of banks under its supervision and may vet and approve the appointment of bank senior managers and board members during normal periods of bank operations as well as when the bank is subject to remedial orders or plans and/or recovery and resolution plans.

---

24   Regulation (EU) No. 575/2013 of the European Parliament and of the Council of 26 June 2013 on prudential requirements for credit institutions and investment firms and amending Regulation (EU) No. 648/2012 [2013] OJ L176/1 (CRR).
25   Directive 2013/36/EU of the European Parliament and of the Council of 26 June 2013 on access to the activity of credit institutions and the prudential supervision of credit institutions and investment firms, amending Directive 2002/87/EC and repealing Directives 2006/48/EC and 2006/49/EC [2013] OJ L 176/338.
26   Alexander K, 'The EU Single Rulebook: Capital Requirements for Banks and the Maximum Harmonisation Principle', chapter 3 in Hinojosa LM and Beneyto J (eds), *European Banking Union: The New Regime* (Wolters Kluwer 2015).

5.28 To ensure that the Member State supervisory authorities apply the sound and prudent management principle similarly across EU/EEA states, the European Banking Authority (EBA) adopts regulatory technical standards that are binding and supervisory guidelines that are non-binding to promote enhanced harmonisation of supervisory practices across EU/EEA Member States. The EBA seeks to ensure that the exercise of supervisory powers, including the exercise of powers that intervene in the governance of banking and investment firms, is not unduly divergent across EU jurisdictions.

C Sound and Prudent Management of the Bank

5.29 While EU banking law does not define the concept of 'sound and prudent management', it repeatedly emphasises the essential role of the management body in ensuring sound and prudent management. This is to be achieved primarily through robust internal governance arrangements, including clear organisational structures, defined, transparent and consistent lines of responsibility, effective processes to monitor and report risk, adequate internal control mechanisms, including administration and accounting procedures, and remuneration policies consistent with sound and effective risk management.[27]

5.30 It is the management body's role to define, oversee and supervise the implementation of governance arrangements in a manner that ensures effective and prudent management and includes setting out the credit institution's strategic objectives, risk strategy and internal governance, overseeing the process of disclosure and oversight of senior management.[28] As explained above, the management body of a credit institution comprises its supervisory and managerial function. The term 'management body' is used in the European Banking Authority Guidelines on internal governance[29] to embrace all possible governance structures, keeping in mind that EU-wide there is the use of both unitary (where one body e.g. the board of directors, performs both supervisory and management functions) and dual governance structures (where supervisory and management functions are performed by a supervisory board and a management board, respectively). The Guidelines do not advocate any particular structure.

5.31 The management body is required to exercise its powers in a manner which is not just sound and prudent, but also proportionate to the nature, scale and complexity of the credit institution's risk structure.[30] The provisions relating to sound and prudent management by the management body are further fleshed out in the EBA Guidelines on internal governance 2017.[31] These identify specific instances of prudential and sound management that are part

---

27 CRD (CRD IV), Article 74(1).
28 CRD (CRD IV), Article 88(1).
29 European Banking Authority, 'Final Report – Guidelines on Internal Governance under Directive 2013/36/EU' (26 September 2017).
30 CRD (CRD IV), Article 74(2).
31 CRD (n 28).

of the responsibilities of the management body. According to the EBA Guidelines on internal governance 2017 (Guideline 23 in particular), special responsibilities of the management body broadly cover:

1. business strategy and the key policies of the credit institution within the purview of the applicable regulatory framework and the institution's long-term financial interests and solvency;
2. overall risk strategy;
3. an adequate and effective internal governance and internal control frameworks that include a clear organisational structure and well-functioning independent internal risk management, compliance and audit functions;
4. amount, types and distribution of internal and regulatory capital;
5. targets for the liquidity management of the institution;
6. remuneration framework that is in line with the principles set out the CRDIV Directive;
7. arrangements aimed at ensuring that the individual and collective suitability assessments of the management body are carried out effectively and that the composition and succession planning of the management body are appropriate;
8. a selection and suitability process for key function holders;
9. arrangements aimed at ensuring the internal functioning of each committee of the management body;
10. a risk culture in line with EBA's internal governance guidelines, which address the institution's risk awareness and risk-taking behaviour;
11. corporate culture and values, which foster responsible and ethical behaviour;
12. a conflict of interest policy at institutional level;
13. arrangements aimed at ensuring the integrity of the accounting and financial reporting systems, including financial and operation controls and compliance with the law and relevant standards.

5.32 Indicators of whether a bank's 'prudent and sound management' is being safeguarded or not cover a wide area of activity, including bank capital and liquidity management, corporate governance and business strategy, reputation and operational risks (including fraud and money laundering risks). Prudent and sound management also covers non-quantitative governance and legal risks that the bank may be exposed to and the risks arising from its decision-making processes and accountability structures. The bank's overall controls in corporate governance, organisational structure and risk strategy are important features of prudential regulation.

5.33 It is clear from the provisions of EU banking legislation and technical standards and guidelines that the primary responsibility for sound and prudent management lies with the management body. The CRD recognises the power that shareholders exercise and therefore their role in ensuring sound and prudent management. If a competent authority is not satisfied as to the suitability of shareholders, it may refuse authorisation to commence activity of a credit institution in the interests of preserving sound and prudent management of the credit institution.[32]

D Regulating Appointments to the Management Bodies of the Bank

5.34 The CRD establishes that responsibility for appointments to the managing body is within the purview of the credit institution, specifying that such an appointment should be based on knowledge, repute, skill and experience (CRD, Article 91). The EBA Guidelines on the suitability of members of the management body ('EBA Guidelines on management body suitability')[33] put the primary onus of this assessment on the institution both prior to and after appointment,[34] with the requirement to notify the competent authority of appointments. The Guidelines specify suitability requirements not just with regards to credit institutions, but also to investment firms, financial holding companies and mixed financial holding companies.[35] The management body is responsible for the selection and suitability assessment process for key function holders within the institution.[36] EBA Guideline 23 on internal governance also specifies that it is the responsibility of the managing board to appoint its members.[37]

5.35 The EBA Guideline 135 states that, unless otherwise specified in the Guidelines, the management body or the nomination committee should ensure that the assessments of the members of the management body are carried out before they are appointed. Guideline 136, however, specifies two situations when the assessment can occur after the appointment, when (1) the members are appointed by the shareholders and (2) a member needs suddenly to be replaced by a new member.[38]

5.36 The other stage of the assessment process for appointments to the managing body involves evaluation by the competent authority of the institution's appointments. Under the EBA Guidelines, competent authorities are tasked with undertaking an independent assessment of the suitability of proposed or appointed members of the management body.[39] However, it should be emphasised that the EBA Guidelines are legally non-binding and that the ultimate decision on appointments to the management body lies with the competent authority. If a member of the management body is not considered to be suitable, the

---

32 CRD (CRD IV), Article 74(2).
33 European Securities and Markets Authority and European Banking Authority, 'Final Report – Joint ESMA and EBA Guidelines on the Assessment of the Suitability of Members of the Management Body and Key Function Holders under Directive 2013/36/EU and Directive 2014/65/EU' (26 September 2017) www.eba.europa .eu/documents/10180/1972984/Joint+ESMA+and+EBA+Guidelines+on+the+assessment+of+suitability+of +members+of+the+management+body+and+key+function+holders+%28EBA-GL-2017-12%29.pdf accessed 21 February 2018.
34 Ibid., Guidelines 24, 25 and 135. See EBA Guidelines, page 17 recital 8 ('subject matter').
35 Ibid., Guidelines, page 17 recital 8 ('subject matter').
36 Ibid., Guideline 23, letter h (n 28).
37 Ibid., Guidelines on internal governance 2017 (n 28), Guideline 23, letter h.
38 Ibid., Guidelines 135, 136 and 139.
39 Ibid., Executive Summary and Guidelines 170 et seq.

competent authority should require the credit institution either not to appoint the member or, if the member is already appointed, to take appropriate measures for a replacement.[40]

5.37 EBA Guidelines on management suitability, Guidelines 4–9.3, set out criteria to be used by the competent authority in assessing suitability. These are far more prescriptive than the criteria set out for the institutions and broadly focus around three factors: reputation, experience and governance. Elements to assess good reputation include personal and business conduct to ensure sound and prudent management of the institutions, criminal and administrative records, investigations, compliance with professional codes of conduct, dismissal from employment in a position of trust including minor incidents, especially those relating to crimes in the financial sector, tax offences, corporate law and insolvency.[41] Criteria for assessment of experience include banking and financial sector-related education, training, and professional and practical experience gained in previous occupations.[42] Governance criteria include sufficient devotion of time, avoidance of conflict of interests and independence.[43]

5.38 The EBA Guidelines on management body suitability specify that if a member of the management body is not suitable, the credit institution, and, if necessary, the competent authority should take appropriate action.[44] The kind of action that can be undertaken varies. For the credit institution, appropriate action following non-suitability of a prospective member of the managing board involves taking necessary steps to improve the suitability of the individual under consideration, such as training, adjusting responsibilities, etc.[45]

5.39 The competent authority is required to inform the credit institution of non-compliance with any regulatory measures, giving the credit institution the opportunity to correct any such instances of non-compliance. The competent authority may reassess the suitability of members of the management body including through inspection and an interview process.[46] The entire process – both the first stage (assessment by the credit institution) and the second stage (assessment by the competent authority) – is to be completed within six months from the date of receipt of the complete application.[47]

5.40 The EU regulations requiring that bank boards consult regulators before appointing executives and board members were the main issue in an international arbitration case brought by the controlling shareholder of a Polish bank (FM Bank) against the Republic of Poland in 2015 on the grounds that the Polish regulator (the KNF) had acted disproportionately under EU law and inequitably under the terms of a bilateral investment treaty

---

40 Ibid., Guideline 191, letter c.
41 Ibid., Guideline 73 et seq. Guideline 75, letter b and Guideline 76.
42 Ibid., Guideline 58 et seq.
43 Ibid., Guidelines 41 and 79 et seq.
44 Ibid., Executive Summary and Guideline 165.
45 Ibid., Guidelines 168 and 191.
46 Ibid., Guideline 181 et seq.
47 Ibid., Guideline 179.

between Poland and Luxembourg (the home country of the controlling shareholder) when it ordered the controlling shareholder (PL Holdings) to sell all of its 99.5 per cent of shares it held in the unlisted bank as an administrative sanction for the shareholder failing to ensure that the bank's supervisory board had consulted with the regulator before appointing the bank's CEO and other executive managers. The Stockholm Chamber of Commerce arbitration panel that decided the case ruled resoundingly in favour of PL Holdings by holding that although the Polish regulator had the authority to require the bank's supervisory and management board to seek its approval before appointing the bank's CEO, the regulator's administrative sanction – requiring the controlling shareholder to sell all of its interest in the bank – was disproportionate as a matter of EU law and therefore violated the bilateral investment treaty between Poland and Luxembourg, thus entitling the shareholder to over €70 million in compensation.[48] The arbitration panel's decision is important in so far as it acknowledges that EU law allows regulators to impose administrative sanctions on banks and their shareholders for failing to ensure that the bank is managed in conformity with the principle of sound and prudent management but that administrative bodies imposing the sanctions can only impose sanctions that are proportionate to the breach committed and that the decision for imposing sanctions must conform with due process of law under European Union law and the European Convention on Human Rights.

III SHAREHOLDER RIGHTS

5.41 Public international law has addressed the distinction between the rights and interests of shareholders. In the *Barcelona Traction case*, the International Court of Justice (ICJ) observed that a public company with limited liability is founded on the distinction between the rights of the company and those of the shareholders.[49] Although a wrong committed against a company may infringe the shareholders' economic interests, it may not necessarily infringe their rights. The ICJ ruled that whenever a shareholder's interest is harmed by a measure directed at the company, it is the company's legal right, not the shareholders', to take appropriate action.[50] In other words, an act that only infringes the company's rights, and not those of the shareholders, does not involve legal responsibility towards the shareholders, even though the shareholders' economic interests may be harmed. This principle is also known under UK company law as the rule in *Foss* v. *Harbottle*.[51] Therefore, only the company acting by resolution of the board of directors, not the shareholders, could bring an action against the party which had infringed its rights.

---

48 *PL Holdings Sàrl* v. *Republic of Poland*, Partial Award, SCC Case No. V 2014/163, IIC 1265 [2017], 28 June 2017, Arbitration Institute of the Stockholm Chamber of Commerce (SCC).
49 *Barcelona Traction, Light and Power Company Limited*, ICJ Reports [1970], paras. 56–58.
50 Ibid., para. 58 [1843] 2 Hare 461, 67 ER 189.
51 [1843] 2 Hare 461, 67 ER 189. See also *Bamford* v. *Bamford*, [1970], Ch. 212 (CA (Civ Div)).

5.42 Under the laws of most countries with joint stock company legislation, shareholder rights can be divided into (1) economic or pecuniary rights and (2) control or governance rights. Economic rights can include the right to receive the remaining value of a company after it is liquidated or wound-up in insolvency. Control rights can include the right to influence the company's decision-making and strategic direction. In most European jurisdictions, shareholders can usually act in concert without burdensome regulatory reporting requirements to influence the board. For instance, some jurisdictions only require 5 or 10 percent of a class of voting shares to propose resolutions, to put issues on the agenda or to call extraordinary shareholder meetings. In contrast, US law imposes extensive disclosure requirements on the communications and actions of shareholders who act in concert and together control 5 per cent or more of a class of voting shares in a public company.

5.43 More specifically, shareholder rights usually cover the right to vote at general and special meetings to elect directors,[52] to approve the sale of certain company assets and to amend the company articles or charters. Moreover, in many civil law jurisdictions, shareholders would have a right to elect directors to the supervisory board. This is the case, for instance, under French, German and Swiss law.[53] In addition, most jurisdictions require that shareholders vote on important structural changes in the company, such as acquisitions and mergers, and whether the company will be liquidated or not. Shareholders who own the same class of shares have a right to be treated equally, and they are residual claimants who have a right to receive a pro-rata portion of the company's profits and assets, giving them a direct economic interest in the success and profitability of the company. Minority shareholders who vote against company reorganisations or major transactions (e.g. acquisitions and mergers) are entitled to benefits which are approximately equal to those received by controlling shareholders.

5.44 As discussed below, EU Company Law provides shareholders in a public limited liability company with the right to approve any proposal by management or outside party to increase, reduce or alter the capital of the company.[54] Moreover, the Directive lays down procedures for an offer of subscription on a pre-emptive basis which must be offered to the shareholders of a public limited liability company whenever the capital is increased by consideration in cash.[55] This raises the important issue of pre-emptive rights for

---

52   See Dine J, *Company Law* (Sweet & Maxwell 2001), 120–121.

53   See Menjucq M, 'Corporate Governance Issues in France' (2015) 16 *European Business Law Review* 5 101–115 and Schneider UH, 'Corporate Governance Issues in Germany – Between Golden October and Nasty November', in Norton JJ and Rickford J (eds), *Corporate Governance Post-Enron* (British Institute of International and Comparative Law 2006), 143–150.

54   Directive (EU) 2017/1132 of 14 June 2017 relating to certain aspects of company law (2017) OJ L169/46, Article 68 et seq., updating the shareholder rights that had been set forth in the Second Council Directive 77/91/EEC of 13 December 1976 on coordination of safeguards which, for the protection of the interests of members and others, are required by Member States of companies within the meaning of the second paragraph of Article 58 of the Treaty, in respect of the formation of public limited liability companies and the maintenance and alteration of their capital, with a view to making such safeguards equivalent (1977) OJ L 26/1 (no longer in force).

55   Directive (EU) 2017/1132 (n 54), Article 72(3).

shareholders in public companies and how these are regulated under EU law.[56] Pre-emptive rights entitle a shareholder to be offered the right to purchase a proportionate number of shares in order to maintain its percentage of ownership and voting control.[57] By having the right to approve the decision of directors to alter or increase the company's capital, shareholders can decide whether or not the company can issue more equity shares which, if approved, could have the effect of diluting their ownership interest in the company.

Box 5.3 The *Pafitis* case (CJEU 1996)

The European Court of Justice's decision in the *Pafitis* case acknowledges that the regulatory objectives to protect depositors and, more generally, financial stability may justify strict regulatory rules and supervisory actions that could infringe on shareholder rights in certain instances (Case C-441/93 *Panagis Pafitis and others* v. *Trapeza Kentrikis Ellados A.E. and others* [1996] ECR I-1347). However, the exercise of these powers must comply with the principle of proportionality under the EU Treaty and Charter and any secondary legislation. In *Pafitis*, the CJEU ruled that the powers granted by the Greek central bank to a temporary bank administrator to reorganise a heavily indebted bank without shareholder approval violated Articles 25 and 29 of the EU Second Company Law Directive (later re-enacted as Directive 2017) that requires that shareholders approve any change to the financial structure of a public limited liability company and that they have mandatory subscription rights in any recapitalisation. The Court also ruled that the appointment of the administrator with sweeping powers to recapitalise the bank was not an 'execution' measure – in the sense of an insolvency or bank resolution – that would allow the administrator to suspend shareholder governance rights. Instead, the exercise of

regulatory powers granted to the bank administrator had to meet a stricter definition of proportionality under EU law based on a necessity test that would assess whether the regulator could have adopted other regulatory measures or rules, such as having a comprehensive deposit insurance scheme, that could meet its regulatory objectives of depositor protection and banking stability without interfering to such an extent with bank shareholder rights. Crucially, the court stated in para. 57:

> the directive does not, admittedly, preclude the taking of execution measures intended to put an end to the company's existence and, in particular, does not preclude liquidation measures placing the company under compulsory administration with a view to safeguarding the rights of creditors. However, the directive continues to apply where ordinary reorganization measures are taken in order to ensure the survival of the company, even if those measures mean that the shareholders and the normal organs of the company are temporarily divested of their powers.

---

56   Ibid., Article 72(1).
57   See Article 57 bis para. 4 of the Law of 22 March 1993 relating to the statute and supervision of credit institutions (Loi du 22 mars 1993 relative au statut et au contrôle des établissements de crédit) (BE).

The court held that the appointment of a temporary administrator under Greek law did not resemble an 'execution measure' or even a 'liquidation measure', even though all the powers and competencies of the company organs were transferred to the administrator. The court made a distinction between the measures that could have been taken under Greek law that would have resulted in the withdrawal of the bank's licence and its liquidation, and the appointment of a temporary administrator that would allow the bank to continue its operations as before. Indeed, the vesting of all powers and competencies of the organs of the company with the administrator was only temporary and all subsequent capital increases following the initial one directed by the temporary administrator were approved by the new shareholders. This proved that the company was not executed into insolvency and that the appointment of the temporary administrator was to ensure the company's survival and therefore could not justify extinguishing the rights of the original shareholders and thus violating shareholder rights under EU law.

A Human Rights and Shareholders

5.45 The European Court of Human Rights (the Strasbourg Court) has also addressed the nature of shareholder rights. In *Olczak* v. *Poland*, the Court recognised that a share was 'a complex object' and that a shareholder in a company had corresponding rights which encompassed 'a share in the company's assets in the event of its being wound up, and other unconditioned rights, especially voting rights and the right to influence the company's conduct'.[58] In *Olczak*, the Court observed that shares in a public company have economic value and therefore can be regarded as 'possessions' within the meaning of Article 1 of Protocol 1 of the European Convention on Human Rights.[59] The share is not only an indirect claim on company assets, but can include other rights as well, especially voting rights and the right to influence the company.[60]

5.46 Under US law, the primary source for shareholder rights is state law.[61] As with most European jurisdictions, common shareholders are viewed as residual claimants of the corporation because of their claim on profits and assets upon liquidation.[62] Regarding control rights, common shareholders can vote for directors to act on their behalf. However, the legal relationship between the shareholders and directors is not legally one of agency, as the 'principals (the shareholders) do not control the decisions of the agent (the directors)'.[63] Upon election, the directors have fiduciary duties to act in the best economic interests of the company and all its shareholders, not simply for the shareholders who elected them. Under

58 *Olczak* v. *Poland* App no 30417/96 (ECtHR, 7 November 2002), 12; *S and T* v. *Sweden* (1986) 50 DR 158.
59 *Olczak* v. *Poland* (n 50).
60 *Sovtransavto Holding* v. *Ukraine* 2002-VII-95, 4–5; *S and T* v. *Sweden* (1986) 50 DR 158.
61 See, generally, Eisenberg MA, 'The Structure of Corporation Law' (1989) 89 *Columbia Law Review* 1461–1525.
62 See Revised Model Business Corporation Act 2016 (RMBCA), section 6.03(c) (requiring that outstanding shareholders have unlimited voting rights and are entitled to receive the net assets of the corporation upon dissolution).
63 Pinto AR and Branson DM, *Understanding Corporate Law* (Matthew Bender 1999), 93.

the majority of state statutes, ordinary business decisions are made by the board, while structural or governance decisions are made by the shareholders. In certain circumstances, however, the board can take governance decisions as well. A majority of state statutes permit the board to decide matters which are also listed as shareholder rights, but the shareholders have a right to override the decision taken by the board.[64]

5.47 Regarding pre-emption rights under US law, the federal securities laws do not afford shareholders with pre-emption rights. US commentators rationalise this by arguing that shareholders in a publicly traded corporation are less concerned with pre-emptive rights 'because they are passive investors and have no expectation of maintaining their percentage ownership'.[65] The stock exchange rules of several major US exchanges, however, provide strong shareholder voting rights which corporations must adhere to in order to keep their listing. For example, the New York Stock Exchange requires shareholder voting and approval for a company to issue new shares if the new shares significantly dilute the existing value of shares.[66] Nevertheless, US state law pre-emption rights are generally more limited than the pre-emption rights offered under the company laws of most EU states. For example, under the Delaware General Corporation Law, there is a presumption of no pre-emption rights unless they are provided expressly in the articles.[67] Other states, such as New York, provide for pre-emption rights unless a company expressly opts-out in its articles.

5.48 The availability of pre-emption rights for shareholders in public limited liability companies under Article 72 of EU Directive 1132/2017 suggests that shareholders in European companies have stronger legal protections than shareholders of US companies against being diluted of their ownership interest in a public company through the exercise of pre-emption rights. However, as discussed below in paragraph 5.50, EU Member States are allowed to enact legislation that allows shareholders to opt-out of their pre-emption rights for a maximum period of five years by passing a resolution at a general meeting.[68]

5.49 Generally, shareholders in US companies exercise a more limited number of substantive powers that include the election of directors and approval of amendments to the charter or bylaws, acquisition and mergers, the sale of substantial corporate assets and voluntary dissolution. Shareholders in European companies, by contrast, are statutorily mandated to vote on more strategic matters, such as whether to spin-off divisions, or, in the case of capital raising, whether to alter or increase the company's capital, including whether to waive pre-emptive rights related to an increase in company capital. It appears, therefore, that the rights of shareholders under European law are more solidly entrenched than under US law. US corporation law allows the articles and bylaws to be written in a way that places

---

64 See RMBCA (n 62), 10.20.
65 See Pinto and Branson (n 63), 73.
66 New York Stock Exchange Listed Company Manual http://wallstreet.cch.com/LCM/ accessed 18 May 2018, section 312.03.
67 Delaware General Corporation Law (DGCL) section 102(b)(3).
68 Article 72, Directive /2017/1132 (n 54).

most governance power with the board.[69] For instance, the limitation of shareholder rights under some US state laws can be demonstrated in the case of Delaware, a popular state for registration and as headquarters for many major US corporations.[70] The Delaware General Corporation Law provides that the articles of incorporation may contain 'any provision creating, defining, limiting and regulating the powers of the corporation, the directors, and the shareholders'. Thus, the board typically holds all powers that are not explicitly reserved for the shareholders.

5.50 In contrast, under most European jurisdictions, the shareholders' meeting is the source of most governance powers that are not given by statute to the board. Company charters or shareholder resolutions are prohibited from delegating powers to the board that are statutorily mandated to be exercised in the shareholders' meeting (except if the statute specifically provides for such a delegation). For example, shareholder rights to approve (or not) any change in the financial structure of a public limited liability company cannot be delegated to the board. Similarly, the Court of Justice of the European Union has recognised that shareholders have an inherent right to maintain their proportionate equity holdings in the issued capital of a public limited liability.[71] As discussed in paragraph 5.48, EU law, however, allows shareholders to opt-out of their pre-emption rights for a maximum period of five years by passing a resolution at a general meeting.[72] The resolution can be renewed without limit based on one of two types of majority vote: (1) two-thirds of the shares represented at the meeting or (2) if a majority is present, a simple majority of the voting shares present.[73] Thus, EU law empowers shareholders in EU-based public limited liability banking companies to exercise a broader range of governance powers over the internal operations of a bank than do the laws and regulations of other non-EU jurisdictions, including the United States.

5.51 Another means for shareholders to exercise their rights is to bring a derivative action against directors on behalf of the company in which they own shares for negligence or mismanagement of the company that resulted in losses to the company and/or the shareholders. The UK Companies Act 2006 provides such a remedy for aggrieved shareholders and was the legal basis for shareholders in the Royal Bank of Scotland to institute proceedings in 2010 against three former RBS directors, including its former CEO, the then Sir Fred Goodwin, for negligence and misrepresentation in a prospectus, contrary to section 80 of the Financial Services and Markets Act 2000, that was distributed in the market in May 2008 as part of the bank's emergency rights issue document (capital raising) a few months before the bank

---

69   See DGCL (n 67), section 141(a).

70   The Delaware General Corporation Law provides that the articles of incorporation may contain '*any provision creating, defining, limiting and regulating the powers of the corporation, the directors, and the shareholders*'. Thus, the board typically holds all powers that are not explicitly reserved for the shareholders – Delaware Code title 8: Corporations, chapter 1 – General Corporation Law.

71   C-42/95 *Siemens AG* v. *Henry Nold* [1996] I-6017, opinion of 19 September 1996, para. 15.

72   Directive (EU) 2017/1132 (n 54), relating to certain aspects of company law (2017) OJ L169/46, Articles 68(2) and 72(5). Ibid., Article 83.

73   Ibid.

collapsed and was taken over by the UK government in October 2008. The so-called RBS Shareholder Action Group alleged that in the prospectus, the RBS board members had misrepresented the bank's financial position as being strong when in fact the board was aware at the time the prospectus was issued that the bank had serious financial problems arising from extraordinary high levels of debt based on its misjudged decision in 2007 to acquire the Dutch bank ABN AMRO and substantial investment losses from structured finance products. The RBS Shareholder Action Group consisted of several sets of shareholders' proceedings, which were only fully settled in 2017, after the former bank board members and CEO agreed to pay substantial settlements to the RBS Shareholder Action Group.

B Regulatory Action and Shareholder Rights

5.52 A financial crisis can lead to a sudden loss of investor confidence in a bank's securities and may require a regulator to act quickly outside of normal corporate governance rules to recapitalise or restructure it. Europe and the US take different approaches. Under EU law, regulators are restricted from acting quickly in restructuring a bank which is not insolvent without *ex ante* shareholder approval. For instance, if a regulator requires a bank to recapitalise itself by issuing new shares, the EU Directive of 2017 relating to certain aspects of company law requires that any increase in capital shall be decided upon by the general meeting and in respect of the pre-emptive rights of shareholders over the newly issued shares.[74] Although most EU state regulators have authority to take measures that may affect shareholder control or economic rights, they must ordinarily obtain majority approval by shareholders. In contrast, US federal banking law allows the regulator broad discretion to order an ailing bank to take prompt corrective action to recapitalise itself or to take some other action that could alter the governance rights of shareholders without their approval. These different approaches present various degrees of regulatory intrusiveness into the corporate governance of banks and will be discussed below.

1 Limiting Shareholder Rights to Reduce Moral Hazard

5.53 Agency problems and moral hazard can lead to excessive financial risk-taking because there is a failure of responsibility on the part of the risk-taker. This arises in a situation when a market participant decides to engage in a risky but profitable transaction, even though doing so could increase systemic risk. The risk-taker does not fully absorb the expected costs of the transaction because the harm or costs from a possible systemic collapse has been externalised onto society. Although regulation can theoretically require all harm to be internalised, such a requirement may not be politically or pragmatically feasible as systemic harm is caused indirectly and affects a wide range of third parties in unpredictable ways.

5.54 This vulnerability is exacerbated by the corporate law regime of limited liability. Limited liability gives investor-managers strong incentives to take risks that could generate out-size

---

74 Ibid., Articles 68(1) and 72.

personal profits, even if that increases the firm's chance of failure. This is a serious problem with bank corporations because their shareholders benefit from the upside gains of bank risk-taking but do not absorb fully the downside risks of failure as most of these costs are externalised onto society. The same is true of highly leveraged shadow banking firms who not only engage in financial intermediation on which the real economy is dependent but also are highly interconnected with traditional banks, and so the costs of their failure are likely to have systemic consequences.

5.55 In the 1970s, US public regulatory law began to address this externality problem by extending the regulatory requirements applicable to corporate entities to any investors who were defined under the federal regulatory regime as owning a controlling interest, or exercising control in some other way, in a regulated firm or institution.[75] This has had the effect of limiting the application of the principle of limited liability by exposing certain investors in regulated companies to potential liability that exceeds the value of their investments for regulatory breach against both the government and private claimants. For instance, in US banking and thrift regulation, US regulators have imposed prudential regulatory requirements on parent companies, affiliates or individuals who own or control at least 5 per cent of the shares of a regulated financial institution.[76] Specifically, the US Supreme Court held in *Board of Governors* v. *First Lincolnwood Corp.*,[77] that the board of governors had the authority to assess the financial and managerial soundness of a company which had applied to purchase a controlling interest in a bank corporation.[78] The court upheld the board's denial of the application on the grounds that the prospective investor was, in the board's view, financially unsound and 'would not be a sufficient source of financial and managerial strength to its subsidiary bank'.[79]

5.56 In addition, another aspect of the source of strength doctrine occurs when US regulators determine that a bank is failing, or has failed, in which case they have authority to compel existing controlling shareholders to downstream additional capital into the ailing bank.[80] In other words, the board of governors has authority to issue directives requiring shareholders to invest substantial amounts in addition to what they have already invested in a

---

75   See Blumberg P, Strasser K, Georgakopoulos N and Gouvin EJ, *The Law of Corporate Groups: Jurisdiction, Practice, and Procedure* (first published 1992, 2nd edn, Aspen Publishers Online 2007).
76   See Jackson HE, 'The Expanding Obligations of Financial Holding Companies' (1994) 107 *Harvard Law Review* 507 517–525.
77   *Board of Governors* v. *First Lincolnwood Corp.*, 439 US 234 [1978].
78   See Schinski M and Mullineaux D, 'The Impact of the Federal Reserve's Source of Strength Policy on Bank Holding Companies' (1995) 35 *Quarterly Review of Economics and Finance* 485–496; Bierman L and Fraser DR, 'The "Source of Strength" Doctrine: Formulating the Future of America's Financial Markets' (1993) 12 *Annual Review of Banking Law* 269–316.
79   *Board of Governors* v. *First Lincolnwood Corp.* (n 77); see also *Irving Bank Corp* v. *Board of Governors*, 845 F.2d 1035 (1988).
80   The board adopted Regulation Y in 1984 which provides: 12 CFR section 225.4 Corporate Practices (a) *Bank holding company policy and operations*. (1) A bank holding company shall serve as a source of financial and managerial strength to its subsidiary banks and shall not conduct its operations in an unsafe or sound manner.

banking institution if the regulator determines that the investors should provide further financial support.

5.57 The limitation on the principle of limited liability that occurs under US regulatory law in the form of the source of strength doctrine and other regulations does not have an equivalent in European regulatory practice. Institutional investors in EU companies and banks are largely protected from regulatory liability or other private civil claims for regulatory breach against the company to the extent of the value of their investment in the company. As special resolution regimes are amended in light of the present financial crisis, it is submitted that regulators outside the US may seek broader powers, similar to the source of strength doctrine, in order to require existing shareholders in banks to demonstrate their capacity beyond what they have invested in the bank to be a source of strength. In exceptional circumstances, policymakers may find it necessary, in order to protect depositors and maintain financial stability, to pierce the corporate veil of an ailing bank so as to compel some of its shareholders to downstream capital to the bank.

5.58 For most countries, the doctrine of limited liability as it applies to shareholders in bank joint stock companies should ideally be redesigned to better align investor incentives with societal interests. For instance, limitations on limited liability might be appropriate involving the imposition of multiple – or double – liability on an equity investor-manager liable to lose its investment plus an additional amount equal to its investment, depending on what level of control it exercised or had the capacity to exercise over a banking institution. This creates an irony of sorts: that regulation to improve microeconomic goals (limiting investor liability to encourage equity investment) can impair the financial stability goal, such as limiting systemic risk-taking.

2 Legal Principles to Constrain Regulatory Powers

5.59 Shareholder rights have been recognised as rights to property under the European Convention on Human Rights (ECHR) and given protective status under the European Union Treaties and primary legislation. A shareholder's ownership interest in a company's capital stock has been recognised as protected 'possessions', and thus a property right under Article 1 of the First Protocol of the European Convention on Human Rights.[81] The European Court of Human Rights (ECtHR) has ruled that shares in a company have economic value and therefore constitute 'possessions' within the meaning of Article 1 of Protocol 1.[82] In *Sovtransavto Holding* v. *Ukraine*, the applicant company initially held a 49 per cent stake in a Ukrainian company, Sovtransavto-Lugansk. Following the decision of a state agency ordering the company to raise significantly more outside share capital, the percentage held by the applicant company was reduced to 20.7 per cent. The relative decline in the applicant's shareholdings in the company had the result of limiting its ability to influence

---

81 Article 1 ECtHR Protocol.
82 *Sovtransavto Holding* v. *Ukraine* ECHR 2002-VII-95, 937.

the direction and management of the company and protect its investment. The Court held that the manner in which the domestic court proceedings were conducted and resolved, and the uncertainty in which the applicant shareholder was left, upset the 'fair balance' that was required to be struck between the demands of the public interest and the need to protect the applicant shareholder's right to the enjoyment of its possessions. Consequently, the state failed to comply with its obligation to secure to the applicant shareholder the effective enjoyment of its property right. The case supports the view that Article 1 of Protocol 1 protects shareholders against direct and indirect forms of property deprivation and interference by governmental authorities.

5.60 A company share is not only an indirect claim on the company's assets, but can include other rights as well, especially voting rights and the right to influence the company.[83] In the *Marini* v. *Albania* case, the ECtHR found that shares held by the applicant had an economic value and constituted 'possessions' within the meaning of Article 1 of Protocol No. 1.[84] It proceeded to observe that a company share is 'a complex thing. It certifies that the holder possesses a share in the company together with corresponding rights. That is not only an indirect claim on company assets, but other rights, especially voting rights and the right to influence the company, may stem from the share.'[85]

5.61 In the *Marini* case, the applicant held a 50 per cent stake in a company. Repeated actions by the state left the applicant with no decision-making power in the company. Consequently, there were changes in the powers the applicant exercised as a shareholder; that is to say, in his ability to run the company, control its assets and receive its profits. The ECtHR found that the state measures at issue had rendered the applicants' shareholding 'inactive' and had 'upset the "fair balance" that has to be struck between the demands of the public interest, and the need to protect the applicant's right to the peaceful enjoyment of his possessions'. Consequently, the state had failed to comply with its obligation to secure the applicant's effective enjoyment of his right of property, as guaranteed by Article 1 of Protocol No. 1.[86]

5.62 Nevertheless, the exercise of shareholder rights is subject to a number of qualifications and conditions as set forth under national laws and regulatory regimes. As analysed in more detail in Chapter 14, the ECHR has been interpreted as balancing these competing interests while recognising legitimate expectations in property rights and the state's prerogative to regulate the economy and to take extraordinary action during a crisis. State oversight of the banking sector and the exercise of regulatory authority should be anchored in certain legal principles. In designing financial regulation, incentives structures should be developed for both *ex ante* prudential regulation and *ex post* crisis management measures that emphasise market-based solutions to financial sector failures while providing adequate state resources

---

83 Ibid., 4–5 (citing *S and T* v. *Sweden* 50 DR 158).
84 *Marini* v. *Albania*, ECtHR No. 3738/02, Judgment (18 December 2007), paras. 161 and 164.
85 Ibid., para. 165.
86 Ibid., para. 174.

to manage a crisis effectively and to contain any spillover effects onto the broader economy. The regulatory regime should also incentivise shareholders to take on more responsibility for recapitalising a troubled bank and redesigning compensation for management so that the bank's risks are more efficiently allocated between long- and short-term investments.

IV SUPERVISORY TOOLS FOR BANK GOVERNANCE

5.63 Banking supervision involves the supervisor monitoring the financial health of the bank and in certain circumstances calling upon bank managers to strengthen the bank's position by enhancing its regulatory capital, changing the composition of its assets, reducing the concentration of its asset exposures, or replacing management or the board. Such supervisory guidance may be in the first instance voluntary and merely an effort by the supervisor to inform the bank of perceived regulatory weaknesses. Under US prompt corrective action, the regulator may, before deciding whether to impose mandatory measures, exhort bank management to increase regulatory capital by, for instance, recapitalising itself.[87] In this scenario, it would be the decision of management and in some states it would require shareholder approval to increase the bank's capital. Similarly, the Chairman of the French Banking Commission can invite the bank managers or shareholders to take corrective action to cure any perceived regulatory weaknesses.[88] The UK regulatory authorities have followed a flexible risk-based approach in which supervisors engage in a dialogue with bank management and use voluntary guidance to influence the bank's prudential practices.[89] Through dialogue and veiled pressure, most banks are likely to take corrective measures to satisfy the concerns of their supervisor. In certain cases, however, more forceful regulatory action may be necessary.

A The Basel Committee and Bank Governance

5.64 The Basel Committee has adopted an array of standards and principles to govern bank corporate governance, including the Principles of Bank Corporate Governance (2010), the Core Principles of Banking Supervision (2012) and the Basel Capital Accord's Pillar 2, providing standards of supervisory review for bank corporate and risk governance (2013). This section summarises the most relevant standards and principles of these international regulatory frameworks.

---

87   Section 38(a) of the Federal Insurance Corporation Act of 1991 sets forth the statutory requirements for a well-capitalised bank and the various stages of regulatory intervention, all the way from voluntary guidance to a cease and desist order, and sanctions.
88   Article L511–42 of the Monetary and Financial Code (FR).
89   See Financial Services Authority, 'Financial Stability and Depositor Protection: FSA Responsibilities' (CP08/23) (December 2008), 5 www.fsa.gov.uk/pubs/cp/cp08_23.pdf accessed 19 December 2018.

5.65 The Core Principles of Banking Supervision recommend that supervisors have the authority to establish fit and proper requirements for bank directors, which limits who shareholders can vote for as directors, and to be consulted on appointments to the supervisory and management boards.[90] The Core Principles also restrict the acquisition of controlling interest in a banking institution to those investors who can demonstrate compliance with prudential safeguards (i.e. source of strength requirements).[91] Regulatory restrictions on management may also include large exposure limits on the bank's lending portfolio and asset allocation rules for the bank's proprietary trading.

B Pillar 2: Basel IIII Supervisory Review

5.66 The supervisory review process, together with Pillar 3 (market discipline), complements Pillar 1 (minimum capital requirements) for ensuring that the bank holds a level of capital and has adequate governance structures in place along with robust risk management processes and that it communicates its risk exposure to the market to ensure market discipline. Basel III Pillar 2 enhances the supervisory review process by allowing the supervisors to have wide powers of oversight to test the bank's corporate governance structures and its risk management practices from both a micro-prudential and macro-prudential perspective.[92] Pillar 2 provides for early intervention by supervisors if bank capital does not appear to the supervisor to cover sufficiently the risks inherent in their business activities. Increased capital should not be viewed as the only alternative to addressing a corresponding increase in risks confronting banks. This means that the supervisor has discretion to require the bank to adjust its governance practices and strategic business plans if they prove to be a source of unsustainable risk for the bank itself or – especially in the case of a SIFI – the broader financial system in which it operates. Further, capital should not be regarded as a substitute for fundamentally inadequate governance or risk management processes.

5.67 Pillar 2 introduces the supervisory review enhancement process (SREP), which enhances the bank supervisor's oversight and implementation of the *four key principles* of sound corporate governance and specific guidance relating to risk management and measurement. Principle 1 states that banks should have a process for assessing their overall capital adequacy in relation to their risk profile and a strategy for maintaining their capital levels.[93] Significantly, the bank's board of directors has the responsibility for setting the bank's tolerance for risks and for ensuring that management establishes a process for

---

90 Basel Committee on Banking Supervision, 'Core Principles for Effective Banking Supervision (Basel Core Principles)' (September 1997) www.bis.org/publ/bcbsc102.pdf accessed 21 February 2018, Principle 3.
91 Ibid., Principle 4.
92 Basel Committee on Banking Supervision, Basel III: A Global Regulatory Framework for More Resilient Banks and Banking Systems (December 2010, revised June 2011) (Basel III Accord), Pillar 2, Credit Risk, Articles 733–735 www.bis.org/publ/bcbs189.pdf accessed 21 February 2018; Operational Risk, Articles 736–737; Market Risk, Articles 738–738(v); Interest Rate Risk, Articles 739–740; Liquidity Risk, Article 741.
93 Basel II (as amended) (Basel III), Pillar 2, generally paras. 720, 721; specifically paras. 726–745.

assessing risks and developing a system relating how its risk level corresponds to the bank's capital level. Pillar 2, para. 730 states:

> The bank's board of directors has responsibility for setting the bank's tolerance for risks. It should also ensure that management establishes a framework for assessing the various risks, develops a system to relate risk to the bank's capital level, and establishes a method for monitoring compliance with internal policies. It is likewise important that the board of directors adopts and supports strong internal controls . . . .[94]

It is responsible for monitoring compliance with internal policies and is also responsible for establishing '[p]olicies and procedures designed to ensure that the bank identifies, measures, and reports all material risks'.[95]

5.68 Banks are required to establish adequate systems 'for monitoring and reporting risk exposures'[96] that allow senior management to '[e]valuate the level and trend of material risks and their effect on capital levels'; as well as '[e]valuate the sensitivity and reasonableness of key assumptions used in the capital assessment measurement system'.[97] With regard to the internal control review, the 'bank should conduct periodic reviews of its risk management process to ensure its integrity, accuracy, and reasonableness' to allow for the '[i]dentification of large exposures'.[98]

5.69 Principle 2 provides that supervisors should review and evaluate banks' internal capital adequacy assessments and strategies, as well as their ability to monitor and ensure their compliance with regulatory capital ratios. Specifically Pillar 2, para. 748 provides:

> Supervisors should also review the adequacy of risk measures used in assessing internal capital adequacy and the extent to which these risk measures are also used operationally in setting limits, evaluating business line performance, and evaluating and controlling risks more generally. Supervisors should consider the results of sensitivity analyses and stress tests conducted by the institution and how these results relate to capital plans.[99]

Supervisors should take appropriate action if they are not satisfied with the results of this Internal Capital Adequacy Assessment Process (ICAAP). The ICAAP was the most common means of implementing the corporate and risk governance principles. It was adopted under Basel II and remains in effect under Basel III by requiring supervisors to examine a bank's stress-testing results as part of a supervisory review of both the bank's internal capital assessment and its internal liquidity adequacy assessment programme (ILAAP). In

---

94 Ibid., para. 730.
95 Ibid., para. 731.
96 Ibid., para. 743.
97 Ibid.
98 Ibid., para. 745.
99 Ibid., paras. 748–750.

particular, supervisors should consider the results of forward-looking stress-testing for assessing the adequacy of the bank's capital and liquidity adequacy plans.[100]

5.70 Principle 3 provides that supervisors should expect banks to operate above the minimum regulatory capital ratios and should have the ability to require banks to hold capital in excess of the minimum based on an assessment of the bank's governance and risk-management practices.[101] Regulatory capital buffers are to provide for reasonable reassurance that the bank has 'good internal systems and controls, a well-diversified risk profile and a business profile well covered by the Pillar 1 regime ...'.[102] It is expected that in the normal course of business, 'the type and volume of activities will change, as will the different risk exposures, causing fluctuations in the overall capital ratio'.[103] And Principle 4 provides that supervisors should seek to intervene at an early stage to prevent capital from falling below the minimum levels required to support the risk characteristics of a particular bank and should take rapid remedial action if capital is not maintained or restored.[104] This principle supports the practice of prompt corrective action that allows supervisors to intervene in bank managerial decision-making if problems begin to emerge in the bank's operation and allows the supervisor to take pre-emptive measures if they determine that they are proportionate and necessary (i.e. capital raising or restriction of bank distributions).

5.71 The SREP provides more exacting standards for bank supervisors to test the risk-management practices of bank risk officers and to incorporate into their stress tests the financial stability risks of hypothetical scenarios involving the bank's exposures to structural or systemic risks. In the case of British banks, the UK Prudential Regulation Authority (PRA) is concerned with the near-term risks to British banks of a growing bubble in UK housing prices. The PRA is also encouraging bank risk officers to run scenario stress-testing involving a Eurozone sovereign default or Eurozone-based bank default. Also, key risk areas of concern include the implications for British banks of a sharp reversal of accommodative monetary policies. These types of stress tests are part of a forward-looking stress-testing approach that is an important element of a bank's internal capital assessment process. Pillar 2 stress-testing is essentially concerned with short-term crisis scenarios that could occur in three to five years. In contrast, longer-term risks to the financial sector are generally not subject to stress-testing because the availability of data is limited and the assumption underlying the forecasts lacks specificity.

---

100 Basel Committee on Banking Supervision, 'Peer Review of Supervisory Authorities' Implementation of Stress Testing Principles' (April 2012) www.bis.org/publ/bcbs218.pdf accessed 21 February 2018.
101 Basel II (as amended) ('Basel III') paras. 757–758.
102 Ibid., para. 757.
103 Ibid., para. 757b. The article goes on to state that '[t]here may be risks, either specific ... or more generally to an economy at large, that are not taken into account in Pillar 1'. Para. 757e.
104 Ibid., paras. 759–760. The Basel Committee acknowledges that the 'permanent solution to banks' difficulties is not always increased capital' (para. 760). Other specified measures may be necessary, but not effective immediately.

5.72 This could be a major weakness in Pillar 2 stress-testing because supervisor and bank risk officers are overly concerned with near-term crisis and are not engaged in planning for longer-term crisis that may occur because of the cumulative build-up of risk across the system and markets. For example, some experts have suggested that the effects of climate change on the economy may lead to the accumulation of high carbon assets in the financial system that might lead to banking sector instability through bank credit exposures. This type of longer-term scenario testing is not presently emphasised in the Pillar 2 framework. Although Pillar 2 provides a flexible framework for bank supervisors to engage with bank risk officers to assess and measure the financial stability risks of macro-prudential risks, its effectiveness in preparing banks for longer-term systemic or macro-prudential risks across the financial system remain to be tested.

5.73 In addition, despite the flexibility of approach afforded to the supervisor under the SREP, the UK PRA has had some challenges turning the latter into an effective supervisory practice. Under the existing Pillar 2 regime there is, in theory, an explicit link between the SREP and the PRA's evaluation of risks arising from the oversight, governance and risk management of the firm. This risk is expressed in the form of a governance scalar, which is applied to firms' Pillar 1 and Pillar 2 capital requirements. It is expressed overall as part of a firm's Individual Capital Guidance (ICG). The Pillar 2 governance scalar policy has been applied differently between supervisory areas. PRA teams worked closely in 2009 to refine the governance scalar policy; however, an agreement could not be reached. Failure to reach a common policy has resulted in inconsistencies between large, small and international firms.

5.74 In contrast, US regulators assess the financial health of a bank by reviewing its capital adequacy, asset quality, management, earnings, liquidity sensitivity to market risk (so-called 'CAMELS'). Banks are rated on each component, and a composite rating is also computed with a range from one to five as follows: 1 is 'strong', 2 is 'satisfactory', 3 is 'less than satisfactory', 4 is 'deficient', and 5 is 'critically deficient'. The main US federal banking agencies (the Office of the Comptroller of the Currency (OCC), the Federal Deposit Insurance Corporation (FDIC) and the Federal Reserve) all assign examination CAMELS ratings to banks. As part of that process, they evaluate governance and risk management within each of the CAMELS components, but then also assign an overall rating to governance and risk management. These ratings are not tied directly to capital. Instead, they are likely to lead to more intrusive supervision as well as restrictions on business activities and capital distributions. These measures are expected to provide an incentive for firms to improve their governance and risk management processes.

5.75 Additional capital can be imposed under the US Comprehensive Capital Analysis and Review (CCAR). Under this stress-testing regime, the US assesses not only the quality of a bank's capital adequacy assessment process, but also its corporate governance, controls, and risk measurement and management practices. The extent to which its ability to determine its risk exposures falls short of expectations can result in the bank being required to hold more capital. It should be emphasised that this assessment is undertaken under the

US Pillar 1 framework and so the decision to impose higher capital is based on a narrower set of criteria than the broader set of criteria used by the UK Prudential Regulation Authority in its Pillar 2 assessment of a bank's governance and risk management.

5.76 The enhanced supervisory oversight of bank corporate governance and risk management, and linking the determination of regulatory capital to sustainable corporate governance and risk management practices, provides another aspect of how bank capital has taken on a more social dimension, in addition to its earlier primary role of signalling solvency to the market.

C Pillar 3: Market Discipline (Enhanced Disclosure)

5.77 The purpose of Pillar 3 – market discipline – is to complement the minimum capital requirements (Pillar 1) and the supervisory review process (Pillar 2). The market discipline approach largely focuses on developing a set of disclosure requirements which will allow market participants to assess key pieces of information to investors on the scope of application, capital, risk exposures, risk assessment processes and hence the capital adequacy of the institution. Such disclosure requirements have particular relevance for investors because so much of the risk measurement process relies on the bank's internal methodologies and gives substantial discretion in determining their capital requirements, which are ordinarily only communicated to the bank supervisor.

5.78 In principle, banks' disclosures should be consistent with how senior management and the board of directors assess and manage the risks of the bank. Under Pillar 1, banks use specified approaches/methodologies for measuring the various risks they face and the resulting capital requirements. By providing disclosures to the capital markets, it is intended that investors should learn fully the risks to which banking institutions are exposed. A fuller disclosure regime under Pillar 3 departs from the earlier practice under Basel II of banks making more limited disclosure to the markets about the quality of their capital and riskiness of their assets. Public disclosure to reduce information asymmetries in assessing bank risk-taking is another important social function of bank capital.

CONCLUSION

5.79 This chapter analyses the legal and regulatory dimension of bank corporate governance, with particular emphasis on the board of directors and the role of shareholders. It also considers the legal structure of banks as corporate entities that are owned by shareholders who are protected by limited liability and the duties of directors of banking institutions. The chapter considers how the duty of care and fiduciary duties are interpreted in different jurisdictions. It then considers the special position of banks in the economy and how this affects the interpretation of bank director duties to take account of the social impact of the banking business and the importance of the principle of sound and prudent management under European Union law. The role of shareholders in bank governance and their legal rights, particularly in respect of the exercise of regulatory powers is then evaluated. The chapter analyses how regulatory law governs shareholder rights in the context of the externalities imposed by banks on society and considers how bank governance should oversee risk management to ensure sustainable returns for bank shareholders. It reviews the relevant areas of the Basel Accord that regulate bank corporate governance – specifically, Pillar 2 – supervisory review and Pillar 3 – market discipline. How bank governance is supervised under the Pillar 2 regimes by US and UK regulators in terms of prudential assessments of bank capital and managerial strength is then explored.

QUESTIONS

1. Describe weaknesses in bank governance before the crisis.
2. Should the fiduciary duty of board directors include a duty to protect society from bank risk-taking?
3. How does EU law define the sound and prudent management of a bank and in what areas of corporate decision-making can regulators influence bank management?
4. How do regulators oversee banks to ensure adequate capital and management practices?
5. How are shareholder rights and interests affected by a regulator's decision that a bank should be recapitalised?

Further Reading

Darbellay A, *Regulating Credit Rating Agencies* (Edward Elgar 2013)

de Bos A, Galle A and Jans M, 'Reshaping the Governance of the Dutch Banking Sector: Impact of the Dutch Banking Code', *Journal of Banking Regulation* 101–117

Hannigan B, 'Statement of Directors' Duties and Duties Owed to the Company', in *Company Law* (5th edn, Oxford University Press 2018)

Mulbert PO, 'Managing Risk in the Financial System', in Moloney N, Ferran E and Payne J (eds), *The Oxford Handbook of Financial Regulation* (Oxford University Press 2015), 364–408

Thiessen R, *EU Banking Supervision* (Eleven International Publishing 2013)

6

Deposit Insurance and Bank Resolution

Banks 'were international in life, but national in death'.

Lord King of Lothbury (former Governor of the Bank of England)

Table of Contents

INTRODUCTION

6.1 This chapter discusses the main principles of deposit insurance and bank resolution. It analyses the rationale and importance of depositor protection regulation with a particular focus on UK and EU regulations, comparison with the United States and reference to a few other jurisdictions. The inadequacy of deposit protection schemes in Europe became apparent during the crisis and led to substantial reforms of bank deposit guarantee regulation in the European Union. The bank run precipitated by the collapse of the British bank Northern Rock in September 2007 demonstrated the inadequacies of the UK's pre-crisis depositor guarantee system. The chapter will discuss the conceptual basis of deposit guarantee schemes and how some have evolved to incorporate risk-based metrics as a basis to calculate deposit guarantee premiums. It will explore how the European Union has required Member States to move away from post-pay schemes where participating banks pay into a fund after a bank defaults to a pre-pay scheme where banks pay about 0.5 per cent of covered deposits into a segregated fund that can later be used to repay depositors after bank defaults. The chapter will also consider whether bank deposit guarantee schemes are complementary to achieving regulatory objectives and the relationship between deposit guarantee schemes and bank resolution.

6.2 The main principles of bank resolution regimes will be explored. The chapter reviews the Financial Stability Board's 'Key Attributes of Effective Resolution Regimes for Financial Institutions' which sets forth principles and recommended tools that countries should adopt to ensure that systemically important financial institutions can fail without creating a systemic financial crisis and without resort to public funds. It also analyses the main elements of the US Organised Liquidation Authority's bank resolution rules under the Dodd-Frank Act 2010. And it examines the European Union's Bank Recovery and Resolution Directive (BRRD) and the United Kingdom's special resolution regime. The EU Bank Recovery and Resolution Directive and the UK resolution regime provide discretion to resolution authorities to utilise certain 'tools' from a resolution 'toolkit' to take a bank into resolution, while taking into account the impact on investors and creditors.

6.3 Prior to the crisis, most countries did not have formal legal and regulatory frameworks for the resolution of banking and financial institutions experiencing financial distress. Since the crisis, most advanced economies, including the European Union and the United States, have implemented some version of the Financial Stability Board's Key Attributes of Effective Resolution containing resolution tools such as bail-in. This chapter suggests that for banks that operate on a cross-border basis and have significant cross-border exposures, the decision to use certain resolution tools should be coordinated with the resolution authorities of other states to ensure that a cross-border bank failure does not undermine regulatory objectives. It finally explores the shortcomings and potential downfalls of using resolution tools, particularly the bail-in tool, and how their use can impinge on property rights and other legal rights.

I THE RATIONALE OF DEPOSIT GUARANTEE SCHEMES

6.4 The banking literature suggests that banks possess superior information regarding the viability of assets and that their primary function is to serve as delegated monitors of borrowers on behalf of depositors with surplus capital.[1] Since depositors lack sufficient information to assess the riskiness of assets in the bank's portfolio, they are not able adequately to monitor banks. This information advantage in favour of banks leads to moral hazard between the bank and depositors. This means that bank owners acting through their managers have strong incentives to increase risk because they can transfer some of the expected costs of their risks to third-party creditors, such as depositors, while receiving the upside gains that might arise from their risky behaviour. To address the risk to depositors, most developed countries provide some sort of deposit insurance protection. Since the crisis of 2007–2008, many deposit insurance schemes have increased the amount of their coverage for individual deposit accounts to provide more depositor confidence in the banking system. For instance, the United States increased the amount of coverage for depositors for each account they hold with a depository institution from $100,000 to $250,000 per account.[2] The European Union requires Member States to

---

1 Ellis DM and Flannery MJ, 'Does the Debt Market Assess Large Banks' Risks?' (1992) 30 *Journal of Monetary Economics* 481 483–485, discussing the function of banks as monitors of borrowers who act on behalf of savers.

2 The Wall Street Reform and Consumer Protection Act of 2010 (The Dodd-Frank Act).

establish deposit guarantee schemes that protect up to €100,000 for one account at each bank.[3]

6.5 Deposit guarantee schemes are deemed to be necessary not only to protect individual bank depositors, but also to protect financial stability. Banks generally have leveraged balance sheets with illiquid assets that are usually invested over the medium to longer term, and short-term liquid liabilities – mainly to depositors and other short-term creditors – which can be realised at short notice. This maturity mismatch between illiquid longer-term assets and liquid short-term liabilities creates a fragile, leveraged funding structure for banks which requires depositor confidence so that they can fulfil their intermediary role of borrowing short term and lending longer term, thereby supporting the broader economy.[4] Depositor confidence, however, can dissipate rapidly, in part because the legal basis upon which a depositor can assert a claim against the bank for repayment of its deposit is vulnerable to a bank default – at common law the depositor's claim for money held in a bank account consists of a *chose in action* or unsecured claim to enforce the deposit account contract and to compel the bank to pay over the balance owed in the account (in cash or upon instructions transferring funds to a third party).[5]

6.6 The account holder is in a legally weak position because if they pay cash (coins or notes) into their bank account, legal and beneficial ownership of those funds vests absolutely and unconditionally in the bank which may use the money for its own purposes. In return, the bank undertakes – upon demand and subject to the banking contract – to pay the amount deposited by the customer plus any contractual interest (in cash or as instructed to a third party). The customer's deposit of coins, notes or of incorporeal money by transfer from another bank thus consists of a personal obligation against their bank. If the bank defaults and is in insolvency or resolution, the account holder is merely an unsecured creditor who would have to share equally and on a pro-rata basis in any proceeds paid by the bank to it and other unsecured creditors. Deposit guarantee schemes, however, prioritise depositors for repayment over other unsecured creditors and allow them to be repaid as soon as possible by the guarantee scheme. This enhances depositor confidence in the banking sector so that depositors do not perceive the necessity to withdraw their funds immediately, which avoids the bank having to sell off its assets in a 'fire sale' in order to repay depositors and other short-term creditors, and this protects the wider economy from indirect losses.[6]

---

3 Directive 2014/49/EU of the European Parliament and of the Council of 16 April 2014 on deposit guarantee schemes (2014) OJ L 173/149, increasing deposit insurance coverage for one account at each bank.
4 See Diamond DW and Dybvig PH, 'Bank Runs, Deposit Insurance, and Liquidity' (1983) 91 *Journal of Political Economy* 401.
5 See *Libyan Arab Foreign Bank* v. *Bankers Trust* [1989] QB 728, 750–751 (Staughton J.); *Lipkin Gorman* v. *Karpnale Ltd* [1991] 2 AC 548 (HL), 573–574 (Lord Goff); *R* v. *Preddy* [1996] AC 815, 841 (Lord Jauncy); *Foskett* v. *McKeown* [2001] 1 AC 102, 127–128 (Lord Millett).
6 Garcia G and Prast H, 'Depositor and Investor Protection in the EU and the Netherlands: Past, Present and Future' (2004) De Nederlandsche Bank Occasional Studies Vol. 2/Nr. 2 www.dnb.nl/en/binaries/OSVolNr2_tcm47-146642.pdf accessed 21 February 2018.

6.7 Moreover, market failure can occur in the banking sector based on asymmetric information between depositors and banks regarding the amount of information and expertise available to depositors to assess the riskiness of the bank's balance sheet. The potential negative externalities caused by a bank run for the broader economy justifies both *ex ante* prudential regulation and *ex post* bailout mechanisms for depositors such as deposit guarantees.[7] Similarly, the negative externality of bank failure sometimes justifies the central bank to provide 'lender of last resort' support to ailing deposit institutions which are illiquid but solvent and which can provide the central bank good collateral for the value of the central bank's liquidity support.

6.8 The resulting view, that financial markets can be subject to inherent instability, induces governments to intervene to provide depositor protection in some form or other. Explicit deposit insurance is one approach, while an explicit or implicit deposit guarantee is another. In either case, general prudential supervision also occurs to limit the risk incurred by insurers or guarantors. To control the incentives of bank owners who rely heavily on government-subsidised deposit insurance, governments typically enforce some control over bank owners. These can involve limits on the range of activities (structural regulation); linking deposit insurance premiums to the riskiness of the deposit-taking institution; and aligning capital adequacy requirements to the riskiness of bank assets.

6.9 While such controls may overcome the agency problem between government and bank owners, it must be asked how significant this problem is in reality. A cursory review of recent banking crises would suggest that many causes for concern relate to management decisions which reflect agency problems. Management may have different risk preferences from those of other stakeholders including the government, owners, creditors, etc., or have limited knowledge in assessing the risks involved in its decisions, and yet have significant freedom of action because of the absence of adequate control systems able to resolve agency problems. Nevertheless, government-subsidised risk-taking for financial institutions can lead to excessive risk-taking and significant externalities for the economy. For many years, the US deposit insurance system provided the same level of deposit insurance coverage for all retail depositors at insured depository institutions, regardless of the riskiness of the institutions. The *ex ante* premiums paid by banks into the deposit insurance fund provided a fund against which depositor claims could be made when an institution failed to meet a depositor's claim for repayment of its deposited funds. The amount of premium paid by an institution was not risk-based, that is, it did not depend on the riskiness of the bank's portfolio or trading activities. The absence of any risk-based price for determining premiums on deposit insurance created an incentive for bank management to take greater risks with depositors' funds because they could attract the same priced deposit insurance coverage regardless of the riskiness of the banks' portfolio. This created incentives for US banks and savings and loans institutions in the 1980s to make many more risky loans than they would have made without such generous deposit guarantee coverage. This deposit guarantee policy was an important factor that contributed to the

---

7 See Goodhart CAE, Hartmann P, Llewellyn DT, Rojaras-Suarez L and Weisbrod S, *Financial Regulation: Why, How, and Where Now?* (Routledge 1998).

eventual failure of hundreds of banks and savings and loans institutions in the 1980s and 1990s, resulting in massive payouts by the US deposit insurance fund.

II DEPOSIT GUARANTEE SCHEMES, MORAL HAZARD AND BANKING CRISES

6.10 The Icelandic banking crisis in 2008–2010, and its aftermath, demonstrated major weaknesses in the European Union/European Economic Area deposit guarantee scheme arrangements. The EU Deposit Guarantee Directive 1994 had provided a minimum amount of coverage of €20,000 for each depositor at an EU-based bank that was registered with its Member State deposit guarantee scheme. Each state was given discretion as to whether they would use *ex ante* or *ex post* funding arrangements and whether these arrangements would be industry or state funded. Each state, therefore, was not required to be responsible for guaranteeing payments to depositors in the event that a deposit fund had inadequate resources to pay out on depositor claims. As a result, the EU legislation was unable to ensure that a large number of depositors could receive payouts in a banking crisis.

6.11 In 2008, Iceland's banking system collapsed with the failure of the three largest Icelandic banks. The largest of these banks was *Landsbanki*, which had significant cross-border operations across EU states in both wholesale and retail banking. Landsbanki had over 345,000 retail deposit account holders both in the United Kingdom and the Netherlands who held their accounts in Landsbanki's online branch, Icesave. The Landsbanki collapse caused the Icesave dispute when Iceland's government declared that its deposit protection fund was inadequate to pay the depositor claims of the Icesave account holders. Iceland adopted resolution legislation in 2009 to restructure its banking system in which the liabilities and assets of the three failed Icelandic banks were restructured and sold off respectively, with some of the proceeds used to pay the depositors of Landsbanki (the vast majority of whom were Icelandic residents) but not the claims of depositors in Landsbanki's online branch Icesave, most of whom were residents of the UK and the Netherlands.

6.12 When the Icelandic government refused to pay the claims of the Icesave account holders, the UK government imposed terrorist financing sanctions on Iceland under the UK Anti-Crime, Terrorist and Security Act 2001 that treated Iceland as a pariah state resulting in asset freeze orders against the Icelandic government, Iceland's central bank, and the assets of the restructured Icelandic banks located in the UK. While the dispute continued, the UK and Dutch governments paid the claims in full of UK and Dutch deposit account holders of Icesave who had lost their savings.

6.13 The UK and Dutch governments then asserted a claim for repayment of these amounts directly against the Icelandic government. The Icelandic state proposed bilateral loan guarantees for repayment but they were rejected by Icelandic voters. The UK and Dutch governments brought an action against the Icelandic government before the European Free Trade

Association (EFTA) court for violating its obligations under the 1994 Deposit Guarantee Directive and provisions of the European Economic Area Agreement. The EFTA Court ruled in favour of Iceland on all claims brought against it by the UK and Dutch governments, causing surprise to many legal experts. The UK and Dutch governments were then subrogated as claimants of their nationals' claims against the Landsbanki receivership, and in 2016 the receivership under Icelandic law repaid all priority claims, including all claims to the UK Financial Services Compensation Scheme (FSCS) and the Dutch deposit guarantee scheme.

Box 6.1: *The UK v Iceland* – the *Landsbanki* case

On the afternoon of 7 October, after Landsbanki had been placed into receivership – but before the head of the Central Bank of Iceland made his live public television appearance about how the Icelandic state would respond to its foreign debt obligations, the UK Chancellor of the Exchequer Alistair Darling had a telephone conversation with his counterpart, Iceland's Finance Minister.

DARLING: Do I understand that you guarantee the deposits of Icelandic depositors?

MATHIESEN: Yes, we guarantee the deposits of the banks and branches here in Iceland.

DARLING: But not the branches outside Iceland?

MATHIESEN: No, not what was outside of the letter that was already sent.

DARLING: But is that not in breach of the EEA Treaty?

MATHIESEN: No, we don't think so and think this is actually in line with what other countries have been doing over recent days.

The next day, Alistair Darling announced that he was taking steps to freeze the assets of Landsbanki in the UK. Under the Landsbanki Freezing Order 2008, passed at 10 a.m. on 8 October 2008, the UK Treasury went on to freeze the assets of Landsbanki and assets belonging to the Central Bank of Iceland, and the government of Iceland. The freezing order was based on provisions in Part 2 of the Anti-terrorism, Crime and Security Act 2001, and was made 'because the Treasury believed that action to the detriment of the UK's economy (or part of it) had been or was likely to be taken by certain persons who are the government of or resident of a country or territory outside the UK'.

Over 80,000 people signed an online petition against Britain's use of 'anti-terrorism legislation' against Landsbanki, under the theme 'Icelanders are NOT terrorists'.

A International Association of Deposit Insurers

6.14 The International Association of Deposit Insurers (IADI)[8] is a forum where deposit insurers from around the world meet to discuss best practice for the regulation of deposit insurance

---

8 International Association of Deposit Insurers: 'About IADI' (IADI Objectives, Bank for International Settlements 2018) www.iadi.org/en/about-iadi/ accessed 19 December 2018.

schemes. The IADI was founded in May 2002 as a non-profit organisation under Swiss law and is domiciled at the Bank for International Settlements in Basel, Switzerland. The IADI provides training and educational programmes for its members and research guidance on deposit insurance issues. The IADI's objectives are '[t]o contribute to the stability of financial systems by promoting international cooperation in the field of deposit insurance and providing guidance for establishing new, and enhancing existing, deposit insurance systems, and to encourage wide international contact among deposit insurers and other interested parties'. The IADI has undertaken three strategic goals for the period of 2015–2020: (1) to promote deposit insurance system compliance with the IADI Core Principles; (2) to advance deposit insurance research and policy development; (3) to provide members with technical support to modernise and upgrade their deposit insurance systems.

6.15 The crisis demonstrated that there were inconsistencies in the legal and regulatory frameworks across countries for deposit guarantee schemes. As discussed above, the Icelandic banking crisis represented a serious lack of understanding, even by policymakers regarding the extent and scope of deposit guarantee laws. As a result, the IADI adopted in 2009 the Core Principles for Deposit Insurance Schemes and, after further consultation and feedback from members, revised the core principles in 2014.[9] For the purposes of this chapter, the most significant principles are the following: Principle 3 provides that the deposit insurer should be operationally independent, well governed, transparent, accountable and insulated from external interference.

6.16 Regarding cross-border issues, Principle 5 provides that information sharing and coordination arrangements are in place for jurisdictions where foreign banks operate (Principle 5 (1)). The coverage of deposits in a branch bank in a foreign jurisdiction should be governed by bilateral or multilateral agreements to determine which deposit insurer(s) are responsible for reimbursement (Principle 5(2)). Principle 7 recommends compulsory membership in a deposit insurance system for all banks (including state-owned banks, see Principle 7(1)).

6.17 Principle 9 addresses sources and uses of funds by recommending that funds should be readily available and provided on an *ex ante basis* (Principle 9 (1)). Principle 14 provides that an 'effective failure resolution regime should enable the deposit insurer to provide for protection of depositors and contribute to financial stability' and the legal framework should include a bank resolution regime. Principle 15 recommends prompt reimbursement of depositors' insured funds within seven working days, while the Financial Stability Board also recognises the seven working-day rule for depositor reimbursement when the bank is put into resolution.[10] Principle 16 entitled 'Recoveries' provides that 'The deposit insurer

---

9   See 'The Revised Core Principles for Effective Deposit Insurance Systems' (2014).
10   See IADI Principle 15(1) provides that '[t]he deposit insurer is able to reimburse most insured depositors within seven working days'. See also Financial Stability Board, 'Key Attributes of Effective Resolution Regimes for Financial Institutions' (Financial Stability Board 15 October 2014), Key Attribute 3.2 xii, p. 8, stating in relevant part '[[r]esolution authorities should have the power to] [e]ffect the closure and orderly wind-down

should have, by law, the right to recover its claims in accordance with the statutory creditor hierarchy.'

B European Union Deposit Guarantee Directive 2014

6.18 The European Union adopted Directive 2014/49/EU,[11] establishing minimum standards for bank deposit guarantee schemes in order to address the severe moral hazard problems that had become apparent in most Member States' deposit guarantee arrangements during the crisis of 2007–2008. The Directive's main aim was twofold: (1) to ensure financial stability in Europe with regard to the prevention of bank runs, and (2) to ensure that depositors are eligible to recover a certain minimum amount of their deposits from a separate fund financed *ex ante* by mandatory bank contributions, regardless of whether the bank individually has adequate resources to meet depositor claims. Under the Deposit Guarantee Scheme (DGS), certain deposits are deemed eligible, while other deposits are ineligible, such as, among other things, the bank's own funds, bank deposits with other banks and deposits that are connected to criminal offences resulting in a conviction for money laundering.[12] The DGS aims primarily to protect retail depositors who might otherwise, in the absence of a reliable deposit guarantee scheme, precipitate a run on a bank.

6.19 For eligible deposits, the DGS sets a coverage level of €100,000 for each depositor of a regulated credit institution.[13] The €100,000 limit per depositor of an individual credit institution, and not for each individual deposit account at a credit institution, was designed to incentivise depositors to spread their deposits around different banks if their aggregate deposits exceed €100,000 at an individual institution. There are exceptions to the €100,000 limit per bank rule, in which a deposit in excess of €100,000 is eligible for coverage if (i) the source of the deposit is related to a transaction of private residential property, (ii) the deposit serves a social purpose, and (iii) deposits have been made by the state to provide insurance benefits or compensation for criminal injuries or wrongful conviction.[14] The rationale for these exceptions is to ensure that temporary deposit increases in the accounts are protected, but for only a limited period of at least three months and no longer than twelve months, so that depositors with unexpected increases in their deposit balances will have enough time to decide how to use the sum in excess of the €100,000 limit.

6.20 The DGS financing consists of two approaches. First, the *ex ante* funding approach in which banks which are members of the deposit scheme make contributions so that the available

---

(liquidation) of the whole or part of a failing firm with timely payout or transfer of insured deposits and prompt (for example, within seven days) access to transaction accounts and to segregated client funds)'.

11   Directive 2014/49/EU of the European Parliament and of the Council on deposit guarantee schemes (2014) OJ L 173/149, Article 4(1).

12   Ibid., Article 5(1)(a–k).

13   The EU Capital Requirements Regulation No. 575/2013, Article 4(1)(1) defines 'credit institution' as an institution that accepts deposits from the public and which invests those deposits into assets on its balance sheet.

14   Ibid., Articles 6(1) and 7(1).

funds of the scheme cover at least 0.8 per cent of the covered deposits of the institution members of the scheme.[15] The second approach is *ex post* funding, which can occur if a bank fails or is otherwise not able to meet depositor claims, and the sources of the deposit guarantee scheme are inadequate to repay depositors. In this scenario, the banks that are members of the scheme are obliged to make extraordinary contributions, up to 0.5 per cent of their covered deposits per calendar year.[16] In addition to these two approaches, Member States are also obliged to introduce alternative short-term funding arrangements,[17] which are generally understood to be government credit lines;[18] for example, short-term loans from the Treasury to the scheme. Another funding approach that is not yet legally required for Member States would allow a national deposit scheme that is underfunded because of an excessive number of depositor claims to attempt to borrow from other willing Member State guarantee schemes up to a maximum of 0.5 per cent of the covered deposits of the borrowing DGS.[19]

6.21 However, the DGS Directive's impact on the moral hazard of depositors should be considered in the context of a bank that could be taken into resolution and wound-up. In this context, the EU Bank Recovery and Resolution Directive introduces a mandatory 'super-preference' for deposits protected by EU deposit guarantee schemes, such as the Financial Services Compensation Scheme in the UK, for amounts below €100,000. This means that in insolvency, the FSCS is in the most senior class of unsecured creditors. The BRRD also provides mandatory preference in the creditor hierarchy for depositors in EU and non-EU-based banks who are individuals, and small and medium-sized and micro businesses whose deposits exceed the deposit protection limit of €100,000 (£85,000).

6.22 The DGS Directive also provides for judicial review of measures taken by officials of deposit guarantee schemes. Member States are obliged to ensure that the claims of depositors can be brought before the courts if their claims are rejected by deposit guarantee authorities.[20] In addition, once a deposit scheme makes a payment to depositors, it is entitled to be subrogated to the rights of the depositors against the bank, which means that the deposit guarantee scheme can become a creditor of a bank in a resolution.[21]

6.23 In 2015, the European Commission proposed a White Paper on a European Deposit Insurance Scheme (EDIS), which would serve as a single deposit guarantee scheme to

---

15 Ibid., Article 10(2).
16 Ibid., Article 10(8).
17 Ibid., Article 10(9).
18 Colaert V, 'Deposit Guarantee Schemes in Europe: Is the Banking Union in Need of a Third Pillar?' (2014) *European Company and Financial Law Review* 2 27.
19 Directive 2014/49/EU (n 11), Article 12. See Colaert (n 18), 27. This aspect of the Directive had been drafted as obligatory initially, but Member States have not yet agreed to adopt this requirement as binding the DGS Directive.
20 Directive 2014/49/EU (n 11), Article 9(1). The rights of investors and other third parties to seek judicial review will be discussed in Chapter 14.
21 Ibid., Article 9(2).

improve the efficiency of the process of deposit protection and repayment.[22] Yet, as of 2018, no legislation has been proposed. One reason for this is that Member States have different views regarding the benefits of a single EU-wide deposit guarantee scheme. Regarding such a scheme, some Member States can claim that their economies and financial systems are stronger and more stable than other Member States, and therefore they are less willing to contribute to an EU-wide scheme that would probably not be drawn upon by their own banks but instead by banks who are members of DGS schemes in other economically weaker Member States.

C Deposit Insurance and Moral Hazard: The US FDIC

6.24 The US Federal Deposit Insurance Corporation (FDIC) was established by Congressional statute during the Great Depression in 1931 to provide deposit insurance for depositors of failed US banking institutions. During its first sixty years, the FDIC assessed the insured institutions at the same flat rate for deposit insurance coverage. Although the FDIC's deposit insurance system was crucial for restoring depositor confidence in the US banking system in the 1930s and 1940s, and undoubtedly played an important role in the recapital-isation of US banks, it was subsequently criticised for creating moral hazard among bank managers, owners and depositors who perceived the generous deposit insurance coverage to be a subsidy for risk-taking because depositors would be bailed out regardless of the riskiness of the bank's lending and business activities. For instance, Robert Merton showed that before 1991 (when FDIC deposit insurance became risk-based) the FDIC insurance premium rates were calculated on a fixed-price basis for all insured deposits; and that this created a put-option-like subsidy for bank shareholders who were protected against down-side losses by limited liability and thus were incentivised to encourage management to engage in riskier (higher expected value return) lending and trading activities.[23]

1 The Need for Risk-Based Deposit Insurance

6.25 In 1991, as a response to the savings and loan crisis of the 1980s, Congress sought to mitigate the moral hazard problem by enacting the Federal Deposit Insurance Corporation and Institutions Act 1991 (FDICIA). Under FDICIA, the Federal Deposit Insurance Corporation (FDIC) has been vested with discretionary authority to make determinations of unsafe and unsound banking practices in violation of the FDICIA that would place the insurance fund at risk. FDICIA established a risk-based assessment system under which the premiums paid by federally insured financial institutions are based on risks the institutions pose to the insurance fund. Specifically, section 302(a) of the FDICIA requires the FDIC to establish final risk-based assessment regulations. In section 302(a) of the FDICIA, Congress defined a 'risk-based assessment system' as:

---

22 Van Roosebeke B, 'EU Deposit Guarantee Scheme in the European Parliament: Some Progress, Need for Improvement' (cepAdhoc 2016) https://www.cep.eu/fileadmin/user_upload/cep.eu/Studien/cepAdhoc_Einlagen sicherung/cepAdhoc_Deposit_Guarantee_Scheme.pdf accessed 19 December 2018.
23 See Kane EJ, *The S&L Insurance Mess: How Did It Happen?* (Urban Institute Press 1989), discussing how US deposit insurance created a moral hazard that was a major contributor to the US savings and loans crisis.

a system for calculating a depository institution's semi-annual assessment based on –

  (i) the probability that the deposit insurance fund will incur a loss with respect to the institution, taking into consideration the risks attributable to –
    (I) different categories and concentrations of assets;
    (II) different categories and concentrations of liabilities, both insured and uninsured, contingent and non-contingent; and
    (III) any other factors the [FDIC] determines are relevant to assessing such probability;
  (ii) the likely amount of any such loss; and
  (iii) the revenue needs of the deposit fund.[24]

6.26 Under the FIDICIA regime, the FDIC has issued a risk-based classification system based on detailed reports and expert evaluations of the financial condition of an institution. The FDIC's regulations require the agency to analyse objective 'capital' factors as well as subjective 'supervisory' factors.[25] Institutions are divided into 'small institutions' and 'insured branches of foreign banks' and are assigned to risk categories I, II, III or IV and are then sorted into the supervisory groups A, B or C.[26] Institutions categorised as 'large and highly complex institutions' are assessed using a scorecard. For 'large institutions', the initial base assessment rate is determined according to the scorecard for large institutions, whereas for 'highly complex institutions' the rate is determined according to the scorecard for highly complex institutions. These two categories of scorecards differ in their components and measures, and in the weighting of these measures.[27]

6.27 The US FDICIA 1991 approach demonstrates that the regulator can influence the risk preferences of the bank manager by adjusting the insurance premium rates for insured deposits. Despite the FDIC's new powers to devise premium charges that more truly reflect the underlying risk of a bank's assets, some experts argue that deposit insurance premiums at US depository institutions remain under-priced.[28] Nevertheless, most regulators are in agreement that the reduction of moral hazard in bank risk-taking requires, in part, a more efficient pricing of deposit insurance premiums based on risk-based factors along with a level of coverage that creates an incentive for depositors to engage in some monitoring and in bearing some of the risks of bank managers.

D The Lender of Last Resort, Bank Manager and Fixed Claimants

6.28 Moral hazard can also exist between the regulator and bank manager. The issue that arises is whether the regulator can design governance structures to reduce the social costs of bank

---

24 12 USC section 1817(b)(l)(C).
25 *FDIC* v. *Coushatta* 930 F. 2d 122 (5th Cir.), cert. denied, 502 U.S. 857 (1991).
26 12 CFR section 327.9(a), 12 CFR section 327.9(c).
27 12 CFR section 327.9(b).
28 Flannery MJ, 'Pricing Deposit Insurance when the Insurer Measures Bank Risk with Error' (1991) 15 *Journal of Banking and Finance* 975 975–998.

risk-taking. According to Arrow,[29] it is impossible to allocate risk efficiently between the regulator and bank because of asymmetric information. For instance, the lender of last resort (LOLR) mechanism provides a safety net that allows the bank to shift risk to the regulator (insurer) or to depositors. This is especially the case when the bank is perceived as too big to fail. The LOLR mechanism provides a safety net for banks that allows them to discount the cost of their risk-taking. On the other hand, in regard to deposit insurance, it has been argued that the insurer-regulator is assumed to manage the trade-off between the social costs of bank default and the economic benefits of bank risk-taking when the bank avoids default.[30]

6.29 Moreover, various devices are used to protect fixed claimants against excessive risk-taking in the firm. However, according to Macey et al.,[31] what makes banks primarily different from other types of firms is the lack of discipline exerted by fixed claimants (e.g. depositors and other banks). According to Hellmann, Murdock and Stiglitz,[32] monitoring financial institutions is a public good, which will give rise to a free-rider problem. For example, deposit insurance reduces the incentive for insured depositors to monitor the bank's risk-taking because their deposits are protected regardless of the success of the bank's investments. Furthermore, in a world without deposit insurance, depositors would be incentivised to demand a higher interest rate to compensate for the extra risk due to the bank's risk-taking. This would increase the cost of capital in the banking sector and thus inhibit economic development objectives. Therefore, it is necessary that the regulator plays an appropriate role in designing an incentive compatible deposit insurance system and addresses other sources of market failure.

6.30 Although moral hazard will always exist in financial markets where there is asymmetric information and misaligned incentives between the owner of assets (the principal) and the manager of those assets (the agent), *ex ante* regulation can play an important role in reducing moral hazard by aligning the economic incentives of the bank with those of the depositor, and by providing more information for the depositor to monitor the operations and behaviour of the bank as well. Nevertheless, moral hazard will always be a significant problem in banking where the deposit protection scheme provides a 100 per cent guarantee against risk, in effect serving as an indemnity against all losses. However, as investors' understanding of risk and regulation becomes more sophisticated, the problem of moral hazard is becoming increasingly a factor in the design of deposit guarantee schemes.

---

29 Arrow KJ, *Aspects of the Theory of Risk Bearing* (Yrjö Jahnssonin Säätiö 1965).
30 See Flannery (n 28), 981–987.
31 Macey JR and O'Hara M, 'The Corporate Governance of Banks' (April 2003) 9 *FRBNY Economic Policy Review* 1 91; Mehran H, 'Introduction – Critical Themes in Corporate Governance' (April 2003) 9 *Federal Reserve Bank of New York Economic Policy Review* 1 www.newyorkfed.org/medialibrary/media/research/epr/2003/EPRvol9no1.pdf accessed 21 February 2018.
32 Hellmann TF, Murdock KC and Stiglitz JE, 'Liberalization, Moral Hazard in Banking, and Prudential Regulation: Are Capital Requirements Enough?' (2000) 90 *American Economic Review* 1 147.

1 Prompt Corrective Action

6.31 Prompt corrective action is an important principle that is applied by some states to govern the relationship between bank shareholders, management and the regulator or deposit guarantee scheme when the bank is in danger of meeting minimum prudential requirements. Under the US prompt corrective action regime, the FDIC has five categories to classify bank soundness, and it has discretion to intervene in bank management decision-making if the bank's capital level drops into the lower three categories. If the bank's capital drops to the lowest category designated as 'critically undercapitalised', the FDIC is required to appoint a conservator or receiver. The FDIC may exercise forbearance in exceptional circumstances where it has agreed with the relevant federal bank regulator that receivership or conservatorship would likely result in significant market turbulence and would further damage depositors' interests.

6.32 The US prompt corrective action (PCA) regime for depository institutions provides detailed rules governing PCA proceedings by providing trigger points that determine when a particular regulatory action can be taken, thereby enhancing legal certainty while allowing the regulator the flexibility not to apply an enhanced regulatory measure if it might exacerbate market conditions (i.e. a financial crisis) or worsen depositors' interests. Shareholder expectations are thus enhanced by having their property rights subject to a prescriptive legislative and regulatory regime in which there are clear expectations about what will happen to their control and economic interests if the bank's conditions deteriorate. The expectation of the loss of control or the dilution of share value acts to discipline shareholders to exercise more effective oversight of bank management and to influence management to take less socially risky behaviour. Moreover, if the bank cannot be salvaged, the regulations providing for receivership or conservatorship allow for an efficient winding-up of the bank, with depositors being reimbursed from the deposit insurance fund and the FDIC acting as residual claimant for any surplus assets in the estate.

6.33 US courts have examined whether FDIC procedures for issuing capital directives to banks which have been classified as financially unsound violate the due process requirements of the US Constitution. The Fifth Circuit Court Appeals held in *FDIC* v. *Coushatta*[33] that the FDIC must adhere to a three-factor inquiry that courts are required to use in determining what type of FDIC procedures satisfy due process before the government may deprive an entity of a property interest protected by the Due Process Clause of the Fifth or Fourteenth Amendments.[34] The three factors are: (1) the private interest that will be affected by the official action; (2) the risk of an erroneous deprivation of such interest through the procedures used, and the probable value, if any, of additional or substitute procedural safeguards; and (3) the government's interest, including the function involved and the fiscal

---

33 *FDIC* v. *Coushatta* 930 F. 2d 122 (5th Cir.), cert. denied, 502 U.S. 857 (1991).
34 See *Matthews* v. *Eldridge*, 424 U.S. 319, 333 [1976].

and administrative burdens that the additional or substitute requirement would entail.[35] Essentially, due process is flexible and calls for such procedural protections as the particular situation demands.[36]

6.34 In assessing prudential supervisory practices, the Fifth Circuit in *Coushatta* concluded that procedures for determining capital adequacy and risk-based supervisory ratings satisfied due process. The court reasoned that the private interest of accurate capital directives is significant but that the risk of an erroneous deprivation of property because of the application of a directive is marginal. The court noted that a pre-deprivation evidentiary hearing (as opposed to an informal hearing) was not warranted because a bank has adequate opportunity to respond to the notice through written procedures. Also, the court found that the government's interest is substantial because delay would considerably weaken the benefits from a prompt directive, which seeks to rectify a bank's undercapitalisation. Similarly, in *Doolin*, the Fourth Circuit reviewed the procedures allowing a bank to challenge a FDIC determination of risk-based capital ratings, and found the procedure to be in compliance with constitutional standards of due process.[37] The FDIC procedure allowing banks to contest their risk-based capital ratings meets the due process test because it provides banks with notice of their risk classifications and an opportunity to challenge the classification through the review procedures established in the regulations.

6.35 Similar to the EU requirement that each Member State maintain a deposit guarantee scheme, the FDIC also has a crucial role to play in protecting retail bank depositors in the US by insuring deposits up to US$250,000.[38] The coverage is similar to the concept seen in the DGS Directive, so that each depositor is protected per bank, per deposit. The FDIC, however, has a system in which there are different account ownership categories, and the US$250,000 level of protection applies to each deposit account at a FDIC-insured institution, along with the same level of coverage for other account categories including trust accounts and employee benefit plan accounts.[39]

III BANK RESOLUTION

6.36 Prior to the crisis of 2007–2008, most countries did not have bank resolution regimes to unwind or restructure a bank in financial difficulties. Rather, authorities used insolvency law or taxpayer bailouts to manage distressed banks. Insolvency law proved inadequate

---

35 *FDIC* v. *Coushatta* (n 33) [335].
36 Ibid. [334].
37 12 CFR section 327.3. Accordingly, the courts have held that the due process clause does not require a pre-deprivation evidentiary hearing before a particular risk-based weighting is applied to banks' capital position; *Doolin Security Savings Bank, F.S.B.* v. *Federal Deposit Insurance Corporation* 53 F.3d 1395 at 1403.
38 12 CFR section 330.1(o).
39 Federal Deposit Insurance Corporation, 'Your Insured Deposits' (online brochure, FDIC 2018) www.fdic.gov/deposit/deposits/brochures/your-insured-deposits-english.html accessed 19 December 2018.

because wind-downs were focused on legal entities and administered by judicial authorities. Also, insolvency was destructive of the going concern value of the bank and disruptive of its critical economic functions, and it applied to multiple financially and operationally interconnected entities in many jurisdictions. Insolvency also involved little if any advance planning and created cross-border frictions with other authorities where the institution had subsidiaries or branches operating, and where some jurisdictions engaged in ring-fencing local assets of the cross-border entity.

6.37 In contrast, bank resolution regimes are controlled by administrative authorities and they aim to preserve the going concern value of the bank and maintain continuity of its critical functions. Resolution frameworks involve advanced planning that identifies one or a few financial entities that are subjected to potential intervention in a crisis or market distress scenario, and there is cross-border coordination with other resolution authorities regarding at which level – single point of entry or multiple point of entry – the resolution authority will intervene to impose losses on creditors and shareholders. Cross-border resolution planning also ensures coordination regarding recognition of contractual and statutory bail-in mechanisms.

6.38 Bank resolution laws have been deemed vital for maintaining the stability of the financial system, especially during times of crisis. For instance, Goodhart (2014) states that they should involve regulators and resolution authorities asking 'themselves how to protect the system of banks, conditional on another bank, perhaps one of the biggest and most inter-connected, having already failed'.[40] Following the crisis, many jurisdictions adopted bank resolution laws that allow regulators to suspend shareholder corporate governance rights and procedures in order to protect depositors and to restore a bank's financial health. For example, the Italian special administrative regime suspends many of the powers of the shareholders' general meeting. Appointed by the Bank of Italy, the special administrators may convene the general meetings and establish the agenda. However, the approval of the bank's capital structure remains with the shareholders' general meeting.[41] Similarly, the German supervisory authority (Bafin) may suspend current management and appoint a temporary administrator to manage a failing bank.[42] Under French law, the Banking Commission can appoint a temporary administrator with powers to manage and act on behalf of the bank.[43] Similarly, the Belgian Banking, Finance and Insurance Commission (BFIC), now replaced by the Financial Services and Markets Authority (FSMA) since 2011, can appoint a special

---

40   See Goodhart CAE, 'Bank Resolution in Comparative Perspective: What Lessons for Europe?' (2014) paper on file with author.

41   Italian Consolidated Banking Law (*Decreto legislativo 1° settembre 1993, n. 385* – Testo Unico *Bancario*), Article 72(6).

42   See section 46(1) of German Banking Act (*Gesetz über das Kreditwesen*) as amended by the Gesetz zur Abschirmung von Risiken und zur Planung der Sanierung und Abwicklung von Kreditinstituten und Finanzgruppen vom 7 August 2013.

43   Articles L613–18 and L. 613–22 of the French Monetary and Financial Code (*Code monétaire et financier*) as amended by the Loi no. 2013–672 du 26 juillet 2013 de Séparation et de Régulation des Activités Bancaires.

inspector with enhanced administration powers. Swiss law also provides the regulator with powers to appoint a special administrator to govern the bank's affairs and more extended powers.[44] Moreover, the Swiss regulator can likewise impose a forced reorganisation, with changes to the capital structure that are not subject to shareholder approval.[45] Norwegian law provides for a public administration regime that allows for a compulsory reorganisation and overriding of the shareholders. The Norwegian supervisor may stipulate that the share capital should be increased by a new subscription for shares and designate eligible investors to subscribe for the shares, thus diluting existing shareholders.[46] Similarly, the French Banking Commission may request the courts to order the transfer of shares to another entity.[47]

6.39 Special resolution procedures for banks may provide for a conservatorship whereby the regulator or central bank appoints an official to take control of the bank's operations. Such action may interfere with shareholder control rights and may also lead to a suspension of more fundamental rights, such as the right to elect directors, or to call a special shareholder meeting and to submit resolutions to elect new – or remove existing – directors.

6.40 The value of the shareholders' interest may be further depleted or eliminated if the conservator or other official decides to transfer some or all of the bank's viable assets to a state-owned bridge bank or to sell them to a private purchaser, such as another bank, while leaving the original bank with mostly unviable assets. In some cases, regulatory action may lead to the bank's financial health being restored, in which case pre-resolution shareholder rights would be restored.

A The FSB's Key Attributes of Effective Resolution Regimes

6.41 As discussed in Chapter 3, the Financial Stability Board (FSB) plays an important role in monitoring and making recommendations about the global financial system and it also plays the lead role in adopting principles to govern bank resolution regimes. The Financial Stability Board published the 'Key Attributes of Effective Resolution Regimes for Financial Institutions' that sets forth principles and recommended tools that countries should adopt to ensure that systemically important financial institutions can fail without creating a systemic financial crisis and without resort to public funds. The FSB's Twelve Key Attributes were endorsed by G20 Leaders in 2011 and now are largely implemented by the home jurisdictions of the Global Systemic Important Banks (G-SIBs) on a harmonised basis at the level of general principles, but the specific rules that

---

44   Article 23 quarter of the Swiss Banking Act (*Bundesgesetz über die Banken und Sprakassen (SR 952.0)*).
45   Ibid., Article 29 section 3.
46   Sections 3–5 of the Norwegian Act on Guarantee Schemes for Banks and Public Administration, etc. of Financial Institutions (Guarantee Schemes Act) of 6 December 1996 (as amended per 1 July 2004) (*Lov om finansforetak og finanskonsern (finansforetaksloven)*). Article L613–25 of the Monetary and Financial Code (n 43).
47   Ibid., Article L613–25.

govern when authorities apply certain resolution tools and to what extent vary considerably between jurisdictions. The main pillars of the Twelve Attributes are: a proactive approach to systemic bank failures through resolution planning and resolvability assessment. Resolution plans set out preferred resolution strategies for G-SIBs. Resolvability assessments identify barriers to implementing preferred resolution strategies and authorities have powers to remove barriers. For example, the FSB Attributes state that '[t]o improve a firm's resolvability, supervisory authorities or resolution authorities should have powers to require, where necessary, the adoption of appropriate measures, such as changes to a firm's business practices, structure or organization' and, as discussed in Chapter 7, '[t]o enable the continued operations of systemically important functions, authorities should evaluate whether to require that these functions be segregated in legally and operationally independent entities that are shielded from group problems'.

6.42 The FSB Attributes also emphasise the clear identification of a resolution authority with a broad range of powers: a comprehensive and common toolkit of supervisory and resolution measures; a credible funding source for resolution authorities so that taxpayers are not called upon to bail out a bank or to subsidise its restructuring; and resolution funding should be provided through privately financed deposit insurance or resolution funds. In 2014, the Key Attributes were complemented by two annexes providing: (1) additional guidance on specific Key Attributes relating mainly to information sharing for resolution purposes; and (2) sector-specific guidance on how the Key Attributes should be applied for insurers, financial market infrastructures (FMIs) and the protection of client assets held by investment firms that go into resolution.

6.43 Also, enhanced international cooperation is necessary to ensure that resolution planning covers the major activities of the bank and provides a communication channel when in crisis. Cooperation is achieved through the establishment of Crisis Management Groups (CMGs) bringing together the major authorities and jurisdictions where the bank is active. CMGs focus on resolution planning and hold regular meetings, typically twice a year. Cooperation and information sharing are governed by firm-specific cooperation agreements (CoAg). As discussed below, the FSB's Total Loss-Absorbing Capacity (TLAC) standard for G-SIBs was agreed in 2015, comprising both external and internal TLAC provisions and designed to foster cooperation in resolution.

6.44 The FSB principles are designed for national authorities to adopt adequate resolution tools, such as bail-in (discussed below), to shift the costs of a bank's failure away from society at large to certain bank stakeholders, such as bondholders and shareholders, who should bear the primary economic burden of the bank's failure. A bank recovery and resolution framework has been seen as necessary to provide a mechanism that allows financial institutions to restructure their debts and in some cases to go into administration or liquidation without threatening the stability of the banking sector and broader financial system.

B Bank Resolution Regimes: The Rationale

6.45 The core objectives of a resolution framework are: protection of financial stability, continuity of critical functions and no (or very limited) use of public funds. The social costs that banks pose for the economy demonstrate the need for resolution regimes that provide a legal framework for authorities to decide whether to attempt to save a bank by recapitalisation or other restructuring pre-insolvency, and, if this fails, to oversee in insolvency the unwinding of the bank's multiple positions and to sell off its viable assets to other banks or investors in order to repay creditors, including depositors.[48] For many countries, ordinary insolvency law procedures for non-bank companies also apply to the administration and liquidation of a failing bank.[49] Generally, corporate insolvency law applies an elaborate framework to rank the economic claims of creditors and other stakeholders against a firm which is unable or unwilling to honour its financial obligations.

6.46 Insolvency law may prove socially costly, however, for certain firms, such as banks, because insolvency procedures may result in restrictions on a bank performing its essential intermediary function in providing payments and borrowing and lending for the economy. For instance, insolvency law may result in a stay on payments and a balance sheet freeze, which would make it difficult, if not impossible, for the bank to rely on the wholesale funding markets and to manage its counterparty exposures through netting. The inadequacies of general insolvency law to address the risks which banks pose to the broader economy has led many countries to enact special bank resolution regimes in which the restructuring of creditor claims and the reorganisation of the bank is done in a way that does not unduly limit the bank in performing functions for the economy.

6.47 An important element of these resolution regimes is that they permit the resolution authority to take certain measures pre-insolvency which may alter or reduce shareholder rights and the claims of other third parties, such as creditors, in order to protect depositors in the weakened bank and to maintain overall financial stability. The rationale for a pre-insolvency intervention regime is that the authority should have the power to take certain measures in response to a rapid loss of market confidence which may result in the bank losing access to the inter-bank loan market and wholesale debt markets which may result in increased systemic risk. Through the resolution authority's intervention, a market-based solution may become possible. If a market solution is not possible, however, the intervention may be the first step by the authority to take control of the failing bank and transfer its shares and other property, including contractual rights and obligations, to a state-owned

---

48   See Bank of England, HM Treasury and the Financial Services Authority, 'Financial Stability and Depositor Protection: Special Resolution Regime' (July 2008) www.gov.uk/government/uploads/system/uploads/attachment_data/file/238704/7459.pdf accessed 21 February 2018.
49   See Financial Services Authority, 'Financial Stability and Depositor Protection: Strengthening the Framework' (January 2008), 2–4 www.fsa.gov.uk/pubs/cp/JointCP_banking_stability.pdf accessed 21 February 2018.

bridge bank or a private purchaser. Further steps may involve the bank being declared insolvent and being subject to administration or liquidation.

6.48 For resolution regimes to work effectively, however, it is necessary that the regulator has the authority to act quickly and in certain circumstances to set aside the normal corporate governance rules that usually involve obtaining shareholder approval if the bank is required to take a course of action that may diminish shareholder control rights or their economic rights. In other words, the regulator's exercise of resolution powers pre-insolvency may have the effect of compromising shareholder control rights and any regulatory decision to inject state capital into the bank or to require the bank to raise additional capital from external sources, or to transfer the bank's property to another investor without shareholder assent, could significantly reduce the shareholders' economic rights. This should be contrasted with what might happen if the authority does not intervene and the bank is declared insolvent. In this scenario, a conservator or administrator could be appointed to manage the bank's assets and business operations or, alternatively, a receiver or trustee could be appointed to liquidate the bank's operations.[50] Essentially, insolvency would mean that shareholder control and governance rights would terminate and the shareholder would be left with only a residual monetary claim against the assets of the bank's estate.[51] The exercise of regulatory powers in a special resolution regime raises a number of important legal and regulatory issues regarding how to balance prudential regulatory objectives and shareholder rights. This will involve an analysis of the substance and scope of shareholder rights under the European Convention on Human Rights and European Community law.

6.49 The crisis of 2007–2008 demonstrated the importance of having effective bank resolution regimes that can balance the competing interests of investor rights (both shareholders and creditors) with the regulatory objectives of financial stability and depositor protection. As mentioned above, the constraints of corporate insolvency regimes are too cumbersome for the effective resolution of a universal banking group, especially during a financial crisis when a failing bank within a banking group needs to maintain open lines of credit with other financial institutions and to manage its balance sheet while achieving regulatory objectives. Bank resolution regimes must be designed not only to protect shareholders and creditors, but also to achieve other regulatory objectives that are vital for the efficient operation of the economy.

C UK Bank Resolution Regime

6.50 Prior to the crisis, general insolvency law applied to the winding-up or restructuring of a UK bank. The potential systemic risk to the financial system posed by the insolvency of a

---

50 See Olson GN, 'Government Intervention: The Inadequacy of Bank Insolvency Resolution – Lessons from the American Experience', in Lastra RM and Schiffman HN (eds), *Bank Failures and Bank Insolvency Law in Economies in Transition* (Kluwer Law International 1999), 134–136.

51 See Hüpkes EHG, *The Legal Aspects of Bank Insolvency: A Comparative Analysis of Western Europe, the United States and Canada* (Kluwer Law International 2000).

British bank was considered a threat to financial stability with serious implications for the bank's capacity to continue providing payment services for its customers and counterparties. When Northern Rock bank collapsed in September 2007, the lack of an effective bank resolution regime left the UK Treasury with the untenable choice of putting Northern Rock into insolvency, thereby possibly setting off a systemic crisis in the UK banking sector, or bailing it out by guaranteeing its liabilities, particularly liabilities to depositors. After the Bank of England refused to provide it with extraordinary loans in August 2007, a full-blown bank run had begun by late August 2007. The run intensified at Northern Rock branches across the UK throughout September until the then UK Chancellor of the Exchequer, Alistair Darling, announced in September 2008 that the UK Treasury would guarantee all of Northern Rock's depositor liabilities, even beyond what was covered at the time by the UK's deposit guarantee scheme.

6.51 At the time, the UK deposit guarantee scheme covered only up to £32,000 in customer deposits per bank and the customer incurred a 10 per cent excess charge per bank, thereby reducing the maximum payout to each depositor to less than £29,000 per bank. Moreover, depositors would have to apply for repayment from HM Treasury and wait an estimated few months before actually being repaid the value of the deposit minus the 10 per cent excess. Given such constraints, it is understandable why there was a run on Northern Rock.[52]

6.52 By January 2008, the UK Chancellor decided to inject taxpayer money into Northern Rock by purchasing all its shares at their estimated market price of 1 pence per share. The UK Parliament then adopted temporary resolution legislation in February 2008 that ratified the government's effective nationalisation of Northern Rock and also served as a legal basis to take other failing banks and building societies into resolution in 2008, including Bradford and Bingley bank (2008) and the Dunfermline Building Society (2008). After the restructuring, selling off viable operations and winding-up of these institutions, the UK Treasury in October 2008 responded to the global financial turbulence caused by the Lehman Brothers collapse by injecting 45 billion pounds through purchasing 82 per cent of the common equity shares in the Royal Bank of Scotland at £5.02 per share, whilst injecting 23 billion pounds by purchasing 42 per cent of the common equity shares of Lloyds Banking Group. RBS had incurred substantial debt by agreeing a takeover of the Dutch bank ABN-AMRO in 2007 just as the financial crisis was starting. Later, after the crisis had begun, the UK Treasury pressured Lloyds Banking Group in October 2008 to take over the weakened Halifax Bank of Scotland that was on the edge of collapse.[53]

---

52   See House of Commons Treasury, 'The Run on the Rock: Fifth Report of Session 2007–08' (volume I, report, together with formal minutes, The Stationery Office Limited 26 January 2008) https://publications.parliament.uk/pa/cm200708/cmselect/cmtreasy/56/56i.pdf accessed 19 December 2018. See also volume 2: House of Commons Treasury Committee, 'The Run on the Rock: Fifth Report of Session 2007–08' (volume II, oral and written evidence, The Stationery Office Limited 1 February 2008) https://publications.parliament.uk/pa/cm200708/cmselect/cmtreasy/56/56ii.pdf accessed 19 December 2018.
53   The UK Treasury announced in its 2017 Autumn Budget that it would sell its remaining 71 per cent stake in the Royal Bank of Scotland. In June 2018, 925 million shares worth over £2.5 billion were sold at £2.71, reducing the Treasury's stake in RBS by 7.7 per cent to 62.4 per cent. For a discussion of the events surrounding

6.53 With this as the background, the Parliament received the Royal Assent in February 2009 for the Banking Act 2009 that granted the Treasury and the Bank of England sweeping powers to restructure failing banks and to transfer their shares and property to a government-owned bridge bank or to a private purchaser.[54] The Act also provides a mechanism to compensate shareholders, depositors and third-party creditors of a bank taken into resolution.[55] The Banking Act was amended by the Financial Services Act 2012 to expand the use of resolution powers to systemically important investment banks.

6.54 The Banking Act Special Resolution Regime applies to UK-incorporated banks and investment banks that have permission from the UK regulator to accept deposits and banking group holding companies incorporated in the UK which own bank subsidiaries operating in other jurisdictions. The regime does not apply to foreign-owned branches of banks incorporated in other EEA states (including Icelandic banks). The Bank of England Resolution Directorate serves as resolution authority and can utilise stabilisation powers in three areas: (1) pre-insolvency stabilisation powers; (2) a bank insolvency procedure; and (3) a bank administration procedure. The Bank of England has the sole responsibility for exercising the stabilisation powers that include: transfers of shares and any other property (including partial property transfers) owned by the failing bank to either a private sector purchaser, a bridge bank or into temporary public ownership. In exercising these powers, the Bank of England would have authority to appoint a temporary administrator to manage the affairs of a bank taken into public ownership, or to administer the residual assets of a bank from which shares and property were transferred to a government-owned bridge bank or to a private purchaser.

6.55 The Prudential Regulation Authority (PRA) would have the responsibility for determining whether the preconditions for use of the stabilisation powers and the bank insolvency procedures have been met and deciding after consultation with the Bank of England and the Treasury whether to take the bank into resolution.[56] Section 7 sets out the two main conditions that trigger the special resolution regime (SRR): (1) the bank is failing, or is likely to fail, and has failed to satisfy the threshold conditions for permission to carry on regulated activities set out in the Financial Services and Markets Act 2000;[57] and (2) it is not reasonably likely that without the stabilisation powers the bank can take action to satisfy the threshold conditions.[58] The FSA would have to determine that the threshold conditions[59] have been met before the SRR can become operational, with the result that the Bank of England can then exercise the stabilisation powers. The Treasury is responsible for

the UK Treasury injecting taxpayer money to buy the majority of shares of RBS and Lloyds, see Darling A, *Back from the Brink* (London: Atlantic Books), 140–174.
54 Banking Act 2009, sections 11 and 12.
55 Ibid., section 27.
56 Ibid., section 12.
57 Financial Services and Markets Act 2000, section 41(1).
58 The Banking Act 2009, section 7(3).
59 See also ibid., Threshold Conditions, Instrument 2009.

any decision involving the use of public funds which might be required as a result of the Bank's exercise of special resolution tools. The Treasury can also use public funds to compensate shareholders or third-party creditors who can demonstrate that they have suffered losses by having their shares or property transferred fully or partially to a bridge bank or to a private purchaser.[60]

6.56 The resolution regime applies to UK-incorporated banks that have permission from the UK regulator to accept deposits and banking group holding companies incorporated in the UK which own bank subsidiaries operating in other jurisdictions. The regime does not apply to foreign-owned branches of banks incorporated in other EEA states.

6.57 The resolution regime provides for certain departures from general corporate governance arrangements. The bank administration procedure allows for special administration or conservatorship under which all corporate bodies – the board and management – are suspended and an appointed official temporarily takes control of the bank's operations. The powers of the temporary administrator, however, also extend to the shareholders' power to determine changes to the bank's capital structure by suspending all such shareholder rights during administration.

6.58 Under the UK resolution regime, the special administrator would appear to have strong powers to use resolution tools that would have the effect of setting aside corporate governance rights and impinging on the ownership rights of owners and creditors of a distressed bank. The effect of this may not be so deleterious for shareholders, as they often have accepted a dilution of control and share value in connection with capital raisings during crises. This was the case with some British banks – Barclays, the Lloyd's Banking Group and Halifax Bank of Scotland in November and December 2008 – during the crisis when their shareholders voted to accept substantial increases in capital, resulting in substantial dilution of their equity interests.[61]

6.59 Yet, it may be more legitimate for policy reasons to allow a regulatory authority to impose a capital raising without shareholder approval if the decision is based on clear criteria and agreed regulatory standards. A regulator or other state authority could ensure that shareholders are afforded due process and the decision is based on coherent and legitimate requirements. If shareholders suffer losses, they should be compensated, as is required under the UK Banking Act, based on principles of equal treatment. Under this approach, the shareholders' control and economic rights may be significantly reduced, but they would retain a diluted interest in the bank along with an upside gain if the bank recovers and leaves administration. The alternative would be shareholders insisting on full adherence to

---

60   Ibid., sections 54–56.
61   See Ferran E, 'Bailouts of Ailing Banks through Capital Injections' (2008), unpublished paper on file with author, 6–8.

their right of approval to any capital change, but with the risk that without the protections of the resolution regime the shareholders will lose all their interests in a collapsed bank.

6.60 The Court of Justice of the European Union (CJEU) has addressed this issue in the context of EU Company Law and the efforts of a national authority to require a bank to be recapitalised without shareholder approval. Generally, EU Company Law requires that measures affecting a bank's capital structure, such as a capital increase or a merger with another bank, are to be decided by shareholders.[62] As discussed in Chapter 5, the CJEU ruled in *Pafitis*[63] that the Second Company Law Directive (now replaced by Directive (EU) 2017/1132) precluded national legislation which allowed an administrator to order a recapitalisation of an undercapitalised bank without a shareholder resolution and approval at a general or specially called meeting. The ECJ however further ruled in *Pafitis* that the Directive does not preclude the taking of resolution or insolvency measures intended to put an end to a bank's existence by stating the following:

> does not preclude the taking of execution measures intended to put an end to the company' s existence and, in particular, does not preclude liquidation measures placing the company under compulsory administration with a view to safeguarding the rights of creditors. However, the directive continues to apply where ordinary reorganization measures are taken in order to ensure the survival of the company, even if those measures mean that the shareholders and the normal organs of the company are temporarily divested of their powers.[64]

6.61 Similarly, the CJEU ruled in the *Kefalas* case[65] that 'the decision-making power of the general meeting' provided for by EU Company Law applies even 'where the company is experiencing serious financial difficulties'. A reorganisation involving a change in capital structure for a bank that has not been taken into compulsory administration or winding-up therefore requires a vote of approval by shareholders at a general or special meeting.

D US Bank Resolution Regime

6.62 The US bank resolution regime underwent significant changes with the Dodd-Frank Act of 2010. The purpose of the Dodd-Frank Act is to ensure the financial stability of the US and to end the practice of governments and central banks bailing out too-big-to-fail financial institutions by creating rules to govern the orderly winding-up of failing banks. To this end, Section II of the Dodd-Frank Act establishes the Orderly Liquidation Authority (OLA). The OLA is operated and administered by the FDIC throughout the process of putting a bank

---

62 Company Directive (EU) 2017/1132 of the European Parliament and of the Council of 14 June 2017 relating to certain aspects of company law OJ L 169/46.
63 Case C-441/93 *Panagis Pafitis and others* v. *Trapeza Kentrikis Ellados A.E. and others* [1996] ECR I-1347.
64 Ibid.
65 C-367/96, *Kefalas and Others* v. *Elliniko Dimosio (Greek State) and Organismos Oikonomikis Anasygkrotisis Epicheiriseon AE (OAE)* [1998] ECR I-2843.

into an orderly liquidation.[66] The purpose of the OLA is to maintain financial stability and prevent the moral hazard caused by taxpayer-funded bailouts by requiring an orderly liquidation of a failing bank.[67] It is important to mention that the Dodd-Frank Act regards the orderly liquidation procedure set forth in Section II of the Act as *lex generalis*, which applies only when the FDIC is appointed as the OLA to take a bank into an orderly liquidation. If the FDIC does not invoke resolution powers, the bank in question will be subject to US bankruptcy law.[68]

6.63 The Dodd-Frank Act emphasises that for a bank that is taken into orderly liquidation its shareholders and creditors must bear the losses incurred by the bank before the taxpayer is called upon to cover its losses. Also, the management of a failing bank that is taken into orderly liquidation is required to be dismissed with the possibility that individual members of management or the board of directors may be held liable for losses or damages incurred by the deposit guarantee fund or other taxpayer-supported guarantees arising from the bank's losses, or possibly have their compensation (i.e. bonuses) recouped or clawed back by those who have suffered losses caused by their mismanagement. Further, a bank taken into orderly liquidation should under no circumstances receive direct public funding, as it should ultimately be liquidated. This reinforces the Act's objective of promoting financial stability by reducing taxpayer subsidies to banks, thereby strengthening market discipline by reducing moral hazard.[69] The OLA's resolution of a bank includes imposing losses on shareholders in order to liquidate its going concern value and to ensure that the institution is treated as a 'gone concern' to be restructured and sold off to private purchasers.[70]

6.64 The triggering of the OLA's rules of orderly liquidation involves a mandatory procedure to be followed for each institution. First, the Board of Governors of the Federal Reserve System are required to prepare a written recommendation approved by a two-thirds majority of the Board that an institution should be taken into liquidation. Following this, a two-thirds majority of the managing board of the FDIC is required to prepare a written recommendation in support of the liquidation. The Secretary of the Treasury receives these two recommendations, and prepares a separate recommendation in consultation with the President.[71] The Treasury Secretary's recommendation must be based on the systemic risks posed by the institution, which requires the application of the rules under Section II concerning the objectives of an orderly liquidation. Based on this recommendation, a notification is made to the board of directors of the bank subject to the potential resolution, in which it is requested to acquiesce or consent to the appointment of the FDIC (under its authority as OLA) as the receiver of the bank. Should the board agree, then the Secretary

---

66   The Wall Street Reform and Consumer Protection Act, 2010, section 204(b), Dodd-Frank Wall Street Reform and Consumer Protection Act 2010 section 204, 12 USC section 5384.
67   Ibid., section 204(a).
68   Ibid., section 202(c).
69   Ibid., section 206(1).
70   Ibid., section 296(6).
71   Ibid., sections 203(a) and (b).

appoints FDIC as the receiver; if not, then the Secretary is obliged to file a petition before the District Court for the District of Columbia in order to obtain a court order granting the FDIC the receivership of the bank.[72]

1 Single Point of Entry (SPOE) and Multiple Points of Entry (MPOE)

6.65 The Dodd-Frank Act Section II adopts the single point of entry (SPOE) approach for the application of its orderly liquidation provisions.[73] The SPOE approach involves the home country authority of the banking group (usually the jurisdiction where the controlling holding company is registered) controlling the resolution process and having the tools to impose losses on shareholders and creditors at the holding or top operating company level. This allows the subsidiaries of the holding company, or top operating company, to be recapitalised through writing down the claims of the holding company or top operating company on the subsidiaries. This avoids the need for operating subsidiaries in home and key host jurisdictions to enter resolution and reduce the incentives of host authorities to seize the local assets of subsidiaries in order to satisfy the claims of local creditors. The FDIC and Bank of England published a joint paper in 2012 discussing their respective SPOE resolution strategies.[74] The SPOE is particularly popular in jurisdictions where most of the largest global banks are headquartered because the resolution authorities in these countries would be largely responsible for deciding how to restructure most of the global SIB's liabilities and assets with effect on its subsidiaries and branches operating in multiple jurisdictions.

6.66 In contrast to SPOE, the multiple point of entry approach is preferred by many jurisdictions that do not host the headquarters of large global banking groups. Under the MPOE approach, a globally systemic bank is subject to resolution procedures by the home country of the G-SIFI and the key host authorities where the G-SIFI has systemically important operating subsidiaries or branches. The MPOE allows for a regional break-up or resolution of a G-SIFI that would be coordinated by the home authority but with subsidiaries in host jurisdictions subject to resolution tools exercised by host authorities. The MPOE approach can lead to creditors of subsidiaries in home and key host jurisdictions suffering losses, as opposed to imposing losses only on creditors and shareholders of the holding company under the SPOE approach. Also, the resolution tools applied to different parts of the global banking group need not be the same. For the MPOE to be effective requires close cooperation between home and host authorities to avoid competing resolution or insolvency proceedings and ring-fencing of local assets.

---

72 Ibid., section 202 (a)(1)(A)(i).
73 'Resolution of Systemically Important Financial Institutions: The Single Point of Entry Strategy' (2013) FDIC, Federal Register Vol. 78/243 76616.
74 Federal Deposit Insurance Corporation and Bank of England, 'Resolving Globally Active, Systemically Important, Financial Institutions' (December 2012) www.fdic.gov/about/srac/2012/gsifi.pdf accessed 22 March 2018, paras. 24–29 (discussing US SPOE strategy) and 30–37 (discussing UK SPOE strategy).

6.67 The US SPOE approach involves the FDIC's appointment as the receiver of the controlling US holding company that owns the banking institution subject to resolution. The FDIC should ensure that the exercise of its powers as receiver of the bank holding company should not hinder the operations of subsidiaries within the holding company that perform critical financial functions for their customers as well as for the financial system as a whole. Once appointed as the receiver of the holding company, the FDIC is entitled to merge the ailing bank with another institution, or transfer the assets and liabilities of the bank to another institution, or to establish a 'bridge financial company'.[75] In exercising its powers, the FDIC is entitled to terminate all rights and claims of shareholders and creditors that can be asserted against the bank holding company or against an ailing depository institution that is controlled by the holding company, but it cannot terminate the rights of employees to assert certain compensation claims against the holding company or individual banking institution. Generally, however, the FDIC's role as receiver involves it in writing down or converting the liabilities of the bank holding company or individual bank subsidiary within the holding company in order to achieve an orderly liquidation or resolution.[76]

6.68 Another function of the FDIC as resolution authority is in establishing a bridge financial company (bridge bank) to which the healthy assets of the bank can be transferred, while the claims of the shareholders and creditors remain in the receivership, which can incur losses imposed by the receivership, including the writing down or conversion of debt claims into equity.[77] The FDIC then attempts to find a private sector purchaser of the bridge bank within a reasonable time. If a private sector purchaser cannot be found for the bridge bank, the Dodd-Frank Act envisions the utilisation of the Orderly Liquidation Fund (OLF),[78] which aims to provide liquidity support for the bridge bank while the FDIC administers it in resolution.

6.69 The principle of no creditor worse off in resolution than in liquidation requires that the maximum liability of the FDIC as the OLA receiver in the resolution of a bank cannot exceed its maximum liability if it was acting as a subrogated creditor of a bank that was undergoing liquidation under Chapter 7 of the US Bankruptcy Code. The comparison of the FDIC's liability as OLA receiver or as a subrogated creditor under the Bankruptcy Code depends on a valuation of the claims of the creditors and shareholders, as required in section 210(d) of the Dodd-Frank Act. Section 210(d) requires that the maximum liability of the FDIC as the OLA receiver must be assessed and cannot exceed the expected sum the creditors and shareholders would have received if the bank was subjected to liquidation under the Bankruptcy Code.

---

75 Dodd-Frank Act (n 2) section 210(a)(1)(F–G).
76 Ibid., section 201(a)(3).
77 Federal Register (n 73) 76617.
78 Dodd-Frank Act (n 2) section 204(m).

E Loss-Absorbent Capital

6.70 The FSB adopted a total loss-absorbent capital (TLAC) standard which recommends that countries require that systemically important banks hold between 16–20 per cent total loss-absorbent capital calculated against their risk-based assets. TLAC is a minimum capital requirement on the liability side of the bank's balance sheet that is in addition to the minimum capital requirements of the Basel III Agreement. The TLAC requirement can be met with equity or debt capital or other unsecured long-term liabilities that absorb losses and allow a bank in difficulty to recapitalise itself (or its successors) if in resolution. It also helps ensure continuity of critical functions and an orderly wind-down and restructuring. TLAC is a firm-specific minimum requirement – with a common minimum level recommended at 16–20 per cent of risk-based assets. The FSB TLAC requirement is a political commitment for jurisdictions to implement where global systemically important banks operate. The TLAC standard is implemented in the EU and UK through the minimum required eligible liabilities standard (MREL) as discussed below (see Figure 6.4).

6.71 Section 165 of the Dodd-Frank Act mandates the Board of Governors of the Federal Reserve and the Treasury to introduce prudential standards for banking and other financial insti-tutions, including the requirement that banks hold a minimum amount of loss-absorbent capital. Similar to the EU and other jurisdictions, the loss-absorptive capacities of banks play a crucial role in determining whether a bank is taken into insolvency or resolution. If a

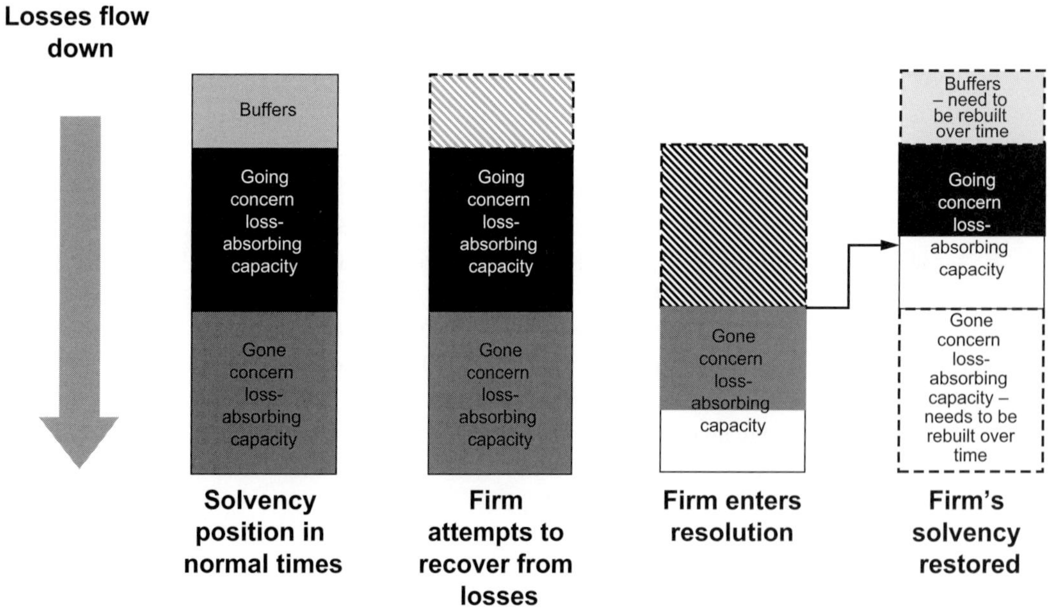

Figure 6.1 FSB Total Loss-Absorbent Capital standard (TLAC)

bank has adequate loss-absorbent capital to cover its losses, it may be considered less risky to the stability of the financial system and therefore may avoid being taken into resolution or, alternatively, insolvency. However, if it does not have adequate loss-absorbent capital, the bank can be taken into resolution if its insolvency would be considered a threat to the stability of the financial system.

6.72 Based on the above, the Board of Governors and the Treasury have published a final rule regarding the definition of loss absorption, in which the loss-absorbent capacity standard in the US is different from other jurisdictions, including the EU. As discussed below, the EU follows a requirement that defines loss-absorbent capital based on an MREL. In contrast to the MREL standard, the US uses the TLAC standard that is recommended by the FSB.[79] The US TLAC requirement consists of a minimum amount of long-term debt (consisting of subordinated bonds and Cocos) and Tier 1 capital of at least 18 per cent of risk-weighted assets, and 7.5 per cent of its total leverage exposure. This level is to be effective for all systemically important US banks as from 1 January 2019.[80] The long-term debt requirement of 18 per cent of the bank's risk-weighted assets is in addition to the minimum required Tier 1 and Tier 2 capital requirements of Basel III, as set forth in US 'Regulation Q'.[81] The US TLAC requirement applies only to systemically important banks. As of 2018, the ratio of the TLAC requirement (i.e. long-term bonds) and Tier 1 and Tier 2 capital requirements of Basel III to a bank's risk-weighted assets is approximately 30 per cent. This represents a significant increase compared with the pre-crisis level of around 5 per cent. This amounts to an increase in bank loss-absorbent capital of around US$2 trillion since the crisis.[82]

F Creditor Hierarchy under US OLA

6.73 The issue of creditor hierarchy in a bank resolution is addressed by section 210(b)(1) of the Dodd-Frank Act. Federally insured deposits as defined under the Federal Deposit Insurance Act 1991 have priority over all other unsecured creditors of a bank. The creditor hierarchy mandated under US law is significantly different from the EU BRRD. The Dodd-Frank Act lists the claimant with the highest priority first, with other creditors listed afterwards according to descending priority, whereas the BRRD lists the first type of liability bail-in that is to be applied before imposing losses on a list of creditors with descending priority. The US creditor hierarchy in a bank resolution is as follows:

---

79 Federal Reserve System, 'Total Loss Absorbing Capacity, Long-Term Debt, and Clean Holding Company Requirements for Systemically Important U.S. Bank Holding Companies and Intermediate Holding Companies of Systemically Important Foreign Banking Organizations' (2017) FDIC, Federal Register Vol. 82/14 8269.
80 Federal Reserve System (n 79), 8270.
81 Federal Reserve System (n 79), 8266.
82 The Department of the Treasury, 'Orderly Liquidation Authority and Bankruptcy Reform' (21 February 2018) Report 16 https://home.treasury.gov/sites/default/files/2018-02/OLA_REPORT.pdf accessed 21 December 2018.

1. The FDIC costs incurred administratively for the resolution (including subrogated claims for reimbursement of deposit insurance payments to depositors of banks in FDIC receivership).
2. Claims of the US states. It is also possible for the state to withdraw its claims so that the latter claimants have the opportunity to receive more.
3. The claims of individual employees from the bank, which are under the categories of wages, payments for vacation, severance and absence for sickness, yet a maximum of only US$11,725, and the claims that have not arisen 180 days before the transfer of receivership may be claimed per claimant.
4. The contributions owed to employee benefit plans, arising from services rendered not later than 180 days before the date of appointment of the FDIC as the receiver. The extent of this class is that the number of employees covered by each such plan, multiplied by 11,725, minus the aggregate amount paid to such employees (under the aforementioned class 3), plus the aggregate amount paid by the receivership on behalf of such employees to any other employee benefit plan.
5. Any general or senior liability of the bank.
6. Any subordinated liability.
7. Any wages, salaries or commissions that are owed to the senior executives and directors of the bank.
8. Any obligation to the shareholders or persons with regard to interests in equity of the bank.

6.74 Under section 210(b)(4) of the Dodd-Frank Act, the general standard of treatment for the creditors of the same class is based on the principle of *pari passu*, so that they are awarded proceeds of the liquidation of the bank on a pro-rata basis and absorb losses equally on a pro-rata basis. The legislation however grants discretion to the FDIC to depart from the *pari passu* rule under certain circumstances. For example, it is possible for the FDIC to treat claimants of the same class in a different manner if the FDIC determines that such action is necessary to (i) maximise the value of the assets of the bank, (ii) ensure the continuity of operations essential to the receivership or the bridge bank, (iii) maximise the value of the returns from the sale or transfer of ownership of the assets of the bank, and (iv) minimise the amount of loss on the sale or transfer of ownership of the assets of the bank. The FDIC also has to ensure that all claimants that are in the same class do not receive less than they would have received if the bank in question had been subjected to liquidation under Chapter 7 of the US Bankruptcy Code.[83]

6.75 The FDIC's discretion to depart from the *pari passu* rule if one of the above exceptions in section 210(b)(4) is met is limited however by a regulation which provides that the FDIC's discretion does not apply[84] to the holders of long-term senior debt instruments, to holders of subordinated debt instruments, or to shareholders, which would result in the claimants of these instruments receiving less than what they would have received under Chapter 7

---

83   See Dodd-Frank Act, section 210(d) (valuation criterion).
84   12 CFR 380.27(b)(1–3).

liquidation proceedings, except that the FDIC may exercise its discretion to treat these claimants of the same class differently if they belong in the general class of debt instrument holders, and if the majority of the FDIC's board of directors approve of the differential treatment.[85]

6.76 Moreover, the FDIC has proposed in an interim rule that, among other types of unsecured creditors, only those that the FDIC decides in its discretion to be 'essential vendors' can receive preferential treatment (i.e. payment for services).[86] Essential vendors are defined as those who render services essential for the continuity of the activities of the receivership or the bridge bank, such as providers of utility services.

IV EUROPEAN UNION BANK RESOLUTION

6.77 The European Union's Bank Recovery and Resolution Directive (BRRD)[87] that became effective on 1 January 2016 provides the only legally binding transnational bank resolution regime. The BRRD requires the resolution authorities of the twenty-eight Member States to have use of four resolution tools that are enumerated in Article 37(3), namely, the sale of the business tool, the bridge institution tool, the asset separation tool and the bail-in tool. Resolution authorities may execute the resolution tools individually or in any combination.[88] The design of the BRRD bail-in tool requires covered institutions to issue minimum required eligible liabilities (MREL) as loss-absorbent capital.[89] Resolution authorities have discretion over whether or not to use the resolution tools, or in what combination to use them, including use of the bail-in tool to impose losses on bank liabilities, such as bondholders, when an institution is experiencing financial difficulties.

6.78 The adoption of the bail-in tool was a response to one of the main causes of the crisis of 2007–2008, that banks and other institutions had not engaged in adequate resolution planning with the result that when markets froze in late 2007 and again in 2008 public authorities had no mechanism outside of a formal restructuring or insolvency for allocating losses to an institution's creditors when it was in financial distress. Although the experience of the last crisis in Europe has led policymakers to adopt resolution tools that are designed

---

85   FDIC Regulatory Information (n 79) (4).
86   The Department of the Treasury Report (n 82), 33.
87   Directive 2014/59/EU of the European Parliament and of the Council of 15 May 2014 establishing a framework for the recovery and resolution of credit institutions and investment firms and amending Council Directive 82/891/EEC, and Directives 2001/24/EC, 2002/47/EC, 2004/25/EC, 2005/56/EC, 2007/36/EC, 2011/35/EU, 2012/30/EU and 2013/36/EU, and Regulations (EU) No. 1093/2010 and (EU) No. 648/2012, of the European Parliament and of the Council (2014) OJ L 173, 12.6.2014, 190–348 (BRRD).
88   Ibid., Article 37(4).
89   Minimum Requirement for own Funds and Eligible Liabilities (MREL) in the BRRD and total loss-absorbing capacity (TLAC) from Basel III. See European Banking Authority, 'Regulatory Technical Standards on Minimum Requirement for Own Funds and Eligible Liabilities (MREL)', EBA/CP/2014/41 (28 November 2014), London; see also Basel Committee on Banking Supervision, 'Standard: TLAC holdings: Amendments to the Basel III Standard on the Definition of Capital' (October 2016) www.bis.org/bcbs/publ/d387.pdf accessed 18 May 2018.

to address the particular types of risks that caused the last crisis, it is questionable whether these tools will be effective in addressing the fallout from the next crisis.

A The BRRD

6.79 The BRRD requires Member States to make the necessary changes in their legal regimes so that the national legislation contains a special resolution regime for credit institutions and certain systemically important investment banks. Article 1(2) provides that the Directive is a minimum harmonisation Directive, meaning that Member States are permitted to adopt stricter legislative or regulatory requirements in addition to the minimum requirements in the Directive. Stricter requirements at the Member State level are permitted, as long as the additional requirements do not violate the Directive itself or other areas of EU law.

6.80 Article 31 BRRD provides the main objectives which include preserving financial stability and protecting public funds through the prevention of extraordinary financial support for financial institutions (i.e. bailout) by the taxpayers. Another important objective is protecting depositors.[90] However, it should be emphasised that the overriding objective is maintaining financial stability and ending public financing for banks during periods of market distress. The protection of depositors is intended to be a derivative objective from these two more fundamental objectives.

6.81 The Directive requires a list of factors to be fulfilled before the resolution authority can utilise its resolution tools.[91] The resolution authority must make a determination that the bank is (i) either failing or likely to fail, (ii) that no other alternative from the private sector could effectively provide a similar solution, and (iii) there is a public interest in the resolution of the bank. The Directive also makes reference to general principles of law that apply under the BRRD and EU law to resolutions so that Member States must ensure that any resolution action or measure to impose losses on third-party creditors or shareholders is subject to the constraints of the BRRD legal framework and other applicable EU law (including the EU Treaty).[92]

1 Creditor Hierarchy

6.82 Figure 6.2 shows the order in which claimants are required to absorb losses when a resolution authority utilises a resolution tool. Bank shareholders should be the first class to bear losses when a bank is taken into resolution. Following shareholders, creditors are next in line to bear losses and they are classified into the following categories: subordinated debt holders, who are next in line to bear losses after shareholders, followed by creditors holding unsecured senior liabilities, followed by depositors and, finally, creditors whose claims are secured by the value of collateral. Members of the same class must bear losses

---

90 Directive of the European Parliament and of the Council 2014/59/EU (n 87).
91 Ibid., Article 32.
92 Ibid., Article 34(1)(a–i).

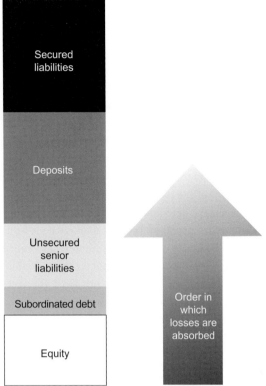

Liabilities and capital
('Sources of funds')

Secured liabilities

Deposits

Unsecured senior liabilities

Subordinated debt

Equity

Order in which losses are absorbed

Figure 6.2 BRRD creditor hierarchy for absorbing losses in a bank resolution

equally or share in the proceeds of any distribution from the bank on an equal basis (the *pari passu* rule).

6.83 Another important principle is that the creditors should not incur heavier losses in a bank resolution than they would otherwise incur if the bank was taken into insolvency.[93] This requires that the resolution authority ensure that an accurate valuation of the assets and liabilities of the bank in resolution is received because the valuation determines the amount that the creditors are eligible to claim, through the resolution process. Article 36 BRRD requires that there has to be a 'fair, prudent and realistic' valuation of the assets and liabilities of the bank by an independent valuer, who is not part of the resolution or governmental authority.[94] The valuation must take into account the priority classification of the creditors of the bank, and also compare the treatment that the creditors would receive

---

93   De Serière V and van der Houwen D, "No Creditor Worse Off" in Case of Bank Resolution: Food for Litigation?' (2016) 7 *Journal of International Banking Law and Regulation Issue* 7 376.
94   Directive 2014/59/EU (n 87), Article 36(1).

(i.e. compensation) under normal insolvency procedures.[95] Article 36(5) provides that the valuation shall be prudent, so that the rates of default and the amount of losses are represented in a realistic manner. Moreover, the valuation may not take into account the potential value of public financial support such as a bailout.[96]

B Resolution Tools

6.84 The BRRD mentions four different tools in resolution, namely: (1) the sale of business, (2) the bridge institution, (3) asset separation, and (4) bail-in.[97] The sale of business tool is the method in which the bank is completely or partially sold to another entity. The bridge institution tool is the method where the essential and functioning parts of a bank in resolution are transferred to another bank that (usually owned by the state) is established for this purpose until a buyer for the bank can be found. The bridge institution tool does not require the approval of the bank shareholders to be used. The asset separation tool aims to distinguish between the deteriorating assets and the viable assets of a bank in resolution, and to transfer the bad assets to an asset management vehicle (AMV, also called the 'bad-bank'), so that the bank may continue to function (also called a 'good-bank'). It is important to note that this option is only possible in combination with other tools. Finally, as discussed below, the bail-in tool stands out from the rest of the tools, as it is arguably the one that has the most impact on the rights of creditors particularly as it involves a mandatory debt restructuring.[98]

1 Bail-In

6.85 Bail-in provisions are generally intended to address the moral hazard problem of so-called too-big-to-fail financial institutions and the unfairness of having taxpayers subsidise excessive private sector risk-taking. The BRRD contains a bail-in feature, in which creditors and shareholders of a distressed financial institution must 'suffer appropriate losses and bear an appropriate part of those costs arising from the failure of the institution . . . [to] give shareholders and creditors of institutions a stronger incentive to monitor the health of an institution during normal circumstances'.[99] The bail-in provisions include replacing management at the failing institution, and implementing a 'restructuring plan' as compatible as possible with the recovery plan submitted by the corporation prior to its failing.

6.86 The BBRD, however, leaves much to the discretion of resolution authorities, allowing them to keep in place the institution's management where 'appropriate and necessary' and to

---

95 Ibid., Article 36(8).
96 Ibid., Article 36(5).
97 Ibid., Article 37; Lazcano MH, 'The Sale of Business Tool', in *Understanding Bank Recovery and Resolution in the EU: A Guidebook to the BRRD* (2012) World Bank Group (April 2017), 121–131.
98 Zhou J, Rutledge V, Bossu W, Dobler M, Jassaud N and Moore M, 'From Bail-Out to Bail-In: Mandatory Debt Restructuring of Systemic Financial Institutions' (2012) IMF Staff Discussion Note 6.
99 See generally Alexander K and Schwarcz SL, 'Macroprudential Quandary: Unsystematic Efforts to Reform Financial Regulation', in Buckley RP, Avgouleas E and Arner DW (eds), *Reconceptualising Global Finance and Its Regulation* (Cambridge University Press 2015), 127–158, 153–154.

exclude 'certain kinds of unsecured liability' from bail-in. Further, in 'extraordinary cir- cumstances',[100] resolution authorities may request funding from alternative financing arrangements – which could even include a taxpayer-funded loan. When it comes to the scope of the bail-in tool, the authorities are granted discretion to apply the bail-in tool to all liabilities of a bank; yet certain types of liabilities are exempted from the tool. Among the exempt liabilities from bail-in are retail depositors whose deposits are protected by the EU deposit guarantee scheme[101] and creditors with secured liabilities such as covered bonds,[102] or other similar liabilities used for hedging purposes, or other liabilities that a bank may owe arising from employment, liabilities to tax and social security authorities.

6.87 The BRRD also sets the order of the liabilities to which the bail-in tool is applied. Article 48(1) BRRD requires the following order of liabilities for bail-in:[103]

1. The Common Equity Tier 1 capital.
2. Additional Tier 1 capital.
3. The principal amount of Tier 2 capital instruments.
4. The principal amount of subordinated debt (that is not included in classes mentioned in (2) or (3) above).
5. The rest of the eligible claims.

6.88 Figure 6.3 illustrates how a bail-in can be used to absorb the losses of a failing bank and to recapitalise it. In panel A, the bank which has a total balance sheet of £300 suffers £10 loss. This could be because some of the loans it has made are not repaid. As a result of the loss, the bank will have insufficient capital to continue to operate so it enters resolution. It is assumed that the bank will need to be recapitalised to the same amount as before the firm entered resolution.

6.89 In Figure 6.3, the conversion of eligible liabilities into common equity shares has been structured in such a way that each class in the order of hierarchy is required to be fully bailed-in before the liabilities in the next class can be bailed-in. After all liabilities in that class are totally written down and converted into equity, the next class of creditors becomes available to be bailed-in if there are further losses to be absorbed.[104] However, the resolution authority can exempt certain creditor liabilities from bail-in.

6.90 The BRRD observes the general principle that shareholders have to bear the initial losses in a bail-in, and once all shares are written down, the creditors begin to share the burden

---

100 Ibid., 156.
101 Article 44(2) of the Directive 2014/59/EU (n 87).
102 The Directive 2014/59/EU has a reference to the Article 52(4) of the Directive 2009/65/EC for the definition of a 'covered bond' in Article 1(96). In this Directive, a covered bond has been defined as a bond that is subject to special public supervision by law to protect bondholders.
103 Directive 2014/59/EU (n 87), Article 48(1).
104 Ibid., Article 48(5).

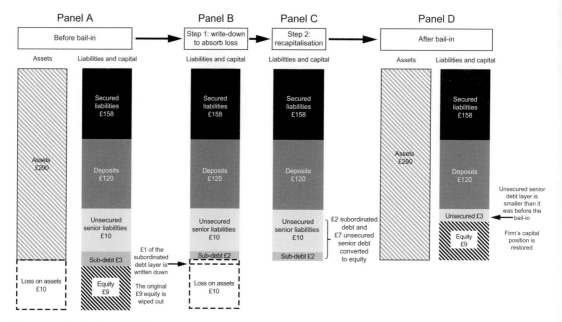

Figure 6.3 Stylised model of bail-in

according to the order of priority in Article 48(1). It may be considered prudent to impose losses first on shareholders because they stand to reap any upside gain from bank profits, whereas they should correspondingly be exposed to any downside loss involving the risk of bankruptcy or default.

6.91 Certain bank liabilities, however, are exempted from bail-in, including deposits that are covered by the Directive on Deposit Guarantee Schemes, secured liabilities (including covered bonds), client assets or client money that is segregated from the bank balance sheet, liabilities that arise because of a fiduciary relationship, liabilities to institutions (excluding entities that are part of the same group) with an original maturity of fewer than seven days, liabilities with a remaining maturity of fewer than seven days (owed to payment systems or securities settlement systems), salaries, pension benefits or other fixed remuneration of employees, operational liabilities (IT services, utilities and the rental, etc.), tax and social security authorities (if preferred under the applicable law) and Deposit Guarantee Scheme contributions that are due.

6.92 Moreover, in exceptional circumstances, the BRRD allows the resolution authority to exclude certain liabilities from bail-in.[105] The conditions for this are established in four scenarios: (1) it is not possible to apply bail-in tool to the liability in a timely manner, (2) the functioning of the bank is dependent on that liability, so that the application of bail-in would result in the disruption of the critical functions and core business areas of the bank,

---

105 Ibid., Article 44(3).

(3) the presence of the liability supports financial stability, and in its absence, the effect of contagion would have a negative impact on the stability of the whole market (which could particularly be the case when non-covered deposits are concerned, by triggering bank runs for example), and (4) the bailing-in would cause a decrease in the value of the bank to the extent that the application of bail-in becomes more costly than exclusion for the other creditors. However, if the resolution authority decides to exclude certain types of liabilities, the extent of bail-in applied to other eligible liabilities may be increased but subject to the no creditor worse off principle (NCWO).

6.93   Notwithstanding the assets and liabilities that are exempted from the bail-in tool, once a specific class of liabilities is subjected to bail-in, then the losses of the creditors will be determined and accrued on a pro-rata basis,[106] so that the burden on the creditors in the same class will be in accordance with the *pari passu* principle. The BRRD also recognises the status of derivatives as financial instruments that are subject to bail-in as to the value of the derivative position at a specific point in time. Thus, creditor positions in derivatives contracts can be written down and converted into an equity position on the condition that the necessary close-out in the contract has been performed.[107]

6.94   Some have argued that this wide regulatory discretion may increase, rather than decrease, moral hazard.[108] The chance that the institution's creditors and shareholders will ultimately be bailed out by taxpayer funds or other public support may justify a decision by the institution's management to engage in high-risk, potentially profitable, activity.[109] Some commentators have observed, however, that some discretion should always be associated with a bail-in/bailout decision.[110] Quantitative factors do not necessarily fit every situation. Indeed, if used as an automatic trigger, they could create an unnecessary panic when a firm nears the trigger.

6.95   The bail-in itself, therefore, might trigger a contagion effect, in which 'the failure of one institution either causes the creditors of others to withdraw funding in a manner akin to a classic bank run or sets off a general panic leading debt markets to freeze'.[111] News of a bail-in might also lower market confidence in the value of assets held by the bailed-in bank (if such assets might be subject to a forced sale), spreading market uncertainty to other institutions holding the same or similar assets. Bail-ins will also impose losses on the

---

106   Ibid., Article 48(2).
107   Ibid., Article 49(2).
108   See Krauskopf B, Langner J and Rötting M, 'Some Critical Aspects of the European Banking Union' (2014) 29 *Banking & Finance Law Review* 2 241–269.
109   Boyd AS, 'Bail-Ins: Just Another Self-Fulfilling Prophecy?' (2012) 27 *Banking & Finance Law Review* 559.
110   See Anabtawi I and Schwarcz SL, 'Regulating Ex Post: How Law Can Address the Inevitability of Financial Failure' (2013) 92 *Texas Law Review* 75 117; Schwarcz SL, 'Controlling Financial Chaos: The Power and Limits of Law' (2012) 3 *Wisconsin Law Review* 815 837.
111   Scott HS, 'Interconnectedness and Contagion: Financial Panics and the Crisis of 2008' (2014) Working Paper.

bailed-in bank's shareholders and creditors, some of which may themselves be banks or other systemically important financial institutions.[112]

6.96 Thus, an inconsistent application of the bail-in tool bears many risks. Some of these risks have already taken their toll on financial markets, contributing to volatility in Eurozone bank share prices and the unexpected increase in the cost of bank debt financing due to the uncertainty surrounding the effect of the bail-in measures. Moreover, the uncertainty surrounding several recent court cases in Austria Portugal, Italy and Spain created legal uncertainty about the scope of application of bail-in measures and to what extent they can be imposed on bank creditors, thus contributing to volatility in Eurozone bank bond markets.

6.97 The bail-in resolution tool is particularly problematic in a legal sense because it grants vast discretion to Member State competent authorities to impose losses on the property rights of investors (both equity and debt) in a covered financial institution. The discretionary use of powers by authorities to restrict property rights – and other fundamental legal rights – in order to achieve regulatory or other public policy objectives must conform with the proportionality principle under EU law (interpreted both by the CJEU and ECHR). However, the discretionary *ad hoc* exercise of resolution powers (i.e. bail-in) can not only potentially infringe on the fundamental rights of shareholders and creditors of financial institutions, but can also result in substantial moral hazard in the financial system, which can potentially lead to financial system disturbances and even breakdown. For example, the use of the bank resolution tool of 'bail-in' in the European Union affords authorities with sweeping discretion as to when and to what extent bank creditors can be bailed into a bank's losses during periods of market distress outside of bankruptcy.

6.98 Although this litany of 'tools' represents a range of diverse approaches, it provides no guidance as to which tools should be used in which circumstances, or as to how they should be calibrated.

6.99 The misapplication of resolution tools – such as imposing losses on certain groups of bondholders but not others – without providing concrete guidance in advance as how losses would be allocated and to what extent they would be imposed, could potentially create substantial moral hazard in the financial system and may be as likely to cause or exacerbate financial problems as solve them.

2 Minimum Required Eligible Liabilities (MREL)

6.100 As mentioned above, to ensure that the application of the bail-in tool is effective, and that the banks subject to the tool have the necessary amount of liabilities that may be used to absorb losses, the BRRD contains requirements for banks to hold a minimum amount of its

112 See Anabtawi and Schwarcz (n 110), 117.

$$\frac{MREL}{Total\ liabilities\ and\ own\ funds}$$

Figure 6.4 MREL to be expressed as % of total liabilities and own funds

own funds and eligible liabilities measured against the total value of the bank's assets and liabilities.[113] The purpose of MREL is to ensure that banks hold sufficient amounts of regulatory capital instruments and eligible liabilities for loss absorption and recapitalisation. The BRRD does not foresee a harmonised minimum level of bail-in eligible instruments at the level of individual banks.

6.101 EU Member State resolution authorities are required to consider a list of criteria when determining the amount of MREL, including: (i) does the minimum MREL amount ensure that the institution can be resolved, (ii) ensure that losses can be absorbed and that core equity (Tier 1) capital levels can be restored, (iii) reflect the size, business model, risk appetite and funding sources, (iv) potential Deposit Guarantee Scheme contribution, and (v) extent of adverse effect on financial stability. The resolution authority should determine MREL after consulting with the regulatory authority and for cross-border institutions there should be consultation and joint decision by the resolution college and in the absence of agreement, the EBA should mediate a final decision (see Figure 6.4).

6.102 The MREL requirement is represented in terms of a percentage which is calculated by the ratio of own funds and eligible liabilities (numerator) to the total liabilities and own funds (denominator) of the bank. The conditions for instruments to be included in the MREL definition are set forth in Article 45(4) BRRD and include that the instrument is: (a) issued and fully paid up; (b) not owed to, nor secured or guaranteed by, the institution in question; (c) purchase of the instrument is not funded by the institution; (d) remaining maturity over one year; (e) does not arise from a derivative; and (f) does not arise from a deposit that benefits from a preference in the national insolvency law in accordance with DGS. Where a liability is governed by the law of a third country, resolution authorities may require the institution to demonstrate that any decision of a resolution authority to write down or convert that liability would be effective under the law of that third country (a country outside the EU/EEA).[114] The BRRD does not set a specific percentage that is applicable to all banks, but instead mandates the resolution authority to calculate it on a case-by-case basis.[115]

6.103 The MREL standard concept is very similar to the Total Loss-Absorbing Capacity (TLAC) standard adopted by the FSB and the United States, although there are significant differences.[116] The main difference is that the TLAC concept only applies to banks that are deemed

---

113   Directive 2014/59/EU (n 87), Article 45(1).
114   Ibid., Article 45(4).
115   Ibid., Article 45(6).
116   Deutsche Bundesbank, 'Monthly Report' (Vol. 68, No. 7, July 2016), 74.

global systemically important, whereas the MREL requirement applies to all European banks and systemically important investment banks. Another difference lies within the different denominators in determining the loss absorption; the TLAC uses a risk-weighted asset (RWA) percentage whereas the MREL uses the ratio of eligible liabilities and own funds to the total liabilities and own funds of the bank.[117] The European Commission has proposed legislation to implement the TLAC standard into the BRRD for global systemically important banks, but as of 2018 this proposal is still being debated by the EU legislative bodies.

6.104 Further, the BRRD mandates the European Banking Authority (EBA) to draft technical implementing standards for the determination of the amount of capital necessary to ensure adequate loss absorption.[118] Based on the EBA proposed technical standards, the Commission implemented them into EU law by adopting Commission Delegated Regulation (EU) 2016/1450, wherein two separate calculations are set forth: (1) the amount necessary to ensure loss absorption; and (2) the amount necessary to recapitalise the bank so that it may meet minimum capital requirements and therefore continue to operate as a going concern. The resolution authority shall therefore determine the amount of MREL by considering (i) the minimum capital requirements (Basel III) set in Regulation No 575/2013, (ii) the additional capital requirements set by the Directive 2013/36/EU, (iii) the combined buffer requirements as defined in the Article 128(6) of the same Directive 2013/36/EU. These three requirements should constitute the minimum amount, and the authority may choose to add any applicable leverage ratio requirement or the Basel III floor pursuant to the Article 500 of the Regulation No 575/2013 as well. For the recapitalisation, any additional amount that the resolution authority considers necessary for market confidence may also be included.

6.105 Finally, the European Banking Union's Single Resolution Mechanism regulation provides that the Single Resolution Board – representing the resolution authorities of the participating nineteen EU states – adopt a consistent approach for determining the level and definition of MREL liabilities, thereby enhancing the predictability of resolution across these Member States.[119]

V EU BANK RESOLUTION AND DEPOSIT GUARANTEE SCHEMES POST-BREXIT

6.106 As discussed in Chapter 14, Brexit will have a dramatic impact on banking and financial regulation in the European Union and the United Kingdom, with implications for

---

117   Financial Stability Board, 'Principles on Loss-Absorbing and Recapitalisation Capacity of G-SIBs in Resolution; Total Loss-Absorbing Capacity (TLAC) Term Sheet' (Report, 2015), 10.
118   Directive 2014/59/EU (n 87), Article 45(2).
119   Single Resolution Board, 'Minimum Requirement for Own Funds and Eligible Liabilities (MREL): SRB Policy for 2017 and Next Steps' (Report, 2017), 10.

cross-border resolution and deposit guarantee schemes as well. Indeed, the resolvability of new banking group structures may become more difficult post-Brexit because of the complexities and uncertainties of the effect of UK banking regulation under EU law and vice versa. Regarding the outsourcing of key technical functions in recovery and resolution planning for large cross-border banks, there will be significant regulatory challenges post-Brexit. In the context of Brexit, firms may outsource activities (including data systems or information technology infrastructure) to a separate EU or UK operation with a view to maintaining existing structures and minimising costs.

1 Bank Outsourcing Plans

6.107 Banks will need to assess whether their outsourcing plans would have an adverse effect on the continuity of critical services in recovery, resolution and post-resolution restructuring. The UK Prudential Regulation Authority (PRA) expects that firms outsourcing critical services will continue to remain responsible for functions that require senior management judgement or decision-making that could affect the prudential soundness or risk appetite of the firm. For this reason, the PRA expects these functions to be retained within the firm. The EU27 competent authorities are likely to have similar expectations on outsourcing. The European Securities and Markets Authority (ESMA) adopted guidance that it is necessary to ensure that the conditions for outsourcing do not generate supervisory arbitrage risks. Any outsourcing or delegation arrangement from entities authorised in the EU27 to third-country entities should be strictly framed and consistently supervised. Certain key activities and functions should be present in the EU27 Member States.

2 Recognising Cross-Border Resolution Decisions

6.108 Regarding recognition and enforcement of bank resolution decisions, the EU and UK post-Brexit will potentially lose automatic recognition of cross-border resolution decisions and powers. The BRRD ensures that resolution actions by EU resolution authorities are automatically recognised and enforced by resolution authorities of other Member States. Post-Brexit, resolution actions by EU27 resolution authorities in relation to assets, liabilities or contracts located or booked in the UK, or subject to UK law, may not be effective. The same will hold true for resolution actions taken by UK resolution authorities in relation to assets, liabilities or contracts located or booked in EU27, or governed by EU27 law. While recognition of EU27 Member States' use of resolution tools has already been implemented into UK law, it is unclear whether it will be maintained and whether reciprocal recognition arrangements can be negotiated with EU27 to apply between the UK and EU27 post-Brexit.

6.109 Article 93 of BRRD contemplates that the European Commission may produce proposals for contingency agreements with third countries governing cooperation between resolution authorities in the event of resolution of third-country banks which have branches, subsidiaries or parent undertakings in the EU, and vice versa. Pending such agreements, Article 94 of BRRD provides general mechanisms for recognition by EU Member States of third-country resolution measures. These include joint recognition decisions by a resolution college or, if there is no resolution college (or it does not reach a decision), each Member State's resolution authority can make its own decision. Such decisions are subject to public interest exclusions which may reduce the likelihood of recognition of UK resolution actions in respect of UK banks.

6.110 There may need to be alternative legal requirements for own funds and eligible liabilities to constitute MREL and to be subject to bail-in. This would include English law governed by the International Swaps and Derivatives Association (ISDA) master agreements after Brexit that apply to certain bank liabilities. These alternative require-ments do not apply where the resolution authority determines that liabilities could be bailed-in under the law of the third country or a binding agreement between the Member State and the third country. Therefore, in a post-Brexit scenario, the UK and EU27 resolution authorities may rely on their statutory recognition regimes imple-mented as a result of BRRD. Moreover, resolution authorities may not count as MREL, liabilities governed by third-country law for which they are not satisfied that any resolution decision would be effective. The BRRD2 includes proposed changes to Article 55, where contractual recognition is a condition for a debt instrument's qualification to satisfy the MREL.

3 Membership in Deposit Guarantee Schemes and Resolution Financing Arrangements

6.111 The key considerations are that new group structures may lead to changes to resolution financing and depositor protection arrangements. The EU27 branches of UK firms will have to contribute to local resolution funds, or the Single Resolution Fund where relevant and, accordingly, UK branches of EU27 firms will have to contribute to the UK resolution arrangements as necessary. The UK is now increasing contributions by all banks that are subject to UK resolution arrangements by imposing a bank balance sheet levy based on the bank's net profits.

6.112 Equally, on depositor protection, third-country branches will join the local deposit guarantee scheme unless the EU27 designated authority or the UK designated authority (i.e. the PRA) determines that the home scheme provides equal protection. Firms will need to engage with regulators and assess whether changes to IT systems disclosures, procedures and contributions are required. It is likely that UK branches of EU27 firms and EU27 branches of UK firms will no longer be covered by the home deposit guarantee scheme and will have to join the local scheme. In general, authorisations for third-country branches are carried out in accordance with national law. Firms will need to consider regulators' risk appetite for third-country branches. For example, the PRA will be content for third country branches undertaking retail banking activities beyond *de minimis* levels only if there is a very high level of assurance from the home state supervisor over resolution. The PRA also expects new third-country branches to focus on wholesale banking and to operate at a level that is not critical to the UK economy.

6.113 Under the BRRD, non-EEA-covered deposits will be preferred but not super-preferred in the creditor hierarchy in insolvency. This will have an impact on the amount the relevant deposit guarantee scheme will recover from the insolvency estate as well as the amount that the scheme would be able to contribute in resolution. Firms will need to have an understanding of where the deposit guarantee scheme would rank in the creditor hierarchy in a home state insolvency.

CONCLUSION

6.114 The financial crisis demonstrated the importance of having strong bank deposit guarantee schemes and bank resolution regimes. This chapter discussed the main principles, theories and rationales of deposit guarantee schemes and how they differ from each other in major jurisdictions such as the European Union and the United States. The crisis led to new legislation that increased the amount of coverage in deposit protection schemes but seemed to ignore the moral hazard problems that such increases in coverage for depositors and bank managers caused. Moreover, the implementation of certain principles of deposit guarantee schemes (e.g. prompt corrective action) designed to protect depositors and to restore a bank's financial health can lead to the suspension of shareholder corporate governance rights and to other limitations on bank managerial autonomy.

6.115 The chapter also discussed the main principles, concepts and rationales of bank resolution regimes. Prior to the crisis, most countries did not have resolution regimes, so when a bank experienced financial difficulties the choice was either insolvency, liquidation or bailout. During the crisis, most failed banks were bailed out, resulting in fiscal retrenchment and global economic recession. Bailouts were hugely inefficient and morally hazardous. Authorities focused on financial stability in their own jurisdictions and adopted idiosyncratic and uncoordinated national approaches to unwinding and protecting stakeholders against failed cross-border banks. For instance, resolution procedures for banks may provide for a conservatorship whereby the regulator or central bank appoints an official to take control of the bank's operations. Such action may interfere with shareholder control rights and may also lead to a suspension of more fundamental rights, such as the right to elect directors, or to call a special shareholder meeting and to submit resolutions to elect new – or remove existing – directors. The value of the shareholders' interest may be further depleted or eliminated if the regulator decides to transfer some or all of the bank's viable assets to a state-owned bridge bank or to sell them to a private purchaser, such as another bank, while leaving the original bank with mostly unviable assets. In some cases, regulatory action may lead to the bank's financial health being restored, in which case pre-resolution shareholder rights would be restored.

6.116 Although resolution regimes are generally designed to provide a more comprehensive legal and regulatory framework for a bank to be taken into administration or liquidation without causing a severe disruption to the banking system, they have important legal implications as they suspend corporate governance rules for shareholders and thus interfere with shareholder rights. The chapter analyses the EU Bank Recovery and Resolution Directive (BRRD) and raises concerns with the absence of specific criteria for determining when certain resolution tools can be used or how and when they should be calibrated. It also discusses some of the regulatory risks in using bail-in, as it is defined and applied in the BRRD, to impose losses on bank creditors and thereby limit the taxpayer's direct financial exposure for having to bail out a systemically important institution.

QUESTIONS

1. Would the BRRD allow a resolution authority to take a bank into resolution if the bank's net assets are worth €100 million to the bank's creditors in insolvency but worth €60 million to the bank's creditors in resolution? What is the relevant principle to be applied and what should the resolution authority do?
2. Under EU and US law, is there a government backstop if deposit guarantee funds are insufficient?
3. What is the *pari passu* rule and what are the conditions in which the FDIC can depart from the *pari passu* rule in a bank resolution?
4. Should foreign branches and subsidiaries be covered by the home deposit guarantee scheme? Why or why not?
5. Is the deposit guarantee limit sufficient to provide adequate protection?
6. Describe what bail-in is under the BRRD? Are there any legal concerns regarding its use?

Further Reading

Busch D, 'Governance of the Single Resolution Mechanism', in Busch D and Ferrarini G (eds), *European Banking Union* (Oxford University Press 2015)

De Serière V, 'Recovery and Resolution Plans of Banks in the Context of the BRRD and the SRM', in Busch D and Ferrarini G (eds), *European Banking Union* (Oxford University Press 2015)

Gardella A, 'Bail-In and the Financing of Resolution Within the SRM Framework', in Busch D and Ferrarini G (eds), *European Banking Union* (Oxford University Press 2015)

Kleftouri N, *Deposit Protection and Bank Resolution* (Oxford University Press 2015)

Simon S, 'The Architecture of the BRRD: A UK Perspective', in Busch D and Ferrarini G (eds), *European Banking Union* (Oxford University Press 2015)

7

Bank Organisation and Structural Regulation

Table of Contents

INTRODUCTION

7.1 Since the 1970s, the liberalisation of financial markets has allowed banks to expand their activities across states and national borders and to become multi-functional institutions with global reach that can provide their customers with a wide variety of financial services. This has created substantial synergies for banks, their customers and the broader economy, yet it has introduced risks which, if not managed efficiently, can create substantial social costs. An example of how banks failed to manage such risks was the market turmoil of 2007–2008 that resulted in the collapse and bailout of many large and systemically important financial institutions in a number of countries. This called into question the effectiveness of the universal banking model and the validity of risk-based models for estimating and pricing risks (discussed in Chapter 4). The universal banking model and the risk-based models for estimating economic and regulatory capital were accepted by regulators as essential features of the banking business. Banks were incentivised to grow larger through mergers and acquisitions and to expand across financial sectors into merchant banking, insurance and asset management and by doing so were deemed by bank management and regulators to have diversified their risks across multiple product lines and market sectors.

7.2 The crisis demonstrated how large multi-functional banking and financial institutions that followed the universal banking model could fail catastrophically in managing their risks and the inadequate response of regulators and policymakers in bailing out these institutions rather than imposing any sort of meaningful market discipline on their management, creditors and shareholders. This chapter discusses the regulatory and legal response to the failure of bank managers to manage risks in large multi-functional banking institutions and to the inadequacies of risk-based models of prudential regulation. It addresses how structural regulation has come to play an important role in some jurisdictions to support prudential regulatory objectives and bank resolution regimes. The chapter first analyses the UK's ring-fencing regime as set forth in the Financial Services (Banking Reform) Act 2013. It then analyses the European Commission's 2014 legislative proposal for structural regulation of the banking industry. This proposal was the subject of much debate and criticism and was later withdrawn in 2018. Although the EU withdrew the proposal, it provides an interesting model for other countries to consider in deciding how and whether to regulate the institutional structure of banking groups. The chapter also discusses structural legislation in Germany, France and Belgium and compares these approaches with the US structural regulation proposals that have become known as the Volcker Rule.

7.3 The question of whether structural reform or ring-fencing may hinder the effectiveness of bank resolution regimes and what can be done to enhance coordination between both frameworks is also considered. It suggests that ring-fencing proposals may enhance prudential regulation and bank resolution procedures by requiring banking groups to be more transparent in their group structures and by protecting the bank's systemic functions from excessive risk-taking. The chapter concludes that although ring-fencing proposals may enhance prudential regulation and bank resolution procedures by requiring banking groups to be more transparent in their group structures and protecting the bank's systemic functions, this raises the issue that compliance with these structural regulatory controls will significantly limit the economic and risk diversification benefits of the universal banking model and could lead to the most risky trading activity (i.e. currency, credit and commodity derivatives) being transferred off bank balance sheets into the shadow banking sector (discussed in Chapter 10) where it can still pose significant risks to financial stability.

I UNIVERSAL BANKING MODEL

7.4 Structural regulation calls into question the efficacy of the universal banking model for systemically important banks as it seeks to limit or segregate the risks that large banks or banking groups are exposed to. It is premised on the notion that the economic and risk diversification benefits of the traditional universal banking model – involving a single bank offering a variety of financial services across the main financial sectors of commercial banking, securities trading and insurance – are not justified due to the potential systemic risks that large and medium-sized banking groups pose to society. In theory, universal banking aims to achieve synergies in the provision of financial services through cross-selling of products and investments and reduced overall risks through diversification.[1] The universal banking model arose to dominance in continental Europe, and in many Asian countries and developing countries which had relied historically on bank funding as the main source of credit for economies. For example, European companies (including small and medium-sized enterprises) in 2016 relied on bank funding for 76 per cent of all financing, whereas US companies relied on banking funding for about 27 per cent of all financing.[2] The

---

1   European Central Bank, 'Consolidation and Diversification in the Euro Area Banking Sector', Monthly Bulletin (May 2005) www.ecb.europa.eu/pub/pdf/mobu/mb200505en.pdf accessed 21 February 2018.
2   See G30, 'Shadow Banking and Capital Markets: Risks and Opportunities' (November 2016), 6 http://group30.org/images/uploads/publications/ShadowBankingCapitalMarkets_G30.pdf accessed 26 March 2018; and Anderson N, Brooke M, Hume M and Kürtösiová M, 'A European Capital Markets Union: Implications for Growth and Stability' (February 2015) Financial Stability Paper No. 33, 6 www.bankofengland.co.uk/-/media/

large contribution of bank funding in Europe derives mainly from large global banking groups, which provide around half of bank credit for European companies.[3]

7.5 Although bank-originated credit is the predominant source of finance for companies in most European countries, the European Commission has proposed legislation that would promote increased financing from companies from the capital markets.[4] The Commission's proposed legislation aims to enhance long-term financing of the European economy by (i) mobilising private sources of long-term financing, (ii) making better use of public finance, (iii) developing capital markets, (iv) improving SMEs' access to financing, (v) attracting private finance to infrastructure, and (vi) enhancing the overall environment for sustainable finance.[5] These and other initiatives will take some time before they result in companies sourcing significantly more of their financing from the capital markets.

A Multi-Functional Banking Groups: The Benefits

7.6 In most economies where bank financing is predominant, banks will continue to play a vital role as intermediaries in providing most of the funding for companies and other businesses. This means that the universal banking model will continue in most jurisdictions to allow large banking groups and individual standalone banks to engage in an array of financial activities ranging from mortgage lending and credit cards to underwriting and selling securities and insurance.[6] In some jurisdictions, such as Germany, they take equity stakes in non-financial firms and vote their shares to influence management, while often appointing their agents and employees as board members of firms in which they own shares. This is the classic operational strategy of large universal banks in Europe and Japan. Indeed, the largest universal banks in terms of asset size continue to use the size and scope of their balance sheets to leverage their trading positions in the derivatives markets and to offer a number of other financial products.[7] As discussed in Chapter 1, multi-functional banking groups provide universal banking services through a corporate group or conglomerate[8]

boe/files/financial-stability-paper/2015/a-european-capital-markets-union-implications-for-growth.pdf?la=en&thash=26629651BA24F7590B3EA31632CF09EE4DF0B7B2 accessed 28 March 2018.

3   European Commission, 'Green Paper – Building a Capital Markets Union' (18 February 2015) SWD (2015) 13 final, 7 http://ec.europa.eu/finance/consultations/2015/capital-markets-union/docs/green-paper_en.pdf accessed 28 March 2018.

4   See European Commission, Communication from the Commission to the European Parliament and the Council on 'Long-Term Financing of the European Economy' (27 March 2014) COM(2014) 168 final, 10–12 www.ec.europa.eu/internal_market/finances/docs/financing-growth/long-term/140327-communication_en.pdf accessed 21 February 2018.

5   Ibid.

6   See Canals J, *Universal Banking* (Oxford University Press 1997), 8–11.

7   The seven largest banking groups in the world are: Industrial and Commercial Bank of China (US$3.473 trillion), the China Construction Bank Corporation (US$3.017 trillion) and the Agricultural Bank of China (US$2.816 trillion). Fourth is Mitsubishi (US$2.723 trillion), Bank of China (US$2.612 trillion), JP Morgan Chase & Co. (US$2.491 trillion), HSBC (US$2.375 trillion) and BNP Paribas (US$2.190 trillion) See Alem Husain, 'Top Global Banks' (S&P Global Market Intelligence, 14 December 2017) https://marketintelligence.spglobal.com/our-thinking/ideas/top-global-banks accessed 28 March 2018.

8   See Tripartite Group of Bank, Securities and Insurance Regulators, 'The Supervision of Financial Conglomerates' Report (July 1995), 69 www.bis.org/publ/bcbs20.pdf accessed 21 February 2018.

structure by offering a wide range of financial services through a network of companies and firms that are controlled by a holding company or affiliated banking or financial entity. For instance, international regulatory bodies have defined a 'financial conglomerate' as 'any corporate group under common control whose exclusive or predominant activities consist of providing a significant level of services in at least two of the financial sectors of banking, securities, and insurance'.[9] Multi-functional banking and financial groups are usually international in character either through their cross-border operations through foreign subsidiaries and branches or their interconnections with foreign financial institutions and other market participants through the securitisation markets, securities lending and repurchase agreement (repo) markets, and the derivatives and swaps markets. The growing operations of universal banks in corporate group and conglomerate structures is a response to the globalisation of financial markets, the competitive pressures of providing financial services to corporate clients with cross-border operations and the pooling of capital and investment services to achieve greater returns for clients.

7.7 In this regard, these large banking and financial groups are multi-functional in their operations. They provide the entire financial system with liquidity and, therefore, play a central role for the economy by providing funding to institutions and individuals to invest in viable assets that might otherwise not obtain funding in a difficult economic climate. The array of financial services which they provide can also facilitate and enhance cross-border trade and investment and assist local companies with more competitive terms of finance for their cross-border operations, not to mention the competitive financing arrangements that a large universal bank group could make available for the cross-border operations of a large multinational company.[10]

B Multi-Functional Banking Groups: The Risks to Society

7.8 The financial crisis of 2007–2008, however, called into question the efficacy of the universal banking model and the soundness of large multi-functional banks and how they manage their risks. Large financial institutions operating in corporate groups or conglomerate structures expanded their cross-border operations in the 1990s and 2000s in order to compete in foreign markets and to diversify their risk exposures.[11] In 2007 and 2008, however, large banks and financial institutions – including many universal banking groups – experienced severe financial distress and were either rescued with taxpayer-funded bailouts or supported with central bank and government guarantees.[12] Large

---

9   Ibid.
10   Eiteman DK, Stonehill AI and Moffett MH, *Multinational Business Finance* (10th edn, Pearson 2004), 696–701.
11   See Basel Committee on Banking Supervision, Committee on Global Financial System, 'Principles for the Supervision of Financial Conglomerates' Final Report (September 2012) www.bis.org/publ/joint29.htm accessed 21 December 2018, 1. See ibid., and see also The Joint Forum, 'Review of the Differentiated Nature and Scope of Financial Regulation, Key Issues and Recommendations' (January 2010), 14.
12   *See BaFin Journal*, 'Systemrelevante Finanzunternehmen – G20 sehen Fortschritte bei nationalen und internationalen Lösungsansätzen zum "Too Big to Fail" Problem' (October 2013), 30. See also Darling A, *Back from the Brink: 1,000 Days at No. 11* (Atlantic Books Limited 2011), 130–149.

banking groups and conglomerates were criticised for investing in high-risk structured finance assets and for speculating in credit default swaps and other credit-linked derivatives which recklessly increased their risk exposure at the expense of their depositors, creditors, shareholders and ultimately the taxpayers.[13] The collapse of these institutions, the extent of the taxpayer bailouts and the subsequent impact on the economy have led to a re-evaluation of the benefits of the universal banking model and to calls for structural regulation of financial groups that would require, *inter alia*, legal separation – or ring-fencing – into a subsidiary of the group's retail deposit-taking and small business lending activities, or alternatively ring-fencing the risky trading activities of a banking group in a separate subsidiary.[14]

II RING-FENCED BANKING: THE UK APPROACH

7.9 Historically, the organisational structure of British banking evolved differently from the universal banking model of other European states because of legal restrictions on the size and operations of domestic and multinational banks. By the twentieth century, British banking groups had grown dramatically in size and scope with their cross-border operations in far-flung former colonies.[15] By the late twentieth century, British banking groups, such as Barclays Banking Group, HSBC PLC and the Royal Bank of Scotland PLC, had become some of the largest banking groups in the world. Although retail banking was generally conducted in a separate subsidiary from investment banking activities in these institutions, the retail banking subsidiary provided capital and credit to the investment banking subsidiaries on favourable, non-market terms that allowed the investment banking subsidiaries to use funds from retail depositors and generous central bank liquidity support to speculate in risky investments and to take large positions in derivatives. The synergies brought about by such conglomerations of banking and financial activity contributed to the dramatic growth of the banking sector relative to the rest of the British economy with the value of banking assets constituting about 500 per cent of UK GDP.[16] However, large British banking groups with cross-border operations, such as the Royal Bank of Scotland, Lloyds TSB, and Halifax Bank of Scotland, received direct taxpayer bailouts during the crisis that took the form of equity capital injections and guarantees of their liabilities. The bailouts involved the UK Treasury injecting capital directly into some of Britain's largest banks.[17]

---

13   See *BaFin Journal* (n 12), 31.

14   See the recommendations of the Independent Commission on Banking, 'Final Report – Recommendations' (September 2011), 252 http://webarchive.nationalarchives.gov.uk/20131003105424/https:/hmt-sanctions.s3. amazonaws.com/icb%20final%20report/icb%2520final%2520report%5B1%5D.pdf accessed 21 February 2018. See also European Commission, 'Report of the High-Level Expert Group on Reforming the Structure of the EU Banking Sector', chaired by Erkki Liikanen, 105 (the 'Liikanen Report') (2 October 2012) www.ec.europa .eu/internal_market/bank/docs/high-level_expert_group/report_en.pdf accessed 21 February 2018.

15   See Jones G, *British Multinational Banking 1830–1990* (Oxford University Press 1993), 297.

16   See Independent Commission on Banking (n 14), 17.

17   HM Treasury, 'RBS Share Sale Returns 2.5 Billion to UK Taxpayers' (2018) www.gov.uk/government/news/ rbs-share-sale-returns-25-billion-to-uk-taxpayers accessed 21 December 2018.

7.10 To manage this capital, the UK Treasury created in 2008 UK Financial Investments Ltd, which took an 82 per cent equity ownership interest in the Royal Bank of Scotland PLC in October 2008 and a 27 per cent ownership in Lloyds Banking Group. In 2018, the Treasury closed UK Financial Investments Ltd and transferred its remaining ownership interest in UK banks to UK Government Investments Ltd, which in 2018 owned approximately 70 per cent of the Royal Bank of Scotland PLC. On 4 June 2018, the Treasury announced that it was placing 925 million shares worth over £2.5 million sold to institutional investors at 271 pence per share, reducing the government's stake by 7.7 per cent to 62.4 per cent.

7.11 In response to the British banking failures, the Independent Commission on Banking (ICB) conducted a study in 2010–2011 on how British banks could be made safer and more competitive while still performing their vital economic functions. The ICB (also known as the Vicker's Commission) issued its report in 2011 making a number of recommendations, the most important of which was that certain British banking groups should be institutionally restructured so that their retail deposit-taking and payment services, along with services for small and medium-sized businesses, would be segregated into a separate body that would be prohibited from engaging in risky trading activities and other investment banking business that would now have to take place in a separate subsidiary of the group.[18] The ICB also proposed that banks create more efficient account transfer services that would allow customers to change accounts between banks, thereby enhancing competition in the retail banking sector.[19] The ICB asserted that separation or 'segregation' of the retail banking operations from the rest of the banking group would make the group easier to resolve in a crisis because the assets and liabilities of the group could be separated from the assets and liabilities of the ring-fenced bank, and the latter could continue to provide vital deposit and payment services for the economy. For ring-fencing to be effective, the ICB argued that it was necessary for the barrier separating the retail bank from the group to be high so that state-insured deposits could not cross-subsidise risky trading activity in other entities of the group. This would lead over time to a shrinking of the group's risky activities (for example, fixed-income derivatives and currency trading) to a more sustainable level that would not, it was argued, pose as much risk to the financial sector. The ICB concluded that ring-fencing would have the overall effect of making large banking organisations easier to resolve while maintaining critical banking services during distressed markets, and while limiting excessive risk-taking in other parts of the group that could undermine financial stability.

7.12 The UK government accepted the ICB's ring-fencing proposals by proposing primary legislation in 2012 that received the Queen's assent in 2013 as the Financial Services (Banking Reform) Act 2013. The Banking Reform Act establishes the concepts of ring-fenced bodies, and core and excluded activities. The precise details of which banking groups would be subject to the ring-fencing requirement and the definition of core and excluded

18   Independent Commission on Banking, Final Report (n 14).
19   Ibid.

activities were set forth by the Treasury in secondary legislation made under the Act. Under the secondary legislation, ring-fencing was defined as applying to banks with 'core deposits' of £25 billion or more.[20] 'Core' deposits are defined as those of individuals (other than high-net-worth individuals (HNWIs) and their families) and small businesses. HNWIs and larger organisation depositors will have the option (but not the obligation) to deposit outside the ring-fence if they so choose.[21]

7.13 The legislation sets forth a strict separation between banking services deemed essential for individuals and small and medium-sized enterprises (SMEs) *and* the risky trading activities of investment banks, which is vital for reducing structural complexity and enhancing the resolvability of banking groups in a crisis or other distressed scenario, where speed of execution is vital.[22] The ring-fencing policy aims to insulate banking services critical to individuals and SMEs from shocks elsewhere in the financial group or wider system by making it easier to ensure continuous provision of those services and to maintain vital financial services to the economy during periods of banking sector stress. Indeed, the UK ring-fencing legislation has influenced the ongoing debate in many countries about whether retail banking and payment system activities of banks should be separated in a subsidiary that would operate independently of other subsidiaries in the banking group that conducts capital market functions and riskier trading activities, such as dealing in derivatives and other risky financial contracts.

7.14 The UK ring-fencing approach is important in two ways: (1) the structural separation is mandated prior to a crisis event. This assures that the separation is, indeed, enforceable and does not fail because the mere planning for such a separation turned out to be incomplete or to neglect the dynamics and time constraints of a crisis; and (2) the legislative framework gives clear and compelling specifications on what assets and services are vital and how they will be shielded from contagion. Put differently, the regime leaves less room for interpretation for supervisors, banks and creditors. This view that structural regulation should be less flexible and more predictable was asserted by the then Governor of the Bank England Sir Mervyn King (now Lord King) in 2012 when he stated before the Parliamentary Commission on Banking Standards:

> [b]ut if judgment ends up simply as a negotiation between the regulator and the regulated bank, there is only one winner in that, and that will be a very bad outcome. Clarity is crucial to enable the regulator to exercise judgment within a very well defined framework, and the regulator needs to be able to tell Banks, 'This

---

20 See The Financial Services and Markets Act 2000 (Ring-Fenced Bodies and Core Activities) Order 2014 SI 2014/1960.
21 Ibid.
22 See HM Treasury, Department for Business Innovation and Skills, 'Banking Reform: Delivering Stability and Supporting a Sustainable Economy' (14 June 2012), 4 www.gov.uk/government/uploads/system/uploads/attachment_data/file/32556/whitepaper_banking_reform_140512.pdf accessed 18 March 2018.

is the capital requirement you will have', as opposed to merely entering into a negotiation.[23]

7.15 The two most important elements of the UK ring-fence approach are: (1) the scope of the ring-fencing policy (or what the ICB labelled as the 'location'); and (2) the legal, economic and operational independence of the ring-fenced bank (or what the ICB labelled the 'height'). The details of the height and location are mostly defined in secondary legislation.[24] The purpose of defining the ring-fence in the legislative framework, rather than leaving it to be defined by regulators in their rulebook, allows the regulator to devote its resources to implementing the legislation and supervising compliance while avoiding constant negotiations and lobbying efforts by the banks to change the ring-fence in terms of its location and height. Former Bank of England Governor Lord King further elaborated on this view by stating:

> Our strong view is that as far as possible this should be done in legislation and not left to the regulator. I say that because the difficulty that will arise with this approach is that the Banks and their lawyers will have enormous amounts of money, time and resources to come up with all kinds of clever ways to try to get round the rules set out in legislation. Unless those rules are pretty clear the regulator will be chasing the Banks round in a circle and will come under enormous pressure . . . It should be for Parliament to define the ring-fence for retail Banking. The definition may need adjusting from time to time and therefore should not be enshrined in primary legislation. Instead it should be set out in secondary legislation so it can be more easily reviewed and adjusted. It should not be left to the Bank or the regulators to define the ring-fence.[25]

A The Location of the Ring-Fence

7.16 The UK ring-fencing requirements took effect in April 2018 and apply to banking groups with more than £25 billion in liabilities. Five UK banking groups are subject to the ring-fenced requirements: Barclays Bank UK PLC, the Royal Bank of Scotland PLC, HSBC Bank PLC, Lloyds Bank PLC and Santander Bank PLC. The ring-fencing requirements cover the provision of day-to-day retail banking services and payment services. For instance, to comply with the ring-fencing requirements, Barclays Group has established a new bank, Barclays Bank UK PLC, which will conduct retail banking operations alongside, but

23 See Lord King's evidence in House of Lords, House of Commons, Parliamentary Commission on Banking Standards, 'First Report of session 2012–13', para. 74 (21 December 2012) https://publications.parliament.uk/pa/jt201213/jtselect/jtpcbs/98/98.pdf accessed 22 March 2018.
24 See The Financial Services and Markets Act 2000 (Ring-Fenced Bodies and Core Activities) Order 2014 SI 2014/1960 (n 20).
25 See Lord King of Lothbury's oral evidence before the Parliament's Joint Select Committee on the Financial Services Act 2012. See House of Lords, House of Commons, Joint Committee on the Draft Financial Services Bill, 'Draft Financial Services Bill – Session 2010–12', paras. 186–187 (December 2011) www.publications.parliament.uk/pa/jt201012/jtselect/jtdraftfin/236/236.pdf or www.publications.parliament.uk/pa/jt201012/jtselect/jtdraftfin/236/23602.htm accessed 21 February 2018.

independently from, Barclays Bank PLC, which will conduct investment banking and proprietary and other trading activity. These two banks will operate with separate boards of directors from each other under the listed entity, Barclays PLC, which will operate under the group structure of Barclays Banking Group.

Core Activities/Core Services

7.17 The ring-fence is designed to be erected around the activities for which even temporary interruption could have systemic or severe implications for the economy. These so-called 'core activities' under the Banking Reform Act 2013 are mandated services that a ring-fenced bank is required to provide, including accepting deposits, providing facilities for withdrawing money or making payments from deposit accounts and overdraft facilities in connection with such accounts.[26] Only a ring-fenced bank may engage in such 'core activities', as follows:

1 Accepting Deposits

7.18 The Banking Reform Act (section 142B) provides that only the acceptance of deposits from individuals and small and medium-sized enterprises (SMEs)[27] (whether carried on in the UK or elsewhere) will be considered a core activity. Section 142C provides that the following deposit services are 'core activities': (a) facilities for the accepting of deposits or other payments into an account which is provided in the course of carrying on the core activity of accepting deposits; (b) facilities for withdrawing money or making payments from such an account; and (c) overdraft facilities in connection with such an account. The Treasury acknowledges that, besides accepting deposits, other banking services might be of systemic importance. In particular, the provision of domestic credit to households and SMEs and payment and transaction services are included in the list of core activities.[28]

2 Exemptions

7.19 The Act authorised the Treasury to propose secondary legislation providing criteria which, if met by the deposit-taking institution, would exempt them from the ring-fencing requirement. Thus far, Parliament has approved secondary legislation adopting the following exemption criteria:[29] £25 billion *de minimis* rule, exempting banking institutions that take deposits amounting to less than £25 billion from the ring-fencing requirement. Other exemptions include allowing deposits from larger companies and certain high net worth individuals to be placed outside the ring-fence upon explicit customer request. Moreover, building societies will not be considered a ring-fenced bank. Also, UK branches of foreign

26 See The Financial Services and Markets Act 2000 (Ring-Fenced Bodies and Core Activities) Order 2014 SI 2014/1960 (n 20).
27 Ibid. The Treasury uses a quantitative limit to define SMEs.
28 Ibid.
29 Ibid.

(non-EEA) institutions will be exempt from the ring-fenced requirements but only if they accept deposits amounting to less than the *de minimis* threshold of £25 billion. If deposits, however, exceed this threshold the non-EEA headquartered parent will be required to incorporate a subsidiary and to comply fully with the ring-fencing requirements in order to accept further deposits in the UK.[30]

B Excluded Activities

7.20 On the other hand, there are certain activities which are not allowed to be in the same entity as the core activities. The legislation designates these activities as 'excluded activities'.[31] For instance, section 142D of the Act provides that 'dealing in investments as a principal' (whether carried on in the UK or elsewhere) is an excluded activity. Dealing in investments as a principal is defined as '[b]uying, selling, subscribing for or underwriting securities or contractually based investments as principal is a specified kind of activity'.[32] This will affect vast areas of both investment and wholesale banking activities. Moreover, the Treasury has broad power to propose secondary legislation excluding other activities as well. For instance, Parliament approved in 2014 secondary legislation that makes trading in physical commodities an excluded activity, and prohibits ring-fenced bodies from having exposures to financial institutions, other than in specified circumstances (for example, provision of trade finance to non-financial customers).[33]

7.21 The exemptions from excluded activities are set forth in Treasury secondary legislation that allows ring-fenced banks to undertake certain activities or create additional prohibited activities. In this context, secondary legislation passed in July 2014 creates specific exemptions to allow a ring-fenced bank to manage its own risks (for example, interest rate risk on its lending portfolio), and to sell a limited range of simple risk management products (for example, simple interest rate swaps, currency forwards) to customers, subject to limits on the size and riskiness of the ring-fenced entity's derivative portfolio.[34] Specifically, the secondary legislation prohibits the ring-fenced banks from dealing in investments as principal and commodities trading, subject to the following exemptions: (1) managing the risks associated with its business including: changes in interest rates, exchange rates or commodity prices; changes in any index of retail prices or of residential or commercial property prices; changes in any index of the price of shares; default risk; or liquidity risk; (2) buying, selling or subscribing for investments which are liquid assets for the purpose of managing its liquidity; (3) selling derivatives to account holders that are traded on trading venues subject to certain restrictions. These restrictions relate to the complexity of the

---

30 Ibid.
31 Ibid. (Excluded Activities and Prohibitions) Order 2014 SI 2014/2080.
32 Ibid., Article 14 (Regulated Activities) Order 2001 (other than investments of the kind specified by Article 87, or Article 89 so far as relevant to that article). See Financial Services and Markets Act 2000, Schedule 2 contains a definition of 'dealing in investment' that includes both agents and principals.
33 See The Financial Services and Markets Act 2000 (Ring-Fenced Bodies and Core Activities) Order 2014 SI 2014/1960 (n 20).
34 Ibid.

derivatives, the types of risks to which the ring-fenced bank can expose itself when selling derivatives, and two caps on the derivatives trading activity: a 'net' cap and a 'gross' cap; (4) trading in liquid assets for the purpose of managing liquidity risk; (5) acquiring investments in exchange for a loan write-off; (6) acquiring debentures issued by itself, one of its subsidiaries or its parent undertaking.

7.22 The exemption allowing the sale of derivatives to clients as principals has become one of the most controversial areas in the secondary legislation: the Independent Commission on Banking had previously recommended in 2011 that ring-fenced banks should not be allowed to sell derivatives to clients as principals because the complicated nature of derivatives trades and counterparty exposures would make the retail bank more difficult to resolve. On the other hand, the same statutory instrument also provides that dealing in commodities is an excluded (i.e. prohibited) activity.[35] This prohibition aims to insulate ring-fenced banks against swings in global commodity prices.

C Prohibitions

7.23 Finally, the Act authorises the Treasury to propose, and for Parliament to approve, secondary legislation that imposes prohibitions on ring-fenced banks. Such prohibitions work in a similar way to the excluded activities orders, but the prohibition orders are intended to capture transactions with specified types of counterparties or transactions in particular jurisdictions.[36] In other words, exclusions target activities, whereas prohibitions target people and places.

7.24 For example, there are exposure limits vis-à-vis third parties in order to prevent external contagion of losses across the banking system. The Treasury intends to restrict 'any economic exposure' (with exceptions applying for payment arrangements, liquidity and risk management) vis-à-vis institutions that (i) engage in financial intermediation, and (ii) may be highly leveraged, have a high degree of maturity or liquidity mismatch or have a high degree of financial interconnectedness. Examples of institutions that comply with those criteria are non-ring-fenced banks, investment firms, funds and insurance companies.[37]

7.25 Generally, the ring-fenced bank is not permitted to have exposures to 'financial institutions', apart from where such exposures relate to certain exempted activities that include: (1) entering into transactions for risk management purposes, intra-group transactions and payments exposures; (2) facilitating trade finance; (3) issuing securitisation and covered bonds; (4) conducting conduit lending; (5) conducting repurchase (repo) transactions; and (6) performing ancillary activities.

35 Ibid.
36 Ibid.
37 Ibid.

7.26 The ring-fencing regime also contains geographical limits that restrict the possibility for UK ring-fenced banks to establish branches or subsidiaries outside the EEA. The UK bank entity must ensure that cross-border activities do not present a barrier to the resolution of ring-fenced assets (for example, by creating multiple jurisdictions or coordination difficulties with multiple resolution authorities). In fact, the intention is quite clear that a ring-fenced bank shall not carry out any banking activity through non-EEA branches or subsidiaries. Instead, non-EEA operations will have to be undertaken in separate subsidiaries of the group.[38] Thus, the regime implements some features of a geographical subsidiarisation requirement. In addition, the Treasury and the Prudential Regulation Authority require that all major service and credit contracts be written under the laws of an EEA Member State, though this requirement will likely change after Brexit.[39]

7.27 The geographical limitation also mitigates the problem of a potential unequal treatment of foreign creditors, such as bondholders and depositors, and facilitates cross-border resolution. The limitation is based on the UK policy of not protecting deposits in the non-EEA operations of UK banks, nor providing vital services to their non-EEA operations. The geographic limitation on the ring-fenced bank's operations, however, is transparent and will have only a limited effect on the bank's operations because most of their depositors and assets are booked in EEA jurisdictions. Indeed, Randell[40] suggests that the geographic limitation of the ring-fenced bank's operations provides resolution synergies that outweigh the unfairness to potential non-EEA creditors. In the case of resolution he observes that '[i]n addition, if a decision is taken to transfer only part of the business of this subsidiary or subsidiaries to a private sector purchaser or bridge bank, the exercise should also be considerably simpler than' under the pre-2013 regime because the asset side of the subsidiary's balance sheet will consist predominantly of UK/EEA assets.[41] Moreover, geographical limitations may mitigate similar concerns with regard to the requirement under EU and UK law that depositors are preferred in priority to unsecured bondholders in a resolution.[42] As the Treasury noted, limiting depositor preference should not have a significant impact: 'in creating a perception that overseas creditors will be disadvantaged, as a substantial majority of insured deposits are expected to be in ring-fenced banks, which will not be able to branch outside of the EEA – only non-ring-fenced banks can do this'.[43]

---

38   See House of Lords, House of Commons, Joint Committee on the Draft Financial Services Bill (n 25), para. 177. See also House of Lords, House of Commons, Parliamentary Commission on Banking Standards, 'Changing Banking for Good' Final Report (19 June 2013), Volume II: 'Chapters 1 to 11 and Annexes, together with formal minutes', 178–179, paras. 238–239 www.parliament.uk/documents/banking-commission/Banking-final-report-vol-ii.pdf accessed 21 February 2018.

39   See HM Treasury, Department for Business Innovation and Skills, 'Banking Reform: Delivering Stability and Supporting a Sustainable Economy' (14 June 2012) www.gov.uk/government/uploads/system/uploads/attachment_data/file/32556/whitepaper_banking_reform_140512.pdf accessed 18 March 2018.

40   Randell C, 'The Great British Banking Experiment: Will the Restructuring of UK Banking Show Us How to Resolve G-SIFIs?' (2012) 6 *Law and Financial Markets Review* 1 17.

41   Ibid.

42   See HM Treasury, Department for Business Innovation and Skills (n 39), paras. 2.22–2.25 and Annex, 70.

43   Ibid., para. 3.64.

D The Height of the Ring-Fence

7.28 The Banking Reform Act requires the regulator to make rules to ensure that the ring-fenced bank can act independently from the rest of its group while providing services. The Act further specifies the areas in which rules should be made, including holding shares in other corporate entities, entering into contracts with other members of the group, governance of the ring-fenced bank, restricting payments that a ring-fenced bank may make to other members of the group and disclosure. These requirements are designed to ensure that a ring-fenced bank interacts with the rest of its group on a third-party basis, and that it remains legally, economically and operationally independent.

7.29 The relationship between a ring-fenced body and the rest of its corporate group will be governed by rules made by the regulators (Prudential Regulation Authority (PRA) and Financial Conduct Authority (FCA)). The Banking Reform Act requires the regulators to make rules, where reasonably practicable, to ensure that ring-fenced bodies are independent of other group members, and specifies particular areas where rules must be made (e.g. intra-group financial dealings). The precise content of rules will be determined by the regulators.

1 Legal and Operational Links[44]

7.30 The ring-fence shall provide for legal separability in times of financial distress and operational independence at all times. If the ring-fenced activity is carried out in a larger group, the ring-fenced bank must be established as a separate legal entity and is not allowed to hold shares of non-ring-fenced entities. In principle, banking groups remain free to organise their operational structures as they choose. However, if the regulator finds that a group's management information systems, including information technology and employment structures, present a barrier to the separation of a ring-fenced bank and continuous provision of its services, the regulator shall require the group to make appropriate changes to their operations. Moreover, ring-fenced banks should not be permitted to use non-ring-fenced banks to access business-critical UK payment systems and networks.

7.31 The operational independence of the ring-fenced bank is defined according to the following principles: independent capitalisation and funding for any operational subsidiaries; an effective service-level agreement between group entities; the provision of services by operational subsidiaries on an arm's length basis; and operational assets used for critical economic functions should be owned by the operational entity providing those services.

2 Economic Links[45]

7.32 The restrictions on economic links between the ring-fenced bank and other group entities are not as 'high' or as strict as the requirements for legal and operational independence

---

44 Ibid., paras. 2.56–2.60.
45 Ibid., paras. 2.61–2.69.

between the ring-fenced bank and group entities. Indeed, restrictions on economic links have been referred to as semi-permeable to a large extent. In principle, this means there should be few restrictions on the ability of the holding company or other affiliates in the group structure from down-streaming capital to the ring-fenced bank to support it in times of difficulty. On the other hand, safeguards should exist restricting the ability of the ring-fenced bank to upstream or transfer capital or other financial support to the holding company or other group affiliates respectively.[46]

7.33 These restrictions on economic links mean that ring-fenced banks will have to comply with capital and liquidity requirements on a standalone basis. Obviously, limiting economic links necessarily includes regulating internal group exposures as well. The Treasury agreed with the ICB that internal exposures should be treated as if those exposures were between third parties on an arms' length basis. The Capital Requirements Directive IV (CRD IV)[47] governs large exposures within banking groups and sets a cap of 25 per cent of the institution's Tier 1 capital in respect of exposures to other entities in the group.[48] Secondary legislation is likely to govern certain types of intra-group exposures more explicitly (for example, cross-default clauses, intra-group guarantees and netting arrangements) as well as to establish rules on how to ensure that intra-group transactions are disclosed and undertaken under market conditions.

3 Governance and Disclosure[49]

7.34 The independence of a ring-fenced bank must be underpinned by strong governance. The key to independent governance will be: (i) the composition of the board; and (ii) a requirement on board members to act in the interests of the ring-fenced bank (as opposed to the group as a whole) and to protect the ring-fence. The final regulations submitted as secondary legislation recommended that at least half of the board as well as the chair of the ring-fenced bank are independent and that no more than one-third of the ring-fenced bank board may be representatives of the rest of the group. In essence, the latter requirement permits the board members from the rest of the group to have the opportunity to influence a group-wide strategy, while the former requirement would allow the majority of the ring-fenced bank board to veto any strategy that might undermine the ring-fenced bank's future prospects and stability.

7.35 In addition, ring-fenced banks should have their own board committees – providing that independence in selecting the board, in setting a risk appetite for the firm and in setting its pay structures is primarily a matter for the ring-fenced bank. The ICB also suggested that the

---

46   Ibid., paras. 2.60–2.61.
47   Directive 2013/36/EU of the European Parliament and of the Council of 26 June 2013 on access to the activity of credit institutions and the prudential supervision of credit institutions and investment firms, amending Directive 2002/87/EC and repealing Directives 2006/48/EC and 2006/49/EC [2013] OJ L 176/338.
48   Directive 2013/36/EU of the European Parliament and of the Council of 26 June 2013 on access to the activity of credit institutions and the prudential supervision of credit institutions and investment firms, amending Directive 2002/87 EC and repealing Directives 2006/48/EC and 2006/49/EC [2013] OJ L176/338.
49   See generally HM Treasury/BIS (n 42), paras. 2.70–2.74.

boards of the ring-fenced bank and of its parent company should have a duty to maintain the integrity of the ring-fence, and to ensure that the ring-fence principles are followed at all times.[50] In order to strengthen the market signal (as well as to mitigate reputational damage), the ring-fenced bank should be able to demonstrate publicly that it is independent. The precise content and scope of these disclosures that the ring-fenced bank is independent are controversial and will likely be subject to future change through secondary legislation.

7.36 Finally, UK ring-fencing differs from measures to prohibit proprietary trading (such as the Volcker Rule in the US which restricts proprietary trading) under the laws of certain EU Member States in that it does not distinguish between proprietary trading and other economically similar forms of trading such as market-making. All dealing in investments as principal, i.e. on the bank's own balance sheet, is excluded from the UK ring-fence (except where covered by one of the exemptions described earlier), but can be conducted by other entities or subsidiaries within the group.

III THE EU COMMISSION PROPOSAL ON OTHER STRUCTURAL REFORMS

7.37 In 2014, the European Commission proposed a Regulation[51] on structural reform, which was later withdrawn after much debate and criticism.[52] Nevertheless, the Commission's proposal merits discussion in this chapter as a possible model for other countries outside Europe. The Commission's proposal was based on the proposals of the High Level Expert Group chaired by Erkki Liikanen[53] (former Central Bank Governor of Finland), and it followed various structural reforms enacted in the United States (the Volcker Rule), the United Kingdom, France and Germany. The proposed Regulation sought to address the risks from intra-group exposures associated with certain trading activities and to enhance a banking group's resolvability.[54] The Commission proposal stated that: '[t]he separation of trading activities from a deposit-taking entity within a banking group would considerably facilitate bank resolution', and that '[b]etter structured groups make it easier to isolate the problem than when the group structure is opaque'.[55] The draft Regulation intended to

50   See discussion in Independent Commission on Banking (n 14), 72.
51   European Commission, Proposal for a Regulation of the European Parliament and of the Council on 'structural measures improving the resilience of EU credit institutions' (29 January 2014) COM(2014), 43 final https://eur-lex.europa.eu/legal-content/EN/ALL/?uri=CELEX%3A52014PC0043 accessed 21 March 2018.
52   See Annex IV: Withdrawals, point 3 in European Commission, 'Communication from the Commission to the European Parliament, the Council, the European Economic and Social Committee and the Committee of Regions – Commission Working Programme 2018 – An agenda for a more united, stronger and more democratic Europe' and Annexes (24 October 2017) COM (2017), 650 final http://eur-lex.europa.eu/legal-content/EN/TXT/HTML/?uri=CELEX:52017DC0650&from=EN accessed 23 March 2018.
53   The Liikanen Report (n 14).
54   In MEMO/14/64 of 29 January 2014.
55   See European Commission, Memo on 'Structural Measures to Improve the Resilience of EU Credit Institutions – Frequently Asked Questions' http://europa.eu/rapid/press-release_MEMO-14-63_en.htm accessed 21 March 2018.

safeguard core financial activities, such as lending to clients and accepting deposits, by separating them from risky trading activities (i.e. derivatives trading). This separation would also limit the cross-subsidisation of trading activities by retail deposits that are eligible for deposit guarantees. By not being able to transfer capital from retail deposits to the bank's securities trading activities, the retail bank would have an incentive to lend more to the real economy. The Commission's draft Regulation combined two general approaches that were associated with the US Volcker Rule and the EU Liikanen Report, namely: (1) banning specific trading activities defined as proprietary and (2) requiring certain trading activities to be carried out by separated entities. These approaches are outlined below.

A General Ban on Certain Trading Activities

7.38 The US Dodd-Frank Act 2010 contains a general ban on proprietary trading (the Volcker Rule), which applies to any insured US depository institution as well as their controlling companies or affiliates.[56] The US federal regulators have implemented this requirement by defining the scope of the Volcker Rule as subject to extensive conditions. For example, the final regulations contain a list of exempted activities, including risk-mitigating hedging activities,[57] underwriting activities[58] and market-making-related activities.[59]

7.39 The Commission's withdrawn draft Regulation, in contrast, imposed a more narrow ban on proprietary trading and on specific investment transactions that do not qualify as proprietary trading per se.[60] The Commission defined proprietary trading as 'using own capital or borrowed money to take positions in any type of transaction to purchase, sell or otherwise acquire or dispose of any financial instrument or commodities for the sole purpose of making a profit for own account, and without any connection to actual or anticipated client activity or for the purpose of hedging the entity's risk as result of actual or anticipated client activity, through the use of desks, units, divisions or individual traders specifically dedicated to such position taking and profit making'.[61]

7.40 Significantly, the wording of the draft Regulation's ban on proprietary trading, however, did not include underwriting activities, market-making-related activities or transactions to hedge risks resulting from client activity.[62] The draft Regulation further exempted specific trading of commodities from the ban and certain sovereign bonds.[63]

---

56 Federal Deposit Insurance Corporation 12 US Code section1851(a)(1)(A), section1851(h)(1).
57 Ibid., (d). The four US federal regulators have adopted proposed rules to define conditions and exemptions of the Volcker Rule. See SEC Final Rule, 17 CFR section 255.5 – Proprietary Trading and Certain Interests in and Relationships with Covered Funds.
58 Securities and Exchange Commission, SEC Final Rule, 17 CFR section 255.4(a).
59 SEC Final Rule, 17CFR section 255.4(b).
60 Commission Proposal, n 51, Article 6(1)(b).
61 Ibid., (1)(a); Article 5(4).
62 Ibid., Article 5(4).
63 Ibid., Article 6(2)(a) and 6(6).

7.41 The proposed ban on proprietary trading would have applied to EU banks, EU parent banks, their branches and subsidiaries, as well as EU branches of non-EU banks, provided any of these institutions (a) were identified as a global systemically important institution (G-SIIs) under EU banking law[64] or (b) had assets and trading activities exceeding certain limits.[65] An estimated thirty banking groups would have been subject to the draft Regulation's coverage, which included banking groups with a balance sheet size of €30 billion and trading assets exceeding either €70 billion or 10 per cent of total assets for three consecutive years.[66] Moreover, to assist enforcement, financial institution remuneration policies were prohibited from encouraging or rewarding activity involving such proscribed and restricted activities.[67]

B Trading Activities Triggering Separation

7.42 Prior to this proposal, some EU states had already adopted structural reform legislation to address the risks associated with proprietary trading and intra-group exposures that requires some degree of separation between the insured deposit-taking and trading entities or subsidiaries within the financial group structure. It was intended that such structural separation or subsidiarisation within the group would facilitate a resolution of the group if its solvency were threatened and would have allowed public authorities to confine taxpayer support to the retail deposit-taking subsidiary and the inter-bank payment system. Based on other EU state practice, and the Liikanen proposal, two other subsidiarisation approaches could be applied to the separated entity.

1 Subsidiarisation and Ring-Fencing Requirements in National Legislation

7.43 The Liikanen Report proposed a subsidiarisation approach that consisted in allowing proprietary trading only in so far as it is carried out by a legally, economically and operationally separate trading subsidiary, which is then prevented from deposit-taking activities. The structural reform legislation enacted in Germany[68] and France[69] follows this model.

7.44 The German reform legislation applies to 'credit institutions', as defined under Article 4(1)(1) of the Capital Requirements Regulation (CRR),[70] which may only carry out certain trading

---

64   Ibid., 3(1)(a), applying to a Global SIBI under Article 131 of the Capital Requirements Directive IV.
65   Ibid., Article 3(1)(b), namely, when having total assets of at least €30 billion and trading activities exceeding either €70 billion or 10 per cent of total assets for three consecutive years.
66   MEMO/14/64 (n 54).
67   European Commission Proposal (n 51), Article 7.
68   *Gesetz über das Kreditwesen* (KWG; German Banking Act), section 3 and 25f, as amended by the Gesetz zur Abschirmung von Risiken und zur Planung der Sanierung und Abwicklung von Kreditinstituten und Finanz-gruppen vom 7 August 2013.
69   Code Monétaire et Financier (Monetary and Financial Code) Article L511–47ff as amended by the Loi no. 2013–672 du 26 juillet 2013 de Séparation et de Régulation des Activités Bancaires.
70   section 1(3d) KWG and Regulation (EU) No. 575/2013 of the European Parliament and of the Council of 26 June 2013 on prudential requirements for credit institutions and investment firms and amending Regulation (EU) No. 648/2012 [2013] OJ L 176/1.

activities through a legally, economically and operationally separate 'financial trading institution' (*Finanzhandelsinstitut*).[71] The subsidiarisation requirement applies either when
trading activities by the entity or the group exceed certain thresholds,[72] or when the German
regulator deems the trading activities too risky for the credit institution's solvency.[73] In the
former case, the requirement applies to transactions for the institution's own account, which
may only be carried out by the trading subsidiary,[74] while market-making activities[75] and
transactions to hedge client activity[76] are exempted from subsidiarisation; in the latter case,
the requirement imposed by the German regulator applies not only to transactions for own
accounts, but may extend to any financial transaction deemed to entail comparable risks.[77]

7.45 The French reform similarly subjects credit institutions, financial companies and mixed
financial holding companies to a subsidiarisation requirement should their trading activities exceed certain limits, defined further in a Council of State decree.[78] The French regime
defines proprietary trading as financial transactions 'involving' the credit institutions' own
account,[79] but explicitly exempts the provision of investment services to clients,[80]
hedging[81] and market-making activities[82] for which no subsidiarisation is required. Once
subsidiarised, the trading entities are prohibited from providing deposit-taking services.[83]

7.46 In contrast, Belgium adopted legislation in 2014 on the status and supervision of credit
institutions that imposes restrictions on the activities of banking groups and credit

71 Section 25f(1) KWG.
72 Section 3(2)(1)(1) and 3(2)(1)(2) KWG, namely, when trading assets exceed €100 billion for the past
financial year, or when such assets exceed 20 per cent of (at least €90 billion) total assets for the past three
financial years.
73 Section 3(4) KWG.
74 Ibid., (2)(2) KWG.
75 Ibid., (2)(2)(3) KWG.
76 Ibid., (2)(3)(1) KWG.
77 Ibid., (4)(1)(2) KWG. Regardless of whether they entail comparable risks, the regulator may also prohibit
market-making activities (section 3(4)(1)(1) KWG).
78 Code monétaire et financier, Article L511–47(I), supplemented by Article R511–16 created by Council of
State decree number 2014–785 of 8 July 2014.
79 Ibid., (1).
80 Ibid., (1)(a): 'Les activités de négociation sur instruments financiers faisant intervenir leur compte propre, à
l'exception des activités relatives a) *A la fourniture de services d'investissement à la clientèle*' (emphasis added).
81 Ibid., (1)(c) and (IV) stating in part: 'Les activités de négociation sur instruments financiers faisant
intervenir leur compte propre, à l'exception des activités relatives c) A la couverture des risques de l'établissement de crédit ou du groupe . . . à l'exception de la filiale mentionnée au présent article' (coverage of credit risks
of the credit institution or the group . . . except the subsidiary mentioned in this article) and Article L511–47(VI):
'Au sens du présent article, on entend par "couverture" l'activité d'un établissement mentionné au I qui se porte
partie à des opérations sur des instruments financiers dans le but de réduire ses expositions aux risques de toute
nature liés aux activités de crédit et de marché. Les instruments utilisés pour ces opérations de couverture
doivent présenter une relation économique avec les risques identifiés . . .'. (Author's translation: 'coverage'
(hedging) denotes the activity of the institution mentioned in art. L511-47(I) which refers to operations on
financial instruments whose purpose it is to reduce its exposure to risks of all nature related to activities of credit
and market. The instruments used for these operations of coverage must present an economic relationship with
the identified risks.).
82 Code monétaire et financier, Article L511–47(I)(1)(d) and (V).
83 Ibid., Article L511–48(I), second indent.

institutions.[84] The Belgian legislation prohibits credit institutions from conducting proprietary trading, either directly or through Belgian or foreign-controlled subsidiaries. This is known as prohibiting proprietary trading within the bank or banking group's consolidated perimeter. However, some proprietary trading is permitted by the credit institution or by entities or subsidiaries within the credit institution's controlled group perimeter if it is conducted for one of the following reasons: (1) for clients, (2) for market-making purposes, (3) to cover the bank's own risk if necessary to fulfil the bank's role as an intermediary with clients, (4) to achieve sound and prudent liquidity management or (5) long-term holding of financial instruments if these activities are considered necessary to the bank's business plan. Also, credit institutions can transfer their proprietary trading activities to a separate legal entity (i.e. stockbroking firm) outside the bank's controlled consolidation perimeter.

7.47 Commentators have criticised the generally defined nature of these five exceptions as being so broad that they swallow the prohibition itself. Also, banks can circumvent the prohibition by transferring proprietary trading activities to a separate legal entity outside the banking group's controlled perimeter that specialises in trading activities. Although the Belgian law is arguably 'more ambitious' than similar measures adopted in France and Germany, there is criticism that the ban on proprietary trading under Belgian law is watered down by the numerous exceptions. Moreover, since the banks are required to demonstrate that their proprietary trading falls under one of the exceptions, a 'grey zone' of legal uncertainty has arisen because the bank supervisor has the discretion to decide whether the particular credit institution can engage in proprietary trading. This undermines regulatory transparency and legal certainty.[85]

7.48 As discussed above, the UK's ring-fencing approach, in contrast, consists in making the deposit-taking entity a legally, economically and operationally independent entity from the rest of its group,[86] ensuring that it remains unaffected by the activities of other members, especially by their insolvency.[87] The ring-fenced banks are then prohibited from carrying out proprietary trading activities ('dealing in investments as principal').[88]

2 Separation Requirements in the EU Proposal

7.49 The Commission proposal went beyond the Liikanen Report's proposals by linking separation requirements not to proprietary trading (which is subject to an outright ban) but to

84 Ibid., Law of 25 April 2014 on the status and supervision of credit institutions ('l'activité de négociation pour compte propre').
85 Finance Watch, 'The Continuous Fling with Investment Banking', 26 February 2015 www.finance-watch .org/the-continuous-fling-with-investment-banking/ accessed 21 December 2018.
86 HM Treasury, 'Sound Banking: Delivering Reform' (October 2012) para. 2.36 www.gov.uk/government/ uploads/system/uploads/attachment_data/file/211866/icb_banking_reform_bill.pdf accessed 21 March 2018.
87 Financial Services and Markets Act 2000, section 142H(4) as amended by the Financial Services (Banking Reform) Act 2013.
88 Ibid., section 142D(2) as amended by the Financial Services (Banking Reform) Act 2013.

trading activities in general. The proposal defined trading activities in a negative way by specifying what they are not: any activity that does not consist of deposit-taking, lending or other enumerated services.[89]

7.50 The competent supervisory authority would regularly review specific metrics linked to the trading activities of (1) EU banks taking EU-eligible deposits, so-called 'core credit institutions', (2) EU parent banks having deposit-taking banks in their group, and (3) EU branches from non-EU banks.[90] If the metrics exceed certain limits, the authority will need to initiate the separation.[91] Should the metrics remain under the relevant limits, the regulator would have the discretion to decide whether to initiate the separation.[92] Once the separation has been triggered, the trading activities can only be carried out by a group entity that is legally, economically and operationally separate from the deposit-taking bank.[93] Such a trading entity would be prohibited from taking deposit guarantee-eligible deposits or providing retail payment services, except when necessary for the exchange of collateral related to trading activities.[94] Conversely, the deposit-taking bank may then only carry out trading activities for the purpose of prudently managing its capital, liquidity and funding[95] and may continue selling derivative instruments only under certain conditions.[96] The draft Regulation, however, would have allowed the Commission to approve certain structural reforms previously adopted by Member States, including those discussed above in the UK, Belgium, France and Germany.[97]

7.51 In summary, the Commission proposal was not calling for a break-up of European universal banking groups. Universal banks would have continued to serve clients with a broad set of services and financial products. The measures proposed would instead have simplified the way that the too-big-to-fail (TBTF) banks operated and would have facilitated their resolvability. This is partly why, under Article 4(2) of the proposal, the draft Regulation would have allowed the national competent authority (or the European Central Bank) to exempt non-EU subsidiaries of EU banks from the ring-fencing requirements of the proposal (even if the host country had not provided any equivalent ring-fencing rules), as long as a sufficiently robust group-level resolution strategy between the host country and the European Union was in place.

---

89 European Commission Proposal (n 51), Article 8.
90 Ibid., Article 9.
91 Ibid., Article 10(1); the relevant limits will be specified in delegated Acts by the Commission (Article 10(4)).
92 Ibid., Article 10(2). Query the role of the ECB in exercising such discretion to decide which banking group has engaged in excessive risk-taking to justify the ECB to separate certain trading activities.
93 Ibid., Article 13.
94 Ibid., Article 20.
95 Ibid., Article 11.
96 Ibid., Article 12.
97 Ibid., Article 21.

Table 7.1 Comparison of structural regulation requirements of Belgian law and the draft EU Regulation (the latter legislation was withdrawn in 2018)

	Belgium	EU
	Applies to all credit institutions under Belgian law (and subsidiaries)	Applies to European G-SIBs and banks with total assets over €30 billion and trading activities over €80 billion or 10% of total assets
Proprietary trading	Prohibition of proprietary trading with exceptions, including:	Proprietary trading prohibited for G-SIBs and other large credit institutions
	• investment services for customers, market-making, hedging, treasury management, long-term investing	• No exceptions unless threshold not met • Narrow definition. Proprietary trading if: (1) sole purpose is making profit for own account and (2) no link to client activity (actual or anticipated)
	Possibility to transfer/split-off to special entities (stockbroker companies)	

7.52 The Commission's proposal was different from the Belgian legislation because it defined what type of (proprietary) trading was not allowed, whereas the Belgium legislation defined what type of trading is allowed. Moreover, regarding the French and German laws, both structural reforms were part of a broader legislative package that included implementation of bank recovery and resolution regimes (Mise en Place du Régime de Résolution Bancaire and Planung der Sanierung and Abwicklung von Kreditinstituten and Finanzgruppen respectively). Improved resolution was therefore an important objective of these legislative packages; however, resolvability was not expressly mentioned in either country's legislation on structural reform (see Table 7.1).

7.53 That said, it seems that any separation of risky activity is arguably a step towards enhanced resolvability, including the separation rules under both the French and German regimes. Nevertheless, this view is questioned by the Belgian National Bank in its 2013 Report[98] on structural reform, which assesses whether these regimes actually 'improve resolvability'. It states that, in France and Germany, the amount of trading book activity allowed in the banking group is a barrier to improved resolvability – perhaps because the threshold of assets and activity triggering subsidiarisation is too high, or because the definition of proprietary trading requiring subsidiarisation is too narrow. Nevertheless, generally, the European Union approach – both the Commission's former proposal and the UK, French, German and Belgian ring-fencing regimes – view resolvability as an important objective of ring-fencing.

98 See National Bank of Belgium, 'Structural Banking Reforms in Belgium: Final Report' 2 (July 2013) www.nbb.be/doc/ts/publications/NBBReport/2013/StructuralBankingReformsEN.pdf accessed 21 March 2018.

IV THE PROS AND CONS OF STRUCTURAL REFORMS

7.54 The debate over the advantages and disadvantages of structural reforms consists of a wide range of opinions.[99] For the industry and others the reforms are obviously too strict and disproportionate, whilst others view the reforms as inadequate and far-reaching enough in creating a Glass-Steagall-like or narrow banking separation. And yet others believe that regulating the institutional structure will simply lead to other forms of evasion and arbitrage that will allow risks to shift to other parts of the financial system outside of the financial group structure, thereby creating other types of systemic risk presently unperceived by regulators.[100]

A Advantages

7.55 Ring-fencing can enhance resolvability and limit the potential government guarantee. Most commentators agree that there are four main advantages to regulating structure.[101] First, the structure enhances separability, and therefore the resolvability, of financial institutions. It is simpler to transfer the ownership of an existing legal entity than it is to identify from within a large integrated balance sheet all of the retail assets and liabilities and to transfer them. When activities are completely integrated there is also no assurance that individual activities, or groups of activities, will be viable on their own. The key benefit of separation is, thus, that it would make it easier for the authorities to require creditors of failing retail banks, failing wholesale/investment banks, or both, to bear losses, instead of the taxpayer. The evident transparency of the entire regime to all creditors would substantially reduce any expectation by market participants that they would be bailed out and, thus, reduce perceived government guarantees. More generally, ring-fencing may also improve market discipline because of a greater degree of transparency around the financial resources available to each business line.

7.56 Second, different activities may enjoy different levels of perceived government guarantee. Retail deposit-taking, at one extreme, is partially backed by explicit insurance, while proprietary trading of financial instruments is not justified in receiving a government guarantee or other taxpayer support. Combining financial activities in a single entity makes it harder for the authorities to treat each activity differently in resolution while extending the scope of perceived government guarantees to activities that would ordinarily not merit protection. Importantly, separation would also allow the authorities to distinguish between creditors of the retail bank and creditors of other entities in the banking group in a way that they cannot do if activities are conducted in the same legal entity.

7.57 Third, structural change could help to address a time inconsistency problem in addressing the TBTF problem – authorities in the heat of a crisis will always face enormous pressure to

---

99   Ibid.
100   Thiessen R, *Are EU Banks Safe?* (Eleven International Publishing 2014), 169–170.
101   See Independent Commission on Banking (n 14), 9 and paras. 2.25 and 4.78–4.80.

support banks despite the negative consequences this has for moral hazard. Separating retail banks, where the political pressure will always be greatest, from other activities should help to alter the incentives of the authorities so that they are less likely to support these other activities.

7.58 Fourth, ring-fencing reduces complexity as well as the single entity's size, which again enhances supervision, resolvability and market discipline by providing more than an 'all-or-nothing' option for the authorities.[102] Indeed, Sir John Vickers, former Chairman of the British Independent Commission on Banking, observed that a ring-fence could help reduce this risk, but not necessarily because retail banking is less risky than wholesale or investment banking. Rather, ring-fencing allows the authorities to maintain the continuous provision of retail services through resolution of a smaller and simpler entity. Similarly, Erkki Liikanen argued that '[s]eparation of these activities into separate legal entities is the most direct way of tackling banks' complexity and interconnectedness'. And as separation would make banking groups 'simpler and more transparent, it would also facilitate market discipline and supervision and, ultimately, recovery and resolution'.[103]

B Disadvantages

7.59 On the other hand, ring-fencing can result in arbitrage and shifting much of the riskiest bank behaviour off-balance sheet and away from supervisory scrutiny. This could create the opportunity for many under-regulated non-bank financial firms (for example, asset management firms) to take on much of the trading that European banks are beginning to shift off their balance sheets to comply with stricter bank capital regulations and structural reforms.[104] Moreover, the fundamental assumption of the ring-fencing policy is that investment banking activities are riskier as well as less beneficial to social welfare (and, thus, also less worthy of protection) than more traditional retail banking activities. Not surprisingly many arguments in favour of ring-fencing are an indirect form of critique on the pre-crisis behaviour and the disproportionate role that certain high-risk investment banking activity had come to play in the economy.[105] This critique, however, fails to take account fully of the important synergies and economies of scale and scope that the provision of universal banking services provides for the economy in the form of lower cost provision of retail financial services and risk mitigation for the bank itself in offering a broader range of products and services.

102   Ibid., para. 4.63.
103   The Liikanen Report (n 14), 100.
104   See PricewaterhouseCoopers, 'Asset Management 2020: A Brave New World' (2014) www.pwc.com/gx/en/asset-management/publications/pdfs/pwc-asset-management-2020-a-brave-new-world-final.pdf accessed 22 March 2018.
105   See Wolf M, 'Why Curbing Finance is Hard To Do' (*Financial Times* Opinion, 22 October 2009) www.ft.com/content/0a8a6362-bf3d-11de-a696-00144feab49a accessed 22 March 2018 and Kay K, '"Too Big To Fail" is Too Dumb an Idea to Keep' (*Financial Times* Opinion, 27 October 2009) www.ft.com/content/375f4528-c330-11de-8eca-00144feab49a accessed 22 March 2018.

V DOES THE EU RESOLUTION REGIME MAKE RING-FENCING UNNECESSARY?

7.60 The UK Banking Act 2013 and the Commission's proposed Regulation (which was withdrawn in 2018) emphasised the importance of the ring-fencing requirement as a tool to enhance the resolvability of large complex banking organisations. Ring-fencing is potentially beneficial to bank resolution in two ways. First, it may make post bail-in restructuring easier to execute because of the transparency of the group's ring-fenced structure that allows bail-in to be imposed on the group's investment banking liabilities before being applied to the liabilities of the retail bank. Second, it may provide for fall-back options for the resolution authority where losses are greater than the gone concern loss-absorbing capacity (GLAC) of the holding company (although any fall-back measure is likely to be disruptive and disorderly).

7.61 First, ring-fencing can facilitate post-bail-in restructuring by providing separability between core business lines and functions that are conducted by the ring-fenced bank (RFB) against those tasks and functions that are conducted by the non-ring-fenced bank (NRFB). The effectiveness of the separability will depend on ring-fencing delivering some or all of the following in respect of the degree of separation between the RFB and the NRFB.

1. the RFB and NRFB should not depend on each other operationally (for example, they should depend on a separate group service company);
2. they do not book risk onto each other's balance sheets;
3. they each have distinct franchise value and client relationships;
4. they each have stand alone access to financial market infrastructures, including payment and settlement systems; and
5. they have distinct and separate human resource and governance arrangements.

7.62 These considerations, however, are not unique to banks subject to ring-fencing; there are ways to deliver these outcomes without ring-fencing; and post-bail-in restructuring may require splitting business lines and functions within either the RFB or the NRFB, in which case ring-fencing may not be helpful.

7.63 Second, resolution authorities may also find ring-fencing beneficial because it provides fall-back options where losses are greater than the gone concern loss-absorbing capacity (GLAC) of the banking group's holding company. For instance, if losses are greater than GLAC at holding company level, but losses are confined to either the RFB or NRFB, ring-fencing may be beneficial in two ways: by insulating or, in certain circumstances, transferring to a bridge bank, or a private sector purchaser (PSP), the non-loss generating part of the group; and in respect of bailing-in operating liabilities of the loss-generating part of the group (whether the RFB or the NRFB), it should be relatively less disruptive to bail-in operating liabilities of either the RFB or the NRFB than to bail-in those operating liabilities had both the RFB and NRFB functions been conducted via a single legal entity. Both these options, however, are likely to be highly disruptive and disorderly. In addition, ring-fencing is unlikely to deliver standalone viability of either the RFB or NRFB (where the other part of the group is failing), although meeting the separability conditions listed above should help.

7.64 Where losses are spread more evenly across both the RFB and NRFB, ring-fencing may not deliver much in the way of fall-back resolution options. But ring-fencing may reduce the likelihood that both the RFB and NRFB are simultaneously loss making (for example, because of reduced cross-booking of risk, distinct management or governance arrangements, and higher capital and leverage ratio requirements for the RFB).

7.65 On the other hand, the single point of entry (SPE) resolution process itself can achieve the key outcomes that ring-fencing was designed to achieve.[106] Notably, SPE ensures continuity of core retail functions, along with all other critical functions in a group (whether they are located in the RFB, NRFB or other parts of the group); and by reducing the TBTF subsidy for a bank as a whole, it achieves the same outcome as trying to reduce, through ring-fencing, the TBTF subsidy derived from the integration of the wholesale and investment banking businesses with the retail bank business (where the retail business is deemed TBTF). Furthermore, it is highly doubtful whether these outcomes could be been by ring-fencing alone, i.e. without a credible, group-wide resolution strategy.

7.66 In addition, ring-fencing may also have certain second order benefits for resolution. For instance, the transfer of debt from the bank operating company to the holding company may become cheaper if the operating company is separated into an RFB and NRFB entity. Such separation may also simplify collateral arrangements, therefore making liquidity provision to the RFB more manageable if the rest of the group or other entities in the group are in resolution.

7.67 Finally, in the European Union, the efficacy of any Member State's structural regulation regime can be called into question if the primary purpose of structural regulation is to facilitate banking group resolution. This is because the Bank Recovery and Resolution Directive[107] (BRRD) provides broad powers for resolution authorities to require banks or banking groups to change their organisational structure if the authority determines *ex ante* that the bank as an institution or the banking group's structure is a substantial impediment to a feasible and credible resolution of the institution or banking group.[108] Under Article 17(5) of the BRRD, the resolution authority is empowered to conduct a resolvability

---

106 See Federal Deposit Insurance Corporation and Bank of England, 'Resolving Globally Active, Systemically Important, Financial Institutions', joint paper by the Federal Deposit Insurance Corporation and the Bank of England (10 December 2012) www.fdic.gov/about/srac/2012/gsifi.pdf accessed 22 March 2018.
107 Directive 2014/59/EU of the European Parliament and of the Council of 15 May 2014 establishing a framework for the recovery and resolution of credit institutions and investment firms and amending Council Directive 82/891/EEC, and Directives 2001/24/EC, 2002/47/EC, 2004/25/EC, 2005/56/EC, 2007/36/EC, 2011/35/EU, 2012/30/EU and 2013/36/EU, and Regulations (EU) No. 1093/2010 and (EU) No. 648/2012, of the European Parliament and of the Council [2014] OJ L 173/190 (BRRD).
108 Ibid., Article 17(5).

assessment to identify whether or not there are substantial impediments to the implementation of a credible and feasible resolution plan. If the authority determines that there are substantial impediments to the implementation of the plan, it may order the institution to remove the impediments, including changing its organisational structure or business activities. Indeed, this could involve changes to the legal, operational and financial structure of the institution or the group itself and their business activities. In ordering the removal of such organisational impediments, Article 17 of the BRRD sets out procedural and substantive rules about how the institution or group can be required to reduce or remove these impediments.

7.68 Articles 15 and 16 of the BRRD provide that the resolution authority must consult the competent supervisory authority when it determines whether or not there are substantial impediments to the resolvability of a firm.[109] The resolution authority is required to notify the firm in writing of any substantial impediments they have identified, and the firm or group will have the opportunity to address these concerns and propose measures to eliminate these impediments. Article 17(5) of the BRRD provides that if the firm's or group's proposals are considered inadequate, the resolution authority will have the power to take specific actions that address or remove the impediments to resolvability.[110] In selecting the appropriate measure to remove them, resolution authorities have wide discretion to choose a measure based on the nature of the impediments. These measures can be classified in three categories – structural, financial and information-related, or data management.

7.69 Under Article 17(8) of the BRRD, the European Banking Authority has developed guidelines specifying further details on the measures and the circumstances in which each measure may be applied in order to support a consistent application of such measures by Member States.[111] And Article 85 of the BRRD requires that there is a right of appeal against a decision to take a crisis prevention measure,[112] which includes a requirement to remove impediments to resolvability.

7.70 Similarly, the Single Resolution Mechanism Regulation[113] (SRMR) for the Member States participating in the Banking Union requires the Single Resolution Board (SRB) to draw up resolution plans after consultation with the national competent authorities (including the

---

109 Ibid., Article 15 applies this requirement to individual credit or investment institutions and Article 16 applies the requirement to banking groups subject to consolidated supervision.

110 Ibid., Article 17(5).

111 European Banking Authority, 'Guidelines on the Specification of Measures to Reduce or Remove Impediments to Resolvability and the Circumstances in which Each Measure May Be Applied under Directive 2014/59/EU' (19 December 2014) www.eba.europa.eu/documents/10180/933988/EBA-GL-2014-11+%28Guidelines+on+Impediments+to+Resolvability%29.pdf/d3fa2201-e21f-4f3a-8a67-6e7278fee473 accessed 22 March 2018.

112 See BRRD, Article 2(1)(101) (defining what a 'crisis prevention measure' is that can be challenged on appeal).

113 Regulation (EU) No. 806/2014 of the European Parliament and of the Council of 15 July 2014 establishing uniform rules and a uniform procedure for the resolution of credit institutions and certain investment firms in the framework of a Single Resolution Mechanism and a Single Resolution Fund and amending Regulation (EU) No. 1093/2010 (2014) OJ L 225/1.

European Central Bank) and national resolution authorities (including the group resolution authority). Article 10(11) of the SRMR is equivalent to Article 17(5) of the BRRD in so far as the SRB, when drafting and revising the resolution plan, shall identify any material impediments to resolvability and, based on the EU legal principles of necessity and proportionality, propose relevant measures to the resolution authorities to address those impediments.[114] The SRB can then require the relevant national resolution authority to take specific measures to require the institution to remove the impediments to resolvability if the institution can potentially draw on funds from the Single Resolution Fund.[115]

7.71 Based on these provisions of the BRRD and SRMR, the *raison d'être* of the Commission's structural regulation proposal can be called into question because if the primary purpose of the draft Regulation was to facilitate bank recovery and resolution by proposing or permitting a particular set of *ex ante* organisational structures for banking groups, then the utility of this proposal is substantially undermined by empowering Member State resolution authorities with broad discretionary powers to require banking groups to reorganise themselves or change their institutional structures in any way (subject to the EU legal principle of proportionality) that the resolution authority believes is necessary to promote a more effective resolution of the banking group during times of distress. These substantial powers for resolution authorities certainly raise questions about the need for any EU legislation permitting or disallowing, *ex ante*, particular organisational structures for banks and banking groups and were probably the ultimate reason why the Commission withdrew its structural regulation proposal.

CONCLUSION

7.72 The global financial crisis has led several jurisdictions to propose legislation to regulate the organisational structure of banks and banking groups. This chapter analysed the UK's ring-fencing regime as set forth in the Banking Reform Act 2013, which focuses on protecting ring-fenced retail banking from excessively risky trading in other parts of the banking group. Second, the chapter considered the European Commission's 2014 structural regulation proposal and compared it with similar legislative initiatives in France, Germany and Belgium. Although the European Commission's proposed Regulation aimed to limit risky trading and related activities in banking groups, EU states eventually withdrew the proposal because of the view that it would hinder the ability of resolution authorities to require certain organisational structures to support bank resolution planning. The chapter finally addressed the question of whether structural reform or ring-fencing may hinder the effectiveness of bank resolution regimes and what can be done to enhance coordination between both frameworks.

---

114 Ibid., Article 10(11).
115 Ibid.

7.73 Moreover, Article 17(5) of the BRRD and Article 10(11) of the SRMR provide that the resolution authority can decide that a bank's or banking group's organisational structure is an impediment to the feasible and credible implementation of its resolution powers, thereby justifying a demand by the resolution authority that the bank or group change its organisational structure. Although these legislative measures have the aim of improving the resolvability of banks and depositor protection and limiting excessive risk-taking, they may also have the unintended effect of reducing the economic benefits of risk diversification and limiting financial product offerings that universal banks have traditionally provided to their customers. Moreover, the various limitations and prohibitions on bank trading will probably not lead to a reduction of harmful risk-taking in the financial sector, but to a shift of risk-taking away from the banking sector (where it can be monitored by supervisors) to under-regulated areas of the financial system. The experience of the US savings loan crisis of the 1980s, and later the collapse of the British banks Northern Rock, Bradford and Bingley and Alliance and Leicester suggest that banking crises can arise from poor under-writing and weak regulation in traditional bank lending and not from risky securities and derivatives trading. All of this should call for caution in considering proposals for structural regulation of the EU banking sector that have as a primary focus the limitation of excessive bank risk-taking in securities and derivatives trading.

7.74 Finally, other proposals for structural regulation should be mentioned in brief. Guynn and Kenadjian (2014) advocate that structural solutions should be complementary to other more targeted measures (i.e. higher capital requirements) and more targeted solutions should be promoted in order to ensure financial stability. Also, Goodhart (2014) appears to regard ring-fenced solutions with some scepticism and instead argues for higher capital require-ments of up to 15 per cent, including a higher core equity Tier 1 ratio, supported by a ladder of administrative sanctions when capital levels fall beneath 15 per cent subject to counter-cyclical adjustment.

QUESTIONS

1. What is the Volcker Rule?
2. What is ring-fenced banking?
3. Will ring-fenced banking solve the too-big-to-fail problem?
4. How is structural regulation related to bank resolution?
5. Besides the UK, discuss the structural regulation approaches of other countries.

Further Reading

Brea VLEC, *The Legal Structure of Commercial Banks and Financial Regulation: Does Organizational Form Matter?* (Erasmus University, Rotterdam, PhD dissertation 2017)

Busch D and van Rijn MBJ, 'Towards Single Supervision and Resolution of Systemically Important Non-Bank Financial Institutions in the European Union', *European Business Organisation Law Review* (March 2018) (Springer)

Chow TS and Surti J, 'Making Banks Safer: Can Volcker and Vickers Do It?' (2011) IMF Working Paper WP 11/236 www.imf.org/en/Publications/WP/Issues/2016/12/31/Making-Banks-Safer-Can-Volcker-and-Vickers-Do-it-25289 accessed 18 December 2018

ECB Working Paper Series, 'Commercial Bank Failures during the Great Recession: The Real (Estate) Story', Macroprudential Research Network, Working Paper No. 1779/ April 2015

Goodhart CAE, 'The Optimal Financial Structure', March 2013, LSE Financial Markets Group Paper Series

Guynn RD and Kenadjian PS, 'Structural Solutions: Blinded by Volcker, Vickers, Liikanen, Glass Steagall and Narrow Banking' (November 2014), in *Too Big to Fail III: Structural Reform Proposals – Should We Break Up the Banks?*, edited by Kenadjian PS and Dombret A (March 2015), Institute for Law and Finance Series

Huertas TF, 'Six Structures in Search of Stability' (July 2015), Special Paper No. 236, LSE Financial Markets group paper series

Lehmann M, 'Volcker Rule, Ring-Fencing or Separation of Bank Activities: Comparison of Structural Reform Acts Around the World', LSE Law Society and Economy Working Papers 25/2014, London School of Economics and Political Science, Law Department

UK Independent Commission on Banking, Final Report, September 2011, the Vickers Report

Viñals J, Pazarbasioglu C, Surti J, Narain N, Erbenova M and Chow J, 'Creating a Safer Financial System: Will the Volcker, Vickers and Liikanen Structural Measures Help?' (May 2013) IMF Staff Discussion Note www.imf.org/~/media/Websites/IMF/imported-full-text-pdf/external/pubs/ft/sdn/2013/_sdn1304.ashx accessed 20 December 2018

8

Bank Mis-Selling

Table of Contents

INTRODUCTION

8.1 The financial crisis and ensuing economic slowdown resulted in many legal and regulatory claims against banking institutions by their customers and third parties for mis-selling financial products and rendering inadequate advice and disclosure regarding their risks. The pre-crisis approach to regulating the marketing, sale and distribution of financial products was based on the notion that the disclosure of more information was adequate for retail investors to assess the expected returns and risks of different financial products and investments. The regulatory focus on mandatory disclosure of information imposed few, if any, *ex ante* limits on the offer and design of financial products. There were largely no constraints on selling processes and on the design and distribution of financial products. Banks and other intermediaries were encouraged to know their customers to support their business strategy of selling more innovative products and investments designed to allow their customers exposure to the potential gains of liberalised financial markets, yet exposing them as well to the downside risks of these volatile and unpredictable markets.

8.2   The crisis demonstrated, however, that many retail, professional and wholesale institutional investors had failed to understand the risks associated with complex financial products and that investor reliance on mandatory regulatory disclosure was inadequate for investors to understand and assess the relevant risks. Huge losses by large numbers of customers and professional investors were attributed in part to cognitive heuristics; that is, reliance on 'rule of thumb' approaches to deciding which products to purchase, rather than formal techniques of risk assessment. Moreover, bank and investment firm governance was too weak to address the incentives of brokers and customer advisers who were incentivised to promote 'tied' products that paid disproportionately high commissions or 'retrocessions' that were usually not disclosed to the customer.

8.3   This chapter analyses the law and regulation of bank mis-selling. It discusses how the main rationale for regulating the sale of financial products has evolved in response to the crisis. It also considers the main legal and regulatory principles that apply across major market economies, with a particular focus on the European Union and the main principles of contract and tort law that apply to the sale of financial products by banks. The English common law principles will attract close attention because English law is often the choice of law of many banks and financial institutions for the sale of financial products. The chapter will analyse how English courts have interpreted bank civil liability for alleged mis-selling of financial products. Generally, at common law, liability rules tend to favour banks and impose a heavy burden on investors and customers to prove breach of any statutory, common law or fiduciary duties. A major hurdle for a claimant bank customer to overcome is to show that the bank owed it a duty of care in the sale of a product or the rendering of advice regarding the risks associated with the bank's products and investments. For example, English common law (and other common law jurisdictions) generally allows a bank and its customer to contract out of the duty of care, resulting in an arm's length relationship between the bank and the customer in which the bank has no obligation to inform or advise its client, nor to reveal any of the risks associated with its product nor to assess the suitability of its customer for the products it sells. Without a duty of care, the bank merely has an obligation not to make explicit material misrepresentations to its customers regarding its products.

8.4 The chapter will also analyse how UK financial regulation has applied principles of regulatory law to give bank customers additional legal protections against banks which have sold them questionable financial products. It suggests that regulatory law should be utilised more by jurisdictions seeking to provide additional protections for bank customers who have been mis-sold financial products and for whom private law remedies in contract and tort are inadequate. Although the courts of other jurisdictions (e.g. civil law jurisdictions such as Germany) make it much more difficult for banks to contract out of the duty of care, bank customers still find it very difficult to prevail in claims for mis-selling against banks. As a result, the European Union has adopted legislation to strengthen the regulatory laws of Member States that require banks to review the design of financial products and assess the suitability of retail and professional customers for certain financial products. The main legislation considered in this chapter will be the Markets in Financial Instruments Directive II (MiFID II). It also discusses generally the draft legislation proposed by the European Commission to create a collective redress regime for bank customers and investors who were mis-sold financial products in violation of EU consumer protection laws. The chapter concludes that regulatory law has an important role to play in re-balancing the legal relationship between banks and their customers concerning the sale and distribution of financial products and that the principle of treating customers fairly should be applied more robustly by regulators.

I INFORMATION DISCLOSURE PARADIGM

8.5 Prior to the crisis, regulators deemed bank customers to be 'well-informed' investors who could make rational, wealth-maximising investment decisions. The rational investor was empowered by the information that was disclosed to them by financial intermediaries and issuers to make efficient and wealth-maximising investments. Most consumer or retail financial regulation was based on the assumptions of neo-liberal classical theory, which held that investors are rational agents who seek to maximise their wealth by allocating their investments according to their risk appetites to obtain the highest risk-adjusted return.[1] Based on this assumption of the rational wealth-maximising investor, policymakers designed a model of retail or consumer financial regulation that was based on more and relevant information disclosure for investors to make their own rational calculations and assessments of risk to fit their unique circumstances. Despite widespread dissemination of information to the customers of financial institutions, there were many instances of systematic and intentional mis-selling of financial products and related investment services by institutions and their brokers in the 1990s and 2000s. Systematic and widespread mis-selling continued post-crisis despite the adoption of extensive international and EU regulatory reforms.

---

1 Kingsford Smith D and Dixon O, 'The Consumer Interest and the Financial Markets', in Moloney N, Ferran E and Payne J (eds), *The Oxford Handbook of Financial Regulation* (Oxford University Press 2015), 707.

8.6 This led policymakers and regulators in many countries to adopt alternative theories of regulation that are based on behavioural finance models, which emphasise the bounded rationality or capability barriers of investors. These models hold that the rationality of investors is bounded because of the complexity and inherent asymmetric information barriers in financial markets and that investors often do not act rationally in their best interests and are subject to irrational behaviour, such as herding, that can lead to more volatile and lower investment returns over time.[2]

8.7 Other regulators have emphasised the importance of financial literacy, defined as 'awareness, knowledge, skill, attitude and behaviour necessary to make sound financial decisions'.[3] Studies suggest that financial literacy is very low among most retail financial customers. The crisis demonstrated that many retail, professional and wholesale institutional investors had failed to understand the risks associated with complex financial products and that investor reliance on mandatory regulatory disclosure was inadequate for them to understand and assess the relevant risks. Huge losses by large numbers of customers and professional investors were attributed in part to cognitive heuristics; that is, reliance on 'rule of thumb' approaches to deciding which products to purchase, rather than formal techniques of risk assessment. Behavioural bias, including overconfidence, risk tolerance, social influence and framing effects (highlighting positive features, downplaying potential losses) proved to be a significant influence on the investments and financial products subscribed to by many bank customers and investors.

8.8 The European Commission recognised these market failings in a 2011 Decision that attributed the systematic mis-selling of financial products by financial institutions, and the massive losses of institutional and retail investors to market failures, to information asymmetry and agency costs and to behavioural biases and cognitive heuristics. The Commission's Decision in Retail Investment Services[4] stated that retail investors in the EU struggled to make optimal investment decisions; that they were influenced by behavioural weaknesses, and that the efficacy of disclosure requirements was very much dependent on the context of the markets in which decisions were made. Other market failures identified by the Commission included retail customer confusion, very limited searching for information, difficulties in processing conflict of interest disclosure and heavy reliance on trust in investment advice.[5] The result was that, pre- and post-crisis, despite the adoption of

---

2 See Shiller R, *Irrational Exuberance* (Princeton University Press 2000), 14–17. See also Armour J, et al., *Principles of Financial Regulation* (Oxford University Pres, 2016) 255, discussing rationales for financial product regulation including information for consumer choice and the behaviour or conduct of selling firms.
3 Organisation for Economic Co-operation and Development, International Network on Financial Education, 'Measuring Financial Literacy: Questionnaire and Guidance Notes for Conducting an Internationally Comparable Survey of Financial Literacy' (OECD financial literacy questionnaire 2011), 3 www.oecd.org/finance/financial-education/49319977.pdf accessed 21 December 2018.
4 Chater N, Huck S and Inderst R, 'Consumer Decision-Making in Retail Investment Services: A Behavioural Economics Perspective' Final Report to the European Commission/SANCO (November 2010) www.ec.europa.eu/consumers/financial_services/reference_studies_documents/docs/consumer_decision-making_in_retail_investment_services_-_final_report_en.pdf accessed 21 February 2018.
5 Ibid.

extensive regulatory reforms, such massive mis-selling of financial products – both to retail and sophisticated investors – was endemic to the markets.

8.9 For many countries, the pre-crisis approach to regulating the marketing of financial products was based on the information paradigm that imposed few, if any, *ex ante* limits on the offer and design of investment products. Moreover, there were largely no constraints on selling processes and how products were distributed. Banks and other intermediaries were encouraged to know their customers and to support their business strategy of selling more and innovative and risky financial products designed to allow their customers exposure to the potential gains of liberalised financial markets, while also allowing them to assess the risks of managing and hedging the accompanying risks themselves.

II PRE-CRISIS REGULATORY FRAMEWORK

8.10 The implementation of the information disclosure paradigm was a fundamental assumption in the adoption of legislation to promote the liberalisation of financial markets in many market-based economies. This was particularly true in the European Union, where the EU Council of Ministers adopted a Decision at Lisbon in June 1999 that approved the Financial Services Action Plan (FSAP). The FSAP consisted of over forty pieces of EU legislation to support the EU internal market for financial services and to make European financial markets more competitive and innovative in order to compete globally, particularly with US capital markets.

8.11 The sale of financial products by banks was governed by the Markets in Financial Instruments Directive I (MiFID I 2004/39/EC 2004). Legally in force since 2007, MiFID I contained the overarching principle of best execution and applied to investment services and trading venues, including official exchanges and multilateral trading facilities (MTFs). MiFID I also contained the important objective of investor protection and was regarded as a milestone in the EU's regulation of financial markets. MiFID I set out specific provisions for harmonising the regulation of investment services across the EU by guaranteeing a minimum level of investor and financial consumer protection. It also contained the important objective of protecting the customers of banks and other financial firms in the purchase of certain financial products. For example, Article 19(2) MiFID I required that information addressed to clients, including marketing communications, should be fair, clear and not misleading.[6]

8.12 Regarding the distribution of financial products, banks and other financial intermediaries were required to disclose the risks to clients, but there was no obligation for firms to advise clients. Investors were expected to assume the risks based on information and guidance

---

6   Article 27(2–8) of the MiFID I Implementation Directive (Commission Directive 2006/73/EC of 10 August 2006) defines the requirements for marketing communications with respect to the obligation under Article 19(2) of MiFID I.

provided. Furthermore, it was relatively straightforward for a bank or other firm to reclassify customers as professional clients who were not subject to heightened disclosure of risks standards or to any type of duty of care from the selling institution. Although MiFID I addressed conduct of business concerns in the sale of financial products (including marketing, disclosure and suitability requirements), there were inadequate controls regarding conflict of interests, product design and order execution. Moreover, the widespread and pervasive nature of mis-selling of financial products in most EU states following MiFID I's implementation deadline of January 2007 suggests that most Member States and some firms failed to implement it adequately into domestic law and regulation.[7] For instance, a 2011 study on the implementation of MiFID I found that firms gathered insufficient information on clients' backgrounds and abilities to invest; that firms focused more on the amount of the potential investment rather than on due diligence; and that investment advice provided was largely based on superficial information.[8]

8.13   Between 2005 and 2010, the gaps and weaknesses of the EU approach to regulating retail investor protection that relied primarily on a disclosure paradigm were becoming more apparent as episodes of mis-selling were growing more common across Europe. Moreover, the impact of the global financial crisis of 2008 further exposed weaknesses in consumer financial protection in many other jurisdictions outside the European Union. Serious financial market risks for retail financial clients were caused in part by financial institutions engaging in regulatory arbitrage due to the sectoral approach to regulation. Under MiFID and other EU legislation governing the sale of insurance and more complex financial products, there were very limited regulatory powers for product intervention, and ambiguities and gaps in EU legislation allowed Member State regulators to engage in light touch regulation along with passive supervision which allowed banks to avoid investor safeguards. Despite the reforms brought about by MiFID I and other EU legislation (i.e. the Insurance Mediation Directive), the crisis demonstrated weaknesses in EU regulation of financial product distribution and the disclosure of risks. The crisis and its aftermath resulted in massive losses for retail customers and investors, which were exacerbated by systematic mis-selling practices that understated the risks for retail investors but were very profital for the banks and other institutions which sold them.

8.14   Persistent mis-selling was also demonstrated during the transition from MiFID I to MiFID II.[9] Indeed, some of the more egregious mis-selling practices in the sale of structured products and proprietary products (particularly in Spain) and of complex interest rate hedging products (particularly in the UK) were designed to shore up financial institutions' balance sheets by generating more profits during the post-crisis economic slowdown and to

---

7   See discussion below of massive mis-selling of financial products by UK banks between 2008 and 2013, and Kupšys K, 'The Index-linked Bond Case involving Luminor (ex. DNB) is Referred to the Court of Justice of the European Union' (press release, sazininga-bankininkyste, 2017).
8   See Moloney N, *EU Securities and Financial Markets Regulation* (3rd edn, Oxford University Press 2014), 795.
9   Ibid., 805.

offset some of the costs associated with compliance with new prudential regulatory requirements, such as the Basel III Capital Accord.

8.15 In the UK, structured products that were guaranteed by the US investment bank Lehman Brothers were sold based on significant advice failures and serious disclosure deficiencies. The UK Financial Services Authority (FSA) brought numerous enforcement actions;[10] and the German regulator *Bundesanstalt für Finanzdienstleistungsaufsicht* (BaFin) brought actions against banks and investment firms in relation to the marketing and sale of Lehman debt certificates.[11] Across other states, regulators brought many mis-selling actions, complaints were filed with Ombudsmen services, and alternative dispute resolution methods were frequently used in many states to address major mis-selling problems that were exacerbated because of substantial losses which materialised during the crisis.[12]

8.16 In addition, other regulatory weaknesses associated with mis-selling included the vulnerability of the investment product distribution market to market failures derived from the dominance of complex packaged products such as household investments; the persistent conflict of interest risk arising from the '*financial supermarket*' model or commission-based adviser business model; proliferation of complex products; incomplete disclosure; and the limited ability of investors to understand complex products.[13]

8.17 The predominant approach for most countries was process-based, quality-of-advice rules which struggled to ensure that customers had adequate information and were offered suitable products. Also, regulatory arbitrage was a problem, as MiFID I principles and rules did not apply to insurance-based investment products or deposit-based investment products. Bank governance was too weak to address the incentives of brokers and customer advisers who were incentivised to promote *tied* products, which paid disproportionately high commissions or *retrocessions*, which were usually not disclosed to the customer and were designed to generate related revenue streams to increase profits for financial institutions following their huge losses during the crisis.[14] Arbitrage also arose from segmentation and classification of investors and products.[15] The financial crisis revealed the great

10 Financial Supervisory Authority, 'FSA Takes Action to Help Investors with Lehman-Backed Structured Products' (press release, FSA/PN/144/2009) (27 October 2009) www.fsa.gov.uk/pages/Library/Communication/PR/2009/144.shtml accessed 21 February 2018.

11 Hopper M and Buckingham P, 'A Changing Landscape: Regulatory Developments in the Distribution of Retail Investment Products' Herbert Smith Freehills key issues and themes, Herbert Smith Gleiss Lutz Stibbe 2010) www.lexology.com/library/detail.aspx?g=9833fe22-38b4-4b83-a8b9-e30341b8e0fc accessed 20 December 2018.

12 European Commission, Commission Staff Working Paper 'Executive Summary of the Impact Assessment Accompanying the Document: Proposal for a Directive of the European Parliament and of the Council on Markets in Financial Instruments [Recast] and the Proposal for a Regulation of the European Parliament and of the Council on Markets in Financial instruments' (SEC (2011) 1226 final, European Commission, 20 October 2011) www.ec.europa.eu/internal_market/securities/docs/isd/mifid/SEC_2011_1227_en.pdf accessed 21 February 2018.

13 Moloney (n 8), 788.

14 Ibid.

15 Ibid.

risks for customers – regardless of whether they were wholesale or retail investors – without adequate market experience, who were allowed to invest in complex financial products by accessing the products on the wholesale market.

III UK MIS-SELLING AND CASE LAW

8.18 The United Kingdom provides an exceptional case study of how an EU Member State can implement the requirements of EU financial legislation, such as MiFID I, into its domestic law and regulatory framework, yet still suffer from a massive and widespread mis-selling crisis instigated largely because of weak governance practices in financial firms, light touch supervisory practices and inadequate enforcement action by the regulator. Customer complaints for mis-selling against UK banks and financial services firms received much attention during the pre- and post-crisis periods, especially following the British banking crisis of 2007–2008.

8.19 Under English common law, all banks that sell financial products and services to clients and customers are generally subject to a *duty of care* in the sale of these products and services. The duty of care, however, is subject to limitations imposed by the principle of freedom of contract (*contractual estoppel*), which allows the parties in the contractual agreement to dispense with the duty of care, resulting in a *caveat emptor* (buyer beware) relationship between the bank and its customer. Parties are free to negotiate their own terms, which are generally upheld by the courts to ensure commercial certainty and that a bank does not generally owe a duty of care to its customers to advise on the merits of transactions unless it has expressly undertaken to do so – in which case the bank would be required to advise with reasonable care and skill.[16] In *Thornbridge Limited* v. *Barclays Bank PLC*, the court ruled that a bank does not have a duty of care to advise a customer on the merits of a transaction unless it has undertaken to do so. *Thornbridge* also reaffirms a strict application of the doctrine of *contractual estoppel*, so that a bank customer that has signed an undertaking that it has not received advice from a bank on a particular transaction cannot later sue the bank for negligent advice, even if the latter in fact had rendered erroneous advice or information about the transaction.

8.20 The buyer beware relationship, however, does not negate the bank's duty of care to avoid carelessly mis-stating facts – which means that the bank's affirmative representations or statements cannot be inaccurate or false without attracting potential liability. Nevertheless, a bank's duty of care to advise its clients of the risks or about the suitability of a product 'should not be readily inferred in a commercial relationship'.[17] Depending on the financial product or investment sold, the duty of care could entail a duty to investigate the suitability

16 *Thornbridge Limited* v. *Barclays Bank PLC* (2015) EWHC 3430 (QB); *JP Morgan Chase Springwell Navigation Corp* (2010) EWHC Civ 1221.
17 *Bankers Trust International PLC* v. *PT Dharmala Sakti Sejahtera* (1996) CLC 518 at 531, per Mance J; *Camerata Property Inc.* v. *Credit Suisse Securities (Europe) Ltd (No. 2)* (2012) EWHC 7 (Comm).

of the products sold to customers and, if appropriate, to warn customers of the risks of investing in these products. English courts, however, have overwhelmingly ruled against bank customers who have claimed that their banks owed them a duty of care to assess their suitability for the sale of certain financial products when the parties have agreed in writing to dispense with the duty of care. Under English law, when parties dispense with the duty of care, it is almost impossible for the customer to prevail on a mis-selling claim absent some showing of fraud or affirmative misrepresentation.

8.21 As a result, claims against banks for breach of a duty of care or fiduciary duties under English law rarely succeed. Nevertheless, the impact of the financial crisis resulted in unexpected and crippling losses for millions of individuals and small businesses in addition to substantial losses for professional investors, all of which resulted in an unprecedented number of civil lawsuits against banks for breach of the duty of care – in particular, claims for misrepresentation, negligent advice and failure of the duty to warn and investigate. Moreover, several million complaints have been filed with the UK financial regulator – the Financial Conduct Authority and its predecessor the Financial Services Authority – against banks for failing to treat their customers fairly and for breach of other regulatory principles in the sale of financial products.

8.22 UK court decisions demonstrate that, despite the growth of statutory and regulatory obligations for banks, 'party autonomy is at the heart of English commercial law'.[18] In the absence of statutory or regulatory intervention, the courts give effect to the contractual terms which parties have freely agreed in writing and are reluctant to imply terms into a contract. The courts respect the freedom of parties to agree terms of their own choosing, as expressed by the 'plain words' of the contract, and they are reluctant to interpret the words by using assumptions as to what they were purportedly intended to achieve without clear support from the natural and ordinary meaning of the words themselves.[19] This is particularly relevant for banks involved in the sale of complex financial instruments.[20] Moreover, the absence of any principle of good faith or unconscionability in English law further protects banks from a high volume of claims.[21]

8.23 Similarly, the UK statutory and financial regulatory regime has also struggled to provide adequate avenues of redress in cases involving vulnerable retail customers – including individuals and small businesses – who were mis-sold financial products. After having failed to supervise the sales practices of regulated financial institutions (especially banks) in

---

18   See *Belmont Park Investments Pty Ltd* v. *BNY Corporate Trustee Service Ltd (Revenue and Customs Commissioners intervening)* [2011] UKSC 38; [2012] 1 AC 383, per Lord Collins at [103].
19   See *Anthracite Trade Investments (Jersey) Ltd* v. *Lehman Brothers Finance SA* (In Liquidation) [2011] EWHC 1822 (Ch.); [2011] 2 Lloyd's Rep. 538 (the Court determined the meaning and effect of early close-out provisions in two cash settled put options incorporating the 1992 ISDA Master Agreement, which were part of larger investment structures devised and marketed by Lehman Brothers).
20   See *Belmont Park Investments Pty Ltd* (n 18) per Lord Collins at [104].
21   Cranston R, 'The (Non)-Liability of Banks under English Law', in Gordon L, Kleineman J and Wibom H (eds), *Functional or Dysfunctional: The Law as a Cure?* (Stockholm Centre for Commercial Law 2014), 205.

the early 2000s, which resulted in massive mis-selling of financial products to individual and small business customers, the former Financial Services Authority (FSA) and the Financial Conduct Authority (FCA, established in 2013) both played a more active role in encouraging customers and financial institutions to allow the Financial Ombudsman Service (FOS) to settle disputes between institutions and retail clients and small business customers. The FOS was established in 2000 to provide a scheme to allow customer complaints to be adjudicated against financial services firms in cases involving general insurance, banking and credit, and investment services. Consumer credit later came under its remit on 6 April 2007, based on the Consumer Credit Act 2006.[22]

8.24 The Ombudsman regime has been extensively utilised to file millions of claims against banks for mis-selling financial products, including payment protection insurance (PPI) and derivative products such as interest rate swaps. The Ombudsman Service is much easier and less expensive for claimants to bring mis-selling claims compared to the courts. Since the early 2000s, borrowers who purchased PPI to insure against the risk that they may be unable to maintain loan repayments have sought redress for mis-selling through the FOS and the courts. The courts have clarified the law on PPI mis-selling in several decisions assessing the lawfulness of PPI mis-selling regulations[23] and the unfair relationship between lenders and borrowers.

8.25 The case of *Harrison & Harrison* v. *Black Horse Limited*[24] involved the legal question of whether a lender's failure to disclose the existence or amount of commission from an insurer on their sale of PPI to a customer amounts to unfairness in the relationship between the parties pursuant to section 140A of the Consumer Credit Act 1974 (CCA). Both the High Court and Court of Appeal decided the claim against the borrower claimants and their appeal to the Supreme Court was subsequently withdrawn by consent.

8.26 The borrowers had also claimed that an unfair relationship was created by the lender's breach of the regulator's intermediary conduct of business rules (ICOB rules) and the PPI policy was unsuitable owing to the length of the cover and its cost.[25] The facts of the case involved two loans obtained by the borrowers from the lender, both taken out with PPI. The second loan was then discharged by refinance in 2009 and the PPI was cancelled. The PPI was sold by the lender to the borrower as the agent for the actual insurer, Lloyds TSB General Insurance Limited; therefore, it was an insurance intermediary acting on an advised basis in relation to the specific PPI offered. The lender earned 87 per cent of the premium in commission from the insurer on the sale of the PPI, which was not at all disclosed to the

---

22 Consumer Credit Act 2006, section 59.
23 *R (on application of the British Bankers Association)* v. *Financial Services Authority and Financial Ombudsman Service* [2011] EWHC 999, [2011] All ER (D) 222 (April).
24 *Harrison & Harrison* v. *Black Horse Limited* [2011] EWCA Civ. 1128.
25 The applicability of the ICOB rules to the bank's duty of care in the sale of PPI and other regulated financial products to commercial and individual customers has been reaffirmed in *Saville* v. *Central Capital Ltd* [2014] EWCA Civ. 337, [2014] All ER (D) 216 (March).

borrowers. This decision has raised the bar of proof even higher for borrowers seeking compensation in the courts for alleged PPI mis-selling – in particular, it cannot be argued that a lender's failure to disclose their commission created an unfair relationship under section 140A of the CCA.

8.27 Alternatively, borrowers can seek redress through the FOS, which applies a *fairness test* based on the UK regulator's treating customers fairly principle to decide cases. The use of the Ombudsman has tended to result in more favourable outcomes for borrowers than pursuing actions in court.[26] As a result, the vast bulk of mis-selling claims against British banks has been brought before the Ombudsman based on the regulatory law principle of treating customers fairly, rather than asserting a breach of contract or tort law claim in court. The British Bankers Association (BBA) challenged in court the regulator's use of the Financial Ombudsman Service, rather than the courts, for binding resolution of mis-selling complaints as beyond the regulator's powers under law.

8.28 The lawfulness of the FSA's PPI mis-selling policy statement and guidelines were upheld by the English High Court against a legal challenge by the BBA.[27] The main legal issue raised by the BBA was whether the FSA had the authority to issue a policy that included a statement that the FSA's main Principles (general statements of conduct required of financial services firms[28]) would be taken into account when the Financial Ombudsman Service made decisions on whether compensation would be 'fair and reasonable' under section 228(2) of Financial Services and Markets Act 2000. The court (per Ouseley J.) issued a judgment in 2011 rejecting the BBA legal challenge and upholding the regulator's authority under FSMA to issue a policy that its main principles could be relied on by the Ombudsman to decide with legally binding effect whether compensation was 'fair and reasonable'.

8.29 In summary, following the mis-selling scandals, the UK regulatory authorities have adopted legally binding regulatory principles and standards to ensure that banks treat their customers fairly and afford them fair and reasonable adequate compensation for violations of statute and regulation. This has had the effect of expanding the scope of a bank's potential liability for mis-selling.[29] As discussed above, the most prominent application of UK regulatory principles to banks' mis-selling of financial products came in respect of the sale

---

26 Financial Ombudsman Service (UK) has stated: 'What we consider to be fair and reasonable redress will depend on the individual circumstances of the complaint.'

27 See *R (on application of the British Bankers Association)* v. *Financial Services Authority and Financial Ombudsman Service* [2011] (n 23) (per Ouseley J.).

28 See chapter 2 of 'Principles for Business' (PRIN) in the FSA Handbook, including: Integrity; Skill, care and diligence; Customers' interests; Communications with clients; and Customers: relationships of trust www.handbook.fca.org.uk/handbook/PRIN/2/1.html accessed 7 January 2019.

29 UK Financial Supervisory Authority Policy Statement, 'The assessment and redress of Payment Protection Insurance Complaints: Feedback on the further consultation in CP10/6 and final Handbook text' (Policy Statement PS10/12, Financial Services Authority August 2010) www.fca.org.uk/publication/policy/ps10_12 .pdf accessed 7 January 2019, 3.

of payment protection insurance (PPI). The UK regulator adopted regulatory guidelines and a policy statement on PPI complaints handling that reflects a more aggressive approach to ensuring that bank customers have an adequate remedy to resolve their mis-selling claims before the Financial Ombudsman, which should serve as a precedent for customers in bringing future claims.

8.30 Post-Brexit, it remains to be seen to what extent the UK will transpose the requirements of MiFID II and MiFIR into UK law.[30] In particular, policymakers are considering whether MiFID II will allow UK credit institutions and investment firms to contract out of their duty of care to retail and wholesale customers and to use the doctrine of *contractual estoppel* to limit their liability to both consumer and commercial customers.[31]

IV A CHANGE IN FOCUS

8.31 The post-crisis regulation reforms for the marketing and sale of financial products and related investment services focus on three main areas: distribution, disclosure and product intervention. Under these legislative and regulatory reforms, a different precautionary *ex ante* approach is taken to retail markets and product distribution.[32] This approach adopts a different rationale for the regulation of the sale and distribution of financial products, which moves away from the disclosure paradigm to a behavioural finance paradigm. As mentioned in Chapter 1, pre-crisis the regulation of the sale of retail financial products and investment services was based on a disclosure paradigm that assumed that investors can rationally assess information that is disclosed to them and then, based on this and other information widely available in the market, decide in which financial products to invest in order to maximise their individual utilities and achieve the greatest risk-adjusted returns. In contrast, the behavioural paradigm suggests that bank clients and investors are not able to process all the relevant information and to calculate the risks, and that regulation should be designed to play a more interventionist role to limit, for example, the potential downside losses of risks for customers and to take account of behavioural biases that arise from social and biological factors.[33]

A MiFID II/MiFIR

8.32 MiFID II has the stated objective of making European financial markets safer, fairer and more transparent, and restoring investor confidence after the financial crisis. Following the

---

30 The Financial Services and Markets Act 2000 (Qualifying EU Provisions) (Amendment) Order 2016, amending the Qualifying EU Provisions Order 2013 to make MiFIR a qualifying EU provision for various parts of FMSA, and to ensure that the FCA and PRA have the appropriate powers to perform their roles under MiFIR.
31 HM Treasury, 'A New Approach to Financial Regulation: Judgement, Focus and Stability', Report presented by HM Treasury to Parliament by Command of Her Majesty (July 2010), 15–16.
32 Moloney (n 8), 789.
33 See Coates JM and Herbert J, 'Endogenous Steroids and Financial Risk Taking on a London Trading Floor' (2008), 105 *Proceedings of the National Academy of Sciences* 16 6167, 6169.

regulatory reforms which took place worldwide after the 2007–2008 financial crisis, the European Commission attempted to address gaps and weaknesses in MiFID I by replacing it with Directive 2014/65/EU (MiFID II) and adopting Regulation No 600/2014 (MiFIR)[34] to close the gaps created between MiFID II and EMIR (Regulation (EU) 648/2012). The European Commission has issued a number of delegated acts further specifying the rules under MiFID II[35] and MiFIR.[36] MiFID II was required to be transposed into Member State law by July 2017 and, together with MiFIR, became legally enforceable on 3 January 2018.[37] The Commission launched nineteen infringement actions in October 2017 against Member States who had failed to transpose the legislation by the deadline.[38]

8.33 MiFID II applies to all financial institutions and infrastructure including banks, investment firms, fund managers, exchanges and other trading venues, high-frequency traders, brokers and pension funds and retail investors. It widens the scope of the application of provisions, including the conduct of business rules to cover a broad range of markets such as equities, fixed income, commodities and foreign exchange; and products, including futures, exchange traded products, retail derivatives such as contracts for differences and structured deposits (Article 1(4) MiFID II).[39] MiFID II aims to require most trading to take place on regulated markets, including exchanges, Multilateral Trading Facilities (MTFs), Organised Trading Facilities (OTFs) and Systematic Internalisers. MiFID II empowers regulators to require more transparency for off-exchange markets and volume caps for equity 'dark pools'. Banks and other financial intermediaries are required to unbundle client payments for analyst research and trading commissions, and provide stricter standards for investment products.

34   Directive 2014/65/EU (Markets in Financial Instruments Directive/MiFID II), Regulation (EU) No. 600/2014 (Markets in Financial Instruments Regulation/MiFIR).
35   Commission Delegated Regulation of 25 April 2016 supplementing Directive 2014/65/EU; Commission Delegated Directive of 7 April 2016 supplementing Directive 2014/65/EU.
36   Commission Delegated Regulation of 18 May 2016 supplementing Regulation (EU) No. 600/2014 of the European Parliament and of the Council with regard to definitions, transparency, portfolio compression and supervisory measures on product intervention and positions [2016] OJ L87/90; European Commission, 'Overview and State of Play of RTS and ITS Relating to MiFID/MiFIR' (policies, information, and services website, European Commission 2018) https://ec.europa.eu/info/files/mifid-mifir-its-rts-overview_en accessed 20 December 2018.
37   Regulation (EU) 2016/1033 of the European Parliament and of the Council of 23 June 2016 amending Regulation (EU) No. 600/2014 on markets in financial instruments, Regulation (EU) No. 596/2014 on market abuse and Regulation (EU) No. 909/2014 on improving securities settlement in the European Union and on central securities depositories [2016] OJ L175/1; Regulation (EU) No. 596/2014 of the European Parliament and of the Council of 16 April 2014 on market abuse (market abuse regulation) and repealing Directive 2003/6/EC of the European Parliament and of the Council and Commission Directives 2003/124/EC, 2003/125/EC and 2004/72/EC [2014] OJ L173/1; Directive (EU) 2016/1034 of the European Parliament and of the Council of 23 June 2016 amending Directive 2014/65/EU on markets in financial instruments [2016] OJ L175/8.
38   See European Commission, 'European Commission – Fact Sheet, January Infringements Package: Key Decisions' (press release, 25 January 2018) europa.eu/rapid/press-release_MEMO-18-349_en.pdf accessed 21 December 2018.
39   Annex I, Section C MiFID II lists all financial instruments covered by MiFID II – Directive 2014/65/EU of the European Parliament and of the Council of 15 May 2014 on markets in financial instruments and amending Directive 2002/92/EC and Directive 2011/61/EU [2014] OJ L173/349.

8.34 The unbundling of client payments for analyst research and trading commissions is likely to affect how financial products are sold and how investment advice is rendered. Indeed, it is an important part of the MiFID II regime that regulates how asset managers pay for the research they use to make investment decisions. It was a major concern to what regulators saw as a conflict of interest at the heart of trading that hurts asset managers' clients, including pension funds, ordinary savers and retail investors, because banks that were acting as brokers for asset managers were able to pass the cost of research to the asset managers, who would then pass the costs on to their clients without disclosure. Basically, pre-MiFID II, asset managers received research, including written reports and phone calls with analysts, for free from banks and other financial firms, although the cost of this service was built into trading fees, which are usually paid by fund managers' clients. For the first time, fund managers will have to budget separately for research and trading costs, otherwise known as unbundling.

8.35 The unbundling and organisational requirements are expected to have an impact beyond the EU. EU demands for the personal details of traders are already creating tensions with the privacy rules of other jurisdictions outside the EU, such as Hong Kong and Singapore. The new regime on research payments also poses a significant challenge for US brokers. Under US regulations, brokers cannot receive direct payments for research unless they are formally registered as investment advisers. This means, in theory, that they will not be able to provide research for European clients – who will be obliged to make direct payments for this service – from 2018, unless they are registered with the US Investment Advisers Act 1940. The Securities and Exchange Commission (SEC), the US regulator, has the power, however, to waive the rules and allow brokers to receive direct payments for research from investors who are subject to MiFID II. The SEC is expected to make a decision in 2019, but, in the meantime, US banks and other institutions that employ these brokers will come under pressure to comply with the MiFID II rules and if they do so they will agree to register with the SEC as investment advisers in order to be able to continue servicing clients with EU operations.

8.36 MiFID II also addresses the selling processes of financial institutions by adopting rules governing the organisational requirements and conduct of business provisions. As to the investment firms' organisational requirements, reference is made to the new provisions on product governance arrangements relating to firms which develop financial products and to those which sell them.[40] The purpose of such provisions is to enhance the firms' understanding of the products they develop or sell and to ensure that they are suitable for the clients they are being sold to.[41] To this end, investment firms are required to maintain, operate and review the process for approval of each financial instrument – and significant

---

40 See Busch D, 'Product Governance and Product Intervention under MiFID II/MiFIR', in Busch D and Ferrarini G (eds), *Regulation of the EU Financial Markets: MifID II and MiFIR* (Oxford University Press 2017), 124.
41 MiFID II, Article 16.

adaptations of existing financial instruments – before it is marketed or distributed to clients.[42] Moreover, specific record-keeping provisions have been laid down in the context of the organisational requirements. In particular, records will include the recording of telephone conversations or electronic communications relating to, at least, transactions concluded when dealing on an institution's own account and the provision of client order services that relate to the reception, transmission and execution of client orders. Investment firms must also notify new and existing clients that telephone communications or conversations between the investment firm and its clients that result, or may result, in transactions will be recorded.[43]

8.37 Sales targets and remuneration rules are also applicable to banks and other covered financial intermediaries. These rules are based on the European Securities and Markets Authority's (ESMA) Guidelines on Remuneration Policies and Practices and aim at ensuring that staff incentives do not result in a conflict of interest or impinge upon the firm's obligation to act in the best interest of the client.[44] Finally, as to conduct of business, Articles 25 and 27 of MiFID II narrow the list of execution-only products and broaden the list of information investment firms have to provide with regard to best execution.[45]

8.38 The MiFID II/MiFIR closed the exception for non-advice, execution-only financial products, including for structured Undertakings for Collective Investment in Transferable Securities (UCITS) products that are marketed to retail customers, and made it more difficult for a retail client to be opted-up to professional client status. MiFID II creates high-level requirements for the distribution of insurance-based investment products. It prohibits firms from offering lending (margin) services in conjunction with execution-only services. It creates a new category of '*independent investment advice*', in which advice labelled as independent must advise clients on a cross-market selection of financial instruments. There is also a prohibition on commission payments for independent advice and a prohibition on commission payments for discretionary asset management.

8.39 MiFID II contains a stronger principle of fair treatment that includes a fiduciary-style obligation on the investment firm to act fairly in the client's best interests (Article 24(1) MiFID II), and a duty to act honestly, fairly and professionally in accordance with the best interests of the firm's clients. This is known more generally as a duty of loyalty that is designed to address the weaknesses in the previous information disclosure regime, which did not take account of the disadvantages affecting clients who often suffer from asymmetric information problems and behaviour biases.[46] Also, regarding marketing,

---

42   Ibid., (3).
43   Ibid., (6) and (7).
44   Ibid., Article 24(10).
45   Ibid., Articles 25 and 27.
46   Moloney (n 8), 800.

Article 24(3) requires that all information addressed by a firm to clients is 'fair, clear and not misleading'.[47]

8.40 MiFID II regulates the quality of advice rendered to clients by requiring financial advisers to undergo training and have a minimal education in finance and related fields before they can be authorised as agents who can advise clients. This involves demonstrating that the products they sell to their clients are suitable: the suitability assessment must be based on a '*know your customer*' (KYC) assessment. Advisers are required to state whether the advice is provided on an independent basis or not.

8.41 Regarding a firm's execution-only regime, there are more prescriptive rules regarding when clients can be used only for trade execution purposes, and there are limitations regarding which products can be sold on an execution basis only. However, MiFID does not apply these restrictions to a number of other structured investment products that can be sold by asset management firms under the UCITS directive, which can be sold on an execution-only basis.

8.42 Regarding product intervention, MiFID II/MiFIR confers on ESMA and Member State regulators in consultation with ESMA the power to prohibit or restrict the marketing, distribution or sale of a particular financial instrument or type of activity. MiFID II also makes a stricter distinction between eligible counterparties,[48] professional and retail investors, and the ability of retail clients to opt-up to the professional client level, which provides fewer safeguards for the client. It should be noted that 'eligible counterparties' (usually other financial and investment institutions) have the least protection under MiFID II and impose the fewest duties on banks regarding customer protections.

8.43 Compared to MiFID I, MiFID II aims to enhance the level of protection of different categories of clients. However, there will be room for further analysis once the implementation process is completed in accordance with the Commission's ongoing level 2 rule-making process and the final level 3 compliance and enforcement stage. Before the Brexit referendum, the UK competent authorities were considering the necessary changes for transposing MiFID II into domestic legislation.[49] In particular, they were assessing the impact that the new EU legislation might have on the ability of UK credit institutions and investment firms to contract out of their duty of care to retail and wholesale customers, and to limit their liability to both consumer and commercial customers.[50]

47   See Enriques L and Gargantini M, 'The Overarching Duty to Act in the Best Interest of the Client in MiFID II', in Busch D and Ferrarini G (eds.), *Regulation of the EU Financial Markets: MiFID II and MiFIR* (Oxford University Press 2017).
48   '[E]ligible counterparties' have the least protection under MiFID II and impose the fewest duties on the investment firms.
49   The Financial Services and Markets Act 2000 (Qualifying EU Provisions) (Amendment) Order 2016.
50   HM Treasury (n 31).

B MiFID II Shortcomings

8.44 The reform of the provision of independent advice was an attempt to resolve the conflict of interest problem, but the reforms are apparently having limited effect, as they target only independent investment advice and therefore will affect only a very small segment of the EU product distribution market. MiFID II also seems to lack specific requirements for strict supervision of organisational governance requirements to prevent a conflict of interest in the design and sale of financial instruments and products.

8.45 Moreover, MiFID II has been criticised for not going far enough in regulating the marketing or promotion of financial products. As with MiFID I, MiFID II contains a requirement that marketing materials are required to be 'fair, clear and not misleading'.[51] However, MiFID II goes further, with additional requirements regarding the distribution of research and marketing materials in Articles 36 and 37 of Commission Delegated Regulation 2017/565. Furthermore, MiFID II cross-references the Market Abuse Regulation (MAR) by requiring MAR principles to be adhered to regarding what information goes into marketing and research documents.

8.46 Although MiFID II covers a wide range of financial instruments, it does not comprehensively address distribution of insurance-based products (governed by the Insurance Distribution Directive (IDD)).[52] However, MiFID II has made targeted reforms to the distribution of insurance-based products by imposing additional conflict of interest and disclosure-related obligations on the direct sales and distribution and advice of insurance-based investment products. MiFID II provides high-level requirements for the distribution of insurance-based products by insurance companies; but the IDD remains a lighter touch regime that imposes less strict standards regarding how advice is rendered by insurance firms and also allows for commissions and inducements for the sale of insurance-based products.[53]

8.47 MiFID II also contains incomplete disclosure requirements on the distribution of financial instruments and products covered by the Directive. For instance, it does not address standardisation or format, or how retail-oriented summary disclosures should be designed. Moreover, the regulation of financial products is a new and untested tool for the EU and may have unexpected effects. Particularly the power to impose product bans may lead to an intrusive and heavy-handed regulatory approach. It places a great deal of authority with the regulator to find the optimum levels of risk and choice in the retail market.[54] Nevertheless,

---

51   MiFID II, Article 24(3).
52   See Colaert V, 'MiFID II in Relation to Other Investor Protection Regulation: Picking Up the Crumbs of a Piecemeal Approach', in Busch D and Ferrarini G (eds), *Regulation of the EU Financial Markets: MifID II and MiFIR* (Oxford University Press 2017).
53   Moloney (n 8), 778.
54   Ibid., 834.

the new regulatory framework has merits in seeking to impose controls on the distribution of extremely risky financial products to retail customers whose principal value can be lost.

8.48 Other weaknesses with MiFID II include the concern that although it aims to protect clients, it does not accomplish this because of the lack of standardised information disclosed to customers and the lack of any consistent format to present information on costs, charges and risks between different financial services providers.[55] As a result, industry bodies have attempted to fill the gap by encouraging member firms to prepare a European MiFID Template (EMT) that attempts to provide standardised information for customers, but this is not compulsory.

8.49 Moreover, regarding advice, MiFID II does not differentiate between client groups with different levels of financial literacy.[56] Effective advice requires different advice for different client groups with different investment objectives. Also, it is argued that MiFID II uses too many rules and instruments to achieve identical goals, thereby generating excessive compliance costs. This would potentially drive banks out of some segments of the retail business. Also, the MiFID II inducement regime does not include a ban on commissions across all sales channels, but only applies the ban to independent advisers. Where the bank discloses to its customer that it is not providing independent advice, it can receive commissions or retrocessions from third-party product providers as long as the bank discloses that it is receiving such payments to its customer.[57] It raises the question of whether commission or tied products should be prohibited or restricted for all types of advisory and sales arrangements facilitated by banks.

8.50 MiFID II requires extensive disclosure of the risks associated with financial products and the compensation arrangements around the distribution of such products. These disclosure requirements have been criticised because they may lead to long, complex disclosures for customers, which is especially challenging for retail clients.[58] Such complex and extensive disclosures may benefit the firm more than the customer. Also, it is not clear whether MiFID II restrictions on investment products sold execution-only may enhance investor protection.[59]

---

55   Franke G, Mosk T and Schnebel E, 'Fair Retail Banking: How to Prevent Mis-selling by Banks' (SAFE white paper series No. 39, 2016), 1 http://safe-frankfurt.de/fileadmin/user_upload/editor_common/Policy_Center/Franke-Mosk-Schnebel-Fair_Retail_Banking.pdf accessed 18 March 2018.
56   However, MiFID II does provide different levels of protection between retail investors (highest protection), professional clients (mid-level protection and eligible counterparties (low to no protection).
57   MiFID II, Article 11.
58   See Conradi P, 'Funds Flout Law by Charging Billions in Hidden Fees, Says Gina Miller', *The Sunday Times* (London, 4 February 2018), 39.
59   House of Lords European Union Committee, 'The Post-Crisis EU Financial Regulatory Framework: Do the Pieces Fit?' (2 February 2015) 5th Report of Session 2014–2015, Paper 103, 50 www.publications.parliament.uk/pa/ld201415/ldselect/ldeucom/103/103.pdf accessed 21 February 2018.

8.51 Finally, MiFID II's restriction on conflicts of interest, especially concerning the disclosure and inducement rules, only applies to the sale of MiFID-scope instruments. This has created the incentive to promote products not subject to regulatory controls under MiFID, thereby leading to the possibility of firms arbitraging the marketing and the sale of unit-linked investments, insurance-based and deposit-based investments.[60] Investors confronted with Packaged Retail and Insurance-based Investment Products (PRIIPs) (Regulation (EU) No. 1286/2014) may assume that similar regulatory protections apply to other products as well. Member States have the discretion to require stricter standards and requirements than the MiFID II regime requires. For example, the UK Retail Distribution Review resulted in the extension of the MiFID II regime to other structured and insurance-based products. The UK super-equivalence approach could also be utilised by other EU states and other non-EU/EEA countries who would like to apply these controls to other financial products and instruments.

V REGULATORY AGENCY DESIGN FOR RETAIL FINANCIAL PROTECTION

A Institutional Models

8.52 As discussed in Chapter 2, the institutional design of financial regulation has historically differed between states and jurisdictions. Generally, four main supervisory models of financial regulation provide the canvas on which states develop their institutional structures of financial regulation and supervision. These models are known as the *functional, institutional, integrated* and *Twin Peaks* approaches.[61] According to the *functional* approach, supervisors are responsible for the type of financial business or function of a firm or institution. Different supervisors would have responsibility for different lines of financial business. In contrast, the *institutional* model of supervision attributes competences or powers to a regulatory body depending on the type of financial institution subject to supervision. The *integrated* approach generally involves a regulator with full or consolidated authority to supervise all financial institutions and approved individuals in the financial sector regarding their discharge of all functions in the financial services industry. And the *Twin Peaks* approach involves the division of supervisory powers between (usually) two regulators: one with responsibility for prudential supervision of all financial institutions and financial stability, and the other responsible for conduct of business and investor and consumer protection in the marketing and sale of securities and other financial products.

---

60 Moloney N, 'Regulating Retail Investment Products: The Financial Crisis and the EU Challenge' (2010) 11 *ERA Forum* 3 329, 337.
61 See Ferran E, 'Institutional Design: The Choices for National Systems', in Moloney N, Ferran E and Payne J (eds), *The Oxford Handbook of Financial Regulation* (Oxford University Press 2015), 99–128. See also Group of Thirty, 'The Structure of Financial Supervision: Approaches and Challenges in a Global Marketplace' (Group of Thirty report, 2008).

B Institutional Design at National Level

8.53 Although some states have adopted a version of one of the above models in practice, most states have experimented with hybrid institutional forms that are the product of historical evolution and the design of constitutional structures (i.e. federalism), and the design of economic and financial institutions.[62] States are continuing to experiment with different institutional structures of supervision post-crisis, as they did prior to the crisis. No one size appears to be optimal for all countries, as financial, legal and political systems vary between states.

8.54 The European Union embarked on a major institutional restructuring of financial regulation by creating a European System of Financial Supervision (ESFS) consisting of three micro-prudential supervisory authorities – the European Banking Authority, the European Securities and Markets Authority, and the European Insurance and Occupational and Pension Authority – and a European Systemic Risk Board (ESRB) to conduct macro-prudential oversight of the European financial system.[63] Although the sectoral approach to financial regulation may be appropriate for the European Supervisory Authorities, it is not necessarily an adequate approach at the national level for most countries. One lesson that seems to have emerged from the crisis is that the supervisors responsible for prudential oversight and financial stability should be independent – and institutionally separate – from the supervisors responsible for investor and consumer protection. This is because the objectives of financial stability and investor or consumer protection can diverge and in some cases become conflicting. Accordingly, it could be argued that national authorities should, as a principle, and barring other compelling circumstances to the contrary, separate institutionally the consumer financial protection agency from the supervisory agency responsible for prudential supervision or financial stability. This principle is justified for the same reasons that in many countries the competition authority should be separate from the financial stability agency because, on occasion, their objectives may conflict.

8.55 In the United States, the Dodd-Frank Act of 2010 created an independent Consumer Financial Protection Bureau (CFPB) with enforcement powers, while in the UK the new Financial Conduct Authority (FCA) also has consumer protection in its remit. However, in most EU Member States, and in many other countries, the prudential supervisor is typically also responsible for consumer protection. It is suggested that most countries should create an independent agency along the lines of the US CFPB with independent enforcement powers, but whose governance would be independent of other supervisory bodies, including the central bank.

---

62 Ibid., 100.
63 Regulation (EU) No. 1092/2010 of the European Parliament and of the Council of 24 November 2010 on European Union macro-prudential oversight of the financial system and establishing a European Systemic Risk Board OJ L 331. See Green PJ and Jennings-Mares JC, 'Regulatory Reform in Europe: What to Expect in 2014' (Client Alert, Morrison & Foerster, 2014), 3.

VI ADJUSTING REGULATION TO PROTECT BANK CUSTOMERS

8.56 The widespread mis-selling practices of banks that led to massive losses for both retail and professional customers before and after the crisis, and the relative unavailability of viable legal remedies for bank customers to hold banks to account for the sale of such products, suggest that private law remedies in many countries are inadequate to hold banks to account for mis-selling. Moreover, bank mis-selling that resulted in such widespread losses was generally in conformity with the regulatory requirements that were in place at the time. Banks were generally permitted to design risky financial products for retail and professional investors without having to undertake suitability assessments of their customers for such products. The pervasiveness of bank mis-selling across Europe, the UK and US and in other countries further suggests that regulatory disclosures were insufficient to solve information asymmetries and conflicts of interest. In addition, they were not adequate to enable customers to process and understand the risks associated with the volume and complexity of information for these products. Indeed, policymakers' reliance on the disclosure of information through mandatory disclosures failed to equip bank customers with the knowledge and understanding to assess and manage the risks to which they were exposed by the sale of risky financial products. Regulators in Europe, the UK and other countries are now adjusting their regulatory philosophy and approach to bank selling practices that requires banks to engage in more comprehensive suitability assessments and stronger adherence to the principle of 'treat customers fairly'. This new focus on suitability and treating customers fairly implies that regulators should occasionally intervene in the market and adjust or ban certain products. Indeed, the need for product intervention in response to complex products acknowledges the limits of disclosure and financial literacy in addressing market failures.

8.57 For many countries, including the European Union and the United Kingdom, the post-crisis regulatory reforms for the marketing and sale of financial products and related investment services focus on three main areas: distribution, disclosure and product intervention. Under these legislative and regulatory reforms, a different precautionary *ex ante* approach is taken to retail markets and product distribution.[64] This approach adopts a different rationale for the regulation of the sale and distribution of financial products, which moves away from the disclosure paradigm and towards a behavioural finance paradigm. As mentioned above, pre-crisis, the regulation of the sale of retail financial products and investment services was based on a disclosure paradigm that assumed that investors can rationally assess information that is disclosed to them and then, based on this and other information widely available in the market, decide which financial products they will invest in to maximise their individual utilities and achieve the greatest risk-adjusted returns. In contrast, the behavioural paradigm suggests that bank clients and investors are not able to process all the relevant information and calculate the risks, and that regulation should be designed to play

---

64 Moloney (n 8), 789.

a more interventionist role to limit, for example, the potential downside losses of risks for customers while taking account of behavioural biases that arise from social or biological factors.

A The European Commission's Draft Legislation on Representative Actions

The European Commission proposed draft legislation, entitled a 'New Deal for Consumers' in April 2018 in several areas.[65] The Commission's draft legislation is relevant to retail financial services regulation in the EU because it would create a new collective redress regime, allowing consumers to seek redress against banks and other financial firms if EU financial consumer legislation (including MiFID II) is violated. The Commission's proposals include a new draft Directive on representative actions for the protection of the collective interests of consumers in which 'qualified entities' would be authorised to bring a representative action before a Member State court or administrative authority on behalf of classes of consumers who have suffered losses for a trader's violation of EU consumer protection laws. If the trader is found liable, it would be required to compensate the consumers who suffered losses or take other redress measures to make them whole again. Redress for retail customers of banking or financial institutions would be available where the bank or financial services firm was shown to have breached prescribed EU financial services legislation. The draft Directive would provide financial consumers with an additional procedural avenue to have their rights asserted under EU financial services law, to compensate them for losses and to provide any other relief, including injunctive relief.

8.58 The aims and advantages of the proposed Directive on representative action include ensuring increased access to justice and safeguarding against abusive litigation. It would complement public enforcement of consumer financial services legislation by creating private enforcement avenues for aggrieved investors and other financial customers, which are currently undermined by the MiFID II legislation. The Commission and Parliament underline that public enforcement will remain key, but private enforcement is important as well as a complementary tool to enforce consumer rights. However, the proposal provides a hybrid enforcement framework involving public authorities who can bring claims in the private interest of consumers. It is envisioned that it will supplement existing national enforcement remedies and not supplant them. It will be important for achieving deterrence: companies will face a more realistic prospect of potentially very high fines. The Directive further aligns the rights of EU consumers with US consumers in permitting damages to be sought from a large corporate group for any violation of consumer protection law that results in losses for EU residents. Consumer organisations, along with public authorities, have incentives to bring claims on behalf of a group of numerous claimants. The Directive requires Member States to take steps to ensure that financial obstacles do not deter entities in bringing claims.

---

65 European Commission, Explanatory memorandum of the Commission's proposal for a directive on representative actions for the protection of the collective interests of consumers, and repealing Directive 2009/22/EC COM/2018/0184 final – 2018/089 (COD).

B Shortcomings and Potential Challenges

8.59 The draft Directive creates the risk of fragmentation and gives Member States discretion to implement procedural rules differently, including rules on the standard proof for misconduct. Although the draft Directive attempts to create more uniformity in the bringing of civil actions in breach of EU consumer law, it allows a diversity of remedies to be brought under private and regulatory law against malfeasants. Despite attempting to achieve a one-size-fits-all approach across Member States, it largely concerns the procedural aspects of bringing claims for violations of EU consumer law. The different approaches to civil procedural law may result in forum shopping and regulatory arbitrage.

8.60 Public authorities (e.g. the Financial Conduct Authority) may not be proactive enough, due to the potential to focus on other tasks and so private lawyers will be required to give advice and initiate claims. Moreover, the potential lack of expertise of national judges to hear these types of cases will be important in giving effect to final decisions of courts and tribunals designated under the Directive that become irrefutable as evidence of a violation of the claimants' rights, which can be enforced in the Member State jurisdiction court where the action was brought. And if an action results in damages for claimants in one Member State, it will be given a rebuttable presumption of being recognised and enforced in the courts of other Member States. However, this can be challenged by the judgment defendant who can provide evidence to rebut the presumption. The representative actions draft Directive introduces a number of powerful remedies that will constitute another source of legal and operational risk which derives from bank misconduct, and which will have to be addressed by senior management and the boards of banks in the European Union.

CONCLUSION

8.61 This chapter provides an overview of the law and regulation of bank mis-selling. In doing so, it analyses legal and regulatory developments in the European Union and the United Kingdom, along with general observations of other jurisdictions. It analyses the viability of various legal remedies and regulatory principles designed to protect bank customers. The crisis demonstrated that regulatory disclosures were insufficient to solve information asymmetries and conflicts of interest, and could not adequately address the risks associated with the volume and complexity of information. This showed the need to move away from a primary reliance on the information disclosure paradigm that enshrines the notion of the empowered investor and confident consumer to a new philosophy of *consumer protection* and the need to *treat customers fairly*. This new focus on suitability and treating customers fairly implies that regulators should occasionally intervene in the market and adjust or ban certain products. Indeed, the need for product intervention in response to complex products acknowledges the limits of disclosure and financial literacy in addressing market failures.

8.62 The Market in Financial Instruments Directive II (MiFID & MiFIR) is designed to reform the marketing, sale and distribution of financial products. MiFID II focuses on three main areas: distribution, disclosure and product intervention, and has wide application to all financial institutions and infrastructure including banks, investment firms, fund managers, exchanges and other trading venues, high-frequency traders, brokers and pension funds, and retail investors. Regarding financial products, its requirements apply to designated MiFID financial instruments and products that relate to equities, fixed income, commodities and foreign exchange and products. Although MiFID II covers a wide range of financial instruments, it does not comprehensively address the distribution of insurance-based products and depository-based investments. Also, the MiFID II inducement regime does not include a ban on commissions across all sales channels, but only applies the ban to independent advisers. It raises the question – especially for other jurisdictions – of whether commission or tied products should be prohibited or restricted across all sales channels. MiFID II imposes costly compliance obligations on banks.

8.63 The chapter also considers what type of institutional structure is appropriate for the supervision of consumer financial protection. After reviewing the main supervisory models – *functional, institutional, integrated and Twin Peaks* – it recommends that the institutional design of financial regulation should be based on the principle that consumer financial protection cannot be discharged efficiently and effectively if it is conducted within the same agency as banking supervision. The rationale for this is similar to where the competition authority is separated from the financial stability agency because, on occasion, their objectives may conflict. In the United States, the Dodd-Frank Act 2010 created an independent Consumer Financial Protection Bureau (CFPB) with enforcement powers whose governance and decision-making authority is separate from the agencies responsible for banking supervision. However, in most European countries, the prudential supervisor is typically also responsible for consumer financial protection. The chapter concludes that the CFPB model should be followed by all countries, but that the agency's independence should be clearly based in law.

QUESTIONS

1. How has the rationale of regulation for bank selling of financial products changed since the crisis?
2. Do you think the legal remedies for bank customers against banks for mis-selling financial products are adequate?
3. How does MiFID II regulate bank mis-selling?
4. How does MiFID II regulate the compensation of bankers for selling financial products?
5. How does MiFID II regulate the design of financial products?
6. Will MiFID II regulatory requirements limit the ability of banks to serve their customers with the most efficient and profitable products?

Further Reading

De Pascalis F, 'Sales Culture and Misconduct in the Financial Services Industry: An Analysis of Cross-Selling Practices' (2018) 5 *Business Law Review* 39 150

European Commission, Explanatory Memorandum of the Commission's Proposal for a Directive on Representative Actions for the Protection of the Collective Interests of Consumers, and Repealing Directive 2009/22/EC COM/2018/0184 final – 2018/089 (COD)

European Commission, Inception Impact Assessment on the Targeted Revision of EU Consumer Law Directives, June 2017

Gortsos CV, 'Public Enforcement of MiFID II', in Busch D and Ferrarini G (eds), *Regulation of the EU Financial Markets: MiFID II and MiFIR* (Oxford University Press 2017)

Independent Directors of the Board of Wells Fargo & Company, Sales Practices Investigation Report (10 April 2017) https://www08.wellsfargomedia.com/assets/pdf/about/investor.../board-report.pdf

9

Misconduct and Financial Crime

Table of Contents

INTRODUCTION

9.1 Banks and bankers are responsible for complying with business rules that apply to a wide variety of financial market activity. Banker misconduct took the form of fraud in misrepresenting the risks associated with the marketing and sale of asset-backed and mortgage-backed securities.[1] Banks were also engaged in widespread and systematic manipulation of market benchmarks and, in some cases, insider dealing and market abuse. As a result, conduct risk has become an important concern of regulators, defined as 'the risk of losses to an institution arising from an inappropriate supply of financial services' because of intentional or negligent misconduct.[2] Banks have incurred huge administrative and criminal fines for misconduct both before and after the crisis. By the end of 2015, the twenty largest banking groups in the world had incurred €324.3 billion in fines.[3] The US banks had incurred the largest fines, with Bank of America the leader at €69.4 billion, JP Morgan Chase at €41.10 and Morgan Stanley at €28.96. European banks incurred less in overall fines, but still paid substantial penalties, with British banks paying the most: Lloyds €25.94 billion, Barclays €20.07and the Royal Bank of Scotland €19.81.[4] The National Bank of Australia was in the top twenty, with €4.64 billion in fines.

9.2 More than 55 per cent of the fines imposed on the top twenty banks arose from misconduct in traditional areas of the banking business, such as commercial and retail lending. Misconduct continues to plague the US and European banking industries. Wells Fargo was fined $85 million by US regulators when it admitted in 2011 that it systematically and intentionally billed millions of US customers for account services that they did not request.[5] Misconduct constitutes an important and growing source of operational risks for banks and represents a significant ratio of bank total assets.

9.3 Moreover, banks (including Citi, Barclays and UBS) were systematically abusing financial markets by deliberately manipulating interest rate and exchange rate benchmarks and indices, such as the London Inter-Bank Offered Rate (LIBOR) and exchange rate indexes that set daily interest rates and foreign exchange rates respectively. This chapter addresses misconduct risk involving banks and how this has become a major source of reputation and operational risk for the banking industry. It also discusses international standards of

---

1   See 'Barclays Agrees to Pay $2 Billion in Civil Penalties to Resolve Claims for Fraud in the Sale of Residential Mortgage-Backed Securities', and 'Two Former Barclays Executives (Paul K. Menefee and John T. Carroll) Agree to Pay $2 Million to Resolve Claims Brought Against Them Individually' (29 March 2018) (E.D.N.Y. Docket No. 16-CV-7057 (KAM/JO)).
2   Resti A, 'Fines for Misconduct in the Banking Sector: What is the Situation in the EU?' (Brussels: EU Parliament) (March 2017), 5 www.europarl.europa.eu/RegData/etudes/IDAN/2017/587400/IPOL_IDA(2017) 587400_EN.pdf accessed 21 December 2018.
3   See CCP Research Foundation, 'Conduct Costs Project Report 2016' (LSE 2016), 13.
4   Ibid.
5   Board of Governors of the Federal Reserve System, 'Federal Reserve Issues a Consent Cease and Desist Order and Assesses Civil Money Penalty Against Wells Fargo', (20 July 2011) www.federalreserve.gov/newsevents/pressreleases/enforcement20110720a.htm accessed 21 December 2018.

financial regulation and national and European legislative and regulatory initiatives to control and limit bank misconduct. Part I discusses the International Organization of Securities Commissions (IOSCO) principles and the Core Principles for Banking Supervision. Part II illustrates how the European Union regulates and disciplines market abuse and manipulation. Part II also discusses the UK market abuse legislation and how UK authorities have become more proactive in disciplining bankers in recent years for market abuse. Part III discusses the bank rate-rigging scandal involving the LIBOR and regulatory initiatives for bank rate-setting practices. It discusses, in particular, the MAR's wide scope of application to cover most trading of over-the-counter (OTC) derivatives contracts in Europe and the trading of derivatives outside Europe that reference assets booked or held in EU-based trading systems.

I INTERNATIONAL STANDARDS RESTRICTING BANK MISCONDUCT

9.4 International policymakers addressed these regulatory concerns at the G20 Heads of State Summit in Pittsburgh in September 2009 by adopting an international regulatory reform agenda to improve financial market transparency, mitigate systemic risk and protect against market abuse in the context of the OTC derivatives markets.[6] To achieve these objectives, the G20, among other proposals, introduced reporting obligations capturing all OTC derivative contracts, and obligations to trade standardised derivative contracts on exchanges or electronic trading platforms, and to clear these contracts with central counterparties or clearing houses along with mandatory margining requirements and higher capital requirements for those contracts that would not be subject to the clearing obligation.[7] The G20 also emphasised the importance of stricter enforcement against insider dealing, market manipulation and other market misconduct.[8] This ambitious reform programme has led to a number of legislative and regulatory reforms in many national jurisdictions that have involved not only stricter rules of conduct but also important structural changes for financial markets which have been introduced and implemented across multiple jurisdictions led by the European Union and the United States.

A International Organization of Securities Commissions (IOSCO)

9.5 The International Organisation of Securities Commissioners (IOSCO) has adopted standards and principles for countries to protect investors against misleading, manipulative or fraudulent practices. IOSCO adopts a broad definition of 'manipulative or fraudulent' conduct, which includes insider trading, front running or trading ahead of customers and the misuse of client assets. Indeed, IOSCO recognises market abuse and insider dealing to be

---

6   G20, 'G20 Leaders Statement: The Pittsburgh Summit' (2009) Pittsburgh Summit, University of Toronto G20 Research Group www.g20.utoronto.ca/2009/2009communique0925.html accessed 16 May 2018.
7   Ibid., para. 13, 7.
8   Ibid., para. 28.

a threat to the integrity and good governance of financial markets which can, in certain circumstances, undermine systemic stability and investor protection, and therefore has adopted international standards for the regulation of securities markets that contain recommended prohibitions on market abuse and insider dealing.[9]

9.6 IOSCO has designated the principle of full disclosure of material information to be the primary principle for ensuring investor protection. Full disclosure reduces information asymmetries in the marketplace and thereby improves the investor's ability to assess the potential risks and rewards of their investments. However, as discussed in Chapter 8, full disclosure does not address behavioural biases or psychological influences on investor behaviour that could lead to inefficient or suboptimal investment decisions, especially by retail investors. Nevertheless, IOSCO places primary reliance on the principle of disclosure of material information as the main regulatory means through which to protect investors and to ensure that they are in a position to make wealth-enhancing decisions.

9.7 As part of full disclosure, IOSCO also asserts that a key component of full disclosure is adequate accounting and auditing standards, which should be of a high and sufficiently robust standard to inspire international confidence. Moreover, only duly licensed or authorised persons should be allowed to offer themselves to the public to provide investment services. This should also apply in the case of banks and other financial intermediaries. IOSCO also encourages national authorities to adopt strict standards of supervision for the securities and market trading activities of banks and other intermediaries for the purpose of achieving investor protection by setting minimum standards. Investors should be treated in a just and equitable manner by financial intermediaries, based on standards that should be established in rules of business conduct. An effective system of surveillance is needed which would entail inspection, oversight and internal compliance programmes for investment firms and intermediaries.

9.8 Nevertheless, IOSCO recognises that in securities markets, investors are particularly vulnerable to misconduct by banks and other financial intermediaries, and that in most cases they will have limited capacity to take the necessary means to protect themselves. Further, the complex character of securities transactions and fraudulent schemes requires strong enforcement of laws to protect investors and bank customers. In the event that a violation occurs, investors and bank customers should be able to rely on regulatory intervention to assist and support the enforcement of their rights.

9.9 IOSCO sets out the principle that investors should have access to neutral fora, such as courts or administrative tribunals, to seek redress for damages and other injuries arising from market abuse and other misconduct. Remedies should include adequate compensation and/ or restitution. The network of mutual assistance agreements that IOSCO has encouraged

---

9   International Organization of Securities Commissions, 'Objectives and Principles of Securities Regulation' (June 2010), paras. 33–38 www.iosco.org/library/pubdocs/pdf/IOSCOPD323.pdf accessed 21 February 2018.

national regulators to adopt should lead to more effective enforcement. Effective cross-border supervision and enforcement will depend on close cooperation with and coordination by national regulators.

B Core Principles for Banking Supervision

9.10 The Basel Committee's Core Principles for Banking Supervision were revised in 2012 to strengthen regulatory principles for both prudential regulation and misconduct risk. The Core Principles now recognise that misconduct risk is a major factor influencing the stability of banks as well as the protection of their customers. The Core Principles address misconduct risk specifically in several principles, but the most emphasis is placed in Principle 28, Disclosure and Transparency, which requires bank supervisors to determine that banks and banking groups 'regularly publish information on a consolidated and, where appropriate, solo basis that is easily accessible' (Basel Committee's Core Principles for Banking Supervision, Principle 28). In doing so, bank supervisors and banks may reference the pillar market discipline disclosure requirements of Basel III (see Chapter 4). The essential disclosure requirements may be found in applicable accounting, stock exchange listing or other similar reporting rules.

9.11 Principle 29, entitled 'Abuse of Financial Services', states that the supervisor 'determines that banks have adequate policies and processes, including strict customer due diligence (CDD) rules to promote high ethical and professional standards in the financial sector and prevent the bank from being used, intentionally or unintentionally, for criminal activities' (Basel Committee's Core Principles for Banking Supervision, Principle 29). This includes ensuring that banks comply with international standards against money laundering and terrorist financing in conformity with the Financial Action Task Force Recommendations. The Core Principles emphasise the FATF Recommendations that banks report suspicious activities involving cases of potential money laundering and terrorist financing to the relevant national financial crime intelligence unit or centre, which is established either as an independent governmental authority or within an existing authority, or authorities, that serves as an Financial Intelligence Unit.

9.12 As misconduct risk is increasingly viewed by bank supervisors and bank risk management as a material factor influencing the soundness of a banking institution, it will play a growing role in prudential supervisory assessments and will be referenced increasingly by prudential supervisors and risk management teams.

II MARKET ABUSE LAWS

9.13 Market abuse laws generally consist of prohibitions on insider dealing, market manipulation and other types of financial fraud, including mis-selling of financial products. The regulation of insider dealing has traditionally had the objective of protecting shareholders from the misuse of privileged or confidential information belonging to the company by corporate insiders who were in a position to utilise the information for their gain at the expense of the company and shareholders. In contrast, regulatory controls on market manipulation were designed to prevent misleading statements and practices concerning issuers and their securities, and behaviour that would distort the markets.

9.14 Insider dealing laws are considered necessary to reduce the occurrence of insiders – within the issuing firm or the bank advising the firm – misusing privileged, material or non-public information that belongs to the issuing firm by trading on the basis of such information to make a profit or avoid a loss before the information is disclosed to the public through ordinary market channels. Market manipulation involves deliberate acts or statements intended to create false or misleading impressions about issuers of securities, or to engage in behaviour that would distort the functioning of the market, which could lead to unusual and sharp price swings in securities and related volatility that can undermine investor confidence and financial stability. As discussed below, the importance of insider dealing and market manipulation laws for banks and bankers is demonstrated by a number of regulatory actions and criminal prosecutions brought against them for failure to manage inside information appropriately in conformity with legal requirements. Examples are members of a bank's board of directors failing to disclose negative information as soon as possible about a bank's financial health, even during market turbulence, or a bank insider leaking inside information to a third party, even though the banker did not make a profit or avoid a loss in disclosing the inside information.

9.15 Some countries have adopted strict legal and regulatory frameworks to control and prevent market abuse. The United Kingdom adopted legislation creating a civil (or administrative) offence of market abuse pursuant to the Financial Services and Markets Act 2000 (FSMA),[10] which was a forerunner to later market abuse legislation adopted by the European Union and other states. The UK FSMA also created separate criminal offences for market manipulation (misleading statements and misleading acts), which were later expanded under the Financial Services Act 2012 to include three separate offences, namely: 'Misleading statement' (section 89), 'Misleading impressions' (section 90) and 'Misleading statements in relation to benchmarks' (section 91). The FSMA Act 2000 authorises the regulator to impose administrative penalties for violation of the market abuse regime and to prosecution in court for criminal offences of insider dealing and market manipulation.[11]

---

10 Financial Services and Markets Act 2000, sections 118–123.
11 Ibid., 'Penalties for Market Abuse', section 402 (authorising the FSA to bring insider dealing prosecutions which may result in a fine or seven years of imprisonment under Part V of the Criminal Justice Act of 1993). See also Financial Services Act 2012, containing specific offences for 'Misleading Statement' (section 89), 'Misleading Impressions' (section 90) and 'Misleading Statements etc. in Relation to Benchmarks' (section 91).

9.16   After the 2007–2008 crisis, policymakers and regulators recognised the importance of controlling market abuse, not only to protect shareholders against the misuse of inside information belonging to the company and other firms, but also to promote a more efficient functioning of capital markets by fostering minimum standards of fair dealing and best practice.[12] Indeed, the crisis demonstrated how quickly markets react to price-sensitive information and how this can undermine investor confidence and financial stability. In the European Union and other jurisdictions, market abuse laws, such as the EU Market Abuse Directive 2003[13] (replaced by the Market Abuse Regulation 2014), had only prohibited abusive behaviour and conduct in the trading of securities and other covered financial instruments in regulated markets, such as on stock or derivatives exchanges or on multi-lateral trading facilities. The prohibitions on market abuse did not apply to most alternative trading systems, nor to many types of financial instruments, such as OTC derivatives, that were not based on underlying investments in regulated markets. For instance, during the 2010–2012 European sovereign debt crisis, the existing regulatory framework permitted the use of certain derivative instruments, such as sovereign credit default swaps, in a way that might have contributed to extreme volatility in EU sovereign bond markets involving certain sovereign issuers. This raised concerns about whether sovereign bonds and related derivative instruments should be subject to the same anti-abusive trading restrictions as qualifying investments on regulated markets under the EU Market Abuse Directive. EU policymakers thus amended and eventually replaced the Market Abuse Directive of 2003. This Directive had defined market abuse more narrowly to be one of seven types of behaviour involving the trading of financial instruments on regulated markets or linked to regulated markets with the Market Abuse Regulation in 2014. The latter contained a much broader offence of market abuse which covered many more types of financial instruments that are traded off regulated markets (i.e. over-the-counter) or in off-exchange trading networks.[14]

---

12   See European Commission, 'Green Paper – Building a Capital Markets Union' (18 February 2015) SWD (2015), 13 final http://ec.europa.eu/finance/consultations/2015/capital-markets-union/docs/green-paper_en .pdf accessed 28 March 2018.

13   Council Directive 2003/6/EC on insider dealing and market manipulation (market abuse) (2003) OJ L96/16. See also Commission Directive 2003/124/EC implementing Directive 2003/6/EC of the European Parliament and of the Council as regards the definition and public disclosure of inside information and the definition of market manipulation (2003) OJ L339/70; Commission Directive 2003/125/EC implementing Directive 2003/6/EC of the European Parliament and of the Council as regards the fair presentation of investment recommendations and the disclosure of conflicts of interest (2003) OJ L339; Directive 2004/72/EC implementing Directive 2003/6/EC of the European Parliament and of the Council as regards accepted market practices, the definition of inside information in relation to derivatives on commodities, the drawing up of lists of insiders, the notification of managers' transactions and the notification of suspicious transactions (2004) OJ L162/70, and a Commission Regulation 2273/2003/EC implementing Directive 2003/6/EC of the European Parliament and of the Council as regards exemptions for buy-back programmes and stabilisation of financial instruments (2003) OJ L336, providing implementing measures in relation to exemptions for buy-back plans and stabilisation of financial instruments.

14   See also Article 8 of Regulation (EU) No. 596/2014 of the European Parliament and of the Council on Market Abuse (Market Abuse Regulation) and repealing Directive 2003/6/EC of the European Parliament and of the Council and Commission Directives 2003/124/EC, 2003/125/EC and 2004/72/EC (2014) OJ L173/1.

A The European Union Market Abuse Regulation (MAR)

9.17 The EU Market Abuse Regulation (MAR)[15] replaced the EU Market Abuse Directive[16] – and its related implementing legislation in 2014 – with an implementation deadline for EU states of July 2016. MAR requires EU Member States to prohibit and/or restrict behaviour that is defined by the Regulation as insider dealing or market manipulation, and to create administrative and civil sanctions for its enforcement. MAR's stated purpose is to establish a more uniform and stronger framework in order to preserve market integrity, avoid potential regulatory arbitrage and provide more legal certainty and less regulatory complexity for market participants.[17] MAR was accompanied by a separate Directive imposing an obligation on all Member States to create criminal sanctions for market abuse (MAD 2).[18] MAD 2 was introduced to harmonise administrative sanctions in each EU Member State and also to introduce for the first time a requirement to establish criminal offences for market abuse in Member States where it had thus far been only enforced with administrative sanctions. MAD 2 also required Member States to adopt a criminal offence for the manipulation of market indices or benchmarks, such as LIBOR. To this end, the MAR/MAD 2 sets out a framework that aims to place all investors 'on an equal footing' as to the availability of valuable information concerning issuers of financial instruments or transactions involving covered derivative instruments.

9.18 The MAR defines the following categories as constituting market abuse: (1) behaviour (by one or more persons) which (a) occurs in relation to a qualifying investment traded or admitted to trading on a prescribed market or in respect of which a request for admission to trading on the market has been made,[19] and (b) falls within any one or more types of behaviour as follows: (2) insider dealing (trading in covered instruments to make a profit or avoid a loss);[20] (3) improper disclosure of inside information;[21] (4) misuse of relevant information where the behaviour falls below the standard of behaviour reasonably expected by a regular user of the market or a person in the position of the alleged abuser;[22] (5) manipulating transactions in the relevant market unless for legitimate reasons and in conformity with accepted market practices on the relevant market;[23] (6) manipulating devices; (7) information dissemination that gives or is likely to give a false or misleading impression; or (8) misleading behaviour or distortion of the market where the behaviour falls below the standard.[24]

---

15 Council Regulation (EU) 596/2014 on Market Abuse (Market Abuse Regulation) and repealing Council Directive 2003/6/EC and Commission Directives 2003/124/EC, 2003/125/EC and 2004/72/EC (MAR, Market Abuse Regulation) (2014) OJ L173/1.
16 Directive 2003/6/EC of the European Parliament and of the Council on insider dealing and market manipulation (market abuse) (2003) OJ L 96/16 (MAD 1).
17 Market Abuse Regulation, recital 4.
18 Council Directive 2014/57/EU of the European Parliament and of the Council of 16 April 2014 on criminal sanctions for market abuse (market abuse directive) (2014) OJ L173/179 (MAD 2).
19 Market Abuse Regulation, Article 2.
20 Ibid., Article 8.
21 Ibid., Article 10.
22 Ibid., Articles 8 and 9.
23 Ibid., Articles 12 and 13.
24 Ibid.

9.19 The MAR defines 'inside information' as information which is (i) 'of a precise nature', (ii) has not been made public, (iii) relates to one or more issuers of financial instruments, and (iv) if the information were made public, it would be likely to have a considerable effect on the prices of those financial instruments. Significantly, these elements must coexist for any information to qualify as 'inside information' under the MAR. However, it should be noted that the criteria of information of a precise nature and having a significant price effect are very much linked to each other and hence it is important not to consider each criterion in isolation. Nevertheless, it is possible to identify separately the factors which should be taken into account in respect of each criterion.[25]

9.20 The MAR defines what is meant by the term 'information of a precise nature' in Article 7 as follows:

> ... information shall be deemed to be of a precise nature if it indicates a set of circumstances which exists or which may reasonably be expected to come into existence, or an event which has occurred or which may reasonably be expected to occur, where it is specific enough to enable a conclusion to be drawn as to the possible effect of that set of circumstances or event on the prices of the financial instruments or the related derivative financial instrument, the related spot commodity contracts, or the auctioned products based on the emission allowances.
>
> MAR 2014 Article 7(2)[26]

9.21 The precise nature of information depends on what the information is and its context and will be assessed on a case-by-case basis. For the information to be precise, it must be based on firm and objective evidence, not mere rumour or speculation, and 'specific enough to enable a conclusion to be drawn as to the possible effect or event on the prices of financial instruments'.[27] The UK adopted the requirement that inside information must be 'specific or precise' in section 56(b) of the Criminal Justice Act 1993, Part V. Under UK law, information is precise when it is exact. Moreover, the use of the word 'specific' can eliminate more than mere rumour and untargeted information from the definition of inside information.

9.22 An Australian case[28] held that the phrase 'specific information' meant not merely that the information was precisely definable, but that its entire content could be precisely and 'unequivocally expressed and discerned'.[29] The court concluded that specific information had to be specific in itself and not based on a process of deduction.[30] Similarly, in another

---

25 Committee of European Securities Regulations, 'Market Abuse Directive: Level 3 – Second Set of CESR Guidance and Information on the Common Operation of the Directive to the Market' CESR/06-562b (July 2007), 4 www.cesr-eu.org/data/document/06_562b.pdf accessed 17 May 2018.
26 Market Abuse Regulation, Article 7.
27 Ibid., 7(2).
28 *Ryan* v. *Triguboff* [1976] 1 NSWLR 588.
29 *Ryan* v. *Triguboff* 596.
30 *Ryan* v. *Triguboff* 597.

Australian case, but not involving an insider dealing prosecution, the court exonerated company directors from allegedly violating the stock exchange's timely disclosure rules by failing to make an announcement that the company was facing significant losses, when the actual amounts lost had not yet been assessed and finalised.[31]

9.23 In this context, it is logical and reasonable to submit that information that is speculative or equivocally expressed and discerned, including contingent events or occurrences whose certainty or finality depends on the decisions of third parties, including government agencies, is not *precise* or *specific* to constitute one of the criteria of the definition of inside information under EU law. When considering which market developments may reasonably be expected to come into existence and have a significant impact on price, a crucial issue will be whether it is reasonable to draw a conclusion based on *ex ante* information available at the time.

9.24 In addition to the requirement that the information is precise, not disclosed to the public and related to covered financial instruments, it must also satisfy the fourth criterion that the information 'would be likely to have a significant effect on the prices of financial instruments' and therefore does not constitute inside information.

9.25 Article 7(4) of the Market Abuse Regulation elaborates on what is meant by the concept of information 'likely to have a significant effect on prices of financial instruments'.

> . . . information which, if it were made public, would be likely to have a significant effect on the prices of financial instruments, derivative financial instruments, related spot commodity contracts, or auctioned products based on emission allowances shall mean information a reasonable investor would be likely to use as part of the basis of his or her investment decisions.

9.26 To determine whether information is specific enough to allow a conclusion to be drawn about its impact on prices, EU authorities believe that this can happen in two situations. First, when the 'information is such as to allow the reasonable investor to take an investment decision without, or at very low, financial risk – i.e. the investor would be able to assess with confidence how the information, once publicly known, would affect the price of the relevant financial instrument and related derivative financial instruments'; and, second, 'when the piece of information was such that it is likely to be exploited immediately on the market – i.e. that as soon as the information became known, market participants would trade on the basis of it'.[32]

9.27 Moreover, Article 7(4) MAR specifies that for information to be 'inside information', it must be information 'a reasonable investor would be likely to use as part of the basis of his

---

31 See P.D. Connolly QC in his *Report Parliament of Queensland into the Affairs of Queensland Syndication Management Pty Ltd and Ors* (1974). See also *Thorold Mackilin* v. *HM Advocate* 1994 JC 132, 1995 SLT 110.
32 Committee of European Securities Regulations (n 25).

investment decisions'. This so-called 'reasonable investor test' for determining whether the information has an impact on the price of financial instruments depends on whether the reasonable investor would be likely to use the information as part of the basis for their investment decision. There is no uniform interpretation and application of Article 7(4) MAR across EU Member States. In the UK, the Upper Tribunal in the *Hannam* case in 2014 regarded the reasonable investor test as simplistic and ruled that the reasonable investor, while in the process of making an investment decision, would only rely on information which is likely to have an impact on the price of the security. Under UK law, the *Hannam* case confirms the reasonable investor test supplements (and does not replace) the significant price effect test.

9.28 In addition, the UK courts have considered evidence of whether information is likely to have a significant effect on the price of securities to be what a reasonable investor would have done. In other Commonwealth jurisdictions, judges have adopted a reasonable investor test and held that information will be price sensitive if it is information which would influence the ordinary reasonable investor about whether to buy or sell the security in question. In *R* v. *Sanders and others*,[33] Mr Justice Simon of the English High Court accepted the prosecution's contention that if a movement of about 10 per cent in the price of a security could be reasonably anticipated, then it would be significant. The UK courts have adopted a similar approach in subsequent cases. Obviously, a hard and fast rule of 10 per cent would be problematic in a public policy sense in markets where high-frequency traders can use algorithms to trade multiple times in micro-seconds in order to profit from very small price differences. However, the UK courts have also accepted the proposition that it is necessary for the prosecution to show that the movement in price is not accounted for by normal market movements; in other words, the price movement of the relevant securities has to be exceptional.[34]

9.29 In considering the above, insiders at banking institutions should take into account the fact that the significance of the information in question will vary widely from institution to institution, depending on a variety of factors such as the institution's size, interconnectedness and the market sentiment about the firm and the sector in which it operates. In addition, what is likely to have a significant price effect can vary according to the asset class of the financial instrument. For example, a piece of information which may be price sensitive for an equity issuer may not be so for an issuer only of debt securities.

1 Bank Insiders Who Leak Inside Information

9.30 EU law has afforded Member States some discretion in defining the term 'insider'. This has particular relevance for banking institutions, as a number of professionals within the bank

33 (Unreported) Southwark Crown Court (20 June 2012), see UK Financial Services Authority case summary, FSA/PN/060 2012.
34 See prosecution evidence in *R* v. *Mustafa and others* (Unreported) Southwark Crown Court (5 March to 23 July 2012), Financial Services Authority, 'Six Sentenced for Insider Dealing' (27 July 2012) www.fsa.gov.uk/library/communication/pr/2012/080.shtml accessed 17 May 2018; and *R* v. *Richard Joseph* (Unreported) Southwark Crown Court, 30 January to 11 March 2013, FSA/PN/023/203.

will have responsibility for managing and utilising inside information and in some cases disseminating that information to third-party customers or business associates. The UK legislation defines *insider* in section 118B of the Financial Services and Markets Act as any person who has inside information, amongst other things, 'as a result of having access to the information through the exercise of his employment, profession or duties'. The term 'insider' applies to any person who has inside information as a result of his membership of the administrative, management or supervisory bodies of an issuer of qualifying investments, as a result of his holding in the capital of an issuer of qualifying investments, as a result of his criminal activities, or obtained by other means and which he knows, or could reasonably expect to know, is inside information. In this respect, the UK Financial Conduct Authority's Code of Market Conduct (MAR) sets out the following factors as indicators of whether a person is an insider: (1) if a normal and reasonable person in the position of the person who has inside information would know or should have known that the person from whom he received it is an insider; and (2) if a normal and reasonable person in the position of the person who has inside information would know or should have known that it is inside information.[35]

9.31 The MAR prohibits insiders from leaking inside information to third parties, even though the insider or the party to whom the information was leaked did not benefit financially from the leaked information. In a case involving a British banker who had worked at JP Morgan's London office, the UK regulator brought an enforcement action against the banker (Ian Charles Hannam who at the time was Chairman of Capital Markets at JP Morgan and Global Co-Head of UK Capital Markets at JP Morgan Cazenove) in 2012 and imposed a fine of £450,000 for violating section 118(3) of FSMA because he leaked inside information through two emails to a third-party foreign government official.[36] Mr Hannam argued that the information was not inside information and, alternatively, if it was, he was acting legitimately according to his employment and professional duties. In May 2014, the Upper Tribunal upheld the FCA's decision imposing liability for market abuse and the fine because Mr Hannam had in fact leaked inside information by sending two emails to an unauthorised third party.[37] Even though both the FCA and the Tribunal acknowledged that Mr Hannam did not act deliberately or recklessly, and that no profit was generated consequently to the disclosure, it was claimed that because of his senior position and experience he could not ignore the 'inside' nature of the disclosed information. Hence, he should have taken the necessary measures to keep it confidential.[38]

B The Market Abuse Regulation and the OTC Derivatives Markets

9.32 European policymakers addressed the need to reform the OTC derivatives markets in a twofold manner: first, the EU Regulation on OTC Derivatives, Central Counterparties and

---

35 Financial Conduct Authority Handbook, Market Conduct MAR 1.2 Market Abuse: general, section 1.2.8 www.handbook.fca.org.uk/handbook/ accessed 18 May 2018.
36 See Financial Conduct Authority, 'Final Notice to Ian Charles Hannam' (17 July 2014), ICH01012 www.fca .org.uk/publication/final-notices/ian-charles-hannam.pdf accessed 18 May 2018.
37 Ibid.
38 *Ian Charles Hannam* v. *The Financial Conduct Authority* [2014] UKUT 0233 (TCC).

Trade Repositories (known as the European Market Infrastructure Regulation or EMIR) was adopted and entered into force on 16 August 2012.[39] EMIR required that standardised derivative contracts are traded on exchanges or on transparent electronic trading platforms and that they are cleared by a third party, central counterparty or clearing house.[40] Second, EU policymakers sought to address the problem of market abuse in the OTC derivatives markets by extending the scope of the market abuse regime under the MAR to include a wider range of financial instruments, including all OTC derivative contracts traded by EU counterparties or on EU markets or trading platforms.

9.33 By applying market abuse laws to trading in the derivatives markets – both on-exchange and off-exchange – policymakers had intended to fill gaps in the regulation of certain instruments and markets that had allowed market participants using sophisticated trading systems to trade instruments in 'dark pools' and systematic internalisers or organised trading facilities that were away from regulated markets. Such trading was not subject to the same reporting requirements as trading on regulated markets, and certain restrictions on misconduct did not apply to such trading. In these opaque areas of financial markets, price-sensitive information could spread quickly and impact financial stability, especially in the case of fragile financial institutions and sovereign debtors.

1 MAR's Application to Derivatives

9.34 The scope of application of the previous Market Abuse Directive was limited to activity relating to financial instruments admitted to trading on a regulated market (RM) or for which a request for admission to trading on such a market had been made. The view taken now by the EU authorities is that financial instruments are increasingly traded on other venues and the scope of MAR should therefore cover these new trading facilities. The new trading facilities have been defined in Article 4 of the Markets in Financial Instruments Directive (MiFID II).[41] As a result, MAR applies not only to financial instruments admitted to trading on a regulated market but also to any financial instruments traded on a multilateral trading facility (an MTF)[42] – admitted to trading on an MTF or for which a request for admission to trading on an MTF has been made – and to financial instruments traded on an organised trading facility (an OTF).[43] It also applies to financial instruments not covered by any of the above, the price or value of which depends on or has an effect on the price or value of a financial instrument otherwise covered by MAR. This effectively

---

39   Council Regulation (EU) 648/2012 of 4 July 2012 on OTC derivatives, central counterparties and trade repositories (EMIR) [2012] OJL 201/1, recital 18.

40   EMIR, Article 4 'Clearing obligation', see Regulation (EU) No. 648/2012 of the European Parliament and of the Council of 4 July 2012 on OTC derivatives, central counterparties and trade repositories [2012] OJ L201/1 (EMIR).

41   Directive 2014/65/EU on markets in financial instruments (MiFID 2) [2014] OJ L 173/349 and Council Regulation 600/2014 on markets in financial instruments (MiFIR) (2014) OJ L 173/84. MiFID 2 and MiFIR together replace Dir 2004/39/EC of the European Parliament and Council of 21 April 2004 on markets in financial instruments (MiFID I) which had been in force since November 2007.

42   MiFID II, Article 4(22).

43   Ibid. (23).

broadens the scope of MAR to various instruments traded over-the-counter (OTC instruments), such as credit default swaps and contracts for differences.

9.35 In addition, MAR now also covers behaviour which occurs outside any of the trading venues, acknowledging the fact that a financial instrument may be manipulated through behaviour that does not occur on any them.[44] By broadening the scope to cover instruments traded on an MTF or OTF, the rules now apply to very diverse markets and instruments. While the regulated market and MTF are categories covering markets where financial instruments are traded continuously, an off-exchange trading facility (OTF) is a category that covers a number of fixed-income broker crossing systems, wholesale inter-dealer markets and voice-hybrid systems that do not rely on continuous trading. By extending the application of the rules to other trading venues, the European market abuse rules now apply to a number of securities that are listed on markets outside the EU, as many of them are also traded on an EU MTF or OTF. This significantly extends the extra-territorial reach of the market abuse regulation to insider dealing and market manipulation taking place entirely outside the EU simply because the trading relates to an instrument which happens also to be admitted to trading on a trading facility in the EU. There is no need for any EU entity to be involved or for there to be any impact on markets in the EU.

2 Market Manipulation

9.36 Article 12 of MAR sets out what constitutes market manipulation and Annex I provides details of indicators that will be taken into account when transactions or orders to trade are examined. Most importantly, due to the broadened scope of MAR, the market abuse provisions now apply to any financial instruments traded, admitted to trading, or for which a request for admission to trading on a RM or MTF has been made, any financial instrument traded on an OTF, OTC derivatives (including contracts for differences (CFDs), credit defaults swaps (CDS)) and spot commodity contracts (if the price of such a commodity contract is based on that of a derivative or if certain financial instruments are referenced to such spot commodity contracts). Following the information on LIBOR rigging, the initial MAR proposal was amended in 2012 to also cover manipulation of calculation of benchmarks.[45] In its report containing the final technical advice on possible delegated acts concerning MAR (the 'FR 2015/224'[46]), the European Securities and Markets Authority (ESMA) has prepared a non-exhaustive list of examples of practices that could be considered as market manipulation, linking the examples to the indicators set out in Annex I. The report clarifies the point that market manipulation can occur across products if, for example, a transaction in a derivative results in undue influence on the price of the underlying financial instrument.

---

44   Market Abuse Regulation, Article 2(3).
45   Ibid., Article 12(1)(d).
46   ESMA, 'Final Report: ESMA's Technical Advice on Possible Delegated Acts Concerning the Market Abuse Regulation' (3 February 2015).

9.37 Notwithstanding such a non-exhaustive list, ESMA confirmed that an example of a practice that is deemed illicit could be justified by legitimate reasons if otherwise in compliance with the applicable rules and regulations. A person entering into a transaction that could be deemed to constitute market manipulation may be able to establish that his reasons for entering into the transaction were legitimate and in conformity with accepted practice on the relevant market.[47] However, the current proposal in FR 2015/224 does not give any further guidance on what would constitute 'legitimate reasons' in this context.

9.38 On the other hand, ESMA did state that absence of an intent to manipulate the market does not necessarily imply that particular conduct may not still fall within the scope of market manipulation. A person may therefore commit market abuse unintentionally by engaging in practices that have a certain manipulative effect, even without realising that such activity may have such consequences.

9.39 MAR also extends the discretion afforded to Member States under MAD 1 to decide what are accepted market practices in the OTC markets and thus do not constitute market manipulation. Under MAD 1, accepted market practice (the AMP) is a specific market practice that could fall under the definition of market manipulation but is accepted by the competent authority of a Member State if carried out for a legitimate reason; it therefore does not constitute market manipulation. Since MAR also applies to OTC transactions, AMP may be established in the context of OTC markets. ESMA left it to the competent authority to decide when approving an AMP whether it can be conducted only by regulated entities or also by any unregulated entities participating in the market.

3 Public Disclosure of Inside Information and Delays

9.40 Issuers of financial instruments traded on an RM or on an MTF or OTF (provided that the issuer has requested admission to trading on an MTF or has approved trading on an MTF or OTF) have to disclose any inside information to the public at the time such information is being disclosed to any third party not owing duties of confidentiality. The transparency directive No. 2004/109/EC (the TD) sets out the appropriate channels of such disclosure with respect to issuers of instruments admitted to trading on an RM. ESMA is now proposing that similar channels of dissemination of information are used for issuers only issuing MTF- or OTF-traded instruments without any distinction between the different issuers. Publishing information on the issuer's website without any announcement to the media is not sufficient to comply with the disclosure obligation.[48]

9.41 Article 19 of MAR sets out the requirements for persons discharging managerial responsibilities (PDMRs Disclosure) within an issuer of a financial instrument, as well as persons closely associated with them, to notify the issuer of every transaction conducted on their own

---

47   Market Abuse Regulation, recital 42.
48   ESMA (n 46), para. 234.

account relating to the shares or debt instruments of that issuer. The scope of the notification obligation is broader than in MAD 1, as it applies to any transactions on instruments (including derivatives linked to such instruments) issued by an issuer who has either requested or approved admission of its financial instruments to trading on an RM, approved trading of its financial instruments on an MTF or an OTF, or has requested admission to trading of its financial instruments on an MTF. Article 19(3) specifies that it is the issuer's duty to ensure that the notified information 'is made public promptly and no later than three business days after the transaction in a manner which enables fast access to this information on a non-discriminatory basis'. Article 19(7) specifies that notifiable transactions should include pledging or lending of financial instruments and transactions undertaken by any person professionally arranging or executing transactions, including where discretion is exercised. The venue or place where that transaction has been conducted is not relevant for the purposes of determining whether a transaction has to be reported. In the FR 2015/224, ESMA clarified that 'transaction' should include gifts, inheritances and donations involving a PDMR. Any acquisition of financial instruments as a result of a conversion, even if such a conversion is an automatic conversion not requiring any exercise of discretion by the PDMR (such as would be the case for the automatic exercise of warrants), has to be reported as well. This relates to the fact that there is no requirement to report a transaction that is dependent on the occurrence of a condition until the condition has been satisfied.

9.42 When setting out the disclosure obligation, ESMA concluded in the FR 2015/224 that the notification should set out the gross amount of cash received or paid for the transaction executed. This approach was selected over a more sophisticated approach that would have required, for instance, disclosure on a Delta-adjusted basis, which would take into account the Delta of the instrument at any particular point in time. The 'Delta' of a derivative instrument refers to the rate of change of the price of the instrument compared with the price of the underlying asset or instruments.[49]

9.43 Where PDMR engages in a transaction involving an index, basket of instruments or an investment fund, ESMA proposes that the reporting obligation should apply only if the relevant financial instrument constitutes at least 20 per cent of the value of the index, basket or investment fund at the time of the transaction. ESMA initially proposed that disclosure will also be required in a situation where a collective investment manager is entering into transactions relating to the financial instruments. This was picked up by the industry in the comment letters as problematic in practice as the portfolio manager will be making investment decisions without any involvement or knowledge of the PDMR, who may as a result become subject to such disclosure obligation. It was pointed out that in its proposal, ESMA has interpreted the Level 1 text as being broader than what, strictly speaking, is required to achieve the stated goals. The final text in FR 2015/224 amends the approach and rather than requiring disclosure of any transaction effected by the

---

49 See Hull JC, *Options, Futures, and Other Derivatives* (8th edn, Pearson Education International 2012), chapter 18.

portfolio manager without the PDMR's knowledge, the disclosure is now limited to transactions by the PDMR in shares or units of a collective investment scheme where the underlying fund has exposure to the financial instruments above the minimum thresholds set by ESMA. This disclosure obligation will only apply if PDMR is aware of the fund composition or could have obtained the necessary information about the exposure of a fund to a particular financial instrument before making a decision to invest in the fund. If the fund was invested in the relevant financial instrument above the threshold set by ESMA, the investment by the PDMR in the fund would be subject to the disclosure requirement. Disclosure regarding investment decisions by an unrelated third-party portfolio manager should be irrelevant from a market integrity point of view, as the portfolio manager is making its investment decisions irrespective of whether a PDMR has made any investments in the fund. Any such disclosure based on the original proposal could result in giving the market misleading signals, as the PDMR would have to make disclosure with respect to exposure that would not be changing as a result of its own investment decisions.

III LIBOR: MANIPULATION BENCHMARKS

A What was LIBOR and How Did It Work?

9.44 The London Inter-Bank Offered Rate (LIBOR) was calculated each day by the British Bankers' Association (BBA), a London-based trade group whose members included large UK and foreign banks. The BBA licensed the use of LIBOR rates to other institutions, publishers and media outlets. The setting of LIBOR rates began in 1986 in response to the banking industry's desire to adopt a virtually risk-free interest rate to serve as a benchmark for almost all bank lending. The unexpected volatility in interest rates following the breakdown of the Bretton Woods system in the 1970s had resulted in significant risks for banks in making long-term fixed-rate loans. The risk was that market interest rates could increase and leave a bank exposed to borrowers who were already paying a fixed interest rate, over a fixed period of time, to the bank that was less than what it had cost the bank to borrow in the market (from depositors or other lenders) to finance the loan. Short-term loans could solve that problem, but at the risk that the borrower might be forced to repay at any time a loan that was taken out for a long-term project. LIBOR solved this problem by allowing a loan to be long term, but with a rate that was periodically reset based on the cost of funds to banks. If a loan were priced at, say, three percentage points above the three-month LIBOR, the bank would be getting a reasonable risk premium, and would face no risk from changing market rates, since the interest rate would be reset every three months. The borrower would still receive a stable interest rate for a long-term loan. There were two implicit assumptions in LIBOR. One was that banks were virtually risk-free, or at least that their risk was small and would not vary much over time. The other was that there was a way to calculate what the rate was. Both assumptions turned out to be wrong.[50]

---

50   Norris F, 'The Myth of Fixing the Libor' *New York Times* (New York, 27 September 2012) www.nytimes.com/2012/09/28/business/the-myth-of-fixing-the-libor-high-low-finance.html accessed 18 May 2018.

9.45 The LIBOR rates grew to be the most important interest rate benchmark used by thousands of banks and other financial firms around the world to set interest rates for mortgage, small business, consumer and student loans and many other financial products. They were also used as reference benchmarks for the pricing of derivatives contracts, such as interest rate swaps and some credit default swaps. By 2013, it was estimated that a total notional exposure to LIBOR was about US$240 trillion, in the form of mortgage and consumer loans, credit card rates and derivatives and bonds. For over thirty years, most banks, companies and consumers have used LIBOR to provide a basis for calculating the interest rates and payment schedules of financial products.

9.46 Each day under LIBOR, a bank that was a member of a LIBOR panel would submit its rate for the relevant period, or 'tenor'. The bank's rate was intended to be without reference to the rates submitted by other banks on the panel. The submitted rates were hypothetical rates that were not based on the bank's actual borrowings in the market. The resulting submissions made by the various panel banks were then collated by Thomson Reuters and calculated based on the mean average – after excluding the highest quartile and bottom quartile submissions – of the submissions resulting in the day's LIBOR rate. As the rates were hypothetical, and not based on actual rates at which banks were borrowing, these rates could not be verified by actual market data. From 1998 to 2010, the British Banking Association provided the operative definition of LIBOR as: '[t]he rate at which an individual Contributing Panel Bank could borrow funds, were it do so by asking for and then accepting inter-bank offers in reasonable market size, just prior to 11.00 London time'. It should be emphasised that a submission which was not a genuine assessment for the purposes of this definition could significantly impact on the LIBOR rate selected.

9.47 Regulatory investigations showed that the rates were being manipulated on a regular basis between 2004 and 2011 by bank rate submitters with the knowledge and approval of senior management. Sometimes the motive was to make the bank look better in the eyes of the market – for example, submitting low rates so that the market would think that the bank was healthier or less risky than it really was. However, the motive was also simply to rig the benchmark rate set by each panel in order to manipulate the prices and interest rates charged by the banks in their favour for a variety of investments and loans that they sold to their customers or, alternatively, to rig the rate in favour of the trading positions of individual traders who were similarly conspiring with rate submitters to rig the rates to their individual trading positions. By conspiring to rig the rates, the traders and rate submitters would gain personally through increased status at the bank and increased compensation.

1 LIBOR Rate-Rigging Prosecutions

9.48 On 3 August 2015, after an extended jury trial, former UBS and Citigroup trader Tom Hayes was convicted in Southwark Crown Court (London) on eight counts of conspiracy to defraud the market in relation to the manipulation of the Japanese Yen London Interbank

Offered Rate (Yen LIBOR) and was sentenced to fourteen years in prison. He was prosecuted by the UK Serious Fraud Office (SFO) along with a group of traders and rate submitters and their managers from other well-known global banks such as Barclays and Deutsche Bank for entering into agreements with them, between 2006 and 2010, to manipulate Yen LIBOR while employed as a trader and LIBOR rate submitter with UBS Securities Japan Limited (2006–2009) and later with Citigroup Global Markets Japan Inc. His case was later separated from the other defendants because he had entered into agreement with UK authorities to provide assistance to the SFO in its LIBOR investigations and made admissions of dishonesty in order to avoid extradition to the United States to stand trial on similar criminal charges of manipulating LIBOR. The court concluded that Hayes's motive for manipulating LIBOR was to advance his trading interests, specifically to increase UBS's (and later Citigroup's) trading profits, to receive rewards in the form of bonuses and status within both banks and to disadvantage UBS's and Citigroup's respective counterparties.

9.49 The judge instructed the jury that they had to consider three issues: (1) Did the defendant Hayes agree to work with the others who were accused of manipulating LIBOR to procure the making of the bank's LIBOR submission of a rate that was not the bank's genuine understanding of its borrowing rate in accordance with the LIBOR definition, but instead a rate that was intended to advantage the trader and/or the bank's trading? (2) Was what the defendant agreed to do with the others dishonest by the ordinary standards of reasonable and honest people? And (3) did the defendant realise that what he agreed to do was dishonest by the ordinary standards of reasonable people? The defendant Hayes argued that even if he had agreed to influence the LIBOR rate submission process to his and the bank's advantage, it was not dishonest of him to have done so as his bank managers and other superiors within the organisation were aware of and had condoned his activity and had rewarded and encouraged his practices. Hayes argued that according to the objective or standard of ordinary and honest people, what he had done was not dishonest because it was accepted practice within the banks where he had worked – UBS and Citigroup – and it appeared to be accepted practice with other banks who were members of the LIBOR panels on which he had participated. Indeed, there was evidence from regulatory investigations that the manipulation of LIBOR was not an exceptional practice that only a few rogue bankers were involved in, but rather was a systematic and generally condoned practice at the cash desks and proprietary trading desks and up to the level of senior management in the liquidity departments of some of the largest and most recognised global banks. These banks were fined mainly by UK and US regulators for systematically engaging in massive manipulation of the LIBOR benchmark to benefit themselves at the expense of their customers. The defendant Hayes argued that because of the demonstrated disregard by bank management and the compliance department of LIBOR rate-rigging within the bank, he did not appreciate that his behaviour of manipulating LIBOR was – according to the standards of ordinary and honest people – dishonest and therefore it was not fraudulent as the prosecution had alleged. The jury reached a verdict that Hayes was guilty of all eight counts of conspiracy to defraud the market by manipulating LIBOR and he was sentenced to fourteen years in prison for not only participating in LIBOR manipulation but also for condoning, implicitly encouraging and acquiescing manipulation, including by some members of the board of directors.[51]

9.50 However, UK SFO LIBOR prosecutions were not successful in other criminal trials involving the same charges (conspiracy to defraud) against LIBOR rate submitters and their trader colleagues from other banks. Two Barclays traders, Stylianos Contogoulas and Ryan Michael Reich, were both acquitted of conspiring to manipulate the LIBOR interest rate. The two defendants used a similar defence to Tom Hayes – that the business practice and culture of Barclays bankers completely acceptied rate submitters and traders deliberately rigging the LIBOR rates. The jury decided that the defendants did not have the requisite knowledge in the first place to enable them to have 'deliberately disregarded' the proper basis for Barclays' LIBOR submissions.

9.51 In addition, given the lack of 'red flags' or any intervention from the compliance team, or more senior colleagues, telling them that what they were doing was wrong, the jury found that the defendants did not think at that time that they were doing anything dishonest.

9.52 In contrast, the banks themselves were not prosecuted for conspiracy to defraud under criminal law and instead were subjected to administrative regulatory enforcement actions that resulted in substantial civil penalties imposed on the banks over several years. The most active investigations and enforcement actions were undertaken by UK and US regulators. For example, the UK FSA imposed a fine of £59.5 million on Barclays for LIBOR manipulation and the US authorities also imposed US$360 million in fines on Barclays for manipulating LIBOR and EURIBOR along with another US$450 million fine in June 2012. The US imposed a US$1.5 million fine on UBS for LIBOR, while the UK imposed an £87.5 million fine on the Royal Bank of Scotland for LIBOR manipulation and £14 million on the inter-bank derivatives dealer ICAP Europe Ltd in September 2013. The US also imposed a US$325 million fine on the Dutch bank Rabobank for LIBOR manipulation. Later, fifteen other banks paid substantial fines, including: Citigroup Inc., HSBC, Bank of America, JP Morgan, Deutsche Bank, Credit Suisse, Lloyds, etc. Even the European Commission prosecuted the banks for their roles in EURIBOR and LIBOR rate-rigging as part of a criminal cartel in violation of EU competition law. Barclays' and UBS's behaviour was egregious and systematic across the banking institution and both banks agreed to provide evidence of rate-rigging by other banks in return for reduced fines and deferred prosecution arrangements.

B The Wheatley Review[52]

9.53 The then chief executive of the UK Financial Conduct Authority, Martin Wheatley, proposed reforms of LIBOR in 2013 that would have involved subjecting the rate-setting

---

51 Final Judgment by Court of Appeal (Criminal Division) on Appeal form the Crown Court at Southwark Crown Court (per J. Cooke), Case No. 201504027 C£ (21.12.2015).
52 HM Treasury, 'The Wheatley Review of LIBOR: Final Report' (September 2012) https://assets.publishing. service.gov.uk/government/uploads/system/uploads/attachment_data/file/191762/wheatley_review_libor_finalreport_280912.pdf accessed 18 May 2018.

process to regulatory oversight and reducing its activities by limiting the number of currencies and maturities involved. The proposal would have lowered the number of LIBOR reference rates – from 150 to 20 – where the regulator would be 'confident there is a real market to underpin the rates'.[53] More specifically, the Wheatley Review reached three fundamental conclusions that underpin its recommendations: (1) There is a clear case in favour of comprehensively reforming LIBOR rather than replacing the benchmark. (2) Transaction data should be explicitly used to support LIBOR submissions. A number of the Review's recommendations are intended to establish strict and detailed processes for verifying submissions against transaction data and limiting the publication of LIBOR to those currencies and tenors that are supported by sufficient transaction. (3) Market participants should continue to play a significant role in the production and oversight of LIBOR. While LIBOR needs to be reformed to address the weaknesses that have been identified, it would not be appropriate for the authorities to completely take over the process of producing a benchmark which exists primarily for the benefit of market participants.

9.54 The Wheatley Review's ten-point plan[54] for comprehensive reform of LIBOR included the following:

1. *Regulation of LIBOR.* The authorities should introduce statutory regulation of administration of, and submission to, LIBOR, including an Approved Persons regime, to provide the assurance of credible independent supervision, oversight and enforcement, both civil and criminal (Wheatley Review chapter 2).
2. *Institutional reform.* The BBA should transfer responsibility for LIBOR to a new administrator, who will be responsible for compiling and distributing the rate, as well as providing credible internal governance and oversight. This should be achieved through a tender process to be run by an independent committee convened by the regulatory authorities (see chapter 3, paragraphs 3.5 to 3.16).
3. *New rate administrator.* The new administrator should fulfil specific obligations as part of its governance and oversight of the rate, having due regard to transparency and fair and non-discriminatory access to the benchmark. These obligations will include surveillance and scrutiny of submissions, publication of a statistical digest of rate submissions, and periodic reviews addressing the issue of whether LIBOR continues to meet market needs effectively and credibly (see paragraphs 3.17 to 3.38).
4. *The rules governing LIBOR.* Submitting banks should immediately look to comply with the submission guidelines presented in this report, making explicit and clear use of transaction data to corroborate their submissions (see paragraphs 4.5 to 4.13).
5. *Code of Conduct.* The new administrator should, as a priority, introduce a code of conduct for submitters that should clearly define: guidelines for the explicit use of transaction data to determine submissions; systems and controls for submitting firms; transaction record-

---

53 Ibid.
54 Financial Services Authority, 'The Regulation and Supervision of Benchmarks' Policy Statement PS 13/6 (March 2013).

keeping responsibilities for submitting banks; and a requirement for the regular external audit of submitting firms (see chapter 4, paragraphs 4.14 to 4.31).

6. *Immediate improvements to LIBOR.* The BBA should cease the compilation and publication of LIBOR for those currencies and tenors for which there is insufficient trade data to corroborate submissions, immediately engaging in consultation with users and submitters to plan and implement a phased removal of these rates (see chapter 5, paragraphs 5.3 to 5.13).

7. *LIBOR submissions.* The BBA should publish individual LIBOR submissions after three months to reduce the potential for submitters to attempt manipulation, and to reduce any potential interpretation of submissions as a signal of creditworthiness (see paragraphs 5.14 to 5.18).

8. *Banks.* Banks that were not previously submitting to LIBOR should be encouraged to participate as widely as possible in the LIBOR compilation process, including, if necessary, through new powers of regulatory compulsion (see paragraphs 5.19 to 5.28).

9. *Market participants.* Market participants using LIBOR should be encouraged to consider and evaluate their use of LIBOR, including a consideration of whether LIBOR is the most appropriate benchmark for the transactions that they undertake, and whether standard contracts contain adequate contingency provisions covering the event of LIBOR not being produced (see paragraphs 5.29 to 5.39).

10. *International coordination.* The UK authorities should work closely with the European and international community and contribute fully to the debate on the long-term future of LIBOR and other global benchmarks, establishing and promoting clear principles for effective global benchmarks (see chapters 6 and 7).

9.55 In response to the Wheatley proposals, the UK government proposed legislation that administration of, and submission to, LIBOR should become regulated activities under the Financial Services and Markets Act 2000 (FSMA). Subsequently, the Treasury amended the Regulated Activities Order to make administration of, and provision of information to, specified benchmarks regulated activities. The UK rules now call for better governance of financial benchmarks such as LIBOR, with efforts made to assure there is no manipulation by traders. The new British rules, as proposed, call for auditors to certify bank LIBOR policies every year, and allow private lawsuits by persons or institutions who believe they have been harmed by manipulative and inaccurate LIBOR submissions. But banks have complained that regular audits cost too much and would 'adversely affect the incentives for firms to participate in the benchmark'. When the final rules came out in March 2013, a couple of important changes were made: (1) audits may be less frequent than every year; and (2) private rights of action in the form of lawsuits for LIBOR manipulation are not allowed.

9.56 In July 2013 the BBA announced that they would transfer responsibility for the administration of LIBOR from the BBA to the New York Stock Exchange/Euronext (NYSE/Euronext). The appointment of a new administrator – a London-based, UK registered company, regulated by the UK's Financial Conduct Authority – was one of the key recommendations of the Wheatley Review. Later, NYSE/Euronext transferred responsibility for administration of LIBOR to the Intercontinental Exchange (ICE). ICE administers LIBOR through its unit, IBA. Rather than discarding LIBOR, IBA has attempted to reform it because there is continued support for its use as a benchmark. Many financial companies and firms are wary of moving away from LIBOR to a new benchmark because it could suddenly change payment exposures for millions of transactions and loan exposures.

9.57 The UK Financial Conduct Authority began supervising the LIBOR administrator and the rate-setting process as of 1 April 2013. Since August 2013, only five currencies and seven maturities have been quoted every day (thirty-five rates), making it more likely that the rates submitted are underpinned by real trades. The Danish, Swedish, Canadian, Australian and New Zealand LIBOR rates were ended, without disruption to the financial markets. Under section 91 of the Financial Services Act 2012, knowingly or deliberately making false or misleading statements in relation to benchmark setting was made a criminal offence. Under the new regime, each individual submission that comes in from the banks is embargoed for three months. As LIBOR should be reflective of the rate at which contributor banks can borrow funds, embargoing individual submissions reduces the motivation to submit a false rate to portray a falsely positive picture of creditworthiness. A new code of conduct requires banks to have systems and controls in place regarding LIBOR. For example, each bank must now have a named person responsible for LIBOR rate submissions who is accountable if there is any wrongdoing. The banks must keep records so that they can be audited by the regulators if necessary. The administration of LIBOR has itself become a regulated activity.[55]

9.58 In 2018, the LIBOR administrator ICE announced that it would begin trading a three-months futures contract based on the Sterling Overnight Index Average (SONIA), a measure at which banks and building societies can borrow from each other on a short-term basis.[56] SONIA is an alternative benchmark intended to supplant LIBOR[57] and is based on actual transactions rather than on estimated quotes made by banks, which could be manipulated.[58] The use of the SONIA benchmark is part of a broader international effort by banks and regulators to move the market away from the tainted LIBOR rates. In April 2018, the Bank of England began publishing the SONIA rates, which regulatory authorities have found to be more attractive as a benchmark for market transactions, in part because SONIA

55   Browne A, 'Libor Now Has a New Administrator – But Our Reforms Have Gone Much Further' (*City A.M.*, 11 July 2013) www.cityam.com/article/libor-now-has-new-administrator-our-reforms-have-gone-much-further#sthash.L3qpkU6i.dpuf accessed 18 May 2018.

56   Bank of England, 'SONIA Key Features and Policies' (May 2018) Section 2 'Definition of SONIA' www.bankofengland.co.uk/-/media/boe/files/markets/benchmarks/sonia-key-features-and-policies.pdf accessed 21 December 2018.

57   Bailey A, 'The Future of LIBOR' (27 July 2017), Speech at Bloomberg London www.fca.org.uk/news/speeches/the-future-of-libor accessed 21 December 2018.

58   Jones H, 'Bank of England Expects Big Libor Switch to Start in Earnest' (*Reuters*, 18 April 2018) https://uk.reuters.com/article/us-boe-markets-sonia/bank-of-england-expects-big-libor-switch-to-start-in-earnest-idUKKBN1HP1GB accessed 21 December 2018.

is an overnight rate that can fluctuate while LIBOR rates are held steady for a term. The move away from LIBOR has been reinforced by the statement of the UK FCA executive that LIBOR will be discontinued in the near future.[59]

IV FINANCIAL CRIME AND AML/CTF

9.59 Prior to 2001, there was not a high priority for banks and regulators to monitor and control money laundering and terrorist financing. Although banks had begun to adopt 'Know Your Customer' and 'Suspicious Transaction Reporting' practices in the 1990s in response to the Financial Action Task Force's 1990 Forty Recommendations against money laundering, most countries did not apply strict anti-money laundering regulatory and administrative controls. The Financial Action Task Force's Forty Recommendations grew to Forty-Nine in 2002 to include specific measures aimed at terrorist financing.[60] Most state efforts to control money laundering and terrorist financing had taken the form of criminal law enforcement that was handled by prosecutors and other enforcement authorities, usually against criminal enterprises which were profiting from the proceeds of crime. However, little emphasis was placed on holding third-party banks and professionals responsible for facilitating and assisting economic crime. The criminal law standard of proof for obtaining convictions made it difficult for prosecutors to bring enforcement actions against banks and other financial firms for facilitating or assisting money laundering. What's more, money laundering was difficult to prosecute because in the 1980s and 1990s most countries had only adopted a limited number of predicate offences upon which a money laundering offence could be based. A successful money laundering prosecution required proof beyond reasonable doubt that a predicate offence (i.e. drug trafficking or prostitution) had been committed along with a separate financial transaction that was connected to the underlying predicate offence. This was extremely difficult to prove and so only a few high-profile prosecutions, such as those against the Bank of Credit and Commerce International (BCCI), were brought.

9.60 The terrorist attacks on the United States on 11 September 2001, however, dramatically shifted the focus of policymakers from using the criminal law to enforce anti-money laundering measures against banks and other financial firms to utilising civil and administrative law measures – including administrative sanctions – against banks, financial firms and other third-party intermediaries, such as accountants, lawyers and trust company service providers, who had played a significant role in facilitating and assisting

---

59 See Bailey (n 58), final paragraph.
60 Financial Action Task Force, 'FATF 40 Recommendations' (October 2003) and 'FATF IX Special Recommendations' (October 2001), and Financial Action Task Force, FATF (October 2001), 'FATF' IX Special Recommendations, see Financial Action Task Force, FATF (2012–2018), International Standards on Combating Money Laundering and the Financing of Terrorism & Proliferation, FATF, Paris, France www.fatf-gafi.org/recommendations.html accessed 9 January 2019.

transactions involving criminal organisations and terrorist groups. Financial sector industry bodies, such as the Wolfsberg Group, an association of thirteen global banks which aims to develop frameworks and guidance for the management of financial crime, have played a role in adopting guidance for bank compliance with anti-financial crime measures, particularly with respect to 'Know Your Customer' standards.

9.61 Indeed, the 9/11 terrorist attacks triggered a significant modification of anti-financial crime (AFC) laws across the world.[61] While national and international anti-financial crime regulations and laws were already in place prior to September 2001,[62] it is since the 9/11 attacks that a materially large volume of laws, regulations, technical guidance and recommendations have been issued by governments and international economic organisations imposing increasingly higher standards on banking institutions across the world. International organisations such as the Basel Committee on Banking Supervision (discussed in Chapters 3 and 4) and the Wolfsberg Group have issued documents, whether in the form of principles, guidance, frequently asked questions (FAQs) or statements, with the aim of helping banks to design and implement AFC programmes.

9.62 Similarly, national and international regulators have regularly amended their regulatory frameworks by expanding and strengthening anti-money laundering (AML), anti-bribery & corruption (AB&C) and economic sanctions rules. The European Union, for example, recently published its fourth AML directive,[63] whereas the UK Financial Conduct Authority (FCA) and its predecessor, the Financial Services Authority (FSA), have published in the last eighteen years a significantly high number of consultation papers, reports, reviews and new regulations. In the UK, the enactment of new regulatory rules led to the expansion of the UK financial crime regulatory framework and imposed additional requirements on UK-based banks and financial firms. Changes in the UK regulatory regime also prompted the engagement of the FCA with AFC concerns in a more timely manner than before; nevertheless, it is not yet possible to affirm whether the changes have been effective.

9.63 Since 2001, banks have undertaken substantial and costly compliance efforts to safeguard the banking system against money laundering and terrorist financing. Regulators across Europe, the US and other jurisdictions have adopted comprehensive, risk-based approaches to control financial crime.[64] Banks and financial institutions have also adopted a more

---

61   United States Department of State, International Narcotics Control Strategy Report Bureau for International Narcotics and Law Enforcement Affairs, March 2003 Report, 'Money Laundering and Financial Crimes'.

62   See Financial Action Task Force (n 60).

63   Directive 2015/849 of the European Parliament and of the Council on the prevention of the use of the financial system for the purposes of money laundering or terrorist financing, amending Regulation (EU) No. 648/2012 of the European Parliament and of the Council, and repealing Directive 2005/60/EC of the European Parliament and of the Council and Commission Directive 2006/70/EC [2015] OJ L 141/73.

64   Financial Conduct Authority, 'Anti-Money Laundering – Annual Report 2016/17' (2017), 6 www.fca.org.uk/publication/annual-reports/annual-anti-money-laundering-report-2016-17.pdf accessed 21 December 2012.

holistic approach to compliance, moving away from a tick-the-box culture to emphasising a risk-based approach that complements an institution's business objectives and strategy. A robust and embedded compliance culture is seen as a prerequisite for a successful and sustainable business strategy which allows institutions to detect and prevent criminals from using the financial system to launder the proceeds of crime or to finance terrorist activities. Financial institutions are spending, on average, US$60 million per year to meet their AML compliance costs, but some larger firms are spending up to US$500 million annually to comply with Know-Your-Customer and customer due diligence (CDD) rules.[65] Although banks have spent millions on improvements to their financial crime programmes, and have more than doubled the recruitment of AML/CFT professionals, financial crime still poses a major threat to economies and societies.

9.64 According to a study published by the Transparency International (TI) organisation in June 2016, the UK Treasury estimated in 2007 that each year £10 billion of illicit funds pass through the UK 'regulated sector' of banks, high-value dealers and other firms.[66] In 2013, this figure had increased to between £23 billion and £57 billion of illicit wealth laundered through the formal financial sector of London each year. Similarly, in a study published by the United Nations Office on Drugs and Crime (UNODC)[67] in 2011, the International Monetary Fund (IMF) estimated that there has been an increasing trend of money laundering across the globe since 1996. According to the IMF, whilst at least US$0.6 trillion was laundered in 1996, the figure doubled to US$1.2 trillion in 2009.[68]

9.65 In addition, as mentioned earlier in this chapter, the volume and figures of fines enforced against banks in the last twenty years have increased at a similar rate. A recently published study from the Conduct Cost Project's (CCP) Research Foundation states that the world's top twenty banks were fined conduct charges totalling £264 billion between 2012 and 2016,[69] an increase of almost a third compared to 2008–2012. For the five years between 2012 and 2016, Bank of America was the most fined bank, incurring £45.6 billions-worth of charges.[70] JP Morgan came in second, with £33.6 billions-worth of charges, followed by Morgan Stanley, which was fined £24.4 billion.

---

65 Accenture Consulting, 'Evolving AML Journey – Leveraging Machine Learning Within Anti-Money Laundering Transaction Monitoring' (2017), 2 www.accenture.com/_acnmedia/PDF-61/Accenture-Leveraging-Machine-Learning-Anti-Money-Laundering-Transaction-Monitoring.pdf accessed 20 December 2018.
66 HM Treasury, Home Office, 'The Financial Challenge to Crime and Terrorism' (February 2007), para. 2.44 https://webarchive.nationalarchives.gov.uk/+/http:/www.hm-treasury.gov.uk/d/financialchallenge_crime_280207.pdf accessed 21 December 2018.
67 UNODC, 'Estimating Illicit Financial Flows Resulting from Drug Trafficking and Other Transnational Organized Crimes' (October 2011),18 www.unodc.org/documents/data-and-analysis/Studies/Illicit_financial_flows_2011_web.pdf accessed 21 December 2018.
68 Ibid.
69 CCP Research Foundation. Conduct Costs Project Report 2017, International Results Table (2012–2016) http://ccpresearchfoundation.com/noticeboard?item=32056-conduct-costs-project-report-2017 accessed 21 December 2018.
70 *United States* v. *HSBC Bank USA, NA and HSBS Holdings PLS*, Deferred Prosecution Agreement (10 December 2012).

9.66 In the UK, HSBC became the record-holder in 2012 for the largest sanctions fine ever paid in history (£1.2 billion) as part of a deferred prosecution agreement (DPA), and an additional £492 million in civil penalties.[71] In 2009, Lloyds was fined £231 million due to transactions with Iranian customers, and in 2010 Barclays paid £190 million due to the facilitation of wire transfers of customers in Cuba, Iran and elsewhere.[72] Similarly, Standard Chartered paid £187 in December 2012 for removing information from wire transfers for customers in Iran, Sudan, Libya and Burma.[73]

9.67 In addition to AML/CTF liability, banks were also investigated and admitted liability for misrepresentation in the marketing and sale of mortgage-backed securities. For example, Credit Suisse (CS) reached a settlement in January 2017 with the US Department of Justice (DOJ) regarding its misrepresentations in the marketing and sale of residential mortgage-backed securities (RMBS). The settlement released CS from potential civil claims by the DOJ related to its securitisation, underwriting and issuance of RMBS. CS agreed to pay a substantial US2.46 billion fine to the DOJ. In addition, CS must provide compensation payments totalling SD2.8 million within five years following the settlement to investors who suffered losses as a result of their fraudulent misrepresentations. The DOJ and CS agreed to the appointment of an independent monitor to oversee the implementation of the related 'consumer relief' requirements of the settlement.[74] Similarly, Wells Fargo entered into a civil settlement with the Department of Justice in 2018 to pay administrative penalties of US$2.09 billion for misrepresentation in the marketing and sale of residential mortgage-backed securities prior to the crisis. The Justice Department press release states that it 'holds Wells Fargo responsible for originating and selling tens of thousands of loans that were packaged into securities and subsequently defaulted'. This caused investors, including financial institutions, to lose billions of dollars investing in residential mortgage-backed securities originated by Wells Fargo. The settlement agreement stated that Wells Fargo misrepresented the quality of the mortgage-backed securities it packaged and sold to investors by knowingly relying on mis-stated income and incomplete documentation in order to increase the volume of loans. US authorities have entered settlement agreements with other large global banks, including a 2018 settlement with Barclays PLC for US$2 billion, for misrepresentation in the marketing and sale of residential

71 US Department of Justice, 'Lloyds TSB Bank PLC Agrees to Forfeit $350 Million in Connection with Violations of the International Emergency Economic Powers Act' (9 January 2009) www.justice.gov/opa/pr/lloyds-tsb-bank-plc-agrees-forfeit-350-million-connection-violations-international-emergency accessed 21 December 2018.
72 US Department of Justice, 'Barclays Bank PLC Agrees to Forfeit $298 Million in Connection with Violations of the International Emergency Economic Powers Act and the Trading with the Enemy Act' (18 August 2010) www.justice.gov/opa/pr/barclays-bank-plc-agrees-forfeit-298-million-connection-violations-international-emergency accessed 21 December 2018.
73 US Department of Justice, 'Standard Chartered Bank Agrees to Forfeit $227 Million for Illegal Transactions with Iran, Sudan, Libya, and Burma' (10 December 2012) www.justice.gov/opa/pr/standard-chartered-bank-agrees-forfeit-227-million-illegal-transactions-iran-sudan-libya-and accessed 21 December 2018.
74 Credit Suisse, 'Credit Suisse Reaches Settlement with U.S. Department of Justice Regarding Legacy Residential Mortgage-Backed Securities Matter' (press release, 18 January 2017) www.credit-suisse.com/corporate/en/articles/media-releases/cs-reaches-settlement-us-doj-legacy-rmbs-201701.html accessed 21 December 2018.

mortgage-backed securities (RMBS). Also, the Justice Department settled with the Royal Bank of Scotland for US$4.9 million for mis-selling RMBS. Under the Trump administration, the Justice Department has settled for much less on average than the settlement agreements of the Obama administration, which included a US$16.5 billion settlement with Bank of America in 2014 for RMBS claims, and settlements in 2013 of US$13.7 billion with JP Morgan Chase & Co. and US$7 billion with Citi.

CONCLUSION

9.68 Banker misconduct has become a major source of reputation and operational risk for banks. Before and after the crisis, many traders and their managers at some of the world's largest and most recognised banks (i.e. Citi, Barclays and UBS) engaged in systematic manipulation of market benchmarks and indices. These episodes of misconduct led to hundreds of millions in fines on the banking industry and demonstrated how misconduct risk has implications for system-wide risk when they involve banking industry benchmarks and systematic fraud across many institutions that can result in disorderly operation of the markets. This raises important policy issues about how banker misconduct is regulated and how the criminal law has been used to discipline misconduct, as seen with the UK prosecution of bankers for fraud in the manipulation of LIBOR.

QUESTIONS

1. How does the LIBOR scandal represent weaknesses in bank governance?
2. How did LIBOR work and how was it manipulated?
3. Discuss the breadth and scope of the Market Abuse Regime and explain why it is relevant for bankers.
4. Were the fines imposed on banks for misconduct adequate? If not, what sanctions do you think would have been more effective?
5. Do regulations adopted after 9/11 impose unrealistic requirements on banks?
6. Why have banks committed so many regulatory breaches?

Further Reading

Alexander K, *Economic Sanctions: Law and Public Policy* (Macmillan 2009), especially chapters 10–12.
Alldridge P, *Money Laundering Law* (Hart Publishing 2003), 1–42, 89–107
Barnes P, *Stock Market Efficiency, Insider Dealing and Market Abuse* (Gower 2009)
Berhporsson AF, *What is Market Manipulation?* (University of Copenhagen, published PhD dissertation 2017)

Ellinger EP, Lomnicka E and Hare CVM, *Banking Law* (Oxford University Press 2011), 3–77, 92–112

Tuveson M and Ralph D, 'Is Regulation of Risk Culture the Missing Piece? Civil Actions Reconsidered. Banking and Financial Services Policy Report', *Wolters Kluwer Law & Business* (2016) 35 1

Weinstein S and Wild, C, *Legal Risk Management, Governance and Compliance* (Globe Law and Business 2013), 11–44, 111–124, 145–164

10

Shadow Banking

Table of Contents

INTRODUCTION

10.1 The chapter analyses the phenomenon of shadow banking and why it is relevant to banking regulation. Banking regulation has traditionally been concerned with regulating legal entities that are engaged in borrowing callable funds from the public which are then leveraged on the institution's balance sheet into longer-term loans and credits for businesses and individuals. For many regulators, this type of credit intermediation – or 'maturity transformation' (borrowing short and lending long) – attracted regulatory concern because the funds raised from the public were owed to retail depositors who could, if they lost confidence in their bank or banking system, precipitate a 'bank run'. As discussed in Chapter 4, to meet this concern, regulators have generally required that retail deposit-taking banks hold minimum amounts of capital and liquid assets and are subject to governance requirements. However, financial institutions which raise their funding from bond issuance, securitisation structures and non-deposit loans provided by wholesale or professional investors, or other banks were generally not subject to these requirements. As regulatory requirements for deposit-taking banks became more costly in the 1990s and 2000s, more and more credit was channelled through the so-called 'shadow banking' sector. The growth of the shadow banking sector was identified as one of the factors that caused the crisis of 2007–2008.[1] Since the adoption of the post-crisis regulatory reforms (i.e. Basel III), there have been further regulatory concerns about the continued growth of credit intermediation in the shadow banking sector in relation to the growth of lending in the regulated banking sector.

10.2 This chapter suggests that the financial stability risks associated with the growth of shadow banking raise fundamental questions about the overarching objectives of banking regulation. It suggests that financial innovation and technology advances in the provision of credit through alternative channels outside the regulated banking sector necessitate a more systematic approach to financial regulation that involves the management of the underlying economic functions of the financial system – the provision, allocation and deployment of financial capital – as well as the financial system's capacity to serve as a network within which those functions can be conducted. By focusing on the underlying functions of the financial system, and not on specific legal entities, regulators will be able to address the effects of change and innovation on financial markets and the implications for financial stability.

10.3 To illustrate the difficulty of regulating change and innovation in financial markets, this chapter considers the specific problem of regulating shadow banking. Shadow banking involves collecting surplus funds from multiple investors and allocating the funds to borrowers who can productively use them. Shadow banking essentially involves the traditional function of banking – borrowing short and lending long – but conducted outside or partially outside the formal banking sector. The Financial Stability Board has defined shadow banking as 'credit intermediation involving entities and activities (fully or partially) outside the regular banking system' or 'non-bank credit intermediation in short'.[2]

10.4 Shadow banking has grown rapidly in response to the increased cost of regulation in the formal banking sector. The US Federal Reserve estimates that the 'gross size of the industry was nearly $20 trillion in March 2008, significantly larger than the liabilities of the traditional banking system, while others estimated it at three times that level – $60 trillion

---

1 Financial Crisis Inquiry Commission, 'Financial Crisis Inquiry Report – Final Report of the National Commission on the Causes of the Financial Crisis in the United States' Official Government Edition (January 2011), 427 www.gpo.gov/fdsys/pkg/GPO-FCIC/pdf/GPO-FCIC.pdf accessed 21 February 2018.
2 See Financial Stability Board, 'Shadow Banking: Strengthening Oversight and Regulation – Recommendations of the Financial Stability Board' (October 2011), 3.

in December 2011'.[3] The Financial Stability Board estimated in 2014 that the shadow banking sector had grown to US$36 trillion globally.[4] In the EU area, the broad measure of shadow banking accounted for €31 trillion in total assets at the end of the fourth quarter of 2016.[5] The European Systemic Risk Board (ESRB) found that the broad measure of shadow banking in the euro area expanded by almost 40 per cent over the period 2012–2016.[6] Although shadow banking constitutes a large and growing portion of the credit market, it is not well defined and it largely takes place outside the formal banking sector and, therefore, is not subject to prudential controls and oversight. This chapter suggests that there is a need to define shadow banking by identifying its overall scope and its basic characteristics. Based on this definition and conceptual understanding, shadow banking can be regulated in a manner that maximises its efficiencies while minimising its risks to the financial system.

I WHAT IS A BANK?

10.5 As discussed in Chapter 1, the business of banking has traditionally involved at its core credit intermediation; that is, the collection of callable savings from depositors and other lenders and the making of longer-term loans to borrowers while providing liquidity to customers in the form of payment facilities. The financial risks associated with credit intermediation, also known as 'maturity transformation', constitute a major concern for bank regulators because the practice of borrowing short and lending long can pose risks to society if banks fail to manage their risks effectively. Moreover, the scope and application of the laws which regulate and supervise credit institutions contain a much narrower definition of what constitutes a bank that consists primarily of taking retail deposits and providing longer-term loans and payment services. For instance, EU banking law states that banks are defined as undertakings, 'whose business it is to receive deposits or other repayable funds from the public and to grant credits for its own account'.[7] This narrow legal definition excludes a large number of credit intermediaries that are involved in the business of borrowing short and lending long and which pose financial stability risks to society.

---

3   See Halstrick P, 'Tighter Bank Rules Give Fillip to Shadow Banks', *Reuters* (London, 19 December 2011) https://uk.reuters.com/article/uk-regulation-shadow-banking/tighter-bank-rules-give-fillip-to-shadow-banks-idUKLNE7BJ00T20111220 accessed 26 February 2018, and Schwarcz SL, 'Regulating Shadow Banking' (2011) 31 *Review of Banking & Financial Law* 63 610.
4   Financial Services Authority, 'Global Shadow Banking Monitoring Report 2015' (November 2015), 9 www.fsb.org/2015/11/global-shadow-banking-monitoring-report-2015/ accessed 21 December 2018.
5   European Systemic Risk Board, 'EU Shadow Banking Monitor' No. 2 (May 2017), 2 www.esrb.europa.eu/pub/pdf/reports/20170529_shadow_banking_report.en.pdf accessed 6 March 2018.
6   Ibid.
7   See Article 3(1) of Directive 2013/36/EU of the European Parliament and of the Council of 26 June 2013 on access to the activity of credit institutions and the prudential supervision of credit institutions and investment firms, amending Directive 2002/87/EC and repealing Directive 2006/48/EC and 2006/49/EC [2013] OJ L176/338.

The blurring of the distinction between banks and non-bank financial institutions has resulted in a clear need for regulators to be able to identify and supervise firms that are engaged in the banking business. For instance, some non-bank financial institutions provide services similar to those provided by banks and could be easily confused for banks, such as building societies and credit unions in the UK which provide services very similar to banking as they accept deposits and provide loans.

10.6 The prevailing argument is that banks require a higher level of regulation than other financial institutions, thereby necessitating the need for regulators to identify banks by setting out a satisfactory legal framework for the definition of banking and what constitutes the banking business. Without such a framework, much of what constitutes banking would escape regulation and pose undue risks to the financial sector and the economy. This phenomenon is sometimes called the 'shadow banking' problem, a concept discussed in more detail in this chapter.

10.7 Internationally, the importance of defining banks and the permissible activities in which they can engage is captured in Core Principle 4 of the Basel Revised Core Principles For Effective Banking Supervision, which provides that '[t]he permissible activities of institutions that are licensed and subject to supervision as banks are clearly defined and the use of the word "bank" in names is controlled'.[8] Moreover, Basel Core Principle 1 recommends that 'a primary objective of banking regulation' is 'to promote the safety and soundness of banks and the banking system'. This means that supervisors should be monitoring both the 'safety and soundness' of individual banks as well as systemic risks that arise across the financial system and that may threaten the stability of individual banks.[9] This suggests that bank supervisors should have the competence to identify and monitor overarching, system-wide risks across financial markets that are material to the stability of individual banking institutions.

10.8 Despite the Core Principles' potentially broad scope of supervisory oversight, most jurisdictions do not provide legal competence for bank supervisors to oversee the broader financial system, but rather the focus of supervisory competence is directed to individual institutions that are defined as credit or banking institutions under domestic law. The judicial decisions of several countries have not adopted a universal definition of a bank. For instance, English common law historically defined banks as businesses that accepted deposits for their customers' accounts while negotiating cheques on behalf of their customers that either drew on, or credited, their accounts vis-à-vis third parties.[10] In contrast, the Australian courts have defined the essential elements of banking business more broadly as 'the collection of money by receiving deposits upon loan, repayable when and as expressly or

---

8   See Basel Committee on Banking Supervision, Revised 'Core Principles for Effective Banking' (September 2012), Core Principle 4 www.bis.org/publ/bcbs230.pdf accessed 21 February 2018.

9   Ibid. Core Principle 1 states as an essential criterion that '[t]he primary objective of banking regulation is to promote the safety and soundness of banks and the banking system', Core Principle 1, Essential criteria 2.

10   *United Dominion Trust LTD* v. *Kirkwood* [1966] 2 QB 431, 453 (per Denning).

impliedly agreed upon, and the utilisation of the money so collected by lending it again in such sums as are required'.[11] The different legal definitions across jurisdictions suggests, as Lord Denning observed, that 'a banker is easier to recognise than to define'.[12]

10.9 The problem of defining banks has been made more difficult by the emergence of multi-functional banks that operate in complex financial groups providing a variety of financial services, including commercial banking, merchant banking and securities broker-dealers. Rather, regulators in different jurisdictions have adopted quite different approaches to defining banks. Internationally, state practice appears to have converged on three approaches: (1) a bank is an institution defined as such by a governmental authority; (2) a bank engages in one or more activities listed as banking by a regulatory or governmental authority; and (3) a bank is defined in terms of some generalised characteristics such as the 'taking of deposits from the public', and 'the use of the word "bank" is limited to licensed and supervised institutions in all circumstances where the general public might otherwise be misled'.[13]

10.10 The United Kingdom has adopted a definition under Part 4 of the Financial Services and Markets Act 2000 (FSMA) (as amended) that the carrying on of the business of banking is a regulated activity for which permission must be obtained from the UK regulators, the Prudential Regulation Authority and the Financial Conduct Authority.[14] The business of banking includes accepting deposits (within the meaning of section 22 of FSMA 2000, taken with Schedule 2 and any order under section 22). Under the FSMA 2000 (Regulated Activities) Order 2001, accepting deposits is a specified kind of activity if:

a. money received by way of deposit is lent to others; or,
b. any other activity of the person accepting the deposit is financed wholly, or to a material extent, out of the capital of or interest on money received by way of deposit.

10.11 The Banking Act 2009 goes further to exclude certain institutions, such as building societies and credit unions, from being classified as banks even though they perform similar functions to banks, such as accepting money by way of deposit and lending the money to others.[15]

10.12 The UK statutory approach to defining banks, however, provides the Treasury with discretion to expand the definition to include other financial firms engaged in the banking

11 *Commissioners of the State Savings Bank of Victoria* v. *Permewan, Wright & Co. Ltd* [1915] 19 CLR 457, 470.
12 *Kirkwood* (n 10) [1966] 2 QB 431, 453.
13 See Basel Committee on Banking Supervision (n 8), Core Principle 4, 31. See also discussion in Cranston R, *Principles of Banking Law* (Oxford University Press 2002), 5.
14 Financial Services and Market Act 2000 (FSMA), section 19 (as amended).
15 The Act expressly states that a bank does not include: (a) a building society (within the meaning of section 119 of the Building Societies Act 1986), (b) a credit union within the meaning of section 31 of the Credit Unions Act 1979, or (c) any other class of institution excluded by an order made by the Treasury.

business; that is, borrowing short term from depositors and other lenders and making longer-term credits available to borrowers. This approach, though not without its problems, is preferred to the legally and politically more cumbersome approach followed by many jurisdictions of requiring primary legislation to change the definition of banks. The adoption of primary legislation or statutes for many countries can be a complicated and lengthy process that is not necessarily the most effective or efficient way to regulate evolving 'risks in financial markets.

10.13 Despite the different approaches to defining which financial institutions are banks and thereby subject to prudential regulation, the question of whether an institution is a bank or not in a particular jurisdiction can be quickly resolved by inquiring whether it has been licensed by a regulatory body or not. The variety of national approaches for determining whether a financial institution is licensable is not universal and lacks symmetry with the cross-border nature of international finance in which credit flows across borders more or less seamlessly and is legally bound by national law and regulation. The lack of effective coordination between states in defining banks and other financial institutions has resulted in regulatory arbitrage internationally, in which credit flows through different legal entities and structures that are not defined as regulated banking institutions. This results in a lower common denominator of regulation that allows the generation of high levels of debt and leverage across the financial system that is technically outside the regulated banking sector, but for which the banking sector has in many cases a contingent liability. This is the shadow banking system, which is analysed below along with some observations concerning how it might be regulated in the future.

II A FUNCTIONAL APPROACH TO BANKING REGULATION

The function of the financial system as a whole is to serve as a *network* within which its component elements, firms and markets, can achieve their *economic functions*. Law is integral to achieving this end and the financial system can be characterised as a *law-related system*. Regulation of a law-related system, as a system, should have two purposes: 'to prevent harmful conduct' that can impair the system's ability to serve as a network and to 'avoid harmful consequences' of conduct that cannot be prevented.[16]

A Designing Functional Banking Regulation

10.14 Designing *functional* banking regulation should focus on preventing harmful conduct and avoiding harmful consequences. In reality, that focus should be broadened beyond 'conduct' as non-conduct-related vulnerabilities of the financial system can also impair economic functions. Accordingly, banking regulation should aim to limit the triggers of

---

16 See Schwarcz SL, 'Regulating Financial Change: A Functional Approach' (2016) 100 *Minnesota Law Review* 1441.

systemic shocks. Ideally, banking regulation would act *ex ante* to limit the triggers of systemic shocks caused by structural vulnerabilities. As discussed below, shadow banking can increase vulnerabilities due to maturity transformation; for example, the asset-liability mismatch that results from the short-term funding of longer-term projects. This mismatch creates a 'liquidity default risk' that borrowers will be unable to repay their lenders. A bank 'run' is the typical example of maturity transformation leading to a liquidity default, but money market mutual funds also provide short-term loans, essentially withdrawable on demand, to fund longer-term investment projects, usually arranged by banks.

10.15 Although maturity transformation is a vulnerability of the financial system, it is also a benefit. Using short-term debt to fund long-term projects is attractive because it allows banks who use their information and risk management skills to assess the creditworthiness of projects and to extend funds derived from surplus savers who would otherwise not have the same capacity to channel their savings to viable projects. The bank's intermediary role can generate a positive externality for the economy and result in lower default rates and a lower cost of borrowing. Regulation should not, therefore, attempt to prohibit or unduly limit maturity transformation. In a traditional banking context, the standard regulatory solution is not to require banks to match-fund their assets. Rather, governments often provide deposit insurance that limits the likelihood that depositors will panic.

10.16 The liquidity default risk that inevitably remains can trigger systemic shocks. As discussed below, the failure of pre-crisis regulation to adequately address liquidity default risk resulting from the maturity transformation in shadow banking networks is widely believed to have contributed to the build-up of risks in the financial system in the period leading up to the 2007–2008 crisis.[17]

B Responding to Institutional and Market Innovations

10.17 The design and structure of banking regulation is tied to the current institutional and market architecture. The current institutional and market structure for financial markets is constantly changing. Banking – and financial – regulation should together aim to support the main functions of financial markets and firms. Regulation, however, can quickly become outmoded and obsolete because of market and institutional innovations and evolution that respond to innovation in financial products and investment structures, advances in technology and regulatory requirements.

10.18 Prior to the 2007–2008 crisis, the financial regulatory regime was mainly focused on the risks posed by bank-intermediated funding. This regulatory framework had failed to adequately address a collapsing financial system in which the majority of funding was

---

17　See Alexander K, Eatwell J, Persaud A and Reoch R, 'Financial Supervision and Crisis Management in the EU' (2007) Policy Study IP/A/ECON/IC/2007–069, Brussels: European Parliament, 13–15 www.augurproject.eu/IMG/pdf/JEatwellEtAl_FinancialSupervisionYCrisisManagement_EUreport-2.pdf accessed 21 February 2018.

derived from non-bank intermediated sources. Despite the international regulatory reforms (discussed in Chapter 3), similar systemic risks are returning to the financial markets and some regulators have responded by identifying regulatory 'tools' to fix defects in the design and structure of today's financial firms and markets. These regulatory tools, if not recalibrated, will likely lose their utility over time.

10.19 Rather, financial regulation should embrace change, by protecting the ongoing functions of the financial system: the provision, allocation and deployment of capital. A fundamental task of financial regulation should be to correct failures that impair the ability of firms and markets to perform these economic functions. That necessarily includes protecting against systemic risk.

10.20 It is submitted that a 'functional' approach to regulating finance is necessary to provide a set of regulatory ordering principles with which real-world banking regulation can be compared, whatever the existing financial architecture. That, in turn, could help to inform the uses and limits of regulatory tools and could also provide perspective on deciding between competing regulatory objectives and reducing the potential for regulatory arbitrage. By adopting a functional approach to regulation, financial regulation can transcend the constantly evolving institutional structures of finance that are tied to the design and operations of financial firms and markets. Because present-day regulation can quickly become outmoded, it should be designed around the basic functions of financial markets and firms.

III THE CHALLENGE OF SHADOW BANKING

10.21 The shadow banking sector has grown dramatically in recent years and is estimated at US$36 trillion in assets on a global basis.[18] Although shadow banking plays an important role in the provision of credit to the economy, it is not well defined.[19] As mentioned earlier, a broader definition of 'shadow banking' refers to 'financial intermediaries that conduct maturity, credit, and liquidity transformation without access to central bank liquidity or public sector credit guarantees' (see Figure 10.1).[20]

10.22 A more limited definition would focus on what shadow banks do. This raises two questions: first, should the concept of shadow banking refer to the provision of *any* financial product and services by shadow banks, or should it focus only on the financial products and services provided by traditional banks? Second, should shadow banking be limited to financial products and services provided by shadow banks, or should it also embrace the intermediaries used by shadow banks to provide those products and services through the financial

---

18   In 2016, the Financial Stability Board estimated the gross size of the shadow banking sector to be US$36 trillion. Financial Stability Board, 'Global Shadow Banking Monitoring Report 2015' (November 2015), 9.
19   Ibid.
20   Pozsar Z, Tobias A, Ashcraft A and Boesky H, 'Shadow Banking' (July 2010) Federal Reserve Bank of New York Staff Report No. 458, abstract www.newyorkfed.org/medialibrary/media/research/staff_reports/sr458_July_2010_version.pdf accessed 5 March 2018.

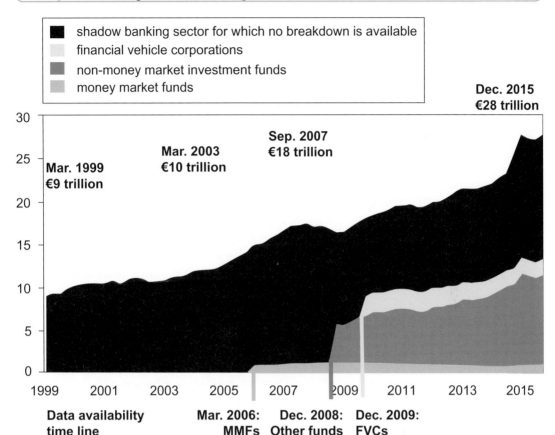

Figure 10.1 Shadow banking sector assets (Q1 1999–Q4 2015)
Source: European Central Bank, 'Financial Stability Review' (May 2016), 91 www.ecb.europa.eu/pub/pdf/other/ financialstabilityreview201605.en.pdf accessed 5 March 2018.

markets, for example, by way of securitisation, special purpose vehicle (SPE) issuance of securities and repurchase agreement lending?

A The Nature of Shadow Banking

10.23 While traditional banks tend to be highly regulated, shadow banks tend to be less regulated. Since shadow banks tend to be less regulated than traditional banks, regulatory arbitrage drives the demand for shadow banking to some extent. Therefore, increasing bank regulation requirements will almost always increase shadow banking demand. If driven exclusively by regulatory arbitrage, shadow banking may not represent a public good, as regulatory arbitrageurs might use deal structures that carry higher transaction costs. Also, regulatory arbitrage disadvantages market participants that lack the wealth and expertise to create legal structures to take advantage of it.

10.24 If it is not driven by regulatory arbitrage, shadow banking can constitute a public good by helping to achieve efficiencies. This is because it includes a range of intermediation activities with significant economic value outside the traditional banking system, including 'disintermediation', which removes the need for banks to act as intermediaries between the sources of funds (capital and other financial markets) and the users of funds (e.g. corporations that operate in the real economy), thus lowering the cost of capital for firms and individuals.

10.25 If shadow banking does not provide efficiencies in intermediation, and is instead primarily motivated by regulatory arbitrage, it can pose systemic risks to the financial system. This is because maturity transformation in the shadow banking system contributed significantly to asset bubbles in the US residential and commercial real estate markets prior to the 2007–2008 financial crisis. Shadow banking provides short-term funding of long-term capital needs, creating the risk of liquidity discontinuities. However, short-term funding of long-term capital needs is a problem not of shadow banking per se but of the financial system. Even traditional banks fund themselves through short-term deposits, with resulting liquidity discontinuities called 'bank runs'. To some extent, shadow banking delivers more diverse and, arguably, more innovative financial products than traditional banking.

B Assessing the Benefits and Costs of Shadow Banking

10.26 Shadow banking's disintermediation of traditional banks from the provision of credit increases economic efficiency by enabling companies to borrow without paying an interest rate mark-up charged by traditional banks. Shadow banking transactions involving non-deposit-taking financial firms, such as investment banks, finance companies and hedge funds, often perform the intermediation function in the place of banks and produce fewer efficiencies. Nonetheless, because operating in the non-bank context can create greater efficiencies (i.e. lower spreads than traditional bank loans on debt) for the economy as a public good (along with lower regulatory compliance costs), non-bank intermediation can optimise social welfare, so long as regulatory risks, such as systemic risks, are adequately addressed.

10.27 By decentralising lending, shadow banking can result in both positive and negative externalities. Decentralisation can increase consumer welfare by expanding the variety of funds and financial products available to individual investors. It can also make the financial system more robust in the face of negative shocks, as losses are distributed among smaller financial institutions and the 'too-big-to-fail' problem is mitigated. Decentralisation can also increase risk. For instance, market failures may occur more frequently in shadow banking than in the traditional banking system. Shadow banking might also increase the likelihood that systemic risk is triggered and transmitted. Awrey argues that, due to decentralisation, shadow banking creates market fragmentation, interconnectedness and opacity, making it difficult for market participants to process information, allowing risks to accumulate unnoticed and causing panic when hidden risks suddenly become apparent.[21]

---

21 Awrey D, 'Complexity, Innovation and the Regulation of Modern Financial Markets' (2012) 2 *Harvard Business Law Review* 2 235, 238 ff, 245 f.

Gorton and Metrick argue that shadow banking might increase the likelihood that systemic risk will be triggered.[22] Schwarcz and Anabtawi argue that two otherwise independent correlations can combine to transform localised economic shocks into broader systemic crises.[23] The first is an intra-firm correlation between a firm's financial integrity and its exposure to risk from low-probability adverse events. The second is a system-wide correlation among financial firms and markets, as shadow banking uses financial markets to provide products and services and increases interconnectedness.

C Regulating Shadow Banking

10.28 The regulation of the shadow banking sector should not necessarily be focused on limiting shadow banking but instead on maximising efficiencies and minimising shadow banking's potential to increase systemic risk. Regulation can maximise economic efficiency by addressing the fundamental sources of financial market failure that have been identified elsewhere in this book that are most likely, individually or in combination, to trigger systemic economic shocks or facilitate their transmission, namely, agency problems that result in moral hazard and adverse selection, conflicts of interest that arise from corporate legal structures (i.e. limited liability) of banking institutions that can create externalities and complexity of financial markets that exacerbates the asymmetric information problems, making it more difficult to assess and manage risks. In considering these fundamental *sources* of market failure, four *types* of market failure can be identified in the shadow banking system: information failure, rationality failure, principal–agent failure and incentive failure. These will be addressed in turn.

10.29 First, complexity of the shadow banking system can undermine disclosure, which is the main regulatory response to information failure. This has been further complicated by regulatory requirements under the Dodd-Frank Act as the shadow banking network's complexity at times makes it incomprehensible. One possibility is to simplify or standardise shadow banking to minimise its complexity. But standardisation can backfire. For instance, standardising derivatives transactions can inadvertently increase systemic risk by concentrating derivatives exposure at the clearing house level.[24] Standardisation may also stifle innovation.

10.30 Second, humans have bounded rationality, which explains why, despite the complexity of shadow banking, market participants acted without full understanding. For instance, some investors based their decisions to purchase financial products or make investments on mathematical models that they did not fully comprehend. Furthermore, many of these mathematical models were based on flawed assumptions regarding the likelihood that past

22 Gorton GB and Metrick A, 'Securitized Banking and the Run on Repo' (2009) NBER Working Paper No. 15223.
23 Schwarcz SL and Anabtawi I, 'Regulating Systemic Risk: Towards an Analytical Framework' (2011) UCLA School of Law, Law-Econ Research Paper No. 10–10.
24 See Balmer A, *Regulating Financial Derivatives – Clearing and Central Counterparties* (Elgar 2018). See also Schwarcz (n 16), 1349, 1395.

data on credit defaults and asset price movements were accurate estimates of future credit and market risks. These flawed value-at-risk statistical models could only serve, at best, as rough approximations of future financial market risks.

10.31 Third, principal–agent failure involves conflicts of interest between managers and owners of banks and financial firms where, because managers who are risk-takers for the bank are paid under short-term compensation schemes that are based on variable compensation (i.e. bonuses), they have an incentive to enter into transactions that have a greater upside payoff but equally a greater downside loss if the risks materialise. As discussed in Chapter 5, banker compensation structures that are largely based on variable compensation that is linked to higher firm revenue or share price performance over the short term can result in a misalignment of interests with the long-term performance of the bank. To prevent this principal–agent failure, banks could pay, including managers and others who take significant risks, under longer-term compensation schemes, such as deferred compensation based on long-term results.

10.32 Fourth, incentive failure can arise because technological advances have enabled investors to diversify their portfolio exposures to risk, which can instil the belief that risk has been minimised and therefore does not need to be monitored as closely. Indeed, technology has enabled the shadow banking network to produce diverse and innovative financial products that can lead to greater risk diversification and increased risk-adjusted returns. And advanced technology, including computerisation, facilitates tracking of allocated cash flows, enabling investment risk to be finely dispersed. In theory, such investment diversification is beneficial. However, risk sometimes can be marginalised by becoming so widely dispersed that rational market participants individually lack the incentive to monitor, which happened prior to the 2007–2008 crisis.

10.33 Regulation should focus on minimising shadow banking's potential to create systemic risk. Specifically, shadow banking might increase that potential by increasing the likelihood that systemic risk will be triggered and, poossibly, transmitted. Shadow banking may increase the likelihood that systemic risk will be triggered by making panics more likely. Targeted regulation is not a possibility, as it is difficult to identify all the causes of panics. Regulation could indirectly reduce fragmentation, interconnectedness and opacity by limiting the factors that give rise to shadow banking. A possible regulatory solution lies with limiting regulatory arbitrage, either by regulating traditional banks less or by regulating shadow banks more. The latter seems to be occurring in the current regulatory reform process. For instance, Scwarcz observes how 'the Dodd-Frank Act subjects non-bank financial firms that are designated as systemically significant to enhanced prudential regulation, including capital requirements, limits on leverage and short-term debt, liquidity requirements and increased regulatory disclosures'.[25]

---

25   Schwarcz (n 3), 619, 639.

10.34 Banking regulation should also address other structural vulnerabilities that can trigger systemic shocks. Regulation cannot realistically eliminate the triggers of systemic shocks, as regulators cannot predict them and therefore the market will be exposed to vulnerabilities. Some examples include failure by a firm or market which can rapidly propagate throughout the financial system in various ways including through financial payment networks and through high-speed computerised algorithmic trading systems. As discussed in 1.42–1.48, corporate finance has become increasingly disintermediated from the traditional banking system, resulting in shadow banking networks increasingly becoming channels for propagation of financial failures. At a micro level, fragility or failure of a systemically important institution can arise from depositor or investor, rationality and information failure, which could trigger a systemic collapse. It is therefore virtually certain that the financial system will face systemic shocks from time to time. An effective regulatory framework should therefore be designed to support the financial system in providing credit and investment capital after a systemic shock is triggered.

10.35 Regulation should also be designed to break the transmission of systemic shocks. This requires identification of transmission mechanisms. For instance, ring-fencing can best be understood as legally deconstructing a firm in order more optimally to reallocate and reduce risk. This is an example of insulating the firm to break the transmission of shocks. Ring-fencing raises questions about when, and how, it should be used as an economic regulatory tool with different approaches, as shown by the Dodd-Frank Act's Volcker Rule (Chapter 7) which prohibits banking groups with more than US$10 billion in assets from engaging in proprietary trading (with some exceptions), and the UK Banking Reform Act 2013, which requires large banking groups with more than £25 billion in retail deposit liabilities to establish a ring-fenced retail banking subsidiary.

10.36 Regulation should also limit the impact of systemic shocks. There are two ways to stabilise systemically important financial institutions (SIFIs) and the financial markets impacted by shocks. First, by requiring firms and markets to be more internally robust. This could be accomplished in various ways. Traditional banking regulation is inflexible, as it subjects banks and systemically important institutions to rigorous capital, solvency and similar requirements (to assure that they can continue operating). The flaw in this approach is that regulation's primary goal should be to protect the financial system's overall capacity to function as a network. Regulation need not, therefore, impose capital or solvency requirements on individual firms so long as it otherwise achieves that goal. This regulatory flexibility is important because capital and solvency requirements do not always efficiently reduce systemic risk. Nevertheless, reducing a shadow bank's leverage, for example, can certainly enable it to withstand economic shocks and reduce its chance of failure.

10.37 Functional regulation could, in theory, impose capital and solvency requirements on systemically important shadow banks. But it need not impose those requirements if it otherwise stabilises those firms, such as by providing liquidity if and when needed to protect the financial system's network functions. This insight enables functional banking regulation to be much more flexible than traditional regulation.

10.38 Second, ring-fencing certain financial activities in a financial institution can help to make traditional banks and systemically important shadow banks more internally viable – and thus more robust – by preventing the firm from engaging in risky activities and investing in risky assets. Some observers are sceptical of any rule that paternalistically substitutes a blanket regulatory prescription for a sophisticated firm's own business judgement.[26]

10.39 The provision of liquidity to firms and markets can be used to stabilise systemically important firms. In order to internalise costs, the source of the liquidity could be partly privatised by creating a systemic risk fund. Such a fund could be based on contributions by firms and institutions that reflect the potential externality they pose to the system. This could be a type of Pigouvian externality tax that would reduce moral hazard by discouraging those who contribute to the fund from engaging in financially risky activities. It would also motivate firms to cross-monitor each other.

CONCLUSION

10.40 In September 2008, the pre-crisis financial regulatory framework, which assumed the dominance of bank-intermediated funding, had failed to identify and control systemic risks and limit the fall-out from a collapsing financial system in which the majority of funding had become non-bank intermediated. Similar risks may be building up again, as regulators are concentrating on identifying regulatory 'tools' to fix defects in the design and structure of today's financial firms and markets without regard to evolving market structures and the types of risks that financial innovation can introduce to the system. These regulatory tools, if not recalibrated, will lose their utility over time and possibly exacerbate systemic financial market risks.

10.41 Rather, financial regulation should embrace change, by also protecting the ongoing functions of the financial system: the provision, allocation and deployment of capital. A fundamental job of financial regulation should be to correct failures that impair the ability of firms and markets to perform these economic functions. This necessarily includes protecting against systemic risk.

10.42 The shadow banking industry represents a particular challenge for functional regulation. This chapter suggests that shadow banking should be regulated to try to maximise its efficiencies while minimising its risks. Traditional financial regulatory agencies tend to be compartmentalised, each focusing on its specific mandate; because shadow banking cuts across these categories, its regulation may well require a more holistic effort or, at least, enhanced cross-agency coordination than currently exists in today's regulatory practice. Efforts to increase the regulation of shadow banks must address the question of whether regulation optimally minimises the risk of systemic harm while preserving shadow banking's efficiency.

26 Schwarcz (n 16), 1441.

11

Regulating Risk Culture

Table of Contents

INTRODUCTION

11.1 This chapter considers to what extent regulation can play a role in facilitating the development of organisational norms to enhance risk culture in financial institutions. Specifically, it assesses the regulatory responses and industry-led initiatives taken since the crisis to address weaknesses in bank risk culture. It reviews recent international, European Union and UK regulatory developments that relate to the regulation of bank risk culture. The chapter discusses some of the regulatory tools adopted to address weaknesses in bank risk culture and how self–regulatory initiatives in the banking and financial services sector are playing an important role in leading reform efforts to improve risk culture in the banking and financial services sector. It discusses how regulatory guidance and binding rules in certain areas (e.g. remuneration) can influence and strengthen risk culture in banking institutions, but that ultimately institutions themselves, acting in coordination with civil society organisations (e.g. universities), are best placed to channel the collective actions of individuals to strengthen risk culture by developing and reaffirming organisational ethics, norms and standards that support overall firm performance and protect against socially costly behaviour.

I BANK GOVERNANCE AND RISK CULTURE

11.2 It is generally accepted that the culture within banking institutions during the period prior to the global financial crisis of 2007–2009 emphasised excessive risk-taking for short-term profits at the expense of longer-term firm performance and sustainable shareholder value.[1] Moreover, the risk culture within institutions was driven by compensation arrangements that relied heavily on variable pay, which was determined by short-term performance metrics that often rewarded behaviour that generated short-term revenue and profits while placing the firm's long-term viability at risk and disadvantaging customers. One of the lessons of the crisis, therefore, was that regulators should play a greater role in judging how culture drives firm behaviour and risk-taking, and how this impacts society as a whole. Indeed, former Chief Regulator of the British Financial Services Authority, Hector Sants, observed that '[t]he end goal should be that firms understand their own culture and the potential risks posed by the wrong culture'.[2]

11.3 However, the problem with regulators judging how culture drives risk-taking within the banking industry has been questioned because there have been no baseline standards in place to define what 'good behaviour' might actually look like. The problem, at least in the public mind, was that the reckless behaviour that helped create the financial crisis was a product of a win-at-all-costs culture, within which bankers felt it was acceptable to use deceptive or unethical methods, or legal or regulatory loopholes, to maximise profit. Indeed, the Governor of the Bank of England Mark Carney, speaking in June 2015, called it an 'ethical drift' in the banking sector, which meant that unethical behaviour 'went unchecked, proliferated and eventually became the norm'.

---

1   See United States Financial Crisis Inquiry Commission, 'Financial Crisis Inquiry Report – Final Report of the National Commission on the Causes of the Financial Crisis in the United States' Official Government Edition (January 2011), 15–17 www.gpo.gov/fdsys/pkg/GPO-FCIC/pdf/GPO-FCIC.pdf accessed 21 February 2018. Awrey D, Blair W and Kershaw D, 'Between Law and Markets: Is There a Role for Culture and Ethics in Financial Regulation?' (2013) 38 *Delaware Journal of Corporate Law* 1, 191–245.
2   Sants H, Chief Executive UK Financial Services Authority, 'Do Regulators Have a Role to Play in Judging Culture and Ethics?' (speech at the Chartered Institute of Securities and Investments Conference, 17 June 2010) www.fsa.gov.uk/pages/library/communication/speeches/2010/0617_hs.shtml accessed 18 May 2018.

11.4 As a result, banking and financial sector industry associations have taken the initiative to develop some common standards to define what 'good behaviour' might look like and to assist institutions in avoiding further scandals, reputational damage and more restrictive regulation, which Governor Carney warned would be 'inevitable' if firms and their staff fail to take the opportunity to develop their own common standards to meet regulatory objectives.

11.5 In many other jurisdictions, regulators and policymakers have urged banks and other financial institutions, in particular those regarded as Systemically Important Financial Institutions (SIIFIs), to develop a sound 'risk culture'. Likewise, supervisors and regulators have been encouraged to have, among other things, a systematic focus on financial institutions' culture. Since then, 'risk culture' has become a central topic in debates on financial regulation at all levels. Regulators, policymakers and practitioners have been devoting their efforts to providing effective strategies to ensure a sound risk culture within financial institutions. However, as some commentators recognise, there is no uniform definition of risk culture.[3] The academic literature regarding the regulation of risk culture in the financial services industry is very limited. But it is possible to identify three areas in which the concept has been addressed.

11.6 First, various definitions of risk culture have been developed and analysed by practitioners in the banking industry. The Basel Committee has defined risk culture as 'a bank's norms, attitudes and behaviours related to risk awareness, risk-taking and risk management and controls that shape decisions on risks'.[4] Indeed, the concept of risk culture has been shaped by referring to individual behaviour, ethics and company governance mechanisms.[5] Specifically, risk culture is considered a subset of the broader company's organisational culture and is thus defined as 'the norms and traditions of behaviour of individuals and of groups within an organization that determine the way in which they identify, understand, discuss, and act on the risks the organization confronts and the risks it takes'.[6] Significantly, firms converge on defining risk culture as everyone's responsibility, from management to employees; in other words, as a system of values and behavioural norms that help foster risk management processes and ensure an adequate level of risk control. In this context, risk culture is seen as an effective tool for reducing a firm's excessive risk-taking.[7]

---

3   Power M, Ashby S and Palermo T, 'Risk Culture: Definitions, Change Practices and Challenges for Chief Risk Officers', in Jackson P (ed.), *Risk Culture and Effective Risk Governance* (Risk Books 2014), 25–46.
4   Basel Committee on Banking Supervision, 'Guidelines: Corporate Governance Principles for Banks' (July 2015) www.bis.org/bcbs/publ/d328.pdf accessed 21 February 2018.
5   See Banks E, *Risk Culture: A Practical Guide to Building and Strengthening the Fabric of Risk Management* (Palgrave Macmillan 2012), 23.
6   Institute of International Finance, 'Reform in the Financial Services Industry: Strengthening Practices for a More Stable System' (December 2009) www.iif.com/system/files/iifreport_reformfinancialservicesindustry_ 1209.pdf accessed 21 February 2018.
7   Ernst & Young, 'Shifting Focus: Risk Culture at the Forefront of Banking', EY Risk Management Survey of Major Financial Institutions (2014) www.ey.com/Publication/vwLUAssets/ey-shifting-focus-risk-culture-at-the-forefront-of-banking/$FILE/ey-shifting-focus-risk-culture-at-the-forefront-of-banking.pdf accessed 21 February 2018.

11.7 Second, risk culture can be influenced by legislative and regulatory reforms. Importantly, the perception of risk culture by practitioners is now being influenced to a considerable extent by the incentives created by policymakers and regulators. Indeed, in 2009, the Basel Committee on Banking Supervision (BCBS) encouraged regulators to strengthen risk culture within the bank risk management function and highlighted the importance of risk culture (as a 'critical focus') in bank business strategies.[8] This was then transposed into some of the main EU post-crisis banking legislation. For instance, the EU Capital Requirements Directive IV invites EU Member States to 'promote a sound risk culture at all levels of credit institutions and investment firms'.[9]

11.8 Third, operationalising an effective risk culture within financial institutions can be achieved most efficiently through an interactive and iterative process of mutual dialogue and guidance between the bank supervisor and bank board. Clearly, regulators now stress that risk culture cannot be ignored as part of a financial institution's broader organisational culture. In this respect, the Group of 30 (G30) declared in 2013 that: 'Boards should identify and deal seriously with risky culture, ensure their compensation system supports the desired culture, discuss culture at the board level and with supervisors, and periodically use a variety of formal and informal techniques to monitor risk culture.'[10] In practice, regulators claim that an effective risk culture is ensured through an appropriate interaction between a firm's board and supervisors.

11.9 Risk culture influences the decisions of management and employees during day-to-day activities and has an impact on the risks they assume. Accordingly, to promote an effective risk culture it is the board's task to set the 'tone at the top'. On the other hand, bank supervisors should liaise with the board, its risk and audit committees, to verify whether the institution has adequate risk governance mechanisms and an effective risk culture.[11] Furthermore, the Financial Stability Board (FSB) has set out clear guidance to help regulators and supervisors assess risk culture in financial institutions. In its 2014 Guidance on Supervisory Interaction with Financial Institutions on Risk Culture, the FSB stated that: 'a sound risk culture bolsters effective risk management, promotes sound risk-taking, and ensures that emerging risks or risk-taking activities beyond the institution's risk appetite are recognized, assessed, escalated and addressed in a timely manner'. The FSB also recommended that supervisors play an active role in assessing good risk culture among financial institutions.[12]

---

8 Basel Committee on Banking Supervision (BCBS), 'Enhancements to Basel II Framework' (July 2009) www .bis.org/publ/bcbs157.htm accessed 21 December 2018.

9 Directive 2013/36/EU of the European Parliament and of the Council of 26 June 2013 on access to the activity of credit institutions and the prudential supervision of credit institutions and investment firms, amending Directive 2002/87/EC and repealing Directives 2006/48/EC and 2006/49/EC [2013] OJ L 176/338, recital 54.

10 G30, 'A New Paradigm: Financial Institution Boards and Supervisors' (October 2013) www.group30.org/ images/uploads/publications/G30_NewParadigm.pdf accessed 21 February 2018.

11 Ibid., 4.

12 See Financial Stability Board, 'Guidance on Supervisory Interaction with Financial Institutions on Risk Culture: A Framework for Assessing Risk Culture' (April 2014) www.fsb.org/wp-content/uploads/140407.pdf accessed 21 February 2018.

11.10 Moreover, the role of ethics and culture in financial institutions' risk management practices is of relevant concern from a supervisory perspective as well. The G30, in its 2015 Banking Conduct and Culture study, drew a line between the roles of the board and management of firms and regulatory authorities in relation to culture and risk culture. While the former have responsibility for the firm's cultural focus, the latter cannot determine culture; they should, instead, perform monitoring functions as to the effectiveness of a firm's own culture to deter, among other things, behaviour that is inconsistent with regulatory norms and standards.[13] It is worth noting that the issue of risk culture from the supervisory perspective has a broader scope than a firm's own vision. In essence, while firms address risk culture from an internal perspective, supervisors should address risk culture from an external perspective in relation to the systemic implications that the firm's conduct can have on the markets and the financial system.

11.11 Recent financial scandals strengthened the view that there is a link between firm culture and prudential regulation. Scandals such as the rigging of the London Inter-Bank Offered Rate (LIBOR), financial sanctions violations and mis-selling of financial products (i.e. Payment Protection Insurance) prompted supervisors to discuss risk culture in the context of so-called misconduct risk. For instance, recently the European Systemic Risk Board (ESRB) analysed misconduct risk in the banking sector from a macro-prudential perspective. Among the reccommendations the ESRB provided to prevent misconduct risk, it encouraged banks to adopt adequate behaviours, practices and governance mechanisms to reduce the potential for misconduct.[14] Significantly, appropriate risk culture ensures adequate risk management and is also regarded by supervisors as a tool for preventing financial institutions' conduct having systemic implications, other than criminal consequences. Similar views have been expressed by regulators, including Danièle Nouy, Chair of the Supervisory Board of the European Central Bank's Single Supervisory Mechanism, who observed that 'culture and ethics' are at the heart of banks' decisions in terms of risk-taking and safe and sound management practices.[15]

11.12 This means that understanding culture – what one does 'when nobody is watching' – and ethics – the line between acceptable and unacceptable decisions – can help us to recognise, and even predict, some behaviours.[16] The challenge of regulating risk culture in the banking sector involves a delicate division of responsibilities between what the industry, including bank boards and managers, should be doing and what tools regulators should be utilising to enhance risk culture.

---

13 G30, 'Banking Conduct and Culture: A Call for Sustained and Comprehensive Reform' (July 2015).

14 See European Systemic Risk Board, 'Report on Misconduct Risk in the Banking Sector' (June 2015) www.esrb.europa.eu/pub/pdf/other/150625_report_misconduct_risk.en.pdf accessed 21 February 2018.

15 See Nouy D, Chair of the Supervisors Board of the Single Supervisory Mechanism, 'Towards a New Age of Responsibility in Banking and Finance: Getting the Culture and the Ethics Right' (speech at the European Central Bank, 23 November 2015) www.bankingsupervision.europa.eu/press/speeches/date/2015/html/se151123.en.html accessed 18 May 2018.

16 Ibid.

II UK REGULATORY INITIATIVES FOR RISK CULTURE

11.13 The United Kingdom has addressed weak risk culture within banking institutions and other financial firms by utilising a combination of legislative and regulatory measures, such as a Remuneration Code,[17] and voluntary initiatives of banking sector and other industry bodies to improve risk culture. Although the UK approach may not be appropriate for all jurisdictions, it provides a useful model for regulators to consider the proper balance to strike between official regulatory tools and voluntary self-regulatory standards and guidelines.

11.14 As part of the post-crisis regulatory reforms, Parliament enacted substantial legislative changes for the regulation of the banking and financial services sectors.[18] As discussed in Chapter 2, the Financial Services Act 2012 (FSA Act 2012) substantially changes the institutional structure of UK financial regulation by creating a Financial Policy Committee in the Bank of England that is responsible for macro-prudential policy and a Prudential Regulation Authority (PRA) responsible for supervising credit institutions, certain investment firms and insurance firms, and controlling the systemic risks that these firms pose to the UK financial system. Under the FSA Act 2012, the PRA and the FCA have broad powers to supervise and regulate the corporate governance and risk management practices of firms and individuals to ensure that they fulfil their regulatory obligations.

11.15 UK regulatory powers to supervise risk culture derive from the Financial Services Act 2010,[19] the Financial Services Act 2012[20] and the Financial Services (Banking Reform) Act 2013.[21] The Financial Services Act 2010 addresses the issue of risk culture by empowering the Treasury to require regulated firms to produce executive remuneration reports and imposed a duty on the regulator to adopt rules requiring authorised persons to implement an appropriate remuneration policy.[22] Based on these powers, the then UK regulator – the Financial Services Authority – adopted a Remuneration Code in 2010 that contained principles and standards governing the remuneration policies of regulated financial firms. The Code was later updated to implement the requirements of EU banking law under the Capital Requirements Directives restricting how variable remuneration (e.g. bonuses) can be paid.[23] More generally, the Prudential Regulation Authority (PRA) declared that even though it does not have any 'right culture' in mind, it will act 'to tackle serious failings

---

17 Financial Conduct Authority, 'Remuneration' (published 9 May 2015, last updated 15 June 2016) www.fca.org.uk/firms/remuneration accessed 18 March 2018.
18 See Walker GA, Purves R and Blair, M Q. C., *Financial Services Law* (Oxford University Press, 2014), chapter 1, 19–56.
19 Financial Services Act 2010 (c. 28).
20 Ibid., 2012 (c. 21).
21 Financial Services (Banking Reform) Act 2013 (c. 33).
22 Financial Services Act 2010, sections 4–7. The FSA was instructed to develop a Remuneration Code.
23 See Alexander K, 'Implementation of Capital Requirements Directive III Remuneration Rules in the UK: Implications, Limitations and Lessons Learned' (2012) Economics and Monetary Affairs, European Parliament, Workshop on Banks' Remuneration Rules (CRD III): Are they implemented and do they work in practice? IP/A/ECON/WS/2012-18, PE 464-465, 55–58.

in culture through its normal activity, through use of its supervisory powers, and through enforcement action'.[24] Similarly, the FCA has stressed the importance of focusing on financial institutions' culture and particularly risk culture to prevent behaviour in violation of regulatory rules and standards.[25]

11.16 The Financial Services (Banking Reform) Act 2013 also addressed weaknesses in bank governance, including bank risk culture. This legislation became the legal basis for implementing the recommendations of the Parliamentary Commission on Banking Standards (PCBS) in its report *Changing Banking for the Good* issued in June 2013, whose main aim was to enhance professional standards and promote sound culture in the UK banking sector. The PCBS 2013 recommendations were adopted in the aftermath of the scandals surrounding the manipulations of the London Inter-Bank Offered Rate (LIBOR) and the foreign exchange rate indices.[26] Also, British regulators had found most UK banks to have been responsible for mis-selling financial products, including Payment Protection Insurance (PPI), in a pervasive and systematic way to their customers. The PCBS was highly critical of most British banks for these abuses, especially the largest and most sophisticated institutions, in particular, criticised bank senior figures who 'have continued to shelter behind an accountability firewall'.[27]

11.17 To this end, the FCA began to conduct a review of UK banking culture in 2015 in order to assess whether risk culture at British banks should be subject to additional regulation. The FCA consultation was intended to determine whether programmes to change culture in retail and wholesale banks were 'driving the right behaviour'. In 2015, however, the FCA closed its review of banking culture in wholesale and retail markets without making any recommendations.[28]

---

24 See Bank of England Prudential Regulation Authority, 'The Use of PRA Powers to Address Serious Failings in the Culture of Firms' Statement of Policy (June 2014) www.bankofengland.co.uk/-/media/boe/files/pruden tial-regulation/statement-of-policy/2014/the-use-of-pra-powers-to-address-serious-failings-in-the-culture-of-firms.pdf accessed 21 February 2018.
25 The Financial Conduct Authority's former Director of Enforcement has stated that 'we believe that a firm's culture is a key driver of staff behaviour and, in many cases, where things have gone wrong in a firm, a cultural issue was a key part of the problem'. See Financial Conduct Authority, 'Culture in Banking' www.fca.org.uk/publication/foi/foi4350-information-provided.pdf accessed 18 March 2018.
26 Foreign Exchange Professionals Association, 'Focus On: Foreign Exchange Benchmarks', 1–2, discussing manipulation of the foreign exchange fix https://fxpa.org/wp-content/uploads/2015/06/fxpa-benchmarks-5–22final.pdf accessed 18 March 2018.
27 See House of Lords, House of Commons, Parliamentary Commission on Banking Standards, 'Changing Banking for Good', Final Report (19 June 2013) www.parliament.uk/business/committees/committees-a-z/joint-select/professional-standards-in-the-banking-industry/news/changing-banking-for-good-report/ accessed 21 February 2018.
28 See Walker P, 'FCA Drops Banking Culture Review' (*Financial Times Adviser*, 4 January 2016) www.ftadviser.com/2016/01/04/regulation/regulators/fca-drops-banking-culture-review-TD3pZ14e2LXNnhNgpk2T HP/article.html accessed 18 March 2018 and Emma Dunkley, 'UK Draws Line Under "Banker Bashing" After Scrapping Assessment', *Financial Times* (London, 30 December 2015) www.ft.com/content/e926e9e2-aef1-11e5-993b-c425a3d2b65a accessed 18 March 2018. Alongside the shelving of the banking culture review, it emerged that the FCA had also set aside two other studies, including one of retail investment advice.

A Senior Managers and Certification Regime

11.18 Despite the FCA closing its banking culture review in 2015, the UK Treasury has adopted important secondary legislation to address weaknesses in bank accountability and risk management that have important implications for the regulation of risk culture. In October 2015, the Financial Services (Banking Reform) Act 2013 authorised the UK Treasury to adopt the Senior Managers and Certification Regime (SM&CR).[29] The SM&CR was adopted based on the PCBS's conclusions that flaws in the regulatory regime governing the conduct of senior management and individuals, namely, the Approved Persons Regime (APR) in Part 5 of the Financial Services and Markets Act 2000 (FSMA 2000), resulted in an inadequate level of accountability at senior management level for systematic malpractice within institutions.[30] The SM&CR replaced the previously applicable Approved Persons Regime (APR) and contains three components: the Senior Managers Regime (SMR), the Certification Regime and Conduct Rules. The SMR concerns the nucleus of senior lines of responsibility, the Certification Regime applies to senior managers plus additional staff whose positions could pose significant harm to the bank or its customers, and the Conduct Rules apply to all senior managers, all certified persons and most other bank employees.[31] The SM&CR aims to enhance the accountability of individuals working in the banking industry with particular emphasis on those in senior management positions and those responsible for managing and taking risks within financial institutions, but it is also applicable through the Conduct Rules to almost all bank employees. The SM&CR addressed the need for regulators to work with regulated institutions in developing adequate risk culture standards to support senior management and other employees and professionals working in the financial sector in meeting their ethical responsibilities to customers and complying with regulatory requirements. The SM&CR came into force on 7 March 2016.[32]

11.19 In light of the serious weaknesses in accountability and business culture identified by the PCBS, the SM&CR framework was initially directed to banking institutions. However, a report commissioned by the UK Treasury entitled 'Fair and Effective Markets Review' proposed that most elements of the SM&CR be extended to other regulated firms active in the wholesale fixed-income, currency and commodities markets (FICC).[33] Subsequently, the UK government accepted this proposal with the view to shaping a 'more rigorous, comprehensive and consistent approach across the financial services industry'.[34] Accordingly, the new regime replaced the APR for all regulated financial firms in 2018 and the

29 The Financial Services (Banking Reform) Act 2013 and HM Treasury, 'Senior Managers and Certification Regime: Extension to All FSMA Authorised Persons' (October 2015) www.gov.uk/government/uploads/system/uploads/attachment_data/file/468328/SMCR_policy_paper_final_15102015.pdf accessed 21 February 2018.
30 Ibid.
31 Ibid., 7.
32 Financial Conduct Authority, 'Senior Managers and Certification Regime' Press Release (published 7 July 2015, last updated 11 January 2018) accessed 21 February 2018.
33 HM Treasury, Bank of England, Financial Conduct Authority 'Fair and Effective Markets Review: Final Report' (June 2015) www.bankofengland.co.uk/-/media/boe/files/markets/fair-and-effective-markets/terms-of-reference.pdf accessed 18 March 2018.
34 HM Treasury (n 29), 5.

final rules are known as the Individual Accountability Regime (IAR) and will apply to banks and financial firms that meet the definition of 'Authorised Person' under section 31 of the Financial Services and Markets Act 2000.

11.20 The SM&CR/IAR is regarded as a milestone for a new era of accountability. However, it will require a complex implementation process through the guidance of the UK regulatory and supervisory authorities. To this end, the FCA and the PRA have been already providing rules, guidance and implementing measures for banks and other regulated institutions. To assist this process, the UK Treasury supported the transition process from the old Approved Persons Regime (APR) to the SM&CR/IAR by conducting several consultations as to its applicability to regulated financial services firms, including its application to UK branches of foreign banks.[35]

11.21 Essentially, the SM&CR/IAR consists of three pillars: (1) the Senior Managers regime; (2) the Certification regime; and (3) the Conduct Rules. Key elements can be summarised as follows. The SM&CR addresses individuals having high decision-making powers within an institution. Non-executive directors and individuals operating outside the UK may also fall into this category. Significantly, for institutions under the oversight of the FCA, the new Conduct Rules will cover senior managers, certified persons, directors and other employees. Individuals holding senior management responsibilities will be subject to supervision and pre-approval procedures by the FCA or PRA. To this end, firms will have to understand and pay considerable attention to concepts such as Senior Management Functions, Prescribed Responsibilities and Overall Responsibilities.[36] In so doing, they are required to set out a 'Governance' or 'Responsibilities Map' indicating names of senior managers, roles and responsibilities, as well as lines of accountability within the firm. In addition, they must ensure that they have adequate procedures to assess the 'fitness' and 'propriety' of senior managers and other staff who might cause harm to the firm or its customers.

11.22 Finally, Conduct Rules are another noteworthy feature of the SM&CR. These are high-level rules applying directly to all staff (with the exclusion of ancillary staff). Firms are expected to incorporate the Conduct Rules in their employment documentation and provide training on them.[37] Senior managers and other individuals subject to the SM&CR will be accountable to the regulator if they breach Conduct Rules prescribed by the FCA or PRA in relation to their own area of responsibility. Among other things, senior managers hold a statutory duty of responsibility to take 'reasonable steps' to prevent the firm from breaching regulatory requirements within a senior manager's area of responsibility.[38]

---

35 Ibid., 8.
36 See Financial Conduct Authority, 'CP15/22 Strengthening Accountability in Banking: Final Rules (Including Feedback on CP14/31 and CP15/5) and Consultation on Extending the Certification Regime to Wholesale Market Activities' (July 2015) www.fca.org.uk/publication/consultation/cp15-22.pdf accessed 21 February 2018.
37 Ibid.
38 Ibid.

11.23 As mentioned above, the SM&CR must be explained in the context of a wider debate on bank culture, which was triggered in the aftermath of scandals that ultimately undermined public confidence in the banking sector and in the financial services industry as a whole. Implementing the SM&CR will be unquestionably a big effort for all the concerned firms. Senior managers will have to show how they take into consideration an effective culture and how this performs within their firm. The SM&CR is considered to be a significant contribution to improving banking culture and thus increasing individual accountability. Indeed, the Head of the Financial Conduct Authority has stated that '[r]esponsibility is the central plank of the new Senior Managers Regime. We do want senior managers to feel this responsibility in all that they do and that includes a responsibility for forming and implementing a positive culture throughout the organisation.'[39]

III SELF–REGULATION AND THE ROLE OF PROFESSIONAL BODIES

11.24 The Parliamentary Commission on Banking Standards (PCBS) report also highlighted that, in addition to official sector regulation, 'a credible set of professional bodies' can help enhance professional standards and culture in the financial sector.[40] In regulatory jargon, the term 'professional bodies' has broad meaning. For instance, Baxter and Megone stress that the term can be generically referred to as bodies providing technical and ethical training in the banking sector or, more specifically, to organisations that elaborate behavioural standards with the view to influencing the conduct of professionals working in the banking and financial sectors.[41] The post-crisis reforms paved the way for the creation of voluntary professional bodies, such as the Chartered Bankers: Professional Standards Body (CB:PSB), the Fixed-Income, Currency and Commodities Market Standards Board (FMSB) and the Banking Standards Board (BSB). These bodies intend to raise the standards, professionalism and accountability of individuals in the financial industry.

A Chartered Bankers: Professional Standards Body

11.25 The Chartered Bankers: Professional Standards Body (CB: PSB) was jointly launched in 2011 by the Chartered Banker Institute and eight UK banks. Its aim is to create a strong culture of ethics and professionalism in the UK banking industry through the development and implementation of sustainable standards. To this end, the most salient initiative is The

---

39 Bailey A, Deputy Governor of the Bank of England, Prudential Regulation and Chief Officer, Prudential Regulation Authority 'Culture in Financial Services – A Regulator's Perspective' (speech at the City Week 2016 Conference, 9 May 2016), 3 www.bankofengland.co.uk/-/media/boe/files/speech/2016/culture-in-financial-services-a-regulators-perspective.pdf?la=en&hash=088A4BBDA75375CCD822EE715A35BC662FCD8A6D accessed 18 May 2018.
40 House of Lords, House of Commons (n 27), Vol. I, para. 18.
41 See Baxter J and Megone C, 'Exploring the Role of Professional Bodies and Professional Qualifications in the UK Banking Sector', Independent Report Commissioned by the Banking Standard Board (October 2016) www.bankingstandardsboard.org.uk/wp-content/uploads/2016/10/160928-Professionalism-in-banking-publication-FINAL-WEB.pdf accessed 21 February 2018.

Chartered Banker Code of Professional Conduct (the Code). This lays down values, attitudes and appropriate behaviours for all professional bankers. Significantly, all CB:PSB member firms are expected to integrate the Code with their own codes of business. The Code conforms to the spirit and letter of the FCA and PRA Individual Conduct Rules. According to the Code, professionalism in banking is evidenced through the following conducts: (1) treating all customers, colleagues and counterparties with respect and acting with integrity; (2) developing and maintaining their professional knowledge and acting with due skill, care and diligence; considering the risks and implications of their actions and advice, and holding themselves accountable for them and their impact; (3) being open and cooperative with the regulators; complying with all current regulatory and legal requirements; (4) paying due regard to the interests of customers and treating them fairly; (5) observing and demonstrating proper standards of market conduct at all times; (6) acting in an honest and trustworthy manner, being alert to and managing potential conflicts of interest; and (7) treating information with appropriate confidentiality and sensitivity.[42]

11.26 In addition, the CB:PSB has recently published a revised version of its 2012 Foundation Standard, which 'sets out the CB:PSB's expectations of all individuals in relation to the Professional Conduct and Professional Expertise required by such individuals to apply the Code on a day-to-day basis'.[43] Following the PCBS inputs towards a better culture and professionalism in banking, the pathway proposed by the CB:PSB has brought some significant results. Over 500,000 bankers in the UK and globally are now covered by a common code of conduct, the Chartered Banker Code of Professional Conduct (the Code) with about 70 per cent of the UK banking workforce covered by this common Code. In total, 246,000 individuals, 93 per cent of the eligible group of bank employees across the UK and globally met the Foundation Standard in 2015. Moreover, the CB:PSB has developed ten Foundation Standard eLearning modules that include knowledge provision and training for the Senior Managers and Certification Regime.[44]

B FICC Markets Standards Board

11.27 The Fixed Income, Currency and Commodities Markets Standards Board (FMSB) was established in 2015 following the recommendations set out in the Fair and Effective Markets Review (FEMR).[45] The FMSB aims to promote good practice standards for wholesale fixed-income, currencies and commodities markets through coordination between domestic and global firms, as well as end users at the most senior level. In November

42 Chartered Banker Professional Standards Board, Code of Professional Conduct (effective 1 September 2016) www.charteredbanker.com/filemanager/root/site_assets/governance/the_chartered_banker_code_of_profes sional_conduct_47494.pdf accessed 18 May 2018.
43 Ibid., Foundation Standard for Professional Bankers (January 2016) www.cbpsb.org/professional-stand ards/foundation-standard.html accessed 18 May 2018.
44 Ibid., 'Progress Report 2016' (May 2016) www.cbpsb.org/filemanager/root/site_assets/progress_report_ 2016/cb_psb_report_2016_final.pdf accessed 18 May 2018.
45 HM Treasury, Bank of England (n 33).

2016, the FSMB published a standard for improving bank transparency so as to guarantee that the interests of investors are a primary concern of banks, investment and trading firms.

11.28 According to the standard: (1) banks' allocation policies should be made available to market participants; (2) issuer preferences in the allocation process should take priority; (3) when a mandate is granted, the lead banks and issuer should agree a document setting out the issuer's aims for the transaction and how the banks will achieve that, including allocation preferences and marketing strategy; (4) banks should disclose to the market their policy on how they select investors for market soundings and investor roadshows; (5) lead banks should agree a strategy on book disclosure frequency with the issuer – book updates should be disclosed publicly and should not be misleading; (6) investors need time to collate their demand for a transaction; (7) investors should put in orders which are a true reflection of their demand and should not be misleading.[46] The FMSB standard is the result of a 'unique joint effort by corporate users of the market, institutional investors and underwriting banks to bring greater clarity to the process for issuing debt and ensure it works fairly and effectively for all concerned'.[47]

11.29 More recently the FMSB's Conduct and Ethics Sub-Committee has also encouraged the strengthening of surveillance and training in wholesale markets to better address the risk of insider dealing and market manipulation. In December 2016, the FMSB issued guidelines accordingly. With regard to surveillance, the guidelines recommend that this function is independent from the front office and the systems are periodically reviewed to adapt to specific types of risks.[48] As to training, this requires more involvement from senior managers ('who understand the business best') to junior levels. In fact, central to the guidelines is a bigger role for managers who must, among other things, engage in face-to-face discussion of conduct issues with staff.[49]

C Banking Standards Board

11.30 The Banking Standards Board (BSB) was launched in 2015 as a result of the PCBS's proposed reforms and the follow-up recommendations of Sir Richard Lambert's Banking Standards Review in 2014.[50] The BSB intend to promote adequate standards of behaviour

---

46 See Fixed Income Currencies and Commodities (FICC) Markets Standards Board, 'New Issue Process Standard for the Fixed Income Markets' (2 May 2017) www.fmsb.com/wp-content/uploads/2017/04/FMSB_NewIssuesProcess_FIMarkets_2-May-FINAL.pdf accessed 21 February 2018.
47 Ibid., 'FICC Markets Standards Board Proposes Greater Transparency in New Issue Process for Debt' (fmsb.com, 18 November 2016) http://fmsb.com/ficc-markets-standards-board-proposes-greater-transparency-in-new-issue-process-for-corporate-debt/ accessed 18 March 2018.
48 Ibid., 'Surveillance Core Principles for FICC Market Participants: Statement of Good Practice for Surveillance in Foreign Exchange Markets' (December 2016) www.femr-mpp.co.uk/wp-content/uploads/2016/12/16-12-08-SoGP_Surveillance-in-FX-Markets_FINAL.pdf accessed 21 February 2018.
49 Ibid., 'Statement of Good Practice for FICC Market Participants: Conduct Training' (December 2016) www.femr-mpp.co.uk/wp-content/uploads/2016/12/16-12-08-SoGP-Conduct-Training_FINAL.pdf accessed 21 February 2018.
50 Lambert R, 'Banking Standards Review' (2014) www.cii.co.uk/knowledge/policy-and-public-affairs/articles/banking-standards-(lambert)-review-final-report/30421 accessed 15 February 2018.

and competence across UK banks and building societies so as to rebuild trust and reputation in the sector.[51] In its 2015–2016 annual review, the BSB set out its key areas of work for the next years: (1) conducting assessment exercises among member firms on key themes; (2) promoting professionalism across all parts of the banking sector and at all levels; (3) exploring the relationship between law, regulation and ethics, and what this means in the specific context of banking and banking culture; and (4) developing voluntary standards that will support a better service for customers and other relevant parties across the sector.[52]

11.31 The BSB assessments involve its member institutions in addressing the following areas: the alignment of a firm's purpose, values and culture; the difference between a focus on culture and on compliance; leadership and key person risk; incentives and reward structures and practices; fostering challenge and speaking up to challenge questionable practices; and the provision, take-up and effectiveness of staff training and support.[53] The BSB aims to become a forum where banking institutions can address issues of trust and reputation and develop voluntary best practice standards to enhance organisational and risk culture in the banking sector.

11.32 The overall progress of industry bodies in addressing weaknesses in bank risk culture suggests that policymakers should in the first instance rely more on industry initiatives, rather than binding regulatory rules, to enhance it. Nevertheless, the following section suggests that regulatory rules and policy can play a useful role in creating incentives for banking institutions to improve their risk governance and culture. In particular, regulatory standards and guidance may be necessary in certain areas, such as remuneration and trusted financial products, to enhance risk culture in banking institutions, but ultimately institutions themselves are best placed to channel the collective actions of individuals to improve the governance and operations of banks.

IV REGULATING BANK CULTURE: WHERE SHOULD THE FOCUS BE?

11.33 With this in mind, the regulation of risk culture in the banking industry should emphasise a balancing of the responsibilities between consumers and firms that takes account of the effect that the perception of regulation might have on moral hazard within the firm and with consumers. A specific area that policymakers and regulators have addressed where such a balance can be struck is the regulation of remuneration structures in banks and financial firms. Several studies have shown that remuneration structures in financial institutions can create morally hazardous behaviour, especially for managers and traders who can be induced by financial and other incentives to engage in risky practices that can

---

51   Ibid.
52   Ibid.
53   See Banking Standards Board, 'Annual Review 2015/2016' (2016) www.bankingstandardsboard.org.uk/wp-content/uploads/2016/03/BSB-Annual-Review-20152016.pdf accessed 21 February 2018.

threaten both the firm's viability as well as create significant social costs. This is because compensation and professional recognition or promotions within the firm are similar to an option contract. The individual in question shares profits (above a certain threshold) with the bank, but not all the losses that can occur because of the individual's conduct. In essence, the employment contract is akin to an asymmetrical bet as the downside is limited (getting fired and suffering damage to reputation). In addition, the promotion or earning of a bonus is presumably tied to extraordinary performance, making it worthwhile to take large risks. 'Going for broke' becomes a viable strategy.[54] More broadly, banks are incentivised to gamble since the behaviour of competitors leads to a 'breakdown of the social order'. To remain profitable and competitive, banks are 'forced' to engage in risky behaviour, even if the individuals within the firm are opposed to such strategies.

11.34 This was illustrated prior to the 2007–2008 crisis by the link between management remuneration and returns on equity that incentivised banks to maintain low levels of equity capital and to increase profits through excessive leverage. This meant that banks had less capital to absorb losses when markets became distressed. Indeed, Lord King told the House of Commons Treasury Committee in 2011:

> I think that the incentives that have been created by linking compensation to the rate of return on equity is clearly a distortion because it gives an incentive built in to raise leverage . . . I have never understood why people thought it was a sensible idea to base compensation in these institutions on the return on equity.[55]

11.35 The regulatory concern with banker compensation being linked to return on equity was one of the driving factors in the European Union's adoption of regulatory reforms in 2009 for how banker bonuses could be paid in the Capital Requirements Directive III. The CRD III banker bonus rules were driven by the findings of the European Commission's High Level Report of February 2009 (the De Larosiere Report) which concluded, among other things, that bank remuneration schemes contributed to excessive risk-taking at banks and other financial firms,[56] while institutional shareholders failed to exercise an effective stewardship role to curb the excessive risk-taking of senior management at leading financial institutions.[57] Later, G20 leaders took the initiative to address the supervision of bank and investment firm remuneration policies. This initiative was, in turn, supported by international supervisory bodies, such as the Financial Stability Board (FSB), who issued

54   Dow J, 'What is Systemic Risk? Moral Hazard, Initial Shocks and Propagation', Institute for Monetary and Economic Studies, Bank of Japan (December 2000), 17–18 www.imes.boj.or.jp/research/papers/english/me18-2-1.pdf accessed 21 February 2018.
55   Ibid. The FCA will also enforce the Remuneration Code with firms covered by the Code but not regulated by the PRA.
56   Ferrarini G and Ungureanu MC, 'Economics, Politics, and the International Principles for Sound Compensation Practices: An Analysis of Executive Pay at European Banks' (2011) 64 *Vanderbilt Law Review* 2 431–502.
57   See Bebchuk LA, Martijn Cremers KJ and Peyer UC, 'The CEO Pay Slice' (2010) The Harvard John M. Olin Center for Law, Economics, and Business Discussion Paper No. 679 9/2010.

recommendations to regulate the remuneration practices of large banks and systemically important financial institutions.

11.36 In parallel to these international initiatives, the EU's CRD III requires EU Member States, as a minimum standard, to require all credit institutions and certain investment firms involved in significant credit intermediation and related risky trading activities to pay no more than 50 per cent of a banker's bonus in cash (the other half must be paid in the bank's shares) and not more than 40 per cent of the bonus can be paid in the year that the bonus was awarded. The remaining 60 per cent of the variable pay award can only be paid over a five-year deferral period, with no more than 20 per cent of the bonus paid in the third year, no more than 20 per cent paid in the fourth year, and no more than 20 per cent paid in the fifth year.[58] The EU restrictions on banker variable pay also prohibit the institution from paying more than 100 per cent of the value of the banker's fixed pay as a bonus, with an exception allowing variable pay up to 200 per cent of fixed salary if the bank's shareholders approve the variable pay package at a general or special meeting.

11.37 The EU regulations governing banker bonuses, first adopted in 2009, led the UK Financial Services Authority to adopt a Remuneration Code in 2010 for senior staff and risk-takers at financial institutions. The PRA and FCA are now responsible for enforcing remuneration regulation in which they 'will be responsible for ensuring that the remuneration policies . . . are aligned with effective risk management and that they do not provide incentives for excessive risk-taking'.[59] Among the Remuneration Code's measures, at least half of variable remuneration should consist of shares rather than cash. The shares awarded in pay packets have to be retained for specified periods. Andrew Procter, Global Head of Government and Regulatory Affairs at Deutsche Bank, said: 'The balance between cash and stock for bonuses has significantly changed in favour of stock.'[60] EU regulation of bank remuneration now requires that deferral periods for at least 60 per cent of cash and stock bonuses are five years at a minimum, while in the UK deferral periods are at seven years. The EU and UK claw-back provisions are much tougher than they have ever been before, either for malice or misconduct or because the profits upon which the bonus decision was made turn out to be illusory. Also, there is a far greater emphasis on indicators of good and bad behaviour being reflected directly in the bonus decision.

11.38 Moreover, the Financial Conduct Authority in 2015 expanded the Code's application to all regulated financial firms, but tailored the main principles and guidelines to apply flexibly to

58 See Capital Requirements Directive III, Directive 2010/76/EU of the European Parliament and the Council of 24 November 2010 amending Directives 2006/48/EC and 2006/49/EC regarding capital requirements for the trading book and for re-securitisations, and the supervisory review of remuneration policies [2004] OJ L 329/3 (no longer in force), recital 7, 9.
59 Ibid.
60 House of Lords, House of Commons, Joint Committee on the Draft Financial Services Bill, Uncorrected Transcript of Oral Evidence Andrew Procter, Sally Dewar and Robert Charnley (8 November 2011) QQ 848–914, Q 880 www.parliament.uk/documents/joint-committees/Draft-Financial-Services-Bill/ucjcdfsb081111ev12.pdf accessed 21 February 2018.

the circumstances of different firms operating across financial sectors.[61] The remuneration policies were further revised and updated in 2016 for commercial banks and certain investment banks, after a consultation of the European Banking Authority that resulted in a set of guidelines on sound remuneration policies under the Capital Requirements Directive IV.[62] These guidelines recognise the link between remuneration and risk-taking in financial firms and how certain remuneration structures can incentivise excessive risk-taking and thus undermine the regulatory objective of financial stability. The EBA Remuneration Guidelines require EU Member State regulators to comply with this guidance when implementing the CRD IV remuneration rules, or explain to the EBA the reasons why they are not complying.[63]

11.39 In early 2016, both the PRA and the FCA published a statement on compliance with the EBA guidelines on Sound Remuneration Policies and have since implemented the guidelines into their oversight tasks.[64] To this end, the PRA in 2017 updated its Supervisory Statement on Remuneration concerning how it requires institutions to designate 'material risk takers' as prescribed by the EBA guidelines on sound remuneration policies.[65] The EBA Guidelines thus provide an important tool for regulators to monitor and influence the incentives in remuneration packages for excessive risk-taking in financial institutions and for excessive risk culture within financial institutions.

Trusted Customer Products

11.40 Another area where regulators may be able to strike a balance between regulating the responsibilities of banks and their customers is in the development of retail financial products. Indeed, it is accepted that complex products combined with a lack of financial literacy is a significant problem in financial markets. Under the Financial Services Act 2012, the FCA is required to have regard to the needs that consumers may have for advice and information from banks that is appropriately presented and provided in a timely,

61   Financial Conduct Authority (n 17).
62   European Banking Authority, 'Guidelines on Sound Remuneration Policies under Articles 74(3) and 75(2) of Directive 2013/36/EU and Disclosures under Article 450 of Regulation (EU) No. 575/2013' (June 2016) www.eba.europa.eu/documents/10180/1314839/EBA-GL-2015-22+Guidelines+on+Sound+Remuneration+Policies_EN.pdf accessed 21 February 2018.
63   Ibid., 6. For an explanation see also Harvard Law School Forum on Corporate Governance and Financial Regulation, Pearce W and Sholem M ((eds), 'Remuneration in the Financial Services Industry 2015' (18 September 2018) https://corpgov.law.harvard.edu/2015/09/18/remuneration-in-the-financial-services-industry-2015/ accessed 18 March 2018.
64   Bank of England news release, 'PRA and FCA Statement on Compliance with the EBA Guidelines on Sound Remuneration Policies' (29 February 2016) www.bankofengland.co.uk/news/2016/february/pra-fca-statement-on-compliance-with-the-eba-guidelines-on-sound-remuneration-policies accessed 15 February 2018 and Financial Conduct Authority, 'PRA and FCA Statement on Compliance with the EBA Guidelines on Sound Remuneration Policies' (published 29 February 2016) www.bankofengland.co.uk/news/2016/february/pra-fca-statement-on-compliance-with-the-eba-guidelines-on-sound-remuneration-policies accessed 18 March 2018.
65   Bank of England Prudential Regulation Authority, Supervisory Statement 'Remuneration' (April 2017) www.bankofengland.co.uk/-/media/boe/files/prudential-regulation/supervisory-statement/2017/ss217.pdf?la=en&hash=71A98E5E2CDD629F9C219C09480AF1CED95E909E accessed 21 February 2018.

accurate, intelligible way. If the FCA is diligent about this duty then it should make progress in helping consumers understand the products they are buying.

11.40 There is, however, more that could be done. Regulators can mandate that banks create trusted consumer products that would be granted a trusted seal of approval by a Trusted Products Board. A Trusted Products Board could create a system of identifying and certifying simple, low-cost financial products. This is not a role that the regulator should take on, but it is something the voluntary sector itself may be well placed to do. The FCA should be prepared to help the voluntary sector in these endeavours by providing information on products and their costs.[66]

11.41 More generally, when considering where the regulatory focus should be, one should bear in mind that most banking crises have arisen from management decisions that reflect agency problems which result in weak risk management and a failure to incorporate a clear and sustainable set of standards and norms adhered to within the organisation. Inadequate risk culture can exacerbate existing agency problems, in which managers have risk preferences that are different from other stakeholders, including owners, customers, creditors and the government representing the public at large. Even if managers' incentives are reasonably aligned with other stakeholders, they may have limited competence in assessing the risks involved in their decisions and yet have significant freedom of action because of the absence of internal control systems that are able to resolve agency problems.

11.42 Adequate corporate governance systems for banking institutions therefore require internal control systems within banks to address the inherent asymmetries of information and the resulting market failures that can arise from the institutional challenges of coordinating the collective activities of many individuals with different risk appetites and professional responsibilities for ensuring that the institution follows and meets its strategic objectives. If a regulatory authority could know all agents' private information and accordingly adjust incentives for each agent based on lump sum transfers between agents, it could achieve a *Pareto* improvement that would reduce the costs associated with the agency problem. However, because governmental regulators cannot in practice observe agents' private information, they can achieve only a constrained or second-best *Pareto* optimum. Reducing the costs associated with agency problems and thereby achieving a second-best solution depends to a large extent on the corporate governance structures of financial institutions and the way information is disseminated to owners, depositors, customers, employees and other stakeholders. In complex banking organisations, the bank itself is the main source of

---

66   House of Lords, House of Commons, Joint Committee on the Draft Financial Services Bill, 'Draft Financial Services Bill – Session 2010–12' Report, together with formal minutes and appendices (December 2011). For related documents, see www.parliament.uk/business/committees/committees-a-z/joint-select/draft-financial-services-bill/ accessed 15 February 2018. In 2011, the UK Treasury announced that a new steering group made up of government, industry, trade and consumer body representatives was established to consider how to bring simple products to market and to report back to the Treasury regarding recommendations.

most information that is relevant for the effective management of financial, strategic and reputational risk. Regulators cannot replace bank managers in successfully managing these risks and ensuring that there is a sound risk culture; rather, regulators can only cajole and pressure institutions to develop a more sustainable risk culture that supports the institution in achieving sustainable profitability that is beneficial for all stakeholder groups while serving the needs of customers and society at large.

11.43 The above discussion suggests that there will be tensions and challenges in attempting to regulate risk culture in banking and financial institutions, and the scope of the regulatory mandate will likely remain uncertain. Nevertheless, banking and financial sector initiatives, whose impetus was provided by the Parliamentary Commission on Banking Standards 2013 report, are beginning to change significantly how banks and other financial institutions address their own agency problems and adopt norms and standards that are designed to enhance their risk culture. These are important self-regulatory initiatives that policymakers and regulators should continue to support.

11.44 Nevertheless, it is unclear whether this is adequate to prevent a future crisis and thus to restore public confidence and trust in banks. Indeed, banks and other financial firms have been tasked with implementing more than 14,000 new regulatory changes since 2011, with the compliance departments of global banks implementing an estimated forty new regulations each day. Although some regulatory reforms address weaknesses in risk culture, they will not be effective unless banking institutions and their leaders initiate changes in their own practices in order to establish and embed sound risk practices that fully apply ethical norms and standards designed to influence an institution's risk culture.

11.45 An effective risk culture facilitates compliance with all regulations and laws and can make a significant contribution to enhancing and retaining corporate value. This is especially important for banks, as their core business involves the measuring and managing of risks. The recent financial crisis demonstrates how credibility and reputation can be lost quickly in a crisis or in similar periods of market distress. For an institution to develop an effective and sustainable risk culture, it should address the following vital areas of its operations. First and foremost, senior management must serve as visible role models who can demonstrate their adherence to and execution of the standards and norms that are set forth in the corporate documents and regulatory codes that are continuously communicated to all members of the organisation.

11.46 In this regard, the structural and organisational parameters of the institution are of particular importance. The board should establish clear guidelines on responsibilities and efficient processes, with recommendations for management about how to develop systematic decision-making processes for identifying and controlling both the bank's own economic risks as well as the risks it poses to society. In large institutions, this process should not be left to the technical specialists in risk management and risk optimisation. Rather, each individual in the institution whose decisions affect the firm's risk profile should consider themselves a risk manager in their particular area of specialisation. This should complement the risk management function that should be fully and independently focused on risk control, while various risk committees at different levels of the institution should monitor individual risk-taking throughout the institution.

11.47 Although technical expertise and continuous training are necessary for risk managers, other skills and talents are also vital, including a thorough and qualitative understanding of the more probable risks, and a cross-departmental understanding (front-to-back office) of different risks and processes for rapid risk identification and mitigation. As banks have placed far too much emphasis on quantitative risk models, risks assessment capabilities should place more weight on qualitative factors. This is especially important in the area of operational risk, which can be measured only to a limited extent with quantitative models.

11.48 In addition, as mentioned above, bank remuneration has often been based mainly on meeting performance targets and the contribution to consolidated earnings on a risk-adjusted basis. Institutions should base compensation models on assessments of risk behaviour, which would also become part of the overall performance evaluation. The assessment of this factor as part of the overall performance evaluation can be based on well-defined key performance indicators (KPIs) that can be used to measure risk behaviour and can be incorporated into the annual performance review.

11.49 It should be emphasised, however, that an effective risk culture should not simply be limited to 'ticking the box' or checking off individual control steps, but should also facilitate and allow an open critical environment for questioning, discussing and even expressing disagreement with senior management and the board. Although complex mathematical models and stress tests are essential tools for some scenario testing, they provide only 'raw results' that do not take account of other key qualitative factors that should influence decision-making. Effective strategic decision-making necessarily requires that critical, qualitative assessments are accompanied by a judgement based on common sense. For instance, with hindsight, it is now recognised that such common sense assessments of risk would have been useful in avoiding some of the losses associated with AAA-rated, asset-backed securities based on subprime mortgages.

11.50 It should be borne in mind that the effective management of risk culture requires that the individual's decision-making be of primary importance within the institution. Even today, most evaluation criteria in the banking and financial services industry focus mainly on quantitative performance metrics, professional expertise and motivation. However, social skills and aspects of character have generally not been emphasised. Character is crucial for assessing and understanding the virtue of the individual. In some market-based economies, certain qualities that are often stigmatised as undesirable – such as greed – are considered desirable. Rather, banks should develop methodologies for assessing and identifying the characteristics of employees and managers. It has been shown that the sustainability and prosperity of firms and individuals are particularly linked to questions of character. Research suggests that successful managers and leaders of organisations are often individuals who are considered to have outstanding character values. It follows that for banks, an essential element in instituting an effective risk culture is the ability for management to assess and judge the character of employees and other agents. Interestingly, character assessments are not yet a crucial component of management practice, especially in the banking industry. It is submitted that the development and use of a systematic 'character assessment' in the selection process for senior management could lead to enhanced risk culture within the firm and to a competitive advantage in the marketplace. For banks, the competitive advantage of incorporating character assessments in assessing and selecting senior management could potentially substantially outweigh the amount that banks have paid in fines in recent years as a result of systematic non-compliance with financial regulations.

11.51 Also, as mentioned above, banking industry bodies have been engaged in developing common standards of good practice. Indeed, the publication of the 'Fair and Effective Markets Review' in 2015 and the report by the Banking Standards Review Council in 2014 made recommendations for improving culture and called for common standards of market practice. These standards or codes of good practice are designed to provide a benchmark against which practitioners and regulators can assess whether behaviour and conduct are acceptable and ethical. From the consumer perspective, knowing that banks are developing a clear picture of the way they should respond to areas where there is no legally binding rule but there is a 'right' way to act will hopefully help address the lack of trust between consumers and the industry.

11.52 It appears that regulators and banking institutions might be well placed to develop common standards of market practice. However, the UK regulator's announcement, in December 2015, that it would not be conducting a planned inquiry into the culture, pay and behaviour of staff in the banking sector might reasonably be described as sending the wrong signal to the industry. Because neither regulators nor banking institutions individually seem likely to drive forward the development of common standards for addressing the 'grey' areas of conduct, the suggestion is that perhaps civil society organisations should take the lead, through initiatives by universities, institutes and other non-governmental bodies, in coordination with banking industry bodies such as the BSB. Banks should see this as an opportunity to prove they are actively seeking to restore public trust in the sector. Indeed, civil society bodies, such as universities and research institutes, are beginning to work with banking and financial sector bodies to develop common standards of acceptable and ethical behaviour. The role of civil society bodies, however, should not lose sight of the fact that developing these standards and norms must involve participation from the personnel employed at all relevant levels of banking institutions and should be shared across all institutions, with industry associations facilitating the sharing of practices and experiences. By drawing on experiences and lessons from across the sector, it will be possible to highlight divergences between firms and risk areas that require more focus. Previously, banks have not known how well they are performing against other banks in terms of conduct. That leads to misperceptions about risks, opportunities and whether the bank's practices meet minimum accepted standards of good practice. Moreover, by knowing how well they are performing, banks should be able to make better business decisions.

CONCLUSION

11.53 This chapter considers the role of regulation in addressing weaknesses in risk culture in banking institutions. It reviews international regulatory developments in the area of risk culture and the main legal and regulatory instruments adopted by the European Union, and particularly by the UK authorities, to enhance risk culture in banking and financial institutions. The chapter suggests that regulation can be most effective in monitoring and facilitating the development of common standards of good practice in the banking industry but not in determining what those standards are. Although regulators can play a role in monitoring risk culture and ethical practices, they are not well equipped to generate common standards to guide behaviour in the industry. Rather, industry-led professional bodies should play an important role by bringing together banking institutions to exchange experiences, report good practices and, possibly, adopt a professional code that would guide the industry. The chapter discusses some of the main industry-led bodies and their objectives, but concludes that a more effective framework for generating common standards of good practice and understanding the relevance of ethical values should involve civil society groups and institutions to facilitate the development of common standards and norms and making them relevant for customers and society. The chapter also suggests that effective self-regulation of risk culture by individual institutions should start with a re-evaluation of the role of the individual within the organisation, along with incorporating character-based assessments into key performance indicators and into selection criteria for senior management. Character building within institutions should be an important focus of strengthening risk culture and should be vital for instilling a broad-based ethical compliance agenda.

QUESTIONS

1. What is risk culture in the banking industry?
2. Does remuneration affect risk culture?
3. What are some of the financial industry initiatives to enhance risk culture?
4. Should regulators try to regulate risk culture?
5. What should the role of self-regulation be?

Further Reading

Black J, 'Seeing, Knowing, and Regulating Financial Markets: Moving the Cognitive Framework from the Economic to the Social' (2013) LSE Legal Studies Working Paper No. 24

Tuveson M and Ralph D, *Risk Culture* (Cambridge University Press 2019)

12

Financial Technology, Digital Currencies and Inclusion

Banks are dinosaurs, they can be bypassed.

Bill Gates (9 January 1995), *The American Banker*

Table of Contents

INTRODUCTION

12.1 Financial technology has begun to disrupt the traditional business model of banking. The mobile smartphone has already transformed consumer financial services along with the growth of internet platform conglomerates. Other disruptive factors provide the potential for radical transformation of the competitive landscape of the banking sector. Some of the factors that are driving institutional change include artificial intelligence, big technology and data management, cloud services for core banking activities, and digital assets and currencies. This chapter discusses some of the issues involving the Fintech challenge for regulators and how regulation itself is changing in response to technological advances. Part I discusses recent developments in financial technology and how it has enhanced banks' capacity to provide credit to the economy (i.e. peer-to-peer lending) and shift risks away from banks to investors who are willing to invest in bank-originated assets. Part II analyses the open banking phenomenon in Europe, the main provisions of the European Union Payment Services Directive 2 and how the latter can facilitate the provision of banking services to bank customers by third-party data companies and the related risks and policy concerns. It also compares EU Payment Services Directive 2 with the United Kingdom's open banking legislation and discusses some of the advantages and disadvantages of these laws and their respective regulations. Part III discusses some of the main issues raised by digital currencies and the Bitcoin phenomenon. Part IV analyses regulation technology (RegTech) by considering its rationale and how it can support banks and regulators in achieving compliance with regulatory requirements. Part V analyses the Fintech phenomenon from an international perspective and reviews the international initiatives that have encouraged countries to utilise Fintech to increase financial inclusion and reduce inequality in societies by ensuring that technology plays a greater role in expanding access to banking and financial services. The chapter concludes that despite the obvious economic benefits of encouraging innovation in banking practices, bank risk officers and regulators should monitor the associated risks of new business practices and how they might contribute to banking sector risks.

I FINTECH AND BANKING

12.2 Financial technology creates the possibility that banking services can be provided without banks. The future of banking and finance is an increasingly converged system where financial service can be provided for consumers and small and medium-sized businesses by technology companies whose origins are in e-commerce and social media. How can traditional banks stay relevant in the fast-moving market for e-financial services and what are the risks for regulators? Moreover, for banks to stay relevant in the face of rapid technological change, they will have to adapt to ongoing changes in technology and the markets that will require updating business models, organisational structure, technological capacity, and a commitment to risk and organisational culture. An important aspect of bank strategy will be the use of artificial intelligence (AI) and digital automation and the overhaul of core banking services that makes greater use of cloud-based services.

12.3 Important areas of financial technology include artificial intelligence, digital currencies or Bitcoin, cloud services for banks and digital assets. From a governance perspective, it is necessary that bank senior management and boards focus on digital transformation and how Fintech tools can support a simpler business mix by geography and product type. In the post-crisis era, as economies recover (albeit slowly in some countries) and monetary policy normalises, bank profits are increasing, which provides an opportunity for management to focus on the longer-term implications of Fintech strategies.

12.4 The role of technology in e-finance in enhancing the provision of banking services for individuals and small businesses is based on making financial services available to those who would normally not have access to efficiently priced or adequate products. Fintech expands the availability of information on financial services, such as investment advice and online and mobile banking services and products. Fintech firms have a market niche in developing products and services for previously under-served markets. All one needs is access to the internet and a mobile network. The spread of mobile technology, smartphones and mobile network coverage will lead to more – and less costly – options for individuals and small and medium-sized enterprises, for example, with peer-to-peer lending, borrowing funds on electronic platforms directly from creditors (direct finance), rather than borrowing indirectly from savers through banks and other financial intermediaries.

A Peer-to-Peer Lending

12.5 Regarding e-banking or peer-to-peer lending, financial technology has facilitated the bringing together of lenders and borrowers, and small businesses and start-ups, with investors. In Europe, over a dozen 'peer-to-peer' lending platforms have been established for small and medium-sized businesses and entrepreneurs to obtain credit: for instance, Zopa and Funding Circle. These Fintech businesses that provide electronic or digital lending platforms are not legally defined as banks; for instance, they do not leverage their balance sheets, nor do they accept deposits. As a result, they are not regulated as banks or other financial intermediaries and thus are not burdened by regulatory costs and therefore can pay higher interest rates to savers (or lenders) and charge lower interest rates to borrowers.

12.6 The advantages of these P2P lenders are as follows. There is no channelling of investment money through traditional banks and therefore it avoids the higher charges of banks as compared to digital lenders that do not have bricks and mortar operations and do not have to comply with costly regulation. Also, by using these e-loan platforms, investors and business borrowers can identify each other and agree their own terms without the intrusion of an intermediary. There is much transparency between lenders and borrowers that does not exist between savers and borrowers of banks. E-lending platforms also provide alternative sources of credit for many small businesses and start-ups who may have difficulty obtaining credit from traditional banks because of stricter regulation and previous lack of access to credit.

12.7 The disadvantages of P2P lending platforms are several, including the creditworthiness and other information about the borrower and lender are more difficult to ascertain. This leads to a higher risk of default, as the lender cannot rely on the veracity of the information provided on the e-lender's platform and it is difficult for the lender to seek compensation for any defaults. These greater risks are not absorbed by the e-lending platform business and instead are covered by individual lenders – many of whom may be unsophisticated in how they assess credit and other market risks. However, the greater risk of default in P2P lending does not appear to pose systemic risks to the banking sector, as the amount of credit provided through e-lending and other P2P platforms is very limited in comparison to the amount of credit provided by the banking sector as a whole.

12.8 However, the number of borrowers is growing rapidly along with limited competition and there is an incentive for some platforms to become too big too quickly. E-lending businesses may not be as sophisticated in managing risks as traditional banks and therefore regulation may have a role to play.

II OPEN BANKING

> All banks do is really data, so when you open that data up to third parties it allows for the first time a separation between the person that manages the customer relationship and the person that provides the balance sheet services.[1]

12.9 The digitisation of banking – particularly in payment services – and the use of access and network technologies has created various opportunities for big data management companies, Fintech firms and challenger banks to increase their respective market share. The European Union adopted Payment Services Directive 2 (PSD2) in January 2016; this introduces a new legal framework to govern the phenomenon of open banking which may transform the provision of banking services. The PSD2 contains an 'access to account rule' which requires all banks and certain other financial intermediaries to provide authorised third-party account providers with access to the bank's customer account records if their customers expressly consent to such third-party access. PSD2 sets out information requirements, rights and obligations of payment service users and providers (PSPs) that facilitate the transfer of funds.

1 Antony Jenkins, former Barclays chief executive. See Arnold M, Binham C and Brunsden J, 'European Banks Brace for Shake-up in Customer Data Access', *Financial Times* (London, 12 January 2018).

12.10 The main objective of PSD2 is to increase competition in the provision of banking services. European policymakers adopted PSD2 because they had concluded that banks had operated with very little competition in their markets for too long.[2] PSD2 requires banks to grant third-party access to their customers' accounts and payment services securely after obtaining customer consent. Prior to PSD2, banks were not required to share customer data with third parties. The third parties who will be granted access to customer accounts under PSD2 are known as *account information service providers* (AISPs). Also, with customer consent, the bank would be required to permit other third parties to initiate payments from a customer's bank account on the customer's behalf to other parties' (i.e. merchants) bank accounts. Under PSD2, these third parties are known as *payment initiation service providers* (PISPs). To access both customers' account information and to initiate payments, a third party must be certified by the financial regulator as an authorised third-party provider (TPP).

12.11 The PSD2 provides the legal basis for the unbundling of banking services in a similar way to how telecom services and some utility services were unbundled in many countries in the 1990s and 2000s. The unbundling of banking services is expected to introduce more competition and efficiencies into the banking sector, especially for retail banking customers. The legislation will require banks to notify their customers that they can consent to have their account records and transaction history transferred to third-party service providers who will then be able to review their records and offer them account services, such as lower charges for credit card or foreign exchange transactions. These AISPs can be other banks, financial data management firms and other non-traditional financial service firms as well as retailers, social media and telecom companies. After reviewing bank customer data, they will be allowed to offer them account information services through an online service that will provide aggregated information on one or more payment accounts held by the customer (e.g. balances and payment history) with other payment service providers.

12.12 AISPs will also be eligible to obtain a licence by the regulator to become a payment initiation service provider (PSP). PSPs can initiate online payment orders at the request of the customer with respect to a payment account held at another PSP. PSPs can be merchants or third-party payment service providers (e.g. PayPal) which, with the consent of the bank's customer, would be allowed to make payments from the customer's account. AISPs and PSPs are expected to transform the provision of banking services by allowing customers to choose to allow them to advise and offer financial services to them, taking away much of this profitable business from the banks. Some bankers predict that AIP technology, along with the legal framework that facilitates the rise of AISPs and PSPs, will result in an unbundling of banking services similar to the unbundling of the telecoms industry. AISPs and PSPs will be in a position to potentially skim off from the banks the

---

2 Ibid., citing Olle Ludvigsson, Member of the European Parliament stating that PSD2 was needed because '[f]or too long banks have existed in an environment without competition'.

marketing, sale and provision of most banking services, leaving banks merely as infrastructure providers that maintain the balance sheets of their customers.

12.13 Although the legislation does not prescribe a particular technology or software program for
AISPs and PISPs to access bank customer accounts, the industry standard is known as
Application Programming Interfaces (APIs). APIs have been deemed the most reliable and
tested technology to facilitate secure and reliable access to customers' accounts, even
though the technology is not directly mentioned in the EU legislation.

12.14 The PSD2 requires banks to open access to their customers' accounts with customer consent
for a wide array of services. For example, the legislation covers the enabling of cash deposits
and withdrawals; execution of credit transfers, standing orders and direct debits; payments
through cards and similar devices; issuing of payment instruments (such as cards or wallets),
money remittances; payment initiation services; and account information services.

12.15 The PSD2 open banking legislation would apply in the following hypothetical situation.
A customer has a savings account with bank A and another financial product (i.e. a
mortgage) with bank B. Prior to PSD2, both banks would have a direct relationship with
the customer about their respective products. However, PSD2 provides that either or both
banks could lose (with customer consent) the customer, as that relationship would be
managed by an AISP. Although the customer would still keep their accounts with both
banks and the banks would provide the balance sheet maintenance, the customer's primary
relationship would be with the AISP or TPP. Essentially, the AISP or TPP would deal with
the bank on the customer's behalf (see Figure 12.1).

A Customer Bank Relationship Today

12.16 The PSD2 provides the basic principles for the regulatory framework that would govern the
functions and responsibilities of account information service providers (AISPs) and payment initiation service providers (PISPs). Each EU Member State will have a designated
regulator that will grant licences to third-party AISPs and PISPs and will ensure that they
comply with the relevant data protection laws and financial regulatory framework, particularly to protect against operational risks and related cyber and financial crime risks. The
European Supervisory Authorities (the EBA, ESMA and EIOPA) will design technical
standards for a risk-based supervisory regime that Member State supervisors can implement
and apply across EU states (see Figure 12.2).

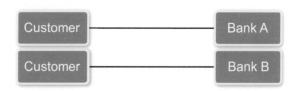

Figure 12.1 Pre-PSD2/open banking

Figure 12.2 Post-PSD2/open banking

12.17 The PSD2, along with other similar legislative and regulatory initiatives in other countries (e.g. UK open banking), could well usher in further disintermediation of retail banking services as third parties take over the relationships that banks currently have with their customers. Established banks might have to reconsider their market position and review their strategy for providing value to their customers. This is expected to increase innovation in the sector and thus provide higher transparency, security, quality of service and lower prices for users, especially for retail customers. In addition, it will promote the further integration of the Eurozone and EU payments system, and support a more efficient EU payments market as well as promote competition.

B UK Open Banking

12.18 The UK Competition and Markets Authority (CMA) issued the Retail Banking Market Investigation Order 2017. This secondary legislation is similar to, but different in key respects from, the EU PSD2. Article 14 of the Order required the nine largest UK-based banks to make available for release personal current account (PCA) and business current account (BCA) datasets to authorised third-party firms by 13 January 2018 as part of the UK open banking policy.

12.19 In late 2017, six of the nine banks informed the CMA that they would not be able to release all the datasets by the specified date. The CMA responded by issuing each of these banks with directions stipulating the timeline for the delivery of the outstanding datasets and the arrangements that each bank must make for reporting progress to the CMA in the meantime. Three of the six banks have complied with the CMA directions as of July 2018, but three have not provided datasets. Although the CMA is responsible for ensuring that covered banks are disclosing the required datasets to authorised third-party firms, the UK financial regulator – the Financial Conduct Authority – is responsible for authorising third-party account service providers and payment service initiators.

12.20 In addition, unlike the PSD2, the UK legislation creates a framework that delegates to the regulator (the FCA) the design of an API standard for digital banking. In designing an API standard, the UK Competition and Markets Authority proposed an implementation entity consisting of the nine largest UK banks to make recommendations for the type of agreed technical standards that would govern the banks' interaction with third-party account providers and the type of API standard to be used for communication and transfer of data between bank customers and third-party service and payment providers. Based on the proposals of the nine banks, the UK adopted regulations that became effective in January 2018 for the use of an API standard and to require that the nine largest UK banks make their customers available to certified third parties.

12.21 The UK regulations make it easier for bank customers to compare details of current accounts and banking services across different banking institutions. Over time, though, it is envisioned that the third-party providers, as well as banks, may develop new online and mobile applications, allowing customers to share data securely across different regulated institutions – both financial firms and data service providers. The Competition and Markets Authority and the Financial Conduct Authority have adopted regulations to certify third-party account service and payment providers that are similar to AISPs and PSPs under the PSD2, but significant differences exist between the two regimes.

12.22 Regarding the API standard, the PSD2 does not require the creation of a common API standard. This allows individual banks to make their data available through different technical standards, which may create additional complexity for the use of account aggregation tools. In contrast, the UK open banking regulation requires the creation of a common API standard across banks and third-party providers.

12.23 For customer data transfer, the PSD2 permits customer account data to take place through a method known as 'screen scrapping', in which customers who agree to provide their account details are required to provide their login details to third-party companies who can subsequently login and obtain their financial information. However, the UK regulations do not require customers who have agreed to provide their account details to provide login details to the third-party providers. Rather, customer data is transferred to the TPP by using a 'plug' and 'socket' approach, in which third-party firms can connect directly to the banks in order to access the data that the customers have consented to provide.

C Covered Institutions and Disintermediation

12.24 The definition of covered institutions that are required to be certified in order to provide third-party account and payment services varies between the UK regulation and the EU PSD2. Under PSD2, third-party providers must be either a certified account information services provider (AISP), a payment initiation provider (PIP), or both (TPP). The UK regulations, however, permit a broader range of third parties to provide these services. They would be authorised through a process called 'white-listing'. For example, price comparison websites that customers might use to compare the prices and services of different banking products do not fall with the coverage of PSD2 and therefore would not be regulated as an

AISP. But the UK open banking regulations would ensure that these web-based information providers were certified and regulated under the regulation's 'white-listing process'.

12.25 The long-term trend caused by the open banking phenomenon is the potential disintermediation of banks from the provision of many retail and some wholesale banking services. Banking industry studies estimate that banks face more disintermediation risk than payment service providers, because payment firms have already adapted to data provision markets.[3] Banks may be forced to compete not merely against other banks but also against many other financial firms and third-party account service providers for account management and products. Also, the increased competition created by PSD2's liberalisation framework for bank account service provision may result in reduced bank profit margins and lead to increased volatility in the value and number of deposit accounts. It could also decrease the volume and sources of bank funding and, in turn, their lending capabilities.

12.26 The short-term trends in open banking are the following: increased regulation driven in part by PSD2 principles-based regulatory standards that are proposed and adopted by the European Supervisory Authorities and later implemented by Member State authorities. The wave of regulation may come before the market converges on any one API standard or particular business practice of third-party account providers. Also, an important question is to what extent will bank customers consent to have their data accessed by these third-party providers? The technical obstacles of implementing the necessary technology infrastructure and account interface protocols for third-party providers with banks and their customers is not yet fully known.

III DIGITAL CURRENCIES AND BITCOIN

12.27 Bitcoin was created in 2009 by an anonymous person named Satoshi Nakamoto, who developed a block-chain technology that allows individuals who access the technology to trade Bitcoin between themselves without the involvement of banks or other intermediaries such as central banks. Bitcoin is an example of a digital or virtual currency – other digital currencies include Ethereum, XRP, Stellar, Cardano – which many users believe will eventually replace central bank currencies ('fiat money') and banks themselves with new virtual currencies that can be traded directly between individuals without the involvement of banks or other intermediaries. The value of Bitcoin, like gold, depends on demand and supply, with the supply limited because Bitcoins must be 'mined' in a complex, virtual system. The growing popularity of Bitcoin, and other virtual currencies, has led to significant increases in its price and to a growing number of individuals buying and selling Bitcoin on unregulated exchanges, often leading to volatile price movements that are

---

3   See Ghose R, *Bank of the Future: The ABCs of Digital Disruption in Finance* (Citi GPS: Global Perspectives & Solutions, March 2018), 60.

vulnerable to financial crime and market manipulation. Although Bitcoin has been associated with drug trafficking, fraud and speculative bubbles, more and more people want to hold Bitcoin as an alternative store of value, including trading futures (derivatives) contracts that use Bitcoin as the reference asset. In this sense, Bitcoin functions more like a commodity rather than a currency.

12.28 Although banks are exposed to the risks of disintermediation because of virtual currencies such as Bitcoin, they are increasingly beginning to provide digital currency services to their customers. Indeed, since 2016, a few banks and a growing number of institutional investors and hedge funds around the world are expressing an interest in virtual currencies as an asset class for their customers. In 2017, the two major US commodities exchanges in Chicago (the Chicago Mercantile Exchange and the Chicago Board Options Exchange) began allowing customers to trade Bitcoin futures contracts. In 2018, Goldman Sachs announced that Bitcoin is not a fraud and does not have the characteristics of a currency, and therefore should be managed as a valuable commodity for its customers.[4] Goldman Sachs has already been bilaterally clearing futures contracts in Bitcoin for its clients who are institutional investors that trade on the two Chicago commodity exchanges. In 2018, Goldman began using its own capital to trade Bitcoin futures contracts on behalf of its customers and has designed a new financial instrument known as a non-deliverable forward contract intended to allow the bank's clients to speculate or hedge against Bitcoin price movements.

12.29 The trading of Bitcoin and other digital assets presents regulatory risks. In the US, banks that use their own capital to trade Bitcoin futures and other digital assets are required to obtain regulatory authorisation from the Federal Reserve Bank of New York and the Commodities Futures Trading Commission (CFTC). Moreover, because Bitcoins are usually traded on electronic exchanges that are not regulated, there are few measures in place to protect investors against market manipulation and theft of Bitcoin by cyber hackers, which has occurred on many Bitcoin exchanges.[5]

12.30 The growing use of Bitcoin and other digital assets could lead to further disintermediation of the banking sector, as more individuals and firms are beginning to acquire and trade directly in digital currencies and do not necessarily need to use the banking system to conduct these transactions. However, banks are playing a growing role in advising endowments and foundations that have received virtual currency donations about how to invest and manage millions of US$ in Bitcoin as an asset class. And other banks are increasingly trading futures contracts referencing digital assets for themselves as well as for their clients. Digital currencies and assets are growing in popularity and offer enormous upside gains,

4 See Popper N, 'Goldman Sachs to Open a Bitcoin Trading Unit' *New York Times* (New York, 4 May 2018) www .nytimes.com/2018/05/02/technology/bitcoin-goldman-sachs.html accessed 28 May 2018.
5 Darbellay A and Reymond M, 'Le régime de responsabilité civile en matière d'émissions publiques de jetons digitaux (ICO)' 2018 *Revue suisse de droit des affaires et du marché financier* 1 48–66.

but present many economic and conduct of business risks that will continue to raise questions about the legitimacy of these markets over time. Moreover, much of the volatility of Bitcoin prices and other digital assets has been driven by the uncertainty surrounding how regulators will treat digital currencies: to what extent they will be approved for trading as an asset class and the related regulatory restrictions on banks that trade contracts which reference digital currency assets and the controls on their distribution to bank customers.

12.31 Moreover, in 2018, some central banks, such as the Swedish and Singapore central banks, have begun exploring whether to issue digital versions of their own currencies. The use of central bank digital currencies was the subject of a report published in March 2018 by the Bank for International Settlements Committee on Payments and Market Infrastructures,[6] which discusses the benefits and risks of issuing such currencies and the effect of central bank digital currencies (CBDCs) on payment systems, monetary policy implementation and financial stability. As mentioned above, central bank money (fiat money) consists of notes and coins which anyone can hold, and of electronic credits recorded in reserve and settlement accounts held by banks at central banks that are used for inter-bank payments. Digital currencies could become a 'new form of central bank money'.[7] The report observes that a central bank could issue a digital currency that is denominated in local or national currency and they could allow anyone to hold such a currency digitally or electronically at the central bank. This would allow CBDCs to be transferred like cash between anyone who held a CBDC account at the central bank. The paper further notes that central banks could regulate whether the accounts were held anonymously (preserving financial privacy) or transparently in aid of tax collection and to control financial crime.[8] The central bank could also decide whether to pay account holders interest,[9] which would affect the incentives for account holders to hold other liquid assets, such as cash, bank accounts or highly rated securities. A higher interest rate on CBDC accounts could result in banks having higher funding costs by having to pay their depositors more to keep them from moving their accounts to CBDC accounts.[10] A central bank could also allow account holders to hold a digital account in a foreign reserve currency, such as the dollar or euro. The use of CBDCs could have significant implications for monetary policy,[11] financial stability[12] and the smooth functioning of payment systems.[13]

12.32 The Swedish central bank – the Riksbank – is considering issuing an e-krona for retail and business payments.[14] However, the BIS report notes that some central banks have only

---

6   Committee on Payments and Market Infrastructures, 'Central Bank Digital Currencies' (Bank for International Settlements, March 2018) www.bis.org/cpmi/publ/d174.pdf accessed 28 May 2018.
7   See Bank for International Settlements Report (n 6), Part 2: Taxonomy, 3.
8   Ibid. (n 6), 6: 'Anonymity'.
9   Ibid. (n 6), 6: 'Interest-Bearing'.
10   Ibid.
11   For more detail, see ibid. (n 6), 10: '4. Monetary Policy Aspects'.
12   For more detail, see ibid. (n 6), 14: '5. Financial Intermediation, Financial Stability and Cross-Border Aspects'.
13   For more detail, see ibid. (n 6), 7: '3. Payment Aspects'.
14   See ibid. (n 6), 7.

found limited benefits in using CBDCs for inter-bank payments.[15] Other risks for central banks in issuing digital currencies could be that depositors might lose confidence in the central bank and there could be a run on the digital currency. In any event, the advent of digital currencies or virtual currencies – whether issued privately or by central banks – raises important policy and regulatory issues for banks and banking.

IV REGULATION TECHNOLOGY (REGTECH)

12.33 Regulation technology (RegTech) involves the provision of services that bring together innovative technology and regulation to enhance compliance with regulatory requirements across industries, including financial services. RegTech was coined by the UK government in 2015 largely as a financial sector response to the Fintech phenomenon.[16] The UK Treasury stated that '[f]intech has the potential to be applied to regulation and compliance to make financial regulation and reporting more transparent, efficient and effective – creating new mechanisms for regulatory technology, Regtech'.[17] Despite its growing importance and widespread applications, RegTech has no commonly accepted definition. As a result, RegTech can be applied in a wide range of contexts, including the potential for continuous monitoring capacity, providing close to real-time information on institutions and transactions, using deep learning and artificial intelligence, and improving the functioning of markets on both a national and cross-border basis.[18]

A The Rationale

12.34 RegTech is a growing phenomenon for banks and financial firms as well as for regulators, and it is driven by the dramatic increase in the costs of risk management and compliance for most financial institutions following the post-crisis regulatory reforms. Indeed, banks on average allocate 10–15 per cent of their staff to regulatory compliance and controls.[19] For example, it is estimated that compliance for European banks with the requirements of the Market in Financial Instruments Directive II (MiFID II) will cost $2.1 billion.[20]

---

15   Ibid.
16   Walport M, 'Fintech Futures: The U.K. as a World Leader in Financial Technologies' (Report by the UK Government Chief Scientific Adviser, 13 March 2015), 5 ff https://bravenewcoin.com/assets/Industry-Reports-2015/UK-Gov-Fintech-Futures.pdf accessed 12 June 2018.
17   HM Treasury, 'Budget 2015' (HC 1093, March 2015), 53 https://assets.publishing.service.gov.uk/govern ment/uploads/system/uploads/attachment_data/file/416330/47881_Budget_2015_Web_Accessible.pdf accessed 12 June 2018: '. . . the FCA, working with the PRA, will also identify ways to support the adoption of new technologies to facilitate the delivery of regulatory requirements – so called Regtech'.
18   See Arner DW, Barberis J and Buckley RP, 'FinTech, RegTech, and the Reconceptualization of Financial Regulation' (2017) 37 *Northwestern Journal of International Law and Business* 371 383.
19   BBVA Research, 'Digital Economy Outlook' (BBVA Digital Regulation Unit, February 2016) www.bbvare search.com/wp-content/uploads/2016/02/DEO_Feb16-EN.pdf accessed 12 June 2018.
20   Noonan L, 'Banks Face Pushback Over Surging Compliance and Regulatory Costs', *Financial Times* (London, 28 May 2015). See also Lewin J, 'MiFID II Preparation Could Cost Firms $2.1 Bn', *Financial Times* (London, 29 September 2016).

12.35 RegTech involves innovative tools and technologies that allow banks and regulators to reduce the costs of regulatory compliance by utilising 'big data' applications, data mining and advanced analytic tools, visualisation tools, biometric and social media analysis, real-time and system embedded compliance and risk evaluation tools, software integration tools, and predictive coding, open platforms and networks.[21] In the banking sector, RegTech solutions are being applied to regulatory reporting, risk management, identity management and control, compliance and transaction monitoring.[22] Specific applications of RegTech involve the use of risk data aggregation, modelling scenario analysis and forecasting, monitoring payments transactions, identification of clients and legal persons, monitoring a bank's internal culture and behaviour, monitoring trading activity and identifying new regulations.[23]

12.36 Risk data aggregation could involve the collection and aggregation of high-quality structured data. Some banks are using modelling scenario analysis and forecasting to comply with stress-testing requirements. For example, Citicorp uses the artificial intelligence (AI) system from a Stanford University spin-off firm Ayasdi to help it pass the US Federal Reserve Bank's stress tests.[24] Banks are able to monitor their internal risk culture and the behaviour of key risk-takers by using advanced analytic tools to learn more about the personalities of traders and risk data aggregation techniques to identify suspicious transactions. Data aggregation tools allow banks to calculate margins on trades in real time, and to select automatically the choice of trading venue and central counterparties based on transaction and regulatory costs.

12.37 RegTech will have an important impact on organisational compliance processes of financial enterprises by using new technologies through, for example, the replacement of analogue by digital processes. Increased automation and aggregation of data will facilitate bank reporting requirements and the supervision of regulated enterprises.

B Regulatory Initiatives

12.38 The UK Financial Conduct Authority has encouraged banks to embrace RegTech in order to facilitate collaboration, knowledge-sharing and communications around new technologies that support better regulation.[25] Regulators in other jurisdictions are also encouraging Fintech innovations within firms to enhance business models and to comply with increasingly stringent and complex regulatory requirements. Some observers foresee a paradigm

---

21 BBVA Research (n 19).
22 Deloitte, 'Reg Tech Universe' (*Deloitte Analysis*, 14 May 2018) www2.deloitte.com/lu/en/pages/technol ogy/articles/regtech-universe.html accessed 12 June 2018.
23 Institute of International Finance, 'Regtech in Financial Services: Technology Solutions for Compliance and Reporting' (IIF, March 2016) www.iif.com/system/files/regtech_in_financial_services_-_solutions_for_com pliance_and_reporting.pdf accessed 12 June 2018.
24 Ibid.
25 See Financial Conduct Authority, 'Call for Input: Supporting the Development and Adoption of Regtech' (FCA, April 2016), 3 www.fca.org.uk/publication/feedback/fs-16-04.pdf accessed 21 December 2018.

shift in financial regulation involving the development of RegTech involving regulators utilising information technology systems and capacities to supervise banking and financial institutions more effectively.[26] RegTech is considered to be an important driver of Fintech. It is argued that RegTech and Fintech should be distinguished, as RegTech represents more than just an efficiency tool, but rather it is a pivotal change leading to a paradigm shift in regulation.[27]

12.39 RegTech may also enable smaller, challenger banks to comply more cost-effectively with regulations and thus promote a more competitive, level playing field between large banks and smaller banks.[28] Indeed, RegTech may be able to assist small banks and financial firms who find it costly and difficult to meet new regulatory requirements in order to comply with the massive volume of regulation that has been adopted. RegTech solutions could foster a more competitive landscape in banking that prevents the creation of even larger banks and which might make the financial system more stable.

12.40 Financial innovation has become more rapid because of advances in financial technology. This means that RegTech should be built into a reconceptualised financial regulatory regime. In the future, it is expected that RegTech will lead to a paradigm shift based on a holistic approach to regulation that will place more emphasis on the nexus of data and digital identity. Effective RegTech solutions for bank compliance require that data needs to be gathered globally on a real-time basis and processed in a coherent way in order to meet the cross-border needs of businesses and regulators.

12.41 RegTech has become an important topic for bank compliance and risk management officers and for regulators as they seek to promote more efficient regulatory frameworks that encourage increased compliance. RegTech has the potential to harness the capabilities of new technologies such as big data, cloud computing and Bitcoin technologies, to design solutions to help banks and financial enterprises and supervisory authorities enhance compliance with evolving financial regulations.[29]

12.42 RegTech's effectiveness depends in part on regulatory and supervisory authorities applying digital technologies for monitoring and ensuring compliance with regulatory standards. It can potentially lead to greater efficiency in regulatory compliance on the part of banks and regulators. It is necessary, however, to have greater interaction between public and private sector technologies that could lead to unified data formats, compatible programming interfaces (API) and machine readable interactions.[30] Some consider RegTech to be a new

---

26   See Arner, Barberis and Buckley (n 18), 376.
27   Ibid., 382 and 383.
28   Arnold M, 'Market Grows for "Regtech" or AI for Regulation', *Financial Times* (London, 14 October 2016).
29   See Weber RH, 'RegTech as a New Legal Challenge' (2017) 46 *Journal of Financial Transformation* 10.
30   Le Brocq N, 'Regtech – The New Paradigm: Recognizing the Potential for Technology to Manage Regulatory Data and Improve Internal Control and Compliance', *Confluence* (13 April 2016).

type of regulatory programme that could deal with everything from digital identity to data sovereignty, thereby extending beyond the financial sphere.[31]

V FINTECH AND FINANCIAL INCLUSION: THE INTERNATIONAL DIMENSION

12.43 Fintech also creates the potential to expand the provision of banking services to people and groups around the world, especially in developing countries and other under-banked markets. The Basel Committee on Banking Supervision has stated that it is a major objective of bank regulators to expand financial inclusion to regions and groups who do not have access to formal banking services.[32] Financial inclusion is measured in three dimensions: (1) in terms of access to financial services, (2) the usage of financial services, and (3) the quality of the financial products provided and the way in which they are delivered. Financial inclusion has become an important international financial policy objective and financial regulatory principle, and has been incorporated into a number of international declarations and codes of good practice. Some of the international initiatives to promote financial inclusion include the Maya Declaration on Financial Inclusion (2011) that was set forth by the Alliance for Financial Inclusion, a network of central banks, financial supervisors and other regulatory authorities from developing and emerging market economies, to improve the economic and social potential of the world's poorest by improving their access to financial services and products. Significantly, the Maya Declaration states that financial inclusion is critical for empowering and transforming the lives of all people, especially the poor, and that policies designed to promote it should also enhance global and national financial stability and market integrity. The G20 has recognised the importance of digital financial services in supporting the objective of financial inclusion. Also, international regulatory bodies, such as the Basel Committee on Banking Supervision, have identified technical guidance for banking supervisors to facilitate the use of digital technologies that enhance financial inclusion.

12.44 Fintech has the potential to facilitate increased financial inclusion by enhancing access to financial services for those individuals and businesses who have been excluded from formal financial markets. Fintech companies are developing digital services that could result in billions of people having greater access to the banking sector and to new investment products. Digital innovations across different areas of the financial sector have had a tremendous impact in enhancing the provision of financial services. Specifically, digital technologies have spread rapidly in many areas of the global economy, yet there is potential for increased use of these technologies.

---

31 Weber (n 29), 11.
32 Basel Committee on Banking Supervision, 'Guidance on the Application of the Core Principles for Effective Banking Supervision to the Regulation and Supervision of Institutions Relevant to Financial Inclusion' (Bank for International Settlements, September 2016), 3–4.

12.45 To support the spread of digital financial technologies, the G20 has adopted High Level Principles for Digital Financial Inclusion (2016) that place great emphasis on using digital technology to enhance financial inclusion. The principles emphasise finding the right balance between innovation and risk in achieving greater financial inclusion and how to utilise legal and regulatory frameworks for using digital technologies to increase this. It involves establishing responsible digital financial practices to protect consumers and to improve financial literacy and awareness so that digital financial products are better understood by users.

12.46 Internationally, the world has 2.5 billion 'unbanked' individuals and 200 million small businesses without formal access to financial services. High percentages of unbanked individuals and businesses are in Africa, Latin America, Asia and the Middle East. Of unbanked individuals, about one billion have mobile phones, meaning for many that financial mobility and enhancements in services could occur in the near future.

12.47 The role of e-finance in enhancing financial inclusion in financial services for individuals and small businesses, especially in developing countries, is based on making financial services available to those who would normally not have access. Fintech expands the availability of information on financial services, such as investment advice and online and mobile banking services and products. Fintech firms have a market niche in developing products and services for previously under-served markets. All people need is access to the internet and mobile network. The spread of mobile technology, smartphones and mobile network coverage will lead to more and less costly options for individuals and small and medium enterprises, for example, with peer-to-peer lending and borrowing funds on electronic platforms directly from creditors (direct finance), rather than borrowing indirectly from savers through banks and other financial intermediaries.

A Barriers for Developing Countries

12.48 Despite the obvious benefits of using digital technology to increase financial inclusion, there are significant barriers, especially for developing countries, involving geographical distances between service providers and users and the lack of market infrastructure (i.e. payment systems and securities settlement). In many countries that rely heavily on agricultural production and services, weather risks are important and can dictate when loans are repaid and whether investments are profitable. Also, in many countries, there is little effective competition in the financial services industry, which leads to higher operating costs and thus high costs and charges for individuals in opening bank accounts. Moreover, in many developing countries, weak regulatory institutions and legal uncertainty for the enforcement of contracts leads to moral hazard among market participants, to adverse selection and thus to unnecessarily higher costs of capital resulting in a misallocation of capital to less efficient projects.

12.49 Each economy is unique and presents its own separate challenges. In the Philippines, the widespread availability of mobile money payments and high demand for international money transfers contrasts with other countries, such as South Africa, where there is less incentive for financially excluded individuals to replace their existing methods of accessing funds. In Mexico, banks have a reputation for poor customer service and are very inefficient relative to banks in other similarly sized Latin American economies. As a result, the availability of smartphones and relatively low barriers to entry are leading to a growing number of Fintech firms entering the Mexican market to provide payment services and lending through smartphones and other digital technology. In Bangladesh, a firm called 'BKash Limited', a subsidiary of BRAC Bank Limited, was launched in 2011 to provide mobile phone financial services, including payments and money transfers, to both unbanked and banked individuals and businesses.[33]

CONCLUSION

12.50 This chapter has reviewed some of the main issues in the financial technology and regulation technology debate and the potential impact on the banking business and the implications for financial inclusion, particularly in developing countries. Financial innovation and technology can enhance the provision of banking services to the economy. Financial technology (Fintech) has, for instance, enabled peer-to-peer lending to become a viable business model that enables surplus savers to invest in loans through an electronic intermediary without the risks of the bank holding the asset on its balance sheet. Fintech also creates risks for investors who provide credit to borrowers on electronic platforms who do not fully understand the credit risks to which they are exposed. Digital currencies (i.e. Bitcoin) raise serious concerns regarding financial crime and the efficacy of the technology to support the trading of digital assets. Digital currencies could also facilitate the disintermediation of banks by allowing parties to deal with each other directly in the digital currency market. Central bank involvement in issuing digital currencies could further threaten the traditional role of banks. In the European Union and United Kingdom, open banking has become a viable business model that threatens the privileged role that banks have had in marketing and selling financial products to their customers. The chapter discusses how open banking could lead to an unbundling of financial services in the banking sector and the role of technology in this process. The chapter also explores how regulation technology (RegTech) can take advantage of financial technologies to increase compliance with regulation and to improve the efficiency and capacity of risk management, thereby enhancing the banking business while achieving regulatory objectives. Finally, international initiatives to increase financial inclusion and how this has become an important objective of international policy and financial regulation are considered. The chapter discusses how Fintech can be used to support financial inclusion but it also considers the business, regulatory and technical challenges.

---

33 Upon registering with BKash, each user receives a mobile wallet that serves as a bank account.

QUESTIONS

1. What changes may third-party data service providers bring to the banking services market?
2. What are the benefits and risks of peer-to-peer banking?
3. How might open banking affect the organisational structure of banking institutions?
4. What type of regulatory risks does open banking pose?
5. What are some of the legal risks that open banking might create for banks?
6. What improvements will APIs bring to the provision of banking services and what are the regulatory concerns?
7. What is the rationale of RegTech?
8. How might RegTech change compliance with banking regulation?
9. How might Fintech enhance access to banking services?
10. What are some of the challenges for banks?

Further Reading

Arner DW, Barberis J and Buckley RP, 'FinTech, RegTech, and the Reconceptualization of Financial Regulation' (2017) 37 *Northwestern Journal of Internation-al Law & Business* 371

Scott Frame WS and White LJ, 'Technological Change, Financial Innovation, and Diffusion in Banking', in Berger AN, Molyneux P and Wilson JOS (eds), *The Oxford Handbook of Banking* (Oxford University Press 2009)

Zachariadis M and Ozcan P, 'The API Economy and Digital Transformation in Financial Services: The Case of Open Banking' (SWIFT Institute Working Paper No. 2016–001, 15 June 2017)

13

Environmental Sustainability

Table of Contents

INTRODUCTION

13.1 This chapter examines the relationship between banking regulation and governance *and* environmental sustainability challenges. Environmental sustainability challenges consist of all man-made environmental risks (not only climate change risks) identified by some scientists as the nine planetary boundaries. If these boundaries are transgressed, humanity cannot continue to develop and thrive in the future.[1] In an important article in the journal *Nature*, a group of distinguished scientists argued that '[t]ransgressing one or more planetary boundaries may be deleterious or even catastrophic due to the risk of crossing thresholds that will trigger non-linear, abrupt environmental change within continental-to-planetary-scale systems'.[2] They asserted that respecting planetary boundaries reduces the risks to human society of crossing these thresholds. Subsequent studies have demonstrated the link between financial and economic risks and environmental sustainability challenges/risks.[3]

13.2 This chapter consists of four parts. Part I will consider the historic links between environmental phenomena and banking, and financial sector stability. Part II will then identify the institutional and market barriers for the banking sector in increasing and allocating credit and investment to more environmentally sustainable sectors of the economy. An important market barrier that will be addressed is the market failure that is associated with what is called the 'Tragedy of the Horizons' (TOH). The TOH concept was emphasised by Governor of the Bank of England, Mark Carney, in a 2015 speech that attracted much attention in regulatory and policy circles. Governor Carney stated that given the scientific evidence and the dynamics of the financial system, climate change could potentially threaten financial resilience in general and economic prosperity over the longer term. The TOH concept is a type of inter-temporal 'tragedy of the commons'.[4] While the benefits of exploiting finite capital resources accrue to a few individual participants, the costs are distributed among many. In the case of environmental risks, the benefits accrue today to those who provide financing for unsustainable economic activities, but most of the costs are imposed on the rest of society inter-temporally over time. Individual market participants therefore who provide financing and capital for fossil fuel-based economic activity have little incentive to

---

1 Rockström J, Steffen WL, Noone A, Persson Å and Stuart Chapin III F, 'Planetary Boundaries: Exploring the Safe Operating Space for Humanity' (2009) 14 *Ecology and Society* 2 32.
2 Rockström J et al., 'A Safe Operating Space for Humanity' (2009) 461 *Nature* 472.
3 See Landon-Lane J, Rockoff H and Steckel RH (eds), 'Droughts, Floods, and Financial Distress in the United States', in Libecap GD and Steckel RH (eds), *The Economics of Climate Change: Adaptations Past and Present* (University of Chicago Press 2009), 73–84. See also Hornbeck R, 'The Enduring Impact of the American Dust Bowl: Short and Long Run Adjustments to Environmental Catastrophe' (2012) 102 *American Economic Review* 4 1477. See also World Economic Forum, 'The Global Risks Report 2016 – 11th edition' (2016) www3.weforum .org/docs/GRR/WEF_GRR16.pdf accessed 21 February 2018.
4 See Carney M, 'Breaking the Tragedy of the Horizon: Climate Change and Financial Stability' (speech at Lloyd's of London, 29 September 2015) www.bankofengland.co.uk/-/media/boe/files/speech/2015/breaking-the-tragedy-of-the-horizon-climate-change-and-financial-stability.pdf?la=en&hash=7C67E785651862457D9 9511147C7424FF5EA0C1A accessed 18 May 2018.

limit the systemic financial risks of their activities today that will likely affect future market participants and society.

13.3 Part III will compare national regulatory approaches in selected developed and developing countries to provide a global perspective to the problem of how banking regulation should address environmental challenges. The chapter suggests that more research is necessary to understand more fully how the different types of environmental and social risks affect countries differently. Part III will also consider the main regulatory and legal principles that are emerging from state practice to address environmental sustainability challenges. Although sound regulation begins at the national level, the risks are global in nature and can only be addressed effectively through cross-border regulatory coordination. Part IV discusses some of the main international and European initiatives to assess the relevance of environmental sustainability risks for banking regulation, while Part V considers some banking policy recommendations for countries to coordinate their regulatory actions in managing the financial risks associated with environmental phenomena.

I ENVIRONMENTAL SUSTAINABILITY RISKS AND BANKING

A Historic Links between the Environment and Banking Stability

Economic historians have demonstrated relationships between weather, agricultural markets and financial markets to show that there are linkages between natural disasters (e.g. drought) and financial market instability.[5] For example, the British economist William Jevons (1884) famously argued that financial crises were produced by sunspots, which could be shown to cause drought and poor harvests in key agricultural producing countries, and which could lead to a downturn in international trade, resulting in significant bank losses and related financial market stresses. During the late nineteenth century and again in the 1930s, the United States suffered from intense windstorms (dust bowls) in the farm belt states which were exacerbated by soil erosion caused by unsustainable farming methods.[6] The ensuing economic downturns during these periods resulted in substantial losses on bank loans and related financial market distress, which spread contagion-like through the regional economy.[7]

More recently, increased hurricane activity in the Caribbean and south-eastern United States caused huge bank losses to businesses and individuals directly impacted by these high wind storms. Hurricane Katrina came ashore in the United States in August 2005, causing in excess of US$200 billion in damages and ranks as one of the costliest natural disasters in US history. In the early twenty-first century, the frequency and intensity of hurricanes have increased significantly, causing much greater damage to coastal economies

---

5 See Landon-Lane et al. (n 3).
6 See Hornbeck (n 3).
7 Ibid. (n 3), 1481–1483.

in the Caribbean, the United States and southeast Asia.[8] The damage led to high loan losses and provisioning for banks that were based in the impacted areas. These bank losses led US regulators to review the adequacy of bank risk models regarding credit risk and hurricane damage.

13.4 The above examples demonstrate historic links between risks arising both from the environment itself (e.g. extreme weather events), from humanity's management of scarce environmental resources (e.g. soil quality and oil) and banking instability. History therefore raises the fundamental question of whether bank regulation should take into account the financial stability risks that can arise from environmentally unsustainable practices.

13.5 Scientists have now identified nine biophysical thresholds for the Earth, which, if crossed, could undermine 'the safe space for human development'. These thresholds – known colloquially as 'planetary boundaries' – represent 'the "planetary playing field" for humanity if we want to be sure of avoiding major human-induced environmental change on a global scale'.[9] Three of these boundaries (namely, climate change, biological diversity and nitrogen input to the biosphere) are thought to have been crossed already (see Figure 13.1).

13.6 Climate change is the boundary about which we know the most. The International Panel on Climate Change (2007, 2013, 2014) has documented the scientific evidence in support of the proposition that global warming and ocean acidification are caused by the carbon-intensive activities of humans. Carbon-intensive activities lead in the longer term to global warming, rising sea levels and ocean acidification. More immediately, they can lead to increasingly volatile weather patterns, including extreme temperatures and intensified flooding of coastal and low-lying areas, water shortages and the health costs of pollution.

13.7 Some believe that these externalities are controlled and even mitigated through adaptations in the economy, such as alternative production processes, or re-directing transport routes to avoid flooded coastlines.[10] According to this view, investors, aware of the scientific evidence on the risks of climate change, would be expected to discount the value of high-carbon assets and increase the value of low-carbon assets, resulting in investment shifting over time to low-carbon assets. Nevertheless, the history of financial crises demonstrates that financial markets suffer from serious over-and underestimation of risks because of asymmetric information and moral hazard. These risks translate into large externalities for the economy and society.[11] Moreover, because financial stability is a

---

8   See Lambert C, Noth F and Schüwer U, 'How Do Banks React to Catastrophic Events? Evidence from Hurricane Katrina' (2017) https://papers.ssrn.com/sol3/papers.cfm?abstract_id=2585521 accessed 18 March 2018.
9   See Rockström (n 2).
10   Nordhaus W, *The Climate Casino: Risk, Uncertainty, and Economics for a Warming World* (Yale University Press 2013).
11   Kindleberger CP and Aliber RZ, *Manias, Panics and Crashes* (6th edn, Palgrave Macmillan 2011), 29–33; Schinasi GJ, *Safeguarding Financial Stability: Theory and Practice* (International Monetary Fund 2006), 47–66; Eichengreen B, *Toward a New International Financial Architecture* (Peterson Institute for International Economics 1999), 80–82.

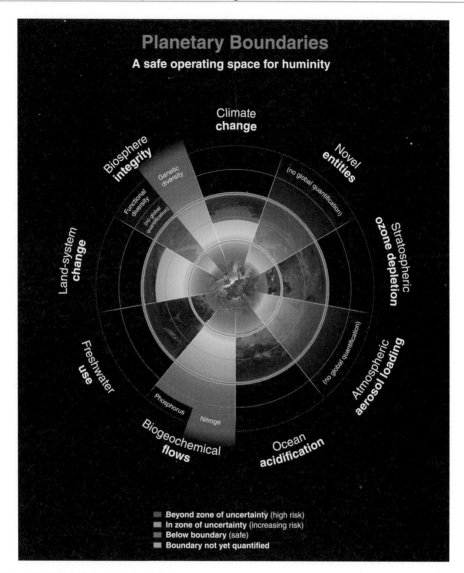

Figure 13.1 Global planetary boundaries
Source: F. Pharand-Deschênes / Globaïa, Stockholm Resilience Centre.

public good, market participants do not have the incentive to invest the necessary capital to provide it themselves, since the benefits of stability spill over to free-riders who do not pay for it.

B The Role of the Banking Sector

13.8 In most countries, banks play a crucial role in providing credit and investment capital for the economy that can be used to mitigate the adverse effects of environmental sustainability risks while enabling the economy to grow and become more resilient to sustainability challenges. Most experts agree that the main environmental sustainability risks – physical, transition and liability risks – potentially create negative externalities for the banking sector and broader economy. But banks are doing more to recognise these risks and support the transition to a more sustainable economy by incorporating or mainstreaming sustainability factors into their risk management models and governance frameworks. In doing so, banks are able to mobilise and reallocate capital away from unsustainable economic activity to more sustainable sectors of the economy.

13.9 While the banking sector is affected by environmental sustainability challenges directly and indirectly, it also plays an important role in supporting the economy's adaptation to environmental changes and building financial resilience to environmental risks.[12] By reallocating credit to more sustainable sectors of the economy and managing credit and market risks, banks contribute, in particular, to (1) reducing environmental sustainability risks, (2) mitigating the impact of these risk when they materialise, (3) adapting to the consequences of environmental change, and (4) supporting recovery when adverse environmental events cause massive disruptions.

13.10 Across many countries, banks have sought to address these risks by adopting different types of green banking practices. Two distinct areas of banking practice have emerged: (1) the development of environmental and social governance guidelines with a particular focus on risk management in the area of project finance and reallocating credit to renewable energy resources. The Equator Principles were established in 2003 to provide banks with voluntary guidance for incorporating environmental and social risks into the bank's assessment of credit and operational risks in large infrastructure investment projects. As a result, many large global banking institutions have mainstreamed environmental governance principles into project finance. (2) Most banks primarily provide short-term credit to large corporations and small and medium-sized firms and savings, and investment products to individuals. They are uniquely positioned to mobilise capital to the green economy, including renewable and clean energy projects by making loans and investments, and structuring specialised transactions.

13.11 The banking sector will play a key role in providing credit and investment for countries as their economies adapt to evolving market structures in response to environmental sustainability challenges. These adaptations may result in volatility in asset prices and in the availability of credit and borrower defaults in economic sectors that the market has determined to be environmentally unsustainable. Where such transition risks are material, they may pose systemic risks to the banking sector. These financial risks associated with environmental sustainability have important implications for the banking sector, as banks are the largest providers of capital for most economies: how they manage the financial risks

---

12 Carney (n 4).

associated with the economy's transition to a more sustainable development path is an important policy concern.

13.12 At the same time, the long-term horizon of the commitment to reduce emissions (2030) combined with the costs of short-term action reduce the credibility of some existing commitments.[13] Some of the constraints or disadvantages for banks in financing environmentally friendly projects concern projects that have comparatively higher capital expenditure and lower operational expenditures, thus leading to a reduced risk-adjusted return in the short term.[14] Also, Weitzman argues that much uncertainty exists regarding the future of technological innovation aimed at reducing sustainability risks. Against this background, there is considerable uncertainty about whether the shift to a more sustainable economy will be gradual and benign – or late and abrupt.[15]

II ENVIRONMENTAL CHALLENGES AND REGULATION

13.13 The 2030 United Nations Sustainable Development Goals' (SDG) development agenda pinpoints environmental sustainability challenges, including climate change, as a major concern to the stability of the global economy. The World Economic Forum Global Risks Report 2016 demonstrates the links between environmental sustainability risks and economic and financial risks (WEF Global Risk Report 2016). The WEF report identified the failure of climate change mitigation and adaptation, along with freshwater availability and diminishing biodiversity, as the most significant environmental sustainability risks. The report also emphasised the second order or 'cascading' risks arising from climate change and other environmental sustainability challenges and how they impact political conflicts, forced migration, food security and economic and financial stability. These challenges will, in turn, have implications for financial institutions in terms of changing risk assessments that will affect the availability and terms of credit and long-term investment returns.

13.14 Since the 1970s, international agreements have addressed a variety of environmental sustainability risks, including awareness of climate change and the associated need to reduce greenhouse gas emissions (GHG). Most recently, the Paris Agreement was adopted at the Paris Climate Change Conference in December 2015 to strengthen the global response to the threat of climate change.[16] Specifically, the Paris Agreement's objectives are:

---

13 As of August 2015, twenty-six countries and territories accounting for more than 55 per cent of global GHG emissions have submitted Intended National Determined Contributions (INDCs) with a 2030 target year (2025 in the case of the US), Morgan Stanley, Global Sustainable + Responsible Investment Research, 'Addressing Climate Change and the Investment Implications: A Primer on Climate Change' (August 2015) (on file with author).

14 Nieto M, 'Banks and Environmental Sustainability: Some Financial Stability Reflections' (2017) International Research Centre for Cooperative Finance.

15 Weitzman ML, 'The Geoengineered Planet', in Palacios-Huerta I (ed.), *In 100 Years* (MIT Press 2013).

16 See United Nations Paris Agreement on Climate Change (2015) http://unfccc.int/files/essential_background/convention/application/pdf/english_paris_agreement.pdf accessed 18 May 2018.

   i. holding the increase in the global average temperature to well below 2°C above pre-industrial levels and pursue efforts to limit the temperature increase to 1.5°C above pre-industrial levels, recognizing that this would significantly reduce the risks and impacts of climate change;

   ii. increasing the ability to adapt to the adverse impacts of climate change and foster climate resilience and low greenhouse gas emissions development . . .; and

   iii. making finance flows consistent towards low greenhouse gas emissions and climate-resilient development.[17]

13.15 Financial policy and regulation are increasingly recognised as important for managing the transition towards a more environmentally sustainable economy that is resilient to environmental risks, such as climate change.[18] On the one hand, the speed and the smoothness of the transition to a green economy and the adjustment costs could affect systemic financial risks. On the other hand, there is a growing recognition that the inculcation of green guidelines and standards into bank lending, trading and investment practices are critical for achieving the core mandates of international financial organisations, such as the International Monetary Fund (IMF 2015a)[19] and the World Bank, which aim to achieve economic growth and financial development that is socially and environmentally sustainable (IMF 2015b).[20] Furthermore, it is widely accepted that most less-industrialised countries (LDCs) are especially vulnerable to the estimated effects of environmental sustainability risks, and will need significant support in the form of concessional finance in order to adapt their economies (IMF 2015c).[21]

13.16 In most countries, institutional and market challenges hinder the provision of bank credit and investment for environmentally sustainable sectors of the economy. In Mexico and India, substantial governmental subsidies for unsustainable agricultural practices have led to a misallocation of capital away from sustainable agricultural and energy sources to unsustainable practices involving, for example, excessive use of fresh water and diesel fuel (Alexander, G20 2016).

13.17 Also, information asymmetries limit the ability of banks to analyse the costs and benefits of environmentally sustainable projects. As a result, banks in most G20 countries have a disproportionately low level of exposure – around 10 per cent of their lending portfolios – to environmentally sustainable projects. This suggests that banks in these countries are not internalising the full costs of socially risky investments and are thereby investing far too

---

17   Ibid., Article 2.

18   See Carney (n 4).

19   International Monetary Fund, 'Financing for Development: Revisiting the Monterrey Consensus' IMF Policy Paper (July 2015) www.imf.org/external/np/pp/eng/2015/061515.pdf accessed 21 February 2018.

20   Fabrizio S et al., 'From Ambition to Execution: Policies in Support of Sustainable Development Goals', IMF Staff Discussion Note SDN/15/18 (September 2015).

21   International Monetary Fund, 'Macroeconomic Developments and Prospects in Low-Income Developing Countries: 2015' (19 November 2015) www.imf.org/external/np/pp/eng/2015/111915.pdf accessed 21 February 2018.

much in unsustainable sectors of the economy. Some countries, such as Mexico, have sought to address these inefficiencies through fiscal reforms and a carbon tax policy. On the other hand, other countries, such as Egypt, have not been confronted with the same types of challenges and have instead relied on large private banks to take the lead in identifying sustainable sectors of the economy and developing risk management strategies for allocating capital to emerging sustainable sectors. This approach has had the effect of influencing other banking institutions – both state-owned and private – to follow suit.

13.18 Based on these countries' experiences, it is clear that more incentives are needed, both market-based and regulatory/fiscal, for banks to address the institutional and market challenges to mobilising more capital and investment for sustainable economic activity. Similarly, enhanced market and policy-based incentives may be needed for banks to mainstream environmental factors across their business strategies, risk management and governance practices. Indeed, the mobilisation of green credit and mainstreaming of environmental factors into banking practice are part of a growing trend to support sustainable banking practices that involve banks in managing the environmental and social risks associated with their financial activities. The overriding objective is to avoid or mitigate financial losses and reputation risks arising from bank exposures to unsustainable economic activity. The question for policymakers is the extent to which governmental or regulatory intervention is necessary to guide the banking sector in allocating more credit and investment to sustainable activity and in protecting the economy against the related financial risks. Because G20 countries have different institutional and market structures, they use different combinations of market-based, regulatory and official sector guidance for the banking sector in supporting the economy's transition to more sustainable development.

13.19 The analysis of the complexity of the potential risks to the financial sector is still at an early stage. For instance, the Financial Stability Board has classified climate-related risks into three broad categories: physical, liability and transition risks (FSB 2015).[22] Physical risks include natural disasters that not only create massive loss of life but also impose substantial costs in damages each year. A growing number of natural disasters and extreme weather events that are more frequent and severe have increased these losses. The physical consequences of climate change extend beyond the direct impact of natural disasters. Physical risks also refer to the impact on insurance liabilities and the value of financial assets that may arise from climate-related events that damage property or disrupt trade. In the financial sector, these losses have consequences most immediately for the insurance and reinsurance sectors, but also extend more widely (e.g. banks). For instance, Swiss Re Sigma Economic Research and Consulting suggests that climate change is increasingly posing a financial threat to the industry, with insured losses from weather events up globally by 6.6

---

22 See Alexander K, 'Stability and Sustainability in Banking Reform: Are Environmental Risks Missing in Basel III?', United Nations Environment Programme and University of Cambridge Institute for Sustainability Leadership (2014) www.unepfi.org/fileadmin/documents/StabilitySustainability.pdf accessed 21 February 2018.

per cent on average in the past twenty-five years and a record number of natural catastrophes in 2014.[23]

13.20 Liability risks arise, for example, when parties who have suffered loss or damage from the effects of climate change seek compensation from those whom they hold responsible. Such claims could come decades in the future, creating liabilities for carbon extractors and emitters and their insurers. Also, in the financial sector, these losses have consequences most immediately for the insurance sector, but also extend more widely to banks and other financial institutions.

13.21 Transition risks are the financial risks which could result from the transition to a more environmentally sustainable economy. Changes in regulation, technology and physical risks could prompt a reassessment of the value of a large range of assets. The abruptness with which such re-pricing occurs could influence financial stability. In the financial sector, these losses have consequences most immediately for the banking and asset management sectors but also extend to the insurance sector.

13.22 While the banking sector is affected by environmental sustainability challenges directly and indirectly, it also plays an important role in supporting the economy's adaptation to environmental changes and building financial resilience to environmental risks. For instance, Mark Carney, Governor of the Bank of England and Chairman of the Financial Stability Board, observed that given the scientific evidence and dynamics of the financial system, climate change could potentially threaten financial resilience in general and economic prosperity over the longer term.[24] By reallocating credit to more sustainable sectors of the economy and managing credit and market risks, banks contribute, in particular, to (1) reducing environmental sustainability risks, (2) mitigating the impact of these risks when they materialise, (3) adapting to the consequences of environmental change, and (4) supporting recovery when adverse environmental events cause massive disruptions.

13.23 Across many countries, banks have sought to address these risks by adopting different types of green banking practices. Two distinct areas of banking practice have emerged. (1) Development of environmental and social governance guidelines with a particular focus on risk management in the area of project finance and reallocating credit to renewable energy resources.[25] For example, the Equator Principles were established in 2003 to provide banks with voluntary guidance for incorporating environmental and social risks into the

23 Swiss Re Sigma, 'Natural Catastrophes and Man-Made Disasters in 2014: Convective and Winter Storms Generate Most Losses', Study No. 2/2015 (2015), 2, 14 http://media.swissre.com/documents/sigma2_2015_en_final.pdf accessed 21 February 2018.
24 See Carney (n 4).
25 See United Nations Environment Programme, 'Greening the Banking System: Taking Stock of G20 Green Banking Market Practice' UNEP Inquiry Working Paper 16/12 (2016) 13, 18–19 www.unepinquiry.org/publication/greening-the-banking-system/ accessed 21 February 2018.

bank's assessment of credit and operational risks in large infrastructure investment projects. As a result, many large global banking institutions have mainstreamed environmental governance principles into project finance. (2) Banks are uniquely positioned to mobilise capital to the green economy, including renewable and clean energy projects, by making loans and investments, and structuring specialised transactions. For example, in 2014, non-recourse bank lending for renewable energy project finance was approximately US$54 billion.[26]

13.24 Mitigating or reducing environmental sustainability risks, however, may require more than voluntary initiatives on the part of the banking sector to promote a more decisive shift away from fossil fuel energy and related physical capital. The role of financial regulation in supporting the transition to a more sustainable economic path has been deemed critical by international organisations.[27] In January 2014, former World Bank President Jim Yong Kim, speaking at the World Economic Forum, recognised the regulatory gap in this area by stating that 'financial regulators must take the lead in addressing climate change risks', and that they should use pricing mechanisms to more effectively control negative externalities or systemic risks associated with global warming.[28]

III BANKING REGULATION AND ENVIRONMENTAL SUSTAINABILITY RISKS

13.25 The overriding objective of banking regulation is to safeguard financial stability and build resilience to shocks, wherever the shocks may come from, and provide a sustainable source of credit, savings products and payment services to the broader economy. Banking regulation can potentially play an important role in mitigating institutional and market impediments to the banking sector's ability to provide adequate capital and liquidity for the economy in meeting environmental sustainability challenges. As discussed in Chapter 2, economic theory holds that policy and regulatory intervention in the banking sector is justified by market failures, which can arise from negative externalities resulting from asymmetric information and competitive distortions. Some evidence suggests that market discipline, on its own, cannot adequately control the externalities in financial markets associated with environmental sustainability challenges.[29] Accordingly, policy or regulatory intervention may be necessary to prevent a misallocation of resources to unsustainable economic activity and to support a reallocation of capital to sustainable sectors of the economy. Policy intervention, however, if not calibrated properly, can also produce its own distortions in the market that can result in further externalities and misallocations of capital

---

26 See G20 Green Finance Study Group, 'G20 Green Finance Synthesis Report' (5 September 2016) www
.unepinquiry.org/wp-content/uploads/2016/09/Synthesis_Report_Full_EN.pdf accessed 21 February 2018.
27 Sullivan R, Bordon A, Feller E and Martindale W, 'Fiduciary Duty in the 21st Century' (September 2015)
Report, UNEP Inquiry.
28 See World Bank Group President Jim Yong Kim Remarks at Davos Press Conference (23 January 2014).
29 Alexander (n 22).

and investment. A careful combination of market innovation and policy frameworks that suit national circumstances may be desirable for some countries in using banking regulation to support the integration of environmental factors into banking practice. In this way, banking regulation can support the efficient operation of the economy by encouraging banks to harness more credit and investment for profitable and sustainable economic activity.

13.26 The priority of banking regulation and financial policy should be to complete implementation of the extensive financial sector reforms introduced following the global financial crisis.[30] Sound legal and institutional frameworks, effective information dissemination, high standards for disclosure and transparency, regulation of business conduct and consumer education can all support financial stability. At the same time, policymakers can use a systemic approach to identifying, assessing and managing the potential risks that environmental sustainability risks, such as climate change, could pose to financial stability.

13.27 For instance, some regulators have put a particular focus on ensuring that connected institutions are sound, adequately capitalised and supervised with effective risk management and disclosure systems incorporating climate risks. Other countries are moving in this direction. It is becoming more common for insurers to conduct regular stress-testing and supervisors to specify scenarios including natural disasters. Some countries require additional reserves against possible catastrophe events. Solvency requirements may impose capital requirements corresponding to catastrophe risk. Some insurers adjust premiums periodically based on loss experience.

13.28 The European Systemic Risk Board (ESRB) in 2015 recommended policy action in response to the potential systemic risk involved in the transition to a more environmentally sustainable and green economy that could involve the use of short- and medium-term regulatory measures. A short-term regulatory response would heavily rely on a better understanding of: (i) banks' and other connected financial firms' direct exposures to non-financial firms with immediate and emerging elevated environmental risks and (ii) the consequences of a disorderly transition to a low-carbon economy. For example, enhanced disclosure of bank exposures to sustainability risks would facilitate a timely assessment of potential risks to financial stability and promote a 'smooth rather than an abrupt transition towards a lower-carbon economy'.[31]

13.29 Some countries have already begun to address these issues by engaging in a variety of regulatory and market practices to assess systemic environmental risks. In doing so, they have

---

30   G20, 'G20 Leaders Statement: The Pittsburgh Summit' (2009) Pittsburgh Summit, University of Toronto G20 Research Group www.g20.utoronto.ca/2009/2009communique0925.html accessed 16 May 2018; see also G20, 'The G20 Seoul Summit Leaders' Declaration' (2009) Seoul Summit, University of Toronto G20 Research Group www.g20.utoronto.ca/2010/g20seoul.html accessed 30 August 2017.

31   See Financial Stability Board, Task Force on Climate-Related Financial Disclosures, 'Recommendations of the Task Force on Climate-Related Financial Disclosures' (2016), iii.

adopted some practices to reduce the banking sector's exposure to environmentally unsustainable activity. As discussed below, regulators in some countries are incorporating environmental sustainability factors into prudential banking regulation in the following areas: disclosure, bank governance, regulatory capital, risk management and financial products.

A Disclosure

13.30 Bank disclosure of risks to investors is an important regulatory tool to support market discipline that can encourage banks to mainstream economically relevant environmental sustainability criteria into their business practices and to reallocate capital to more sustainable sectors of the economy. In many countries, banks and other listed companies are already required to disclose to investors all material financial risks regarding their economic performance. Some environmental risks can be classified as material financial risks (i.e. lender liability for toxic waste clean-up) but most environmental and social risks are not considered by regulators to be material financial risks, and therefore are not required to be disclosed to the market. However, there is a growing demand by investors and other market participants for useful information on bank and other company exposures to environmental sustainability challenges.

13.31 Globally, there are over 400 initiatives and voluntary disclosure frameworks across countries to encourage companies and financial institutions to report environmental and social risk factors. But the information is not consistent across markets and countries, lacks comparability and is often unreliable. Some countries already use the Basel III Pillar 3 market discipline disclosure regime which entails extensive disclosure obligations for banks covering quantitative and qualitative aspects of overall capital adequacy and capital allocation, as well as risk exposures and assessments. This disclosure regime was enhanced after the global financial crisis, resulting in the adoption of stricter disclosure requirements and greater consistency and comparability across jurisdictions for bank disclosures (Basel Committee Disclosure Document on Disclosure, 2014 and Basel Core Principles 27 and 28).

13.32 Industry sector groups and policymakers are considering, however, whether further enhanced disclosures are necessary for banks and other financial institutions regarding their exposures to environmental sustainability risks to assist investors in assessing the links between sustainability challenges and potential risks to financial stability.[32] In June 2017, the Financial Stability Board's industry-led Task Force published recommendations for improving principles and practices for voluntary corporate disclosures that can promote a smooth rather than an abrupt transition towards a lower-carbon economy. The Task

---

32 The G20 Energy Efficiency Investor Statement and a new Green Infrastructure Coalition, both launched in 2015, illustrate investors asking for supportive policy frameworks for green investment. See G20, 'G20 Energy Efficiency Investor Statement' (2015) UNEP Finance Initiative www.unepfi.org/fileadmin/documents/EnergyEfficiencyStatement.pdf accessed 30 August 2017, and UN Principles for Responsible Investment, 'Green Infrastructure Investment Coalition Launched at COP21' (10 December 2015) www.unpri.org/news/green-infrastructure-investment-coalition-launched-at-COP21/ accessed 30 August 2017.

Force (also known as the Bloomberg Commission) consisted of representatives from the private sector, including investors, preparers and other market participants from a variety of industries and regions. The Task Force issued its report in June 2017 and recommended that all listed companies, including banks and financial institutions, make certain voluntary disclosures of climate change risks to investors.

13.33 In addition, European Union policymakers adopted the Disclosure Directive in 2014 that requires Member States to require listed companies, banks and certain financial groups to disclose to the market non-financial information, including environmental sustainability risks and environmental sustainability information related to renewable and non-renewable energy, land use, water use, air pollution, greenhouse gas emissions and the use of hazardous materials. The obligation to disclose applies only to large listed credit institutions and large listed insurance companies which are parent undertakings of a large group, in each case having an average number of employees in excess of 500, in the case of a group on a consolidated basis. The legislation does not prevent EU states from requiring disclosure of non-financial information from undertakings and groups other than those subject to this requirement by the Directive. As a result, there is a wide diversity of institutions covered by this disclosure requirement across EU countries.

13.34 Some countries have implemented the minimum requirements, but others, implicitly or explicitly, have included a number of other entities such as investment companies, large non-listed companies according to precise size criteria, state-owned companies, pension funds, etc. For instance, France has adopted disclosure requirements that all listed companies (including listed banking companies) should disclose their carbon exposures as part of broader climate change reporting requirements. More and more firms in G20 countries are beginning to require environmental and social risk reporting in their company reporting requirements. For instance, Russia now requires that all listed companies (including listed banking companies) report environmental and social risk exposure to investors (Alexander, 2016).

13.35 These national approaches can inform other countries regarding how disclosure of environmental sustainability risks can be applied flexibly in different countries and should accord with current best practices at the national level and in conformity with international reporting standards. While disclosure is an important regulatory tool to inform the market about the financial stability risks associated with climate change, other policy instruments to assess the risks associated with environmental sustainability challenges should be considered as well.

B Bank Governance

13.36 International policymakers are considering the role of bank and financial institution governance as a medium-term policy response to support enhanced financial sustainability business practices. Indeed, bank governance mechanisms are necessary to reduce the incentives for banks to take on financial risks that are environmentally unsustainable and can threaten the stability of the banking sector. Therefore, an effective prudential regulatory framework is necessary to oversee bank risk governance in addressing environmental sustainability risks.

13.37 The main elements for designing bank governance frameworks that promote environmental and social sustainability are intrinsic to good corporate governance on two levels. First, good corporate governance calls on the use of ethical judgement of what is acceptable and what is not. Second, corporate governance has an important role in overseeing and ensuring effective risk management for the bank and ensuring sustainable returns for owners and shareholders. It is widely recognised that there is a strong correlation between good corporate governance and effective environmental and social risk management.

13.38 Bank governance is also affected by stewardship codes and international efforts to recognise whether bank boards should consider environmental and social governance issues in reviewing bank management and whether failing to do so is a failure of the board's fiduciary duty to the bank and investors. The concept of stewardship has been informed by the efforts of institutional investors to harmonise a global understanding of fiduciary duty.[33] Similarly, under Article 69 of the Russian Code of Corporate Governance,[34] the boards of directors of joint stock companies are required to assess the financial and non-financial risks that relate to environmental risks, as well as social, ethical, operational and other risks, and to establish tolerable levels of risk in these areas.[35]

13.39 The EU Disclosure Directive can play a role in improving bank governance by improving bank transparency for investors regarding its involvement in unsustainable economic activity. Institutional investors are already beginning to ask banks about their efforts to mainstream sustainability challenges into their business models and their strategies to mobilise capital for sustainable economic activity.

13.40 Most countries do not require banks to incorporate environmental sustainability risks into the bank's risk governance and management strategy. However, China and Brazil do regulate bank corporate governance regarding environmental risks. China adopted the 'Green Credit Guidelines' in 2012, which require banks to adopt green governance strategies. Brazil has incorporated green governance into its Basel III Pillar 2 supervisory review assessments. Specifically, Brazil has adopted the principle of proportionality for

---

33   Sullivan R and others, 'Fiduciary Duty in the 21st Century' (2015) Report, UNEP Inquiry www.unepfi.org/fileadmin/documents/fiduciary_duty_21st_century.pdf accessed 30 August 2017.
34   Bank of Russia, Letter No. 06–52/2463 (10 April 2014) www.cbr.ru/StaticHtml/File/12105/Inf_apr_1014_en.pdf accessed 1 March 2018, citing Central Bank of Russia Answers to Questionnaire on Banking Policy and Green Finance (29 April 2016), 4 (on file with author).
35   See Alexander K, 'Greening Banking Policy' (September 2016), input paper in support of the G20 Green Finance Study Group 'Greening Banking Policy' www.rwi.uzh.ch/dam/jcr:cd6d77ff-6075-4045-8da0-55eb89824f7a/10_Greening_Banking_Policy.pdf accessed 1 March 2018.

individual banks to decide – based on the bank's particular risk exposures – the extent to which environmental sustainability risks should be incorporated into their governance and risk strategies.

C Risk Management

13.41 Environmental sustainability risks pose a major challenge for banks in assessing how such risks will affect the banking business. In risk management, the US Office of the Comptroller of the Currency (OCC) has issued guidelines for supervisors in connection with the supervision of banks' 'Oil and Gas Exploration and Production Lending'.[36] These are guidelines on prudent credit, interest rates, liquidity, and operational and reputational risks management. In Brazil, the industry body, the Brazilian Banking Association (Febraban), has adopted voluntary standards to enhance bank assessments of environmental risks. Based on this, the Central Bank of Brazil published in 2014 a mandatory Resolution 4327 on the Social and Environmental Responsibility for Financial Institutions that requires banks to incorporate socio-economic factors into their risk governance frameworks. In doing so, each bank is required to do an assessment of its environmental risk exposure based on the principles of proportionality and relevance. Similarly, the China Banking Regulatory Commission (CBRC) adopted the 'Green Credit Guidelines' in 2012 to encourage banks to conduct environmental and social risk assessments and to originate more green loans. By 2015 the majority of Chinese banks, controlling over 80 per cent of Chinese banking assets, have adopted environmental and social risk management practices. France adopted legislation in 2015 that requires financial institutions to incorporate environmental sustainability risks into the institution's risk management strategy.[37] The Russian Central Bank issued recommendations[38] in 2014 to listed joint stock companies that they take into account the environmental risks that they are exposed to. Indonesia has taken a step in this direction with its regulatory body – the Financial Services Authority – announcing a Sustainable Finance Roadmap in 2014 that would require all financial firms and banking institutions to develop business plans and risk management strategies to offer green financial products and lending guidelines.

D Regulatory Capital

13.42 Most countries generally do not require banks to incorporate environmental sustainability risks into their regulatory capital calculations. For example, the United Kingdom and

---

36 See Office of the Comptroller of the Currency 'Oil and Gas Exploration and Production Lending' (2016), OCC Comptroller's handbook booklet, Office of the Comptroller of the Currency www.occ.gov/publications/publications-by-type/comptrollers-handbook/pub-ch-og.pdf accessed 30 August 2017.
37 See '2015 Energy Transition Law' (Law No. 2015–992 of 17 August 2015, related to energy transition for a green growth), *Journal officiel de la République francaise* (2015), art. 173.
38 Shvetsov SA, 'To Joint-Stock Companies, State Corporations and Companies: On Corporate Governance Code' (2014), Letter of the First Deputy Governor of the Central Bank of the Russian Federation No. 06–52/2463, Bank of Russia www.cbr.ru/StaticHtml/File/12105/Inf_apr_1014_en.pdf accessed 30 August 2017.

Switzerland have followed a policy that Basel III provides adequate flexibility for bank supervisors to work with banks in identifying sustainability risks that are material risks to the stability of the banking sector. Although the Basel Accord does encourage banks to calculate regulatory capital for credit and operational risk exposures to borrowers who are in violation of environmental regulations (Basel Capital Accord, para. 510), there is no broader recognition that regulatory capital risk-weights should be adjusted to include environmental sustainability risks. More data and stress-testing are needed before most G20 countries will act in this area.

13.43 However, under Pillar 1 of Basel III, the Central Bank of Brazil has begun to investigate whether environmental and social risks can serve as proxies for credit and other types of financial risks. Brazil and China are also utilising Pillar 2 of Basel III to require banks to assess whether additional capital is required for a bank because of its exposures to environmental sustainability risks. These assessments can involve forward-looking stress-testing of bank portfolios against macro-prudential or system-wide risks associated with unsustainable economic activity.

E The Role of the Basel Core Principles for Effective Banking Supervision

13.44 The Basel Core Principles' (BCPs) last revision in 2012 aimed to promote best practices in bank prudential regulation and supervision. The BCPs are used as a benchmark for assessing the quality of bank supervisory systems and for identifying future work to achieve a common ground of sound supervisory practices.[39] The compliance assessment of BCPs is part of the regular financial sector stability assessments of the IMF and World Bank. Along these lines, it is suggested that the Basel Core Principles should be further revised to require bank regulators to consider banking sector stability risks associated with the transition to a more environmentally sustainable economy and what regulatory tools and practices should be incorporated into banking regulatory frameworks to address these risks.

13.45 Based on the above, growing evidence suggests that environmental sustainability risks have important implications for financial stability in the banking sector, although the analysis of the complexity of the potential risks to the financial sector is still at an early stage. The banking sector is most immediately affected by the financial risks associated with the transition to a more sustainable economy (i.e. a low-carbon economy), which could affect banks' exposure to systemic risk both via impaired GDP growth and via banks' exposure to elevated environmental risk assets. Banks are slowly becoming aware of these considerations.

---

[39] See Basel Committee on Banking Supervision, 'Core Principles for Effective Banking Supervision' (2012) Bank for International Settlements www.bis.org/publ/bcbs230.pdf accessed 30 August 2017.

F Financing Products

13.46 Financial innovation in products and investments will play an important role in stimulating more demand for 'green' investment assets and providing more liquidity for green assets. However, many countries with large banking sectors, with the exception of China, have not begun assessing which financing structures for banks might be conducive to providing more credit to sustainable sectors of the economy. Banking policy and regulation can play an important role in facilitating the creation of new financial products and investments that will attract capital to more sustainable sectors of the economy. For example, the use of simple and transparent financial instruments and investment structures, such as sustainable asset-backed securities, to facilitate more investment in 'green' assets could stimulate increased investment in 'green' credit and other sustainable assets.

13.47 Central banks may also have a role to play by developing new instruments of monetary policy that can encourage banks to bundle loans together into transparent asset classes which can issue highly rated securities that can be used by banks as collateral for central bank funding. National authorities should have discretion to experiment with innovative financing structures that incentivise more investment in green assets and thus provide an impetus for further development of a sustainable economy.

13.48 In applying the above criteria, national approaches demonstrate that successful banking regulation should be tailored to national circumstances. For instance, China's Green Credit Guidelines suggest a particular approach that involves a combination of 'carrots' and 'sticks' to induce banks to make more credit available to sustainable sectors of the Chinese economy. In contrast, Brazil's regulatory approach reflects the growing recognition that environmental risks and sustainability challenges pose risk management and strategic business risks for banks but each bank is different and should assess its own risk exposures based on the principles of proportionality and relevance.

13.49 The experiences of countries suggest that banking policy can play an important role in reducing the institutional and market obstacles to providing more bank credit for the green economy. Many bank supervisors have the flexibility under the Basel Capital Accord and Core Principles for Banking Supervision to begin assessing the environmental risks that are material to their banking and financial sectors. Advanced developed countries in the EU and the United States focus on creating sound market-based economic frameworks that promote the efficient pricing of assets and the reduction of fiscal subsidies for unsustainable economic activity. Other countries – mainly large emerging market countries – use state-owned banks and national development banks to take the lead in investing in renewable and clean energy projects. In addition, some countries have begun considering and using certain regulatory measures to encourage banks to address the institutional and market challenges to providing green finance.

IV INTERNATIONAL INITIATIVES

A Sustainability Network

13.50 Some developing country central banks, regulators and global banks have formed an international body – the Sustainability Banking Network (SBN) – located at the International Finance Corporation of the World Bank to address issues of bank environmental and social governance (E&S governance) and to enhance banking regulation and governance to address the risks and challenges associated with environmental sustainability.[40] The SBN consists of a group of thirty-four emerging market and developing countries and a group of financial market regulators and banking associations from emerging markets whose agenda and meetings are coordinated by the International Finance Corporation of the World Bank.[41] It makes recommendations on national sustainability financial policies and regulatory principles in an effort to influence the environmental and social governance practices of banks and other financial institutions and to promote the recognition of environmental and sustainability risk in financial regulation.[42] In most SBN member countries, SBN policies and regulatory principles are not legally binding regulations but rather strategic and technical 'how to' guidance to assist financial institutions in integrating sustainability considerations into business strategy and operations.[43]

13.51 In February 2018 the SBN released their Global Progress Report. The main aim of the report is to support its less advanced members in establishing or refining their sustainable finance policies and regulatory principles by developing a better understanding of the common barriers and challenges confronting countries in addressing climate change and other environmental concerns.[44]

13.52 The SBN's Global Progress Report assesses the current status of sustainable finance of the participating countries on the basis of the SBN measurement framework, built upon three pillars:

   i. *The E&S Risk Management Pillar* allows evaluation of the extent to which national policies or principles provide financial institutions with comprehensive and detailed guidelines and requirements for the management of E&S risks – also with regard to climate risk and the degree to which these guidelines are applied by financial market participants.
  ii. *The Green Finance Flows Pillar* concerns the introduction of market infrastructures which aim to encourage financial institutions to lend to projects and companies with a climate-friendly effect and impact on capital flows.

---

40   Sustainable Banking Network (SBN), 'Global Progress Report' (February 2018) www.ifc.org/wps/wcm/connect/topics_ext_content/ifc_external_corporate_site/sustainability-at-ifc/publications/publications_report_sbnglobalprogress2018 accessed 21 December 2018.
41   Ibid., 1.
42   Ibid., 2.
43   Ibid., x.
44   Ibid., 5.

iii. *The Enabling Environment Pillar* assesses factors that have proved to be multiplying or undermining in achieving the first two pillars.[45]

13.53 The SBN found that all participating countries initiated programmes supporting sustainable finance, but are at different stages of development. While fifteen countries have already introduced policies or principles, the other nineteen members, as of June 2017, were at the stage of initiation.[46]

13.54 The key findings regarding E&S risk management were that a policy needs to be accompanied by operational guidelines in the form of detailed application guides, key performance indicators or case studies. Also, policies are most effective when applied as broadly as possible to an adequate approach, depending on the underlying risks.[47] The definition of the institutional capacity to be developed and maintained is crucial.[48] The SBN further recommends monitoring E&S risks after disbursement and identifying, assessing and mitigating risks as they are prerequisites for any sustainable finance management system.[49]

13.55 The Global Progress Report will be updated on a regular basis and while the focus of the current report lies on the assessment of the adopted policies and principles by the participating countries, future reports will discuss behavioural changes of banks operating within the countries and their impact.[50] The report concludes that regulatory monitoring efforts must be commensurate with E&S risks associated with borrowers and that a combination of legal and regulatory measures, on the one hand, and softer guidance and technical assistance, on the other, is necessary for an effective E&S regulatory and bank governance framework.

B European Commission High Level Expert Group on Sustainable Finance

13.56 The European Commission appointed a High Level Expert Group on Sustainable Finance in 2016 to conduct a study and issue a report regarding the role of policy and regulation in sustainable finance. The HLEG issued its final report in December 2017, making a series of recommendations about how financial policy and regulation can steer the European economy on to a more sustainable development track. The HLEG report makes important recommendations for the banking sector regarding how bank lending and financing can be aligned more fully with the EU's sustainability objectives. It took the view that further development of best practice on Environmental and Social Governance (ESG) and longer-term sustainability risk assessments are still needed to ensure that sustainability is better integrated into the banking sector, while at the same time ensuring financial stability.

45   Ibid., xi.
46   Ibid., xii.
47   Ibid., 16.
48   Ibid., 17.
49   Ibid., 18 and 19.
50   Ibid., 37

13.57 Bank supervisors should also ensure that banks appropriately include ESG risks in their risk management systems. This could be pursued under Pillar 2 of Basel III. In some cases, it might also lead to changes in an individual bank's capital requirements if risk management has not taken into account the financial risks associated with environmental sustainability.[51] The report observes that two issues are notable as potential constraints on long-term and sustainable bank financing:

1. The current capital framework charges some 'traditional', non-complex lending operations and long-term exposures more than is warranted by risk considerations.[52]
2. The complexity of EU banking regulation – the thrust of which has been designed for large banks and which, in the United States, is applied solely to the largest banks (about twenty) – creates a burden for smaller banks.

13.58 The HLEG has also debated the merits of lowering capital requirements for lending to the green or more sustainable sectors of the economy in order to create incentives for lenders to finance transactions involving green assets. But the HLEG concluded that capital requirements must remain risk-based.

13.59 The European Commission announced at the One Planet Summit in Paris, in December 2017, that European regulators view positively the possible introduction of a 'green supporting factor' to boost lending and investments in low-carbon assets. The HLEG considered this and concluded that certain conditions for a green supporting factor should be in place for it to be used in banking regulation.

- Definitions of a 'green', and also 'brown', asset classes are needed to which differential capital requirements could be applied. The definition of green assets eligible for lower potential capital charges will have to be set by official public bodies and not by banks themselves.
- Evidence of significantly lower risk for lending and financing 'green' assets at the micro level is needed.
- A cap on lower capital requirements on green assets, to prevent the economy from any 'green bubble', under capitalisation or less prudent lenders.
- It might well be that there is a valid risk differential between green and other (brown) assets that is not currently reflected in the capital framework, this way differentiated capital requirements could be justified.

13.60 More generally, banks need to ensure that their assessment of material risks covers financial and non-financial risks. In many banks, ESG issues are already a core part of

---

51 European Commission High Level Experts Group on Sustainable Finance, 'Financing a Sustainable European Economy', Brussels, January 2018, 12–15.
52 See Monteiro DP and Priftis R, 'Bank Lending Constraints in the Euro Area', Brussels: European Commission, 2017.

the process of risk management; in banks where ESG issues are not already a core part of the process of risk management, urgent improvement is needed. The HLEG report made the following recommendations:

- The Commission supports the development, coordination and sharing of best practice on ESG and longer-term sustainability risk assessments for banks. Therefore, all European supervisors should ensure that all national supervisors encourage their banks to have and use such instruments of risk management.
- To implement a green supporting factor, initially it must be investigated whether there is a risk-differential justifying such a factor (this investigation should include subsidies, taxes and public guarantees, which are not mentioned in the whole report).
- With overall EU regulation, the HLEG recommends that the Commission explicitly consider the impact on (sustainability) lending in its impact assessment before transposing the Basel recommendations of December 2017.
- The HLEG also urges the Commission to consider greater proportionality in applying the Basel III framework to different banks.

13.61 The HLEG recommendations have been criticised on the grounds that the 'green supporting factor' will create regulatory arbitrage opportunities for banks to create complex financing structures involving 'green' assets that could undermine regulatory capital objectives and financial stability. Further, it has been argued that 'green' is not necessarily safer than 'brown', and that there is no evidence that lower capital requirements will encourage greater lending and investment. Also, the green supporting factor would have to be very large (i.e. involve a large a reduction in capital requirements for a 'green' loan) in order to significantly increase credit for sustainable sectors of the economy.[53]

13.62 These initiatives suggest the usefulness of certain regulatory measures and governance practices that can be explored by countries on a voluntary basis to determine their efficacy: enhanced disclosure, risk management, bank governance, capital adequacy and financing structures. The Financial Stability Board and other international standard-setting bodies can support national efforts in addressing the linkages between financial risks and environmental sustainability by encouraging the exchange of information between national supervisors and regulators and the development of common definitions of green finance and data registries for banks and bank supervisors to draw on to develop a better understanding of environmental and social risks in the banking sector. Brazil and China incorporate environmental risk assessments into prudential bank regulation and link up regulatory practices with market-based reforms and government-supported finance for renewable and clean energy projects. Financial innovation and market developments will encourage countries to develop forward-looking strategies assessing the financial risks

---

53 See www.lse.ac.uk/GranthamInstitute/news/eu-green-supporting-factor-bank-risk/ accessed 11 July 2018; http://finance-watch.org/hot-topics/blog/1506-green-supporting-factor accessed 11 July 2018.

related to environmental sustainability challenges and to adopt appropriate regulatory measures to control and mitigate these risks.

V THE WAY FORWARD FOR BANKING POLICY

13.63 Countries have taken significant steps to develop banking policy instruments to address the environmental challenges associated with a more sustainable economy. However, no common definitions of key terms, such as 'green assets' or 'green finance' are accepted by countries or banking associations. Without basic definitions of green banking and sustainable economic activity, it will be very difficult – if not impossible – for policymakers, regulators and bankers to agree standards for measuring whether a country or individual banks and market sectors are progressing towards a more sustainable economic path.

13.64 National regulators can share data with one another on green finance and greening sectors of the economy; they could develop data registries providing information on how countries define certain terms such as green assets and to measure the impact of policy measures on a country's transition to a more sustainable economy. Data registries could also contain surveys and industry indices to show baselines for measuring progress in achieving sustainability objectives. The Financial Stability Board and international financial standard-setting bodies should continue further work in measuring financial risks associated with environmental sustainability challenges and adopt voluntary frameworks in the areas outlined below.

13.65 The variety of institutional approaches and policy levers used by countries to address sustainability challenges in banking suggests that policymakers and banking practitioners are in uncharted areas in a world of increasing environmental sustainability risks and their consequences for economic growth and development. Generally, these initiatives aim to reduce environmental risks, transform our economies into environmentally sustainable ones, and build economic and financial resilience against the systemic risks caused by unsustainable economic activity. Regulators are given the important task of adopting guidelines and standards to encourage increased bank lending and funding for more sustainable sectors of the economy. However, it is vital that such regulatory initiatives avoid the potential unintended consequences and market distortions. Rather than direct intervention in the financial sector, banking policies should focus on providing an enabling environment for the system to mitigate climate and other environmental sustainability risks.

13.66 Based on the foregoing, some general regulatory principles and practices can be suggested for further consideration by countries attempting to control and limit the financial market risks associated with environmental sustainability challenges as follows:

- Assess environmental risks and their increasing impact on financial stability and the sustainability of the economy and identify institutional and market challenges to achieving more durable links between banking and other financial sectors and sustainable sectors of the economy.

- Mandate that bank regulators explore the feasibility of incorporating forward-looking risk assessments into bank risk management of scenarios where environmental risks appear to have become embedded in the financial system and how they may affect bank performance and banking sector stability.
- Develop industry-led voluntary disclosure frameworks for environmental risks that are standardised across countries, possibly building on international financial reporting standards (IFRS).
- Encourage banks and regulators to work together to develop simple and transparent investment products to attract more stable investment in 'green' bank assets.
- Encourage banks to build capacity for mainstreaming green finance into bank business practices and strategies across most countries.
- Ensure effective transparency by banks in how they manage environmental sustainability challenges as part of their strategies for green banking.

CONCLUSION

13.67 Environmental sustainability risks are becoming systemic and a potential threat to financial stability.[54] Both growing environmental sustainability challenges, such as complying with international environmental standards (i.e. the Paris Climate Change Agreement), and social inclusion are vital for ensuring that economies move to a more sustainable development path. This will require adaptation to evolving market structures that may result in risks and dislocations that could threaten economic and financial stability. This has important implications for banking policy and regulation because banks are the largest providers of capital for most countries and how they manage these sustainability risks and support national economies in meeting environmental targets is an important policy concern.

This chapter has sought to identify some of the main institutional and market barriers to increased bank lending and investment for environmentally sustainable economic activity and to assess what regulatory, legal and policy instruments are necessary to facilitate the transition to a more sustainable economy. Also, it explores potential regulatory policy responses, on a cross-border and international basis, which could contribute to managing the financial stability risks associated with environmental sustainability challenges that are relevant to both banks and their supervisors. Many countries have begun to utilise flexible institutional approaches and policy levers to use banking policy and regulation to support the economy in achieving sustainable outcomes. Recent reports demonstrate the linkages

---

54   World Bank, 'World Development Report 2014: Risk and Opportunity – Managing Risk for Development' (2013) http://siteresources.worldbank.org/EXTNWDR2013/Resources/8258024–1352909193861/8936935–1356011448215/8986901–1380046989056/WDR-2014_Complete_Report.pdf accessed 21 February 2018.

between environmental sustainability challenges and banking and financial market risks and the relevance of environmental and social risks to banking policy.

The chapter suggests that the usefulness of certain areas of regulation can be explored by countries on a voluntary basis to determine their efficacy: enhanced disclosure, risk management, bank governance, capital adequacy and financing structures. The Financial Stability Board and other international standard-setting bodies can support national efforts to address the linkages between financial risks and environmental sustainability by encouraging the exchange of information between national supervisors and regulators and the development of common definitions of green finance and data registries for banks and bank supervisors to draw on to develop a better understanding of environmental and social risks in the banking sector. Brazil and China incorporate environmental risk assessments into prudential bank regulation and link up regulatory practices with market-based reforms and government-supported finance for renewable and clean energy projects. Financial innovation and market developments will encourage countries to develop forward-looking strategies that assess the financial risks related to environmental sustainability challenges and adopt appropriate regulatory measures to control and mitigate these risks.

QUESTIONS

1. Environmental and social issues (such as climate change, water scarcity, land degradation, income equality), or a disorderly market response to them, represent a material threat to banking stability. Do you agree, or disagree, and why?
2. To what extent should bank regulators consider environmental sustainability risks?
3. How should bank governance address environmental sustainability risks?
4. Should international standard-setting bodies attempt to set standards governing environmental risks?
5. How have some countries applied regulatory tools to address environmental risks?

Further Reading

Alexander K, 'Stability and Sustainability in Banking Reform: Are Environmental Risks Missing in Basel III?' (2014) United Nations Environment Programme (UNEP)/Cambridge University

Landon-Lane J, Rockoff H and Steckel RH, 'Droughts, Floods, and Financial Distress in the United States', in Libecap GD and Steckel RH (eds), *The Economics of Climate Change: Adaptations Past and Present* (University of Chicago Press 2009), reviewing the literature of the linkages between the economy and environmental phenomenon.

14

Administrative Sanctions and Regulatory Enforcement

Table of Contents

INTRODUCTION

14.1 This chapter considers some of the main legal principles and regulatory frameworks in some major jurisdictions for imposing administrative sanctions on banks and related issues of regulatory enforcement. Part I considers European Union law and how Member States are required to adopt and impose proportionate administrative sanctions on a harmonised basis across the EU. It also considers the relevant EU Treaty and legislative principles that govern the type of sanctions that can be imposed on banks and their shareholders for regulatory breach. For instance, bank management and the board of directors can be disciplined for failing to ensure that the bank has sound and prudent management. Part II addresses the UK regulatory enforcement regime and discusses the enforcement action against the Halifax Bank of Scotland and its senior finance officer for regulatory violations prior to the crisis. Part III addresses the challenges for regulatory enforcement and the application of European Human Rights law principles – particularly the proportionality principle and procedural requirements for due process and transparency of regulatory requirements. The chapter analyses these principles of administrative sanctions by discussing recent enforcement cases in Europe, the UK and US.

14.2 In addition, the chapter deals with the growing impact of banking and financial regulation on fundamental legal rights (i.e. property rights) and how judicial review can be used to challenge the adoption of onerous regulatory measures that impinge unduly on individual rights.

I ADMINISTRATIVE SANCTIONS FOR REGULATORY BREACH

A EU Capital Requirements Directive IV

14.3 European banking law and regulation authorises the imposition of an array of administrative and regulatory sanctions, including penalties, on credit institutions and covered investment firms that violate sound and prudent management principles of EU banking legislation. The Capital Requirements Directive IV (CRD IV) consists of a Directive (CRD) and a Regulation (CRR).[1] Both the CRD and the CRR expressly support a maximum harmonisation approach to EU-wide banking regulation and supervision that aims to promote a level playing field for all EU-based credit institutions and covered investment firms.

14.4 Regarding administrative sanctions and orders, CRD article 26(2) specifies that where the influence exercised by the so-called 'proposed acquirer' of a bank or covered investment

---

1 See Directive 2013/36/EU of the European Parliament and of the Council on access to the activity of credit institutions and the prudential supervision of credit institutions and investment firms, amending Directive 2002/87/EC and repealing Directives 2006/48/EC and 2006/49/EC; and Parliament Regulation (EU) 575/2013 of 26 June 2013 on prudential requirements for credit institutions and investment firms and amending Regulation (EU) No. 648/2012 (Capital Requirements Directive IV, CRD IV) [2013] OJ L 176/105.

firm in an acquisition or takeover is likely to operate to the detriment of the prudent and sound management of the institution, the competent authorities shall take appropriate measures to put an end to that situation. The CRD allows supervisors wide discretion in determining what appropriate measures are. Article 26(2) provides that such measures 'may consist in injunctions, penalties, subject to Articles 65 to 72, against members of the management body and managers, or the suspension of the exercise of the voting rights attached to the shares held by the shareholders or members of the credit institution in question'. Save in the most egregious of situations, the supervisor should consider applying one or more of the lesser measures listed in Article 67 (see below) before applying the more severe sanctions listed under Article 26(2).

14.5 Under the CRD, the bank supervisor is given a wide range of powers to intervene in the activity of institutions, as is necessary for the exercise of their function.[2] However, as mentioned above, those powers are subject to Articles 65 to 72. Article 65 of the CRD provides that penalties and measures can be imposed if they are provided for in law, conform to the procedural and substantive principles set forth in Articles 66–72, and are proportional and necessary to meet the general interest of the EU. The procedural and substantive principles of Articles 66–72 embed the principles of proportionality, right to appeal and legality.

14.6 The responsible national regulator would have at its disposal two kinds of action for the failure of a bank to procure 'prudent and sound management'. The first is corrective, through procedural actions, and the second is more in the nature of punitive action. Generally, administrative sanctions consist of measures that can be classified as 'corrective' and/or 'punitive'. Under EU law, both types of measures must be proportionate. Specifically, Article 65 of the CRD requires Member States to lay down rules on administrative penalties and administrative measures in respect of breaches of national provisions, which 'shall be effective, proportionate and dissuasive'.[3]

14.7 The administrative sanctions provided for in Article 67 consist of both corrective and punitive measures. Corrective measures are those that provide for redress of a wrong through compensation, damages for loss or an order to stop violating the law or regulation. For example, Article 67 of the CRD requires Member States to adopt administrative sanctions that are corrective in nature and which provide, among other things, 'compensation' or damages for loss, or an order to stop violating the law or regulatory rules.[4] Specifically, Article 67(a) authorises the bank supervisor to issue a public statement of censure which identifies the natural person, institution, financial holding company or mixed financial holding company responsible and the nature of the breach. Article 67(b) provides for corrective measures in the form of orders requiring the natural

---

2 CRD IV, Article 64(1).
3 Ibid., V, Articles 65(1) and (2).
4 Ibid., Article 68 sets out the conditions, content and format for the publication of administrative penalties.

or legal person responsible to cease specified conduct and to desist from a repetition of that conduct.[5]

14.8 Article 67 also sets out an illustrative list of applicable administrative penalties. It identifies the kind of institutions and breaches that would attract the specified penalties, including institutions which fail to have in place governance required by the competent authorities in accordance with the national provisions transposing Article 74 (internal governance and resolution and recovery plans).[6]

14.9 Under Article 67(c), punitive measures are those which are additional to corrective measures, such as a fine or penalty or loss of licence, and in the case of an institution, withdrawal of the authorisation of the institution in accordance with Article 18. Article 67(d) provides that, subject to Article 65(2), the supervisor can impose a temporary ban against a member of the institution's management body or any other natural person who is held responsible, from exercising functions in institutions. Article 67(e) provides that, in the case of a legal person, administrative pecuniary penalties of up to 10 per cent of the total annual net turnover, including the gross income consisting of interest receivable and similar income, income from shares and other variable or fixed-yield securities, and commissions or fees receivable of the undertaking in the preceding business year. Article 67(f) provides in the case of a natural person, administrative pecuniary penalties of up to €5 million, or equivalent in currency of in the Member State where the misfeasance occurred or individual is based.

14.10 Article 67(g) provides for sanctions that are both punitive and corrective in the form of measures that are penalties, fines or orders that are unrelated or partially related to losses incurred by depositors, investors or the public. In such cases, the penalties or fines can amount to up to twice the amount of the profits gained or losses avoided because of the breach; if profits or losses avoided cannot be determined, the regulator can still assess a fine, penalty or order that serves, in the regulator's view, to deter future misconduct.

14.11 It is clear throughout the CRD, however, that the application of both punitive and corrective measures by the bank supervisor and any regulatory bodies must meet the proportionality test established in EU law. Article 70 relates to the effective application of penalties and exercise of powers to impose penalties by competent authorities. It specifies that when determining the type of administrative penalties to impose, the competent authorities shall take into account all relevant circumstances, including (a) the gravity and the duration of the breach; (b) the degree of responsibility of the natural or legal person responsible for the breach; (c) the financial strength of the natural or legal person responsible for the breach; (d) the importance of profits gained or losses avoided by the natural or legal person

5   Ibid., Article 69 relates to exchange of information on penalties and maintenance of a central database by the European Banking Authority.
6   Ibid., Article 67(1).

responsible for the breach, in so far as they can be determined; (e) the losses for third parties caused by the breach, in so far as they can be determined; (f) the level of cooperation of the natural or legal person responsible for the breach with the competent authority; (g) previous breaches by the natural or legal person responsible for the breach; and (h) any potential systemic consequences of the breach.

14.12 Article 71 relates to the reporting of breaches. It places the onus of establishing effective and reliable mechanisms to encourage reporting of potential or actual breaches on the competent authority. Article 72 provides for a right of appeal, requiring Member States to ensure that decisions/measures taken pursuant to laws/regulations in accordance with the Directive/Regulation are subject to a right of appeal as follows:

> Member States shall ensure that decisions and measures taken pursuant to laws, regulations and administrative provisions adopted in accordance with this Directive or to Regulation (EU) No. 575/2013 are subject to a right of appeal. Member States shall also ensure that failure to take a decision within six months of submission of an application for authorisation which contains all the information required under the national provisions transposing this Directive is subject to a right of appeal.[7]

14.13 As discussed above, Article 67 provides a ladder of administrative sanctions to be applied depending on the egregiousness and persistence of the violation in question. The facts of each case will determine the type and nature of sanction to be imposed; for example, any relatively minor breach of the sound and prudent management principles or other principle or rule in the CRD or CRR should be addressed in a proportionate way by relatively less stringent administrative sanctions that can serve to either dissuade an institution (i.e. the bank board or individual) from engaging in the violation, or to correct its conduct, or as a punitive measure to deter future misconduct. The proportionality principle is crucial for determining whether the administrative sanction in question is appropriate given the facts of each violation. For example, a bank's board of directors that does not have a persistent record of violating banking regulation requirements, but nevertheless in an isolated incident violates a regulatory rule (i.e. failing to consult the supervisor when appointing its chief executive officer) should be subjected to a relatively minor sanction so long as it was willing to address the violation by taking corrective action (i.e. consulting with the supervisory authority) within a reasonable period of time if the appointment of the bank executive was found to be inappropriate and in violation of EBA Guidelines and generally accepted supervisory practice.

14.14 Above all else, the supervisor's intervention into the board's legal authority to appoint a senior manager of a bank or other regulated institution should be proportionate and based on transparent regulatory rules and accepted supervisory practices in effect at the time of

---

7   Ibid., Article 72.

the supervisor's decision to intervene in the exercise of control rights of shareholders and the board of directors whom they elect to exercise their control powers. This exercise of authority – that is, control rights over the appointment of senior management – should be guided by the circumstances of each case, whether the supervisor's exercise of power is serving corrective or punitive function *and* whether it complies with EU Treaty and constitutional principles of proportionality, due process and legality under EU law.

14.15 Under the CRD IV, Member States and their supervisory authorities are explicitly required to ensure that their conduct complies with the proportionality principle. Several provisions of the CRD IV allude to the principle. The CRR sets out an interpretation of the principle of proportionality in the context of the EU's financial sector. Preamble paragraph 46 provides that:

14.16 'The provisions of this Regulation respect the principle of proportionality, having regard in particular to the diversity in size and scale of operations and to the range of activities of institutions. ... Member States should ensure that the requirements laid down in this Regulation apply in a manner proportionate to the nature, scale and complexity of the risks associated with an institution's business model and activities. The Commission should ensure that delegated and implementing acts, regulatory technical standards and implementing technical standards are consistent with the principle of proportionality, so as to guarantee that this Regulation is applied in a proportionate manner. The EBA should therefore ensure that all regulatory and implementing technical standards are drafted in such a way that they are consistent with and uphold the principle of proportionality.'

14.17 As discussed above, Article 70 of the CRD makes specific provision about the effective application of penalties and the exercise of powers to impose penalties by competent authorities. It sets limits on the imposition of sanctions by national supervisory authorities. In particular, it requires Member States and their supervisory authorities, while deciding administrative penalties and measures, to take account of all relevant circumstances, including, where appropriate:

a) 'the gravity and the duration of the breach;
b) the degree of responsibility of the natural or legal person responsible for the breach;
c) the financial strength of the natural or legal person responsible for the breach, as indicated, for example, by the total turnover of a legal person or the annual income of a natural person;
d) the importance of profits gained or losses avoided by the natural or legal person responsible for the breach, insofar as they can be determined;
e) the losses for third parties caused by the breach, insofar as they can be determined;
f) the level of cooperation of the natural or legal person responsible for the breach with the competent authority;
g) previous breaches by the natural or legal person responsible for the breach;
h) any potential systemic consequences of the breach'.

14.18 The EBA Guidelines also have an implied element of proportionality by specifying that credit institutions should make suitability assessments of the managing body, keeping in mind the nature, scale and complexity of the business of the credit institution.[8] There is therefore a clear and express requirement for national authorities to apply the principle of proportionality in their supervisory conduct as a matter of EU law generally, and under CRD IV specifically.

B The EU Charter of Fundamental Rights (EU Charter) and the European Convention on Human Rights (ECHR)

14.19 The EU Treaty and ECHR case law (ECtHR) recognise certain principles, such as proportionality, due process and the right to appeal and legality, as applicable to the exercise of public law powers. Administrative law has incorporated these principles to develop a series of tests for measuring the lawfulness of the exercise of public law powers. Any exercise of public law powers that infringes on ECHR treaty rights, such as the right to property, must be compatible with Convention rights and EU law and must follow a proper reasoning process that comes to a reasonable conclusion. Accordingly, EU bank supervisory authorities exercising powers under the CRD IV are required to be mindful of EU Treaty principles and secondary legislation, and ECtHR jurisprudence.

14.20 Forty-four countries are members of the Council of Europe and signatories to the ECHR, including all EU member states, and are subject to the ECtHR. The Charter of Fundamental Rights of the European Union came into force in 2009 through Article 6 of the Treaty of Lisbon. The Charter applies to the institutions of the EU and its Member States. Much of the Charter is based on the ECtHR case law, European Social Charter, jurisprudence of the Court of Justice of the European Union (CJEU), general principles of law common to EU Member States and pre-existing provisions of EU law.

14.21 An EU Member State bank supervisor's duty to apply the principle of proportionality is triggered by the broad reach of bank supervisory powers which often involve taking measures against a bank that limit the property rights of bank owners and creditors, such as shareholders and bondholders. In particular, the property rights of shareholders and bondholders are guaranteed as a fundamental right, both under EU law, the Charter and the ECtHR. Article 17(1) of the Charter protects the right to property. It provides that property may only be deprived in the public interest or as provided for by law, subject to the payment of fair compensation.[9] The Charter is addressed to EU institutions and bodies as well as national authorities implementing EU law, requiring such bodies to apply the provisions of the Charter in their implementation or direct application of EU directives/regulations into national law.[10]

---

8 EBA, 'Guidelines on the Assessment of the Suitability of Members of the Management Body and Key Function Holders' (22 November 2012), Article 5, Guideline 7 https://eba.europa.eu/-/guidelines-on-the-assessment-of-the-suitability-of-members-of-the-management-body-and-key-function-holders-eba-gl-2012-06- accessed 21 December 2018.

9 Convention for the Protection of Human Rights and Fundamental Freedoms (European Convention on Human Rights, as amended) ECHR, Article 17(1).

10 Ibid., Article 51(1).

14.22 In general, while a Member State supervisor has a reasonably wide canvas for the exercise of its supervisory powers, these powers are required to be exercised in line with CRD IV and keeping in mind the key EU legal principles – that of proportionality, right to appeal and due process and legality, as recognised by the EU Treaty (Treaty of Lisbon). Article 6(3) of the Treaty of Lisbon provides that '[f]undamental rights, as guaranteed by the European Convention for the Protection of Human Rights and Fundamental Freedoms and as they result from the constitutional traditions common to the Member States, shall constitute general principles of the Union's law'.[11] The ECHR is adjudicated by the domestic courts of the signatory states of the Council of Europe and by the European Court of Human Rights (ECtHR) in Strasbourg. The supervisory powers of competent authorities and their powers to impose sanctions are therefore contained by ECHR and EU Treaty principles and wider EU legislation and the ECtHR's ECHR case law.

1 Proportionality and Regulatory Decisions

14.23 The principle of proportionality is embedded in EU law and the ECHR. It requires, *inter alia*, national authorities to give effect to the principle in their implementation of national legislation. The principle of proportionality requires that there be a reasonable relationship between a particular objective to be achieved and the means used to achieve that objective. A decision that is proportional is also likely to be rational, evidence-based and reasonable. Furthermore, for EU states, any limitations on rights and freedoms guaranteed by the Charter are required to be proportional and made only if it is necessary and meets the general interest of the EU (Article 52(1) of the Charter).[12] The Charter specifies that any exception to the rights and freedoms of the Charter – including the right to property under Article 17(1) – must be provided for by law. The jurisprudence of the European Court of Human Rights (ECtHR) holds that proportionality applies in the context of justifying any interference with rights on the basis of such interference being 'necessary in a democratic society'.[13] For instance, the ECtHR has held that the principle of legality under ECHR prevents the state from taking arbitrary and capricious action and requires that any action depriving a person or entity of its property be a proportionate measure that achieves the public interest.

14.24 The central idea is of striking a fair balance, which finds its expression in sub-principles such as less restrictive alternatives; avoidance of absolute rules, which allow for no exceptions; inappropriate reasons; flawed or inadequate procedural protections and safe-guards; or decisions, which undermine the 'essence' of a right.[14]

---

11   See Council of Europe, European Convention for the Protection of Human Rights and Fundamental Freedoms, as amended by Protocols Nos. 11 and 14, ETS 5, 4 November 1950 www.echr.coe.int/Documents/Convention_ENG.pdf accessed 21 December 2018.
12   ECHR, Article 52(1).
13   *Beyeler* v. *Italy*, ECtHR No. 33202/96, Judgment (5 January 2000), page 27, paragraph. See also *Hasan and Chaush* v. *Bulgaria*, ECtHR (Judgment of 26 October 2000).
14   *Sovtransavto Holding* v. *Ukraine*, ECtHR No. 48553/99, Judgment (25 July 2002). *Offerhaus* v. *the Netherlands*, No. 35730/97 (16 January 2001).

2 The Right to Property and Proportionality

14.25 In the ECHR, the right to property is recognised in Article 1 of the First Protocol. It provides that 'no one shall be deprived of his possessions except in the public interest and subject to the conditions provided for by law and the general principles of international law'. Article 1 of the First Protocol states in relevant part:

14.26 'Every natural or legal person is entitled to the peaceful enjoyment of his possessions. No one shall be deprived of his possessions except in the public interest and subject to the conditions provided for by law and by the general principles of international law. The preceding provisions shall not, however, in any way impair the right of a State to enforce such laws as it deems necessary to control the use of property in accordance with the general interest or to secure the payment of taxes or other contributions or penalties.'

14.27 According to the case law of the ECtHR, the term 'possessions' in Article 1 of the First Protocol includes matters of financial value such as stocks and shares in a company (*Bramelid and Malmström* v. *Sweden* [1983] 5 EHRR 249). In *Olczak*, the Court observed that shares in a public company have economic value and therefore can be regarded as 'possessions' within the meaning of Article 1 of the First Protocol.[15]

14.28 Consequently, an investor's shareholding in an EU-based credit institution or investment firm clearly constitutes a 'possession' for the purposes of Article 1 of the First Protocol of the ECHR. Particularly, a shareholder's voting rights in its shares also constitute 'possessions' for the purposes of Article 1 of the First Protocol. That is, the shareholder's right to elect members of the bank board of directors and to exercise other control rights in influencing the sound and prudent management of a bank or covered investment constitutes a fundamental property right.

14.29 The Treaty of Lisbon, as it relates to the right to property, would through Article 6(3) apply the ECtHR jurisprudence to the exercise of supervisory powers by an EU/EEA Member State that infringe on the property rights of bank shareholders and creditors, including the shareholders' control rights to influence the sound and prudent management of a bank. Decisions which affect or impinge on individual shareholdings in a bank, therefore, must comply with the 'proportionality' principle, as it is applied through the Treaty of Lisbon by ECtHR case law.

3 Due Process in Appealing the Imposition of Administrative Sanctions

14.30 The imposition of administrative sanctions requires that Member States establish fair and impartial tribunals to adjudicate regulatory disputes whose conduct and decision-making

---

15 *Olczak* v. *The Republic of Poland*, ECtHR No. 30417/96, Final Decision on Admissibility (7 November 2002), page 60 (citing ECHR [decision] App No. 11189/84, *S and T* v. *Sweden* (11 December 1986), DR 50, 158). For a more detailed discussion, see Alexander K, 'The EU Single Rulebook: Capital Requirements for Banks and the Maximum Harmonisation Principle', in Hinojosa LM and Beneyto J (eds), *European Banking Union: The New Regime* (Wolters Kluwer 2015), chapter 3.

are governed by Article 6 of the Convention of Human Rights. A difficult area for some Member States has been fulfilling their duty to provide adequate procedural avenues of appeal and judicial oversight for investors and regulated financial institutions subjected to administrative sanctions. Establishing a transparent and fair process that respects the right to appeal and adequate judicial oversight must respect the 'doctrines of legality and due process' under EU law.

14.31 Supervisory decisions that infringe on property rights must also respect the doctrines of legality and due process. The principle of legality involves public law acts that are within the scope of any powers that are taken for a proper purpose. Procedural fairness requires that individuals or business entities have the right to be heard before a decision is made by a public law authority that impacts their rights. Any decision involving the exercise of public law powers that impacts rights must follow a proper reasoning process leading to a reasonable conclusion.[16]

14.32 Further, the Charter (Article 47) guarantees the right to an effective remedy for anyone whose rights are guaranteed by EU law. Article 47 further specifies that such a right to an effective remedy includes the right to a fair trial within a reasonable period of time by an independent tribunal. More specifically, Article 72 of the CRD provides that Member States shall ensure that decisions and measures taken pursuant to laws, regulations and administrative provisions in accordance with the CRD or the CRR are subject to a right of appeal.[17] Therefore, any decision by a member state regulatory authority that infringes on fundamental possessions or other property rights (i.e. shareholdings or bond holdings of banks) are subject to appeal and should not take effect until such a reasonable time for appeal has lapsed. Given that the right to appeal is guaranteed under EU law (and, specifically, the CRD), then Member State regulatory authorities are required to provide credit institutions and institutions covered under the CRD IV to an effective remedy and a fair trial in the form of an appeal process.

14.33 In addition, the principles of procedural fairness (due process) and proportionality are also relevant for determining whether any deadline imposed by a supervisor for complying with an administrative order that shareholders sell their interests in a bank or other institution should comply with reasonable time periods given the urgency of the situation (i.e. whether the order is made during a financial crisis). Also, any supervisory sanctions should not be imposed until the bank or the bank's shareholders (if shareholders are the subject of the sanction) have had the opportunity to appeal and any reconsideration by the supervisory authority of the sanction due to an appeal or request for rehearing should lead to a postponement of the imposition of the sanction or penalty. For instance, a supervisor's

16 *Olczak* v. *Poland*, ECtHR No. 30417/96, Final Decision on Admissibility (7 November 2002). See also *Capital Bank AD* v. *Bulgaria*, ECtHR No. 49429/99, Judgment (24 November 2005), page 137.
17 Article 55 of the 2006 Capital Requirements Directive I contained an equivalent provision. Directive 2006/48/EC of the European Parliament and of the Council relating to the taking up and pursuit of the business of credit institutions (recast) (2006) OJ L 177/1 (no longer in force).

postponement or delay in reconsidering its decision to impose sanctions based on a request for rehearing or appeal of the original decision until after a time following date of imposition of the sanctions (if the imposition of such sanctions cannot be effectively or practically reversed) would potentially constitute a violation of the doctrines of legality and due process under EU law, together with the specific requirements of Article 72 of the CRD. As a general matter, the bank board or its shareholders (if shareholders are subjected directly to the sanction) should have the opportunity to exhaust their appeal through all administrative and judicial channels before the supervisor's order to impose sanctions goes into effect.

II UK SANCTIONS FOR BREACHES OF PRUDENTIAL REGULATION

14.34 Under the UK Financial Services and Markets Act 2000 (FSMA) the regulator can prohibit an individual from performing functions in financial services, remove an individual's approval to perform one or more controlled functions or reject an application to assume controlled functions. In deciding to impose sanctions, the Financial Conduct Authority can rely on section 66 of the Financial Services and Markets Act 2000 (FSMA) which allows a penalty to be imposed on a person found to have engaged in misconduct if it is appropriate in all the circumstances. Misconduct is defined as failure of an Approved Person to comply with the Statements of Principle and Code of Practice for Approved Persons (APER)[18] under section 64 FSMA 2000 (as amended by the Financial Services Act 2012) or if a person is knowingly concerned in a contravention by the relevant authorised person of a relevant statutory requirement. The APER contains a list of the relevant factors in assessing reasonableness of an approved person's conduct, including: nature, scale and complexity of the business; role and responsibility in performing a significant influence function; and knowledge they had or should have had of regulatory concerns in the business under their control. Moreover, UK regulations contain APER Principle 6, prohibiting an approved person with a significant influence function from failing to take reasonable steps to be adequately informed about the business for which they are responsible through, for example: permitting transactions and business expansion without understanding sufficiently the risks, inadequately monitoring highly profitable or unusual transactions and business practices, and not challenging subordinates' implausible or unsatisfactory decisions.[19]

A Bank Director Misconduct and Regulatory Enforcement

14.35 The case of the British bank Halifax Bank of Scotland (HBOS) raised important issues about the accountability of directors for misconduct in bank failures.[20] A British Parliamentary

18 Financial Conduct Authority, 'Statements of Principle and Code of Practice for Approved Persons' Release 29 (July 2018).
19 Ibid., section 4.6: Statement of Principle 6, para. 4.6.4.
20 See the House of Lords, House of Commons, Parliamentary Commission on Banking Standards, 'An Accident Waiting to Happen: The Failure of HBOS', 4 April 2013 www.publications.parliament.uk/pa/jt201213/jtselect/jtpcbs/144/144.pdf accessed 21 February 2018. See also Financial Services Authority, 'The Failure of the Royal Bank of Scotland: FSA Board Report' (December 2011) www.fca.org.uk/publication/corporate/fsa-rbs.pdf accessed 21 February 2018.

Commission report (the 'Report') analysed the failure of HBOS and heavily criticised the former members of the HBOS board, including its then chairman Lord Stevenson and the former chief executives Sir James Crosby and Andy Hornby for their roles in the HBOS collapse. The report also criticised the then UK regulator – the Financial Services Authority ('FSA') – for failing to impose administrative sanctions against most of the executive members of the HBOS board. The one member of the HBOS board who was subject to administrative penalties and sanctions was Peter Cummings, the former chief executive of HBOS's Corporate division. The FSA's enforcement action against Cummings raised the issue of whether current regulations reflect an optimal balance between risk and reward for bank directors, such that the deterrent and signalling effect of any sanctions is strong enough to prevent misconduct but not so stringent as to have a chilling effect on entrepreneurial management. It further raises the question whether former directors of failed banks should be banned not only from serving on boards of regulated financial firms but from managing other non-regulated companies.

14.36 The FSA's administrative enforcement action against Cummings resulted in an administrative tribunal decision on 12 September 2012 imposing sanctions for misconduct during the period from January 2006 to December 2008. The sanctions consisted of a financial penalty of £500,000 and a prohibition order against him performing any significant influence function (SIF) in any authorised (regulated) UK firm (that is, a bank, building society, investment firm, insurer or a firm that is part of a group with such firms).

14.37 The FSA ruled that Cummings breached Principle 6 of APER, which requires that an approved person performing a significant influence function (SIF) must exercise due skill, care and diligence in management of their controlled function. The FSA cited the following grounds for Cummings's breach of Principle 6:

1. The Corporate division pursued an aggressive growth strategy under Cummings' direction with a focus on high-risk, sub-investment grade lending, despite deficient controls and systems which failed to provide adequate oversight and this strategy was pursued even as market conditions deteriorated. Cummings failed to take reasonable steps to assess, manage or mitigate the risks involved in the aggressive growth strategy.
2. Cummings failed to take reasonable care to ensure the corporate division adequately and prudently managed high-value transactions which showed signs of stress.

14.38 Furthermore, the FSA found that Cummings was knowingly concerned in the firm's breach of Principle 3 of the FSA's Principles for Business (PRIN), as issued under section 138 of Financial Services and Markets Act 2000 (FSMA), which requires a firm to take reasonable care to organise and control its affairs responsibly and effectively with adequate risk management systems. The FSA made the following findings of breach:

1. HBOS did not have adequate management systems for the high-risk business and lending strategy and aggressive growth strategy it pursued. Cummings was knowingly concerned in these failures by HBOS, albeit he implemented various measures to improve systems.

2. HBOS failed to take reasonable care to organise and control high-value transactions which showed signs of stress. Cummings was also knowingly concerned in these failures.

14.39 The FSA noted that these failings had, or might reasonably be regarded as being likely to have had, a negative effect on UK financial system confidence and the firm's 'fit and proper' classification. The FSA reinforced the financial penalty with a prohibition order under section 56(2) of FSMA, preventing Cummings from performing any significant influence function in any authorised firm on the grounds that he lacks competence and capability, as demonstrated by his breaches under the approved person rules and related principles discussed above.

14.40 Although the FSA found Cummings's conduct to be in breach of the APER and PRIN principles, it accepted the following mitigating factors to reduce the financial penalty: there were pre-existing management deficiencies, Cummings implemented some system improvements, the unexpected severity and speed of the financial crisis, collective decision making was involved and Cummings did not deliberately or recklessly breach the regulations. The FSA also acknowledged that Cummings had voluntarily waived his bonus of £1.3 million when he left the firm in January 2009.

In defence, Cummings made a number of representations:

1. unfairness of being the only individual subject to disciplinary action for the HBOS failure and contribution to the financial crisis generally and the disparity in the penalty compared with other similar cases;
2. danger of considering Cummings's conduct in isolation and assuming the predictability of the financial crisis;
3. management decisions were taken collectively.

14.41 In considering the amount of the penalties for individual directors or managers, the UK regulator will have regard to the following aspects of each case which influence the assessment of the penalty. First, whether the director or manager's behaviour in question was likely to expose the bank to a high level of risk and exposure to the economic cycle, and further to what extent did the director or manager know, or should have known, that under the economic conditions his behaviour would put the bank at risk. Second, was the defendant in question involved in approving and overseeing questionable transactions that unduly increased the bank's risk exposure? Third, once market conditions turned against a bank, did the individual in question continue the aggressive growth strategy instead of adopting a more prudent approach? Fourth, did the bank significantly rely upon the individual's judgement and experience? Fifth, to what extent did the bank's remuneration structure contribute to excessive risk-taking at the bank?

14.42 As a result of the UK regulatory enforcement actions against HBOS and other banks[21] for substantial failings in governance and risk management, the UK Parliament adopted the

---

21 See Financial Services Authority (n 20), describing the governance failures and mismanagement at the Royal Bank of Scotland.

Financial Services (Banking Reform) Act 2013 which set forth the following important reforms in bank corporate governance. First, the Act subjects bank officers and directors to a professional standard of care, which if breached and results in the bank receiving direct taxpayer support (i.e. a bailout) would constitute a regulatory offence that would result in a prohibition from serving as a bank officer or director. Second, all bank employees would be subject to minimum requirements regarding their individual responsibilities defined as standards in performing their key roles. Third, requiring banks explicitly to manage their affairs in a prudent manner and provide a detailed written statement of the responsibilities and duties of officers and directors. Fourth, bank boards are required to notify the regulator when they become aware that there is a significant risk of the bank being unable to meet the threshold conditions for authorisation.

14.43 The Banking Reform Act also creates criminal offences for serious misconduct in the management of a bank, such as (a) negligence (failure in the duty of care which leads to a reasonably foreseeable outcome); (b) incompetence (failure to act in accordance with professional standards or practices); and (c) recklessness (excessive risk-taking, failure to have sufficient regard for the dangers posed to the safety and soundness of the firm concerned or for the possibility that there were such dangers). However, the use of the criminal law to impose liability on bank directors and officers poses a number of complex legal and regulatory questions such as determining causation of the offence in question, the length and cost of investigations and obtaining sufficient evidence to identify individuals to prosecute.

14.44 As discussed in Chapter 5, despite the theoretical possibility of disqualification under the UK Companies Director Disqualification Act (CDDA), no proposals have been put forward to specifically ban directors of failed banks or other regulated firms from becoming directors of other companies. Perhaps the threat of such draconian wide-ranging effects would shift the risk and reward balance for regulation of director duties too much towards stifling entrepreneurial leadership rather than deterring misconduct. Moreover, the result in the Cummings case, and the lack of sanctions against the other directors of HBOS, highlights the inconsistency in enforcement by the financial regulator, which should also be addressed through future regulatory reforms.

III REGULATORY ENFORCEMENT AND HUMAN RIGHTS

14.45 The European Court of Human Rights (the Strasbourg Court) has ruled that a government may expropriate private property, but only on the condition that it pays adequate compensation, and that failure to do so would be a disproportionate interference with property rights.[22] In 1990, a Dutch court ruled that although minority shareholders in Nationale-

---

22 *The Former King of Greece and Others* v. *Greece*, judgment of the European Court of Human Rights ECtHR 2000-XII-119. See also *Offerhaus and Offerhaus* v. *the Netherlands* App No. 35730/97 (ECtHR, 16 January 2001).

Nederlanden and NMB-Postbank respectively were entitled to compensation after they refused to sell their minority interests to the offering purchaser Internationale Nederlanden Groep N.V., they were not entitled to have their compensation determined by a valuation method that was most beneficial to them. Similarly, the temporary UK special resolution legislation enacted in 2008 provided that shareholders are entitled to receive compensation if their shares were transferred by the UK Treasury to a public authority or private party.[23] Under US federal banking law, shareholders were entitled to receive the fair value of their equity interest at the time of the appointment of a receiver. French law also provides that upon the application of the Banking Commission to obtain a court-ordered share transfer, shareholders are entitled to apply for compensation from the Commission.[24]

A Bank Shareholders, Regulatory Discretion and Due Process

14.46 Article 1 of Protocol 1 of the ECHR provides that shareholders should have reasonable opportunity and coherent procedures upon which to act in contesting regulatory actions which interfere with their property rights. As cited above, the Court considered the right to due process in *Olczak* v. *Poland*[25] where the shares held by the complaining shareholder had constituted approximated 45 per cent of the bank's equity capital before the receivers appointed by the National Bank of Poland took control of the bank and reduced the nominal value of its share capital to cover some of the substantial losses which the bank had incurred. Following this, the receivers authorised the bank to issue a new class of non-transferable shares with extra voting rights which were subscribed to and paid for by the National Bank of Poland. The complaining shareholder, whose equity interest dropped to 0.4 per cent, was prohibited from subscribing to any additional shares. The substantial dilution of the shareholder's ownership interest led to a corresponding loss of control over the affairs and management of the bank. The Court ruled that, although the shareholder had standing to allege that its rights under Article 1 of Protocol 1 were infringed, the bank's substantial losses and irregular practices had put its customers' deposits at risk and its possible bankruptcy threatened the public interest by putting the financial system at risk.[26]

14.47 In a financial crisis, a regulator may need to act quickly, which can necessitate the setting aside of normal notice procedures for a party to contest a regulatory action. In *Capital Bank AD* v. *Bulgaria*,[27] the Strasbourg Court ruled that the legitimacy of a regulator's decision to revoke a bank's licence without following normal procedures for notice and a hearing would depend on the nature of the crisis in question and whether it was reasonable and necessary to set aside the respondent party's due process rights before suffering a property

---

23 The Banking (Special Provisions) Act 2008. This temporary UK banking legislation expired in February 2009; it required the Treasury to establish procedures for compensating shareholders or creditors within three months of a property transfer order being made by the Treasury under the regime.

24 French Monetary and Financial Code (*Code monétaire et financier*) as amended by the Loi no. 2013–672 du 26 juillet 2013 de Séparation et de Régulation des Activités Bancaires, Article L613–25.

25 App. no. 30417/96 (ECtHR, 7 November 2002).

26 Ibid.,17.

27 *Capital Bank AD* v. *Bulgaria* ECtHR 2005-XII-37.

deprivation.[28] An important factor would be whether a subsequent hearing held after the regulatory action was taken would not be too late by leading to irreparable damage to the bank's or shareholder's rights. The Court observed that the principle of legality recognised in ECtHR case law prohibits the state from taking arbitrary and capricious state action and requires that any action depriving a person or entity of its property be a proportionate measure that achieves the public interest.[29] Article 1 of Protocol 1 requires that procedural guarantees be in place to allow the individual or entity to contest the state action in question by presenting their views to an independent and impartial tribunal.

14.48 The requirement for an impartial tribunal implicates Article 6 of the ECHR, which provides:

> In the determination of his civil rights and obligations . . . everyone is entitled to a fair and public hearing . . . by an independent and impartial tribunal established by law.

The Strasbourg Court has interpreted property rights to be equivalent to civil rights within the meaning of Article 6(1) ECHR. Therefore, regulatory action that deprives a shareholder of its ownership interest in a company's stock requires that fair procedures are available to the shareholder to object before an impartial tribunal. It is recognised, however, that such procedures can be set aside in exceptional circumstances in which it is necessary for regulatory action to be taken immediately, such as in a banking crisis or other financial market turbulence, where the financial system may be at serious risk.[30]

14.49 In addition, Article 13 ECHR provides:

> Everyone whose rights and freedoms as set forth in [the] Convention are violated shall have an effective remedy before a national authority notwithstanding that the violation has been committed by persons acting in an official capacity.

The right of access to court, however, may be restricted in exceptional circumstances where the state has a legitimate purpose and the means employed to achieve that purpose are proportionate. The determination of a legitimate purpose was at issue in *Camberrow MM5 AD v. Bulgaria*[31] where the Strasbourg Court held that the bankruptcy trustee's sale of an insolvent bank in an expedited manner and as a going concern without court approval was necessary to achieve a higher recovery for creditors and that this justified the setting aside of the consultation and notice requirements of the insolvency procedure. Adhering to the insolvency procedures, which had required full consultations with all creditors and stakeholders over an extended period of time, would have jeopardised the quick sale of the bankrupt bank for a price satisfactory to most creditors. In its decision, the Court reasoned that emergency state measures such as these 'enjoy[ed] a wider margin of appreciation' if

---

28 Ibid.
29 See *Hasan and Chaush* v. *Bulgaria* ECtHR 2000-XI-117.
30 *Olczak* v. *Poland* (n 15), 17–18.
31 *Camberrow MM5 AD* v. *Bulgaria* App No. 50357/99 (ECtHR, 1 April 2004).

they were taken 'in delicate economic areas such as the stability of the banking system'. It concluded that it was not disproportionate for the regulator to restrict the participation of shareholders in the negotiations over the insolvent bank's estate if the result was that the bank could be sold promptly as a going concern while providing a higher recovery for creditors from the bankruptcy estate.

14.50 Shareholder rights can also be implicated by the type and scope of judicial review available to challenge regulatory action. Article 6 ECHR requires judicial review of the exercise of state administrative decisions that interfere with property rights. This means that regulatory action that is upheld by an administrative tribunal must still be subject to judicial review *de novo* on questions of fact and issues of law that relate to the dispute. For example, a violation of Article 6 can occur when courts of first instance rule that they are bound by determinations of material facts by administrative tribunals.[32] In *Credit and Industrial Bank* v. *the Czech Republic*,[33] the Court ruled that the limited scope of judicial review available under Czech law to challenge the insolvency administrator's factual determination of compulsory administration for a Czech bank had violated Article 6(1) on the grounds that the bank's controlling shareholder who had challenged the determination was left with no remedy to appeal the findings to an administrative or judicial tribunal.

14.51 The European Court of Human Rights has interpreted the provision to be composed of three rules. First, the principle of the peaceful enjoyment of property; second, no one shall be deprived of property except subject to conditions prescribed by law and in the public interest; third, the Contracting States are entitled, among other things, to control the use of property according to the general interest. The three rules are not, however, 'distinct' in the sense of being unconnected. The second and third rules are concerned with particular instances of interference with the right to lawful enjoyment of property and should therefore be construed in the light of the general principle enunciated in the first rule.[34] In considering Article 1 Protocol 1, the Court has observed that a 'company share is a complex thing'. It certifies that the holder possesses a share in the company together with corresponding rights. This is not only an indirect claim on company assets 'but other rights, especially voting rights and the right to influence the company, which may follow the share'.[35]

14.52 Moreover, of particular significance to bank holding companies and financial conglomerates, it should be emphasised that the protection of private property under the ECtHR applies to 'every natural and legal person'.[36] Accordingly, the protections of the ECHR are applicable to companies or other business entities who are shareholders in other companies, which means for example that shares in banking companies owned by parent companies would attract property rights protection under the ECHR. Moreover, the

32 See *Obermeier* v. *Austria* App. no. 11761/85 (ECtHR, 28 June 1990).
33 *Credit and Industrial Bank* v. *the Czech Republic* ECtHR 2003-XI-25.
34 *Beyeler* v. *Italy* ECtHR 2000-I 57.
35 *S and T* v. *Sweden* [1986] 50 DR 158.
36 ECHR Protocol Article 1, first sentence.

Strasbourg Court has interpreted Article 1 of Protocol 1 to have broad application to include the rights of shareholders in a public company who, as a result of a merger between their company and another company, were obliged to exchange their shares in the former company for shares in the latter company at an unfavourable rate.[37] The Court held that the protection sought by the shareholder could include a guarantee that the terms of the share exchange were appropriate and did not constitute an unlawful deprivation of property.[38] Nevertheless, the Court recognises that these rights are not absolute and may be restricted in a number of ways provided that certain legal protections are observed.[39]

B Judicial Review of US Regulatory and Resolution Measures

14.53 Judicial review is available for banks and their owners (i.e. shareholders) who are subject to regulatory controls under the Dodd-Frank Act 2010 and other US financial services legislation. Shareholders in US banks, however, have narrower grounds upon which to challenge regulatory decisions and actions taken under US banking law. For instance, federal banking regulators have discretion to determine whether the business activities of banks are 'unsafe or unsound practices' and thus in violation of prudential supervisory standards of federal banking law. Such determinations may only be overruled by a court if it concludes that the agency action was arbitrary, capricious or an abuse of discretion, nor is there sufficient evidence to overcome the presumption of regularity and correctness afforded to the decision. The courts have generally upheld the discretionary authority of US regulators to apply prudential supervisory standards to banks that rely on a combination of objective and subjective standards for determining whether the bank was acting in a prudential manner.[40] These prudential assessments produce specific composite ratings of each bank. Banks may challenge the risk-based assessments that are applied to their activities by the regulator.[41] The review procedure generally involves a three-tier administrative review whereby an institution may challenge its risk-based ratings at the district level, and then may appeal the decision to an administrative panel. Once administrative review is exhausted, an institution may seek review before an administrative law judge.[42]

14.54 Under the above legislation and regulations, US bank regulators have broader discretion than their European counterparts to require a bank to change its corporate governance and business and risk management practices if its activities constitute, in the regulator's view, 'unsafe and unsound' banking practices.[43] The contrasting approaches taken by the Strasbourg Court and US courts regarding the scope of judicial review that shareholders can expect when regulatory action interferes with their property rights suggests that European regulators may be more constrained and limited in the measures they may adopt to achieve

37 *Offerhaus and Offerhaus* v. *the Netherlands* App. no. 35730/97 (ECtHR, 16 January 2001).
38 Ibid.
39 Ibid.
40 *Doolin Security Savings Bank, F.S.B.* v. *Federal Deposit Insurance Corporation*, 53 F.3d 1395.
41 USC chapter 5: 'Administrative Procedure'.
42 Ibid., chapter 7: 'Judicial Review'.
43 12 CFR: Part 337 'Unsafe and Unsound Banking Practices'.

regulatory objectives, which could potentially undermine the standard of banking supervision that is needed in today's turbulent markets. Nevertheless, the Strasbourg Court has also recognised the principle of the margin of appreciation which allows states some discretion in devising their legal and regulatory frameworks so as to comply with the fundamental principles of the ECHR. European law, however, must provide individuals and business entities with remedies to challenge administrative decisions on both factual and legal grounds. Such remedies may lead to tribunals and courts deciding issues involving specialised knowledge and expertise that is beyond their technical capacities. In such cases, it should be considered that European states establish adjudicatory bodies with *de novo* review to examine the decisions and actions taken by regulators to determine whether such regulatory intervention is necessary if it infringes fundamental principles of the ECHR, such as the protection of shareholder property rights. Although the establishment of appropriate tribunals is necessary to comply with Article 6, this should be balanced by the need to have an expedited appeals process with time limits to achieve legal finality.

14.55 The Dodd-Frank Act provided powers to the Financial Stability Oversight Council to designate systemically important financial institutions (SIFI) in accordance with principles set forth by the Financial Stability Board that would result in the institution being subject to stricter oversight by its regulator, including higher capital requirements and subject to a stricter stress-testing regime. However, the FSOC's designation of the Metropolitan Life Insurance company (MetLife) as a SIFI was challenged by MetLife as a violation of due process under the US Constitution because the criteria for designating a SIFI were vague and did not reflect the real financial risks which MetLife posed to the financial system. After taking evidence, the US Federal District Court agreed with MetLife and ruled in 2016 that MetLife's designation as a SIFI under the Dodd-Frank Act was based on vague criteria and not supported by specific evidence of the risks that the firm posed to the financial system and thus was in violation of US administrative law. Moreover, the court found the FSOC's process for designating institutions as systemically important to be 'arbitrary and capricious' and thus in violation of the right to due process under the US Constitution.[44]

14.56 In the area of bank resolution, there are two ways that the use of resolution tools can be challenged by the bank itself or by shareholders under the Dodd-Frank Act. The first concerns the Federal Deposit Insurance Corporation's (FDIC) exercise of resolution powers while acting as the Orderly Liquidation Authority (OLA) under the Dodd-Frank Act. The Dodd-Frank Act requires that when the board of directors of the failing bank refuses to acquiesce or consent to the appointment of the FDIC as the receiver of the bank, the Secretary of the Treasury is required to petition the United States District Court of the District of Columbia for a review and possibly a decision to grant the FDIC the receivership

---

44 See *MetLife, Inc.* v. *Financial Stability Oversight Council*, civil action No. 15–0045 (RMC), unreported decision of US Dist Ct. District of Columbia (30 March 2016), 14 (Judge R. Collyer).

of the bank.[45] The decision of the District Court is to be regarded as final, and is not subject to stays or injunctions.[46] However, it is possible for creditors or shareholders to challenge the decision of the Court by appeal to the Court of Appeals for the District of Columbia Circuit. The scope of review of the Court of Appeals is limited only to whether or not the determination of the Secretary is arbitrary and capricious, considering that (i) the bank is in default or in danger of default, and (ii) the bank satisfies the definition of a 'financial company'.[47] The decision of the Court of Appeals may be appealed to the Supreme Court. The Supreme Court considers the appeal based on the same standard of review as the Court of Appeals.[48] Judicial review affords the claimants the possibility of reversing the FDIC's decision to put the bank into resolution, but this could lead to the bank later being petitioned into bankruptcy.

14.57 The second instance of judicial review relevant for the creditors and shareholders of the bank in resolution is found in section 210(a) of the Dodd-Frank Act. Under this procedure, the FDIC is required to publish a notice for the creditors to present their claims, together with necessary documentation showing proof, within a time limit of at least 90 days after the publication of the Notice.[49] The FDIC is required to post notice to all the creditors listed on the bank's books and records.[50]

14.58 Within 180 days from the submission of a claim, the FDIC is required to notify the claimant whether it allows or disallows the claim in question.[51] If the FDIC disallows the claim, it must provide a statement of the reasons that led to the disallowance, and the procedures for claimants to initiate court proceedings to appeal the FDIC decision.[52] Claimants that wish to bring the case before court then have to file the case within sixty days, starting from the ending of the 180-day period mentioned above, or from the date of their notification of the disallowance.[53] The court with jurisdiction over the petition is the District or Territorial Court of the United States for the district within which the principal place of business of the bank that is being put into resolution.[54]

CONCLUSION

14.59 This chapter analyses the principles governing the application of administrative sanctions and regulatory enforcement. It also considers how administrative sanctions against banks

---

45 Dodd-Frank Act, sections 202(a)(1)(A)(i).
46 Ibid., (a)(1)(B).
47 Ibid., (a)(2)(A)(iv).
48 Ibid., (a)(2)(B)(iv).
49 Ibid., section 210(a)(2)(B).
50 Ibid., (a)(2)(C).
51 Ibid., (a)(3)(A)(i).
52 Ibid., (A)(iii).
53 Ibid., section 210(a)(4)(B).
54 Ibid., (A).

can impinge on legal rights, such as property rights, and for that reason regulatory decisions have to be justified under constitutional law or Treaty principles before a fair and independent tribunal. The chapter reviews the legal framework in the European Union for imposing administrative sanctions on banks and bank management for failing to ensure that a bank is managed in a prudent and sound manner and discusses some of the available remedies of regulators against banks, including disgorging undue profits, correcting unlawful acts and deterring future misconduct. The EU legal principle of proportionality requires that administrative sanctions that impinge on fundamental rights (i.e. property rights or free movement) must conform to the proportionality principle which involves meeting specific criteria as defined by the Court of Justice of the European Union and the European Court of Human Rights. The chapter discusses how the United Kingdom subjects banks and bank management to administrative sanctions and what rights they have to challenge regulatory decisions and enforcement actions. It then discusses the powers under the Dodd-Frank Act to designate financial institutions as systemically important and the rights to procedural due process for institutions designated as systemically important. The chapter finally considers recent developments regarding the enforcement of administrative sanctions under the bank resolution regulations of the US Dodd-Frank Act 2010 and the EU Bank Resolution and Recovery Directive 2014.

QUESTIONS

1. What type of administrative sanctions does EU law allow? How does European law protect bank shareholder rights?
2. What are some of the main legal principles governing the exercise of regulatory power in Europe and the US?
3. What type of judicial review should courts have to review the decisions of regulatory bodies?
4. Are bank shareholders entitled to stronger protections under European law than bank bondholders?
5. Discuss the scope and application of the principle of proportionality with regard to regulatory decision-making.

Further Reading

Everett R, 'Regulation and Financial Disputes in the Civil Courts', in Walker GAE, Purves R and Blair M (eds), *Financial Services Law* (3rd edn, Oxford University Press 2014), 567–588

Gleeson S, 'Regulatory Processes: Authorisation, Supervision, and Enforcement', in Walker GAE, Purves R and Blair M, *Financial Services Law* (3rd edn, Oxford University Press 2014), 245–272 Bank of England, Procedures – The Enforcement Decision Making Committee (August 2018)

15

Future Challenges for Banking Regulation

Table of Contents

INTRODUCTION

15.1 This chapter attempts to analyse some of the main trends in banking regulation considered in this book and to distil some of the principles on which a more effective banking supervisory and regulatory regime can be built. Regulatory reforms adopted following the

2007–2008 crisis require that the banking sector and broader financial markets are subject both to enhanced micro-prudential supervision of individual firms and to macro-prudential supervision of the structure and interconnectedness of the financial system. Moreover, international regulatory reforms encourage countries to redesign the institutional structure of financial regulation to coordinate the pursuit of macro-prudential supervisory and regulatory objectives. The chapter suggests that effective banking supervision and regulation that achieves both macro-prudential and micro-prudential objectives can best be accomplished by adopting a three-pillar approach based on (1) macro-prudential supervision/regulation, (2) micro-prudential supervision/regulation, and (3) monetary policy.

15.2 The chapter also discusses the financial market risks and regulatory issues concerning Brexit and how the British-European Union negotiations may produce regulatory principles – for example, regulatory parity – that could serve as a model for countries internationally to negotiate a more harmonised and effective global financial regulatory regime. It concludes with discussion of the regulatory issues raised in Chapter 13 about environmental and social sustainability and banking regulation; recent initiatives by national authorities to incorporate environmental risks into prudential regulation frameworks; and the issues and challenges this raises for the design of effective banking regulation.

I DEVELOPING A COHERENT MACRO-PRUDENTIAL–MICRO-PRUDENTIAL FRAMEWORK

A Micro-Prudential to Macro-Prudential Supervision

15.3 After the collapse of the International Monetary Fund's Bretton Woods fixed exchange rate regime in 1971, banking and securities regulation in most advanced economies has become locked into an escalating cycle of deregulation, increased competition, financial crises and reregulation.[1] For much of that time, regulatory backlashes have tended to focus largely on how to make individual institutions more sound and transparent for investors while ignoring broader financial system stresses and systemic risks. The justification for prudential regulation of individual banking institutions was linked to the economic importance of banks, how they managed unexpected shocks to their business and how they treated their customers. Prudential supervision was focused on the riskiness of an individual institution's balance sheet and how much capital it was holding against these risks while downplaying risks that were shifted to other off-balance sheet, unregulated entities. This primary focus on risk-based supervision of individual banking institutions ignored systemic risks that were accumulating across the financial system and how they might threaten financial stability.[2]

1   See Eichengreen B and Bordo MD, 'Crises Now and Then: What Lessons from the Last Era of Financial Globalization?' (2002) NBER Working Paper No. 8716.
2   Financial Stability Forum, 'Report of the Financial Stability Forum on Enhancing Market and Institutional Resilience' (7 April 2008) www.fsb.org/wp-content/uploads/r_0804.pdf accessed 21 February 2018.

15.4 Indeed, weaknesses and failings in financial risk management at the firm level have led academics and policymakers to distinguish between 'micro-prudential regulation', which operates to correct 'market failures' by increasing the efficiency of financial firms and markets, and 'macro-prudential regulation',[3] which operates to protect the financial system's stability as a network or system.[4] An important aspect of macro-prudential regulation addresses how 'the nature of regulation applied to an individual institution depends crucially on how "systemic" its activities are', and is 'related ... to its size, degree of leverage, inter-connectedness'.[5]

15.5 In the aftermath of the crisis, a distinction is now made between macro-prudential supervision and micro-prudential supervision. The micro-prudential approach utilised prior to the crisis generally assumed that banks were primarily exposed to exogenous risks (that is, risks that are generated externally to the bank's operations) and that banks could respond to changes in these risks (i.e. an increase in credit or market risks) by making balance sheet adjustments (i.e. buying or selling assets) in a more or less similar manner without affecting asset prices in these markets.[6] Although banks individually might appear to be adjusting their balance sheets prudently in response to changing risks in the market, the cumulative effect of all banks acting in the same or similar manner could be to increase system-wide risks across the financial sector. This can potentially exacerbate market upturns and downturns. Micro-prudential supervision also consisted of a mandate to protect depositors with effective guarantee schemes and designing financial products and investments for retail and professional customers that were appropriate to their individual financial capacities and understanding of financial risks. The failure to coordinate the pursuit of micro-prudential supervisory tasks combined with inadequate macro-prudential supervision of risks across financial markets made it very difficult to fulfil the regulatory objectives of protecting the financial system against systemic risk, ensuring that bank customers, depositors and investors were treated in a manner that was fair, and ensuring that they were sold products and investments that were suitable to their circumstances.

15.6 Moreover, after the crisis the UK Financial Services Authority's Turner Review argued that the lack of macro-prudential regulation and oversight of the financial system was more directly relevant to causing the financial crisis than any specific failure relating to an individual firm.[7] The Review suggested that had there been a better understanding of the link between financial stability and macroeconomic stability, there could have been more

---

3   Borio C, 'Towards a Macroprudential Framework for Financial Supervision and Regulation?' (2003) 49 *CESifo Economic Studies* 2 181–215, 183.
4   See Brunnermeier M, Crockett A, Goodhart CAE, Persaud AD and Shin H, 'The Fundamental Principles of Financial Regulation' (2009) *Geneva Reports on the World Economy* 11 (International Centre for Banking and Monetary Studies), 31–33.
5   Ibid., 11, 18.
6   Ibid., 18.
7   Financial Services Authority, 'The Turner Review: A Regulatory Response to the Global Banking Crisis' (March 2009) www.fsa.gov.uk/pubs/other/turner_review.pdf accessed 21 February 2018.

effective measures formulated to address specific risks of individual banks and firms.[8] The Review cited indicators of macro-prudential risks, such as the liquidity risks manifest in the maturity transformation function of banks, the level of asset prices in property, equity and securitised credit as well as the level of leverage in the financial system as areas where regulators and supervisors could develop a better understanding of how systemic risk can arise.

15.7 The lack of a macro-prudential focus in banking supervision and regulation resulted in massive amounts of leverage building up across the financial system and an overreliance by banks on short-term wholesale funding.[9] Moreover, central bankers failed to understand the linkages between monetary policy and prudential financial regulation and in particular how accommodative interest rate policies can cause asset price bubbles and excessive debt in the financial system.

15.8 The international regulatory reforms adopted by the G20 and the Financial Stability Board following the crisis have emphasised the importance of macro-prudential supervision: that is, monitoring financial stability risks across the financial system, rather than just supervising individual institutions. Although the definition of macro-prudential regulation and supervision is intensely debated, it is suggested that it consists mainly of four main areas: (1) adjusting the application of regulatory rules to institutions according to developments in the broader economy (i.e. counter-cyclical capital requirements); (2) imposing regulatory controls on contractual relationships between market participants (i.e. OTC derivatives counterparties, loan-to-value or loan-to-income ratios); (3) monetary policy controls, such as interest rates, exchange rate controls, regulating money supply and capital controls; and (4) prudential requirements for financial infrastructure or firms providing infrastructure services (i.e. capital requirements for derivative clearing houses).[10]

15.9 Consequently, many countries have adopted macro-prudential regulatory reforms that link up macro-prudential supervision of financial infrastructure and the broader markets with the supervision of individual institutions and understanding the relationship to monetary policy. This three-pillar approach to financial regulation – involving macro-prudential supervision, micro-prudential supervision and monetary policy – has become an important feature in the regulatory reforms of many countries and represents a more holistic and complementary approach to financial regulation. This book suggests that effective banking regulation and supervision must be based on a coherent institutional structure that allows the three pillars to be effectively coordinated. For instance, the European Central Bank has responsibility for micro-prudential supervision and monetary policy, but not macro-prudential or financial stability policy. The importance of coordinating monetary policy

---

8   Ibid., 85.
9   Brunnermeier et al. (n 4), 26–27.
10   See Financial Stability Board, IMF and BIS, 'Macroprudential Policy Tools and Frameworks; Progress Report to G20' (2011) www.imf.org/external/np/g20/pdf/102711.pdf accessed 21 February 2018.

with banking supervision means that those with responsibility for discharging these tasks should work together to exchange information and data and to coordinate their activities to ensure that proportionate measures are adopted. Moreover, the exercise of macro-prudential powers necessarily impinges to a great degree on economic and financial policy, and for that reason those involved in macro-prduential regulation, supervision and policy should be subjected to stronger accountability channels to the public, represented for example by Parliaments and Finance Ministries, regarding how effective regulatory measures are in achieving their objectives and what the trade-off is with other economic policy objectives.

15.10 International standard-setting bodies and the International Monetary Fund – through its Article IV Financial Sector Assessment Programmes – are encouraging countries to design financial regulation to address both micro-prudential risks at the level of the institution and macro-prudential risks across the financial system. The Financial Stability Board and the Basel Committee on Banking Supervision have taken the lead in adopting international regulatory standards to address macro-prudential risks. Since the financial crisis, both international bodies have cooperated in developing proposals for macro-prudential reforms by encouraging countries to assess the risks outside the banking sector that can threaten banking and financial stability. In particular, the FSB has analysed the shadow banking market, involving non-bank financial firms engaged in maturity transformation – borrowing short and lending long – and the systemic risks that this may pose to the financial system. The FSB has also adopted principles that states are encouraged to follow for the orderly resolution of large, systemically important financial institutions. The FSB's principles and objectives are designed to broaden the scope of prudential supervision to include systemic risks that can arise from excessive lending in the shadow banking industry as well as the risks in the trading, clearing and settlement of securities and derivatives. Indeed, these international reforms have been instrumental in leading policymakers and regulators to rethink the objectives of banking and financial regulation in order to identify and control risks both at the level of individual institutions and across the financial system. This means that the concept of prudential regulation has expanded to include not only micro-prudential regulatory and supervisory measures for institutions, but also broader supervision across the financial system that takes account of structured finance and shadow banking markets, centralised trading and clearing of OTC derivatives, and oversight of securities settlement systems.

B Institutional and Supervisory Gaps Remain

15.11 The crisis has led to significant changes in banking regulatory standards, stricter supervisory practices and institutional restructuring of financial regulation based on macro-prudential policies and regulatory concepts for controlling systemic risk. Nevertheless, macro-prudential policy and regulation, their effects and concepts, are not yet fully understood and therefore there is much uncertainty regarding the use and benefits of macro-prudential policy tools.[11] Admittedly, since the financial crisis, the prudential framework has grown in sophistication both substantively and institutionally. Micro- and macro-prudential supervision remains primarily a matter for national authorities. These authorities are central banks, financial authorities and possibly other bodies which bring together representatives from different institutions, including national governments. For example, the Financial Stability Council in Sweden consists of representatives of the Riksbank and the Financial Services Agency. Also, the US Financial Stability Oversight Council (FSOC) consists of the heads of US federal regulatory bodies, while the European Systemic Risk Board is governed by its board members who are the Governors of the Central Banks of EU Member States.

15.12 At the institutional level, some macro-prudential supervisory authorities exercise specific macro-prudential supervisory levers or tools (i.e. counter-cyclical capital requirements and loan-to-income ratios).[12] For example, the use of counter-cyclical capital requirements can be varied depending on the riskiness of assets at points in the economic cycle. Denmark and Switzerland have used counter-cyclical capital buffers to dampen credit booms in their respective housing markets by imposing higher capital requirements on home mortgage loans as opposed to other types of loans. Denmark has also used loan-to-income ratio caps for bank mortgage lending. Other macro-prudential measures include liquidity tools that require financial institutions to hold a certain ratio of liquid assets, i.e. assets that can be easily turned into cash, relative to total assets.[13] Also, leverage ratios could be used to limit the amount of leverage relative to the value of the bank's assets. Forward-looking loss provisions can require financial institutions to set aside provisions against potential future losses on their lending. Also, collateral requirements could be applied, in which lending is limited by the type and value of collateral. An example is a loan-to-value requirement, which would limit the size of a loan relative to the value of the asset. Similarly, 'haircuts' on repurchase agreements would limit the amount of cash that can be lent as a proportion of the market value of a set of securities. Information disclosure and greater transparency could help markets work better. For example, in times of crisis, more information about different institutions' risk exposure could increase the flow of credit as uncertainty is reduced.

15.13 Although the European Systemic Risk Board has been praised for identifying financial stability risks and publishing accessible reports on macro-prudential regulation, it lacks meaningful powers as it can only issue recommendations and warnings, has no binding legal authority and cannot coordinate the macro-prudential policies of EU Member States.

11 Claessens S, 'An Overview of Macroprudential Policy Tools' (2015) 7 *Annual Review of Financial Economics* 397–422. See also Angeloni I, 'Towards a Macro-Prudential Framework for the Single Supervisory Area' (speech at the Belgium Financial Forum, Brussels, 20 April 2015), 18 www.bankingsupervision.europa.eu/press/speeches/date/2015/html/se150420.en.html accessed 23 May 2018.
12 See Bank of England, Financial Policy Committee, 'Financial Stability Report' (2012) www.parliament.uk/business/committees/committees-a-z/commons-select/treasury-committee/other-committee-work-/parliament-2010/bank-of-england-financial-stability-report-/ accessed 21 December 2018.
13 Ibid.

In contrast, the UK macro-prudential regulatory model appears to be more coherent and effective in its operations by vesting macro-prudential supervisory powers in the Bank of England's Financial Policy Committee to issue binding directives or recommendations to the two micro-prudential supervisory authorities – the Prudential Regulation Authority and the Financial Conduct Authority.

15.14 In addition, some of the most important international macro-prudential regulatory reforms are now being criticised as merely incremental improvements on the previous micro-prudential regime. For instance, Basel III continues to allow large global banks to use risk-weighted internal models to estimate credit, market and liquidity risks that rely on historic data and risk parameters that are based on individual bank risk exposures and not on systemic risks across the financial system. Although Basel III contains higher Tier 1 capital requirements, liquidity requirements and a strict floor (Basel IV) on the value of risk-weighted assets, it remains heavily dependent on risk-weighted models that were proven to be unreliable prior to the crisis because of their disproportionate focus on risk management at the level of the individual firm, while not taking into account macro-prudential risks across banking institutions and markets.

15.15 Basel III's Pillar 2 Supervisory Review Enhancement Process (SREP), however, provides the potential for bank supervisors and risk managers to conduct forward-looking macro-prudential risk assessments of systemic risks and stress-testing based on hypothetical scenarios of future crises. Nevertheless, the SREP has not been utilised fully by supervisors and banks to conduct meaningful macro-prudential assessments, in part because the Pillar 2 risk assessments and stress-testing have been largely concerned with shorter-term crisis scenarios of over a 2–3 year period, instead of longer-term risks, such as environmental sustainability risks that could prove to be a threat to financial stability if bank risk managers and policymakers fail to take account of these risks. The Pillar 2 SREP and ICAAP frameworks should be used more systematically to assess forward-looking systemic risks and to ensure that the bank's risk governance framework can manage the impact of such risks on the banking business. In other words, Basel III's Pillar 2 process should be enhanced to consider the effect of bank governance and risk management on broader stakeholders and society.

15.16 The wide scope of macro-prudential regulation will require a broader definition of prudential supervision to include both *ex ante* supervisory powers, such as licensing, authorisation and compliance with regulatory standards, and *ex post* crisis management measures, such as recovery and resolution plans and central bank funding (e.g. lender of last resort). Indeed, the objectives of macro-prudential regulation – to monitor and control systemic risks and related risks across the financial system – will require greater regulatory and supervisory intensity that will necessitate increased intervention in the operations of cross-border banking and financial groups and a wider assessment of the risks they pose. Moreover, systemically important financial instruments (i.e. OTC derivatives), which were traded and cleared bilaterally in non-transparent ways and without adequate guarantees against counterparty credit risk, are now considered to be a concern for macro-prudential regulation. This led to the G20 proposals (now implemented in the EU and US) requiring that most OTC derivative contracts are classified as standardised and thus require to be traded on exchanges or swap execution facilities and centrally cleared by clearing houses or derivatives clearing organisations.[14]

15.17 Recognising that financial crises will inevitably recur, another important focus of macro-prudential regulation concerns the type of *ex post* crisis management measures that can most effectively control the fall-out or spread of a crisis once it begins. As discussed in Chapter 6, the Financial Stability Board has emphasised the importance of resolution regimes that seek to mitigate the taxpayer's exposure to bailing out failing institutions by applying the bail-in principle that imposes losses on creditors and equity holders before an institution is taken into resolution. The FSB recommends that national authorities create temporary or bridge banks to which a failing bank's viable assets can be transferred in times of market distress. Also, resolution powers should be used to restructure and dispose of bank assets and to evaluate whether essential functions of the institution should be carried out in legally and operationally segregated subsidiaries.[15]

15.18 Against this background, one of the major policy lessons from the financial crisis is the profound reconsideration of prudential regulation, in which systemic risk has become the major objective.[16] However, no consent has been reached among regulators or in the literature as to the appropriate scope and tools of macro-prudential regulation, and even the objective of macro-prudential regulations sometimes cannot be agreed upon.[17] Nevertheless, regulators in many countries responded to the crisis by implementing macro-prudential regulations 'as a first line of defence against financial instability risks'.[18] For this, central banks as well as other responsible institutions were in need of clear policies and tools to make sure the tasks and activities could be implemented efficiently as well as effectively.[19] Moreover, a clear and detailed macro-prudential regulation is needed to ensure the resilience of the financial system against shocks and to control and limit systemic risk.[20] It should be emphasised that the optimal use of macro-prudential measures or 'tools' will vary from country to country, depending on the 'country's exposure to shocks

---

14   See Balmer A, *Regulating Financial Derivatives: Clearing and Central Counterparties* (Elgar Financial Law Series 2018), 16–48.

15   See Financial Stability Board, 'Key Attributes of Effective Resolution Regimes for Financial Institutions' (October 2011) www.fsb.org/wp-content/uploads/r_111104cc.pdf accessed 21 February 2018.

16   Servén L, 'Macroprudential Policies in the Wake of the Global Financial Crisis', in Canuto O and Giugale M (eds), *The Day After Tomorrow: A Handbook on the Future of Economic Policy in the Developing World* (The World Bank 2010), 129.

17   Duncan A and Nolan C, 'Objectives and Challenges of Macroprudential Policy' (September 2015) www.gla .ac.uk/media/media_427189_en.pdf accessed 23 May 2018.

18   See Vučinić M, 'Importance of Macroprudential Policy Implementation for Safeguarding Financial Stability' (2016) 3 *Journal of Central Banking Theory and Practice* 79.

19   Ibid.

20   Ibid.

and risks, and its structural, institutional and financial market characteristics that affect the amplification of financial and real-sector cycles and the effectiveness of specific policies'.[21]

C Differences in Regulatory Philosophy

15.19 Developing a coherent and effective macro-prudential regulatory framework will raise significant challenges for most countries because the majority of them followed different regulatory approaches before the crisis and have responded to the crisis with different measures, instruments and levels of intervention. The immediate regulatory responses by the European Union and the United States were designed primarily to address liquidity and capital weaknesses in financial institutions, and the risks posed by cross-border banks. The emergency measures of EU countries and the US generally stabilised their financial systems, but in the aftermath of the crisis global financial markets remain fragile and bank share prices in the EU, US and Japan remain very low relative to other sectors. Indeed, most advanced economies have not fully recovered.

15.20 Across most countries, stricter bank capital and liquidity requirements have driven up the costs of bank intermediation and reduced the attractiveness of securitisation and other forms of wholesale funding because banks are now required to hold more capital against assets that are transferred off their balance sheets – through securitisation structures – and to hold more capital for investments in securitised debt because Basel III has higher capital requirements for investments in securitised debt. Furthermore, unprecedented monetary easing by central banks has resulted in persistently low interest rates for banks that have reduced their margin of profitability (the amount they pay to borrow from creditors/depositors and what they charge for loans) considerably. However, financial innovation could potentially, in the future, permit regulated institutions to circumvent stricter regulatory requirements by channelling capital through alternative financing structures and instruments to support more borrowing in the economy. It remains to be seen whether this will lead to a revival of innovative wholesale finance instruments or to the return of securitisation.

15.21 In this regard, it is informative to consider how EU and US authorities have responded to the systemic risks that arose in asset-backed securities (ABS) and structured finance markets that contributed to the crisis. Their responses are slightly different, but fall into four main categories: (1) increasing disclosure, (2) requiring risk retention, (3) reforming rating agencies, and (4) imposing capital requirements. The EU response, presented in September 2015,[22] is especially notable, and proposes common rules for securitisation and a European framework for simple, transparent and standardised (STS) securitisation. The EU rules are

---

21   Claessens S, Ghosh SR and Mihet R, 'Macro-Prudential Policies to Mitigate Financial System Vulnerabilities' (August 2014) IMF Working Paper WP/14/155 www.imf.org/external/pubs/ft/wp/2014/wp14155.pdf accessed 23 May 2018.
22   Proposal for a Regulation of the European Parliament and of the Council Laying Down Common Rules on Securitisation and Creating a European Framework for Simple, Transparent and Standardised Securitisation and Amending Directives 2009/65/EC, 2009/138/EC, 2011/61/EU and Regulations (EC) No. 1060/2009 and (EU) No. 648/2012, COM (2015) 472 final (2015) OJ.

different from STC (simple, transparent and comparable) securitisation criteria that were proposed in July 2015 by the BCBS and by IOSCO.[23] Specific requirements should ensure that securities remain simple, transparent, standardised and/or comparable. This is closely related to disclosure, since STS reduces asymmetric information problems and opaqueness in the securitisation process.[24] The STS approach of specifically rewarding standardised simplicity is likely to be effective.

15.22 The EU proposal also creates risk-retention requirements to reduce the moral hazard that would be present in an originate-to-distribute system.[25] Risk retention might not be as effective as intended. This is because the risk-retention rules might foster false investor confidence in securities, thus contributing to a potential crisis rather than inhibiting it. It might even create greater risks by leading to a 'mutual misinformation' problem. Similarly, rating agency reforms would require rating agencies to disclose fees charged to their clients. This disclosure requirement might not completely remove the conflict of interest, but it may serve to mitigate it.

15.23 Bank capital requirements corresponding to the Basel III requirements require that higher capital requirements are mandated for investment in ABS. Certain critics argue that this is punitive; instead, they advocate a 'capital-neutrality' approach, arguing that the holding of capital should be based only on the underlying assets.

15.24 In addition, before closing on – and after closing on – structured securities or a securitisation deal, there should be ongoing due diligence requirements including regular stress tests by investors, which would be required for all securitisations, STS included. While these due diligence requirements may be unnecessary and similar to what is typically performed in securities transactions anyway, they might nonetheless help assure due diligence in the case of a rapid expansion of demand for securitisation products, as happened before the last financial crisis.

15.25 Although these regulatory responses provide improvements to some of the risks that contributed to the crisis, they are insufficient in a macro-prudential sense in addressing systemic risk across the financial system. As outlined in Chapter 2, the main causes of market failure are: complexity (makes disclosure insufficient to eliminate information asymmetry and increases the chance of panics); conflicts (principal–agent conflicts); complacency (human irrationality and overreliance on heuristics); change (the difficulty of regulating a constantly changing system); and a type of tragedy of the commons (the

---

23 See Basel Committee on Banking Supervision and Board of the International Organization of Securities Commissions, 'Criteria for Identifying Simple, Transparent and Comparable Securitisations' (July 2015) www.bis.org/bcbs/publ/d332.pdf accessed 23 May 2018.
24 Schwarcz SL and Anabtawi I, 'Regulating Systemic Risk: Towards an Analytical Framework' (2011) UCLA School of Law, Law-Econ Research Paper No.10, 36 and generally.
25 Schwarcz SL, 'Regulating Complexity in Financial Markets' (2009) 87 *Washington University Law Review* 2 256.

benefits of exploiting finite capital resources benefit few while the costs are borne by many). In the context of securitisation, complexity and change are particularly relevant. In the financial crisis, less complex (European) products fared better than their more complex (US) counterparts. STS recognises this and incentivising this form of securitisation is therefore a reasonable compromise. These reform efforts suggest that the ever-evolving financial landscape inevitably leads to failures and crises that cannot be fully predicted and are inevitable. It would therefore seem prudent to supplement *ex ante* regulation of securitisation by mitigating risks through *ex post* regulation, such as resolution, as discussed in Chapter 6.

15.26 These differences in regulatory approach suggest that banking regulation and the use of specific regulatory instruments or 'tools' will vary across jurisdictions, particularly between the world's two largest financial markets: the European Union and the United States. For example, in the immediate aftermath of the crisis, US authorities were (and will continue to be) more reluctant to inject capital into the banking system through direct government holdings. For instance, the US Troubled Asset Relief programme (TARP) provided guarantees for investors in banks' securitised debt exposures in an effort to provide liquidity to the securitisation markets. TARP involved the US government purchasing assets and equity from financial institutions in order to strengthen the US financial sector. It was the largest component of the government's measures in 2008 to address the subprime mortgage crisis.

15.27 Similarly, the Troubled Asset Liquidity Facility (TALF) adopted in November 2008 in the aftermath of the Lehman Brothers collapse authorised the Federal Reserve Bank of New York to lend up to US$1 trillion (originally US$200 billion) on a non-recourse basis to holders of certain AAA-rated, asset-backed securities backed by newly originated consumer and small business loans. Moreover, US regulatory authorities are more sceptical of counter-cyclical capital charges, while favouring regulatory techniques that require banks to take out insurance on their portfolio exposures with private sector counterparties along with state-backed guarantees by the US government for a market-based premium on any residual risks that could potentially topple the financial system. These programmes raise important issues about how US authorities should price the risk insurance (e.g. through the TALF programme) for the guarantees they provide to banks.

15.28 In contrast, EU authorities are more proactive in using counter-cyclical regulatory charges and other types of directly intrusive regulatory measures such as bank provisioning (i.e. Spanish Central Bank provisioning model). Counter-cyclical regulatory capital poses difficult regulatory challenges because finance is by its nature procyclical – both borrowers and lenders pull back in uncertain times. Prudential rules should not exacerbate the trend. Modern accounting rules are strongly procyclical. Risk-based capital is inevitably procyclical, but only reflects the market's perception of risk. In contrast, non-risk-based capital encourages risky lending. The important macro-prudential issue here will be how to determine at what point in an economic or business cycle counter-cyclical charges and provisioning should be imposed by the regulator.

15.29 On the other hand, the US Dodd–Frank Act establishes the Volcker Rule, which prohibits US financial groups that take retail deposits and are eligible for US deposit insurance from engaging in proprietary trading; that is, trading securities or derivatives for the bank's own book. The Volcker Rule will apply in some cases extra-territorially to a non-US financial group if it has a US subsidiary or branch bank that takes deposits eligible for US deposit insurance. Although the European Commission has withdrawn its draft Regulation that would ban large financial groups from engaging in proprietary trading, several EU countries have adopted structural regulation laws (Chapter 7) that separate the bank's retail deposit-taking business from some of the bank's proprietary trading operations, particularly the UK's ring-fenced banking approach, which leaves proprietary trading wholly separate (institutionally and business-wise) in an investment banking subsidiary. These developments in UK, EU and US structural regulation of banking and financial groups portend serious challenges to the global operation of banking groups and how structural regulation will interface with other macro-prudential reforms.

15.30 Based on these different philosophies and approaches to macro-prudential regulation, there are obvious 'frictions' between different countries in their macro-prudential policy in at least two ways. First, prudential policy can be used for competitive purposes, hence other than for regulatory purposes.[26] At any rate, there are – second – market structural differences between countries which might become more important in the future. In most developing countries and advanced economies with a civil law tradition, banks are the dominant providers of industry and company finance, whereas in other countries, such as the US, UK and countries with a common law tradition, capital markets are the primary providers of finance.[27] Even though prudential regulators might share the same overall ambitions (e.g. banking stability), these market structural differences may nevertheless mean that bank-led financial systems and capital market-led financial systems view the world (as it were) through different lenses and adopt different macro-prudential policies and bank regulatory measures, all of which might ultimately create cross-border frictions between one another in terms of competing for financial sector business by adopting accommodating macro-prudential regulations.[28]

15.31 Finally, the integration of the world economy and the expansion of the financial market system have led to an unprecedented interconnectedness among organisations and across countries. Localised financial crises can now cause global losses through the spread of financial contagion; micro-policies can have macroeconomic effects in other countries.[29] The integration of the international and domestic financial markets increases the risks of contagion between financial markets. National financial regulatory controls are less able to

---

26 Salleo C, 'Single Market vs. Eurozone: Financial Stability and Macroprudential Policies', in Allen F, Carletti E and Gray J (eds), *The New Financial Architecture in the Eurozone* (European University Institute 2015), 193.
27 La Porta R, Lopez-de-Silanes F, Shleifer A and Vishny R, 'Investor Protection and Corporate Governance' (2000) 58 *Journal of Financial Economics* 1–2, 3–27, 17.
28 Ibid.
29 Eatwell J and Taylor L, *Global Finance at Risk: The Case for International Regulation* (New Press 2001), 45.

achieve financial stability in liberalised global financial markets than during the Bretton Woods system, when central banks could control their national markets more effectively by maintaining interest rate ceilings, lending limits and binding liquidity ratios. In modern markets, it is too easy for these measures to be circumvented by seeking offshore transactions. This means that an effective, policymaking, international financial regulatory body may be necessary to ensure that macro-prudential measures are adhered to on a cross-border basis.[30]

D Looking to the Future

15.32 Macro-prudential regulation and supervision will require a more holistic regulatory approach that involves linking micro-prudential supervision of individual banks with broader oversight of the financial system and macroeconomic policy. Not only should regulation focus more on macroeconomic factors, such as liquidity risks and leverage requirements for banks – it should also begin to focus on the use of so-called regulatory tools that address specific imbalances in the financial system. For instance, as discussed in Chapter 4, counter-cyclical capital requirements have been developed to address specific asset price movements that are disproportionate to broader asset prices in the rest of the economy. In contrast, some countries may find it more useful to regulate the structure of banks and financial firms (such as the UK and EU). However, macro-prudential regulation will necessarily require a more rules-based approach to controlling systemic risk at both the national and international levels. For instance, this might involve the use of maximum leverage limits across the financial system in which the amount of leverage is capped across a jurisdiction, regional market (i.e. the Eurozone) or sector of the financial system. This could potentially result in a more intrusive approach to regulation, supervision and crisis management that will necessarily require enhanced measures to control excessive risk-taking while mitigating and paying for the tremendous social costs imposed by financial crises. Moreover, effective macro-prudential regulation will require a more proactive posture by host countries to intervene and challenge risk management and measurement models that global banks use and which have been approved by their home regulatory authorities, but which may be inappropriate in a macro-prudential regulatory sense for host country financial markets.

15.33 It is respectfully submitted that, ultimately, whereas the macro-prudential approach focuses on risks across the financial system as a whole, regulatory and policy measures must be introduced at the level of individual banking and financial institutions. The micro-prudential approach is focused on individual institutions and is largely rules-based and backward-looking; it involves regulators asking themselves how best to handle a single bank if it falls into serious trouble.[31] In contrast, the macro-prudential approach is largely

---

30 Ibid., 38.
31 Bank of England Prudential Regulation Authority, 'The Prudential Regulation Authority's Approach to Banking Supervision' (April 2013), 5   www.bankofengland.co.uk/-/media/boe/files/prudential-regulation/approach/banking-approach-2013.pdf accessed 23 May 2018. See also Tucker P, 'Macro and Microprudential

forward–looking and involves the regulator monitoring risks in the market and forecasting how they might evolve in the future; it requires discretionary authority to take measures that apply to all relevant firms across the system to address the build-up of risks that may seriously threaten the market in the future. As Charles Goodhart has noted, it involves the regulator '[asking] themselves how to protect the system of banks, conditional on another bank, perhaps one of the biggest and most inter-connected, having already failed'. Despite these different approaches, micro-prudential regulation and supervision *and* macro-prudential regulation and supervision are not mutually exclusive. Indeed, by recognising the links between micro-prudential and macro-prudential regulation, a more coherent and effective framework can be developed for controlling the types of financial risk-taking that create systemic risks.[32]

II BREXIT AND BEYOND

A Brexit and the EU Internal Market

15.34 Brexit has raised important regulatory and policy issues regarding how cross-border banking will be regulated in Europe and the implications for how third country jurisdictions outside the EU will regulate their financial sectors in order to obtain access to EU financial markets. Moreover, the extent to which Brexit may restrict the access of the UK banks to the EU27 market is of vital economic concern. The UK was due to leave the European Union on 29 March 2019, but there may be a transitional period in which UK banks continue to have full access to the other EU twenty-seven Member State markets with the single passport. It is likely that UK access to the single market, however, will end after the post-Brexit transition period.

15.35 Banks have been asked by regulators to plan for a wide range of possible outcomes, including the 'hard Brexit' scenario, whereby the UK exits the EU without any new trade arrangement. The EU27 market accounts for some 25 per cent of UK banking business – a business which is one of the drives of the UK economy. The ability of UK banks to engage in wholesale banking business and to trade derivatives with EU counterparty banks on a cross-border basis in EU markets will likely require authorisations of the UK banks to trade with EU-based banks and to service open-ended derivatives contracts with EU counterparties. Although UK banks have not needed authorisations for most of their business activities in other EU states, this single market access will end after Brexit. The EU regulatory framework for the UK and other EU banks has been based on membership of the single market and the related 'passporting' privileges that arise from compliance with the EU 'single rulebook'. After Brexit, this passport will no longer be available to

Supervision' (speech at British Bankers' Association Annual International Banking Conference, London, 29 June 2011) www.bis.org/review/r110704e.pdf accessed 18 May 2018.
32   See Goodhart CAE, 'Bank Resolution in Comparative Perspective: What Lessons for Europe?', in Goodhart CAE, Gabor D, Vestergaard J and Ertürk I (eds), *Central Banking at a Crossroads* (Anthem Press 2014), 97.

banks. In the absence of an appropriate EU/UK trade agreement, UK banks could face onerous regulatory costs and barriers. Similar challenges arise for the EU. Some 15 per cent of all banking activity in the EU takes place in the UK. UK banks often provide sophisticated risk management techniques that are necessary to support banking and capital market activity across the EU. Any obstruction to the provision of these services could cause serious disruption to the EU banking sector and potentially to the EU economy.

15.36 Regarding continuity of cross-border financial contracts, banks should review whether any contracts or service-level agreements between UK and EU27 bank could be continued post-Brexit. For example, banks may not be able to perform lifecycle events under existing derivative contracts as a result of the loss of passporting rights. Absent adequate legislation and regulation, banks will have to assess whether contracts necessarily involve regulated activities in their performance and whether activities constitute continued performance of pre-existing contractual obligations or new obligations. New obligations will trigger regulatory authorisation requirements. Banks will have to consider, for example, whether to transfer contractual relationships with EU counterparties from a UK entity to an EU entity by way of individual novations of existing transactions or business transfer schemes.

B Designing a New Trade Arrangement

15.37 While the UK and EU are committed to developing a new and ambitious trading arrangement, these intentions may be obstructed by political interests and technical complexity. Indeed, the banking sector is among the most valuable but also the most heavily regulated sectors of the UK economy. This book has shown (Chapter 3) how banks are not usually permitted to access foreign banking markets unless the bank's home country regulator demonstrates adherence either to international standards or equivalence with the host state's standards. Similarly, non-EU bank access to the EU single financial market requires the bank's home country regulator to demonstrate that its regulatory standards are equivalent to EU standards.

15.38 One of the motivating factors of Brexit, however, was the need to 'take back control', which presupposes a large degree of regulatory autonomy and independence from EU institutional structures. How can this be squared with the EU's equivalence policy without subjecting UK banks to EU regulatory norms and institutional structures, particularly when competitive interests are at stake? Might there be solutions elsewhere? The classic suite of Solutions includes a Free Trade Agreement (FTA), perhaps within the European Free Trade Association (EFTA), which would provide for market access based on some form of mechanism for demonstrating regulatory or equivalence or, if equivalence fails, default reliance on World Trade Organization/General Agreement on Trade in Services (WTO/GATS) rules. Although these potential trading relationships create opportunities, they raise difficult challenges.

C Regulatory Parity and Cross-Border Banking

15.39 It is submitted that the core issue for the EU/UK negotiations over financial market access will be finding agreement on a governing standard for testing regulatory parity. The EU 'equivalence' system is already based on the third country demonstrating a type of parity with EU regulations. Acceptance of EU regulatory norms, however, will probably be resisted by the UK. Accordingly, a bespoke model should be considered which would respond to the mutual interests of the UK and EU in enabling continued reciprocal access through some form of regulatory or supervisory deference based on the parity or similarity of regulatory standards between both jurisdictions. It has been argued that a hybrid standard for regulatory parity offers the most promise. This would rely on the international standards adopted by the international standard Setting bodies (such as the Basel Committee) where appropriate. It is suggested that international standards offer a practical initial benchmark for testing regulatory parity of a third country seeking access to EU financial markets. The success of this approach, however, depends on bespoke EU/UK institutional arrangements for supervisory coordination and dispute resolution and may require a softening of the UK's posture in relation to supranational EU-level dispute resolution.

15.40 Another possibility for EU equivalence, and the potential for regulatory parity, is demonstrated by the EEA/EFTA trading and institutional arrangements. The organisational design and institutional setting of the European Economic Area (the EEA or 'Norway model') exemplifies the challenges which cross-border market access generates. It is respectfully submitted that the EEA does not provide a solution for the UK, as it requires acceptance of EU regulatory norms and institutional structures, but may serve as a short-term fix during an interim period of the single market while a final trading arrangement is negotiated.

15.41 Beyond the EEA, the European Free Trade Association (EFTA) has historically been based on its members entering into FTAs with the EU. Switzerland's experience as an EFTA member is informative. Under the so-called 'Swiss model', Switzerland has negotiated only one FTA with the EU on financial services (the 1989 insurance agreement) which, in effect, requires parity with EU regulation in a narrow area of the provision of insurance services. Since then, Switzerland has struggled to conclude a broader FTA on wider access for its financial services industry, in part because of the uncertainties surrounding the Brexit negotiations.

15.42 As a result, Switzerland is increasingly coming to rely on the EU's third country/equivalence rules and related WTO rules for ensuring access to the EU market, and not on the FTA model. The Swiss experience with the EU equivalence rules has been successful in certain areas (equivalence under Solvency II, but incomplete negotiations under MiFIR/MiFID II). Swiss financial policy has been driven by the political, procedural and regulatory challenges posed by the extent to which the EU retains discretion over equivalence decisions.

15.43 Switzerland has reluctantly embraced equivalence as the most practical means by which Swiss financial firms can gain enhanced access to the EU market, but there are challenges and policy concerns associated with the procedural complexities and contingencies of the equivalence process. This is why Switzerland and the EU are in negotiations over a broader framework treaty between both parties that would provide mutual market access to each other's markets in a broad array of services sectors (including financial services) based on a more harmonised set of legal and regulatory rules to govern financial services. Such a broad framework treaty would be accompanied by binding dispute resolution consisting of arbitration panels with membership from the EU and Swiss judiciaries. It is submitted that the Swiss model (EFTA/equivalence) has limitations for the UK, particularly as Switzerland is seeking more economic convergence and integration and regulatory coordination with the EU, while the UK seems to be moving in the opposite direction.

15.44 EU-UK negotiations over a future trade agreement should focus on the implications of Brexit for cross-border trade in banking and financial services, and exploring the potential regulatory models and institutional governance structures that would be mutually acceptable to both sides in order to achieve enhanced market access. Only by taking this more principled approach can these most important regulations on the organisation of financial regulation between Europe and the United Kingdom achieve a positive and mutually beneficial result.

III BANKING REGULATION AND ENVIRONMENTAL SUSTAINABILITY

15.45 Chapter 13 discussed how environmental sustainability is relevant for banking regulation and how the UN Sustainable Development Goals emphasise the need to generate increased investment in sustainable sectors of the economy in order to address sustainability challenges, including climate change and financial inclusion. Many scientific studies have demonstrated the links between environmental sustainability challenges and economic and financial risks. The main environmental sustainability risks – physical, transition and liability risks – potentially create negative externalities for the banking sector and broader economy. For most countries, banks play a crucial role in providing credit and investment capital that can be used to mitigate these risks while enabling the economy to grow and become more resilient to sustainability challenges.

15.46 The banking sector, however, confronts steep challenges in steering the economy onto a more sustainable path. As economies adapt to evolving market structures in response to environmental sustainability challenges, banks will have to adjust their risk management and business strategies to address potential asset price volatility and increased credit risk in economic sectors that the market has determined to be environmentally unsustainable. These financial risks associated with environmental sustainability challenges have important implications for the banking sector, as banks are the largest providers of capital for most economies: how they manage the financial risks associated with the economy's transition to more sustainable development is an important policy concern.

15.47 Banks are doing more to address these risks by gradually incorporating or mainstreaming sustainability factors into their risk management models and business strategies. This allows banks to mobilise and reallocate capital away from unsustainable economic activity to more sustainable sectors of the economy. In this way, banks can improve their risk management and enhance shareholder value by developing more sustainable financial and investment products and increasing the flows of credit to sustainable sectors of the economy.

15.48 Recent developments in bank governance and regulation suggest that regulation has an important role to play in incentivising banks to address the financial market risks associated with environmental sustainability. An important question that will shape the financial regulatory and policy debate in the near future is to what extent should banking regulation encourage or require banks to address the risks associated with environmentally unsustainable economic activity. The international policy debate is being influenced by a number of proactive regulators and large banking institutions acting within the Sustainability Banking Network to frame some of the main policy issues in this debate. For instance, the Chinese Banking Regulatory Commission adopted the Green Credit Guidelines in 2012 to encourage banks – especially the largest systemically important banks – to enhance their risk management practices in monitoring material financial risks that arise from environmentally unsustainable activity. Chinese regulators also require banks to conduct due diligence on their business customers to ensure that they are complying with environmental regulation and to call-in loans if they become aware of violations of environmental regulations and report such breaches to prosecuting authorities.

15.49 Other countries such as Brazil and Peru have incorporated environmental risk factors into their prudential oversight of banks and financial institutions. As discussed in Chapter 13, Brazil has incorporated environmental sustainability risks into the Pillar 2 supervisory review process of Basel III. Moreover, the European Commission in 2018 adopted an action plan on sustainable finance to examine the extent to which sustainability risks can also carry financial risks, and how sustainability risks can be reflected in bank capital requirements.[33] A European Parliament report concluded in 2018 that more research to assess the extent to which sustainability risks also constitute financial risks should be carried out and:

15.50 'that sustainability risks can also carry financial risks, and that they should therefore be reflected, where substantial, in capital requirements and in the prudential consideration of banks; therefore asks the Commission to adopt a regulatory strategy and a roadmap aimed

---

33 European Commission, 'Action Plan: Financing Sustainable Growth' COM(2018)97 Final (2018) https://ec.europa.eu/info/publications/180308-action-plan-sustainable-growth_en accessed 21 December 2018.

inter alia at measuring sustainability risks within the prudential framework and to promote the inclusion of sustainability risks in the Basel IV framework to ensure sufficient capital reserves; stresses that any capital adequacy rules must be based on and must fully reflect demonstrated risks; aims to initiate an EU pilot project within the next annual budget to begin developing methodological benchmarks for that purpose'.[34]

15.51 Future academic and policy work should assess these regulatory practices and policy proposals carefully to understand more fully what policymakers are attempting to achieve. For example, does involving bank regulators in supporting environmental sustainability objectives constitute an indirect effort to promote a broader state-directed lending policy – a type of financial industrial policy to support achieving environment and social objectives? Or is it part of a narrower regulatory task to support financial stability objectives by requiring or encouraging banks to identify and manage the material financial risks associated with environmentally unsustainable economic activity? It is important that policymakers set clear objectives that do not contradict or undermine the achievement of the main objectives and principles of banking regulation that include financial stability (including macro-prudential regulation), ensuring soundness and integrity in individual financial institutions and protecting depositors, investors and bank customers from market misconduct. By adding additional objectives that do not directly relate to banking and financial sector risks, the achievement of the core objectives could be jeopardised. This book submits that whatever regulatory reforms are adopted, they must be accepted by international standard-setting bodies and fora with implementation coordinated across all countries with significant banking sectors in order to avoid the segmentation of risks in different jurisdictions and regulatory arbitrage. Moreover, a vital concern for bank regulators in all jurisdictions should be that where material risks have been identified, they require a robust application of prudential and conduct of business regulatory standards to protect the financial system as a system, as well as to ensure that bank depositors and customers are protected and that individual institutions do not pose significant externality risks to the financial system and the economy. As banks are the largest providers of credit for most economies, how they manage these risks is an important policy and regulatory concern.

EPILOGUE: TRUST AND BANKING REGULATION

15.52 For regulation to work effectively in the banking sector, there must be trust between regulators and banking institutions. The crisis demonstrated how banks had abused that trust. Bank capital regulation essentially depended on banks to measure their risks by collecting data and building realistic risk models to estimate the amount of regulatory capital they should hold. Chapter 4 discussed how the Basel II framework was essentially

---

34 European Parliament, 'Report on Sustainable Finance' (2018/2007(INI)) (2018) www.europarl.europa.eu/sides/getDoc.do?pubRef=-//EP//TEXT+TA+P8-TA-2018-0215+0+DOC+XML+V0//EN accessed 21 December 2018.

self-regulatory and relied on banks to measure and estimate their risks in a good faith manner. When the mortgage-backed securities market began to deteriorate in early 2007, it became apparent that banks did not understand the risks and, further, had even manipulated their risk-weightings so that they could hold extraordinarily low levels of capital. Chapter 6 discussed how the lack of resolution regimes in most countries before the crisis incentivised banks to take greater risks because they were aware that if their capital deteriorated, the authorities would bail them out to prevent a broader banking sector crisis. The crisis also showed how misconduct risk can be systematic and endemic throughout the banking organisation. As discussed in Chapter 9, bank manipulation of benchmarks such as LIBOR represented a breakdown of the bank's internal controls while the probity of bank management was shown to be lacking because of the acceptance and even encouragement of fraudulent activity across the bank. These failures in bank corporate governance, risk management and compliance culture have resulted in a loss of trust by the regulatory community and the creation of an adversarial relationship between regulators and banks.

15.53 Moreover, the loss of trust can undermine the rule of law and the stability of expectations which are necessary for private parties to enter into agreements and to fulfil their contractual obligations and for the markets to flourish. Indeed, the rule of law underwrites every business transaction and effective institutions should be a beacon to investors, entrepreneurs and businesses. The legal certainty that is necessary for trust to occur in financial markets was hard-won and may have been lost because of the abuse of trust by the banks and the resulting breakdown of financial markets. Indeed, Klaus observes that trust in lending, capital markets, acquisitions, investment and so on only developed over time. In the nineteenth century, stock markets, the insurance business and financial journalism were riddled with scandals and unethical behaviour was endemic. For all businesses, including banking, to verify every transaction is impossible. That is why trust between market participants and trust between regulators and financial institutions is necessary.[35]

15.54 How can this trust be repaired? This is vital for restoring the economic health of the banking industry along with the efficacy of the regulations that bind it. So much of banking regulation relies on trust by the regulator that the banks can assess the risks and price them efficiently without imposing significant costs on society. For commerce – including banking - to function at all in society, there must be trust not only between parties to transactions but also between regulators and the institutions and individuals they regulate. A general assumption of trust should bind all parties to commercial transactions – business owners, employees, suppliers, customers and the authorities who oversee them. For owners of firms and for the regulators who oversee them, it is impossible to verify every transaction, and to confirm that each task has been fulfilled. Delegation of oversight is essential for all businesses – including banking – that have operations of scale. Regulators must have trust and be able to rely on good faith compliance by institutions and individuals or else the system breaks down. Otherwise, 'those

---

35   See Klaus I, 'Forging Capitalism: Rogues, Swindlers, Frauds and the Rise of Modern Finance'.

who are suspicious of everyone have to limit their ambitions, because they assume deceit is endemic'. For them, trust is risky, but what they fail to recognise is that the absence of trust is far worse, and will lead to lower levels of productivity and diminished profits – if not outright market failure. This is why bank managers and regulators must incorporate trust into their operational frameworks, not only so that banks can achieve more sustainable profits and enhanced performance but also to protect society from the risky business of banking. As Emerson observed: 'Our distrust is very expensive.'[36]

QUESTIONS

1. Should the design of banking regulation primarily be based on prescriptive rules or a discretionary application of principles?
2. Discuss the main elements of macro-prudential regulation and its objectives.
3. How will Brexit influence banking regulation?
4. Are environmental and social risks material risks for the banking sector?
5. How can trust be restored between regulators and bankers?

Further Reading

Alexander, K, Barnard C, Ferran E, Lang A and Moloney N, *BREXIT and Financial Services: Law and Policy* (Hart/Bloomsbury 2018)

Brunnermeier M, Crockett A, Goodhart C, Persaud A and Shin H, 'The Fundamental Principles of Financial Regulation' (2009) Geneva Reports on the World Economy 11 (International Centre for Banking and Monetary Studies)

Davies H, 'Comments on Cross-Border Banking Regulatory Challenges', in Caprio G, Evanoff DD and Kaufmann GG (eds), *Cross-Border Banking: Regulatory Challenges* (World Scientific Studies in International Economics 2006)

36 Emerson RW, 'Man the Reformer: A Lecture Read before the Mechanics' Apprentices' Library Association, Boston, January 25, 1841', in Phillips, Sampson & Co. and Emerson RW (eds.), *Nature, Addresses, and Lectures* (5th edn, The Riverside Press 1895).

Bibliography

BOOKS AND BOOK CHAPTERS

Adam A, *Handbook of Asset and Liability Management: From Models to Optimal Return Strategies* (Wiley 2007)

Admati A and Hellwig M, *The Bankers' New Clothes: What's Wrong with Banking and What to Do about It* (Princeton University Press 2013)

Alexander K, 'The EU Single Rulebook: Capital Requirements for Banks and the Maximum Harmonisation Principle', chapter 3 in Hinojosa LM and Beneyto J (eds), *European Banking Union: The New Regime* (Wolters Kluwer 2015)

Alexander K and Schwarcz S, 'Macroprudential Quandary: Unsystematic Efforts to Reform Financial Regulation', in Buckley RP, Avgouleas E and Arner DW (eds.), *Reconceptualising Global Finance and Its Regulation* (Cambridge University Press 2015)

Alexander K, Barnard C, Ferran E, Lang A, and Moloney N, *Brexit and Financial Services: Law and Policy* (Hart Publishing 2018)

Alexander K, Eatwell J and Gosse JB, 'Financial Markets and International Regulation', in Eatwell J, McKinley T and Petit P (eds), *Challenges for Europe in the World, 2030* (Ashgate 2014)

Alexander K, Eatwell J and Persaud A, 'Modern Banking and Securitization', chapter 1 in Alexander K and Dhumale R (eds), *Research Handbook on International Financial Regulation* (Elgar 2012)

Alexander K, Dhumale R and Eatwell J, *Global Governance of Financial Systems: The International Regulation of Systemic Risk* (Oxford University Press 2006)

Allen F and Gale D, *Comparing Financial Systems* (MIT Press 1997)

Aristotle, *Politics* (Benjamin Jowett tr, revised edn, Aeterna Press 2015)

Armour J, et al., *Principles of Financial Regulation* (Oxford University Press 2016)

Arrow KJ, *Aspects of the Theory of Risk Bearing* (Yrjö Jahnssonin Säätiö Helsinki 1965)

Arrow KJ, *Essays in the Theory of Risk-Bearing* (Markham Publishing Co. 1971)

Atiyah PS, *The Rise and Fall of Freedom of Contract* (Oxford University Press 1979)

Avgouleas E, *The Mechanics and Regulation of Market Abuse: A Legal and Economic Analysis* (Oxford University Press 2005)

Bagehot B, *Lombard Street: A Description of the Money Market* (Kegan Paul 1878)

Baker JC, *The Bank for International Settlements: Evolution and Evaluation* (Praeger 2002)

Balmer A, *Regulating Financial Derivatives – Clearing and Central Counterparties* (Elgar Financial Law Series 2018)

Banks E, *Risk Culture: A Practical Guide to Building and Strengthening the Fabric of Risk Management* (Palgrave Macmillan 2012)

Bernegger MP, 'Die digitale Revolution – Neue Geschäftsmodelle für die Finanzindustrie', in *Finanzmärkte im Banne von Big Data* (Zurich Schulthess Juristische Medien AG 2012)

The Bible, Book of Matthew online at www.biblestudytools.com/matthew/ accessed 17 December 2018

Blair M, Purves, R and Walker, GA, *Financial Services Law* (Oxford University Press 2014)

Blumberg PI, Strasser K, Georgakopoulos N and Gouvin EJ, *The Law of Corporate Groups: Jurisdiction, Practice, and Procedure* (first published 1992, 2nd edn, Aspen Publishers 2008)

Brummer C, *Soft Law and the Global Financial System* (1st edn 2012, and 2nd edn, Cambridge University Press 2015)

Busch D, 'Product Governance and Product Intervention under MiFID II/MiFIR', in Busch D and Ferrarini F (eds), *Regulation of the EU Financial Markets: MifID II and MiFIR* (Oxford University Press 2017)

Canals J, *Universal Banking* (Oxford University Press 1997)

Casu B, Girardone C and Molyneux P, *Introduction to Banking* (Pearson Education Limited 2006)

Clapham J, *The Bank of England – A History*, Vol. 1 *1694–1797* (Cambridge University Press 1944)

Cline WR, *The Right Balance for Banks: Theory and Evidence on Optimal Capital Requirements* (Columbia University Press 2017)

Coase R, *The Firm, the Market and the Law* (University of Chicago Press 1988)

Cohen EE, *Athenian Economy and Society: A Banking Perspective* (Princeton University Press 1992)

Colaert V, 'MiFID in Relation to Other Investor Protection Regulation: Picking Up the Crumbs of a Piecemeal Approach', in Busch D and Ferrarini G (eds), *Regulation of the EU Financial Markets; MiFID II and MiFIR* (Oxford University Press 2017)

Collins M, *Money and Banking in the UK: A History* (Beckenham Croom Helm 1988)

Cranston R, 'The (Non)-Liability of Banks under English Law', in Gordon L, Kleineman J and Wibom H (eds), *Functional or Dysfunctional – The Law as a Cure?* (Stockholm Centre for Commercial Law 2014), 205–222

Cranston R, *Principles of Banking Law* (Oxford University Press 2002)

Crick WF and Wadsworth J, *A Hundred Years of Joint Stock Banking* (Hodder & Stoughton 1935)

Darling A, *Back from Brink: 1,000 Days at No. 11* (Atlantic Books Limited 2011)

Davies H, 'Comments on Cross-Border Banking Regulatory Challenges', in Caprio G, Evanoff DD and Kaufmann GG (eds), *Cross-Border Banking: Regulatory Challenges* (World Scientific Studies in International Economics 2006)

Davies P and Worthington S (eds), *Gower and Davies' Principles of Modern Company Law* (9th edn, Sweet & Maxwell 2012)

Davis K, 'Financial Reform in Australia', in Maximilian Hall JB (ed.), *The International Handbook on Financial Reform* (Edward Elgar 2003)

De Pascalis F, *Credit Ratings and Market Over-Reliance: An International Legal Analysis* (Brill-Nijhoff International Trade Law Series 2017)

De Weert F, *Bank and Insurance Capital Management* (Wiley 2011)

Dine J, *Company Law* (Sweet & Maxwell 2001)

Dudley WC and Hubbard G, 'How Capital Markets Enhance Economic Performance and Facilitate Job Creation' (Goldman Sachs Markets Institute 2004)

Duggan A and Lanyon E, *Consumer Credit Law* (Butterworths 1999)

Eatwell J and Taylor L, *Global Finance at Risk: The Case for International Regulation* (New Press 2001)

Eiteman D, Stonehill A and Moffett M, *Multinational Business Finance* (10th edn, Pearson 2004)

Enriques, L and Gargantini M, 'The Overarching Duty to Act in the Best Interest of the Client in MiFID II', in Busch B and Ferrarini G (eds), *Regulation of the EU Financial Markets: MifID II and MiFIR* (Oxford University Press 2017)

Emerson RW, 'Man the Reformer: A Lecture Read before the Mechanics' Apprentices' Library Association, Boston, January 25, 1841', in Phillips Sampson & Co. and Emerson RW (eds.), *Nature, Addresses, and Lectures* (5th edn, The Riverside Press 1895)

Ferran E, 'Institutional Design: The Choices for National Systems', in Moloney N, Ferran E and Payne J (eds), *The Oxford Handbook of Financial Regulation* (Oxford University Press 2015)

Ferran E and Ho LC, *Principles of Corporate Finance Law* (1st edn, Oxford University Press 2007)

Fujii M and Kawai M, *Lessons from Japan's Banking Crisis: 1991–2005* (Edward Elgar 2012)

Galbraith JK, *The Great Crash 1929* (Penguin Press 2009)

Gart A, *Regulation, Deregulation, Regulation: The Future of Banking, Insurance, and Securities Industries* (Wiley 1994)

Golin J and Delhaise P, *The Bank Credit Analysis Handbook: A Guide for Analysts, Bankers and Investors* (2nd edn, Wiley 2013)

Goodhart CAE, 'Bank Resolution in Comparative Perspective: What Lessons for Europe?', in Goodhart, CAE, Gabor D, Vestergaard J and Ertürk I (eds), *Central Banking at a Crossroads* (Anthem Press 2014)

Goodhart CAE, *The Basel Committee on Banking Supervision: A History of the Early Years, 1974–1997* (Cambridge University Press 2011)

Goodhart CAE, 'What Do Central Banks Do?', in Goodhart CAE (ed.), *The Central Bank and the Financial System* (Palgrave Macmillan 1995), 205–215

Goodhart CAE, Hartmann P, Llewellyn D, Rojas-Suarez L and Weisbrod S, *Financial Regulation: Why, How, and Where Now?* (Routledge 1998)

Greenbaum SI and Thakor AV, *Contemporary Financial Intermediation* (2nd edn, Academic Press 2007)

Gros D and Thygesen N, *European Monetary Integration, from the European Monetary System to Economic and Monetary Union* (2nd edn, Addison Wesley Longman 1998)

Hannigan B, *Company Law* (3rd edn, Oxford University Press 2012)

Heffernan S, *Modern Banking* (Wiley 2005)

Hormaeche Lazcano M, 'The Sale of Business Tool', in Lintner P (ed.), *Understanding Bank Recovery and Resolution in the EU: A Guidebook to the BRRD* (World Bank Group April 2017)

Hull J, *Options, Futures, and Other Derivatives* (8th edn, Pearson Education International 2012)

Hull J, *Risk Management and Financial Institutions* (3rd edn, Wiley 2012)

Hunt E, *The Medieval Supercompanies: A Study of the Peruzzi Company of Florence* (Cambridge University Press 1994)

Hüpkes EHG, 'Learning Lessons and Implementing a New Approach – Bank Insolvency Resolution in Switzerland', in Mayes D (eds), *Who Will Pay for Bank Insolvency?* (Palgrave 2003)

Hüpkes EHG, *The Legal Aspects of Bank Insolvency: A Comparative Analysis of Western Europe, the United States and Canada* (Kluwer Law International 2000)

Jones G, *British Multinational Banking 1830–1990* (Oxford University Press 1993)

Kane EJ, *The S&L Insurance Mess: How Did It Happen?* (Urban Institute Press 1989)

Keynes JM, *The General Theory of Employment, Interest and Money* (Palgrave Macmillan 1936)

Kindleberger CP and Aliber RZ, *Manias, Panics and Crashes* (6th edn, Palgrave Macmillan 2011)

Kingsford Smith D and Dixon O, 'The Consumer Interest and the Financial Markets', in Moloney N, Ferran E and Payne J (eds), *The Oxford Handbook of Financial Regulation* (Oxford University Press 2015)

Klaus I, *Forging Capitalism: Rogues, Swindlers, Frauds and the Rise of Modern Finance* (Yale Series in Economic and Financial History) (Yale University Press 2014)

Kurke L, *Coins, Bodies, Games, and Gold: The Politics of Meaning in Archaic Greece* (Princeton University Press 1999)

Landon-Lane J, Rockoff H and Steckel RH, 'Droughts, Floods, and Financial Distress in the United States', in Libecap GD and Steckel RH (eds), *The Economics of Climate Change: Adaptations Past and Present* (University of Chicago Press 2009)

Lastra R, *Central Banking and Banking Regulation* (Financial Markets Group) (London School of Economics 1996)

Lastra R, *International Financial and Monetary Law* (2nd edn, Oxford University Press 2015)

Mauchle Y, *Bail-in and Total Loss-Absorbing Capacity (TLC): Legal and Economic Perspectives on Bank Resolution with Functional Comparisons of Swiss and EU Law* (Kluwer Law International BV 2017)

Menoud V, *Financial Conglomerates* (Schulthess Juristische Medien AG 2010)

Millett P, *Lending and Borrowing in Ancient Athens* (Cambridge University Press 1991)

Mishkin F, *The Economics of Money, Banking and Financial Markets* (11th edn, Pearson 2015)

Moloney N, 'Regulating the Retail Markets', in Moloney N, Ferran E and Payne J (eds), *The Oxford Handbook of Financial Regulation* (Oxford University Press 2015)

Moloney N, *EU Securities and Financial Markets Regulation* (3rd edn, Oxford University Press 2014)

Moloney N, *How to Protect Investors: Lessons from the EC and the UK* (Oxford University Press 2010)

Nieto M, *Banks and Environmental Sustainability: Some Financial Stability Reflections* (International Research Centre for Cooperative Finance 2017)

Nordhaus W, *The Climate Casino: Risk, Uncertainty, and Economics for a Warming World* (Yale University Press 2013)

Norton J, *Devising International Bank Supervisory Standards* (Kluwer 1995)

O'Donovan J, *Lender Liability* (LBC Information Services 2000)

Olson GN, 'Government Intervention: The Inadequacy of Bank Insolvency Resolution – Lessons from the American Experience', in Lastra RM and Schiffman HN (eds), *Bank Failures and Bank Insolvency Law in Economies in Transition* (Kluwer Law International 1999)

Partnoy F, 'Financial Systems, Crises, and Regulationse', in Moloney N, Ferran E and Payne J (eds.), *The Oxford Handbook of Financial Regulation* (1st edn, Oxford University Press 2015)

Pigou AC, *Socialism versus Capitalism* (Macmillan and Co. 1937)

Pigou AC, *The Economics of Welfare* (Macmillan and Co. 1920)

Pinto AR and Branson DM, *Understanding Corporate Law* (Matthew Bender 1999)

Power M, Ashby S, Palermo T, 'Risk Culture: Definitions, Change Practices and Challenges for Chief Risk Officers', in Jackson P (ed.), *Risk Culture and Effective Risk Governance* (Risk Books 2014)

Quinn S and Roberds W, 'An Economic Explanation of the Early Bank of Amsterdam, Debasement, Bills of Exchange and the Emergence of the First Central Bank', in Atack J and Neal L (eds), *The Origins and Development of Financial Markets and Institutions from the Seventeenth to the Present* (Cambridge University Press 2009)

Reinhart CM and Rogoff KS, *This Time is Different: Eight Centuries of Financial Folly* (Princeton University Press 2009)

Renner M, 'Death by Complexity – The Financial Crises and the Crises of Law in World Society', in Kjaer PF, Teubner G and Febbrajo A (eds), *The Financial Crises in Constitutional Perspective: The Dark Side of Functional Differentiation* (Hart Publishing 2011)

Saleh NA, *Unlawful Gain and Legitimate Profit in Islamic Law: Riba, Gharar and Islamic Banking* (Cambridge University Press 1996), 47–48

Salleo C, 'Single Market vs. Eurozone: Financial Stability and Macroprudential Policies', in Allen F, Carletti E and Gray J (eds), *The New Financial Architecture in the Eurozone* (European University Institute 2015)

Schneider UH, 'Corporate Governance Issues in Germany – Between Golden October and Nasty November', in Norton JJ and Rickford J (eds), *Corporate Governance Post-Enron* (British Institute of International and Comparative Law 2006)

Servén L, 'Macroprudential Policies in the Wake of the Global Financial Crisis', in Canuto O and Giugale M (eds), *The Day After Tomorrow: A Handbook on the Future of Economic Policy in the Developing World* (The World Bank 2010)

Sheng A, *From Asian to Global Financial Crisis: An Asian Regulator's View of Unfettered Finance in the 1990s and 2000s* (Cambridge University Press 2009)

Shiller R, *Irrational Exuberance* (Princeton University Press 2000)

Smith A, *The Wealth of Nations* (first published 1776, Bantam Dell 2003)

Spong K, *Banking Regulation: Its Purposes, Implementation, and Effects* (5th edn, Federal Reserve Bank of Kansas City Division of Supervision and Risk Management 2000)

Stiglitz J, 'Principal-Agent', in Eatwell J, Milgate M and Newman P (eds), *The New Palgrave: Allocation, Information and Markets* (Macmillan Press 1989)

Taylor MW, *Twin Peaks: A Regulatory Structure for the New Century* (CSFI 1995)

Thiessen R, *Are EU Banks Safe?* (Eleven International Publishing 2014)

Turner A, *Between Debt and the Devil* (Princeton University Press 2016)

Tyree AL, *Banking Law in Australia* (5th edn, Butterworths 2005)

Von Reden S, *Exchange in Ancient Greece* (Duckworth 1995)

Walker GA, *International Banking Regulation: Law, Policy, and Practice* (Kluwer 2001)

Weitzman ML 'The Geoengineered Planet', in Palacios-Huerta I (ed.), *In 100 Years* (MIT Press 2013)

Wetterberg G, *Money and Power – The History of the Sveriges Riksbank* (Atlantis 2010)

Wood PR, *International Loans, Bonds, Guarantees, Legal Opinions* (2nd edn, Sweet & Maxwell 2007)

CONTRIBUTIONS TO EDITED BOOKS/COMMENTARIES

Watter R and Pellanda K, 'Commentary to art. 717 Code of Obligations', in Honsell H, Vogt NP and Watter R (eds), *Basler Kommentar Obligationenrecht II* (Helbling Lichtenhahn Verlag 2016)

INSTITUTIONAL PUBLICATIONS AND MATERIALS

Accenture Consulting, 'Evolving AML Journey: Leveraging Machine Learning Within Anti-Money Laundering Transaction Monitoring' (Accenture 2017) 2, www.accenture.com/_acnmedia/PDF-61/Accenture-Leveraging-Machine-Learning-Anti-Money-Laundering-Transaction-Monitoring.pdf accessed 20 December 2018

Alexander K, 'Greening Banking Policy' (September 2016) Input paper in support of the G20 Green Finance Study Group 'Greening Banking Policy' www.rwi.uzh.ch/dam/jcr:cd6d77ff-6075-4045-8da0-55eb89824f7a/10_Greening_Banking_Policy.pdf accessed 1 March 2018

Alexander K, 'Stability and Sustainability in Banking Reform: Are Environmental Risks Missing in Basel III?' (2014) United Nations Environment Programme and University of Cambridge Institute for Sustainability Leadership www.unepfi.org/fileadmin/documents/StabilitySustainability.pdf accessed 21 February 2018

Alexander K, 'Implementation of Capital Requirements Directive III Remuneration Rules in the UK: Implications, Limitations and Lessons Learned' (2012) Economics and Monetary

Affairs, European Parliament, Workshop on Banks' Remuneration Rules (CRD III): Are they implemented and do they work in practice? IP/A/ECON/WS/2012–18, PE 464–465

Alexander K, 'The Fund's Role in Sovereign Liquidity Crises' (2008) International Monetary Fund, *Current Issues in Monetary and Financial Law*, Vol. 5

Alexander K, Eatwell J, Persaud A and Reoch R, 'Financial Supervision and Crisis Management in the EU' (2007) Policy Study IP/A/ECON/IC/2007–069, Brussels: European Parliament www.augurproject.eu/IMG/pdf/JEatwellEtAl_FinancialSupervisionYCrisisManagement_EUreport-2.pdf accessed 21 February 2018

Anderson N, Brooke M, Hume M and Kürtösiová M, 'A European Capital Markets Union: Implications for Growth and Stability' (February 2015) Financial Stability Paper No. 33 www.bankofengland.co.uk/-/media/boe/files/financial-stability-paper/2015/a-european-capital-markets-union-implications-for-growth.pdf?la=en&hash=26629651BA24F7590B3EA31632CF09EE4DF0B7B2 accessed 28 March 2018

BaFin Journal, 'Systemrelevante Finanzunternehmen – G20 sehen Fortschritte bei nationalen und internationalen Lösungsansätzen zum "Too Big to Fail" – Problem' (October 2013)

Bank for International Settlements, Committee on Payments and Market Infrastructures, 'Central Bank Digital Currencies' (March 2018) www.bis.org/cpmi/publ/d174.pdf accessed 28 May 2018

Bank of England, Financial Policy Committee, 'Financial Stability Report' (2012) www.parliament.uk/business/committees/committees-a-z/commons-select/treasury-committee/other-committee-work-/parliament-2010/bank-of-england-financial-stability-report-/ accessed 21 December 2018

Bank of England, HM Treasury and the Financial Services Authority, 'Financial Stability and Depositor Protection: Special Resolution Regime' (July 2008) www.gov.uk/government/uploads/system/uploads/attachment_data/file/238704/7459.pdf accessed 21 February 2018

Bank of England Prudential Regulation Authority, Supervisory Statement 'Remuneration' (April 2017) www.bankofengland.co.uk/-/media/boe/files/prudential-regulation/supervisory-statement/2017/ss217.pdf?la=en&hash=71A98E5E2CDD629F9C219C09480AF1CED95E909E accessed 21 February 2018

Bank of England Prudential Regulation Authority, 'The Use of PRA Powers to Address Serious Failings in the Culture of Firms' Statement of Policy (June 2014) www.bankofengland.co.uk/-/media/boe/files/prudential-regulation/statement-of-policy/2014/the-use-of-pra-powers-to-address-serious-failings-in-the-culture-of-firms.pdf accessed 21 February 2018

Bank of England Prudential Regulation Authority, 'The Prudential Regulation Authority's Approach to Banking Supervision' (April 2013) www.bankofengland.co.uk/-/media/boe/files/prudential-regulation/approach/banking-approach-2013.pdf accessed 23 May 2018

Bank of Russia, Letter No. 06–52/2463 (10 April 2014) www.cbr.ru/StaticHtml/File/12105/Inf_apr_1014_en.pdf accessed 1 March 2018

Banking Standards Board, 'Annual Review 2015/2016' (2016) www.bankingstandardsboard.org.uk/wp-content/uploads/2016/03/BSB-Annual-Review-20152016.pdf accessed 21 February 2018

Basel Committee on Banking Supervision, 'Regulatory Consistency Assessment Programme (RCAP): Handbook for Jurisdictional Assessments' (March 2016) www.bis.org/bcbs/publ/d361.pdf accessed 21 February 2018

Basel Committee on Banking Supervision, 'Range of Practice in the Regulation and Supervision of Institutions Relevant to Financial Inclusion' (January 2015) www.bis.org/bcbs/publ/d310.pdf accessed 21 February 2018

Basel Committee on Banking Supervision, 'Guidelines: Corporate Governance Principles for Banks' (July 2015) www.bis.org/bcbs/publ/d328.pdf accessed 21 February 2018

Basel Committee on Banking Supervision, 'Core Principles for Effective Banking Supervision' (2012) Bank for International Settlements www.bis.org/publ/bcbs230.pdf accessed 30 August 2017

Basel Committee on Banking Supervision, 'Peer Review of Supervisory Authorities' Implementation of Stress Testing Principles' (April 2012) www.bis.org/publ/bcbs218.pdf accessed 21 February 2018

Basel Committee on Banking Supervision, Revised 'Core Principles for Effective Banking' (Bank for International Settlements September 2012) www.bis.org/publ/bcbs230.pdf accessed 21 February 2018

Basel Committee on Banking Supervision, Committee on Global Financial System, 'Principles for the Supervision of Financial Conglomerates' Final Report (September 2012) www.bis.org/publ/joint29.pdf accessed 21 February 2018

Basel Committee on Banking Supervision, 'Macroprudential Policy Tools and Frameworks – Progress Report to G20' (October 2011) www.bis.org/publ/othp17.pdf accessed 21 February 2018

Basel Committee on Banking Supervision, The Joint Forum, 'Review of the Differentiated Nature and Scope of Financial Regulation, Key Issues and Recommendations' (January 2010) www.bis.org/publ/joint24.pdf accessed 21 February 2018

Basel Committee on Banking Supervision, 'Principles for Enhancing Corporate Governance' (Bank for International Settlements October 2010) www.bis.org/publ/bcbs176.pdf accessed 19 December 2018

Basel Committee on Banking Supervision, 'Basel III: A Global Regulatory Framework for More Resilient Banks and Banking Systems' (December 2010, revised June 2011) www.bis.org/publ/bcbs189.pdf accessed 21 February 2018

Basel Committee on Banking Supervision, 'Enhancements to Basel II Framework' (July 2009) www.bis.org/publ/bcbs157.pdf accessed 21 February 2018

Basel Committee on Banking Supervision, 'Supervisory Guidance on Dealing with Weak Banks' (March 2002) www.bis.org/publ/bcbs88.pdf accessed 21 February 2018

Basel Committee on Banking Supervision, 'Core Principles for Effective Banking Supervision (Basel Core Principles)' (September 1997) www.bis.org/publ/bcbsc102.pdf accessed 21 February 2018

Basel Committee on Banking Supervision and Board of the International Organization of Securities Commissions, 'Criteria for Identifying Simple, Transparent and Comparable Securitisations' (July 2015) www.bis.org/bcbs/publ/d332.pdf accessed 23 May 2018

Baxter J and Megone C, 'Exploring the Role of Professional Bodies and Professional Qualifications in the UK Banking Sector' Independent Report Commissioned by the Banking Standard Board (October 2016) www.bankingstandardsboard.org.uk/wp-content/uploads/2016/10/160928-Professionalism-in-banking-publication-FINAL-WEB.pdf accessed 21 February 2018

BBVA Research, 'Digital Economy Outlook' (BBVA Digital Regulation Unit, February 2016) www.bbvaresearch.com/wp-content/uploads/2016/02/DEO_Feb16-EN.pdf accessed 12 June 2018

Borio C, 'Towards a Macroprudential Framework for Financial Supervision and Regulation?' (February 2003) BIS Working Papers No. 128 https://www.bis.org/publ/work128.pdf accessed 21 February 2018 also available as Borio C, 'Towards a Macroprudential Framework for Financial Supervision and Regulation?' (2003) 49 *CESifo Economic Studies* 2 181–215

Borio C and Lowe P, 'Asset Prices, Financial and Monetary Stability: Exploring the Nexus' (July 2002) BIS Working Papers No. 114 www.bis.org/publ/work114.pdf accessed 21 February 2018

Briault C, 'The Rationale for a Single National Financial Services Regulator', FSA Occasional Paper No. 2 (May 1999)

CCP Research Foundation, 'Conduct Costs Project Report 2016' (LSE 2016) http://ccpresearchfoundation.com/noticeboard?item=32056-conduct-costs-project-report-2017 accessed 21 December 2018

Chater N, Huck S and Inderst R, 'Consumer Decision-Making in Retail Investment Services: A Behavioural Economics Perspective' Final Report to the European Commission/SANCO (November 2010) www.ec.europa.eu/consumers/financial_services/reference_studies_documents/docs/consumer_decision-making_in_retail_investment_services_-_final_report_en.pdf accessed 21 February 2018

Claessens S, Ghosh SR and Mihet R, 'Macro-Prudential Policies to Mitigate Financial System Vulnerabilities' (August 2014) IMF Working Paper WP/14/155 www.imf.org/external/pubs/ft/wp/2014/wp14155.pdf accessed 23 May 2018

Committee of European Securities Regulations, 'Market Abuse Directive: Level 3 – Second Set of CESR Guidance and Information on the Common Operation of the Directive to the Market' CESR/06–562b (July 2007) www.cesr-eu.org/data/document/06_562b.pdf accessed 17 May 2018

Committee on Payments and Market Infrastructures, 'Central Bank Digital Currencies' (Bank for International Settlements, March 2018) www.bis.org/cpmi/publ/d174.pdf accessed 28 May 2018

Committee on Payments and Market Infrastructures, 'Charter' (Bank for International Settlements, September 2014) paras. 1 and 2, www.bis.org/cpmi/publ/d174.pdf accessed 28 May 2018

Council of Europe, European Convention for the Protection of Human Rights and Fundamental Freedoms, as amended by Protocols Nos. 11 and 14, ETS 5, 4 November 1950 www.echr.coe.int/Documents/Convention_ENG.pdf accessed 21 December 2018

Deloitte, 'Reg Tech Universe' (Deloitte Analysis, 14 May 2018) www2.deloitte.com/lu/en/pages/technology/articles/regtech-universe.html accessed 12 June 2018

Department of the Treasury, 'Orderly Liquidation Authority and Bankruptcy Reform' (21 February 2018) Report 16 https://home.treasury.gov/sites/default/files/2018-02/OLA_REPORT.pdf accessed 21 December 2018

Department of the Treasury, 'Financial Stability Oversight Council Designations' Report to the President of the United States (November 2017) www.treasury.gov/press-center/press-releases/Documents/PM-FSOC-Designations-Memo-11-17.pdf accessed 21 February 2018

Department of the Treasury Office of the Comptroller of the Currency, Federal Reserve System, Federal Deposit Insurance Corporation, Department of Treasury Office of Thrift Supervision, 'Risk-Based Capital Guidelines; Capital Adequacy Guidelines; Capital Maintenance: Domestic Capital Modifications' (October 2005) Draft www.federalreserve.gov/bcreg20061205a1.pdf accessed 21 February 2018

Dow J, 'What is Systemic Risk? Moral Hazard, Initial Shocks and Propagation' (December 2000) Institute for Monetary and Economic Studies, Bank of Japan www.imes.boj.or.jp/research/papers/english/me18-2-1.pdf accessed 21 February 2018

Elliott DJ, Feldberg G and Lehnert A, 'The History of Cyclical Macroprudential Policy in the United States' (2013) Federal Reserve Board of Governors, Finance and Economics Discussion Series No. 2013–29 www.federalreserve.gov/pubs/feds/2013/201329/201329pap.pdf accessed 21 February 2018

European Banking Authority, 'Final Report – Guidelines on Internal Governance under Directive 2013/36/EU' (26 September 2017) www.eba.europa.eu/documents/10180/1972987/Final+Guidelines+on+Internal+Governance+%28EBA-GL-2017-11%29.pdf/eb859955-614a-4afb-bdcd-aaa664994889 accessed 21 February 2018

European Banking Authority, 'Guidelines on Sound Remuneration Policies under Articles 74(3) and 75(2) of Directive 2013/36/EU and Disclosures under Article 450 of Regulation (EU) No 575/2013' (June 2016) www.eba.europa.eu/documents/10180/1314839/EBA-GL-2015-22+Guidelines+on+Sound+Remuneration+Policies_EN.pdf accessed 21 February 2018

European Banking Authority, Regulatory Technical Standards on Minimum Requirement for Determining Own Funds and Eligible Liabilities (MREL), EBA/CP/2014/41 (28 November 2014), London

European Banking Authority, 'Guidelines on the Specification of Measures to Reduce or Remove Impediments to Resolvability and the Circumstances in which Each Measure May Be Applied under Directive 2014/59/EU' (19 December 2014) www.eba.europa.eu/documents/10180/933988/EBA-GL-2014-11+%28Guidelines+on+Impediments+to+Resolvability%29.pdf/d3fa2201-e21f-4f3a-8a67-6e7278fee473 accessed 22 March 2018

European Banking Authority, 'Guidelines on the Assessment of the Suitability of Members of the Management Body and Key Function Holders' (22 November 2012) Article 5, Guideline 7 https://eba.europa.eu/-/guidelines-on-the-assessment-of-the-suitability-of-members-of-the-management-body-and-key-function-holders-eba-gl-2012-06- accessed 21 December 2018

European Central Bank, 'Financial Stability Review' (May 2016) www.ecb.europa.eu/pub/pdf/other/financialstabilityreview201605.en.pdf accessed 5 March 2018

European Central Bank, 'Recent Developments in the Balance Sheets of the Eurosystem, the Federal Reserve System and the Bank of Japan', Monthly Bulletin (October 2009) www.ecb.europa.eu/pub/pdf/other/art2_mb200910_pp81-94en.pdf accessed 21 February 2018

European Central Bank, 'The Concept of Systemic Risk' (June 2009) Financial Stability Review www.ecb.europa.eu/pub/pdf/other/financialstabilityreview200906en.pdf accessed 21 February 2018

European Central Bank, 'Consolidation and Diversification in the Euro Area Banking Sector', Monthly Bulletin (May 2005) www.ecb.europa.eu/pub/pdf/mobu/mb200505en.pdf accessed 21 February 2018

European Commission High Level Experts Group on Sustainable Finance, 'Financing a Sustainable European Economy', Brussels, January 2018

European Commission, 'Overview and State of Play of RTS and ITS Relating to MiFID/MiFIR' (last updated January 2018) www.ec.europa.eu/info/files/mifid-mifir-its-rts-overview_en accessed 21 February 2018

European Commission, 'Action Plan: Financing Sustainable Growth' COM(2018)97 Final (2018) https://ec.europa.eu/info/publications/180308-action-plan-sustainable-growth_en accessed 21 December 2018

European Commission, Proposal for a Directive on Representative Actions for the Protection of the Collective Interests of Consumers, and Repealing Directive 2009/22/EC COM/2018/0184 final – 2018/089 (COD) (11 April 2018) https://eur-lex.europa.eu/legal-content/EN/TXT/?uri=COM%3A2018%3A184%3AFIN accessed 25 May 2018

European Commission, 'Communication from the Commission to the European Parliament, the Council, the European Economic and Social Committee and the Committee of Regions – Commission Working Programme 2018 – An Agenda for a More United, Stronger and More Democratic Europe' and Annexes (24 October 2017) COM(2017) 650 final http://eur-lex.europa.eu/legal-content/EN/TXT/HTML/?uri=CELEX:52017DC0650&from=EN accessed 23 March 2018

European Commission, 'Green Paper – Building a Capital Markets Union' (18 February 2015) SWD(2015) 13 final http://ec.europa.eu/finance/consultations/2015/capital-markets-union/docs/green-paper_en.pdf accessed 28 March 2018

European Commission, Communication from the Commission to the European Parliament and the Council on 'Long-Term Financing of the European Economy' (27 March 2014) COM(2014) 168 final www.ec.europa.eu/internal_market/finances/docs/financing-growth/long-term/140327-communication_en.pdf accessed 21 February 2018

European Commission, Proposal for a Regulation of the European Parliament and of the Council on 'Structural Measures Improving the Resilience of EU Credit Institutions' (29 January 2014) COM(2014) 43 final https://eur-lex.europa.eu/legal-content/EN/ALL/?uri=CELEX%3A52014PC0043 accessed 21 March 2018

European Commission, Memo on 'Structural Measures to Improve the Resilience of EU Credit Institutions – Frequently Asked Questions' (29 January 2014) MEMO/14/64 http://europa.eu/rapid/press-release_MEMO-14-63_en.htm accessed 21 March 2018

European Commission, 'Report of the High-Level Expert Group on Reforming the Structure of the EU Banking Sector', chaired by Erkki Liikanen (2 October 2012) www.ec.europa .eu/internal_market/bank/docs/high-level_expert_group/report_en.pdf accessed 21 February 2018

European Commission, Staff Working Paper, 'Executive Summary of the Impact Assessment Accompanying the Document Proposal for a Directive of the European Parliament and of the Council Amending European Parliament and Council; Markets in Financial Instruments', SEC(2011) 1227 final (20 October 2011) www.ec.europa.eu/ internal_market/securities/docs/isd/mifid/SEC_2011_1227_en.pdf accessed 21 February 2018

European Commission, 'Report of the High-Level Expert Group on Financial Supervision in the EU', chaired by Jacques de Larosière (25 February 2009) www.ec.europa.eu/internal_ market/finances/docs/de_larosiere_report_en.pdf accessed 21 February 2018

European Commission, 'White Paper on Financial Services 2005–10' COM (2005) 629 (1 December 2005) www.europarl.europa.eu/meetdocs/2004_2009/documents/com/com_ com(2005)0629_/com_com(2005)0629_en.pdf accessed 21 February 2018

European Parliament, 'Report on Sustainable Finance' (2018/2007(INI)) (2018) www .europarl.europa.eu/sides/getDoc.do?pubRef=-//EP//TEXT+TA+P8-TA-2018-0215+0 +DOC+XML+V0//EN accessed 21 December 2018

European Securities and Markets Authority, 'Final Report: ESMA's Technical Advice on Possible Delegated Acts Concerning the Market Abuse Regulation' (3 February 2015) www.esma .europa.eu/sites/default/files/library/2015/11/2015-224.pdf accessed 18 May 2018

European Securities and Markets Authority and European Banking Authority, 'Final Report – Joint ESMA and EBA Guidelines on the Assessment of the Suitability of Members of the Management Body and Key Function Holders under Directive 2013/36/ EU and Directive 2014/65/EU' (26 September 2017) www.eba.europa.eu/documents/ 10180/1972984/Joint+ESMA+and+EBA+Guidelines+on+the+assessment+of+suitability +of+members+of+the+management+body+and+key+function+holders+%28EBA-GL-2017-12%29.pdf accessed 21 February 2018

European Systemic Risk Board, 'EU Shadow Banking Monitor' No. 2 (May 2017) www .esrb.europa.eu/pub/pdf/reports/20170529_shadow_banking_report.en.pdf accessed 6 March 2018

European Systemic Risk Board, 'Report on Misconduct Risk in the Banking Sector' (June 2015) www.esrb.europa.eu/pub/pdf/other/150625_report_misconduct_risk.en.pdf accessed 21 February 2018

European Systemic Risk Board, Recommendation of the European Systemic Risk Board of 4 April 2013 on Intermediate Objectives and Instruments of Macro-Prudential Policy (ESRB/2013/1) OJ L 170, 15.06.2013 1 (4 April 2013) www.esrb.europa.eu/pub/pdf/ recommendations/2013/ESRB_2013_1.en.pdf accessed 21 February 2018

Ernst & Young, 'Shifting Focus – Risk Culture at the Forefront of Banking' EY Risk Management Survey of Major Financial Institutions (2014) www.ey.com/Publication/vwLUAssets/ey-shifting-focus-risk-culture-at-the-forefront-of-banking/$FILE/ey-shifting-focus-risk-culture-at-the-forefront-of-banking.pdf accessed 21 February 2018

Fabrizio S and others, 'From Ambition to Execution: Policies in Support of Sustainable Development Goals' IMF Staff Discussion Note (September 2015) www.imf.org/external/pubs/ft/sdn/2015/sdn1518.pdf accessed 21 February 2018

Favara G, 'An Empirical Reassessment of the Relationship Between Finance and Growth' (2003) IMF Working Paper WP/03/123 www.imf.org/external/pubs/ft/wp/2003/wp03123.pdf accessed 21 February 2018

Federal Deposit Insurance Corporation, 'Your Insured Deposits' (online brochure, FDIC 2018) https://www.fdic.gov/deposit/deposits/brochures/your-insured-deposits-english.html accessed 19 December 2018

Federal Deposit Insurance Corporation and Bank of England, 'Resolving Globally Active, Systemically Important, Financial Institutions' A joint paper by the Federal Deposit Insurance Corporation and the Bank of England (10 December 2012) www.fdic.gov/about/srac/2012/gsifi.pdf accessed 22 March 2018

Federal Open Market Committee, 'Transcript of the Federal Open Market Committee Meeting of August 7, 2007' (Federal Open Market Committee meeting transcript, Board of Governors of the Federal Reserve System 2018) www.federalreserve.gov/monetarypolicy/files/FOMC20070807meeting.pdf accessed 3 January 2018

Federal Reserve Bank of Chicago's Annual Conference on Bank Structure, Chicago, IL USA (5 May 2005) www.federalreserve.gov/boarddocs/speeches/2005/20050505/ accessed 21 February 2018

Federal Reserve Bank of Minneapolis, *The Minneapolis Plan To End Too Big To Fail* (November, 2016) Minneapolis: Federal Reserve Bank of Minneapolis

Federal Reserve System, 'Total Loss Absorbing Capacity, Long-Term Debt, and Clean holding Company Requirements for Systemically Important U.S. Bank Holding Companies and Intermediate Holding Companies of Systemically Important Foreign banking Organizations' (2017) FDIC, Federal Register Vol. 82/14 8269

Financial Conduct Authority, 'Principles for Businesses' (FCA Handbook Release 35 January 2019) 2.1 www.handbook.fca.org.uk/handbook/PRIN.pdf accessed 20 December 2018

Financial Conduct Authority, 'Principles for Businesses' Handbook Release 23 (January 2018) www.handbook.fca.org.uk/handbook/PRIN.pdf accessed 21 February 2018

Financial Conduct Authority, 'Meeting Investors' Expectations' (Thematic Review TR 16/3) (April 2016) www.fca.org.uk/publication/thematic-reviews/tr16-3.pdf accessed 21 February 2018

Financial Conduct Authority, 'Call for Input: Supporting the Development and Adoption of Regtech' (FCA, April 2016), 3 www.fca.org.uk/publication/feedback/fs-16-04.pdf accessed 21 December 2018

Financial Conduct Authority, 'CP15/22 Strengthening Accountability in Banking: Final Rules (Including Feedback on CP14/31 and CP15/5) and Consultation on Extending the Certification Regime to Wholesale Market Activities' (July 2015) www.fca.org.uk/publication/consultation/cp15-22.pdf accessed 21 February 2018

Financial Crisis Inquiry Commission, 'Financial Crisis Inquiry Report – Final Report of the National Commission on the Causes of the Financial Crisis in the United States' Official Government Edition (January 2011) www.gpo.gov/fdsys/pkg/GPO-FCIC/pdf/GPO-FCIC.pdf accessed 21 February 2018

Financial Ombudsman Service, 'Consumer Factsheet on Payment Protection Insurance' (March 2014) www.financial-ombudsman.org.uk/publications/factsheets/payment-protection-insurance.pdf accessed 21 February 2018

Financial Reporting Council, 'The UK Corporate Governance Code' (April 2016) www.frc.org.uk/directors/corporate-governance-and-stewardship/uk-corporate-governance-code accessed 7 January 2019

Financial Services Authority, 'Principles for Business' (PRIN) in the FSA Handbook www.handbook.fca.org.uk/handbook/PRIN/2/1.html accessed 7 January 2019

Financial Services Authority, 'Global Shadow Banking Monitoring Report 2015' (November 2015) www.fsb.org/2015/11/global-shadow-banking-monitoring-report-2015/ accessed 21 December 2018

Financial Services Authority, 'The Regulation and Supervision of Benchmarks' Policy Statement PS 13/6 (March 2013) www.fsa.gov.uk/static/pubs/policy/ps13-06.pdf accessed 18 May 2018

Financial Services Authority, 'Retail Distribution Review: Independent and Restricted Advice' (Finalised Guidance) (June 2012) www.fca.org.uk/publication/finalised-guidance/fg12-15.pdf accessed 21 February 2018

Financial Services Authority, 'Six Sentenced for Insider Dealing' (27 July 2012) www.fsa.gov.uk/library/communication/pr/2012/080.shtml accessed 17 May 2018

Financial Services Authority, 'The Failure of the Royal Bank of Scotland – FSA Board Report' (December 2011) www.fca.org.uk/publication/corporate/fsa-rbs.pdf accessed 21 February 2018

Financial Services Authority, 'The Assessment and Redress of Payment Protection Insurance Complaints' (August 2010) Policy Statement 10/12 www.fca.org.uk/publication/policy/ps10_12.pdf accessed 21 February 2018

Financial Services Authority, 'The Turner Review – A Regulatory Response to the Global Banking Crisis' (March 2009) www.fsa.gov.uk/pubs/other/turner_review.pdf accessed 21 February 2018

Financial Services Authority, 'Financial Stability and Depositor Protection: Strengthening the Framework' (January 2008) www.fsa.gov.uk/pubs/cp/JointCP_banking_stability.pdf accessed 21 February 2018

Financial Services Authority, 'Financial Stability and Depositor Protection: FSA Responsibilities' (CP08/23) (December 2008) www.fsa.gov.uk/pubs/cp/cp08_23.pdf accessed 21 February 2018

Financial Stability Board, Task Force on Climate-Related Financial Disclosures, 'Recommendations of the Task Force on Climate-Related Financial Disclosures' (2016)

Financial Stability Board, 'Global Shadow Banking Monitoring Report 2015' (November 2015) www.fsb.org/wp-content/uploads/global-shadow-banking-monitoring-report-2015.pdf accessed 21 February 2018

Financial Stability Board, *Summary of Findings of TLAC Impact Assessment Studies* (November 2015) Basel, BIS www.fsb.org/2015/11/summary-of-findings-from-the-tlac-impact-assessment-studies/ accessed 21 December 2018

Financial Stability Board 'Principles on Loss-Absorbing and Recapitalisation Capacity of G-SIBs in Resolution; Total Loss-Absorbing Capacity (TLAC) Term Sheet' (Report, 2015)

Financial Stability Board, 'Guidance on Supervisory Interaction with Financial Institutions on Risk Culture: A Framework for Assessing Risk Culture' (April 2014) www.fsb.org/wp-content/uploads/140407.pdf accessed 21 February 2018

Financial Stability Board, International Monetary Fund, Bank for International Settlements, 'Macroprudential Policy Tools and Frameworks – Progress Report to G20' (27 October 2011) www.imf.org/external/np/g20/pdf/102711.pdf accessed 21 February 2018

Financial Stability Board, 'Key Attributes of Effective Resolution Regimes for Financial Institutions' (October 2011) www.fsb.org/wp-content/uploads/r_111104cc.pdf accessed 21 February 2018

Financial Stability Board, 'Shadow Banking: Strengthening Oversight and Regulation – Recommendations of the Financial Stability Board' (October 2011) www.fsb.org/wp-content/uploads/r_111027a.pdf accessed 21 February 2018

Financial Stability Board and International Monetary Fund, Report of the Financial Stability Board to the G20, 'The Financial Crisis and Information Gaps' (June 2010) www.fsb.org/wp-content/uploads/r_100627c.pdf accessed 21 February 2018

Financial Stability Board, 'Implementing OTC Derivatives Markets Reform' (25 October 2010).

Financial Stability Board, 'Declaration on Strengthening the Financial System – London Summit' (2 April 2009) www.fsb.org/wp-content/uploads/london_summit_declaration_on_str_financial_system.pdf accessed 21 February 2018

Financial Stability Board, 'Overview of Progress in Implementing the London Summit Recommendations for Strengthening Financial Stability' Report of the Financial Stability Board to G20 Leaders (25 September 2009) www.fsb.org/wp-content/uploads/r_090925a.pdf accessed 21 February 2018

Financial Stability Board, 'FSB Principles for Sound Compensation Practices: Implementation Standards' (25 September 2009) www.fsb.org/wp-content/uploads/r_090925c.pdf accessed 21 February 2018

Financial Stability Board, 'Progress since the Pittsburgh Summit in Implementing the G20 Recommendations for Strengthening Financial Stability' Report of the Financial Stability Board to G20 Finance Ministers and Governors (7 November 2009) www.fsb.org/wp-content/uploads/r_091107a.pdf accessed 21 February 2018

Financial Stability Forum, 'FSF Principles for Cross-Border Cooperation on Crisis Management' (2 April 2009) www.fsb.org/wp-content/uploads/r_0904c.pdf accessed 21 February 2018

Financial Stability Forum, 'Report of the Financial Stability Forum on Addressing Procyclicality in the Financial System' (2 April 2009) www.fsb.org/wp-content/uploads/r_0904a.pdf accessed 21 February 2018

Financial Stability Forum, 'Report of the Financial Stability Forum on Enhancing Market and Institutional Resilience' (7 April 2008) www.fsb.org/wp-content/uploads/r_0804.pdf accessed 21 February 2018

Financial Stability Forum, 'Report of the Follow-up Group on Incentives to Foster Implementation Standards' (31 August 2000) www.fsb.org/wp-content/uploads/r_0009.pdf accessed 21 February 2018

Financial Supervisory Authority, 'FSA Takes Action to Help Investors with Lehman-Backed Structured Products' (press release, FSA/PN/144/2009) (27 October 2009) www.fsa.gov.uk/pages/Library/Communication/PR/2009/144.shtml accessed 21 February 2018

Fixed Income Currencies and Commodities (FICC) Markets Standards Board, 'New Issue Process Standard for the Fixed Income Markets' (2 May 2017) www.fmsb.com/wp-content/uploads/2017/04/FMSB_NewIssuesProcess_FIMarkets_2-May-FINAL.pdf accessed 21 February 2018

Fixed Income Currencies and Commodities (FICC) Markets Standards Board , 'Statement of Good Practice for FICC Market Participants: Conduct Training' (December 2016) www.femr-mpp.co.uk/wp-content/uploads/2016/12/16-12-08-SoGP-Conduct-Training_FINAL.pdf accessed 21 February 2018

Fixed Income Currencies and Commodities (FICC) Markets Standards Board, 'Surveillance Core Principles for FICC Market Participants: Statement of Good Practice for Surveillance in Foreign Exchange Markets' (December 2016) www.femr-mpp.co.uk/wp-content/uploads/2016/12/16-12-08-SoGP_Surveillance-in-FX-Markets_FINAL.pdf accessed 21 February 2018

Galati G and Moessner R, 'Macroprudential Policy – A Literature Review' (February 2011) BIS Working Papers No. 337 www.bis.org/publ/work337.pdf accessed 21 February 2018

Garcia G and Prast H, 'Depositor and Investor Protection in the EU and the Netherlands: Past, Present and Future' (2004) De Nederlandsche Bank Occasional Studies Vol. 2/Nr. 2 www.dnb.nl/en/binaries/OSVolNr2_tcm47-146642.pdf accessed 21 February 2018

Ghose R, *Bank of the Future: The ABCs of Digital Disruption in Finance* (Citi GPS: Global Perspectives & Solutions, March 2018), 60

Green, PJ and Jennings-Mares JC, 'Regulatory Reform in Europe: What to Expect in 2014' (Client Alert, Morrison & Foerster, 2014), 3

Greenspan A, 'Risk Transfer and Financial Stability', Federal Rserve Bank of Chicago's Annual Conference on Bank Structure, Chicago, IL USA (5 May 2005)

G10, 'Report on Consolidation in the Financial Sector' (January 2001) www.bis.org/publ/gten05.pdf accessed 21 February 2018

G20 Green Finance Study Group, 'G20 Green Finance Synthesis Report' (5 September 2016) www.unepinquiry.org/wp-content/uploads/2016/09/Synthesis_Report_Full_EN.pdf accessed 21 February 2018

G20, 'G20 Energy Efficiency Investor Statement' (2015) UNEP Finance Initiative www .unepfi.org/fileadmin/documents/EnergyEfficiencyStatement.pdf accessed 30 August 2017

G20, 'G20 Leaders Statement: The Pittsburgh Summit' (2009) Pittsburgh Summit, University of Toronto G20 Research Group www.g20.utoronto.ca/2009/2009communique0925 .html accessed 16 May 2018

G20, 'The G20 Seoul Summit Leaders' Declaration' (2009) Seoul Summit, University of Toronto G20 Research Group www.g20.utoronto.ca/2010/g20seoul.html accessed 30 August 2017

G30, 'Shadow Banking and Capital Markets: Risks and Opportunities' (November 2016) http://group30.org/images/uploads/publications/ShadowBankingCapitalMarkets_ G30.pdf accessed 26 March 2018

G30, 'Banking Conduct and Culture – A Call for Sustained and Comprehensive Reform' (July 2015) www.group30.org/images/uploads/publications/G30_ BankingConductandCulture.pdf accessed 21 February 2018

G30, 'A New Paradigm: Financial Institution Boards and Supervisors' (October 2013) www.group30.org/images/uploads/publications/G30_NewParadigm.pdf accessed 21 February 2018

G30, 'The Structure of Financial Supervision: Approaches and Challenges in a Global Marketplace' (Group of Thirty report, 2008)

Hawkins J and Turner P, 'Managing Foreign Debt and Liquidity Risks in Emerging Economies: An Overview' (September 2000) BIS Policy Papers No. 8 www.bis.org/publ/ plcy08a.pdf accessed 21 February 2018

Herbert Smith Freehills, 'A Changing Landscape: Regulatory Developments in the Distribution of Retail Investment Products' (2010) www.lexology.com/library/detail .aspx?g=9833fe22-38b4-4b83-a8b9-e30341b8e0fc accessed 2 March 2018

HM Treasury, 'Budget 2015' (HC 1093, March 2015) https://assets.publishing.service.gov .uk/government/uploads/system/uploads/attachment_data/file/416330/47881_Budget_ 2015_Web_Accessible.pdf accessed 12 June 2018

HM Treasury, 'Transposition of the Markets in Financial Instruments Directive II' (March 2015) www.gov.uk/government/uploads/system/uploads/attachment_data/file/418281/ PU_1750_MiFID_II_26.03.15.pdf accessed 21 February 2018

HM Treasury, Bank of England, Financial Conduct Authority 'Fair and Effective Markets Review: Final Report' (June 2015) www.bankofengland.co.uk/-/media/boe/files/report/ 2015/fair-and-effective-markets-review-final-report.pdf accessed 21 February 2018

HM Treasury, 'Senior Managers and Certification Regime: Extension to All FSMA Authorised Persons' (October 2015) www.gov.uk/government/uploads/system/uploads/ attachment_data/file/468328/SMCR_policy_paper_final_15102015.pdf accessed 21 February 2018

HM Treasury, 'Review of HM Treasury's Response to the Financial Crisis' (March 2012) www.gov.uk/government/uploads/system/uploads/attachment_data/file/220506/review_fincrisis_response_290312.pdf accessed 21 February 2018

HM Treasury, Department for Business Innovation & Skills, 'Banking Reform: Delivering Stability and Supporting a Sustainable Economy' (14 June 2012) www.gov.uk/government/uploads/system/uploads/attachment_data/file/32556/whitepaper_banking_reform_140512.pdf accessed 18 March 2018

HM Treasury, 'The Wheatley Review of LIBOR: Final Report' (September 2012) https://assets.publishing.service.gov.uk/government/uploads/system/uploads/attachment_data/file/191762/wheatley_review_libor_finalreport_280912.pdf accessed 18 May 2018

HM Treasury, 'Sound Banking: Delivering Reform' (October 2012) www.gov.uk/government/uploads/system/uploads/attachment_data/file/211866/icb_banking_reform_bill.pdf accessed 21 March 2018

HM Treasury, 'A New Approach to Financial Regulation: Judgment, Focus, Stability' (July 2010) Report presented by HM Treasury to Parliament by Command of Her Majestywww.gov.uk/government/consultations/a-new-approach-to-financial-regulation-judgement-focus-and-stability accessed 7 January 2019

HM Treasury, 'Financial Services and Markets Bill: A Consultation Document' (July 1998) on file with author

Honohan P and Klingebiel D, 'Controlling the Fiscal Costs of Banking Crises' (September 2010) World Bank Policy Research Working Paper WPS 2441 http://documents.worldbank.org/curated/en/109971468741329122/pdf/multi-page.pdf accessed 21 February 2018

Hopper M and Buckingham P, 'A Changing Landscape: Regulatory Developments in the Distribution of Retail Investment Products' (Herbert Smith Freehills key issues and themes, Herbert Smith Gleiss Lutz Stibbe 2010) www.lexology.com/library/detail.aspx?g=9833fe22-38b4-4b83-a8b9-e30341b8e0fc accessed 20 December 2018

House of Commons Treasury Committee, 'The Run on the Rock: Fifth Report of Session 2007–08' (volume I, report, together with formal minutes, The Stationery Office Limited 26 January 2008) https://publications.parliament.uk/pa/cm200708/cmselect/cmtreasy/56/56i.pdf accessed 19 December 2018

House of Commons Treasury Committee, 'The Run on the Rock: Fifth Report of Session 2007–08' (volume II, oral and written evidence, The Stationery Office Limited 1 February 2008) https://publications.parliament.uk/pa/cm200708/cmselect/cmtreasy/56/56ii.pdf accessed 19 December 2018

House of Lords European Union Committee, 'The Post-Crisis EU Financial Regulatory Framework: Do the Pieces Fit?' (2 February 2015) 5th Report of Session 2014–2015 Paper 103 publications.parliament.uk/pa/ld201415/ldselect/ldeucom/103/103.pdf accessed 21 February 2018

House of Lords European Union Committee 'The Future of EU Financial Regulation and Supervision' (17 June 2009) 14th Report of Session 2008–09 Vol. 1 www.publications.parliament.uk/pa/ld200809/ldselect/ldeucom/106/106i.pdf accessed 21 February 2018

House of Lords, House of Commons, Parliamentary Commission on Banking Standards, 'First Report of Session 2012–13' (21 December 2012) Volume I: Report, together with formal minutes https://publications.parliament.uk/pa/jt201213/jtselect/jtpcbs/98/98 .pdf and Volume II: Written evidence https://publications.parliament.uk/pa/jt201213/ jtselect/jtpcbs/98/98vw.pdf accessed 22 March 2018

House of Lords, House of Commons, Joint Committee on the Draft Financial Services Bill, Uncorrected Transcript of Oral Evidence Andrew Procter, Sally Dewar and Robert Charnley (8 November 2011) www.parliament.uk/documents/joint-committees/Draft-Financial-Services-Bill/ucjcdfsb081111ev12.pdf accessed 21 February 2018

House of Lords, House of Commons, Joint Committee on the Draft Financial Services Bill, 'Draft Financial Services Bill – Session 2010–12' Report, together with formal minutes and appendices (December 2011) www.publications.parliament.uk/pa/jt201012/jtselect/ jtdraftfin/236/236.pdf or www.publications.parliament.uk/pa/jt201012/jtselect/ jtdraftfin/236/23602.htm accessed 21 February 2018

House of Lords, House of Commons, Parliamentary Commission on Banking Standards, 'An Accident Waiting to Happen': The Failure of HBOS' Fourth Report of Session 2012–13 (4 April 2013) www.publications.parliament.uk/pa/jt201213/jtselect/jtpcbs/144/144 .pdf accessed 21 February 2018

House of Lords, House of Commons, Parliamentary Commission on Banking Standards, 'Changing Banking for Good' Final Report (19 June 2013) www.parliament.uk/business/ committees/committees-a-z/joint-select/professional-standards-in-the-banking-industry/news/changing-banking-for-good-report/, Volume I: 'Summary, and Conclusions and Recommendations' www.parliament.uk/documents/banking-commission/Banking-final-report-volume-i.pdf and Volume II: 'Chapters 1 to 11 and Annexes, together with formal minutes' www.parliament.uk/documents/ banking-commission/Banking-final-report-vol-ii.pdf accessed 21 February 2018

Independent Commission on Banking, 'Interim Report: Consultation on Reform Options' (April 2011) https://s3-eu-west-1.amazonaws.com/htcdn/Interim-Report-110411 .pdf accessed 21 February 2018

Independent Commission on Banking, 'Final Report – Recommendations' (September 2011) http://webarchive.nationalarchives.gov.uk/20131003105424/https://hmt-sanctions.s3.amazonaws.com/icb%20final%20report/icb%2520final%2520report% 5B1%5D.pdf accessed 21 February 2018

Institute of International Finance, 'Regtech in Financial Services: Technology Solutions for Compliance and Reporting' (IIF, March 2016) www.iif.com/system/files/regtech_in_ financial_services_-_solutions_for_compliance_and_reporting.pdf accessed 12 June 2018

Institute of International Finance, 'Reform in the Financial Services Industry: Strengthening Practices for a More Stable System' (December 2009) www.iif.com/ system/files/iifreport_reformfinancialservicesindustry_1209.pdf accessed 21 February 2018

International Association of Deposit Insurers, 'About IADI' (IADI Objectives, Bank for International Settlements 2018) www.iadi.org/en/about-iadi/ accessed 19 December 2018

International Association of Deposit Insurers, 'IADI Core Principles for Effective Deposit Insurance Systems' (IADI revised core principles, Bank for International Settlements November 2014) 39 www.iadi.org/en/assets/File/Core%20Principles/ cprevised2014nov.pdf accessed 19 December 2018

International Monetary Fund, 'Global Financial Stability Report October 2017: Is Growth at Risk?' (October 2017) www.imf.org/en/Publications/GFSR/Issues/2017/09/27/global-financial-stability-report-october-2017 accessed 21 February 2018

International Monetary Fund, 'World Economic Outlook, October 2017 – Seeking Sustainable Growth: Short-Term Recovery, Long-Term Challenges' (October 2017) www.imf.org/en/Publications/WEO/Issues/2017/09/19/world-economic-outlook-october-2017 accessed 21 February 2018

International Monetary Fund, 'IMF-FSB Early Warning Exercise' Factsheet (ordered November 2008, current as of October 2017) www.imf.org/About/Factsheets/Sheets/ 2016/08/01/16/29/IMF-FSB-Early-Warning-Exercise accessed 21 February 2018

International Monetary Fund, 'Financing for Development: Revisiting the Monterrey Consensus' IMF Policy Paper (July 2015) www.imf.org/external/np/pp/eng/2015/ 061515.pdf accessed 21 February 2018

International Monetary Fund, 'Macroeconomic Developments and Prospects in Low-Income Developing Countries: 2015' (19 November 2015) www.imf.org/external/np/pp/ eng/2015/111915.pdf accessed 21 February 2018

International Monetary Fund, 'Key Aspects of Macro-Prudential Policy' (10 June 2013) www.imf.org/external/np/pp/eng/2013/061013b.pdf accessed 21 February 2018

International Monetary Fund, 'Initial Lessons of the Crisis for the Global Architecture and the IMF' (18 February 2009) www.imf.org/external/np/pp/eng/2009/021809.pdf accessed 21 February 2018

International Monetary Fund, 'Global Financial Stability Report – Navigating the Financial Challenges Ahead' (October 2009) World Economic and Financial Surveys www.imf .org/external/pubs/ft/gfsr/2009/02/pdf/text.pdf accessed 21 February 2018

International Monetary Fund, 'Global Financial Stability Report – Market Developments and Issues' (April 2006) www.imf.org/en/Publications/GFSR/Issues/2016/12/31/Market-Developments-and-Issues3 accessed 21 February 2018

International Organization of Securities Commissions, 'Objectives and Principles of Securities Regulation' (June 2010) www.iosco.org/library/pubdocs/pdf/IOSCOPD323 .pdf accessed 21 February 2018

International Organization of Securities Commissions, Technical Committee, June 2009, *Hedge Funds Oversight – Final Report* www.fsb.org/source/iosco accessed 21 February 2018

Ita A, Head of Group Economic Performance and Capital Optimization, UBS AG, Presentation at the University of Zurich Finance Research Program (9 June 2017)

Kupšys K, 'The index-linked bond case involving Luminor (ex. DNB) is referred to the Court of Justice of the European Union' (press release, sazininga-bankininkyste, 2017)

Laeven L and Valencia F, 'Systemic Banking Crises Database: An Update' (2012) IMF Working Paper WP/12/163 www.imf.org/en/Publications/WP/Issues/2016/12/31/ Systemic-Banking-Crises-Database-An-Update-26015 accessed 21 February 2018

Lloyds Bank, 'Underwriting Byelaw' www.lloyds.com/~/media/files/the-market/operating-at-lloyds/regulation/acts-and-byelaws/byelaws/2014_feb_underwriting-byelaw.pdf? la=en accessed 21 February 2018

Macey JR and O'Hara M, 'The Corporate Governance of Banks' (April 2003) 9 Federal Reserve Bank of New York Economic Policy Review 1 www.newyorkfed.org/ medialibrary/media/research/epr/2003/EPRvol9no1.pdf accessed 21 February 2018

Mehran H, 'Introduction – Critical Themes in Corporate Governance' (April 2003) 9 Federal Reserve Bank of New York Economic Policy Review 1 www.newyorkfed .org/medialibrary/media/research/epr/2003/EPRvol9no1.pdf accessed 21 February 2018

Monteiro DP and Priftis R, 'Bank Lending Constraints in the Euro Area', Brussels: European Commission, 2017

Morgan Stanley, Global Sustainable + Responsible Investment Research. 'Addressing Climate Change and the Investment Implications – A Primer on Climate Change' (August 2015) (on file with author)

National Bank of Belgium, 'Structural Banking Reforms in Belgium: Final Report' (July 2013) www.nbb.be/doc/ts/publications/NBBReport/2013/ StructuralBankingReformsEN.pdf accessed 21 March 2018

Office of the Comptroller of the Currency 'Oil and Gas Exploration and Production Lending' (2016) OCC Comptroller's handbook booklet, Office of the Comptroller of the Currency occ.gov/publications/publications-by-type/comptrollers-handbook/pub-ch-og.pdf accessed 30 August 2017

Oliver Wyman report, 'The Impact of the UK's Exit from the EU on the UK-Based Financial Services Sector' (2016) http://www.oliverwyman.com/our-expertise/insights/2016/oct/ The-impact-of-Brexit-on-the-UK-based-Financial-Services-sector.html

Organisation for Economic Co-operation and Development 'Climate and Carbon – Aligning Prices and Policy' (2013) www.oecdlibrary.org/environment-and-sustainable-development/cimate-and-carbon_5k3z11hjg6r7-en accessed 21 February 2018

Organisation for Economic Co-operation and Development, International Network on Financial Education (2011) 'Measuring Financial Literacy: Questionnaire and Guidance Notes for Conducting an Internationally Comparable Survey of Financial Literacy' (OECD financial literacy questionnaire 2011), 3 www.oecd.org/finance/financial-education/49319977.pdf accessed 21 December 2018

Padoa Schioppa T, 'Central Banks and Financial Stability. Exploring a Land in Between' (October 2002) European Central Bank Second Central Banking Conference 'The Transformation of the European Financial System', 269–310 www.ecb.europa.eu/pub/ pdf/other/transformationeuropeanfinancialsystemen.pdf accessed 21 February 2018

Pozsar Z, Adrian T, Ashcraft A and Boesky H, 'Shadow Banking' (July 2010) Federal Reserve Bank of New York Staff Report No. 458 www.newyorkfed.org/medialibrary/ media/research/staff_reports/sr458_July_2010_version.pdf accessed 5 March 2018

PricewaterhouseCoopers, 'Asset Management 2020: A Brave New World' (2014) https://www.pwc.com/gx/en/asset-management/publications/pdfs/pwc-asset-management-2020-a-brave-new-world-final.pdf accessed 22 March 2018

Rhodes C, 'Financial Services: Contribution to the UK Economy' (House of Commons briefing paper 6193, 25 April 2018) 5, http://researchbriefings.files.parliament.uk/documents/SN06193/SN06193.pdf accessed 1 March 2019

Securities and Exchange Commission, 'Prohibitions and Restrictions on Proprietary Trading and Certain Interests In, and Relationships With, Hedge Funds and Private Equity Funds' (SEC final rule, Release No. BHCA-1; File No. S7-41-11, Securities and Exchange Commission 2013) www.sec.gov/rules/final/2013/bhca-1.pdf accessed 19 December 2018

Shvetsov SA, 'To Joint-Stock Companies, State Corporations and Companies: On Corporate Governance Code' (2014) Letter of the First Deputy Governor of the Central Bank of the Russian Federation No. 06–52/2463, Bank of Russia www.cbr.ru/StaticHtml/File/12105/Inf_apr_1014_en.pdf accessed 30 August 2017

Single Resolution Board, 'Minimum Requirement for Own Funds and Eligible Liabilities (MREL): SRB Policy for 2017 and Next Steps' (Report, 2017), 10

South African Reserve Bank, 'Guidance Note 9/2012 Issued in Terms of s 6(5) of the Banks Act, 1990 – Capital Framework for South Africa based on the Basel III Framework' www.resbank.co.za/Lists/News%20and%20Publications/Attachments/5154/G9%20of%202012.pdf accessed 21 February 2018

South African Reserve Bank, South Africa's implementation of Basel II and Basel III www.resbank.co.za/RegulationAndSupervision/BankSupervision/TheBaselCapitalAccord%28Basel%20II%29/Pages/AccordImplementationForum%28AIF%29.aspx accessed 21 February 2018

Sullivan R, 'Fiduciary Duty in the 21st Century' (2015) Report, UNEP Inquiry www.unepfi.org/fileadmin/documents/fiduciary_duty_21st_century.pdf accessed 30 August 2017

Sustainable Banking Network (SBN), 'Global Progress Report' (February 2018) www.ifc.org/wps/wcm/connect/topics_ext_content/ifc_external_corporate_site/sustainability-at-ifc/publications/publications_report_sbnglobalprogress2018 accessed 21 December 2018

Swiss National Bank, 'Financial Stability Report 2016' www.snb.ch/en/mmr/reference/stabrep_2016/source/stabrep_2016.en.pdf accessed 5 March 2018

Swiss Re Sigma, 'Natural Catastrophes and Man-Made Disasters in 2014: Convective and Winter Storms Generate Most Losses' Study No. 2/2015 (2015) http://media.swissre.com/documents/sigma2_2015_en_final.pdf accessed 21 February 2018

Task Force on Climate-Related Financial Disclosures, 'Recommendations of the Task Force on Climate-Related Financial Disclosures' (2016) Financial Stability Board www.fsb.org/what-we-do/policy-development/additional-policy-areas/developing-climate-related-financial-disclosures/ accessed 30 August 2017

Tripartite Group of Bank, Securities and Insurance Regulators, 'The Supervision of Financial Conglomerates' Report (July 1995) www.bis.org/publ/bcbs20.pdf accessed 21 February 2018

UN Principles for Responsible Investment, 'Green Infrastructure Investment Coalition Launched at COP21' (10 December 2015 www.unpri.org/news/green-infrastructure-investment-coalition-launched-at-COP21/ accessed 30 August 2017

United Nations Environment Programme, 'Greening the Banking System: Taking Stock of G20 Green Banking Market Practice' UNEP Inquiry Working Paper 16/12 (2016) www .unepinquiry.org/publication/greening-the-banking-system/ accessed 21 February 2018

United States Department of State, International Narcotics Control Strategy Report Bureau for International Narcotics and Law Enforcement Affairs, March 2003 Report, 'Money Laundering and Financial Crimes'

UNODC, 'Estimating Illicit Financial Flows Resulting from Drug Trafficking and Other Transnational Organized Crimes' (October 2011),18www.unodc.org/documents/data-and-analysis/Studies/Illicit_financial_flows_2011_web.pdf accessed 21 December 2018

Van Roosebeke B, 'EU Deposit Guarantee Scheme in the European Parliament: Some Progress, Need for Improvement' (cepAdhoc 2016) https://www.cep.eu/fileadmin/user_upload/cep.eu/Studien/cepAdhoc_Einlagensicherung/cepAdhoc_Deposit_Guarantee_Scheme.pdf accessed 19 December 2018

Zhou J, Rutledge V, Bossu W, Dobler M, Jassaud N and Moore M, 'From Bail-Out to Bail-In: Mandatory Debt Restructuring of Systemic Financial Institutions' (2012) IMF Staff Discussion Note 6

UNITED NATIONS PARIS CLIMATE CHANGE AGREEMENT

Walport, M, 'Fintech Futures: The U.K. as a World Leader in Financial Technologies' (Report by the UK Government Chief Scientific Adviser, 13 March 2015), 5 ff https://bravenewcoin.com/assets/Industry-Reports-2015/UK-Gov-Fintech-Futures.pdf accessed 12 June 2018

World Bank, 'World Development Report 2014 – Risk and Opportunity – Managing Risk for Development' (2013) http://siteresources.worldbank.org/EXTNWDR2013/Resources/8258024–1352909193861/8936935–1356011448215/8986901–1380046989056/WDR-2014_Complete_Report.pdf accessed 21 February 2018

World Economic Forum, 'The Global Risks Report 2016 – 11th edition' (2016) www3.weforum.org/docs/GRR/WEF_GRR16.pdf accessed 21 February 2018

JOURNAL ARTICLES AND WORKING PAPER SERIES

Adams RMH, 'Is Corporate Governance Different for Bank Holding Companies?' (April 2003) 9 *FRBNY Economic Policy Review* 1 123

Akerlof GA, 'The Market for "Lemons": Quality Uncertainty and the Market Mechanism' (1970) 84 *The Quarterly Journal of Economics* 3 488–500

Alchian A and Demsetz H, 'Production, Information Costs, and Economic Organization' (1972) 62 *American Economic Review* 5 777–795

Alexander K 'Reforming European Financial Supervision: Adapting EU Institutions to Market Structures', *European Law Academy Forum* (2011) 229–252

Alexander K, 'Global Financial Standard Setting, the G10 Committees, and International Economic Law' (2009) 34 *Brooklyn Journal of International Law* 3 861

Anabtawi I and Schwarcz SL, 'Regulating Ex Post: How Law Can Address the Inevitability of Financial Failure' (2013) 92 *Texas Law Review* 75–131

Anabtawi I and Schwarcz SL, 'Regulating Towards an Analytical Framework' (2011) 86 *Notre Dame Law Review* 1349–1412

Arner DW, Barberis J and Buckley RP, 'FinTech, RegTech, and the Reconceptualization of Financial Regulation' (2017) 37 *Northwestern Journal of International Law and Business* 371

Aronson BE, 'Reconsidering the Importance of Law in Japanese Corporate Governance: Evidence from the Daiwa Bank Shareholder Derivative Case' (2003) 36 *Cornell International Law Journal* 11

Awrey D, Blair W and Kershaw D, 'Between Law and Markets: Is There a Role for Culture and Ethics in Financial Regulation?' (2013) 38 *Delaware Journal of Corporate Law* 1, 191–245

Awrey D, 'Complexity, Innovation and the Regulation of Modern Financial Markets' (2012) 2 *Harvard Business Law Review* 235–294

Bebchuk L, Cremers M and Peyer U, 'The CEO Pay Slice' (2010) The Harvard John M. Olin Center for Law, Economics, and Business Discussion Paper No. 679 9/2010

Bentson GJ, 'Universal Banking' (1994) 8 *Journal of Economic Perspectives* 3 121–143

Berger A, De Young R, Flannery M, Lee D and Öztekin Ö, 'How Do Large Banking Organizations Manage Their Capital Ratios' (2008) 34 *Journal of Financial Service Research* 123–149

Bierman L and Fraser DR, 'The "Source of Strength" Doctrine: Formulating the Future of America's Financial Markets' (1993) 12 *Annual Review of Banking Law* 269–316

Blundell-Wignall A, Atkinson A and Lee SH, 'The Current Financial Crisis: Causes and Policy Issues', (2008) 95 *OECD Journal of Financial Market Trends* 2, 1–21

Boyd AS, 'Bail-Ins – Just Another Self-Fulfilling Prophecy?' (2012) 27 *Banking & Finance Law Review* 559

Brownbridge M and Kirkpatrick C, 'Financial Regulation in Developing Countries' (2000) Finance and Development Research Program Working Papers Series, Paper No. 12/2006

Brunnermeier M, Crockett A, Goodhart C, Persaud A and Shin H, 'The Fundamental Principles of Financial Regulation' (2009) *Geneva Reports on the World Economy* 11 (International Centre for Banking and Monetary Studies)

Claessens S, 'An Overview of Macroprudential Policy Tools' (2015) 7 *Annual Review of Financial Economics* 397–422

Coats JM and Herbert J, 'Endogenous Steroids and Financial Risk-Taking on a London Trading Floor' (2008) 105 *Proceedings of the National Academy of Sciences* 16 6167–6172

Colaert, Verle, 'Deposit Guarantee Schemes in Europe: Is the Banking Union in Need of a Third Pillar?' (2014) *European Company and Financial Law Review* 2, 27

Crockett A, 'Why is Financial Stability a Goal of Public Policy?' (1997) Proceedings – Economic Policy Symposium – Jackson Hole, Federal Reserve Bank of Kansas City, 7–36

Darbellay A and Reymond M, 'Le régime de responsabilité civile en matière d'émissions publiques de jetons digitaux (ICO)' (2018) *Revue suisse de droit des affaires et du marché financier* 1 48–66

de Serière V and van der Houwen D, "No Creditor Worse Off" in Case of Bank Resolution: Food for Litigation?' (2016) 7 *Journal of International Banking Law and Regulation Issue* 7 376

Deakin S, 'What Directors Do (and Fail to Do): Some Comparative Notes on Board Structure and Corporate Governance' (2010) 55 *New York Law School Law Review* 525

Deutsche Bundesbank, 'Monthly Report' (2016) 68, 74

Diamond DW and Dybvig PH, 'Bank Runs, Deposit Insurance, and Liquidity' (1983) 91 *Journal of Political Economy* 3, 401–419

Duncan A and Nolan C, 'Objectives and Challenges of Macroprudential Policy' (September 2015) www.gla.ac.uk/media/media_427189_en.pdf accessed 23 May 2018

Eichengreen B and Bordo MD, 'Crises Now and Then: What Lessons from the Last Era of Financial Globalization?' (2002) NBER Working Paper No. 8716

Eisenberg M, 'The Structure of Corporation Law' (1989) 89 *Columbia Law Review* 1461–1525

Ellis DM and Flannery MJ, 'Does the Debt Market Assess Large Banks' Risks?' (1992) 30 *Journal of Monetary Economics* 481–502

Ferran E, 'Bailouts of Ailing Banks Through Capital Injections' (2008) unpublished paper on file with author

Ferran, E and Alexander K, 'Can Soft Law Bodies be Effective? The Special Case of the European Systemic Risk Board' (2011) 12 *The European Law Review* 751–777

Ferrarini G and Ungureanu MC, 'Economics, Politics, and the International Principles for Sound Compensation Practices: An Analysis of Executive Pay at European Banks' (2011) 64 *Vanderbilt Law Review* 2 431–502

Flannery MJ, 'Pricing Deposit Insurance when the Insurer Measures Bank Risk with Error' (1991) *Journal of Banking and Finance* 975–998

Franke J, Mosk T and Schnebel E, 'Fair Retail Banking: How to Prevent Mis-selling by Banks' (6 July 2016) Sustainable Architecture for Finance in Europe White Paper No. 39 http://safe-frankfurt.de/fileadmin/user_upload/editor_common/Policy_Center/Franke-Mosk-Schnebel-Fair_Retail_Banking.pdf accessed 18 March 2018

Gevurtz FA, 'The Role of Corporate Law in Preventing a Financial Crisis: Reflections on "In Re Citigroup Inc. Shareholder Derivative Litigation"' (2010) 23 *Pac McGeorge Global Business & Development Law Journal* 113 available at SSRN: https://ssrn.com/abstract=1544927 accessed 18 March 2018

Goodhart CAE, 'Bank Resolution in Comparative Perspective: What Lessons for Europe?' (2013) unpublished paper on file with author

Goodhart CAE, 'The Macro-Prudential Authority: Powers, Scope and Accountability' (2011) LSE Financial Markets Group Paper Series, Special Paper 203

Goodhart CAE, Hofmann B and Segoviano M, 'Bank Regulation and Macroeconomic Fluctuations' (2004) 20 *Oxford Review of Economic Policy* 4 591–615

Gorton G and Metrick A, 'Securitized Banking and the Run on Repo' (2009) NBER Working Paper No. 15223

Handorf WC, 'Financial Implications of Transitioning to the Wall Street Reform and Consumer Protection Act 2010' (2017) 18 *Journal of Banking Regulation* 1 1–14

Handorf WC, 'The Cost of Bank Liquidity' (2012) 15 *Journal of Banking Regulation* 1 1–13

Hellmann TF, Murdock KC and Stiglitz JE, 'Liberalization, Moral Hazard in Banking, and Prudential Regulation: Are Capital Requirements Enough?' (2000) 90 *American Economic Review* 1 147–165

Hornbeck R, 'The Enduring Impact of the American Dust Bowl: Short and Long Run Adjustments to Environmental Catastrophe' (2012) 102 *American Economic Review* 4 1477–1507

Jackson HE, 'The Expanding Obligations of Financial Holding Companies' (1994) 107 *Harvard Law Review* 507 517–525

Jackson P, 'Amending the Basel Capital Accord' (unpublished paper, Cambridge Endowment for Research in Finance Seminar, 22 January 2000)

Kleftouri N, 'Rethinking UK and EU Bank Deposit Insurance' (2013) 24 *European Business Law Review* 1 95–125

Klein MA, 'A Theory of the Banking Firm' (May 1971) 3 *Journal of Money, Credit and Banking* 2.1 205–218

Krauskopf B, Langner J and Rötting M, 'Some Critical Aspects of the European Banking Union' (2014) 29 *Banking & Finance Law Review*' 2 241–269

La Porta R, Lopez-de-Silanes F, Shleifer A and Vishny R, 'Investor Protection and Corporate Governance' (2000) 58 *Journal of Financial Economics* 3–27

Lambert C, Noth F and Schüwer U, 'How Do Banks React to Catastrophic Events? Evidence from Hurricane Katrina' (2015, revised 2017) https://papers.ssrn.com/sol3/papers.cfm?abstract_id=2585521 accessed 18 March 2018

La Porta R et al., 'Investor Protection and Corporate Governance' (2000) 58 Journal of Financial Economics 3–27

Lastra R, 'The European Insolvency and Reorganisation Regime' (2008) unpublished paper on file with author

Levine R, 'Bank Regulation and Supervision' (2005) NBER Reporter: Research Summary Fall 2005

Levine R, 'Finance and Growth: Theory and Evidence' (2004) NBER Working Paper No. 10766

Lobban M, 'Contractual Fraud in Law and Equity' (1997) 17 *Oxford Journal of Legal Studies* 3 441–476

Maloney RP, 'Usury and Restrictions on Interest-Taking in the Ancient Near East' (1974) 36 The Catholic Biblical Quarterly 1, 1–20

Macey JR and O'Hara M, 'The Corporate Governance of Banks' (April 2003) 9 *FRBNY Economic Policy Review* 1 91

McLeay M, Radia A and Thomas R, 'Money Creation in the Modern Economy' (2014) 54 Bank of England Quarterly Bulletin 1, 14–27

Menjucq M, 'Corporate Governance Issues in France' (2015) 16 *European Business Law Review* 5 1003–1016

Modigliani F and Miller MH, 'The Cost of Capital, Corporation Finance, and the Theory of Investment' (1958) 48 *American Economic Review* 3 261–297

Moloney N, 'Regulating Retail Investment Products: The Financial Crisis and the EU Challenge' (November 2010) *Era – Forum* 11(3) 329–349

Peltzman S, 'The Effects of Automobile Safety Regulations' (1975) *Journal of Political Economy* 83 677–726

Randell C, 'The Great British Banking Experiment: Will the Restructuring of UK Banking Show Us How to Resolve G-SIFIs?' (2012) 6 *Law and Financial Markets Review* 1

Rockström J, Steffen WL, Noone K, Persson Å and Stuart Chapin III F, 'A Safe Operating Space for Humanity' (2009) 461 *Nature* 472–475

Rockström J et al., 'Planetary Boundaries: Exploring the Safe Operating Space for Humanity' (2009) 14 *Ecology and Society* 2 32

Ross S, 'The Economic Theory of Agency: The Principal's Problem' (1973) 53 *American Economic Review* 2 134–139

Schinski M and Mullineaux D, 'The Impact of the Federal Reserve's Source of Strength Policy on Bank Holding Companies' (1995) 35 *Quarterly Review of Economics and Finance* 485–496

Schwarcz SL, 'Regulating Financial Change: A Functional Approach' (2016) 100 *Minnesota Law Review* 1441–1494

Schwarcz SL, 'Controlling Financial Chaos: The Power and Limits of Law' (2012) 3 *Wisconsin Law Review* 815–840

Schwarcz SL, 'Regulating Shadow Banking' (2011) 31 *Review of Banking & Financial Law* 610–642

Schwarcz SL and Anabtawi I, 'Regulating Systemic Risk: Towards an Analytical Framework' (2011) UCLA School of Law, Law-Econ Research Paper No. 10–10

Scott HS, 'Interconnectedness and Contagion – Financial Panics and the Crisis of 2008' (2014) https://papers.ssrn.com/sol3/papers.cfm?abstract_id=2178475 accessed 18 March 2018

Shin HS, 'Securitisation and Financial Stability' (2009) 119 *Economic Journal* 536 309–332

Simpson AWB, 'The Horwitz Thesis and the History of Contracts' (1979) 46 *University of Chicago Law Review* 3 533–601

Smith LR and Muñiz-Fraticelli VM, 'Strategic Shortcomings of the Dodd-Frank Act' (2013) *The Antitrust Bulletin* 58 617–633

Stigler G, 'The Theory of Economic Regulation' (Spring 1971) *The Bell Journal of Economics and Management Science* 3–21

Stiglitz JE and Weiss A, 'Credit Rationing in Markets with Imperfect Information' (1981) 71 *American Economic Review* 3 393–410

Taylor MW, 'The Road from "Twin Peaks" and the Way Back' (2000) 1 *Connecticut Insurance Law Journal* 16 61

Vučinić M, 'Importance of Macroprudential Policy Implementation for Safeguarding Financial Stability' (2016) 3 *Journal of Central Banking Theory and Practice* 79–98

Walker GA, 'U.K. Regulatory Revision – A New Blueprint for Reform' (2012) 46 *The International Lawyer* 3 787–828

Weber RH, 'RegTech as a New Legal Challenge' (2017) 46 *Journal of Financial Transformation* 10

Werner R, 'A Lost Century in Economics: Three Theories of Banking and the Conclusive Evidence' (2016) 46 *International Review of Financial Analysis* 361–379

Williamson OE, 'Economics of Organization: A Transaction Cost Approach' (November 1981) 87 *American Journal of Sociology* 3 548–577

Woodward S, 'The Liquidity Premium and the Solidity Premium' (1983) 73 *American Economic Review* 3 348–361

WEBSITES AND NEWSPAPERS

Appelbaum B, 'Skepticism Prevails on Preventing Crisis' *New York Times* (New York, 5 October 2015)

Appelbaum B, 'Days Before Housing Bust, Fed Doubted Need to Act' *New York Times* (New York, 18 January 2013) www.nytimes.com/2013/01/19/business/economy/fed-transcripts-open-a-window-on-2007-crisis.html accessed 3 January 2018

Arnold M, 'Market Grows for "Regtech" or AI for Regulation' *Financial Times* (London, 14 October 2016)

Arnold M, Binham C and Brunsden J, 'European Banks Brace for Shake-up in Customer Data Access' *Financial Times* (London, 12 January 2018)

Ashurst Legal Update, 'Remuneration Code for Banking and Financial Services Firms' (1 January 2016) www.ashurst.com/en/news-and-insights/legal-updates/remuneration-code-for-banking-and-financial-services-firms/ accessed 18 March 2018

Bank of England, 'Strengthening Accountability' www.bankofengland.co.uk/prudential-regulation/key-initiatives/strengthening-accountability accessed 18 March 2018

Bank of England, 'SONIA Key Features and Policies' (May 2018) Section 2 'Definition of SONIA'www.bankofengland.co.uk/-/media/boe/files/markets/benchmarks/sonia-key-features-and-policies.pdf accessed 21 December 2018

Bank of England Financial Policy Committee website www.bankofengland.co.uk/financial-stability accessed 18 March 2018

Bank of England News Release, 'PRA and FCA Statement on Compliance with the EBA Guidelines on Sound Remuneration Policies' (29 February 2016) www.bankofengland.co.uk/news/2016/february/pra-fca-statement-on-compliance-with-the-eba-guidelines-on-sound-remuneration-policies accessed 18 March 2018

Bank of England speeches website www.bankofengland.co.uk/publications/Pages/speeches/2016/901.aspx accessed 18 March 2018

Banking Standards Board website www.bankingstandardsboard.org.uk/ accessed 18 March 2018

Belton C, 'VTB Capital Races to the Top in Russia' *Financial Times* (London, 2 August 2010) www.ft.com/content/6f30a4ac-9dbd-11df-a37c-00144feab49a accessed 18 March 2018

Board of Governors of the Federal Reserve System, 'Federal Reserve Issues a Consent Cease and Desist Order and Assesses Civil Money Penalty Against Wells Fargo' (20 July 2011) www.federalreserve.gov/newsevents/pressreleases/enforcement20110720a.htm accessed 21 December 2018

'Breaking: Zopa Will Launch a Bank' (16 November 2016) www.p2p-banking.com/tag/bank/ accessed 18 March 2018

British Bankers Association, 'setting bbalibor', 'Definitions' www.bbatrent.com/explained/definitions accessed 21 December 2018

Browne A, 'Libor Now Has a New Administrator – But Our Reforms Have Gone Much Further' *City A.M.* (11 July 2013) www.cityam.com/article/libor-now-has-a-new-administrator-our-reforms-have-gone-much-further#sthash.L3qpkU6i.dpuf accessed 18 May 2018

Chartered Banker Professional Standards Board, Founding Members www.cbpsb.org/about-us/founding-members.html accessed 18 March 2018

Conradi P, 'Funds Flout Law by Charging Billions in Hidden Fees, Says Gina Miller' *The Sunday Times* (London, 4 February 2018), 39

Credit Suisse, 'Credit Suisse Reaches Settlement with U.S. Department of Justice Regarding Legacy Residential Mortgage-Backed Securities Matter' (press release, 18 January 2017) www.credit-suisse.com/corporate/en/articles/media-releases/cs-reaches-settlement-us-doj-legacy-rmbs-201701.html accessed 21 December 2018

Department of the Treasury, 'Financial Stability Oversight Council – Designations' (last updated 10 February 2017) www.treasury.gov/initiatives/fsoc/designations/Pages/default.aspx accessed 18 March 2018

Dunkley E, 'UK Draws Line under "Banker Bashing" after Scrapping Assessment' *Financial Times* (London, 30 December 2015) www.ft.com/content/e926e9e2-aef1-11e5-993b-c425a3d2b65a accessed 18 March 2018

European Commission, 'Securities Markets' https://ec.europa.eu/info/business-economy-euro/banking-and-finance/financial-markets/securities-markets_en accessed 18 March 2018

European Commission, 'European Commission – Fact Sheet, January Infringements Package: Key Decisions' (press release, 25 January 2018) europa.eu/rapid/press-release_MEMO-18-349_en.pdf accessed 21 December 2018

Financial Conduct Authority, 'Culture in Banking' www.fca.org.uk/publication/foi/foi4350-information-provided.pdf accessed 18 March 2018

Financial Conduct Authority, 'Statements of Principle and Code of Practice for Approved Persons' (press release 29 July 2018)

Financial Conduct Authority, 'Anti-Money Laundering – Annual Report 2016/17' (2017), 6www.fca.org.uk/publication/annual-reports/annual-anti-money-laundering-report-2016-17.pdf accessed 21 December 2012

Financial Conduct Authority, 'PRA and FCA Statement on Compliance with the EBA Guidelines on Sound Remuneration Policies' (published 29 February 2016) www.fca

.org.uk/news/statements/pra-and-fca-statement-compliance-eba-guidelines-sound-remuneration-policies accessed 18 March 2018

Financial Conduct Authority, 'Statement on European Union Referendum Result' (published 24 June 2016) www.fca.org.uk/news/statements/statement-european-union-referendum-result accessed 18 March 2018

Financial Conduct Authority, 'Remuneration' (published 9 May 2015, last updated 15 June 2016) www.fca.org.uk/firms/remuneration accessed 18 March 2018

Financial Conduct Authority, 'Senior Managers and Certification Regime' Press Release (published 7 July 2015, last updated 11 January 2018) www.fca.org.uk/firms/senior-managers-certification-regime accessed 18 March 2018

Financial Ombudsman Service, 'How Does the Ombudsman Approach Redress Where a PPI Policy Has Been Mis-Sold?' and 'What We Consider to be Fair and Reasonable Redress Will Depend on the Individual Circumstances of the Complaint' Online PPI resource www.financial-ombudsman.org.uk/publications/technical_notes/ppi/redress.html accessed 18 March 2018

Financial Ombudsman Service, 'Assessing the Suitability of Investments' Online technical resources www.financial-ombudsman.org.uk/publications/technical_notes/assessing-suitability-of-investment.htm accessed 18 March 2018

Financial Services Authority, 'The Assessment and Redress of Payment Protection Insurance Complaints' (Consultation Paper CP09/23, Financial Services Authority September 2009) www.fsa.gov.uk/pubs/cp/cp09_23.pdf accessed 7 January 2019

Financial Services Authority, 'The Assessment and Redress of Payment Protection Insurance Complaints: Feedback on CP09/23 and Further Consultation' (Consultation Paper CP10/6, Financial Services Authority March 2010) www.fca.org.uk/publication/consultation/cp10_06.pdf accessed 7 January 2019

Financial Services Authority, 'The Assessment and Redress of Payment Protection Insurance Complaints: Feedback on the Further Consultation in CP10/6 and Final Handbook Text' (Policy Statement PS10/12, Financial Services Authority August 2010) www.fca.org.uk/publication/policy/ps10_12.pdf accessed 7 January 2019

Finance Watch, 'The Continuous Fling with Investment Banking', 26 February 2015 www.finance-watch.org/the-continuous-fling-with-investment-banking/ accessed 21 December 2018

Fixed Income Currencies and Commodities (FICC) Markets Standards Board website www.fmsb.com/ accessed 18 March 2018

Fixed Income Currencies and Commodities (FICC) Markets Standards Board, 'FICC Markets Standards Board Proposes Greater Transparency in New Issue Process for Debt' (fmsb.com, 18 November 2016) http://fmsb.com/ficc-markets-standards-board-proposes-greater-transparency-in-new-issue-process-for-corporate-debt/ accessed 18 March 2018

Foreign Exchange Professionals Association, 'Focus On: Foreign Exchange Benchmarks' https://fxpa.org/wp-content/uploads/2015/06/fxpa-benchmarks-5-22final.pdf accessed 18 March 2018

Gates B, *American Banker Magazine*, 9 January 1995

Greenspan A, 'We Need a Better Cushion Against Risk' (*Financial Times* Opinion, 26 March 2009) www.ft.com/content/9c158a92-1a3c-11de-9f91-0000779fd2ac accessed 18 March 2018

Halstrick P, 'Tighter Bank Rules Give Fillip to Shadow Banks' *Reuters* (London, 19 December 2011) https://uk.reuters.com/article/uk-regulation-shadow-banking/tighter-bank-rules-give-fillip-to-shadow-banks-idUKLNE7BJ00T20111220 accessed 18 March 2018

Harvard Law School Forum on Corporate Governance and Financial Regulation, Pearce W and Sholem M (eds) 'Remuneration in the Financial Services Industry 2015' (18 September 2018) https://corpgov.law.harvard.edu/2015/09/18/remuneration-in-the-financial-services-industry-2015/ accessed 18 March 2018

Hesse M, 'Angriff der Finanzzwerge' *Spiegel.dc* (20 October 2015) www.spiegel.de/ wirtschaft/ unternehmen/fintech-fusion-funding-circle-uebernimmt-konkurrenten-zencap-a-1058522.html accessed 18 March 2018

HM Treasury, Bank of England and Financial Conduct Authority, 'Fair and Effective Financial Markets Review – Terms of Reference' www.bankofengland.co.uk/-/media/ boe/files/markets/fair-and-effective-markets/terms-of-reference.pdf accessed 18 March 2018

HM Treasury, 'Disposal of Approximately 7.7% of The Royal Bank of Scotland Group PLC' (News story, UK Government Investments Limited 5 June 2018) www.ukgi.org.uk/2018/ 06/05/disposal-of-approximately-7-7-of-the-royal-bank-of-scotland-group-plc/ accessed 20 December 2018

HM Treasury, Home Office, 'The Financial Challenge to Crime and Terrorism' (February 2007), para. 2.44 https://webarchive.nationalarchives.gov.uk/+/http:/www.hm-treasury.gov.uk/d/financialchallenge_crime_280207.pdf accessed 21 December 2018

Husain A, 'Top Global Banks' (S&P Global Market Intelligence, 14 December 2017) https:// marketintelligence.spglobal.com/our-thinking/ideas/top-global-banks accessed 28 March 2018

Johnson L, 'Trust Can Seem Risky but Its Absence is Perilous', *Financial Times* (London, 2 December 2014)

Jones H, 'Bank of England Expects Big Libor Switch to Start in Earnest' *Reuters* (18 April 2018) https://uk.reuters.com/article/us-boe-markets-sonia/bank-of-england-expects-big-libor-switch-to-start-in-earnest-idUKKBN1HP1GB accessed 21 December 2018

Kay J, '"Too Big to Fail" is Too Dumb an Idea to Keep' (*Financial Times* Opinion, 27 October 2009) www.ft.com/content/375f4528-c330-11de-8eca-00144feab49a accessed 22 March 2018

Lewin J, 'MiFID II Preparation Could Cost Firms $2.1 Bn' *Financial Times* (London, 29 September 2016)

Le Brocq N, 'Regtech – The New Paradigm: Recognizing the Potential for Technology to Manage Regulatory Data and Improve Internal Control and Compliance' (*Confluence*, 13 April 2016)

Monaghan A, 'Seven Things You Need to Know About the UK Economy' *The Guardian* (24 April 2014) www.theguardian.com/business/economics-blog/2014/apr/24/uk-economy-seven-things-need-to-know-ons-g7 accessed 18 March 2018

Noonan L, 'Banks Face Pushback over Surging Compliance and Regulatory Costs' *Financial Times* (London, 28 May 2015)

Norris F, 'The Myth of Fixing the Libor' *New York Times* (New York, 27 September 2012) www.nytimes.com/2012/09/28/business/the-myth-of-fixing-the-libor-high-low-finance.html accessed 18 May 2018

Popper N, 'Goldman Sachs to Open a Bitcoin Trading Unit' (*New York Times International Edition,* 4 May 2018) www.nytimes.com/2018/05/02/technology/bitcoin-goldman-sachs.html accessed 28 May 2018

The Quran, Sura Al-Baqarah (The Cow) 2:275–279 http://islamicstudies.info/reference.php?sura=2&tverse=275&tto=279

Reilly D, 'From Wall Street to Crawl Street' (*Wall Street Journal*, Europe edition, 29 July 2011) www.wsj.com/articles/SB10001424053111904888304576474261732934454 accessed 18 March 2018

Resti A, 'Fines for Misconduct in the Banking Sector – What is the Situation in the EU' (Brussels: EU Parliament) (March 2017), 5 www.europarl.europa.eu/RegData/etudes/IDAN/2017/587400/IPOL_IDA(2017)587400_EN.pdf accessed 21 December 2018

Snider J, 'The New Crowded Derivatives Trade', Real Clear Markets (*Realclearmarkets.com*, 14 June 2013) www.realclearmarkets.com/articles/2013/06/14/the_new_crowded_derivatives_trade_100401.html accessed 18 March 2018

The Economist, 'The Origins of the Financial Crises: Crash Course' (*The Economist*, 7 September 2013) www.economist.com/news/schoolsbrief/21584534-effects-financial-crisis-are-still-being-felt-five-years-article accessed 18 March 2018

The Economist, 'Financial Stability: The Better You Do, the Greater the Risk' (*The Economist*, 26 April 2007) www.economist.com/node/9086520 accessed 18 March 2018

The Economist, 'Subprime Lending: Rising Damp' (*The Economist*, 8 May 2007) www.economist.com/node/8829612 accessed 18 March 2018

US Department of Justice, 'Barclays Bank PLC Agrees to Forfeit $298 Million in Connection with Violations of the International Emergency Economic Powers Act and the Trading with the Enemy Act' (18 August 2010)www.justice.gov/opa/pr/barclays-bank-plc-agrees-forfeit-298-million-connection-violations-international-emergency accessed 21 December 2018

US Department of Justice, 'Lloyds TSB Bank PLC Agrees to Forfeit $350 Million in Connection with Violations of the International Emergency Economic Powers Act' (9 January 2009) www.justice.gov/opa/pr/lloyds-tsb-bank-plc-agrees-forfeit-350-million-connection-violations-international-emergency accessed 21 December 2018

Walker P, 'FCA Drops Banking Culture Review' (*Financial Times Adviser*, 4 January 2016) www.ftadviser.com/2016/01/04/regulation/regulators/fca-drops-banking-culture-review-TD3pZ14e2LXNnhNgpk2THP/article.html accessed 18 March 2018

Wolf M, 'Why Curbing Finance is Hard to Do' (*Financial Times* Opinion, 22 October 2009) www.ft.com/content/0a8a6362-bf3d-11de-a696-00144feab49a accessed 22 March 2018

LEGISLATION AND REGULATION

UK

Act for the Better Regulation of Co-partnerships of Certain Bankers in England 1826 (7 Geo. IV, c. 46)

Bank of England Act 1998

Banking Act 2009

Banking (Special Provisions) Act 2008

Building Societies Act 1986

Company Directors Disqualification Act 1986

Consumer Credit Act 2006

Credit Unions Act 1979

Financial Services Act 2012

Financial Services (Banking Reform) Act 2013

Financial Services and Markets Act 2000

Financial Services and Markets Act 2000 (Qualifying EU Provisions) (Amendment) Order 2013, No. 419

Financial Services and Markets Act 2000 (Qualifying EU Provisions) (Amendment) Order 2016, No. 936

Financial Services and Markets Act 2000 (Ring-Fenced Bodies and Core Activities) Order 2014 No 1960

Financial Services and Markets Act 2000 (Excluded Activities and Prohibitions) Order 2014 No. 2080

House of Commons, Banking Bill 2008

Insolvency Act 1986

Joint Stock Banking Companies Act 1857 (20 and 21 Vict. c. 49)

Joint Stock Banks Act 1844 (7 and 8 Vict. c. 113)

Joint Stock Banks Act 1858 (21 and 22 Vict. c. 91)

Joint Stock Companies Act 1844

Unfair Contract Terms Act 1977

US

Delaware Code: Delaware General Corporation Law (DGLC)

Dodd-Frank Act 2010

Federal Insurance Corporation Act of 1991

Federal Reserve System Regulation Y; Docket Nos. R-0935; R-0936 Bank Holding Companies and Change in Bank Control (Regulation Y)

Revised Model Business Corporation Act (RMBCA) 2016

US Code Title 5 Part I Chapter 7

US Code Title 12 Chapter 16: Federal Deposit Insurance Corporation, section 1817 – Assessments (b)(1)(C)

US Code of Federal Regulations Title 12 Chapter III:

Federal Deposit Insurance Corporation, section 327.9 – Assessment pricing methods (a)

Title 12 of the Code of Federal Regulations, chapter III: Federal Deposit Insurance Corporation, section 327.9 – Assessment pricing methods (c)

Title 12 of the Code of Federal Regulations, chapter III: Federal Deposit Insurance Corporation, section 327.9 – Assessment pricing methods (b)

Federal Deposit Insurance Corporation, 'Prohibitions and Restrictions on Proprietary Trading and Certain Interests In, and Relationships With, Hedge Funds and Private Equity Funds', 12 CFR Part 351

OTHER NATIONAL LEGISLATION

Belgian Law of 2 August 2002(3) on the supervision of the financial sector and on financial services, as modified by Royal Decree of 3 March 2011 (*Loi relative à la surveillance du secteur financier et aux services financiers*)

Belgian Law of 22 March 1993 relating to the statute and supervision of credit institutions (*Loi du 22 mars 1993 relative au statut et au contrôle des établissements de crédit*)

French '2015 Energy Transition Law' (Law No. 2015–992 of 17 August 2015 related to energy transition for a green growth, *Journal officiel de la République française* 2015) Article 173

French Monetary and Financial Code (*Code monétaire et financier*) as amended by the Loi no 2013–672 du 26 juillet 2013 de Séparation et de Régulation des Activités Bancaires

German Banking Act (*Gesetz über das Kreditwesen*) as amended by the Gesetz zur Abschirmung von Risiken und zur Planung der Sanierung und Abwicklung von Kreditinstituten und Finanzgruppen vom 7 August 2013

Italian Consolidated Banking Law (*Decreto legislativo 1° settembre 1993, n. 385* – Testo Unico *Bancario*)

Norwegian Act on Guarantee Schemes for Banks and Public Administration etc., of Financial Institutions (Guarantee Schemes Act) of 6 December 1996 (as amended per 1 July 2004) (*Lov om finansforetak og finanskonsern (finansforetaksloven)*)

Swiss Banking Act (*Bundesgesetz über die Banken und Sprakassen (SR 952.0)*)

EU DIRECTIVES

Commission Delegated Directive 2017/593/EU of 7 April 2016 supplementing Directive 2014/65/EU of the European Parliament and of the Council with regard to safeguarding of financial instruments and funds belonging to clients, products governance obligations and the rules applicable to the provision or reception of fees, commissions or any monetary or non-monetary benefits (2017) OJ L 87/500

Commission Delegated Regulation (EU) 2017/567 of 18 May 2016 supplementing
Regulation (EU) No. 600/2014 of the European Parliament and of the Council with regard
to definitions, transparency, portfolio compression and supervisory measures on product
intervention and positions (2016) OJ L87/90

Commission Delegated Regulation (EU) 2016/1450 of 23 May 2016 supplementing Directive
2014/59/EU of the European Parliament and of the Council with regard to regulatory
technical standards specifying the criteria relating to the methodology for setting the
minimum requirement for own funds and eligible liabilities (2016) OJ L 237/1

Commission Directive 2003/124/EC implementing Directive 2003/6/EC of the European
Parliament and of the Council as regards the definition and public disclosure of inside
information and the definition of market manipulation (2003) OJ L339/70

Commission Directive 2003/125/EC implementing Directive 2003/6/EC of the European
Parliament and of the Council as regards the fair presentation of investment
recommendations and the disclosure of conflicts of interest (2003) OJ L339

Commission Regulation 2273/2003/EC implementing Directive 2003/6/EC of the European
Parliament and of the Council as regards exemptions for buy-back programmes and
stabilisation of financial instruments (2003) OJ L336

Council Directive 2003/6/EC on insider dealing and market manipulation (market abuse)
(2003) OJ L96/16

Directive (EU) 2017/1132 of 14 June 2017 relating to certain aspects of company law (2017)
OJ L169/46

Directive (EU) 2016/1034 of the European Parliament and of the Council of 23 June 2016
amending Directive 2014/65/EU on markets in financial instruments (2016) OJ L 175/8

Directive 2015/849 of the European Parliament and of the Council on the prevention of the
use of the financial system for the purposes of money laundering or terrorist financing,
amending Regulation (EU) No. 648/2012 of the European Parliament and of the Council,
and repealing Directive 2005/60/EC of the European Parliament and of the Council and
Commission Directive 2006/70/EC (2015) OJ L 141/73

Directive 2014/91/EU of the European Parliament and of the Council of 23 July
2014 amending Directive 2009/65/EC on the coordination of laws, regulations and
administrative provisions relating to undertakings for collective investment in
transferable securities (UCITS) as regards depositary functions, remuneration policies
and sanctions (2014) OJ L 257/184

Directive 2014/65/EU of the European Parliament and of the Council of 15 May 2014 on
markets in financial instruments and amending Directive 2002/92/EC and Directive
2011/61/EU (2014) OJ L 173/349

Directive 2014/59/EU of the European Parliament and of the Council of 15 May
2014 establishing a framework for the recovery and resolution of credit institutions and
investment firms and amending Council Directive 82/891/EEC, and Directives 2001/24/
EC, 2002/47/EC, 2004/25/EC, 2005/56/EC, 2007/36/EC, 2011/35/EU, 2012/30/EU and
2013/36/EU, and Regulations (EU) No. 1093/2010 and (EU) No. 648/2012, of the
European Parliament and of the Council (2014) OJ L 173/190

Directive 2014/57/EU of the European Parliament and of the Council of 16 April 2014 on criminal sanctions for market abuse (market abuse directive) (2014) OJ L173/179

Directive 2014/49/EU of the European Parliament and of the Council of 16 April 2014 on deposit guarantee schemes (2014) OJ L 173/149

Directive 2013/36/EU of the European Parliament and of the Council of 26 June 2013 on access to the activity of credit institutions and the prudential supervision of credit institutions and investment firms, amending Directive 2002/87/EC and repealing Directives 2006/48/EC and 2006/49/EC (2013) OJ L 176/338

Directive 2009/65/EC of the European Parliament and of the Council of 13 July 2009 on the coordination of laws, regulations and administrative provisions relating to undertakings for collective investment in transferable securities (UCITS) (2009) OJ L 302/32

Directive 2006/48/EC of the European Parliament and of the Council relating to the taking up and pursuit of the business of credit institutions (recast) (2006) OJ L 177/1 (no longer in force)

Directive 2004/72/EC implementing Directive 2003/6/EC of the European Parliament and of the Council as regards accepted market practices, the definition of inside information in relation to derivatives on commodities, the drawing up of lists of insiders, the notification of managers' transactions and the notification of suspicious transactions (2004) OJ L162/70

Directive 2004/39/EC of the European Parliament and of the Council on markets in financial instruments amending Council Directives 85/611/EEC and 93/6/EEC and Directive 2000/12/EC of the European Parliament and of the Council and repealing Council Directive 93/22/EEC (2004) OJ L 145/1 (no longer in force)

Directive 2004/25/EC of the European Parliament and of the Council of 21 April 2004 on takeover bids (2004) OJ L 142/12

Directive 2010/76/EU of the European Parliament and the Council of 24 November 2010 amending Directives 2006/48/EC and 2006/49/EC as regards capital requirements for the trading book and for re-securitisations, and the supervisory review of remuneration policies (2004) OJ L 329/3 (no longer in force)

Directive 2001/24/EC of the European Parliament and of the Council of 4 April 2001 on the reorganisation and winding up of credit institutions (2001) OJ L 125, 5.5.2001/15

Directive 2001/17/EC of the European Parliament and of the Council of 19 March 2001 on the reorganisation and winding-up of insurance undertakings (2001) OJ L 110/28 (no longer in force)

Second Council Directive 89/646/EEC of 15 December 1989 on the coordination of laws, regulations and administrative provisions relating to the taking up and pursuit of the business of credit institutions and amending Directive 77/780/EEC (1989) OJ L 386/1 (no longer in force)

Sixth Council Directive 82/891/EEC of 17 December 1982 based on Article 54(3)(g) of the Treaty, concerning the division of public limited liability companies (1982) OJ L 378/47 (no longer in force)

Third Council Directive 78/855/EEC of 9 October 1978 based on Article 54(3)(g) of the Treaty concerning mergers of public limited liability companies (1978)OJ L 295/36 (no longer in force)

First Council Directive 77/780/EEC of 12 December 1977 on the coordination of the laws, regulations and administrative provisions relating to the taking up and pursuit of the business of credit institutions (1977) OJ L 322/30 (no longer in force)

Second Council Directive 77/91/EEC of 13 December 1976 on coordination of safeguards which, for the protection of the interests of members and others, are required by Member States of companies within the meaning of the second paragraph of Article 58 of the Treaty, in respect of the formation of public limited liability companies and the maintenance and alteration of their capital, with a view to making such safeguards equivalent (1977) OJ L 26/1 (no longer in force)

Proposal for a Directive of the European Parliament and of the Council of 18 December 2013 on Establishing a Framework for the Recover and Resolution of Credit Institutions and Investment Firms' (2013), COD (2013) 2012/0150

EU REGULATIONS

Commission Delegated Regulation (EU) 2017/567 of 18 May 2016 supplementing Regulation (EU) No. 600/2014 of the European Parliament and of the Council with regard to definitions, transparency, portfolio compression and supervisory measures on product intervention and positions (2016) OJ L 87/90

Commission Delegated Regulation (EU) 2017/565 of 25 April 2016 supplementing Directive 2014/65/EU of the European Parliament and of the Council as regards organisational requirements and operating conditions for investment firms and defined terms for the purposes of that Directive (2016) OJ L 87/1

Directive (EU) 2016/1034 of the European Parliament and of the Council of 23 June 2016 amending Directive 2014/65/EU on markets in financial instruments (2016) OJ L175/8

Regulation (EU) 2016/1033 of the European Parliament and of the Council of 23 June 2016 amending Regulation (EU) No. 600/2014 on markets in financial instruments, Regulation (EU) No. 596/2014 on market abuse and Regulation (EU) No. 909/2014 on improving securities settlement in the European Union and on central securities depositories (2016) OJ L 175/1

Regulation (EU) No. 806/2014 of the European Parliament and of the Council of 15 July 2014 establishing uniform rules and a uniform procedure for the resolution of credit institutions and certain investment firms in the framework of a Single Resolution Mechanism and a Single Resolution Fund and amending Regulation (EU) No. 1093/2010 (2014) OJ L 225/1

Regulation (EU) No. 600/2014 of the European Parliament and of the Council of 15 May 2014 on markets in financial instruments and amending Regulation (EU) No. 648/2012 (2014) OJ L 173/84

Regulation (EU) No. 596/2014 of the European Parliament and of the Council of 16 April 2014 on market abuse (market abuse regulation) and repealing Directive 2003/6/EC of the European Parliament and of the Council and Commission Directives 2003/124/EC, 2003/125/EC and 2004/72/EC (2014) OJ L173/1

Regulation (EU) No. 575/2013 of the European Parliament and of the Council of 26 June 2013 on prudential requirements for credit institutions and investment firms and amending Regulation (EU) No. 648/2012 (2013) OJ L 176/1

Regulation (EU) No. 648/2012 of the European Parliament and of the Council of 4 July 2012 on OTC derivatives, central counterparties and trade repositories (2012) OJ L201/1 (EMIR)

Regulation (EU) No. 1092/2010 of the European Parliament and of the Council of 24 November 2010 on European Union macro-prudential oversight of the financial system and establishing a European Systemic Risk Board (2010) OJ L 331/1

Council Regulation (EC) No. 1346/2000 of 29 May 2000 on insolvency proceedings (2000) OJ L 160/1 (no longer in force)

Proposal for a Regulation of the European Parliament and of the Council on structural measures improving the resilience of EU credit institutions (2014) COM/2014/043 final – 2014/0020 (COD) http://eur-lex.europa.eu/legal-content/EN/ALL/?uri= CELEX:52014PC0043 accessed 23 March 2018

INTERNATIONAL

Basel Committee on Banking Regulation and Supervisory Practices, 1988, Report of the Committee on Banking Regulations and Supervisory Practices, International Convergence of Capital Measurements and Capital Standards (Basel: Bank for International Settlements)

Basel Committee on Banking Supervision, 'Guidance on the Application of the Core Principles for Effective Banking Supervision to the Regulation and Supervision of Institutions Relevant to Financial Inclusion' (Bank for International Settlements, September 2016), 3–4

Basel Committee on Banking Supervision, Standard TLAC holdings (October 2016) https://www.bis.org/bcbs/publ/d387.pdf accessed 18 May 2018

Basel Committee on Banking Supervision, 'Guidelines: Corporate Governance Principles for Banks' (July 2015)

Basel Committee on Banking Supervision, Committee on Global Financial System, 'Principles for the Supervision of Financial Conglomerates' Final Report (September 2012)www.bis.org/publ/joint29.htm accessed 21 December 2018

Basel Committee on Banking Supervision, The Joint Forum, 'Review of the Differentiated Nature and Scope of Financial Regulation, Key Issues and Recommendations' (January 2010), 85

Basel Committee on Banking Supervision, Basel III: A Global Regulatory Framework for More Resilient Banks and Banking Systems (Basel III Accord) (December 2010, revised June 2011) www.bis.org/publ/bcbs189.pdf accessed 18 May 2018

Basel Committee on Banking Supervision, 'Enhancements to Basel II Framework' (July 2009)

Basel Committee on Banking Supervision, *Principles for Sound Liquidity Risk Management and Supervision* (25 September 2008) (Basel: Bank for International Settlements)

Basel Committee on Banking Supervision, International Convergence of Capital Measurement and Capital Standards – A Revised Framework (Basel II Accord) (June 2004, updated November 2005) www.bis.org/publ/bcbs118.pdf accessed 18 May 2018

European Convention for the Protection of Human Rights and Fundamental Freedoms 1950

Protocol to the Convention for the Protection of Human Rights and Fundamental Freedoms (Paris, 20 March 1952), 9 E.T.S., Article 1

United Nations Paris Climate Agreement 2015 http://unfccc.int/files/essential_background/convention/application/pdf/english_paris_agreement.pdf accessed 18 May 2018

OTHER

Angeloni I, 'Towards a Macro-Prudential Framework for the Single Supervisory Area' (speech at the Belgium Financial Forum, Brussels, 20 April 2015) www.bankingsupervision.europa.eu/press/speeches/date/2015/html/se150420.en.html accessed 23 May 2018

Bailey A, Governor of the Bank of England, 'What a Difference a Decade Makes' (speech at the Institute of International Finance's Washington Policy Summit, the Reagan Center, Washington DC, 20 April 2017) www.bankofengland.co.uk/-/media/boe/files/speech/2017/what-a-difference-a-decade-makes.pdf accessed 18 May 2018

Bailey A, 'The Future of LIBOR' (27 July 2017), Speech at Bloomberg Londonwww.fca.org.uk/news/speeches/the-future-of-libor accessed 21 December 2018

Bailey A, Deputy Governor of the Bank of England, 'Culture in Financial Services – A Regulator's Perspective' (speech at the City Week 2016 Conference, 9 May 2016) www.bankofengland.co.uk/-/media/boe/files/speech/2016/culture-in-financial-services-a-regulators-perspective.pdf?la=en&hash=088A4BBDA75375CCD822EE715A35BC662FCD8A6D accessed 18 May 2018

Bank of England, Charter Incorporating the Governor and the Company of the Bank of England (27 July 1694) www.whatdotheyknow.com/request/6134/response/14050/attach/5/1998charter%201.pdf accessed 18 May 2018

Carney M, 'Breaking the Tragedy of the Horizon – Climate Change and Financial Stability' (speech at Lloyd's of London, 29 September 2015) www.bankofengland.co.uk/-/media/boe/files/speech/2015/breaking-the-tragedy-of-the-horizon-climate-change-and-financial-stability.pdf?la=en&hash=7C67E785651862457D99511147C7424FF5EA0C1A accessed 18 May 2018

Chartered Banker Professional Standards Board, Foundation Standard for Professional Bankers (January 2016) www.cbpsb.org/professional-standards/foundation-standard .html accessed 18 May 2018

Chartered Banker Professional Standards Board, 'Progress Report 2016' (May 2016) www.cbpsb.org/filemanager/root/site_assets/progress_report_2016/cb_psb_report_ 2016_final.pdf accessed 18 May 2018

Chartered Banker Professional Standards Board, Code of Professional Conduct (effective 1 September 2016) www.charteredbanker.com/filemanager/root/site_assets/governance/ the_chartered_banker_code_of_professional_conduct_47494.pdf accessed 18 May 2018

Connolly PD, QC, 'Report to Parliament of Queensland into the Affairs of Queensland Syndication Management Pty Ltd and Ors' (1974)

Convention for the Protection of Human Rights and Fundamental Freedoms (European Convention on Human Rights, as amended) (ECHR)

Financial Action Task Force, FATF (2012–2018), International Standards on Combating Money Laundering and the Financing of Terrorism & Proliferation, FATF, Paris, France www.fatf-gafi.org/recommendations.html accessed 9 January 2019

Financial Action Task Force, FATF (October 2001), 'FATF' IX Special Recommendations

Financial Conduct Authority, 'Final Notice to Ian Charles Hannam' (17 July 2014) ICH01012 www.fca.org.uk/publication/final-notices/ian-charles-hannam.pdf accessed 18 May 2018

Financial Conduct Authority Handbook www.handbook.fca.org.uk/handbook/ accessed 18 May 2018

Financial Stability Council in Sweden www.riksbank.se/en-gb/financial-stability/ financial-stability-council/ accessed 23 May 2018

Hassert T, presentation at the Basel Infrastructure Conference, Basel (22 May 2014)

HM Treasury, Bank of England and Financial Services Authority, 'Memorandum of Understanding between HM Treasury, the Bank of England and the Financial Services Authority' (22 March 2006) http://webarchive.nationalarchives.gov.uk/+/http://www .hm-treasury.gov.uk/documents/financial_services/regulating_financial_services/fin_ rfs_mou.cfm accessed 18 May 2018

Ingves S, 'Basel III: Are We Done Now?', 29 January 2018 (Basel: Bank for International Settlements) www.bis.org/speeches/sp180129.htm accessed 21 February 2018

Ingves S, 'Challenges for the Design and Conduct of Macroprudential Policy' (speech at BOK-BIS Conference, Seoul, Korea, 18 January 2011) www.riksbank.se/Upload/ Dokument_riksbank/Kat_publicerat/Tal/2011/110118e.pdf accessed 18 May 2018

Jackson P, 'Beyond Basel II' (presentation at Clare College, Cambridge, 12 September 2010)

King M, Speech at the University of Exeter (19 January 2010) www.bankofengland.co.uk/ archive/Documents/historicpubs/speeches/2010/speech419.pdf accessed 28 August 2015

Lambert S, Sir, 'Banking Standards Review' (2014) www.cii.co.uk/knowledge/policy-and- public-affairs/articles/banking-standards-(lambert)-review-final-report/30421 accessed 15 February 2018

McDermott T, 'Culture in Banking' speech to the British Bankers Association (Financial Conduct Authority, 13 July 2015)

New York Stock Exchange Listed Company Manual http://wallstreet.cch.com/LCM/ accessed 18 May 2018

Nouy D, Chair of the Supervisors Board of the Single Supervisory Mechanism, 'Towards a New Age of Responsibility in Banking and Finance: Getting the Culture and the Ethics Right' (speech at the European Central Bank, 23 November 2015) www .bankingsupervision.europa.eu/press/speeches/date/2015/html/se151123.en.html accessed 18 May 2018

Sants H, Chief Executive UK Financial Services Authority, 'Do Regulators Have a Role to Play in Judging Culture and Ethics?' (speech at the Chartered Institute of Securities and Investments Conference, 17 June 2010) www.fsa.gov.uk/pages/library/communication/ speeches/2010/0617_hs.shtml accessed 18 May 2018

Trichet JC, 'Systemic Risk' (speech at the European Central Bank, 10 December 2009) www.ecb.europa.eu/press/key/date/2009/html/sp091210_1.en.html accessed 18 May 2018

Tucker P, 'Macro and Microprudential Supervision' (speech at British Bankers' Association Annual International Banking Conference, London, 29 June 2011) https://www.bis .org/review/r110704e.pdf accessed 18 May 2018

Wall Street Journal (Europe edition), 29 July 2011, 18 (discussing lower rate of return on equity for banks post-crisis)

World Bank Group President Jim Yong Kim Remarks at Davos Press Conference (23 January 2014) www.worldbank.org/en/news/speech/2014/01/23/world-bank-group-president-jim-yong-kim-remarks-at-davos-press-conference accessed 18 May 2018

Index